Beginning iPhone Development with Swift 4

Exploring the iOS SDK

Fourth Edition

Molly K. Maskrey

Apress®

Beginning iPhone Development with Swift 4: Exploring the iOS SDK

Molly K. Maskrey
Parker, Colorado, USA

ISBN-13 (pbk): 978-1-4842-3071-8
https://doi.org/10.1007/978-1-4842-3072-5

ISBN-13 (electronic): 978-1-4842-3072-5

Library of Congress Control Number: 2017957132

Managing Director: Welmoed Spahr
Editorial Director: Todd Green
Acquisitions Editor: Aaron Black
Development Editor: James Markham
Technical Reviewer: Bruce Wade
Coordinating Editor: Jessica Vakili
Copy Editor: Kim Wimpsett
Compositor: SPi Global
Indexer: SPi Global
Artist: SPi Global

Distributed to the book trade worldwide by Springer Science+Business Media New York, 233 Spring Street, 6th Floor, New York, NY 10013. Phone 1-800-SPRINGER, fax (201) 348-4505, e-mail orders-ny@springer-sbm.com, or visit www.springer.com. Apress Media, LLC is a California LLC and the sole member (owner) is Springer Science + Business Media Finance Inc (SSBM Finance Inc). SSBM Finance Inc is a Delaware corporation.

For information on translations, please e-mail rights@apress.com, or visit www.apress.com.

Apress and friends of ED books may be purchased in bulk for academic, corporate, or promotional use. eBook versions and licenses are also available for most titles. For more information, reference our Special Bulk Sales–eBook Licensing web page at www.apress.com/bulk-sales.

Any source code or other supplementary materials referenced by the author in this text is available to readers at www.apress.com. For detailed information about how to locate your book's source code, go to www.apress.com/source-code/.

Another year, another revision of this book, as well as one of my own personal tribe.

Still around after more than two years of ups and downs, KP stuck beside me during my most difficult times. No matter what I did, her sanity and silliness kept me going. She was, for a long while, my muse...my inspiration to write and to keep it as fun as possible...never taking myself too seriously. Now, as our paths slightly diverge, the qualities she's left permeate my days and make me a better self.

Mellie has been my rock. We've been in and out of being friends, and I hope she knows I consider her the closest friend I've ever had. I probably wouldn't be doing this if it weren't for the love she's shown me.

Tonya came into my life recently and has been such a godsend to help me become more confident in all I say and do, and I can't thank her enough.

She probably has no clue she's in here, but Lauren kept me going for the past year. When I would've preferred to lay in the dark and sleep and zone out, without any aggressiveness Lauren would give me something in her words to keep to going...to not give up. She—I won't say forced, but she was very persuasive—got me into a program that is, this very day, putting me onto a better path for myself and my future and the future of anyone alongside me for my journey.

Finally, to Jennifer...our lives have radically changed over the past year. But, as partners in business and advocates for each other's happy life, our relationship bond, while admittedly very tumultuous, has solidified into something we both see as pretty damn good.

In my personal struggles over the preceding year, these friends kept me from falling into an abyss so deep I might never have returned. Writing can be a lonely thing, and having a support system such as these beautiful, wonderful women are the only reason this endeavor was a success. A special friend told me last year that some friends are only in your life for a season. I pray that these women are friends for a lifetime.

—MM, August 2017

Contents at a Glance

Contents

About the Author

Molly K. Maskrey started as an electrical engineer in her 20s working for various large aerospace companies including IBM Federal Systems, TRW (now Northrup-Grumman), Loral Systems, Lockheed-Martin, and Boeing. After successfully navigating the first dot-com boom, she realized that a break was in order and took several years off, moving to Maui and teaching windsurfing at the beautiful Kanaha Beach Park.

She moved back to Colorado in 2005 and, with Jennifer, formed Global Tek Labs, an iOS development and accessory design services company that is now one of the leading consulting services for new designers looking to create smart attachments to Apple devices.

In 2014 Molly and Jennifer formed Quantitative Bioanalytics Laboratories, a wholly owned subsidiary of Global Tek to bring high-resolution mobile sensor technology to physical therapy, elder balance and fall prevention, sports performance quantification, and instrumented gait analysis (IGA). In a pivot, Molly changed the direction of QB Labs to a platform-based predictive analytics company seeking to democratize data science for smaller companies.

Molly's background includes advanced degrees in electrical engineering, applied mathematics, data science, and business development. Molly generally speaks at a large number of conferences throughout the year including the Open Data Science Conference (ODSC) 2017 West, advancing the topic of moving analytics from the cloud to the fog for smart city initiatives. What fuels her to succeed is the opportunity to bring justice and equality to everyone whether it's addressing food insecurity with her business partner or looking at options for better management of mental health using empirical data and tools such as natural language processing, speech pattern recognition using neural networks, or perfusion analysis in brain physiology.

About the Technical Reviewer

Bruce Wade is a software engineer from British Columbia, Canada. He started software development when he was 16 years old by coding his first web site. He went on to study computer information systems at DeVry Institute of Technology in Calgary; to further enhance his skills, he studied visual and game programming at the Art Institute of Vancouver. Over the years he has worked for large corporations as well as several startups. His software experience has led him to utilize many different technologies including C/C++, Python, Objective-C, Swift, Postgres, and JavaScript. In 2012 he started the company Warply Designed to focus on mobile 2D/3D and OS X development. Aside from hacking out new ideas, he enjoys spending time hiking with his Boxer Rasco, working out, and exploring new adventures.

Acknowledgments

First, I want to acknowledge all my friends who gave me the support to persevere and go through with writing when it would have been so easy to just give up. Thanks to Sam especially, another writer I met more than a year ago, who was always there to provide support, drink tequila, and suggest fun things to do in order to keep it real. He was my cohost at almost a year of rooftop parties at Galvanize.

Thanks to Children's Hospital Colorado and the Center for Gait and Movement Analysis, both of which have been so generous to let me be part of what they do for young adults with cerebral palsy and other gait disorders. The understanding I've gained drives me to focus my efforts on helping the many who truly need it. Thanks to the CEOs of 10.10.10 Health who let me see what they were doing and to provide my annoying feedback.

Thanks to the clients and friends of Global Tek Labs who so generously allowed me to include some of their projects in this book for illustrative purposes. Thanks to the hundreds of people who have attended my talks over the past year and have given me ideas for what to include, such as John Haley who told me of his personal woes in understanding the Auto Layout feature of Xcode. Those actual experiences helped drive the subject matter I chose to include in this book.

Finally, I want to acknowledge all the authors before me who set the stage for my own little work to fit into a much broader landscape.

CHAPTER 1

Getting to Know the iOS Landscape

Coding for Apple mobile devices provides a rewarding and lucrative career path where you might not only change people's lives with your app (see Figure 1-1) but might also have a great time being with bright, like-minded women and men such as yourself. Though you're bound to find some difficulty in learning the language, tools, and processes, these new associates will help you through the landscape of this new world and will challenge you to be your best and to stand out from the mediocre.

Figure 1-1. *One of the greatest feelings you can experience as an iOS developer is seeing other people using your creation out in the real world*

© Molly K. Maskrey 2017
M. K. Maskrey, *Beginning iPhone Development with Swift 4*, https://doi.org/10.1007/978-1-4842-3072-5_1

For now, think of me as one of those friends along your journey of iOS discovery. I'm so proud to be able to help you by providing this initiation into the world of iOS development, whether it is for iPhone, iPod touch, or the iPad. iOS provides an exciting platform that has seen explosive growth since it first came out in 2007. The proliferation of mobile devices means that people are using software everywhere they go, whether it is a phone or a wearable, such as the Apple Watch. With the release of iOS 11, Xcode 9, Swift 4, and the latest version of the iOS software development kit (SDK), things continue to be exciting and generally have become easier for new developers. What's more, you can now bring the world of data science and predictive analytics to your app with CoreML as well as image and natural language processing frameworks.

About the Book

This book guides you down the path to creating your own iOS applications. I want to get you past the initial difficulties to help you understand the way that iOS applications work and how they are built.

As you work your way through this book, you will create a number of small applications, each designed to highlight specific iOS features and to show you how to control or interact with those features. If you combine the foundation you'll gain through this book with your own creativity and determination and then add in the extensive and well-written documentation provided by Apple, you'll have everything you need to build your own professional iPhone and iPad applications.

▓ **Note**   Throughout most of this book, I tend to refer to the iPhone and iPad, as they are the devices that you'll most commonly use in the examples. This does not preclude the iPod touch by any means; it is just a matter of convenience.

▓ **Tip**   The authors of the previous editions of this book have set up a forum, which is a great place to meet like-minded folks, get your questions answered, and even answer other people's questions. The forum is at http://forum.learncocoa.org. Be sure to check it out!

Things You'll Need

Before you can begin writing software for iOS, you'll need a few items. For starters, you'll need an Intel-based Macintosh running Sierra (macOS 10.12) or newer. Any recent Intel-based Macintosh computer—laptop or desktop—should work just fine. Of course, as well as the hardware, you'll need the software. You can learn how to develop iOS applications and get the software tools that you'll need as long as you have an Apple ID; if you own an iPhone, iPad, or iPod, then you've almost certainly already have an Apple ID, but if you don't, just visit https://appleid.apple.com/account to create one. Once you've done that, navigate to https://developer.apple.com/develop. This will bring you to a page similar to the one shown in Figure 1-2.

Develop

Bring Your Ideas to Life

With the power of Xcode, the ease of Swift, and the revolutionary
features of cutting-edge Apple technologies, you have the freedom
to create your most innovative apps ever.

Figure 1-2. *Apple's development resources site*

Click Downloads on the top bar to go to the main resources page (see Figure 1-3) for the current
production release and (if there is one) the current beta release of iOS. Here, you'll find links to a wealth
of documentation, videos, sample code, and the like—all dedicated to teaching you the finer points of
iOS application development. Be sure to scroll to the bottom of the page and check out the links to the
Documentation and Videos sections of the web site. You'll also find a link to the Apple Developer Forums,
where you can follow discussions on a wide variety of topics covering the whole iOS platform, as well as
macOS, watchOS, and tvOS. To post to the forums, you'll need to be a registered Apple developer.

Downloads

Get the latest beta releases of Xcode, macOS, iOS, watchOS, tvOS, and more.

Your use of Apple beta software is subject to and licensed only under the terms and conditions of the Apple Developer Program License Agreement, including any applicable consent
to collect diagnostic data set forth therein. If you have not agreed to the Apple Developer Program License Agreement, you are not permitted to use this software. Refer to the
software installation guides for complete instructions.

Featured Downloads		Build	Date	
Xcode 9 beta 2	Release Notes	9M137d	Jun 21, 2017	Download
Includes the latest beta macOS, iOS, watchOS, and tvOS SDKs.				
macOS High Sierra 10.13 beta 2	Release Notes	17A291m	Jun 29, 2017	Download
Run the macOS Developer Beta Access Utility to download the latest macOS 10.13 beta. As new macOS betas become available you will receive a notification and can install them from the Updates pane in the Mac App Store.				
iOS 11 beta 2 [Preferred]	Release Notes	15A5304i 15A5304j	Jun 26, 2017	Download
Install Configuration Profile directly on any iOS device and receive OTA updates.				
iOS Restore Images				See all
Install via iTunes.				
watchOS 4 beta 2	Release Notes	15R5307f	Jun 21, 2017	Download
Install configuration profile directly on your device to receive OTA updates.				
tvOS 11 beta 2 [Preferred]	Release Notes	15J5310h	Jun 26, 2017	Download

Figure 1-3. *You can download all the production and beta releases of the development tools from the*
Downloads page. You will need to sign in with your Apple ID.

▓ **Note**   At the developer conference WWDC 2016, Apple changed the name of OS X back to the previously used *macOS* to become more in line with the other naming conventions used throughout the four major system platforms.

The most important tool you'll be using to develop iOS applications is Xcode, Apple's integrated development environment (IDE). Xcode includes tools for creating and debugging source code, compiling applications, and performance tuning the applications you've written.

You can download the current beta release of Xcode by following the Xcode link from the developer Downloads page shown in Figure 1-3. If you prefer to use the latest production release, you'll find it in the Mac App Store, which you can access from your Mac's Apple menu.

SDK VERSIONS AND SOURCE CODE FOR THE EXAMPLES

As the versions of the SDK and Xcode evolve, the mechanism for downloading them has changed over the past few years. Apple now publishes the current production version of Xcode and the iOS SDK on the Mac App Store, while simultaneously providing developers with the ability to download preview versions of upcoming releases from its developer site. Bottom line: unless you really want to work with the most recent development tools and platform SDK, you usually want to download the latest released (nonbeta) version of Xcode and the iOS SDK, so use the Mac App Store.

This book is written to work with the latest versions of Xcode and the SDK. In some places, new functions or methods are introduced with iOS 11 that are not available in earlier versions of the SDK.

Be sure to download the latest and greatest source code archive for examples from this book's page at www.apress.com. The code is updated as new versions of the SDK are released, so be sure to check the site periodically.

Your Options as a Developer

The free Xcode download includes a simulator that will allow you to build and run iPhone and iPad apps on your Mac, providing the perfect environment for learning how to program for iOS. However, the simulator does *not* support many hardware-dependent features, such as the accelerometer and camera. To test applications that use those features, you'll need an iPhone, iPod touch, or iPad. While much of your code can be tested using the iOS simulator, not all programs can be. And even those that can run on the simulator really need to be thoroughly tested on an actual device before you ever consider releasing your application to the public.

Previous versions of Xcode required you to register for the Apple Developer Program (which is not free) to install your applications on a real iPhone or other device. Fortunately, this has changed. Xcode 7 started allowing developers to test applications on real hardware, albeit with some limitations that I'll cover in this book, without purchasing an Apple Developer Program membership. That means you can run most of the examples in this book on your iPhone or iPad for free! However, the free option does not give you the ability to distribute your applications on Apple's App Store. For those capabilities, you'll need to sign up for one of the other options, which aren't free.

- *The Standard program costs $99/year*: It provides a host of development tools and resources, technical support, and distribution of your applications via Apple's iOS and Mac App Stores. Your membership lets you develop and distribute applications for iOS, watchOS, tvOS, and macOS.

- *The Enterprise program costs $299/year*: It is designed for companies developing proprietary, in-house iOS applications.

For more details on these programs, visit `https://developer.apple.com/programs` (see Figure 1-4). If you are an independent developer, you can definitely get away with just buying the standard program membership. You don't have to do that until you need to run an application that uses a feature such as iCloud that requires a paid membership, you want to post a question to the Apple Developer Forums, or you are ready to deploy your application to the App Store.

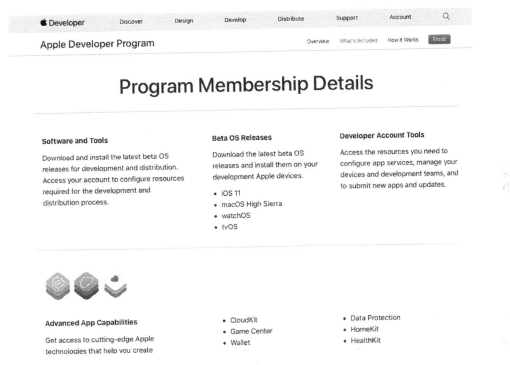

Figure 1-4. Signing up for a paid membership gives you access to beta and OS tools releases

Because iOS supports an always-connected mobile device that uses other companies' wireless infrastructures, Apple has needed to place far more restrictions on iOS developers than it ever has on Mac developers (who are able—at the moment, anyway—to write and distribute programs with absolutely no oversight or approval from Apple). Even though the iPod touch and the Wi-Fi-only versions of the iPad don't use anyone else's infrastructure, they're still subject to these same restrictions.

Apple has not added restrictions to be mean but rather as an attempt to minimize the chances of malicious or poorly written programs being distributed and degrading performance on the shared network. Developing for iOS may appear to present a lot of hoops to jump through, but Apple has expended quite an effort to make the process as painless as possible. Also consider that $99 is still much less expensive than buying, for example, any of the paid versions of Visual Studio, which is Microsoft's software development IDE.

Things You Should Know

In this book, I'm going to assume you already have some programming knowledge in general and object-oriented programming in particular (you know what classes, objects, loops, and variables are, for example). But of course, I don't assume you are already familiar with Swift. There's an appendix at the end of the book that introduces you to both Swift and the Playground feature in Xcode that makes it easy to try the features. If you'd like to learn more about Swift after reading the material in the appendix, the best way to do so is to go directly to the source and read *The Swift Programming Language*, which is Apple's own guide and reference to the language. You can get it from the iBooks store or from the iOS developer site at https://developer. apple.com/library/ios/documentation/Swift/Conceptual/Swift_Programming_Language/index.html.

You also need to be familiar with iOS itself as a user. Just as you would with any platform for which you wanted to write an application, get to know the nuances and quirks of the iPhone, iPad, or iPod touch. Take the time to get familiar with the iOS interface and with the way Apple's iPhone and/or iPad applications look and feel.

Because the different terms can be a little confusing at first, Table 1-1 shows the relationships of IDEs, application programming interfaces (APIs), and languages to the platform operating system for which you are developing.

Table 1-1. *Platform, Tools, Language Relationships*

Develop For...	IDE	API	Language
macOS	Xcode	Cocoa	Objective-C, Swift
iOS	Xcode	Cocoa Touch	Objective-C, Swift

Some Unique Aspects About Working in iOS

If you have never programmed for the Mac using Cocoa, you may find Cocoa Touch—the application framework you'll be using to write iOS applications—a little alien. It has some fundamental differences from other common application frameworks, such as those used when building .NET or Java applications. Don't worry too much if you feel a little lost at first. Just keep plugging away at the exercises and it will all start to fall into place after a while.

■ **Note**   You'll see a lot of reference to *frameworks* in this book. Although the term is a little vague and used in a few different ways depending on the context, a *framework* is a collection of "stuff," which may include a library, several libraries, scripts, UI elements, and anything else in a single collection. A framework's stuff is generally associated with some specific function such as location services using the Core Location framework.

If you have written programs using Cocoa, a lot of what you'll find in the iOS SDK will be familiar to you. A great many classes are unchanged from the versions that are used to develop for macOS. Even those that are different tend to follow the same basic principles and similar design patterns. However, several differences exist between Cocoa and Cocoa Touch.

Regardless of your background, you need to keep in mind some key differences between iOS development and desktop application development. These differences are discussed in the following sections.

iOS Supports a Single Application at a Time—Mostly

On iOS, it's usually the case that only one application can be active and displayed on the screen at any given time. Since iOS 4, applications have been able to run in the background after the user presses the Home button, but even that is limited to a narrow set of situations and you must code for it specifically. In iOS 9, Apple added the ability for two applications to run in the foreground and share the screen, but for that, the user needs to have one of the more recent iPads.

When your application isn't active or running in the background, it doesn't receive any attention whatsoever from the CPU. iOS allows background processing, but making your apps play nicely in this situation will require some effort on your part.

There's Only a Single Window

Desktop and laptop operating systems allow many running programs to coexist, each with the ability to create and control multiple windows. However, unless you attach an external screen or use AirPlay and your application is coded to handle more than one screen, iOS gives your application just one "window" to work with. All of your application's interaction with the user takes place inside this one window, and its size is fixed at the size of the screen, unless your user has activated the Multitasking feature, in which case your application may have to give up some of the screen to another application.

For Security, Access to Device Resources Is Limited

Programs on a desktop or a laptop computer pretty much have access to everything that the user who launched it does. However, iOS seriously restricts which parts of the device your program can use.

You can read and write files only from the part of iOS's file system that was created for your application. This area is called your application's *sandbox*. Your sandbox is where your application will store documents, preferences, and every other kind of data it may need to retain.

Your application is also constrained in some other ways. You will not be able to access low-number network ports on iOS, for example, or do anything else that would typically require root or administrative access on a desktop computer.

Apps Need to Respond Quickly

Because of the way it is used, iOS needs to be snappy, and it expects the same of your application. When your program is launched, you need to get your application open, the preferences and data loaded, and the main view shown on the screen as fast as possible—in no more than a few seconds. Your app should have low latency.

▓ **Note**   By latency, I do not mean speed. Speed and latency are commonly interchanged, but that is not really correct. *Latency* refers to the time between an action is taken and a result happens. If the user presses the Home button, iOS goes home, and you must quickly save everything before iOS suspends your application in the background. If you take longer than five seconds to save and give up control, your application process will be killed, regardless of whether you finished saving. There is an API that allows your app to ask for additional time to work when it's about to go dark, but you've got to know how to use it. So, in general, you want to get things done quickly, which might mean dumping and losing unnecessary information.

Limited Screen Size

The iPhone's screen is really nice. When introduced, it was the highest-resolution screen available on a handheld consumer device, by far. But even today, the iPhone display isn't all that big, and as a result, you have a lot less room to work with than on modern computers. The screen was just 320 × 480 on the first few iPhone generations, and it was later doubled in both directions to 640 × 960 with the introduction of the iPhone 4's Retina display. Today, the screen of the largest iPhone (the iPhone 6/6s Plus) measures 1080 × 1920 pixels. That sounds like a decent number of pixels, but keep in mind that these high-density displays (for which Apple uses the term *Retina*) are crammed into pretty small form factors, which has a big impact on the kinds of applications and interactivity you can offer on an iPhone and even an iPad. Table 1-2 lists the sizes of the screens of all the current commonly used iPhone devices that are supported by iOS 11 at the time of writing.

Table 1-2. iOS Device Screen Sizes

Device	Hardware Size	Software Size	Scaling
iPhone 7	750 × 1334	320 × 568	3×
iPhone 7s	1080 × 1920	375 × 667	3×
iPhone 6s	750 × 1334	375 × 667	3×
iPhone 6s Plus	1080 × 1920	414 × 736	3×
iPhone SE	640 × 1136	320 × 568	2×

The hardware size is the actual physical size of the screen in pixels. However, when writing software, the size that really matters is the one in the Software Size column. As you can see, in most cases, the software size reflects only half that of the actual hardware. This situation came about when Apple introduced the first Retina device, which had twice as many pixels in each direction as its predecessor. If Apple had done nothing special, all existing applications would have been drawn at half-scale on the new Retina screen, which would have made them unusable. So, Apple chose to internally scale everything that applications draw by a factor of 2 so that they would fill the new screen without any code changes. This internal scaling by a factor of 2 applies iPhone 6s and iPhone SE, while the 6s Plus, 7, and 7 Plus use a factor of 3×. For the most part, though, you don't need to worry too much about the fact that your application is being scaled—all you need to do is work within the software screen size, and iOS will do the rest.

The only exceptions to this rule center on bitmap images. Since bitmap images are, by their nature, fixed in size, for best results you can't really use the same image on a Retina screen as you would on a non-Retina screen. If you try to do that, you'll see that iOS scales your image up for a device that has a Retina screen, which has the effect of introducing blur. You can fix this by including separate copies of each image for the 2× and 3× Retina screens. iOS will pick the version that matches the screen of the device on which your application is running.

▨ **Note** If you look back at Table 1-1, you'll see that it appears that the scale factor in the fourth column is the same as the ratio of the hardware size to the software size. For example, on the iPhone 6s, the hardware width is 750 and software width is 375, which is a ratio of 2:1. Look carefully, though, and you'll see that there's something different about the iPhone 6/6s Plus. The ratio of the hardware width to the software width is 1080/414, which is 2.608:1, and the same applies to the height ratio. So, in terms of the hardware, the iPhone 6s Plus does not have a true 3× Retina display. However, as far as the software is concerned, a 3× scale is used, which means that an application written to use the software screen size of 414 × 736 is first logically mapped to a virtual screen size of 1242 × 2208, and the result is then scaled down a little to match the actual hardware size of 1080 × 1920. Fortunately, this doesn't require you to do anything special because iOS takes care of all the details.

Limited Device Resources

Software developers from just a decade or two ago laugh at the idea of a machine with at least 512MB of RAM and 16GB of storage being in any way resource-constrained, but it's true. Developing for iOS doesn't reside in the same league as trying to write a complex spreadsheet application on a machine with 48KB of memory. But given the graphical nature of iOS and all it is capable of doing, running out of memory happens from time to time. Lately, Apple has significantly boosted RAM to a minimum of 2GB.

The iOS devices available right now have either 2GB (iPad, iPad mini 4, iPhone 6s/6s Plus, and iPhone SE), 3GB (iPhone 7s Plus), or 4GB (both iPad Pro models), though this will likely increase over time. Some of that memory is used for the screen buffer and by other system processes. Usually, no more than half of that memory is left for your application to use, and the amount can be considerably less, especially now that other apps can be running in the background.

Although that may sound like it leaves a pretty decent amount of memory for such a small computer, there is another factor to consider when it comes to memory on iOS. Modern computer operating systems like macOS take chunks of memory that aren't being used and write them to disk in something called a *swap file*. The swap file allows applications to keep running, even when they have requested more memory than is actually available on the computer. iOS, however, will not write volatile memory, such as application data, to a swap file. As a result, the amount of memory available to your application is constrained by the amount of unused physical memory in the iOS device.

Cocoa Touch has built-in mechanisms for letting your application know that memory is getting low. When that happens, your application must free up unneeded memory or risk being forced to quit.

Features Unique to iOS Devices

Since I've mentioned that Cocoa Touch is missing some features that Cocoa has, it seems only fair to mention that the iOS SDK contains some functionality that is not currently present in Cocoa—or, at least, is not available on every Mac.

- The iOS SDK provides a way for your application to determine the iOS device's current geographic coordinates using Core Location.

- Most iOS devices have built-in cameras and photo libraries, and the SDK provides mechanisms that allow your application to access both.

- iOS devices have built-in motion sensors that let you detect how your device is being held and moved.

User Input and Display

Since iOS devices do not have a physical keyboard or a mouse, you interact differently with your user than you do when programming for a general-purpose computer. Fortunately, most of that interaction is handled for you. For example, if you add a text field to your application, iOS knows to bring up a keyboard when the user touches that field, without you needing to write any extra code.

▓ **Note** All iOS devices allow you to connect an external keyboard via Bluetooth or the Lightning connector, which provides a nice keyboard experience and saves you some screen real estate. Currently, iOS does not support connecting a mouse.

What's in This Book

When I first started programming applications for iOS, then called iPhone OS, I picked up the original edition of this book based on Objective-C. I became, at least in my mind, a capable and productive app developer, even making some money with my products. So, I want to return the favor by providing this latest and greatest edition to help you achieve that same level of success and more. So, here's what I'm going to be covering:

- In Chapter 2, you'll learn how to use Xcode's user interface (UI) developer tool, Interface Builder, to create a simple visual result, placing some text on the screen.

- In Chapter 3, I'll show you how to start interacting with the user, building an application that dynamically updates displayed text at runtime based on buttons the user presses.

- Chapter 4 continues Chapter 3's topic by introducing you to several more of iOS's standard user interface controls. I'll also demonstrate how to use alerts and action sheets to prompt users to make a decision or to inform them that something out of the ordinary has occurred.

- In Chapter 5, you'll look at handling rotation and Auto Layout, the mechanisms that allow iOS applications to be used in both portrait and landscape modes.

- In Chapter 6, I'll start discussing more advanced user interfaces and explore creating applications that support multiple views. I'll show you how to change which view is shown to the user at runtime, which will greatly enhance the potential of your apps.

- iOS supports tab bars and pickers as part of the standard iOS user interface. In Chapter 7, you'll learn how to implement these interface elements.

- In Chapter 8, I'll cover table views, the primary way of providing lists of data to the user and the foundation of hierarchical navigation–based applications. You'll also see how to let the user search your application data.

- One of the most common iOS application interfaces, the hierarchical list, lets you drill down to see more data or more details. In Chapter 9, you'll learn what's involved in implementing this standard type of interface.

- From the beginning, iOS applications have used table views to display dynamic, vertically scrolling lists of components. A few years ago, Apple introduced a new class called `UICollectionView` that takes this concept a few steps further, giving developers lots of new flexibility in laying out visual components. Chapter 10 introduces you to collection views.

- Chapter 11 shows you how to build master-detail applications and present a list of items (such as the e-mails in a mailbox), allowing the user to view the details of each individual item, one at a time. You'll also work with iOS controls that support this concept, originally developed for the iPad and now also available on the iPhone.

- In Chapter 12, you'll look at implementing application settings, which is iOS's mechanism for letting users set their application-level preferences.

- Chapter 13 covers data management on iOS. I'll talk about creating objects to hold application data and show how that data can be persisted to iOS's file system. I'll present the basics of using Core Data, allowing you to save and retrieve data easily; however, for an in-depth discussion of Core Data, you'll want to check out *Pro iOS Persistence Using Core Data* by Michael Privat and Robert Warner (Apress, 2014).

- Everyone loves to draw, so you'll look at doing some custom drawing in Chapter 14, where I'll introduce you to the Core Graphics system.

- Finally, the appendix introduces the Swift programming language in its current state and covers all the features that you'll need to know to understand the example code in this book.

What's New in This Update?

After the first edition of this book hit the bookstores, the iOS development community grew at a phenomenal rate. The SDK continually evolved, with Apple releasing a steady stream of SDK updates. iOS 11 and Xcode 9 contain many new enhancements. I've been hard at work updating the book to cover the new technologies that you'll need to be aware of to start writing iOS applications.

Swift and Xcode Versions

Though having been out for more than two years now, Swift is still in a state of flux and likely to remain so for some time to come. Interestingly, Apple promised that the compiled binaries for applications written now will work on later versions of iOS, but it is *not* guaranteed that the source code for those same applications will continue to compile. As a result, it is possible that example code that compiled and worked with the version of Xcode that was current when this book was published no longer works by the time you read it. Xcode 6.0 shipped with Swift version 1, Xcode 6.3 had Swift version 1.2, Xcode 7 introduced Swift 2, and Xcode 8 introduced Swift 3. In this book, I'm starting off with a beta 2 release of Xcode 9 and Swift 4.

If you find that some of the example source code no longer compiles with the release of Xcode that you are using, please visit the book's page at `www.apress.com` and download the latest version. If after doing this you are still having problems, please bring it to my attention by submitting an erratum on the Apress web site.

Let's Get Started

iOS provides an incredible computing platform and an exciting new frontier for your development career. You'll likely find programming for iOS to be a new experience—different from working on any other platform. For everything that looks familiar, there will be something alien, but as you work through the book's code, the concepts should all come together and start to make sense.

Keep in mind that the examples in this book are not simply a checklist that, when completed, magically grants you iOS developer expert status. Make sure you understand what you did and why before moving on to the next project. Don't be afraid to make changes to the code. By observing the results of your experimentation, you can wrap your head around the complexities of coding in an environment like Cocoa Touch.

That said, if you've already downloaded and installed Xcode, turn the page and take your next steps to becoming a real iOS app developer.

CHAPTER 2

Writing Your First App

I want to get you started right away with a feel for what this is all about and to motivate your continued progress toward being a great developer, so let's get to it and do something with your iPhone (see Figure 2-1). In this chapter, using Xcode, let's create a small iOS application that will display "Hello, World!" on the screen. You'll look at what's involved in creating the project in Xcode, work through the specifics of using Xcode's Interface Builder to design your application's user interface, and then execute your application on the iOS simulator and an actual device. You'll finish up by giving your application an icon to make it feel more like a real iOS application.

Figure 2-1. *The results of the app you create in this chapter might seem simple, but your work will start you down the road to potential iOS greatness*

© Molly K. Maskrey 2017
M. K. Maskrey, *Beginning iPhone Development with Swift 4*, https://doi.org/10.1007/978-1-4842-3072-5_2

Creating the Hello World Project

By now, you should have installed Xcode 9 and the iOS SDK onto your Mac. You can also download the book's source code archive from the Apress web site (www.apress.com). While you're at it, take a look at the book forums at http://forum.learncocoa.org. The book forums are a great place to discuss iOS development, get your questions answered, and meet up with like-minded people.

▓ **Note**   Even though you have the complete set of project files at your disposal in this book's source code archive, you'll get more out of the book if you create each project by hand, rather than simply running the version you downloaded. By doing that, you'll gain familiarity and expertise working with the various application development tools.

The project you're going to build in this chapter is contained in the Hello World folder of the source code archive.

Before you can start, you need to launch Xcode, the tool you'll be using to do most of what you do in this book. After downloading it from the Mac App Store or the Apple Developer site, you'll find it installed in the /Applications folder, as with most Mac applications. You'll be using Xcode a lot, so you might want to consider dragging it to your dock so you'll have ready access to it.

If this is your first time using Xcode, don't worry; I'll walk you through every step involved in creating a new project. If you're already an old hand but haven't worked with Xcode 7, you may find that some things have changed (mostly for the better, I think).

When you first launch Xcode, you'll be presented with a welcome window like the one shown in Figure 2-2. From here, you can choose to create a new project, connect to a version control system to check out an existing project, or select from a list of recently opened projects. The welcome window gives you a nice starting point, covering some of the most common tasks you might do after starting Xcode. All of these actions can be accessed through the menu as well, so close the window to proceed. If you would rather not see this window in the future, just deselect the "Show this window when Xcode launches" check box at the bottom of the window before closing it.

Figure 2-2. *The Xcode welcome window*

Create a new project by selecting New ➤ Project from the File menu (or by pressing ⌘⇧N). A new project window will open, showing you the project template selection sheet (see Figure 2-3). From this sheet, you'll choose a project template to use as a starting point for building your application. The bar at the top is divided into five sections: iOS, watchOS, tvOS, macOS, and Cross-platform. Since you're building an iOS application, select the iOS button to reveal the application templates.

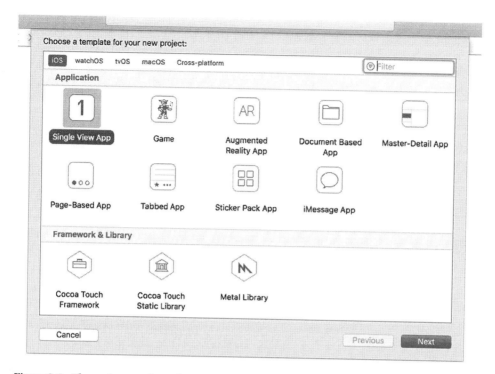

Figure 2-3. *The project template selection sheet lets you select from various templates when creating a new project*

Each of the icons shown in the upper-right pane in Figure 2-3 represents a separate project template that can be used as a starting point for your iOS applications. The icon labeled Single View App contains the simplest template and the one you'll be using for the first several chapters. The other templates provide additional code and/or resources needed to create common iPhone and iPad application interfaces, as you'll see in later chapters.

Click the Single View App (see Figure 2-3) and then click the Next button. You'll see the project options sheet, which should look like Figure 2-4. On this sheet, you need to specify the product name and company identifier for your project. Xcode will combine these to generate a unique bundle identifier for your app. You'll also see a field that lets you enter an organization name, which Xcode will use to automatically insert a copyright notice into every source code file you create. Name your product **Hello World** and enter an organization name and identifier in the Organization Name and Organization Identifier fields, as shown in Figure 2-4. Don't use the same name and identifier as the ones shown in Figure 2-4. For reasons that you'll see when you try to run this application on a real device at the end of the chapter, you'll need to choose an identifier that's unique to you (or your company).

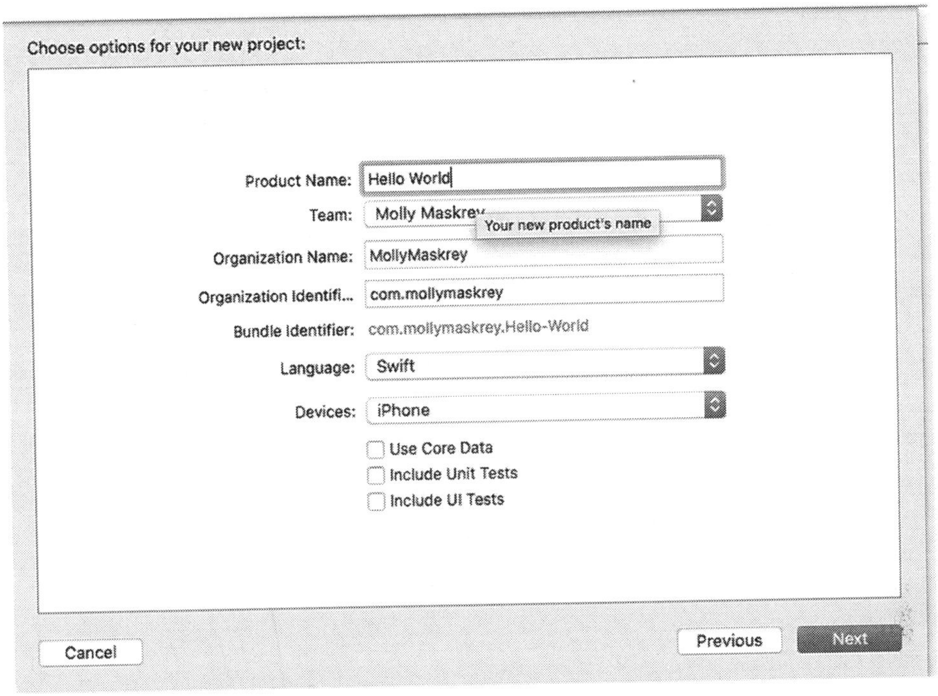

Choose options for your new project:

Product Name: Hello World

Team: Molly Maskrey

Your new product's name

Organization Name: MollyMaskrey

Organization Identifi... com.mollymaskrey

Bundle Identifier: com.mollymaskrey.Hello-World

Language: Swift

Devices: iPhone

☐ Use Core Data
☐ Include Unit Tests
☐ Include UI Tests

Cancel   Previous   Next

Figure 2-4. Selecting a product name and organization identifier for your project

The Language field lets you select the programming language you want to use, choosing between Objective-C and Swift, but since all the examples in the book are in Swift, the appropriate choice here is, of course, Swift.

You also need to specify the devices. In other words, Xcode wants to know if you're building an app for the iPhone and iPod touch, if you're building an app for the iPad, or if you're building a universal application that will run on all iOS devices. Select iPhone in the Devices drop-down menu if it's not already selected. This tells Xcode that you'll be targeting this particular app at the iPhone. For the first few chapters of the book, you'll be using the iPhone device, but don't worry—I'll cover the iPad also.

Leave the Core Data check box unselected—you'll make use of it later. You can also leave the Include Unit Tests and Include UI Tests check boxes unselected. Xcode has good support for testing your applications, but that's outside the scope of this book, so you don't need Xcode to include support for them in your project. Click Next again and you'll be asked where to save your new project using a standard save sheet (see Figure 2-5). If you haven't already done so, use the New Folder button to create a new master directory for these book projects and then return to Xcode and navigate into that directory. Before you click the Create button, take note of the Source Control check box. Git isn't covered in this book, but Xcode includes some support for using Git and other kinds of source control management (SCM) tools. If you are already familiar with Git and want to use it, select this check box; otherwise, feel free to turn it off.

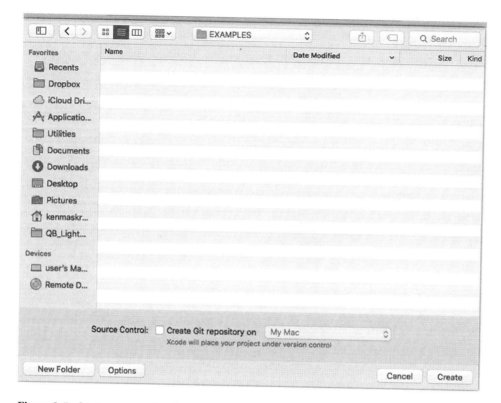

Figure 2-5. *Saving your project in a project folder on your hard drive*

Taking a Look at the Xcode Project Window

After you dismiss the save sheet, Xcode will create and then open your project. You will see a new project window, as shown in Figure 2-6. There's a lot of information in this window; it's where you'll spend a lot of iOS development time.

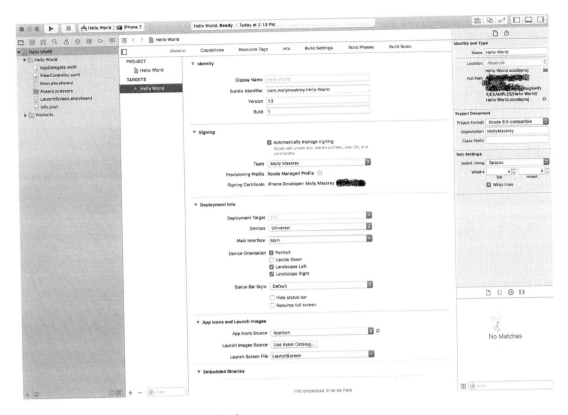

Figure 2-6. *The Hello World project in Xcode*

The Toolbar

The top of the Xcode project window is called the *toolbar* (see Figure 2-7). On the left side of the toolbar you'll see controls to start and stop running your project, as well as a pop-up menu to select the scheme you want to run. A scheme brings together target and build settings, and the toolbar pop-up menus let you select a specific setup quickly and easily.

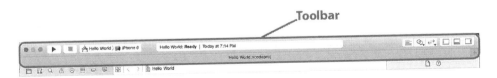

Figure 2-7. *The Xcode toolbar*

The big box in the middle of the toolbar is the *activity view*. As its name implies, the activity view displays any actions or processes that are currently happening. For example, when you run your project, the activity view gives you a running commentary on the various steps it's taking to build your application. If you encounter any errors or warnings, that information is displayed here, as well. If you click the warning or error, you'll go directly to the Issue Navigator, which provides more information about the warning or error, as described in the next section.

On the right side of the toolbar are two sets of buttons. The left set lets you switch between three different editor configurations.

- *Editor Area*: The Editor Area gives you a single pane dedicated to editing a file or project-specific configuration values.

- *Assistant Editor*: The powerful Assistant Editor splits the Editor Area into multiple panes, left, right, top, and bottom. The pane on the right is generally used to display a file that relates to the file on the left or that you might need to refer to while editing the file on the left. You can manually specify what goes into each pane, or you can let Xcode decide what's most appropriate for the task at hand. For example, if you're designing your user interface on the left, Xcode will show you the code that the user interface is able to interact with on the right. You'll see the Assistant Editor at work throughout the book.

- *Comparison view*: The Version Editor button converts the editor pane into a time machine–like comparison view that works with version control systems like Git. You can compare the current version of a source file with a previously committed version or compare any two earlier versions with each other.

To the right of the editor buttons is a set of toggle buttons that show and hide large panes on the left and right sides of the editor pane, as well as the debug area at the bottom of the window. Click each of those buttons a few times to see these panes in action. You'll explore how these are used soon.

The Navigator

Just below the toolbar on the left side of the project window is called the *navigator*. The navigator offers eight views that show you different aspects of your project. Click each of the icons at the top of the navigator to switch among the following navigators, going from left to right:

- *Project Navigator*: This view contains a list of files in your project, as shown in Figure 2-8. You can store references to everything you expect—from source code files to artwork, data models, property list (or .plist) files (discussed in the "Taking a Closer Look at the Hello World Project" section later in this chapter), and even other project files. By storing multiple projects in a single workspace, those projects can easily share resources. If you click any file in the navigator view, that file will display in the Editor Area. In addition to viewing the file, you can edit it, if it's a file that Xcode knows how to edit.

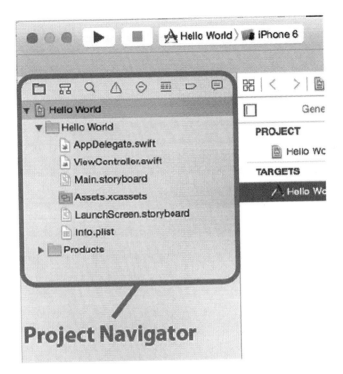

Project Navigator

Figure 2-8. *The Xcode Project Navigator. Click one of the eight icons at the top of the view to switch navigators.*

- *Symbol Navigator*: As its name implies, this navigator focuses on the symbols defined in the workspace (see Figure 2-9). *Symbols* are basically the items that the compiler recognizes, such as classes, enumerations, `struct`s, and global variables.

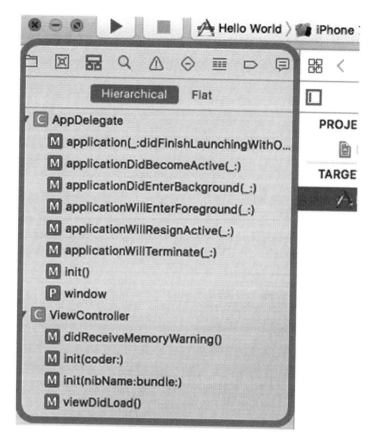

Figure 2-9. *The Xcode Symbol Navigator. Open the disclosure triangle to explore the classes, methods, and other symbols defined within each group.*

- *Find Navigator:* You'll use this navigator to perform searches on all the files in your workspace (see Figure 2-10). At the top of this pane is a multileveled pop-up control letting you select Replace instead of Find, along with other options for applying search criteria to the text you enter. Below the text field, other controls let you choose to search in the entire project or just a portion of it and specify whether searching should be case-sensitive.

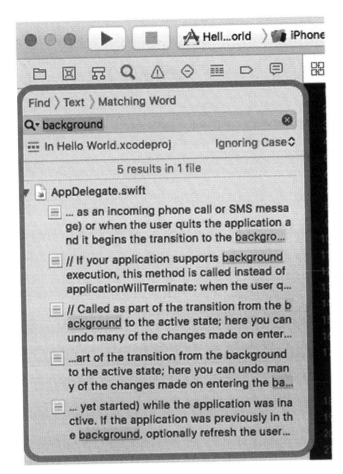

Figure 2-10. *The Xcode Find Navigator. Be sure to check out the pop-up menus hidden under the word Find and under the buttons that are below the search field.*

- *Issue Navigator*: When you build your project, any errors or warnings will appear in this navigator, and a message detailing the number of errors will appear in the activity view at the top of the window (see Figure 2-11). When you click an error in the Issue Navigator, you'll jump to the appropriate line of code in the editor.

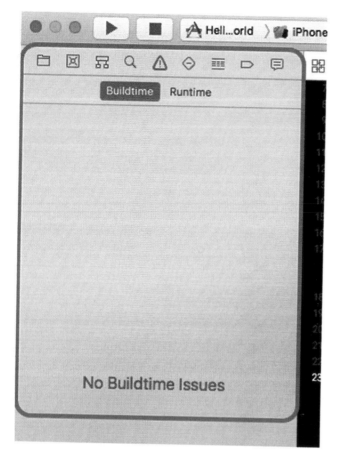

Figure 2-11. *The Xcode Issue Navigator. This is where you'll find your compiler errors and warnings.*

- *Test Navigator*: If you're using Xcode's integrated unit testing capabilities (a topic that isn't covered in this book), this is where you'll see the results of your unit tests. Since you didn't include unit tests in the example project, this navigator is empty (see Figure 2-12).

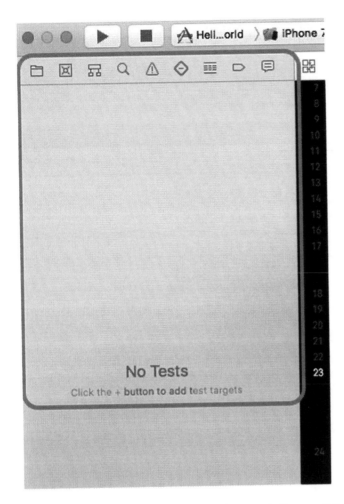

Figure 2-12. *The Xcode Test Navigator. The output of your unit tests will appear here.*

- *Debug Navigator:* This navigator provides your main view into the debugging process (see Figure 2-13). If you are new to debugging, you might check out this part of the Xcode Overview: https://developer.apple.com/support/debugging/. The Debug Navigator lists the stack frame for each active thread. A *stack frame* is a list of the functions or methods that have been called previously, in the order they were called. Click a method, and the associated code appears in the editor pane. In the editor, there will be a second pane that lets you control the debugging process, display and modify data values, and access the low-level debugger. A button at the bottom of the Debug Navigator allows you to control which stack frames are visible. Another button lets you choose whether to show all threads or just the threads that have crashed or stopped on a breakpoint. Hover your mouse over each of these buttons in turn to see which is which.

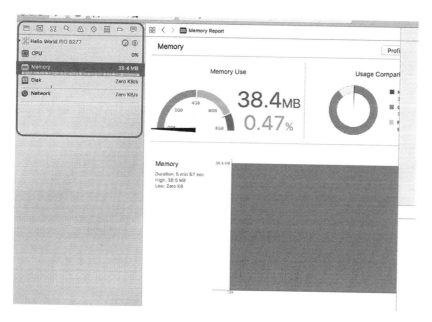

Figure 2-13. *The Xcode Debug Navigator. Controls at the bottom of the navigator let you control the level of detail you want to see.*

- *Breakpoint Navigator*: The Breakpoint Navigator lets you see all the breakpoints that you've set, as shown in Figure 2-14. Breakpoints are, as the name suggests, points in your code where the application will stop running (or *break*) so that you can look at the values in variables and do other tasks needed to debug your application. The list of breakpoints in this navigator is organized by file. Click a breakpoint in the list and that line will appear in the editor pane. Be sure to check out the plus sign (+) button at the lower-left corner of the project window when in the Breakpoint Navigator. This button opens a pop-up that lets you add four different types of breakpoints, including symbolic breakpoints, which are the ones you will use most often.

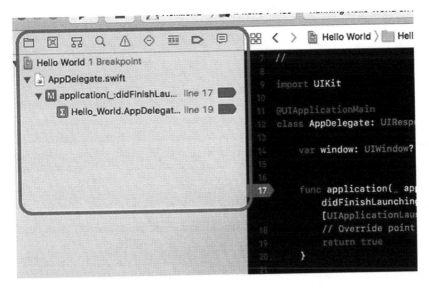

Figure 2-14. *The Xcode Breakpoint Navigator. The list of breakpoints is organized by file.*

- *Report Navigator*: This navigator keeps a history of your recent build results and run logs, as shown in Figure 2-15. Click a specific log, and the build command and any build issues are displayed in the edit pane.

Figure 2-15. *The Xcode Report Navigator. The Report Navigator displays a list of builds, with the details associated with a selected view displayed in the editor pane.*

The Jump Bar

Across the top of the editor, you'll find a control called the *jump bar*. With a single click, the jump bar allows you to jump to a specific element in the hierarchy you are currently navigating. For example, Figure 2-16 shows a source file being edited in the editor pane.

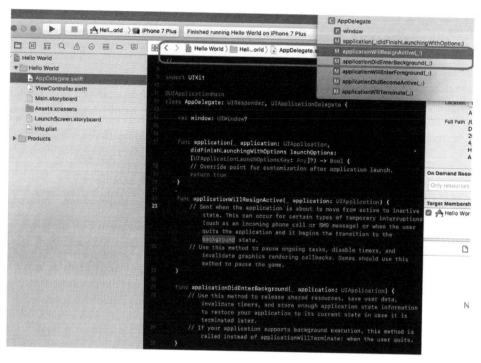

Figure 2-16. *The Xcode editor pane showing the jump bar, with a source code file selected. The submenu shows the list of methods in the selected file.*

The jump bar sits just above the source code. Here's how it breaks down:

- The funky-looking icon at the left end of the jump bar is actually a pop-up menu that displays submenus listing recent files, counterparts, superclasses and subclasses, siblings, categories, includes, and more. The submenus shown here will take you to just about any other code that touches the code currently open in the editor.

- To the right of the menu are left and right arrows that take you back to the previous file and return you to the next file, respectively.

- The jump bar includes a segmented pop-up that displays the hierarchical path to reach the selected file in the project. You can click any segment showing the name of a group or a file to see all the other files and groups located at the same point in the hierarchy. The final segment shows a list of items within the selected file. In Figure 2-16, you see that the tail end of the jump bar is a pop-up that shows the methods and other symbols contained within the currently selected file. The jump bar shows the AppDelegate.swift file with a submenu listing the symbols defined in that file.

Look for the jump bar as you make your way through the various interface elements of Xcode.

▧ **Tip** Like most of Apple's macOS applications, Xcode includes full support for full-screen mode. Just click the full-screen button in the upper right of the project window to try out distraction-free, full-screen coding!

XCODE KEYBOARD SHORTCUTS

If you prefer navigating with keyboard shortcuts instead of mousing to on-screen controls, you'll like what Xcode has to offer. Most actions that you will do regularly in Xcode have keyboard shortcuts assigned to them, such as ⌘**B** to build your application or ⌘**N** to create a new file.

You can change all of Xcode's keyboard shortcuts, as well as assign shortcuts to commands that don't already have one, using Xcode's preferences on the Key Bindings tab.

A really handy keyboard shortcut is ⌘⇧**O**, which is Xcode's Open Quickly feature. After clicking it, start typing the name of a file, setting, or symbol, and Xcode will present you with a list of options. When you narrow down the list to the file you want, hitting the Return key will open it in the editing pane, allowing you to switch files in just a few keystrokes.

The Utilities Area

As mentioned earlier, the second-to-last button on the right side of the Xcode toolbar opens and closes the Utilities area. The upper part of the utilities area is a context-sensitive inspector panel, with contents that change depending on what is being displayed in the editor pane. The lower part of the Utilities area contains a few different kinds of resources that you can drag into your project. You'll see examples of this throughout the book.

Interface Builder

Earlier versions of Xcode included a separate interface design application called Interface Builder (IB), which allowed you to build and customize your project's user interface. One of the major changes introduced in later versions of Xcode integrated Interface Builder into the workspace itself. Interface Builder is no longer a separate stand-alone application, which means you don't need to jump back and forth between Xcode and Interface Builder as your code and interface evolve.

You'll be working extensively with Xcode's interface-building functionality throughout the book, digging into all the various details. In fact, you'll start working with Interface Builder later in this chapter.

Integrated Compiler and Debugger

Xcode has a fast, smart compiler and low-level debugger, which improve with each release.

For many years, Apple used the GNU Compiler Collection (GCC) as the basis for its compiler technology. But over the course of the past few years, it has shifted over completely to the Low Level Virtual Machine (LLVM) compiler. LLVM generates code that is faster by far than that generated by the traditional GCC. In addition to creating faster code, LLVM knows more about your code, so it can generate smarter, more precise error messages and warnings.

Xcode is also tightly integrated with LLVM, which gives it some new superpowers. Xcode can offer more precise code completion, and it can make educated guesses as to the actual intent of a piece of code when it produces a warning and offers a pop-up menu of likely fixes. This makes errors such as misspelled symbol names and mismatched parentheses a breeze to find and fix.

LLVM brings to the table a sophisticated static analyzer that can scan your code for a wide variety of potential problems, including problems with memory management. In fact, LLVM is so smart about this that it can handle most memory management tasks for you, as long as you abide by a few simple rules when writing your code. You'll begin looking at the new feature called Automatic Reference Counting (ARC) in the next chapter.

Taking a Closer Look at the Hello World Project

Now that you've explored the Xcode project window, let's take a look at the files that make up your new Hello World project. Switch to the Project Navigator by clicking the leftmost of the eight navigator icons in your workspace (as discussed in the "The Navigator" section earlier in the chapter) or by pressing ⌘1.

■ **Note** You can access the eight navigator configurations using the keyboard shortcuts ⌘1 to ⌘8. The numbers correspond to the icons starting on the left, so ⌘1 is the Project Navigator, ⌘2 is the Symbol Navigator, and so on, up to ⌘8, which takes you to the Report Navigator.

The first item in the Project Navigator list bears the same name as your project—in this case, Hello World. This item represents your entire project, and it's also where project-specific configuration can be done. If you single-click it, you'll be able to edit a number of project configuration settings in Xcode's editor. You don't need to worry about those project-specific settings now, however. At the moment, the defaults will work fine.

Flip back to Figure 2-8. Notice that the disclosure triangle to the left of Hello World is open, showing a number of subfolders (which are called *groups* in Xcode).

- *Hello World*: The first group, which is always named after your project, is where you will spend the bulk of your time. This is where most of the code that you write will go, as will the files that make up your application's user interface. You are free to create subgroups under the Hello World group to help organize your code. You're even allowed to add groups of your own if you prefer a different organizational approach. While you won't touch most of the files in this folder until the next chapter, there is one file you will explore when you use Interface Builder in the next section. That file is called Main.storyboard, and it contains the user interface elements specific to your project's main view controller. The Hello World group also contains files and resources that aren't Swift source files but that are necessary to your project. Among these files is one called Info.plist, which contains important information about the application, such as its name, whether it requires any specific features to be present on the devices on which it is run, and so on. In earlier versions of Xcode, these files were placed into a separate group called Supporting Files.

- *Hello WorldTests*: This group is created if you enable unit testing for the project (you didn't, so it's not there for this project), and it contains the initial files you'll need if you want to write some unit tests for your application code. I'm not going to talk about unit testing in this book, but it's nice that Xcode can set up some of these things for you in each new project you create if you want. Like the Hello World group, this one contains its own Info.plist file.

- *Products*: This group contains the application that this project produces when it is built. If you expand Products, you'll see an item called Hello World.app, which is the application that this particular project creates. If the project had been created with unit testing enabled, it would also contain an item called Hello WorldTests. xctest, which represents the testing code. Both of these items are called *build targets*. Because you have never built either of these, they're both red, which is Xcode's way of telling you that a file reference points to something that is not there.

▓ **Note**   The "folders" in the navigator area do not necessarily correspond to folders in your Mac's file system. They are just logical groupings within Xcode that help you keep everything organized and make it faster and easier to find what you're looking for while working on your application. Often, the items contained in those groups are stored directly in the project's directory, but you can store them anywhere—even outside your project folder if you want. The hierarchy inside Xcode is completely independent of the file system hierarchy, so moving a file out of the Hello World group in Xcode, for example, will not change the file's location on your hard drive.

Introducing Xcode's Interface Builder

In your project window's Project Navigator, expand the Hello World group, if it's not already open, and then select the Main.storyboard file. As soon as you do, the file will open in the editor pane, as shown in Figure 2-17. You should see something resembling an all-white iOS device centered on a plain white background, which makes a nice backdrop for editing interfaces. This is Xcode's Interface Builder, which is where you'll design your application's user interface.

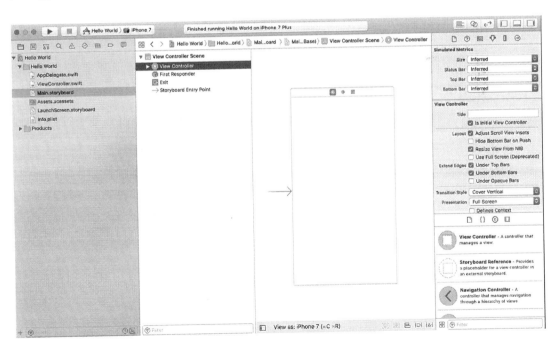

Figure 2-17.   *Selecting Main.storyboard in the Project Navigator opens the file in Interface Builder*

Interface Builder has a long history. It has been around since 1988 and has been used to develop applications for NeXTSTEP, OpenStep, OS X, macOS, and now iOS devices such as the iPhone, iPad, Apple TV, and Apple Watch.

Introducing File Formats

Interface Builder supports a few different file types. The oldest is a binary format that uses the extension .nib, now an XML-based format using the .xib extension. Both of these formats contain exactly the same sort of document, but the .xib version, being a text-based format, has many advantages, especially when you're using any sort of source control software. For the first 20 years of Interface Builder's life, all of its files had the .nib extension. As a result, most developers took to calling Interface Builder files *nib files*. Interface Builder files are often called nib files, regardless of whether the extension actually used for the file is .xib or .nib. In fact, Apple sometimes uses the terms *nib* and *nib file* interspersed through its documentation.

Each nib file can contain any number of objects, but when working on iOS projects, each one will usually contain a single view (often a full-screen view) and the controllers or other objects to which it connects. This lets you compartmentalize your applications, loading the nib file for a view only when it's needed for display. The end result is that you save memory when your app is running on a memory-constrained iOS device. A newly created iOS project has a nib file called LaunchScreen.xib that contains a screen layout that will be shown, by default, when your application launches. I'll talk more about this file at the end of the chapter.

The other file format that IB has supported for the past few years is the *storyboard*. You can think of a storyboard as a "meta-nib file" since it can contain several view controllers, as well as information about how they are connected to each other when the application runs. Unlike a nib file, the contents of which are loaded all at once, a storyboard cannot contain freestanding views, and it never loads all of its contents at once. Instead, you ask it to load particular controllers when you need them. The iOS project templates in Xcode 8 all use storyboards, so all of the examples in this book will start with a storyboard. Although you get only one storyboard for free, you can add more if you need them. Now let's go back to Interface Builder and the Main.storyboard file for the Hello World application (see Figure 2-17).

Exploring the Storyboard

You're now looking at the primary tool for building user interfaces for iOS apps. Let's say you want to create an instance of a button. You could create that button by writing code, but creating an interface object by dragging a button out of a library and specifying its attributes is so much simpler, and it results in the same thing happening at runtime.

The Main.storyboard file you are looking at right now loads automatically when your application launches (for the moment, don't worry about how), so it is the right place to add the objects that make up your application's user interface. When you create objects in Interface Builder, they're instantiated in your program when the storyboard or nib file in which you added them loads. You'll see many examples of this process throughout the book.

Every storyboard gets compartmentalized into one or more *view controllers*, and each view controller has at least one *view*. The view is the part you can see graphically and edit in Interface Builder, while the controller is application code you will write to make things happen when a user interacts with your app. The controllers are where the real action of your application happens.

In IB, you often see a view represented by a rectangle indicating the screen of an iOS device (actually, it represents a view controller, a concept that you'll be introduced to in the next chapter, but this particular view controller covers the whole screen of the device, so it's pretty much the same thing). Near the bottom of the IB window you'll see a drop-down control that begins with *View as*, with a default device type. Click the device type. You can choose which device you'll be creating the layout for, as shown in Figure 2-18.

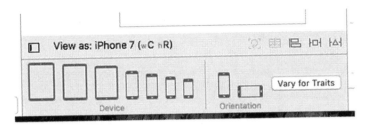

Figure 2-18. *In Xcode 8, IB lets you select the device type and orientation that you work in*

Returning to the storyboard, click anywhere in the outline and you'll see a row of three icons at the top of it, like those shown in Figure 2-17. Move your mouse over each of them and you'll see tooltips pop up with their names: View Controller, First Responder, and Exit. Forget about Exit for now and focus instead on the other two.

- *View Controller*: This represents a controller object that is loaded from file storage along with its associated view. The task of the view controller is to manage what the user sees on the screen. A typical application has several view controllers, one for each of its screens. It is perfectly possible to write an application with just one screen, and hence one view controller, and many of the examples in this book have only one view controller.

- *First Responder*: This is, in basic terms, the object with which the user is currently interacting. If, for example, the user is currently entering data into a text field, that field is the current first responder. The first responder changes as the user interacts with the user interface, and the First Responder icon gives you a convenient way to communicate with whatever control or other object is the current first responder, without needing to write code to determine which control or view that might be.

I'll talk more about these objects starting in the next chapter, so don't worry if it's a bit confusing right now determining when you would use a first responder or how a view controller gets loaded.

Apart from those icons, the rest of what you see in the editing area is the space where you can place graphical objects. But before you get to that, there's one more thing you should see about IB's editor area: its hierarchy view. This view is the Document Outline, as shown in Figure 2-19.

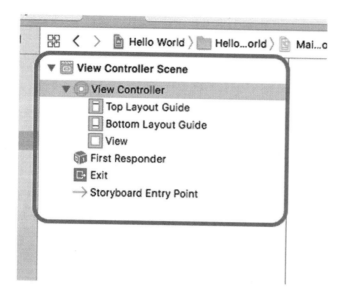

Figure 2-19. *The Document Outline contains a useful hierarchical representation of the storyboard contents*

If the Document Outline is not visible, click the little button in the lower-left corner of the editing area, and you'll see it slide in from the left. It shows everything in the storyboard, split up into *scenes* containing chunks of related content. In this case, you have just one scene, called View Controller Scene. You can see that it contains an item called View Controller, which in turn contains an item called View (along with some other things you'll learn about later). This provides a good way to get an overview of the content where everything you see in the main editing area is mirrored here.

The View icon represents an instance of the UIView class. A UIView object is an area that a user can see and interact with. In this application, you currently have only one view, so this icon represents everything that the user can see in your application. Later, you'll build more complex applications that have several views. For now, just think of this view as an object that the user can see when using your application.

If you click the View icon, Xcode will automatically highlight the square screen outline that I was talking about earlier. This is where you can design your user interface graphically.

Exploring the Utilities Area

The Utilities area makes up the right side of the workspace. If it's not currently selected, click the rightmost of the three View buttons in the toolbar, select View ➤ Utilities ➤ Show Utilities, or press ⌥⌘0 (Option-Command-Zero). The bottom half of the Utilities area, shown in Figure 2-20, is the Library pane, or just plain *library*.

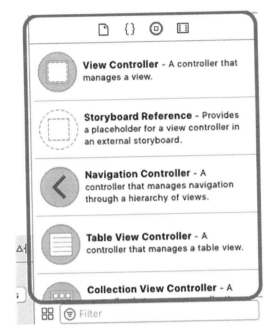

Figure 2-20. *In the library you'll find stock objects from the UIKit that are available for use in Interface Builder. Everything above the library but below the toolbar is known collectively as the inspector.*

The library provides a collection of reusable items for use in your own programs. The four icons in the bar at the top of the library divide it into four sections. Click each icon in turn to see what's in each section.

- *File Template Library*: This section contains a collection of file templates you can use when you need to add a new file to your project. For example, if you want to add a new Swift source file to your project, one way to do it is to drag one type from the File Template Library and drop it onto the Project Navigator.

- *Code Snippet Library*: This section features a collection of code snippets you can drag into your source code files. If you've written something you think you'll want to use again later, select it in your text editor and drag it to the Code Snippet Library.

- *Object Library*: This section contains reusable objects, such as text fields, labels, sliders, buttons, and just about any object you would ever need to design your iOS interface. You'll use the Object Library extensively in this book to build the interfaces for the sample programs.

- *Media Library*: As its name implies, this section is for all your media, including pictures, sounds, and movies. It's empty until you add something to it.

▓ **Note** The items in the Object Library come from the iOS UIKit, which is a framework of objects used to create an app's user interface. UIKit fulfills the same role in Cocoa Touch and as AppKit does in Cocoa on macOS. The two frameworks are similar conceptually; however, because of differences in the platforms, there are obviously many differences between them. On the other hand, the Foundation framework classes, such as NSString and NSArray, are shared between Cocoa and Cocoa Touch.

Note the search field at the bottom of the library. If you want to find a button, type **button** in the search field; the current library will show only items with *button* in the name. Don't forget to clear the search field when you are finished searching; otherwise, not all the available items will be shown.

Adding a Label to the View

Let's start working with IB. Click the Object Library icon (it looks like a circle with a square in the center—you can see it in Figure 2-20) at the top of the Library pane to bring up the Object Library. Just for fun, scroll through the library to find a table view. That's it—keep scrolling and you'll find it. But, there's a better way: just type the words **table view** in the search field and you'll see it appear.

Now find a label in the library. Next, drag the label onto the view you saw earlier. (If you don't see the view in your editor pane, click the View icon in Interface Builder's Document Outline.) As your cursor appears over the view, it will turn into the standard "I'm making a copy of something" green plus sign you know from the Finder. Drag the label to the center of the view. A pair of blue guidelines—one vertical and one horizontal—will appear when your label is centered. It's not vital that the label be centered, but it's good to know that those guidelines are there; when you drop the label, it should appear, as shown in Figure 2-21.

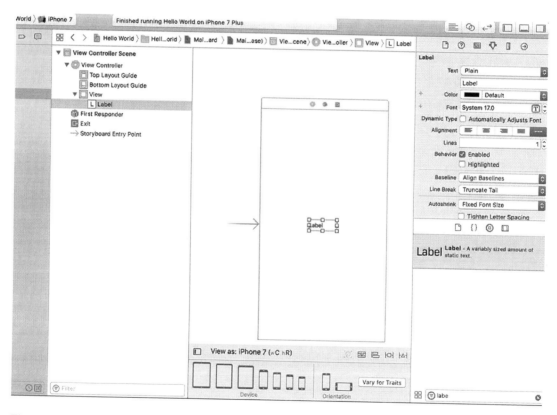

Figure 2-21. *I've found a label in the library and dragged it onto the view*

User interface items are stored in a hierarchy. Most views can contain subviews; however, there are some, like buttons and most other controls, that can't. Interface Builder is smart. If an object does not accept subviews, you will not be able to drag other objects onto it.

By dragging a label directly to the view you're editing, you add it as a subview of that main view (the view named View), which will cause it to show up automatically when that view is displayed to the user. Dragging a label from the library to the view called View adds an instance of UILabel as a subview of your application's main view.

Let's edit the label so it says something profound. Double-click the label you just created and then type **Hello, World!**. Next, click off the label and then reselect it and drag the label to recenter it or position it wherever you want it to appear on the screen.

You've completed this part, so now let's save it to finish up. Select File ➤ Save, or press ⌘S. Now check out the pop-up menu at the upper left of the Xcode project window, the one that says *Hello World*. This is actually a multisegment pop-up control. The left side lets you choose a different compilation target and do a few other things, but you're interested in the right side, which lets you pick which device you want to run on. Click the right side and you'll see a list of available devices. At the top, if you have any iOS device plugged in and ready to go, you'll see it listed. Otherwise, you'll just see a generic iOS Device entry. Below that, you'll see a whole iOS Simulator section listing all the kinds of devices that can be used with the iOS simulator. From that lower section, choose iPhone 7 so that your app will run in the simulator, configured as if it were an iPhone 7.

There are several ways to launch your application: you can select Product ➤ Run, press ⇧R, or press the Run button that's just to the left of the simulator pop-up menu. Xcode will compile your app and launch it in the iOS simulator (see Figure 2-22).

Figure 2-22. *Here's your Hello World program running in the iPhone 7 simulator with iOS 11*

> **■ Note** Prior to the added features of Xcode 8, the text would not automatically center and you would need to work with Auto Layout to add things called *constraints* to make sure that it was centered on any device.

That's really all there is to your first app at its most basic level—and notice that you wrote no Swift code at all!

Changing Attributes

Back in Xcode single-click the Hello World label to select it, and notice the area above the Library pane. This part of the utility pane is called the *inspector*. The inspector is topped by a series of icons, each of which changes the inspector to view a specific type of data. To change the attributes of the label, you'll need the fourth icon from the left, which brings up the Attributes Inspector (see Figure 2-23).

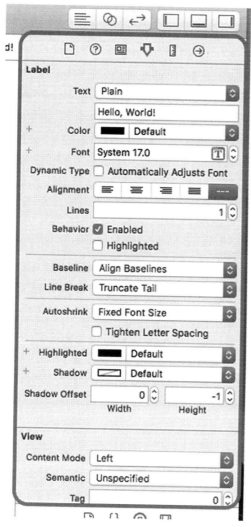

Figure 2-23. *The Attributes Inspector showing your label's attributes*

▓ **Tip** The inspector, like the Project Navigator, has keyboard shortcuts corresponding to each of its icons. The inspector's keyboard shortcuts start with ⌥⌘1 for the leftmost icon, ⌥⌘2 for the next icon, and so on. Unlike the Project Navigator, the number of icons in the inspector is context-sensitive, and it changes depending on which object is selected in the navigator and/or editor. Note that your keyboard may not have a key that's marked ⌥. If it doesn't, use the Option key instead.

Change the label's appearance any way you like, feeling free to play around with the font, size, and color of the text. Note that if you change the font size, you'll need to add an Auto Layout constraint to make sure that it has the correct size at run time. To do that, select the label and then choose Editor ➤ Size to Fit Content from the Xcode menu (see Figure 2-24). Once you've finished playing, save the file and select Run again. The changes you made should show up in your application, once again without writing any code.

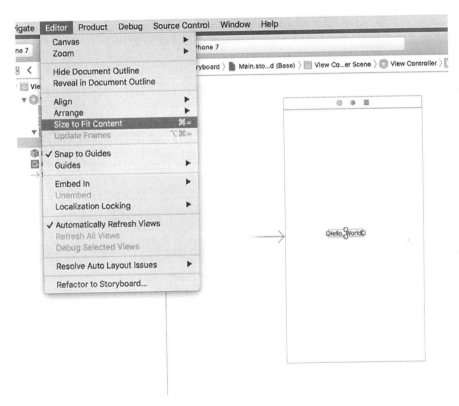

Figure 2-24. *Changing the font size larger will force you to change the layout constraints by selecting Size to Fit Content from the Editor menu*

▓ **Note** Don't worry too much about what all the fields in the Attributes Inspector mean because as you make your way through the book, you'll learn a lot about the Attributes Inspector and what most of the fields do.

By letting you design your interface graphically, Interface Builder frees you to spend time writing the code that is specific to your application, instead of writing tedious code to construct your user interface.

Most modern application development environments have some tool that lets you build your user interface graphically. One distinction between Interface Builder and many of these other tools is that Interface Builder does not generate any code that must be maintained. Instead, Interface Builder creates user interface objects, just as you would in your own code, and then serializes those objects into the storyboard or nib file so that they can be loaded directly into memory at runtime. This avoids many of the problems associated with code generation and is, overall, a more powerful approach.

Adding the Finishing Touches

Let's refine the application by making it feel more like an authentic iPhone app. First, run your project again. When the simulator window appears, press ⌘⇧H. That will bring you back to the iPhone home screen, as shown in Figure 2-25. Notice that the app icon now shows as a plain, default image.

Figure 2-25. The Hello World application shown on the home screen

Take a look at the Hello World icon at the top of the screen. To change from this boring, default image, you need to create an icon and save it as a Portable Network Graphics (.png) file. Actually, for best results, you should create five icons for the iPhone in the following sizes: 180 × 180 pixels, 120 × 120 pixels, 87 × 87 pixels, 80 × 80 pixels, and 58 × 58 pixels. There's another set of four icons that are required if you plan to release your application for the iPad. You'll also need an image that is 187 × 187 pixels for the iPad Pro. The reason for so many icons is because they are used on the home screen, in the Settings app, and in the results list for a Spotlight search. That accounts for three of them, but that's not the end of the story—the iPhone 7/6s Plus, with its larger screen, requires higher-resolution icons, adding another three to the list. Fortunately, one of these is the same size as an icon from the other set, so you actually only need to create five versions of your application icon for the iPhone. If you don't supply some of the smaller ones, a larger one will be scaled down appropriately; but for best results, you (or a graphic artist on your team) should probably scale it in advance.

Do not try to match the style of the buttons that are already on the device when you create the icons; your iPhone or iPad automatically rounds the edges. Just create normal, square images. You'll find a set of suitable icon images in the project archive's Hello World - icons folder.

■ **Note**   For your application's icon, you must use .png images; in fact, you should actually use that format for all images in your iOS projects. Xcode automatically optimizes .png images at build time, which makes them the fastest and most efficient image type for use in iOS apps. Even though most common image formats will display correctly, use .png files unless you have a compelling reason to use another format.

Press ⌘1 to open the Project Navigator, and look inside the Hello World group for an item called Assets.xcassets. This is an *asset catalog*. By default, each new Xcode project is created with an asset catalog, ready to hold your app icons and other resource files. Select Assets.xcassets and turn your attention to the editor pane.

On the left side of the editor pane, you'll see a column with an entry labeled AppIcon. Select this item, and to the right you'll see an area with the text *AppIcon* in the upper-left corner, as well as dashed-line squares for the icons I just talked about (see Figure 2-26). This is where you'll drag all of your app icons.

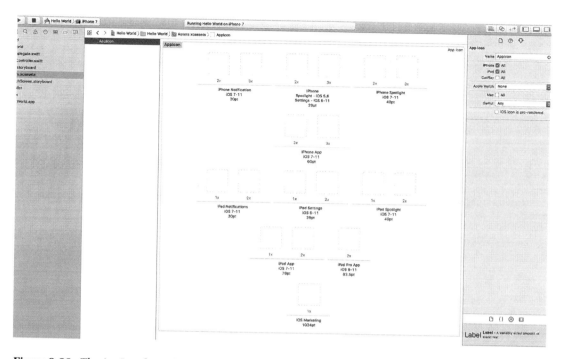

Figure 2-26. *The AppIcon boxes in your project's assets catalog. This is where you set your application's icon.*

In the Finder, open the `Hello World - icons` folder, select all the files, and drag the bunch of them to IB. Most of the icons should automatically fill with the correct name.

___

■ **Note** Early beta releases of Xcode 9 did not support this autofill function at the time of this writing. Also, for now, you don't need to worry about the 1024 iOS Marketing icon.

___

You'll likely have a few empty squares left over where you'll find the right file and drag them individually to make sure that there are no empty squares. You do this by comparing the file size as part of the name to the number of points on the square. Note, Figure 2-27, that you'll need to find the double or triple size file if a square has 2× or 3× below it.

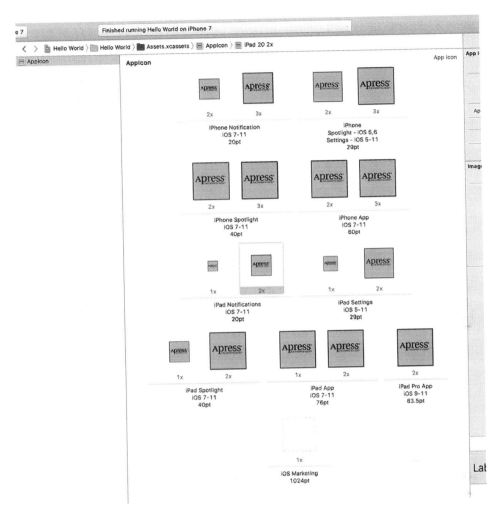

Figure 2-27. *Be sure to match .png files to the proper size requirement for the icon*

Now compile and run your app. When the simulator has finished launching, press ⌘⇧H to go to the home screen, and check out your icon (see Figure 2-28). To see one of the smaller icons in use, swipe down inside the home screen to bring up the Spotlight search field, and start typing the word **Hello**—you'll see your new app's icon appear immediately.

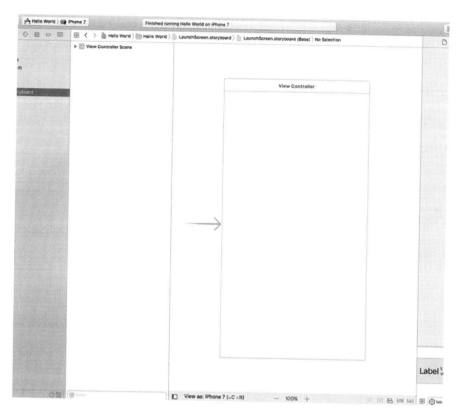

Figure 2-28. *The new app icon for your Hello World app*

■ **Note**   As you work through this book, your simulator's home screen will get cluttered with the icons for the example applications you'll be running. If you want to clear out old applications from the home screen, choose iOS Simulator ➤ Erase All Content and Settings from the iOS simulator's hardware menu.

Exploring the Launch Screen

When you launched your application, you may have noticed the white launch screen that appeared while the application was being loaded. iOS applications have always had a launch screen. Since the process of loading an application into memory takes time (and the larger the application, the longer it takes), the purpose of this screen is to let the user see as quickly as possible that something is happening. Prior to iOS 8, you could supply an image (in fact, several images of different sizes) to act as your app's launch screen. iOS would load the correct image and immediately display it before loading the rest of your application. Starting with iOS 8, you still have that option, but Apple now strongly recommends that you use a launch file instead of a launch image, or as well as a launch image if your application still needs to support earlier releases.

A launch file is a storyboard that contains the user interface for your launch screen. On devices running iOS 8 and newer, if a launch file is found, it is used in preference to a launch image. Look in the Project Navigator and you'll see that you already have a launch file in your project—it's called LaunchScreen.storyboard. If you open it in Interface Builder, you'll see that it just contains a blank view, as shown in Figure 2-29.

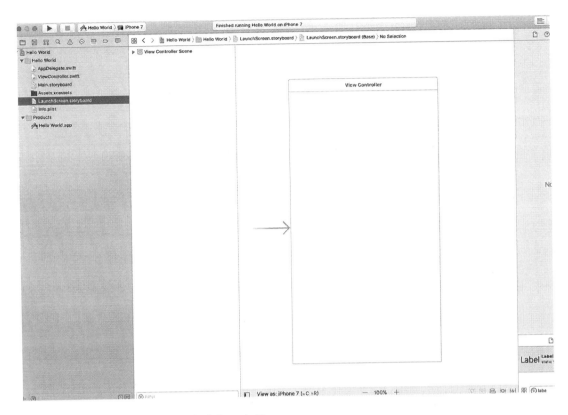

Figure 2-29. *Your application's default launch file*

Apple expects you to build your own launch screen using Interface Builder, in the same way as you would construct any other part of your application's user interface. Apple recommends that you don't try to create a complex or visually impressive launch screen, so follow those guidelines. Here, you're just going to add a label to the storyboard and change the background color of the main view so that you can distinguish the launch screen from the application itself. As before, drag a label onto the storyboard, change its text to **Hello World**, and then use the Attributes Inspector (see Figure 2-23) to change its font to System Bold 32. Making sure that the label is selected, click Editor ➤ Size to Fit Content in the Xcode menu. Now center the label in the view and click Editor ➤ Resolve Auto Layout Issues ➤ Add Missing Constraints to add layout constraints that make sure that it stays there. Next, select the main view by clicking it in the storyboard or in the Document Outline and use the Attributes Inspector to change its background color. To do that, locate the Background control and choose any color you like—I chose green. Now run the application again. You'll see the launch screen appear and then fade away as the application itself appears, as shown in Figure 2-30.

Figure 2-30. *A green launch screen for the Hello World application*

You can read more about the launch file, launch images, and application icons in Apple's *iOS Human Interface Guidelines* document, which you'll find online at https://developer.apple.com/library/ios/documentation/UserExperience/Conceptual/MobileHIG/LaunchImages.html.

Running the Application on a Device

Before bringing this chapter to a close, there's one more thing I will cover. Let's load your app and run it on an actual device. The first step is to connect an iOS device to your Mac using its charging cable. When you do that, Xcode should recognize it and will spend some time reading symbol information from it. You may also see security prompts on both your Mac and your device asking whether you want one to trust the other. Wait until Xcode finishes processing symbol files from the device (check the Activity View to see that) and then open the device selector in the toolbar. You should see your device listed there, as shown in Figure 2-31.

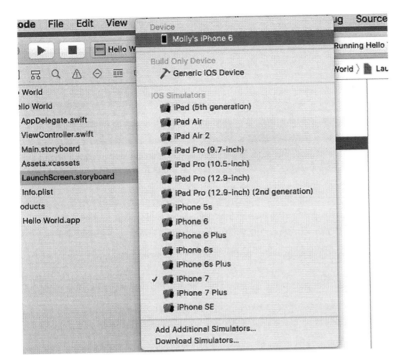

Figure 2-31. *The list of devices and simulators now includes my iPhone 6 running iOS 11 beta*

Select the device and click the Run button on the toolbar to start the process of installing and running the application on it. Xcode will rebuild the application and run it on your device. However, because I'm using an early beta release of Xcode 9, you may see a prompt like the one shown in Figure 2-32.

Figure 2-32. *If the automated provision features fail, you may see this message*

■ **Note**   Apple made improvements to the provisioning system back in Xcode 8, and many of these "fix issue" features have become obsolete. The process has become more seamless and successful. Here, I address the topic in a way to make sure that you complete the provisioning to get the app to run on your actual device.

Before you can install an application on an iOS device, it has to have a provisioning profile, and it needs to be signed. Signing the application allows the device to identify the author of the application and to check that the binary has not been tampered with since it was created. The provisioning profile contains information that tells iOS which capabilities, such as iCloud access, your application needs to have and which individual devices it can run on. To sign the application, Xcode needs a certificate and a private key.

■ **Tip**   You can read about code signing, provisioning profiles, certificates, and private keys in Apple's App Distribution Workflows in the *App Distribution Guide* at https://developer.apple.com/library/ios/ documentation/IDEs/Conceptual/AppDistributionGuide.

In the early days of iOS development, you had to sign in to your developer program account, manually create both of these items, and then register the test devices on which you want to install the application. This was a nontrivial and frustrating process. Xcode 7 was improved to be smart enough to do this for you, and Xcode 8 has improved things even more, so this should all just work; all you need do is to put an app on a device for testing. In some cases, for different specialized builds to be distributed to particular users, you'll want to customize your provisioning process, but for your learning process, the default, easy-to-use mechanisms work just fine.

There are a couple of things that can go wrong. First, if you see a message saying that your app ID is not available, you'll need to choose a different one. The app ID is based on the project name and the organization identifier that you chose when you created the project (see Figure 2-4). You'll see this message if you used com.beginningiphone or another identifier that somebody else has already registered. To fix it, open the Project Navigator and select the Hello World node at the top of the project tree. Then click the Hello World node under the TARGETS section in the Document Outline. Finally, click the General button at the top of the editor area (see Figure 2-33).

Figure 2-33. *Changing your application's bundle identifier*

The app ID that Xcode uses for signing is taken from the Bundle Identifier field in the editor. You'll see that it contains the organization identifier that you selected when you created the project—it's the part of the field that's highlighted in Figure 2-33. Choose another value and try building again. Eventually, you should find an identifier that hasn't already been used. When you've done that, make a note of it and be sure to use it to fill in the Organization Identifier field whenever you create a new project. Once you've done that correctly once, Xcode will remember it so you shouldn't have to do it again.

The other thing that can go wrong is shown in Figure 2-34.

Figure 2-34. Failure to launch in iOS 9, 10, or 11

You'll see this message only if you are not enrolled in the developer program. It means that your iOS device does not trust you to run applications signed with your Apple ID. To fix this, open the Settings application on the device and then go to General ➤ Profile. You'll reach a page with a table that contains your Apple ID. Tap the table row to open another page that looks like Figure 2-35.

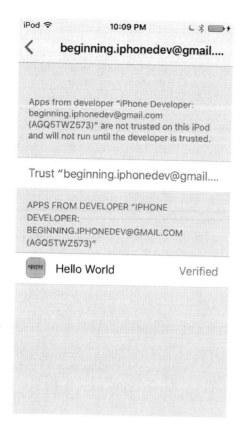

Figure 2-35. *On iOS 9 and newer, developers without a developer program membership are not trusted by default*

Summary

You should be pleased with the progress you've made in this chapter. Although it may not seem like you accomplished all that much, you actually covered a lot of ground. You learned about the iOS project templates, created an application, learned key knowledge about Xcode 9, started using Interface Builder, learned how to set your application icon, and discovered how to run your application on the simulator and on a real device.

The Hello World program, however, is a strictly one-way application. You show some information to the users, but you never get any input from them. In the next chapter, you'll look at how to go about getting input from the user of an iOS device and taking actions based on that input.

CHAPTER 3

Basic User Interactions

Your Hello World app provided a good introduction to iOS development using Xcode and Cocoa Touch, but it lacked a crucial capability—the ability to interact with the user. Without the ability to accept user input, you severely limit the usefulness of your efforts.

In this chapter, you'll write a slightly more complex application—one that will feature two buttons and a label (see Figure 3-1). When the user taps either of the buttons, the label's text changes. This demonstrates the key concepts involved in creating interactive iOS apps. You'll also learn about the NSAttributedString class, which lets you use styled text with many Cocoa Touch visual elements.

Figure 3-1. *In this chapter, you'll develop this simple two-button app.*

© Molly K. Maskrey 2017
M. K. Maskrey, *Beginning iPhone Development with Swift 4*, https://doi.org/10.1007/978-1-4842-3072-5_3

Understanding the MVC Paradigm

If you don't know of MVC, you will. It stands for *model-view-controller* (MVC) and represents a logical way of dividing the code that makes up a GUI-based application. These days, almost all object-oriented frameworks build upon MVC, but few adhere to the MVC model as much as Cocoa Touch.

The MVC pattern divides all functionality into three distinct categories.

- *Model*: The classes that hold your application's data.

- *View*: Made up of the windows, controls, and other elements that the user can see and interact with.

- *Controller*: The code that binds together the model and view. It contains the application logic that decides how to handle the user's inputs.

MVC makes certain that the objects implementing these three types of code are as distinct from one another as possible. Any object you create should be readily identifiable as belonging in one of the three categories, with little or no functionality that could be classified as being either of the other two. An object that implements a button, for example, shouldn't contain code to process data when that button is tapped, and an implementation of a bank account shouldn't contain code to draw a table to display its transactions.

MVC helps ensure maximum reusability. A class that implements a generic button can be used in any application. A class that implements a button that does some particular calculation when it is clicked can be used only in the application for which it was originally written.

When you write Cocoa Touch applications, you primarily create your view components using Interface Builder, although you will sometimes modify, and sometimes even create, parts of your user interface in code.

You create your model by writing Swift classes to hold your application's data. You won't be creating any model objects in this chapter's application because you do not need to store or preserve data. I will introduce model objects as the sample applications get more complex in future chapters.

Your controller component contains classes that you create and that are specific to your application. Controllers are completely custom classes, but more often they exist as subclasses of one of several existing generic controller classes from the UIKit framework, such as UIViewController. By subclassing one of these existing classes, you get a lot of functionality for free and won't need to spend time recoding the wheel, so to speak.

As you get deeper into Cocoa Touch, you quickly start to see how the classes of the UIKit framework follow the principles of MVC. By keeping this concept in the back of your mind as you develop, you will end up creating cleaner, more easily maintained Swift code.

Creating the ButtonFun App

It's time to create your next Xcode project. You'll use the same template that you used in the previous chapter: Single View App. By starting with this simple template again, it's easier to see how the view and controller objects work together in an iOS application. You'll use some of the other templates in later chapters.

Launch Xcode and select File ➤ New ➤ Project or press ⌘⇧N. Select the Single View App template and then click Next.

You'll be presented with the same options sheet that you saw in the previous chapter. In the Product Name field, type the name of your new application, **ButtonFun**. The Organization Name, Company Identifier, and Language fields should still have the values you used in the previous chapter, so you can leave those alone. Once again, you are going to use Auto Layout to create an application that works on all iOS devices, so in the Devices field, this time select Universal. Figure 3-2 shows the completed options sheet.

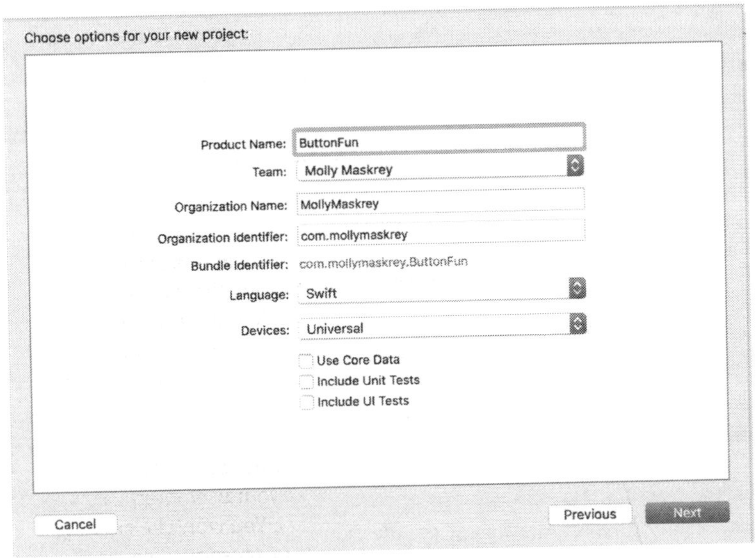

Figure 3-2. *Naming your project and selecting options*

Hit Next. You'll be prompted for a location for your project. You can leave the Create Git repository check box selected or not, whichever you prefer. Click Create and save the project with the rest of your book projects.

Understanding the ViewController

A little later in this chapter, you'll design a view (or user interface) for your application using Interface Builder, just as you did in the previous chapter. Before you do that, let's look at the files that were created for you and then make some changes to them. In the Project Navigator, the ButtonFun group should already be expanded; if it's not, click the disclosure triangle next to it (see Figure 3-3).

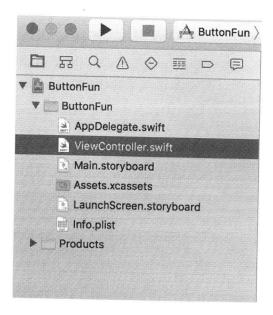

Figure 3-3. *The Project Navigator shows the class files created for you by the project template*

The ButtonFun group should contain two source code files along with the main storyboard file, the launch screen storyboard file, an asset catalog for containing any images your app needs, and an Info.plist file, which I'll discuss in later chapters. The two source code files implement the classes your application needs: your application delegate and the view controller for your application's only view. You'll look at the application delegate a little later in the chapter. First, you'll work with the view controller class that was created for you.

The controller class called ViewController manages your application's view. The name identifies that this class is, well, a view controller. Click ViewController.swift in the Project Navigator and take a look at the contents of the view controller file (see Listing 3-1).

Listing 3-1. ViewController Code Generated by Your Template

```
import UIKit

class ViewController: UIViewController {

    override func viewDidLoad() {
        super.viewDidLoad()
        // Do any additional setup after loading the view, typically from a nib.
    }

    override func didReceiveMemoryWarning() {
        super.didReceiveMemoryWarning()
        // Dispose of any resources that can be recreated.
    }
}
```

Because it was generated by the template, clearly there's not much there yet. `ViewController` exists as a subclass of `UIViewController`, which is one of those generic controller classes mentioned earlier. It is part of the UIKit framework, and by subclassing this class, you get a bunch of functionality included. Xcode doesn't know what your application-specific functionality is going to be, but it does know that you're going to have some, so it has created this class for you to write that specific functionality yourself.

Understanding Outlets and Actions

In Chapter 2 you used Xcode's Interface Builder to design a simple user interface, and in Listing 3-1 you saw the shell of a view controller class. I'll now discuss how the code in this view controller class can interact with the objects (buttons, labels, etc.) in the storyboard. A controller class can refer to objects in a storyboard or nib file by using a special kind of property called an *outlet*. Think of an outlet as a pointer that points to an object within the user interface. For example, suppose you created a text label in Interface Builder (as you did in Chapter 2) and wanted to change the label's text from within your code. By declaring an outlet and connecting that outlet to the label object, you would then be able to use the outlet from within your code to change the text displayed by the label. You'll do that later in this chapter.

Going in the opposite direction, interface objects in your storyboard or nib file can be set up to trigger special methods in your controller class. These special methods are known as *action methods* (or just *actions*). For example, you can tell Interface Builder that when the user taps a button, a specific action method within your code should be called. You could even tell Interface Builder that when the user first touches a button, it should call one action method; and then later, when the finger is lifted off the button, it should call a different action method.

Xcode supports multiple ways of creating outlets and actions. One way is to specify them in your source code before using Interface Builder to connect them with your code, but Xcode's Assistant View gives you a much faster and more intuitive approach that lets you create and connect outlets and actions in a single step, a process you're going to look at shortly. Before you start making connections, let's talk about outlets and actions in a little more detail. Outlets and actions are two of the most basic building blocks you'll use to create iOS apps, so it's important that you understand what they are and how they work.

Outlets

Outlets are ordinary Swift properties that are tagged with the decoration `@IBOutlet`. An outlet looks something like this:

```
@IBOutlet weak var myButton: UIButton!
```

This example depicts an outlet called `myButton`, which can be set to point to any button in the user interface.

The Swift compiler doesn't do anything special when it sees the `@IBOutlet` decoration. Its sole purpose is to act as a hint to tell Xcode that this is a property that you're going to want to connect to an object in a storyboard or nib file. Any property that you create and want to connect to an object in a storyboard or nib file must be preceded by `@IBOutlet`. Fortunately, as you'll see, you can create outlets in Xcode just by dragging from the object to the property that you want to link it to, or even just by dragging to the class in which you'd like to have a new outlet created.

You may be wondering why the declaration of the `myButton` property ends with an `!`. Swift requires all properties to be fully initialized before the completion of every initializer, unless the property is declared to be optional. When a view controller loads from a storyboard, the values of its outlet properties get set from information saved in the storyboard, but this happens *after* the view controller's initializer has been run. As a result, unless you explicitly give them dummy values (which is not desirable), outlet properties have to be declared as optional. That gives you two ways to declare them, using either `!` or `?`, as shown in Listing 3-2.

Listing 3-2. Two Ways to Declare Optional Variables

```
@IBOutlet weak var myButton1: UIButton?
@IBOutlet weak var myButton2: UIButton!
```

Generally, you'll find the second one easier to use because there is no need to explicitly unwrap the optional later when it's used in the view controller's code (see Listing 3-3). Be aware that if you do use the second version, you must make sure that it gets set and does not become `nil` later.

Listing 3-3. Eliminating the Need to Explicitly Unwrap an optional

```
let button1 = myButton1!    // Optional needs to be unwrapped
let button2 = myButton2     // myButton2 is implicitly unwrapped
```

▓ **Note**   The weak specifier attached to the declaration of the outlet property means that the property does not need to create a strong reference to the button. Objects are automatically deallocated as soon as there are no stronger references to them. In this case, there is no risk that the button will be deallocated because there will be a strong reference to it as long as it remains part of the user interface. Making the property reference weak allows deallocation to happen if the view is no longer required and is removed from the user interface at some point. If this happens, the property reference is set to `nil`.

Actions

In a nutshell, actions are methods that are tagged with the decoration @IBAction, which tells Interface Builder that this method can be triggered by a control in a storyboard or nib file. The declaration for an action method will usually look like this:

```
@IBAction func doSomething(sender: UIButton) {}
```

It might also look like this:

```
@IBAction func doSomething() {}
```

The actual name of the method can be anything you want, and it must either take no arguments or take a single argument, usually called sender. When the action method is called, sender will contain a pointer to the object that called it. For example, if this action method was triggered when the user tapped a button, sender would point to the button that was tapped. The sender argument exists so that you can respond to multiple controls using a single action method, which gives you a way to identify which control called the action method.

> ■ **Tip** There's actually a third, less frequently used way to declare an action method that looks like this:
>
> ```
> @IBAction func doSomething(sender: UIButton, forEvent event: UIEvent) {}
> ```
>
> You would use this form if you need more information about the event that caused the method to be called. I'll
> talk more about control events in the next chapter.

It won't hurt anything to declare an action method with a sender argument and then ignore it. You'll
likely see a lot of code that does just that. Action methods in Cocoa and NeXTSTEP needed to accept sender
whether they used it or not, so a lot of iOS code, especially early iOS code, was written that way.

Now that you understand what actions and outlets are, you'll see how they work as you design your user
interface. But first, let's take care of a little bit of housekeeping.

Simplifying the View Controller

Single-click ViewController.swift in the Project Navigator to open the implementation file. As you can see,
there's a small amount of boilerplate code in the form of viewDidLoad() and didReceiveMemoryWarning()
methods that were provided for you by the project template you chose. These methods are commonly
used in UIViewController subclasses, so Xcode gave you stub implementations of them. If you need to use
them, you can just add your code there. However, you don't need either of these stub implementations for
this project, so all they're doing is taking up space and making your code harder to read. You're going to do
yourself a favor and clear away methods that you don't need, so go ahead and delete both of them. When
you've done that, your file should look like Listing 3-4.

Listing 3-4. Your Simplified ViewController.swift File

```
import UIKit

class ViewController: UIViewController {

}
```

Designing the User Interface

Make sure that you save the changes you just made and then single-click Main.storyboard to open your
application's view using Interface Builder (see Figure 3-4). As you'll remember from the previous chapter,
the white window that shows up in the editor represents your application's one and only view. If you look
back at Figure 3-1, you can see that you need to add two buttons and a label to this view.

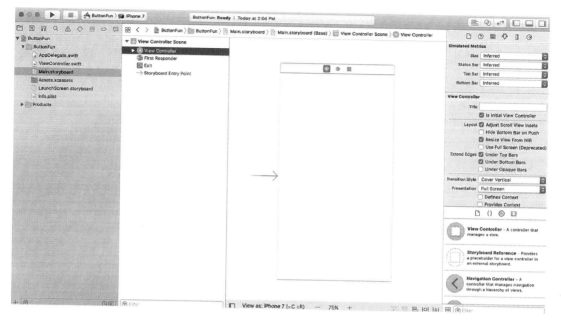

Figure 3-4. *Main.storyboard open for editing in Xcode's Interface Builder*

Let's take a second to think about your application. You're going to add two buttons and a label to your user interface, and that process is similar to what you did to add a label to the application that you built in the previous chapter. However, you're also going to need outlets and actions to make your application interactive.

The buttons will each need to trigger an action method on your controller. You could choose to make each button call a different action method, but since they're going to do essentially the same task (update the label's text), you will need to call the same action method. You'll differentiate between the two buttons using that sender argument discussed earlier. In addition to the action method, you'll also need an outlet connected to the label so that you can change the text that the label displays.

You'll add the buttons first and then place the label, creating the corresponding actions and outlets as you design your interface. You could also manually declare your actions and outlets and then connect your user interface items to them, but Xcode can handle this for you.

Adding the Buttons and Action Method

First you'll add two buttons to your user interface. You'll then have Xcode create an empty action method for you, and you will connect both buttons to it. Any code you place in that method will be executed when the user taps the button.

Select View ➤ Utilities ➤ Show Object Library to open the Object Library. Type **UIButton** in the Object Library's search box. (You actually need to type only the first four characters, **uibu**, to narrow down the list. You can use all lowercase letters to save yourself the trouble of pressing the Shift key.) Once you're finished typing, only one item should appear in the Object Library: Button (see Figure 3-5).

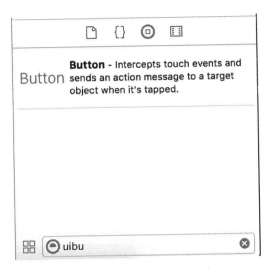

Figure 3-5. A button as it appears in the Object Library

Drag the button from the library and drop it on the white window inside the editing area to add the button to your application's view. Place the button along the left side of the view the appropriate distance from the left edge by using the vertical blue guideline that appears as you move the button toward the left edge of the view. For vertical placement, use the horizontal blue guideline to place the button halfway down in the view. You can use Figure 3-1 as a placement guide, if that helps.

■ **Note**   The little blue guidelines that appear as you move objects around in Interface Builder are there to help you stick to the *iOS Human Interface Guidelines* (HIG). Apple provides the HIG for people designing iPhone and iPad applications. The HIG tells you how you should—and shouldn't—design your user interface. You really should read it because it contains valuable information that every iOS developer needs to know. You'll find it at `https://developer.apple.com/library/ios/documentation/UserExperience/Conceptual/MobileHIG/`.

Double-click the newly added button. This will allow you to edit the button's title. Give this button the title **Left**.

Select View ➤ Assistant Editor ➤ Show Assistant Editor, or press ⌥⌘⏎ to open the Assistant Editor. You can also show and hide the Assistant Editor by clicking the middle editor button in the collection of seven buttons on the upper-right side of the project window (see Figure 3-6).

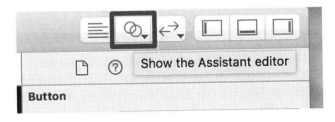

Figure 3-6. The Show the Assistant Editor toggle button (double circles)

The Assistant Editor appears to the right of the editing pane, which continues to show Interface Builder. The Assistant Editor should automatically display ViewController.swift, which is the implementation file for the view controller that "owns" the view you're looking at.

■ **Tip**   After opening the Assistant Editor, you may need to resize your window to have enough room to work. If you're on a smaller screen, like the one on a MacBook Air, you might need to close the Utility View and/or Project Navigator to give yourself enough room to use the Assistant Editor effectively (see Figure 3-7). You can do this easily using the three view buttons in the upper right of the project window (see Figure 3-6).

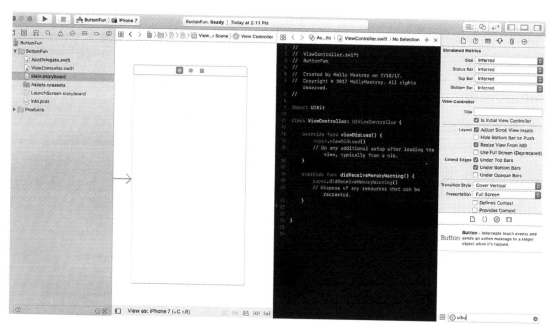

Figure 3-7. *You may have to close other views to see both editing windows on smaller displays*

Xcode knows that your view controller class is responsible for displaying the view in the storyboard, so the Assistant Editor knows to show you the implementation of the view controller class, which is the most likely place you'll want to connect actions and outlets. However, if it is not displaying the file you want to see, you can use the jump bar at the top of the Assistant Editor to fix that. Locate the Automatic segment of the jump bar and click it. In the pop-up menu that appears, select Manual ➤ ButtonFun ➤ ButtonFun ➤ ViewController.swift. You should now be looking at the correct file.

You'll now let Xcode automatically create a new action method for you and associate that action with the button you just created. You're going to add these definitions to the view controller's class extension. To do this, begin by clicking the button that you added to the storyboard so that it is selected. Now, hold down the Control key on your keyboard and then click and drag from the button to the source code in the Assistant Editor. You should see a blue line running from the button to your cursor, as shown in Figure 3-8. This blue line allows you to connect objects in IB to code or other objects. Moving your cursor so it's inside the class definition, as shown in Figure 3-8, a pop-up appears, letting you know that releasing the mouse button will insert an outlet, an action, or an outlet collection for you.

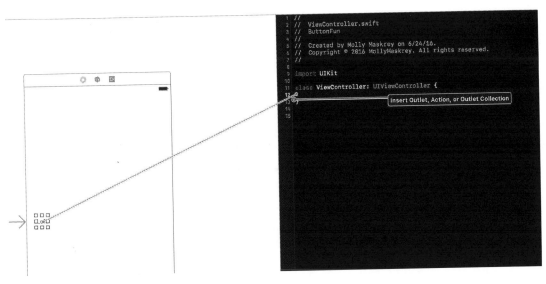

Figure 3-8. *Control-dragging to the source code will give you the option to create an outlet, action, or outlet collection*

▓ **Note** You use actions and outlets in this chapter, and you'll use outlet collections later in the book. Outlet collections allow you to connect multiple objects of the same kind to a single array property, rather than creating a separate property for each object.

To finish this connection, release your mouse button, and a floating pop-up will appear, like the one shown in Figure 3-9.

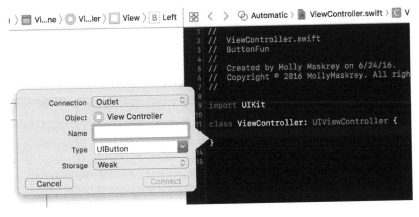

Figure 3-9. *The floating pop-up that appears after you Control-drag to source code*

This window lets you customize your new action. In the window, click the Connection pop-up menu and change the selection from Outlet to Action. This tells Xcode that you want to create an action instead of an outlet (see Figure 3-10). In the Name field, type **buttonPressed**. When you're finished, do *not* hit the Return key. Pressing Return would finalize your outlet; you're not quite ready to do that. Instead, press the Tab key to move to the Type field and type **UIButton**, replacing the default value of AnyObject.

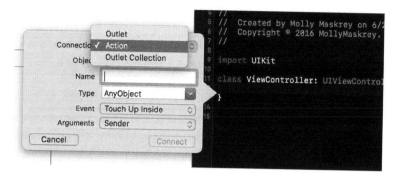

Figure 3-10. *Changing from Outlet to Action*

There are two fields below Type, which you will leave at their default values. The Event field lets you specify when the method is called. The default value of Touch Up Inside fires when the user lifts a finger off the screen if–and only if–the finger is still on the button. This is the standard event to use for buttons. This gives the user a chance to reconsider. If the user moves a finger off the button before lifting it off the screen, the method won't fire.

The Arguments field lets you choose between the three different method signatures that can be used for action methods. You want the sender argument so that you can tell which button called the method. That's the default, so you just leave it as is.

Hit the Return key or click the Connect button, and Xcode will insert the action method for you. The ViewController.swift file in the Assistant Editor should now look like Listing 3-5. You'll come back here to write the code that needs to execute when the user taps either this button or the one you'll add shortly.

Listing 3-5. Your ViewController.swift File with the Added IBAction

```swift
import UIKit

class ViewController: UIViewController {

    @IBAction func buttonPressed(_ sender: UIButton) {
    }
}
```

In addition to creating the method code segment, Xcode connected that button to that method and stored that information in the storyboard. That means you don't need to do anything else to make that button call this method when your application runs.

Go back to `Main.storyboard` and drag out another button, this time placing the button on the right side of the screen. The blue guidelines will appear to help you align it with the right margin, as you saw before, and they will also help you align the button vertically with the other button. After placing the button, double-click it and change its name to Right.

■ **Tip** Instead of dragging out a new object from the library, you could hold down the ⌥ key (the Option key) and drag a copy of the original object (the Left button in this example) over. Holding down the ⌥ key tells Interface Builder to make a copy of the object you drag.

This time, you don't want to create a new action method. Instead, you want to connect this button to the existing one that Xcode created for you a moment ago. After changing the name of the button, Control-click it and drag toward the declaration of the `buttonPressed()` method code in the Assistant Editor. This time, as your cursor gets near `buttonPressed()`, that method should highlight, and you'll get a gray pop-up saying Connect Action (see Figure 3-11). If you don't see it straightaway, move the mouse around until it appears. When you see the pop-up, release the mouse button, and Xcode will connect the button to the action method. That will cause the button, when tapped, to trigger the same action method as the other button.

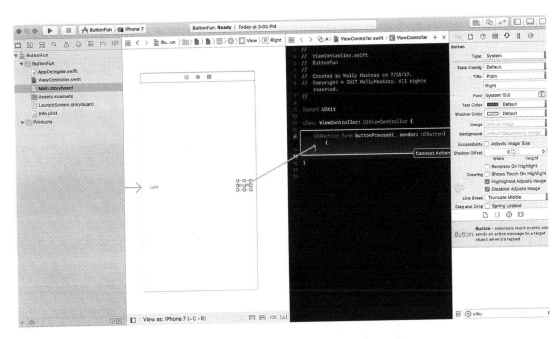

Figure 3-11. *Dragging to an existing action will connect the button to that action*

Adding the Label and Outlet

In the Object Library, type **lab** into the search field to find the Label user interface item (see Figure 3-12). Drag the label to your user interface, somewhere above the two buttons you placed earlier. After placing it, use the resize handles to stretch the label from the left margin (as indicated by the blue guideline) to the right margin. That should give it plenty of room for the text you'll be displaying to the user.

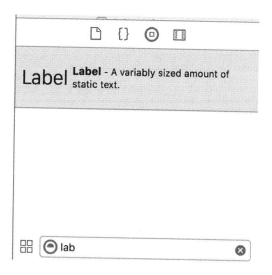

Figure 3-12. *The label as it appears in the Object Library*

The text in a label, by default, is left-aligned, but you want the text in this one to be centered. Select View ➤ Utilities ➤ Show Attributes Inspector (or press ⌥⌘4) to bring up the Attributes Inspector (see Figure 3-13). Make sure that the label is selected and then look in the Attributes Inspector for the Alignment buttons. Select the middle Alignment button to center the label's text.

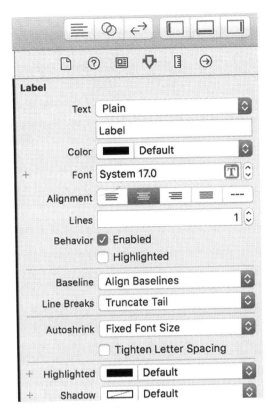

Figure 3-13. *Use the Attributes Inspector to center the label's text*

Before the user taps a button, you want the label blank, so double-click the label (so the text is selected) and press the Delete button on your keyboard. That will delete the text currently assigned to the label. Hit Return to commit your changes. Even though you won't be able to see the label when it's not selected, it's still there.

■ **Tip**   If you have invisible user interface elements, such as empty labels, and want to be able to see where they are, select Canvas from the Editor menu. Next, from the submenu that pops up, turn on Show Bounds Rectangles. If you just want to select an element that you can't see, just click its icon in the Document Outline.

Finally, let's create an outlet for the label. You do this exactly the way you created and connected actions earlier. Make sure that the Assistant Editor is open and displaying ViewController.swift. If you need to switch files, use the pop-up in the jump bar above the Assistant Editor.

Next, select the label in Interface Builder and Control-drag from the label to the header file. Drag until your cursor is right above the existing action method. When you see something like Figure 3-14, let go of the mouse button and you'll see the pop-up window again (shown in Figure 3-9).

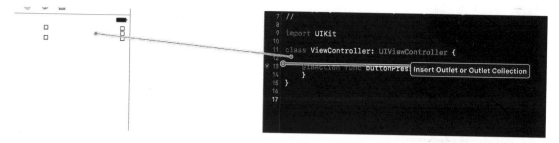

Figure 3-14. *Connecting the UILabel outlet*

Leave the Connection option at the default type of Outlet. You want to choose a descriptive name for this outlet so you'll remember what it is used for when you're working on your code. Type **statusLabel** into the Name field. Leave the Type field set to UILabel. The final field, labeled Storage, can be left at the default value.

Hit Return to commit your changes, and Xcode will insert the outlet property into your code. Your code should now look like Listing 3-6.

Listing 3-6. Adding Your Label Outlet to the View Controller

```
import UIKit

class ViewController: UIViewController {

    @IBOutlet weak var statusLabel: UILabel!

    @IBAction func buttonPressed(_ sender: UIButton) {
    }
}
```

Now you have an outlet where Xcode has "automagically" connected the label to your outlet. This means that if you make any changes to statusLabel in code, those changes affect the label in your user interface. Setting the text property on statusLabel, for example, changes the text that is displayed to the user.

AUTOMATIC REFERENCE COUNTING

If you're familiar with languages like C or C++ where you have to be careful to release memory that you allocate when you no longer need it, you might be somewhat concerned that you seem to be creating objects but not destroying them.

The LLVM compiler that Apple includes with Xcode these days is smart enough to release objects for you, using a feature called Automatic Reference Counting (ARC).

ARC applies only to Swift objects and structures, not to Core Foundation objects or to memory allocated with C-language library functions such as malloc(), and there are some caveats and gotchas that can trip you up. But for the most part, worrying about memory management is a thing of the past.

To learn more about ARC, check out the ARC release notes at this URL:

```
http://developer.apple.com/library/ios/#releasenotes/ObjectiveC/RN-
TransitioningToARC/
```

ARC is helpful, but it's not magic. You should still understand the basic rules of memory management in iOS to avoid getting in trouble with ARC. To learn about the iOS (and macOS) memory management contract, read Apple's *Memory Management Programming Guide* at this URL:

```
https://developer.apple.com/library/ios/documentation/Cocoa/Conceptual/MemoryMgmt/
Articles/MemoryMgmt.html
```

Writing the Action Method

So far, you've designed your user interface and wired up both outlets and actions. All that's left to do is to use those actions and outlets to set the text of the label when a button is pressed. Single-click ViewController. swift in the Project Navigator to open it in the editor. Find the empty buttonPressed() method that Xcode created for you earlier.

To differentiate between the two buttons, you'll use the sender parameter. You'll retrieve the title of the button that was pressed using sender and then create a new string based on that title and assign that as the label's text. Change the buttonPressed() method to that shown in Listing 3-7.

Listing 3-7. Completing the Action Method

```
@IBAction func buttonPressed(sender: UIButton) {
    let title = sender.title(for: .selected)!
    let text = "\(title) button pressed"
    statusLabel.text = text
}
```

This is pretty straightforward. The first line retrieves the tapped button's title using sender. Since buttons can have different titles depending on their current state (although not in this example), you use the UIControlState.selected parameter to specify that you want the title when the button is in its selected state since the user selected it by tapping it. You'll look at control states in more detail in Chapter 4.

■ **Tip** You probably noticed that the argument you used to call the title(for:) method was .selected, not UIControlState.selected. Swift already understands that the argument must be one of the values of the UIControlState enumeration, so you can omit the enumeration name to save typing.

The next line creates a new string by appending this text to the title you retrieved in the previous line: *button pressed*. So, if the left button, which has a title of Left, is tapped, this line will create a string that reads *Left button pressed*. The final line assigns the new string to the label's text property, which is how you change the text that the label is displaying.

Testing the ButtonFun App

Select Product ➤ Run. If you run into any compile or link errors, go back and compare your code changes to those shown in this chapter. Once your code builds properly, Xcode will launch the iOS simulator and run your application. If you run with an iPhone 7 simulator and tap the Left button, you'll see something like Figure 3-15.

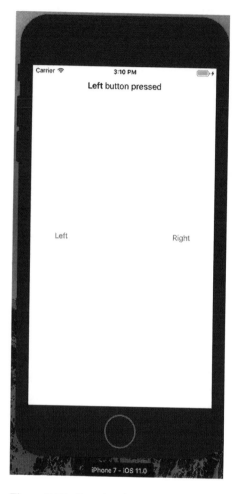

Figure 3-15. *Running the application on an iPhone 6s*

While everything seems to be good with this, the layout of everything needs some work. To see why, change the active scheme, as shown in Figure 3-16, to an iPhone SE and run the application again.

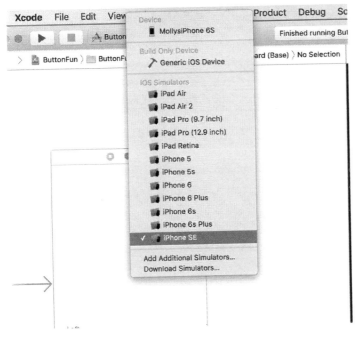

Figure 3-16. *Changing the scheme, and thus the target of execution, to a different size and shape*

The result, displayed in Figure 3-17, shows the problems. Note that while the Left button still works, the label itself is off to the right a bit, and the Right button has completely vanished.

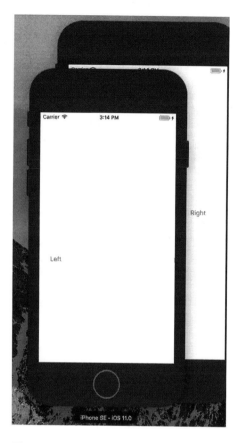

Figure 3-17. *Compared to an iPhone 7, the iPhone SE layout is a little off using a different simulated device*

To start to see why, in Xcode underneath your Interface Builder window, tap the Right button to select it and see the outline, and then below select the "View as" option of iPhone SE, as shown in Figure 3-18. You can see that because you set up your layout to work on a device with a larger screen size, when you move to a smaller device, some of the controls have moved within your new display.

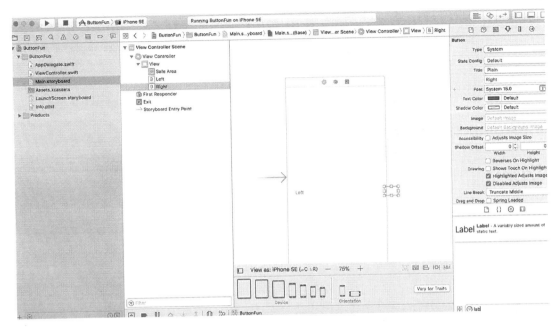

Figure 3-18. *When viewing your layout on a device with a smaller screen area, your Right button shifted so that it is no longer visible*

Fixing Issues Using Auto Layout

The Left button is in the right place, but the label and the other button are not. In Chapter 2, you fixed a similar problem by using Auto Layout. The idea behind Auto Layout is that you use constraints to specify how you want your controls to be placed. In this case, here's what you want to happen:

- The Left button should be vertically centered and close to the left margin of the screen.

- The Right button should be vertically centered and close to the right margin of the screen.

- The label should be horizontally centered, a little down from the top of the screen.

Each of the preceding statements contains two constraints—one of them a horizontal constraint, the other a vertical constraint. If you apply these constraints to your three views, Auto Layout will take care of positioning them correctly on any screen. So, how do you do that? You can add Auto Layout constraints to views in code by creating instances of the NSLayoutConstraint class. In some cases, that's the only way to create a correct layout, but in this case (and in all the examples in this book), you can get the layout that you want by using Interface Builder. Interface Builder lets you add constraints visually by dragging and clicking. First, in the "View as" list under the IB window, reselect 6s as your device so that you see all your controls as you had them. Set the scale to where you can see the whole screen; I'm using 75%. You'll use Auto Layout to fix the other device configurations as well (see Figure 3-19).

71

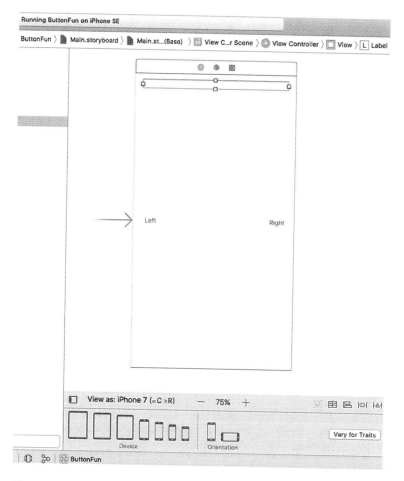

Figure 3-19. *You'll use Auto Layout with the same device you started with to configure for all other device types*

You'll start by positioning the label. Select Main.storyboard in the Project Navigator and open the Document Outline to show the view hierarchy. Find the View icon. This represents the view controller's main view, and it's the one relative to which you need to position the other views. Click the disclosure triangle to open the View icon, if it's not already open, and reveal the two buttons (labeled Left and Right) and the label. Hold down the Control key and drag the mouse from the label to its parent view, as shown on the left in Figure 3-20.

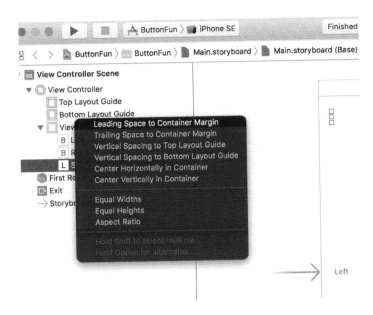

Figure 3-20. *Positioning the label with Auto Layout constraints*

By dragging from one view to another, you are telling Interface Builder that you want to apply an Auto Layout constraint between them. Release the mouse, and a gray pop-up with various choices will appear, as shown on the right in Figure 3-20. Each choice in this pop-up is a single constraint. Clicking any of them will apply that constraint, but you know that you need to apply two constraints to the label, and both of them are available in the pop-up. To apply more than one constraint at a time, you need to hold down the Shift key while selecting them. So, hold down the Shift key and click Center Horizontally in Container and Vertical Spacing to Top Layout Guide. To actually apply the constraints, click the mouse anywhere outside the pop-up or press the Return key. When you do this, the constraints that you have created appear under the heading Constraints in the Document Outline and are also represented visually in the storyboard, as shown in Figure 3-21.

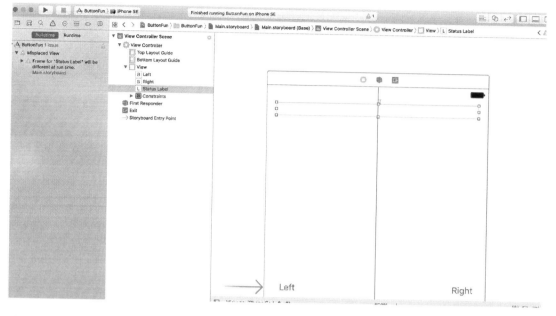

Figure 3-21. *Two Auto Layout constraints have been applied to the label*

■ Tip If you make a mistake when adding a constraint, you can remove it by clicking its representation in the Document Outline, or in the storyboard, and pressing Delete.

You'll probably also see that the label has an orange outline. Interface Builder uses orange to indicate an Auto Layout problem. There are three typical problems that Interface Builder highlights in this way.

- You don't have enough constraints to fully specify a view's position or size.

- The view has constraints that are ambiguous—that is, they don't uniquely pin down its size or position.

- The constraints are correct, but the position or size of the view at runtime will not be the same as it is in Interface Builder.

You can find out more about the problem by clicking the yellow warning triangle in the activity view to see an explanation in the Issue Navigator (see Figure 3-21, far left). If you do that, you'll see that it says "Frame for 'Status Label' will be different at run time"—the third of the problems listed. You can clear this warning by having Interface Builder move the label to its correct runtime position and give it its configured size. To do that, look at the bottom-right side of the storyboard editor. You'll see four buttons, as shown in Figure 3-22.

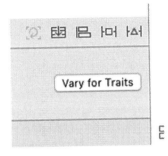

Figure 3-22. *Auto Layout buttons at the bottom right of the storyboard editor*

You can find out what each of these buttons does by hovering your mouse over them. The leftmost shaded button, Update Frames, provides a convenience feature for updating after you make changes. The next button relates to the UIStackView control, which I'll talk about later. Working from left to right, here's what the other three buttons are:

- The Align button lets you align the selected view relative to another view. If you click this button now, you'll see a pop-up that contains various alignment options. One of them is Horizontal Center in Container, a constraint that you have already applied to the label from the Document Outline. There is often more than one way to achieve Auto Layout–related things in Interface Builder. As you progress through this book, you'll see alternate ways to do the most common Auto Layout tasks.

- The pop-up for the Pin button contains controls that let you set the position of a view relative to other views, and to apply size constraints. For example, you can set a constraint that limits the height of one view to be the same as that of another.

- The Resolve Auto Layout Issues button lets you correct layout problems. You can use menu items in its pop-up to have Interface Builder remove all constraints for a view (or the entire storyboard), guess which constraints might be missing, add them, and adjust the frames of one or more views to what they will be at runtime.

You can fix the label's frame by selecting it in the Document Outline or the storyboard and clicking the Resolve Auto Layout Issues button. The pop-up for this button has two identical groups of operations (see Figure 3-23).

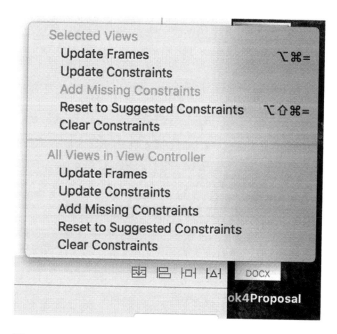

Figure 3-23. The pop-up for the Resolve Auto Layout Issues button

■ **Tip** If none of the items in the pop-up is enabled, click the label in the Document Outline to ensure that it's selected and try again.

If you select an operation from the top group, it's applied only to the currently selected view, whereas operations from the bottom group are applied to all the views in the view controller. In this case, you just need to fix the frame for one label, so click Update Frames in the top part of the pop-up. When you do this, both the orange outline and the warning triangle in the activity view disappear because the label now has the position and size that it will have at runtime. In fact, the label has shrunk to zero width, and it's represented in the storyboard by a small, empty square, as shown in Figure 3-24.

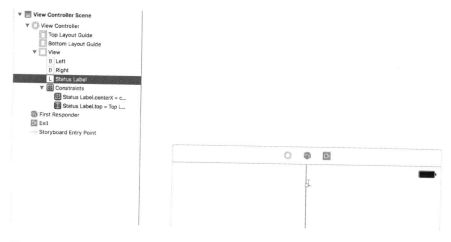

Figure 3-24. After fixing its frame, the label has shrunk to zero size

It turns out that this is actually what you want to see. Many of the views that UIKit provides, including UILabel, are capable of having Auto Layout set their size based on their actual content. They do this by calculating their natural or intrinsic content size. At its intrinsic size, the label is just wide enough and tall enough to completely surround the text that it contains. At the moment, this label has no content, so its intrinsic content size really should be zero along both axes. When you run the application and click one of the buttons, the label's text is set and its intrinsic content size changes. When that happens, Auto Layout will resize the label automatically so that you can see all of the text.

Now that you've taken care of the label, you'll fix the positions of the two buttons. Select the Left button on the storyboard and click the Align button at the bottom right of the storyboard editor (the second button in Figure 3-22, counting from the left). You want the button to be vertically centered, so select Vertical Center in Container in the pop-up and then click Add 1 Constraint (see Figure 3-25).

Figure 3-25. *Using the Align pop-up to vertically center a view*

You need to apply the same constraint to the Right button, so select it and repeat the process. While you were doing this, Interface Builder found a couple of new issues, indicated by the orange outlines in the storyboard and the warning triangle in the activity view. Click the triangle to see the reasons for the warnings in the Issue Navigator, as shown in Figure 3-26.

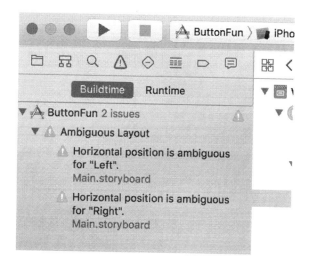

Figure 3-26. *Interface Builder warnings for missing constraints*

Interface Builder warns you that the horizontal positions of both buttons are ambiguous. In fact, since you haven't yet set any constraint to control the buttons' horizontal positions, this should not be a surprise.

■ **Note**   While setting Auto Layout constraints, it is normal for warnings like this to appear. You should use them to help you set a complete set of constraints. You should have no warnings once you have completed the layout process. Most of the examples in this book have instructions for setting layout constraints. While you are adding those constraints, you will usually encounter warnings, but don't be concerned unless you still have warnings when you have completed all of the steps. In that case, you missed a step, you performed a step incorrectly, or possibly there is an error in the book. In the latter case, please let me know by submitting an erratum on the book's page at www.apress.com.

You want the Left button to be a fixed distance from the left side of its parent view and the Right button to be the same distance from the right side of that view. You can set those constraints from the pop-up for the Pin button (the one to the right of the Align button in Figure 3-22). Select the Left button and click the Pin button to open its pop-up. At the top of the pop-up, you'll find four input fields connected to a small square by orange dashed lines, as shown on the left in Figure 3-27. The small square represents the button that you are constraining. The four input fields let you set the distances between the button and its nearest neighbors above it, below it, to its left, and to its right. A dashed line indicates that no constraint yet exists. In the case of the Left button, you want to set a fixed distance between it and the left side of its parent view, so click the dashed orange line to the left of the square. When you do this, it becomes a solid orange line indicating that there is now a constraint to apply. Next, enter **32** in the left input field to set the distance from the Left button to its parent view.

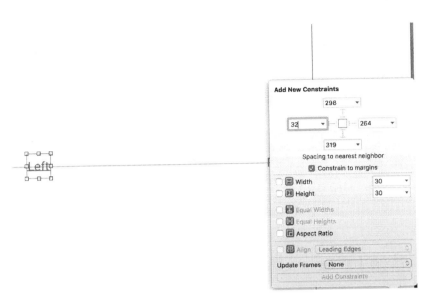

Figure 3-27. *Using the Pin pop-up to set the horizontal position of a view*

To fix the position of the Right button, select it, click the Pin button, click the orange dashed line to the right of the square (since you are pinning this button to the right side of its parent view), enter **32** in the input field, and click Add 1 Constraint.

You have now applied all the constraints that you need, but there may still be warnings in the activity view. If you investigate, you'll see that the warnings are because the buttons are not in their correct runtime locations. To fix that, you'll use the Resolve Auto Layout Issues button again. Click the button (it's the rightmost one) to open its pop-up and then click Update Frames from the bottom group of options. You use the option from the bottom group because you need the frames of all the views in the view controller to be adjusted.

■ **Tip**   You may find that none of the options in the top group is available. If this is the case, select the View Controller icon in the Document Outline and try again.

The warnings should now go away, and your layout is finally complete. Run the application on an iPhone simulator. You'll see a result that's almost like Figure 3-1 at the beginning of this chapter. When you tap the Right button, this text should appear: *Right button pressed.* If you then tap the Left button, the label will change to *Left button pressed.* Run the example on an iPad simulator, and you'll find that the layout still works, although the buttons are farther apart because of the wider screen. That's the power of Auto Layout.

■ **Tip**   When running the application on simulated devices with large screens, you may find that you can't see the whole screen at once. You can fix this by selecting Window ➤ Scale in the iOS simulator menu and choosing a scale that's appropriate for the screen you're using.

If you look back at Figure 3-1, you'll see that one thing is missing. The screenshot of the end result displays the name of the chosen button in bold text; however, what you've made just shows a plain string. You'll bring on the boldness using the NSAttributedString class in just a second; first let's look at another useful feature of Xcode—layout previews.

Previewing Layout

Return to Xcode, select Main.storyboard, and then open the Assistant Editor if it's not already showing (refer to Figure 3-6 if you need a reminder of how to do this). At the left of the jump bar at the top of the Assistant Editor, you'll see that the current selection is Automatic (unless you changed it to Manual to select the file for the Assistant Editor to display). Click to open the pop-up for this segment of the jump bar, and you'll see several options, the last of which is Preview. When you hover the cursor over Preview, a menu containing the name of the application's storyboard will appear. Click it to open the storyboard in the Preview Editor.

When the Preview Editor opens, you'll see the application as it appears on an iPhone in portrait mode. This is just a preview, so it won't respond to button clicks and, as a result, you won't see the label. If you move your mouse over the area just below the preview, where it says *iPhone 6s*, a control will appear that will let you rotate the phone into landscape mode. You can see the control on the left of Figure 3-28 and the result of clicking it to rotate the phone.

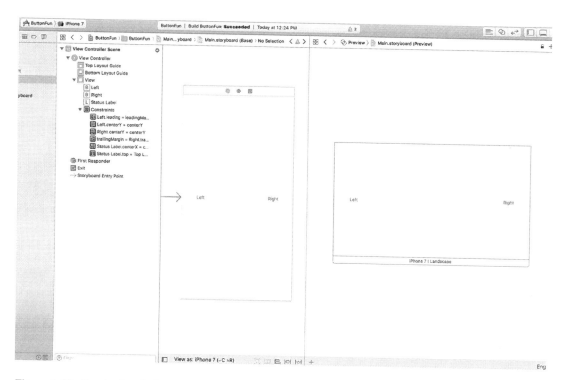

Figure 3-28. *Previewing the layout of the iPhone in landscape mode*

Using Auto Layout, when you rotate the phone, the buttons move so that they remain vertically centered and the same distance away from the sides of the device as in portrait orientation. If the label were visible, you would see that it is in the correct position as well.

You can also use the Preview Assistant to see what happens when you run the application on a different device. At the bottom left of the Preview Assistant (and in Figure 3-28), you'll see a + icon. Click this to open a list of devices and then select iPhone SE to add the new preview to the Preview Assistant. If you still can't see everything, you can zoom the Preview Assistant in a couple of different ways. The easiest is to double-click the Preview Assistant pane—this toggles between a full-size view and a much smaller view. If you'd like more control over the zoom level, you can use a pinch gesture on your trackpad (unfortunately, this is not supported on the magic mouse, at least not at the time of writing). Figure 3-29 shows the two iPhone previews, zoomed out to fit in the space available on my screen. Once again, Auto Layout has arranged for the buttons to be in the correct locations. Rotate the iPhone SE preview to see that the layout also works in landscape mode.

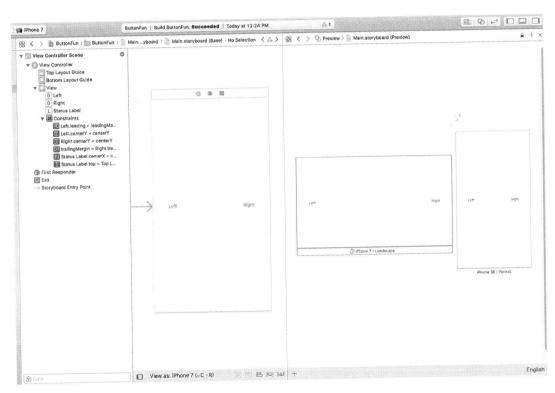

Figure 3-29. *Previewing layouts on two devices at the same time*

▓ **Note**   You can zoom the preview size in the Assistant Editor by clicking in a blank area and then using two fingers to zoom in or out using the pinch gesture.

Changing the Text Style

The NSAttributedString class lets you attach formatting information, such as fonts and paragraph alignment, to a string. This metadata can be applied to an entire string, or different attributes can be applied to different parts. If you think about the ways that formatting can be applied to pieces of text in a word processor, that's basically the model for how NSAttributedString works. Most of the main UIKit controls let you use attributed strings. In the case of a UILabel like the one you have here, it's as simple as creating an attributed string and then passing it to the label via its attributedText property.

So, select ViewController.swift and update the buttonPressed() method, as shown in Listing 3-8.

Listing 3-8. Updated buttonPressed() Method to Add Bold Font Characteristic

```
import UIKit

class ViewController: UIViewController {

    @IBOutlet weak var statusLabel: UILabel!

    @IBAction func buttonPressed(_ sender: UIButton) {
        let title = sender.title(for: .selected)!
        let text = "\(title) button pressed"
        let styledText = NSMutableAttributedString(string: text)
        let attributes = [
            NSFontAttributeName:
                UIFont.boldSystemFont(ofSize: statusLabel.font.pointSize)
        ]
        let nameRange = (text as NSString).range(of: title)
        styledText.setAttributes(attributes, range: nameRange)

        statusLabel.attributedText = styledText
    }
}
```

The first thing the new code does is create an attributed string—specifically, an NSMutableAttributedString instance—based on the string you are going to display. You need a mutable attributed string here because you want to change its attributes.

Next, you create a dictionary to hold the attributes you want to apply to your string. You have just one attribute right now, so this dictionary contains a single key-value pair. The key, NSFontAttributeName, lets you specify a font for a portion of an attributed string. The value you pass in is the bold system font of the same size as the font currently used by the label. Specifying the font this way is more flexible in the long run than specifying a font by name since you know that the system will always have a reasonable idea of what to use for a bold font.

Next, you ask your text string to give you the range (consisting of a start index and a length) of the substring where your title is found. You use the range to apply the attributes to the part of the attributed string that corresponds to the title and pass it off to the label. Let's take a closer look at the line that locates the title string:

```
let nameRange = (text as NSString).range(of: title)
```

Notice that the text variable is cast from the Swift type String to the Core Foundation type NSString. That's necessary because both String and NSString have methods called range(of: String). You need to call the NSString method to get the range as an NSRange object, since that's what the setAttributes() method on the next line expects.

Now you can hit the Run button. You'll see that the app shows the name of the clicked button in bold text, as shown in Figure 3-1.

Examining the Application Delegate

Now that your application works, let's take a minute to look through the source code file you have not yet examined—AppDelegate.swift. This file implements your *application delegate*.

Cocoa Touch makes extensive use of *delegates*, which are objects that take responsibility for doing certain tasks on behalf of another object. The application delegate lets you do things at certain predefined times on behalf of the UIApplication class. Every iOS application has exactly one instance of UIApplication, which is responsible for the application's run loop and handles application-level functionality, such as routing input to the appropriate controller class. UIApplication is a standard part of the UIKit; it does its job mostly behind the scenes, so you generally don't need to worry about it.

At certain well-defined times during an application's execution, UIApplication calls specific methods on its delegate, if the delegate exists and implements the method. For example, if you have code that needs to be executed just before your program quits, you would implement the method applicationWillTerminate() in your application delegate and put your termination code there. This type of delegation allows your application to implement behavior without needing to subclass UIApplication or, indeed, without needing to know anything about the inner workings of UIApplication. All the Xcode templates create an application delegate for you and arrange for it to be linked to the UIApplication object when the application launches.

Click AppDelegate.swift in the Project Navigator to see the stub application delegate that the project template provides. The first couple of lines should look like that shown in Listing 3-9.

Listing 3-9. Application Delegate Initial Code

```
import UIKit

@UIApplicationMain
class AppDelegate: UIResponder, UIApplicationDelegate {

    var window: UIWindow?
```

The code highlighted in bold indicates that this class conforms to a protocol called UIApplication Delegate. Hold down the ⌥ key. Your cursor should turn into crosshairs. Move your cursor so that it is over the word UIApplicationDelegate. Your cursor will turn into a question mark, and the word UIApplicationDelegate will be highlighted, as if it were a link in a browser (see Figure 3-30).

```
 9  import UIKit
10
11  @UIApplicationMain
12  class AppDelegate: UIResponder, UIApplicationDelegate {
13
14      var window: UIWindow?
15
```

Figure 3-30. *When you hold down the ⌥ key (the Option key) in Xcode and point at a symbol in your code, the symbol is highlighted and your cursor changes into a pointing hand with a question mark.*

With the ⌥ key still held down, click this link. A small pop-up window will open, showing a brief overview of the UIApplicationDelegate protocol (see Figure 3-31).

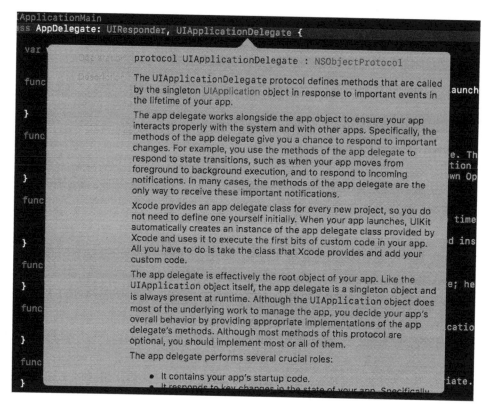

Figure 3-31. *When you ⌥-clicked UIApplicationDelegate from within your source code, Xcode popped up this window, called the Quick Help panel, which describes the protocol*

Scrolling the pop-up to the bottom, you'll find two links (see Figure 3-32).

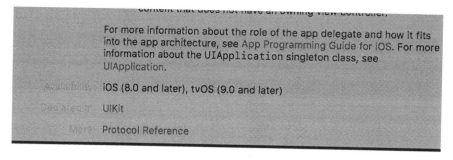

Figure 3-32. *Links to additional information about the selected item*

Notice the two links at the bottom of this new pop-up documentation window; click the More link to view the full documentation for this symbol or click the Declared In link to view the symbol's definition in a header file. This same trick works with class and protocol names, as well as method names displayed in the editor pane. Just Option-click a word, and Xcode searches for that word in the documentation browser.

Knowing how to look up things quickly in the documentation is definitely worthwhile, but looking at the definition of this protocol is perhaps more important. Here's where you'll find which methods the application delegate can implement and when those methods will be called. It's probably worth your time to read the descriptions of these methods.

Back in the Project Navigator, return to AppDelegate.swift to see the implementation of the application delegate. It should look something like Listing 3-10.

Listing 3-10. The AppDelegate.swift File

```swift
import UIKit

@UIApplicationMain
class AppDelegate: UIResponder, UIApplicationDelegate {

    var window: UIWindow?

    func application(_ application: UIApplication, didFinishLaunchingWithOptions
    launchOptions: [NSObject: AnyObject]?) -> Bool {
        // Override point for customization after application launch.
        return true
    }

    func applicationWillResignActive(_ application: UIApplication) {
        // Sent when the application is about to move from active to inactive state. This
        can occur for certain types of temporary interruptions (such as an incoming phone
        call or SMS message) or when the user quits the application and it begins the
        transition to the background state.
        // Use this method to pause ongoing tasks, disable timers, and throttle down OpenGL
        ES frame rates. Games should use this method to pause the game.
    }

    func applicationDidEnterBackground(_ application: UIApplication) {
        // Use this method to release shared resources, save user data, invalidate timers,
        and store enough application state information to restore your application to its
        current state in case it is terminated later.
        // If your application supports background execution, this method is called instead
        of applicationWillTerminate: when the user quits.
    }

    func applicationWillEnterForeground(_ application: UIApplication) {
        // Called as part of the transition from the background to the active state; here
        you can undo many of the changes made on entering the background.
    }
```

```swift
func applicationDidBecomeActive(_ application: UIApplication) {
    // Restart any tasks that were paused (or not yet started) while the application was
    inactive. If the application was previously in the background, optionally refresh
    the user interface.
}

func applicationWillTerminate(_ application: UIApplication) {
    // Called when the application is about to terminate. Save data if appropriate. See
    also applicationDidEnterBackground:.
}
}
```

At the top of the file, you can see that your application delegate has implemented one of those protocol methods covered in the documentation, called application(_: didFinishLaunchingWithOptions:). As you can probably guess, this method fires as soon as the application has finished all the setup work and is ready to start interacting with the user. It is often used to create any objects that need to exist for the entire lifetime of the running app.

You'll see more of this later in the book, where I'll say a lot more about the role that the delegate plays in the application life cycle. I just wanted to give you a bit of background on application delegates and show how this all ties together before closing this chapter.

Summary

This chapter's simple application introduced you to MVC, creating and connecting outlets and actions, implementing view controllers, and using application delegates. You learned how to trigger action methods when a button is tapped. And you saw how to change the text of a label at runtime. Although you built a simple application, the basic concepts used are the same as those that underlie the use of all controls under iOS, not just buttons. In fact, the way you used buttons and labels in this chapter is pretty much the way that you will implement and interact with most of the standard controls under iOS.

It's critical to understand everything you did in this chapter and why you did it. If you don't, make sure to review the parts that you don't fully understand. If things are not completely clear, you will only get more confused as you get into creating more complex interfaces later in this book.

In the next chapter, you'll take a look at some of the other standard iOS controls. You'll also learn how to use alerts to notify the user of important happenings and how to use action sheets to indicate that the user needs to make a choice before proceeding.

CHAPTER 4

■ ■ ■

Adding Intermediate-Level User Interactions

In Chapter 3, I discussed MVC, and you built an application using it. You learned about outlets and actions, and you used them to tie a button to a text label. In this chapter, you'll build an application with a broader set of controls to increase your familiarity with developing a user interface, like the one shown in Figure 4-1.

Figure 4-1. *This chapter's project increases your UI skills by adding several new controls to the mix*

© Molly K. Maskrey 2017
M. K. Maskrey, *Beginning iPhone Development with Swift 4*, https://doi.org/10.1007/978-1-4842-3072-5_4

You'll implement an image view, a slider, two different text fields, a segmented control, a couple of switches, and an iOS button that looks like buttons did before iOS 7. You'll see how to set and retrieve the values of various controls. You'll learn how to use action sheets to force the user to make a choice and how to use alerts to give the user important feedback. You'll also learn about control states and the use of stretchable images to change the appearance of buttons.

Because this chapter's application uses so many different user interface items, you're going to work a little differently than you did in the previous two chapters. You'll break your application into pieces, implementing one piece at a time. Bouncing back and forth between Xcode and the iOS simulator, you'll test each piece before you move on to the next. Dividing the process of building a complex interface into smaller components makes it much less intimidating, as well as more like the actual process you'll go through when building your own applications. This *code-compile-debug* cycle makes up a large part of a software developer's typical day.

Your app uses only a single view and controller, but as you can see in Figure 4-1, there's a lot more complexity in this one view.

The logo at the top of the screen exists in an image view, which, in this app, does nothing more than display a static image. I placed two text fields below the logo: one allowing the entry of alphanumeric text and the other permitting only numbers. A slider sits just below the text fields. As the user moves the slider, the value of the label next to it changes so that it always reflects the slider's current value.

Below the slider are a segmented control and two switches. The segmented control toggles between two different types of controls in the space underneath it. When the application first launches, two switches appear below the segmented control. Changing the value of either switch causes the other one to change its value to match. While this isn't something you would likely do in a real application, it demonstrates how to change the value of a control programmatically and how Cocoa Touch animates certain actions without you needing to do any work.

Figure 4-2 shows what happens when the user taps the segmented control. The switches disappear and are replaced by a button.

Figure 4-2. *Tapping the segmented controller on the left side causes a pair of switches to be displayed. Tapping the right side causes a button to be displayed, as shown here.*

Pressing Do Something causes an action sheet to pop up, asking if the user really meant to tap the button (see Figure 4-3). Notice how the action sheet is now highlighted and in the foreground, while the other controls become dimmed.

Figure 4-3. *An action sheet requests a response from the user*

This provides a standard way of responding to input that is potentially dangerous or that could have significant repercussions, and it gives the user a chance to stop potential problems from happening. If Yes, I'm Sure! is selected, the application displays an alert, letting the user know that everything is OK (see Figure 4-4).

Figure 4-4. *Alerts notify the user when important things happen. This app uses one to confirm that everything went OK.*

Understanding Active, Static, and Passive Controls

Interface controls operate in three basic modes: active, static (or inactive), and passive. The buttons that you used in the previous chapter provide classic examples of active controls. You push them, and something happens—usually, a piece of Swift code you've written executes.

Although many of the controls you use directly trigger action methods, not all controls work this way. The image view that you'll be implementing in this does nothing other than show an image in your application; however, it can be configured to trigger action methods—here, the user doesn't do anything with it. Labels and image controls often work in this manner.

Some controls operate in a passive mode, simply holding on to a value that the user has entered until you're ready for it. These controls don't trigger action methods, but the user can interact with them and change their values. A classic example of a passive control is a text field on a web page. Although it's possible to create validation code that fires when the user tabs out of a field, the vast majority of web page text fields simply contain data that's submitted to the server when the user clicks the submit button. The text fields themselves usually don't cause any code to fire, but when the submit button is clicked, the text field's data gets passed to the associated Swift code.

On an iOS device, most of the available controls function in all three modes, and nearly all of them can function in more than one mode, depending on your needs. All iOS controls exist as subclasses of UIControl, which makes them capable of triggering action methods. Many controls can be used passively, and all of them can be made inactive or invisible. For example, using one control might trigger another inactive control to become active. However, some controls, such as buttons, really don't serve much purpose unless they are used in an active manner to trigger code.

Some behavioral differences exist between controls on iOS and those on your Mac. Here are a few examples:

- Because of the multitouch interface, all iOS controls can trigger multiple actions, depending on how they are touched. The user might trigger a different action with a finger swipe across the control than with just a tap.

- You could have one action fire when the user presses down on a button and a separate action fire when the finger is lifted off the button.

- You could have a single control call multiple action methods on a single event. For example, you could have two different action methods fire on the Touch Up Inside event when the user's finger is lifted after touching that button.

▨ **Note**　Although controls can trigger multiple methods on iOS, the vast majority of the time you're better off implementing a single action method that does what you need for a particular use of a control. You won't usually need this capability, but it's good to keep it in mind when working in Interface Builder. Connecting an event to an action in Interface Builder does not disconnect a previously connected action from the same control! This can lead to surprising misbehaviors in your app, where a control will trigger multiple action methods. Keep an eye open when retargeting an event in Interface Builder, and make sure you remove old actions before connecting to new ones.

Another major difference between iOS and the Mac stems from the fact that, normally, iOS devices do not have a physical keyboard. The standard iOS software keyboard is actually just a view filled with a series of button controls that are managed for you by the system. Your code will likely never directly interact with the iOS keyboard.

Creating the ControlFun Application

Open Xcode and create a new project called **ControlFun**. You'll use the Single View App template again, so create the project just as you did in the previous two chapters.

Now that you've created your project, let's get the image you'll use in your image view. The image must be imported into Xcode before it will be available for use inside Interface Builder, so let's do that now. You'll find three files in the 04 - Logos folder in the example source code archive, named apress_logo.png, apress_logo@2x.png, and apress_logo@3x.png, which are a standard version and two Retina versions of the same image. You're going to add all three of these to the new project's asset catalog and let the app decide which of them to use at runtime. If you'd rather use a set of images of your own choosing, make sure they are .png images sized correctly for the space available. The small version should be less than 100 pixels tall and a maximum of 300 pixels wide so that it can fit comfortably at the top of the view on the narrowest iPhone screen without being resized. The larger ones should be twice and three times the size of the small version, respectively.

In Xcode, select Assets.xcassets in the Project Navigator; then go to the Logos folder in the Finder and select all three images. Now drag the images onto the editor area in Xcode and release the mouse. Xcode uses the image names to figure out that you are adding three versions of an image called apress_logo and does the rest of the work for you (see Figure 4-5). You'll see that there is now an apress_logo entry in the left column of the editing area below the AppIcon entry that you started with. You can now use the name apress_logo in code or in Interface Builder to refer to this image set and the correct one will be loaded at runtime.

Figure 4-5. *Adding the apress_logo images into the Xcode project*

Implementing the Image View and Text Fields

With the image added to your project, your next step is to implement the five interface elements at the top of the application's screen: the image view, the two text fields, and the two labels, as shown in Figure 4-6.

Name:	Type in a name
Number:	Type in a number

Figure 4-6. *The image view, labels, and text fields you implement first*

Adding the Image View

In the Project Navigator, click `Main.storyboard` to open the main storyboard in Interface Builder. You'll see the familiar white background and a single square view where you can lay out your application's interface. As you did in the previous chapter, beneath the IB window select iPhone 7 as your "View as" choice.

Note   This section below the canvas, which came out with Xcode 8 and is known as the *view dimension*, allows you to select how you view the scene you're working with in your IB canvas.

If the Object Library is not open, select View ➤ Utilities ➤ Show Object Library to open it. Scroll about one-fourth of the way through the list until you find ImageView (see Figure 4-7) or just type **image** in the search field. Remember that the Object Library corresponds to the third icon on top of the Library pane.

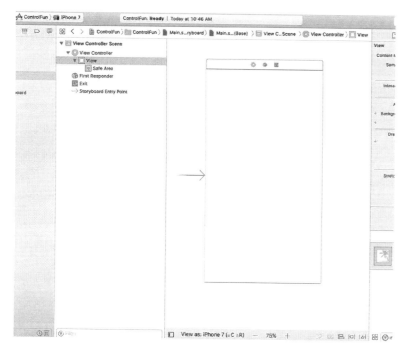

Figure 4-7. *The Image View element in Interface Builder's Object Library*

Drag an image view onto the view in the storyboard editor and drop it somewhere near the top of the view, as shown in Figure 4-8. Don't worry about exactly positioning yet—you'll adjust that in the next section.

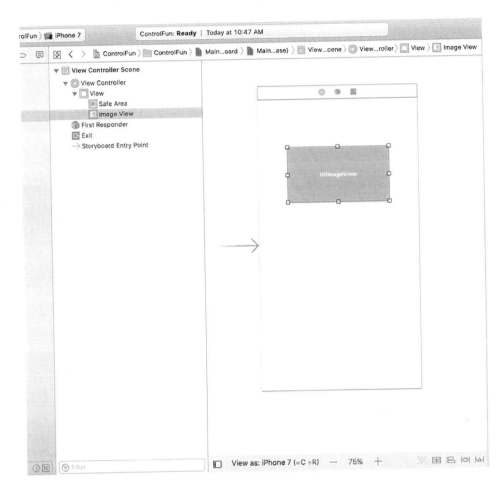

Figure 4-8. *Adding a UIImageView to your storyboard*

With the image view selected, bring up the Attributes Inspector by pressing ⌥⌘ **4**. You should see the editable options of the UIImageView class. The most important setting for your image view is the topmost item in the inspector, labeled Image. Click the little arrow to the right of the field to see a pop-up menu that lists the available images. This list includes any images you added to your project's assets catalog. Select the apress_logo image you added earlier, and it should appear in your image view, as shown in Figure 4-9.

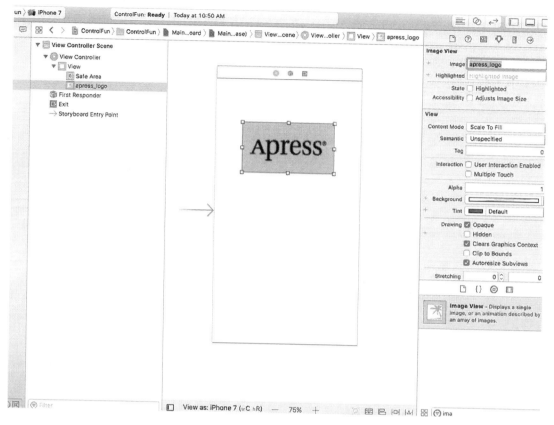

Figure 4-9. *The image view Attributes Inspector. You selected your image from the Image pop-up at the top of the inspector, and this populated the image view with your image.*

Resizing the Image View

The image you used is not the same size as the image view in which it was placed. Xcode, by default, scales the image to completely fill its image view. A big clue that this is so is the Mode setting in the Attributes Inspector, which is set to Scale To Fill. Though you could keep your app this way, it's generally a good idea to do any image scaling that's needed before runtime, as image scaling takes time and processor cycles. In this case, you don't want any scaling at all, so let's resize your image view to the exact size of your image. Start by changing the Mode attribute to Center, which says that the image should not be scaled and should be centered in whatever space is assigned to the image view. Now let's fit the image view to the size of the image. To do that, make sure the image view is selected so that you can see its outline and resize handles and then press ⌘= or select Editor ➤ Size to Fit Content in Xcode's menu. If pressing ⌘= does not work or Size to Fit Content is grayed out, reselect the image view, drag it a little way to the side, and try again.

■ **Tip**   If you encounter difficulty selecting an item in the editing area, you can open the Document Outline by clicking the small rectangular icon in the lower-left corner. Now, click the item you want selected in the Document Outline and, sure enough, that item will be selected in the editor.

To get at an object that is nested inside another object, click the disclosure triangle to the left of the enclosing object to reveal the nested object. In this case, to select the image view, first click the disclosure triangle to the left of the view. Then, when the image view appears in the Document Outline, click it, and it will be selected in the editing area.

Now that the image view is resized, let's move it back to its centered position. You already know how to do that because you did the same thing in Chapter 3. Drag the image view until it's horizontally centered, click the Align icon at the bottom right of the editor area, check the Horizontally in Container check box, and click Add 1 Constraint.

You may notice that Interface Builder shows some solid lines running from an edge of one view to an edge of its superview (not to be confused with the dashed blue lines that are shown while you're dragging things around) or from one side of the superview to another. These solid lines represent the constraints that you have added. If you select the constraint that you just added by clicking it, you'll see that it becomes a solid orange line that runs the entire height of the main view, as shown in Figure 4-10.

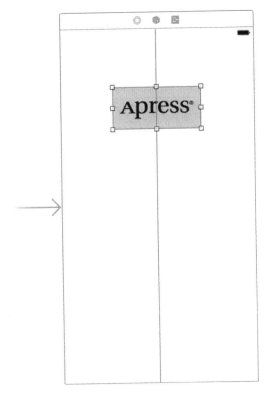

Figure 4-10. *Once you have resized your image view to fit the size of its image, you drag it into position using the view's blue guidelines and create a constraint to keep it centered*

The solid line indicates that you have selected the constraint. The fact that it is orange means that the position or size of the image view is not yet fully specified and so you need to add more constraints. You can find out what the problem is by clicking the orange triangle in the activity view. In this case, Xcode is telling you that you need to set a vertical constraint for the image view. You can either do so now, using the techniques you saw in Chapter 3, or wait until you fix all the constraints for your layout later in the chapter.

■ **Tip**   Dragging and resizing views in Interface Builder can be tricky. Don't forget about the Document Outline, which you can open by clicking the small rectangular icon at the bottom left of the editing area. When it comes to resizing, hold down the ➤ key, and Interface Builder will draw some helpful red lines on the screen that make it much easier to get a sense of the image view's position. This trick won't work with dragging since the ➤ key will prompt Interface Builder to make a copy of the dragged object. However, if you select Editor ➤ Canvas ➤ Show Bounds Rectangles, Interface Builder will draw a line around all of your interface items, making them easier to see. You can turn off those lines by selecting Show Bounds Rectangles a second time.

Setting View Attributes

Select your image view and then switch your attention back over to the Attributes Inspector. Below the Image View section in the inspector is the View section. As you may have deduced, the pattern here is that the attributes that are specific to the selected object are shown at the top, followed by more general attributes that apply to the selected object's parent class. In this case, the parent class of UIImageView is UIView, so the next section is simply labeled View, and it contains attributes that any view class has.

Using the Mode Attribute

The first option in the view inspector is a pop-up menu labeled Mode. The Mode menu defines how the view will display its content. As you've already seen, in the case of the image view, this determines how the image will be aligned inside the view and whether it will be scaled to fit. Feel free to try various options for apress_logo, but remember to reset it to Center when you have finished.

As noted earlier, choosing any option that causes the image to scale will potentially add processing overhead at runtime, so it's best to avoid that whenever possible and size your images correctly before you import them. If you want to display the same image at multiple sizes, generally it's better to have multiple copies of the image at different sizes in your project, rather than force the iOS device to do scaling at runtime. Of course, there are times when scaling at runtime is appropriate and even unavoidable; this is a guideline, not a rule.

Using the Semantic Attribute

Immediately below Mode, you'll find the Semantic attribute. Added in iOS 9, this attribute lets you specify how the view should be rendered in a locale that uses a right-to-left reading order, such as Hebrew or Arabic. By default, the view is unspecified, but you can change this by selecting an appropriate value here. Refer to the description of the semanticContentAttribute property in the Xcode documentation for the UIView class for more details.

Using Tag

The next item, Tag, is worth mentioning, though you won't be using it in this chapter. All subclasses of UIView, including all views and controls, have a property called tag, which is just a numeric value that you can set here or in code. The tag is designed for your use—the system will never set or change its value. If you assign a tag value to a control or view, you can be sure that the tag will always have that value unless you change it.

Tags provide an easy, language-independent way of identifying objects in your interface. Let's say that you have five different buttons, each with a different label, and you want to use a single action method to handle all five buttons. In that case, you probably need some way to differentiate among the buttons when your action method is called. Unlike labels, tags will never change, so if you set a tag value here in Interface Builder, you can use it as a fast and reliable way to check which control was passed into an action method by using the sender argument.

Using Interaction Check Boxes

The two check boxes in the Interaction section have to do with user interaction. The first check box, User Interaction Enabled, specifies whether the user can do anything at all with this object. For most controls, this box will be selected because, if it's not, the control will never be able to trigger action methods. However, image views default to unchecked because they are often used just for the display of static information. Since all you're doing here is displaying a picture on the screen, there is no need to turn this on.

The second check box is Multiple Touch, and it determines whether this control is capable of receiving multitouch events. Multitouch events allow complex gestures such as the pinch gesture used to zoom in on many iOS applications. Since this image view doesn't accept user interaction at all, there's no reason to turn on multitouch events, so leave this check box deselected.

Using the Alpha Value

The next item in the inspector is Alpha. Be careful when using Alpha as it defines how transparent your view is—how much of what's beneath it shows through. It's defined as a floating-point number between 0.0 and 1.0, where 0.0 is fully transparent and 1.0 is completely opaque. If you use any value less than 1.0, your iOS device will draw this view with some amount of transparency so that any objects behind it show through. With a value of less than 1.0, even if there's nothing interesting behind your view, you will cause your application to spend processor cycles compositing your partially transparent view over the emptiness behind it. Therefore, don't set Alpha to anything other than 1.0 unless you have a very good reason for doing so.

Using Background

The next item down, Background, determines the color of the background for the view. For image views, this matters only when an image doesn't fill its view and is letterboxed or when parts of the image are transparent. Since you've sized your view to perfectly match your image, this setting will have no visible effect, so you can leave it alone.

Using Tint

The next control lets you specify a tint color for the selected view. This is a color that some views use when drawing themselves. The segmented control that you'll use later in this chapter colors itself using its tint color, but the UIImageView does not.

Drawing Check Boxes

Below Tint you'll find a series of Drawing check boxes. The first one is labeled Opaque. That should be checked by default; if not, click to select that check box. This tells iOS that nothing behind your view needs to be drawn and allows iOS's drawing methods to do some optimizations that speed up drawing.

You might be wondering why you need to select the Opaque check box when you've already set the value of Alpha to 1.0 to indicate no transparency. The Alpha value applies to the parts of the image to be drawn; if an image doesn't completely fill the image view or there are holes in the image thanks to an alpha channel, the objects below will still show through, regardless of the value set in Alpha. By selecting Opaque, you are telling iOS that nothing behind this view ever needs to be drawn, no matter what, so it does not need to waste processing time with anything behind your object. You can safely select the Opaque check box because you selected Size To Fit earlier, which caused the image view to match the size of the image it contains.

The Hidden check box does exactly what you think it does. If it's selected, the user can't see this object. Hiding an object can be useful at times, as you'll see later in this chapter when you hide your switches and button; however, the vast majority of the time—including now—you want this to remain unchecked.

The next check box, Clears Graphics Context, will rarely need to be selected. When it is selected, iOS will draw the entire area covered by the object in transparent black before it actually draws the object. Again, it should be turned off for the sake of performance and because it's rarely needed. Make sure this check box is deselected (it is likely selected by default).

Clip Subviews is an interesting option. If your view contains subviews and those subviews are not completely contained within the bounds of its parent view, this check box determines how the subviews will be drawn. If Clip Subviews is selected, only the portions of subviews that lie within the bounds of the parent will be drawn. If Clip Subviews is deselected, subviews will be drawn completely, even if they lie outside the bounds of the parent.

Clip Subviews is deselected by default. It might seem that the default behavior should be the opposite of what it actually is so that child views won't be able to draw all over the place. However, calculating the clipping area and displaying only part of the subviews is a somewhat costly operation, mathematically speaking; most of the time, a subview won't lie outside the bounds of its superview. You can turn on Clip Subviews if you really need it for some reason, but it is off by default for the sake of performance.

The last check box in this section, Autoresize Subviews, tells iOS to resize any subviews if this view is resized. Leave this selected, but since you don't allow your view to be resized, it really does not matter whether it's selected or not.

Stretching

Next you'll see a section simply labeled Stretching, which refers to the form of rectangular views being redrawn as they're resized on the screen. The idea is that, rather than the entire content of a view being stretched uniformly, you can keep the outer edges of a view, such as the beveled edge of a button, looking the same even as the center portion stretches.

The four floating-point values set here let you declare which portion of the rectangle is stretchable by specifying a point at the upper-left corner of the view and the size of the stretchable area, all in the form of a number between 0.0 and 1.0 that represents a portion of the overall view size. For example, if you wanted to keep 10 percent of each edge not stretchable, you would specify 0.1 for both X and Y and specify 0.8 for both Width and Height. In this case, you're going to leave the default values of 0.0 for X and Y and 1.0 for Width and Height. Most of the time, you will not change these values.

Adding the Text Fields

With your image view finished, it's time to bring on the text fields. Grab a text field from the Object Library and drag it onto the storyboard. Use the blue guidelines to align it with the right margin and place it a little way below the image view, as shown in Figure 4-11.

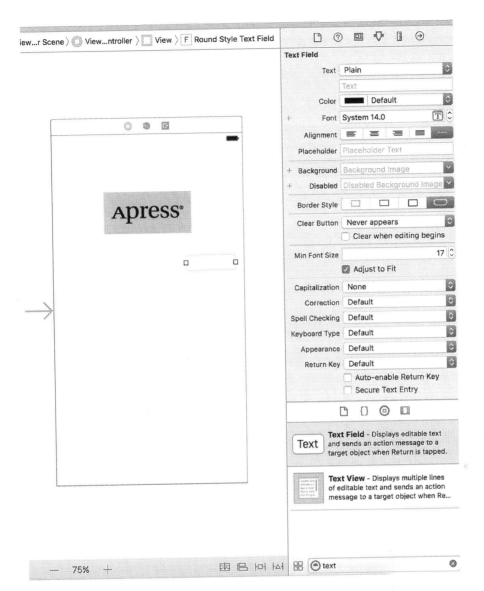

Figure 4-11. *Drag a text field out of the library and drop it onto the view, just below the image view and touching the right side's blue guideline*

Next, grab a label from the library and then drag that over so it is aligned with the left margin of the view and vertically with the text field you placed earlier. Notice that multiple blue guidelines will pop up as you move the label around, making it easy to align the label to the text field using the top, bottom, or middle of the label. You're going to align the label and the text field using the baseline, which shows up as you're dragging around the middle of those guidelines (see Figure 4-12).

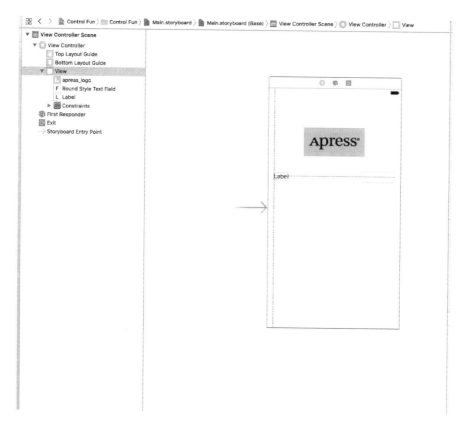

Figure 4-12. Aligning the label and text field using the baseline guide

Double-click the label you just dropped, change it to read **Name:** instead of Label (note the colon character at the end of the label), and press the Enter key to commit your changes.

Next, drag another text field from the library to the view and use the guidelines to place it below the first text field, as shown in Figure 4-13.

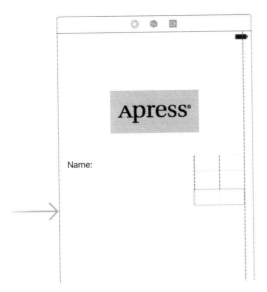

Figure 4-13. *Adding the second text field*

Once you've added the second text field, grab another label from the library and place it on the left side, below the existing label. Again, use the middle blue guideline to align your new label with the second text field. Double-click the new label and change it to read **Number:** (again, don't forget the colon).

Now, let's expand the size of the bottom text field to the left, so it is up against the right side of the label. Why start with the bottom text field? You want the two text fields to be the same size, and the bottom label is longer.

Single-click the bottom text field and drag the left resize dot to the left until a blue guideline appears to tell you that you are as close as you should ever be to the label, as shown in Figure 4-14. This particular guideline is somewhat subtle—it's only as tall as the text field itself, so be sure to look closely.

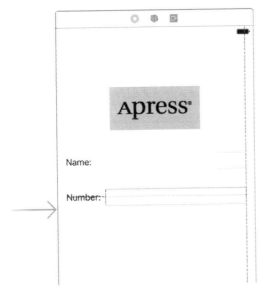

Figure 4-14. *Expand the width of the bottom text field*

Now, expand the top text field in the same way so that it matches the bottom one in size. Once again, a blue guideline provides some help, and this one extends all the way down to the other text field, making it easier to spot.

You're basically finished with the text fields, except for one small detail. Look back at Figure 4-1. Do you see how the Name: and Number: are right-aligned? Right now, yours are both against the left margin. To align the right sides of the two labels, click the Name: label, hold down the ⇧ (Shift) key, and click the Number: label so both labels are selected. Next, press ⌥⌘4 to bring up the Attributes Inspector and make sure the Label section is expanded so you can see the label-specific attributes. If it's not expanded, click the Show button on the right of the header to open it. Now use the Alignment control in the inspector to make the content of these labels right-justified and then make a constraint to make sure that these two fields are always the same width by clicking the Pin icon at the bottom of the editing area, checking the Equal Widths check box in the pop-up that appears, and clicking Add 1 Constraint. At this point, you'll have an orange warning triangle in the activity view and some layout warnings in the Issue Navigator. Ignore these for now—you'll fix them later.

When you are finished, this part of the interface should look very much like Figure 4-1. The only difference is the light-gray text in each text field. You'll add that now. Select the top text field (the one next to the Name: label) and press ⌥⌘4 to bring up the Attributes Inspector (see Figure 4-15). The text field is one of the most complex iOS controls, as well as one of the most commonly used. Let's look through the settings, beginning from the top of the inspector. *Make sure you've selected the text field and not the label or other elements.*

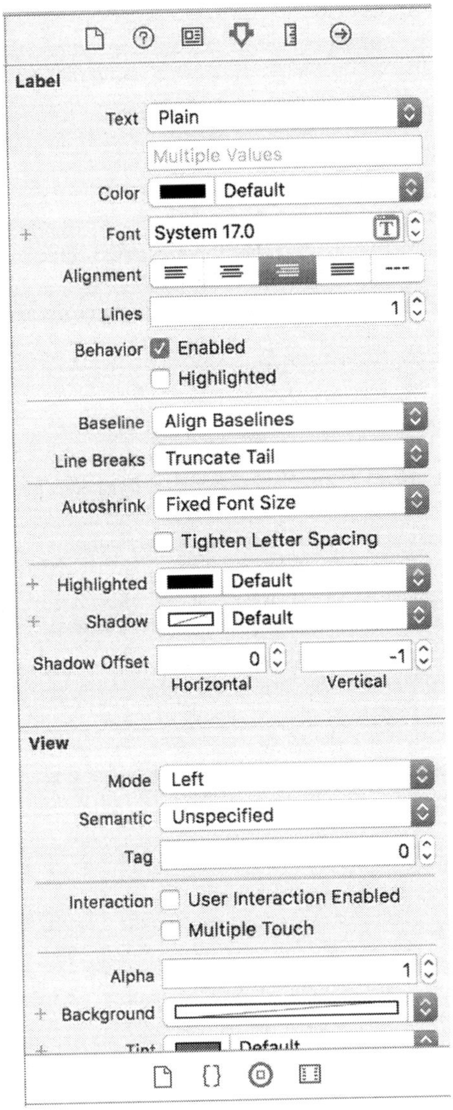

Figure 4-15. *The inspector for a text field showing the default values*

Using Text Field Inspector Settings

In the first section, the Text label is linked to two input fields that give you some control over the text that will appear in the text field. The upper one is a pop-up button that lets you choose between plain text and attributed text, which can contain a variety of fonts and other attributes. You used attributed text to add bold to part of the text in your example in Chapter 3. Let's leave that pop-up button set to Plain for now. Immediately below that, you can set a default value for the text field. Whatever you type here will show up in the text field when your application launches, instead of just a blank space.

After that comes a couple of controls that let you set the font and font color. You'll leave Color at the default value of black. Note that the Color pop-up is divided into two parts. The right side allows you to select from a set of preselected colors, and the left side gives you access to a color picker to more precisely specify your color.

The Font setting is divided into three parts. On the right side is a control that lets you increment or decrement the text size, one point at a time. The left side allows you to manually edit the font name or size. You can click the T-in-a-box icon to bring up a pop-up window that lets you set the various font attributes. You'll leave the font at its default setting of System 14.0 or to whatever size your configuration may be set.

Below these fields are five buttons for controlling the alignment of the text displayed in the field. You'll leave this setting at the default value of left-aligned (the leftmost button).

Rounding out this first section, Placeholder allows you to specify a bit of text that will be displayed in gray inside the text field, but only when the field does not have a value. You can use a placeholder instead of adding a label to the layout (as you did) if space is tight, or you can use it to clarify what the user should type in this text field. Type the text **Type in a name** as the placeholder for your currently selected text field and then hit Enter to commit the change.

The next two fields, Background and Disabled, are used only if you need to customize the appearance of your text field, which is unnecessary and actually ill-advised the vast majority of the time. Users expect text fields to look a certain way. You'll leave these set to their defaults.

Next are four buttons labeled Border Style. These allow you to change the way the text field's edge will be drawn. The default value (the rightmost button) creates the text field style that users are most accustomed to seeing for normal text fields in an iOS application. You may want to look at all four different styles, but when you're finished, put this setting back to the rightmost button.

Below the border setting is a Clear button pop-up button, which lets you choose when the Clear button should appear. The Clear button is the small *X* that can appear at the right end of a text field. Clear buttons are typically used with search fields and other fields where you would be likely to change the value frequently. They are not typically included on text fields used to persist data, so leave this at the default value of "Never appears."

The Clear When Editing Begins check box specifies what happens when the user touches this field. If this box is checked, any value that was previously in this field will be deleted, and the user will start with an empty field. If this box is unchecked, the previous value will remain in the field, and the user will be able to edit it. Leave this deselected.

The next section starts with a control that lets you set the minimum font size that the text field will use for displaying its text. Leave that at its default value for now. The Adjust to Fit check box specifies whether the size of the text should shrink if the text field is reduced in size. Adjusting to fit will keep the entire text visible in the view, even if the text would normally be too big to fit in the allotted space. This check box works in conjunction with the minimum font size setting. No matter the size of the field, the text will not be resized below that minimum size. Specifying a minimum size allows you to make sure that the text doesn't get too small to be readable.

The next section defines how the keyboard will look and behave when this text field is being used. Since you're expecting a name, let's change the Capitalization pop-up to Words. This causes the first letter of every word to be automatically capitalized, which is what you typically want with names.

The next four pop-ups—Correction, Spell Checking, Keyboard Type, and Appearance—can be left at their default values. Take a minute to look at each to get a sense of what these settings do.

Next is the Return Key pop-up. The Return key is on the lower right of the virtual keyboard, and its label changes based on what you're doing. If you are entering text in Safari's search field, for example, it says Search. In an application like this one, where the text fields share the screen with other controls, Done is the right choice. Make that change here.

If the Auto-enable Return Key check box is selected, the Return key is disabled until at least one character is typed into the text field. Leave this deselected because you want to allow the text field to remain empty if the user prefers not to enter anything.

The Secure check box specifies whether the characters being typed are displayed in the text field. You would check this check box if the text field was being used as a password field. Leave it unchecked for your app.

The next section (which you will probably have to scroll down to see) allows you to set control attributes inherited from UIControl; however, these generally don't apply to text fields and, with the exception of the Enabled check box, won't affect the field's appearance. You want to leave these text fields enabled so that the user can interact with them. Leave the default settings in this section.

The last section on the inspector, View, should look familiar. It's identical to the section of the same name in the Image View Inspector you looked at earlier. These are attributes inherited from the UIView class; since all controls are subclasses of UIView, they all share this section of attributes. As you did earlier for the image view, select the Opaque check box and deselect Clears Graphics Context and Clip Subviews—for the reasons discussed earlier.

Setting the Attributes for the Second Text Field

Next, single-click the lower text field (the one next to the Number: label) in the storyboard and return to the Attributes Inspector. In the Placeholder field, type **Type in a number** and make sure Clear When Editing Begins is deselected. A little farther down, click the Keyboard Type pop-up menu. Since you want the user to enter only numbers, not letters, select Number Pad. On the iPhone, this ensures that the users will be presented with a keyboard containing only numbers, meaning they won't be able to enter alphabetical characters, symbols, or anything other than numbers. You don't need to set the Return Key value for the numeric keypad because that style of keyboard doesn't have a Return key; therefore, all of the other inspector settings can stay at the default values. As you did earlier, select the Opaque check box and deselect Clears Graphics Context and Clip Subviews. On the iPad, selecting Number Pad has the effect of bringing up a full virtual keyboard in numeric mode when the user activates the text field, but the user can switch back to alphabetic input. This means that in a real application, you would have to verify that the user actually entered a valid number when processing the content of the Number field.

▓ **Tip**　　If you really want to stop the user from typing anything other than numbers into a text field, you can do so by creating a class that implements the textView(_ textView: shouldChangeTextInRange: replacementText text:) method of the UITextViewDelegate protocol and making it the text view's delegate. The details are not too complex but are beyond the scope of this book.

Adding Constraints

Before you continue, you need to adjust some layout constraints. When you drag a view into another view in Interface Builder (as you just did), Xcode doesn't create any constraints for it automatically. The layout system requires a complete set of constraints, so when it's time to compile your code, Xcode generates a set of default constraints describing the layout. The constraints depend on each object's position within its superview; when it's nearer the left or right edge, it will be pinned to the left or the right, respectively. Similarly, depending on whether it's nearer the top or the bottom edge, it will be pinned to the top or the bottom. If it's centered in either direction, it typically gets a constraint pinning it to the center.

To complicate matters further, Xcode may also apply automatic constraints pinning each new object to one or more of its "sibling" objects within the same superview. This automatic behavior may or may not be what you want, so normally you're better off creating a complete set of constraints within Interface Builder before your app is compiled, and in the previous two chapters, you worked through some examples.

Let's again look at where you're at on this. To see all the constraints that are in play for any particular view, try selecting it and opening the Size Inspector. If you select either of the text fields, you'll see that the Size Inspector shows a message claiming that there are no constraints for the selected view. In fact, this GUI you've been building has only the constraints that you applied earlier, binding the horizontal centers of the image view and the container view and making the labels equally sized. Click the image view and the labels to see these constraints in the inspector.

What you really want is a full set of constraints to tell the layout system precisely how to handle all of your views and controls, just as it would get at compile time. Fortunately, this is pretty simple to accomplish. Select all the views and controls by click-dragging a box around them, from inside the upper-left corner of your container view down toward the lower right. If you start dragging and find that the view starts moving instead, just release the mouse, move it a little bit further inside the view, and try again. When all items are selected, use the menu to execute the Editor ➤ Resolve Auto Layout Issues ➤ Add Missing Constraints command from the All Views in View Controller section of the menu. After doing that, you'll see that all your views and controls now have some little blue sticks connecting them to one another and to the container view. Each of those sticks represents a constraint. The advantage of creating these now instead of letting Xcode create them at compile time is that you have a chance to modify each constraint if you need to do so. You'll explore more of what you can do with constraints throughout the book.

▨ **Tip**   Another way to apply constraints to all the views owned by a view controller is to select the view controller in the Document Outline and then choose Editor ➤ Resolve Auto Layout Issues ➤ Add Missing Constraints.

At this point, with all the necessary constraints in place, you can fix the layout warnings in the Issue Navigator. To do that, select the view controller in the Document Outline and then click Editor ➤ Resolve Auto Layout Issues ➤ Update Frames in the Xcode menu. The layout warnings should be gone.

Creating and Connecting Outlets

For this first part of the interface, all that's left is creating and connecting your outlets. The image view and labels on your interface do not need outlets because you don't need to change them at runtime. The two text fields, however, will hold data you'll need to use in your code, so you need outlets pointing to each of them.

As you probably remember from the previous chapter, Xcode allows you to create and connect outlets at the same time using the Assistant Editor, which should already be open (but if it's not, open it as described earlier).

Make sure your storyboard file is selected in the Project Navigator. If you don't have a large amount of screen real estate, you might also want to select View ➤ Utilities ➤ Hide Utilities to hide the Utilities area during this step. In the Assistant Editor's jump bar, select Automatic. You should see the ViewController. swift file, as shown in Figure 4-16.

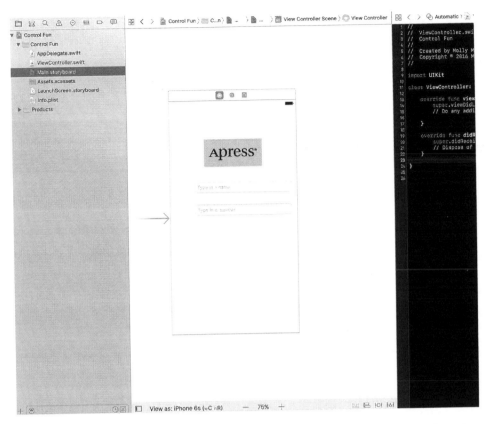

Figure 4-16. *The storyboard editing area with the Assistant Editor open. You can see the Assistant Editor on the right, showing the code from ViewController.swift.*

Let's start connecting things up. Control-drag from the top text field to the `ViewController.swift` file, right below the `ViewController` line. You should see a gray pop-up that reads Insert Outlet, Action, or Outlet Collection (see Figure 4-17). Release the mouse button and you'll get the same pop-up you saw in the previous chapter. You want to create an outlet called `nameField`, so type **nameField** into the Name field and then hit Return or click the Connect button.

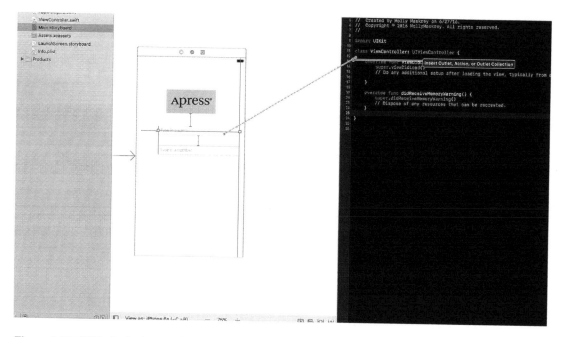

Figure 4-17. *With the Assistant Editor open, you Control-drag over to the source code in order to simultaneously create the nameField outlet and connect it to the appropriate text field.*

You now have a property called nameField in ViewController, and it has been connected to the top text field. Do the same for the second text field, creating and connecting it to a property called numberField. When you've done that, your code should look like Listing 4-1.

Listing 4-1. Your Connected Text Fields

```
class ViewController: UIViewController {
    @IBOutlet weak var nameField: UITextField!
    @IBOutlet weak var numberField: UITextField!
```

Closing the Keyboard

Let's see how the app works so far, select Product ➤ Run. The application should come up in the iOS simulator. Click the Name text field, and the traditional keyboard should appear.

■ **Tip** If the keyboard does not appear, the simulator may be configured to work as if a hardware keyboard had been connected. To fix that, deselect Hardware ➤ Keyboard ➤ Connect Hardware Keyboard in the iOS simulator menu and try again.

Type a name and then tap the Number field. The numeric keypad should appear, as shown in Figure 4-18. Cocoa Touch gives you all this functionality for free just by adding text fields to your interface.

Carrier 📶   8:45 AM   ▬

A Good Friend

123456789

1	2 ABC	3 DEF
4 GHI	5 JKL	6 MNO
7 PQRS	8 TUV	9 WXYZ
	0	⊗

Figure 4-18. *The keyboard comes up automatically when you touch either the text field or the number field*

But there's a little problem. How do you get the keyboard to go away? Go ahead and try. You'll see that nothing happens.

Closing the Keyboard When Done Is Tapped

Because the keyboard is software-based rather than a physical keyboard, you need to take a few extra steps to make sure the keyboard goes away when the user is finished with it. When the user taps the Done button on the text keyboard, a Did End On Exit event will be generated. When that happens, you need to tell the text field to give up control so that the keyboard will go away. To do that, you need to add an action method to your controller class.

Select `ViewController.swift` in the Project Navigator and add the action method in Listing 4-2 at the bottom of the file, just before the closing brace.

Listing 4-2. Method to Close the Keyboard When Done

```swift
@IBAction func textFieldDoneEditing(sender: UITextField) {
    sender.resignFirstResponder()
}
```

As you saw in Chapter 2, the first responder acts as the control with which the user is currently interacting. In your new method, you tell your control to resign as a first responder, giving up that role to the previous control the user worked with. When a text field yields first responder status, the keyboard associated with it goes away.

Save the ViewController.swift file. Let's look back at the storyboard and arrange to trigger this action from both of your text fields.

Select Main.storyboard in the Project Navigator, single-click the Name text field, and press ⌥⌘6 to bring up the Connections Inspector. This time, you don't want the Touch Up Inside event that you used in the previous chapter. Instead, you want Did End On Exit since that event will fire when the user taps the Done button on the text keyboard.

Drag from the circle next to Did End On Exit to the yellow View Controller icon in the storyboard, in the bar that's just above the view you've been configuring, and let go. A small pop-up menu will appear containing the name of a single action, the one you just added. Click the textFieldDoneEditing action to select it. You can also do this by dragging from the circle in the Connections Inspector to the textFieldDoneEditing() method in the Assistant Editor, if you still have it open. Repeat this procedure with the other text field, save your changes, and then run the app again.

When the simulator appears, click the Name field, type something, and then tap the Done button. As expected, the keyboard drops away, but what about the Number field, since there is no Done button, as you can see back in Figure 4-18?

Not all keyboard layouts, including the numeric keypad, include a Done button. You could force the user to tap the Name field and then tap Done, but that's not very user-friendly. And you most definitely want your application to be user-friendly. Let's see how to handle this situation.

Touching the Background to Close the Keyboard

Apple's iPhone applications allow tapping in most text fields—anywhere in the view where there's no active control that causes the keyboard to go away. Let's implement that for your app.

The answer may surprise you because of its simplicity. The view controller includes a property called view that it inherited from UIViewController. This view property corresponds to the main view in the storyboard. The view property points to an instance of UIView that acts as a container for all the items in your user interface. It is sometimes referred to as a *container view* because its main purpose is to simply hold other views and controls. Essentially, the container view provides the background to your user interface. All you need to do is detect when the user taps it. There are a couple of ways to do that. First, there are methods in the UIResponder class, from which UIView is derived, that are called whenever the user places one or more fingers onto a view, moves those fingers around, or lifts them up. You can override one of those methods (specifically the one that's called when the user lifts a finger from the screen) and add your code in there. The other way to do this is to add a *gesture recognizer* to the container view. Gesture recognizers listen to the events that are generated when the user interacts with a view and try to figure out what the user is doing. There are several different gesture recognizers that respond to different sequences of actions. The one that you need to use is the *tap gesture recognizer*, which signals an event when the user puts a finger on the screen and then lifts it up again within a reasonably short time.

To use a gesture recognizer, you create an instance, configure it, link it to the view that you want it to monitor for touch events, and attach it to an action method in your view controller class. When the gesture is recognized, your action method is called. You can create and configure the recognizer in code, or you can do it in Interface Builder. Here, you'll use Interface Builder because it's easier. Return to the storyboard and make sure that the Object Library is showing and then locate a tap gesture recognizer, drag it over the storyboard, and drop it onto the container view. The recognizer is not visible at runtime, so you can't see it in the storyboard, but it appears in the Document Outline, as shown in Figure 4-19.

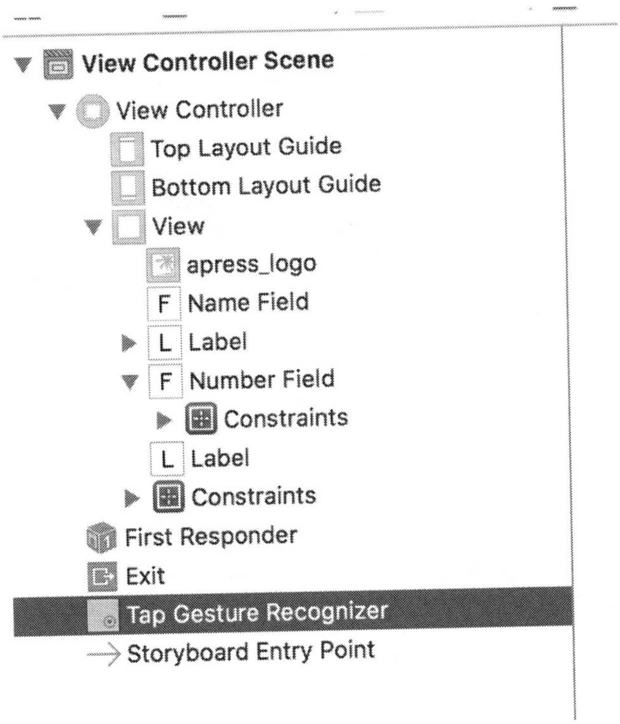

▼ 🖼 **View Controller Scene**

  ▼ ⬭ View Controller

   ⬚ Top Layout Guide

   ⬚ Bottom Layout Guide

   ▼ ⬚ View

    🖼 apress_logo

    F Name Field

    ▶ L Label

    ▼ F Number Field

     ▶ 🖽 Constraints

     L Label

   ▶ 🖽 Constraints

  🗊 First Responder

  ⬀ Exit

  ⊙ Tap Gesture Recognizer

  ⟶ Storyboard Entry Point

Figure 4-19. *Tap gesture recognizer in the Document Outline*

Selecting the gesture recognizer reveals its configurable attributes in the Attributes Inspector, as shown in Figure 4-20.

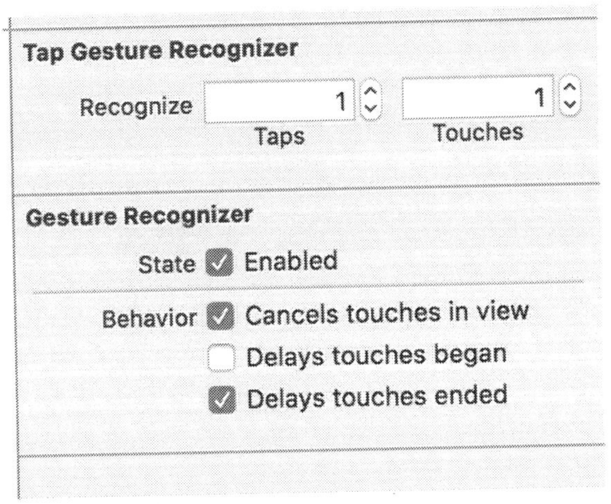

Tap Gesture Recognizer

Recognize	1 ⌃⌄	1 ⌃⌄
	Taps	Touches

Gesture Recognizer

State ☑ Enabled

Behavior ☑ Cancels touches in view

☐ Delays touches began

☑ Delays touches ended

Figure 4-20. *The attributes of the tap gesture recognizer*

113

The Taps field specifies how many times the user needs to tap before the gesture is recognized, and the Touches field controls how many fingers need to be tapped. The defaults of one tap with one finger are exactly what you need, so leave both fields unchanged. The other attributes are fine too, so all you need to do is link the recognizer to an action method. To do that, open `ViewController.swift` in the Assistant Editor and Control-drag from the recognizer in the Document Outline to the line just above the closing brace in `ViewController.swift`. Release the mouse when you see the usual gray pop-up like the one shown in Figure 4-16. In the pop-up that opens, change the connection type to Action and the method name to **onTapGestureRecognized** to have Xcode add the action method and link it to the gesture recognizer. This method will be called whenever the user taps the main view. All you need to do is add the code to close the keyboard, if it's open. You already know how to do that, so change the code to that shown in Listing 4-3.

Listing 4-3. *Your Gesture Recognizer Code to Remove the Keyboard*

```
@IBAction func onTapGestureRecognized(sender: AnyObject) {
    nameField.resignFirstResponder()
    numberField.resignFirstResponder()
}
```

This code simply tells both text fields to yield first responder status if they have it. It is perfectly safe to call `resignFirstResponder()` on a control that is not the first responder so you can call it on both text fields without needing to check whether either is the first responder. Build and run your application again, and this time, the keyboard should disappear not only when the Done button is tapped but also when you tap anywhere that's not an active control, which is the behavior that your users will expect.

Adding the Slider and Label

Let's add a slider and a label, the idea being that the value shown by the label will change as the slider is moved. Select `Main.storyboard` in the Project Navigator so you can add more items to your application's user interface. From the Object Library, bring over a slider and arrange it below the Number text field, using the right side's blue guideline as a stopping point and leaving a little breathing room between the slider and the bottom text field. Single-click the newly added slider to select it and then press ⌥⌘4 to go back to the Attributes Inspector if it's not already visible (see Figure 4-21).

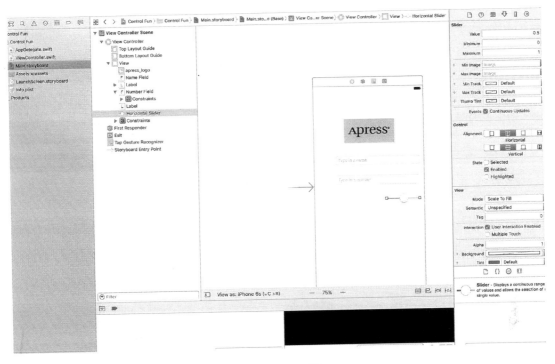

Figure 4-21. *The inspector showing default attributes for a slider*

A slider lets you choose a number in a given range. Use the inspector to set the Minimum value to 1, the Maximum value to 100, and the Current value to 50. Leave the Events Continuous Update check box selected. This ensures a continuous flow of events as the slider's value changes.

Bring over a label and place it next to the slider, using the blue guidelines to align it vertically with the slider and to align its left edge with the left margin of the view (see Figure 4-22).

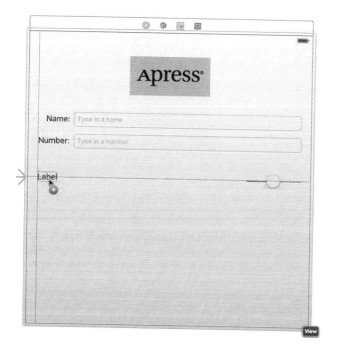

Figure 4-22. *Placing the slider's label*

Double-click the newly placed label, and change its text from Label to **100**. This is the largest value that the slider can hold, and you can use that to determine the correct width of the slider. Since 100 is shorter in length than Label, Interface Builder automatically makes the label smaller for you, as if you had dragged the right-middle resize dot to the edge. Despite this automatic behavior, you're still free to resize the label however you want, of course. If you later decide you want the tool to pick the optimum size for you again, just press ⌘= or select Editor ➤ Size to Fit Content.

Next, resize the slider by single-clicking the slider to select it and dragging the left resize handle to the left until the blue guidelines indicate that you're getting close to the label's right-side edge.

Now that you've added two more controls, you need to add the matching Auto Layout constraints. You'll do it the easy way again this time, so just select the View Controller icon in the Document Outline and then click Editor ➤ Resolve Auto Layout Issues ➤ Add Missing Constraints. Xcode adjusts the constraints so that they match the positions of all of the controls on-screen.

Creating and Connecting the Actions and Outlets

All that's left to do with these two controls is to connect them to an outlet and an action—you need an outlet that points to the label so that you can update the label's value when the slider is used, and you are also going to need an action method for the slider to call as it's changed. Make sure the Assistant Editor is open and showing `ViewController.swift` and then Control-drag from the slider to just below the `onTapGestureRecognized()` method in the Assistant Editor. When the pop-up window appears, change the Connection field to Action, type **onSliderChanged** in the Name field, set Type to UISlider, and then hit Return to create and connect the action.

Next, Control-drag from the newly added label (the one showing 100) over to the Assistant Editor. This time, drag to just below the `numberField` property declaration at the top of the file. When the pop-up comes up, type **sliderLabel** in the Name text field, and then hit Return to create and connect the outlet.

Implementing the Action Method

Though Xcode has created and connected your action method, it's still up to you to actually write the code that makes up the action method so it does what it's supposed to do. Change the onSliderChanged() method to that shown in Listing 4-4.

Listing 4-4. Changing the Label Based on the Slider Position/Value

```
@IBAction func onSliderChanged(_ sender: UISlider) {
    sliderLabel.text = "\(lroundf(sender.value))"
}
```

The call to the lroundf() function (which is part of the standard C library) takes the current value of the slider and rounds it to the nearest integer. The rest of the line converts the value to a string containing that number and assigns it to the label.

That takes care of your controller's response to the movements of the slider; but to be really consistent, you need to make sure that the label shows the correct slider value before the user even touches it. To do that, add the following line of code to the viewDidLoad() method: sliderLabel.text = "50".

This method executes immediately after the running app loads the view from the storyboard file but before it's displayed on the screen. The line you added makes sure that the user sees the correct starting value right away.

Save the file. Next, press ⌘R to build and launch your app in the iOS simulator, and try out the slider. As you move it, you should see the label's text change in real time. Another piece falls into place. But if you drag the slider toward the left (bringing the value below 10) or all the way to the right (setting the value to 100), you'll see an odd thing happen. The label to the left will shrink horizontally when it drops down to showing a single digit and will grow horizontally when showing three. Now, apart from the text it contains, you don't actually see the label itself, so you can't see its size changing, but what you will see is that the slider actually changes its size along with the label, getting smaller or larger. It's maintaining a size relationship with the label, making sure the gap between the two is always the same.

This is simply a side effect of the way Interface Builder works, helping you create GUIs that are responsive and fluid. You created some default constraints previously, and here you're seeing one in action. One of the constraints created by Interface Builder keeps the horizontal distance between these elements constant.

Let's override this behavior by making your own constraint. Back in Xcode, select the label in the storyboard and click the Pin icon at the bottom of the storyboard. In the pop-up, click the Width check box followed by Add 1 Constraint. This makes a new high-priority constraint that tells the layout system, "Don't mess with the width of this label." If you now press ⌘R to build and run again, you'll see that the label no longer expands and contracts as you drag back and forth across the slider.

You'll see more examples of constraints and their uses throughout the book. But for now, let's look at implementing the switches.

Implementing the Switches, Button, and Segmented Control

Let's go back to Xcode once again; this back and forth may seem a bit strange, but it's fairly common to bounce around between source code, storyboards, and nib files in Xcode, testing your app in the iOS simulator while you're developing.

Your application will have two switches, which are small controls that can have only two states: on and off. You'll also add a segmented control to hide and show the switches. Along with that control, you'll add a button that is revealed when the segmented control's right side is tapped.

In the storyboard, drag a segmented control from the Object Library (see Figure 4-23) and place it on the View window, a little below the slider and horizontally centered.

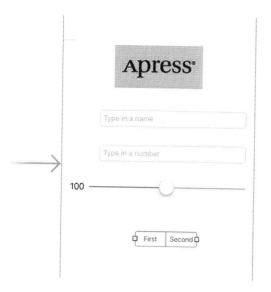

Figure 4-23. *Placing a segmented control onto your storyboard*

Double-click the word *First* on the segmented control and change the title from First to **Switches**. After doing that, repeat the process with the other segment, renaming it **Button** (see Figure 4-24), and drag the control back into its centered position.

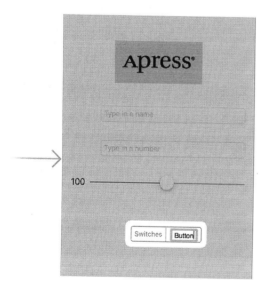

Figure 4-24. *Renaming the segments in the segmented control*

Adding Two Labeled Switches

Next, take a switch from the library and place it on the view, below the segmented control and against the left margin. Then drag a second switch and place it against the right margin, aligned vertically with the first switch, as shown in Figure 4-25.

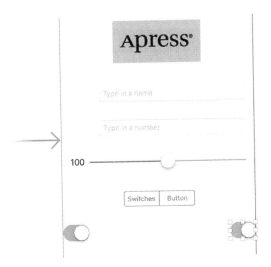

Figure 4-25. *Adding switches to the view*

■ **Tip**   Holding down the ⌥ key and dragging an object in Interface Builder will create a copy of that item. When you have many instances of the same object to create, it can be faster to drag only one object from the library and then Option-drag as many copies as you need.

The three new controls you've added need layout constraints. This time, you'll add the constraints manually. Start by selecting the segmented control and aligning it to the center of the view by clicking the Align icon, checking Horizontally in Container in the pop-up, and clicking Add 1 Constraint. Next, select the segmented control again and Control-drag upward a little until the background of the main view turns blue. Release the mouse and select Vertical Spacing to Top Layout Guide in the pop-up menu to fix the distance from the segmented control to the top of the view.

Now let's adjust the switches. Control-drag from the left switch diagonally left and upward relative to the switch and release the mouse. Hold down the Shift key and select Leading Space to Container Margin and Vertical Spacing to Top Layout Guide from the pop-up, release Shift, and press the Return key or click anywhere outside the pop-up to apply the constraints. Do a similar action with the other switch, but this time Control-drag to the upper right relative and select Trailing Space to Container Margin and Vertical Spacing to Top Layout Guide. When you apply constraints by dragging, Xcode offers you different options depending on the direction in which you drag. If you drag horizontally, you'll have options that let you attach the control to the left or right margins of its parent view, whereas if you drag vertically, Xcode assumes you want to set the position of the control relative to the top or bottom of its parent. Here, you needed one horizontal and one vertical constraint for each switch, so you dragged diagonally to indicate that to Xcode, and you got both horizontal and vertical options.

Connecting and Creating Outlets and Actions

Before you add the button, you'll create outlets for the two switches and connect them. The button that you'll be adding next will actually sit on top of the switches, making it harder to Control-drag to and from them, so you want to take care of the switch connections before you add the button. Since the button and the switches will never be visible at the same time, having them in the same physical location won't be a problem.

Using the Assistant Editor, Control-drag from the switch on the left to just below the last outlet in `ViewController.swift`. When the pop-up appears, name the outlet **leftSwitch** and hit Return. Repeat this process with the other switch, naming its outlet **rightSwitch**.

Now, select the left switch again by single-clicking it. Control-drag once more to the Assistant Editor. This time, drag to just above the brace at the end of the class declaration before letting go. When the pop-up appears, change the Connection field to **Action**, name the new action method onSwitchChanged(), and set the type of its `sender` argument to UISwitch. Next, hit Return to create the new action. Now repeat this process with the right switch, with one change: instead of creating a new action, drag the mouse over the onSwitchChanged() method that was just created and connect to it instead. Just as you did in the previous chapter, you're going to use a single method to handle both switches.

Finally, Control-drag from the segmented control to the Assistant Editor, right below the onSwitchChanged() method. Insert a new action method called toggleControls(), just as you've done before. This time, set the type of its `sender` parameter to UISegmentedControl.

Implementing the Switch Actions

Save the storyboard and let's add some more code to `ViewController.swift`, which is already open in the Assistant Editor. Look for the onSwitchChanged() method, changing it to that, as shown in Listing 4-5.

Listing 4-5. Your New onSwitchChanged() Method

```
@IBAction func onSwitchChanged(_ sender: UISwitch) {
    let setting = sender.isOn
    leftSwitch.setOn(setting, animated: true)
    rightSwitch.setOn(setting, animated: true)
}
```

The onSwitchChanged() method gets called whenever one of the two switches is tapped. In this method, you simply grab the value of the isOn property of sender (which represents the switch that was pressed) and use that value to set both switches. The idea here is that setting the value of one switch will change the other switch at the other time, keeping them in sync at all times.

Now, sender is always going to be either leftSwitch or rightSwitch, so you might be wondering why you're setting them both. You do it that way out of practicality since it's less work to set the value of both switches every time than to determine which the switch made the call and set only the other one. Whichever switch called this method will already be set to the correct value, and setting it again to that same value won't have any effect.

Adding the Button

Next, go back to Interface Builder and drag a button from the library to your view. Add this button directly on top of the leftmost switch, aligning it with the left margin and vertically aligning its top edge with the top edge of the two switches, as shown in Figure 4-26.

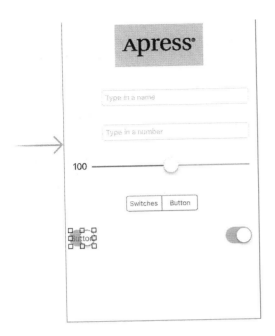

Figure 4-26. *Adding a button on top of the existing switches*

Now, grab the button's right-center resize handle and drag all the way to the right until you reach the blue guideline that indicates the right-side margin. The button should completely overlay the space occupied by the two switches, but because the default button is transparent, you will still see the switches (see Figure 4-27).

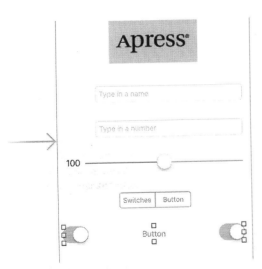

Figure 4-27. *The button, once placed and resized, fills the space occupied by the two switches*

Double-click the newly added button to give it the title **Do Something**.

The button needs Auto Layout constraints. You're going to pin it to the top and to both sides of the main view. Control-drag upward from the button until the view background turns blue and then release the mouse and select Vertical Spacing to Top Layout Guide. Then Control-drag horizontally to the left until the main view background turns blue again and select Leading Space to Container Margin. You'll only get this option if you drag far enough to the left, so if you don't see it, try again by dragging left until the mouse is outside the bounds of the button. Finally, Control-drag to the right until the main view background turns blue and then select Trailing Space to Container Margin. Now run the application to see what you've just done.

Adding an Image to the Button

If you compare your running application to Figure 4-2, you'll immediately notice a difference. Your Do Something button doesn't look like the one in the figure. That's because, starting with iOS 7, the default button displays a very simple appearance: it's just a piece of plain text with no outline, border, background color, or other decorative features. That conforms nicely to Apple's design guidelines for iOS 7 and later, but there are still cases where you'll want to use custom buttons, so I'm going to show you how to do that.

Many of the buttons you see on your iOS device are drawn using images. I've provided images that you can use for this example in the Button Images folder of the source code archive for this book. In the Project Navigator in Xcode, select Assets.xcassets (the same assets catalog that you used earlier when you added images for the Apress logo) and then just drag both images from the Button Images folder in the Finder straight into the editing area in your Xcode window. The images are added to your project and will be immediately available to your app.

Using Stretchable Images

If you look at the two button images you just added, you'll see they're very small and seem much too narrow to fill out the button you added to the storyboard. That's because these graphics are meant to be stretchable. It so happens that UIKit can stretch graphics to nicely fill just about any size you want. Stretchable images are an interesting concept. A stretchable image is a resizable image that knows how to resize itself intelligently so that it maintains the correct appearance. For these button templates, you don't want the edges to stretch evenly with the rest of the image. *Edge insets* are the parts of an image (measured in pixels) that should not be resized. You want the bevel around the edges to stay the same, no matter what size you make the button, so you need to specify how much nonstretchable space makes up each edge.

In the past, this could be accomplished only in code. You'd have to use a graphics program to measure pixel boundaries of your images and then use those numbers to set edge insets in your code. Xcode 6 eliminated the need for this by letting you visually "slice" any image you have in an assets catalog! That's what you're going to do next.

Select the Assets.xcassets asset catalog in Xcode, and inside that select whiteButton. At the bottom right of the editing area, you'll see a button labeled Show Slicing. Click that to initiate the slicing process, which begins by simply putting a Start Slicing button right on top of your image. Click it. You'll see three new buttons that let you choose whether you want the image to be sliced (and therefore stretchable) vertically, horizontally, or both. Choose the button in the middle to slice both ways. Xcode does a quick analysis of your image and then finds the sections that seem to have unique pixels around the edges and vertical and horizontal slices in the middle that should be repeatable. You'll see these boundaries represented by dashed lines, as shown in Figure 4-28. If you have a tricky image, you may need to adjust these (it's easy to do; just drag them with the mouse). However, for this image, the automatic edge insets will work fine.

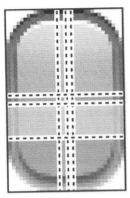

whit...n - 1x

Figure 4-28. *Default slicing for the white button*

Next, select blueButton and do the same automatic slicing for it. Now it's time to put these graphics to use.

Go back to the storyboard you've been working on and single-click the Do Something button. With the button selected, press ⌥⌘4 to open the Attributes Inspector. In the inspector, use the Type pop-up menu to change the type from System to Custom. At the bottom of the Button section in the Inspector, you'll see that you can specify an image and a background for your button. You're going to use the background to show your resizable graphic, so click in the Background pop-up and select whiteButton. You'll see that the button now shows the white graphic, perfectly stretched to cover the entire button frame.

You want to use the blue button to define the look of this button's highlighted state, which is what you see while the button is pressed. I'll talk more about control states in the next section of this chapter; but for now, just take a look at the second pop-up from the top, labeled State Config. A UIButton can have multiple states, each with its own text and images. Right now you've been configuring the default state, so switch this pop-up to Highlighted so that you can configure that state. You'll see that the Background pop-up has been cleared; click it to select blueButton—and you're done.

Using Control States

Every iOS control has five possible control states and is always in one, and only one, of these states at any given moment.

> *Default*: The most common state is the default control state, which is the default state. It's the state that controls are in when not in any of the other states.

> *Focused*: In focus-based navigation systems, a control enters this state when it receives the focus. A focused control changes its appearance to indicate that it has focus, and this appearance differs from the appearance of the control when it is highlighted or selected. Further interactions with the control can result in it also becoming highlighted or selected.

> *Highlighted*: The highlighted state is the state a control is in when it's currently being used. For a button, this would be while the user has a finger on the button.

Selected: Only some controls support the selected state. It is usually used to indicate that the control is turned on or selected. Selected is similar to highlighted, but a control can continue to be selected when the user is no longer directly using that control.

Disabled: Controls are in the disabled state when they have been turned off, which can be done by deselecting the Enabled check box in Interface Builder or setting the control's isEnabled property to NO.

Certain iOS controls have attributes that can take on different values depending on their state. For example, by specifying one image for isDefault and a different image for isHighlighted, you are telling iOS to use one image when the user has a finger on the button and a different image the rest of the time. That's essentially what you did when you configured two different background states for the button in the storyboard.

■ **Note** In previous versions of this book there were four states: Normal, Highlighted, Disabled, and Selected, with the enumerated values in Objective-C as UIControlStateNormal, UIControlStateHighlighted, UIControlStateEnabled, and UIControlStateSelected. You may see older, pre–Xcode 8 and Swift 3 reference these values.

Connecting and Creating the Button Outlets and Actions

Control-drag from the new button to the Assistant Editor, just below the last outlet already in the section at the top of the file. When the pop-up appears, create a new outlet called **doSomethingButton**. After you've done that, Control-drag from the button a second time to just above the closing brace at the bottom of the file. There, create an action method called onButtonPressed() and set Type to UIButton.

If you save your work and try running the application, you'll see that the segmented control will be live, but it won't do anything particularly useful since you still need to add some logic to make the button and switches hide and unhide.

You also need to mark your button as hidden from the start. You didn't want to do that before because it would have made it harder to connect the outlets and actions. Now that you've done that, however, let's hide the button. You'll show the button when the user taps the right side of the segmented control; but when the application starts, you want the button hidden. In the storyboard, select the button and press ⌥⌘4 to bring up the Attributes Inspector. Scroll down to the View section and click the Hidden check box. The button will still be visible in Interface Builder.

Implementing the Segmented Control Action

Save the storyboard and focus once again on ViewController.swift. Look for the toggleControls() method that Xcode created for you and add the new code shown in Listing 4-6.

Listing 4-6. Hide or Unhide the Switches Depending on the Segmented Control

```
@IBAction func toggleControls(_ sender: UISegmentedControl) {
    if sender.selectedSegmentIndex == 0 {  // "Switches" is selected
        leftSwitch.isHidden = false
        rightSwitch.isHidden = false
        doSomethingButton.isHidden = true
    } else {
```

```
        leftSwitch.isHidden = true
        rightSwitch.isHidden = true
        doSomethingButton.isHidden = false
    }
}
```

This code looks at the selectedSegmentIndex property of sender, which tells you which of the sections is currently selected. The first section, called switches, has an index of 0. I've noted this fact in a comment so that when you revisit the code later, you will know what's going on. Depending on which segment is selected, you hide or show the appropriate controls.

Before you run the application, let's apply a small tweak to make it look a little better. With iOS 7, Apple introduced some new GUI paradigms. One of these is that the status bar at the top of the screen is transparent so that your content shines right through it. Right now, that yellow Apress icon really sticks out like a sore thumb against your app's white background, so let's extend that yellow color to cover your entire view. In Main.storyboard, select the main content view (it's labeled View in the Document Outline) and press ⌥⌘4 to bring up the Attributes Inspector. Click in the color swatch labeled Background (which currently contains a white rectangle) to open the standard OS X color picker. One feature of this color picker is that it lets you choose any color you see on the screen. With the color picker open, click the dropper icon at the bottom right to open a magnifying glass. Drag the magnifying glass over the Apress image view in the storyboard and click when it's over a yellow part of the image. You should now see the background color of the Apress image in the color picker next to the dropper icon in the color picker. To set it as the background color for the main content view, select the main view in the Document Outline and then click the yellow color in the color picker. When you're done, close the color picker.

On the screen, you may find that the background and the Apress image seem to have slightly different colors, but when run in the simulator or on a device, they will be the same. These colors appear to be different in Interface Builder because macOS automatically adapts colors depending on the display you're using. On an iOS device and in the simulator, that doesn't happen.

Run the app. You'll see that the yellow color fills the entire screen, with no visible distinction between the status bar and your app's content. If you don't have full-screen scrolling content or other content that requires the use of a navigation bar or other controls at the top of the screen, this can be a nice way to show full-screen content that isn't interrupted by the status bar quite as much.

If you've typed everything correctly, you should also be able to switch between the button and the pair of switches using the segmented control. And if you tap either switch, the other one will change its value as well. The button, however, still doesn't do anything. Before you implement it, you need to talk about action sheets and alerts.

Implementing the Action Sheet and Alert

Action sheets and *alerts* are both used to provide the user with feedback.

- Action sheets are used to force the user to make a choice between two or more items. On iPhones, the action sheet comes up from the bottom of the screen and displays a series of buttons (see Figure 4-3). On the iPad, you specify the position of the action sheet relative to another view, typically a button. Users are unable to continue using the application until they have tapped one of the buttons. Action sheets are often used to confirm a potentially dangerous or irreversible action, such as deleting an object.

- Alerts appear as rounded rectangles in the middle of the screen (see Figure 4-4). Like action sheets, alerts force users to respond before they are allowed to continue using the application. Alerts are usually used to inform the user that something important or out of the ordinary has occurred. Like action sheets, alerts may be presented with only a single button, although you have the option of presenting multiple buttons if more than one response is appropriate.

125

▓ **Note**   A view that forces users to make a choice before they are allowed to continue using their application is known as a *modal view*.

Displaying an Action Sheet

Switch to ViewController.swift and you'll implement the button's action method. Begin by looking for the empty onButtonPressed() method that Xcode created for you and then add the code in Listing 4-7 to create and show the action sheet.

Listing 4-7. Displaying the Action Sheet

```
@IBAction func onButtonPressed(_ sender: UIButton) {
    let controller = UIAlertController(title: "Are You Sure?",
                            message:nil, preferredStyle: .actionSheet)

    let yesAction = UIAlertAction(title: "Yes, I'm sure!",
                        style: .destructive, handler: { action in
                        let msg = self.nameField.text!.isEmpty
                        ? "You can breathe easy, everything went OK."
                        : "You can breathe easy, \(self.nameField.text),"
                        + "everything went OK."
                        let controller2 = UIAlertController(
                            title:"Something Was Done",
                            message: msg, preferredStyle: .alert)
                        let cancelAction = UIAlertAction(title: "Phew!",
                                                    style: .cancel,
                                                    handler: nil)
                    controller2.addAction(cancelAction)
                    self.present(controller2, animated: true,
                                                completion: nil)
    })

    let noAction = UIAlertAction(title: "No way!",
                    style: .cancel, handler: nil)

    controller.addAction(yesAction)
    controller.addAction(noAction)

    if let ppc = controller.popoverPresentationController {
        ppc.sourceView = sender
        ppc.sourceRect = sender.bounds
    }

    present(controller, animated: true, completion: nil)
}
```

What exactly did you do there? Well, first, in the onButtonPressed() action method, you allocated and initialized a UIAlertController, which is a view controller subclass that can display either an action sheet or an alert.

```
let controller = UIAlertController(title: "Are You Sure?",
                    message:nil, preferredStyle: .actionSheet)
```

The first parameter is the title to be displayed. Refer to Figure 4-3 to see how the title you're supplying will be displayed at the top of the action sheet. The second parameter is a message that will be displayed immediately below the title, in a smaller font. For this example, you're not using the message, so you supply the value nil for this parameter. The final parameter specifies whether you want the controller to display an alert (value UIAlertControllerStyle.alert) or an action sheet (UIAlertControllerStyle.actionSheet). Since you need an action sheet, you supply the value UIAlertControllerStyle.actionSheet here.

The alert controller does not supply any buttons by default—you have to create a UIAlertAction object for each button that you want and add it to the controller. Listing 4-8 shows the part of the code that creates the two buttons for your action sheet.

Listing 4-8. Creating the Action Sheet Buttons

```
let yesAction = UIAlertAction(title: "Yes, I'm sure!",
          style: .destructive, handler: { action in
          // Code omitted - see below.
      })

let noAction = UIAlertAction(title: "No way!",
          style: .cancel, handler: nil)
```

For each button, you specify the title, the style, and a handler to be called when the button is pressed. There are three possible styles to choose from.

- UIAlertActionStyle.destructive should be used when the button triggers a destructive, dangerous, or irreversible action, such as deleting or overwriting a file. The title for a button with this style is drawn in red in a bold font.

- UIAlertActionStyle.default is used for a normal button, such as an OK button, when the action that will be triggered is not destructive. The title is drawn in a regular blue font.

- UIAlertStyle.cancel is used for the Cancel button. The title is drawn in a bold blue font.

Finally, you add the buttons to the controller.

```
[controller addAction:yesAction];
[controller addAction:noAction];
```

To make the alert or action sheet visible, you need to ask the current view controller to *present* the alert controller. Listing 4-9 shows how you present an action sheet.

Listing 4-9. Presenting an Action Sheet

```
if let ppc = controller.popoverPresentationController {
    ppc.sourceView = sender
    ppc.sourceRect = sender.bounds
}
present(controller, animated: true, completion: nil)
```

The first four lines configure where the action sheet will appear by getting the alert controller's popover presentation controller and setting its sourceView and sourceRect properties. I'll say more about these properties shortly. Finally, you make the action sheet visible by calling your view controller's present (_:animated:completion:) method, passing it the alert controller as the controller to be presented. When a view controller is presented, its view temporarily replaces that of the view controller that's presenting it. In the case of the alert view controller, the action sheet or alert partially covers the presenting view controller's view; the rest of the view is covered by a dark, translucent background that lets you see the underlying view but makes it clear that you can't interact with it until you dismiss the presented view controller.

Now let's revisit the popover presentation controller configuration. On the iPhone, the action sheet always pops up from the bottom of the screen, as shown in Figure 4-3, but on the iPad, it's displayed in a popover—a small, rounded rectangle with an arrow that points toward another view, usually the one that caused it to appear. Figure 4-29 shows how your action sheet looks on the iPad Air simulator.

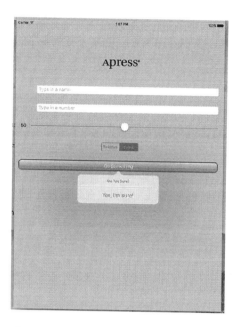

Figure 4-29. *Action sheet presented on an iPad Air*

As you can see, the popover's arrow points to the Do Something button. That's because you set the sourceView property of the alert controller's popover presentation controller to point to that button and its sourceRect property to the button's bounds, as shown in Listing 4-10.

Listing 4-10. Setting the sourceView and sourceRect Properties

```
if let ppc = controller.popoverPresentationController {
    ppc.sourceView = sender
    ppc.sourceRect = sender.bounds
}
```

Notice the if let construction—this is necessary because on the iPhone, the alert controller does not present the action sheet in a popover, so its popoverPresentationController property is nil.

In Figure 4-29, the popover appears below the source button, but you can change this, if you need to, by setting the popover presentation controller's `permittedArrowDirections` property, which is a mask of permitted directions for the popover's arrow. The following code moves the popover above the source button by setting this property to `UIPopoverArrowDirection.down`, as shown in Listing 4-11.

Listing 4-11. Setting the Direction of the Popover

```
if let ppc = controller.popoverPresentationController {
        ppc.sourceView = sender
        ppc.sourceRect = sender.bounds
        ppc.permittedArrowDirections = .down
}
```

If you compare Figure 4-29 and Figure 4-3, you'll see that the No Way! button is missing on the iPad. The alert controller does not use buttons with style `UIAlertStyle.cancel` on the iPad because users are accustomed to dismissing a popover without taking any action by tapping anywhere outside of it.

Presenting an Alert

When the user presses the Yes, I'm Sure! button, you want to pop up an alert with a message. When a button that was added to an alert controller is pressed, the action sheet (or alert) is dismissed, and the button's handler block is called with a reference to the `UIAlertAction` from which the button was created. The code that's executed when the Yes, I'm Sure! button is pressed is shown in Listing 4-12.

Listing 4-12. Popping Up the Alert Message

```
let yesAction = UIAlertAction(title: "Yes, I'm sure!",
                    style: .destructive, handler: { action in
                    let msg = self.nameField.text!.isEmpty
                                ? "You can breathe easy, everything went OK."
                                : "You can breathe easy, \(self.nameField.text),"
                                + "everything went OK."
                    let controller2 = UIAlertController(
                                title:"Something Was Done",
                                message: msg, preferredStyle: .alert)
                    let cancelAction = UIAlertAction(title: "Phew!",
                                            style: .cancel, handler: nil)
                    controller2.addAction(cancelAction)
                    self.present(controller2, animated: true,
                                            completion: nil)
})
```

The first thing you do in the handler block is create a new string that will be displayed to the user. In a real application, this is where you would do whatever processing the user requested. You're just going to pretend you did something and notify the user by using an alert. If the user has entered a name in the top text field, you'll grab that, and you'll use it in the message that you'll display in the alert. Otherwise, you'll just craft a generic message to show.

```
let msg = self.nameField.text!.isEmpty
        ? "You can breathe easy, everything went OK."
        : "You can breathe easy, \(self.nameField.text),"
        + " everything went OK."
```

The next few lines of code are going to look kind of familiar. Alert views and action sheets are created and used in a similar manner. You always start by creating a `UIAlertController`.

```
let controller2 = UIAlertController(
            title:"Something Was Done",
            message: msg, preferredStyle: .alert)
```

Again, you pass a title to be displayed. This time, you also pass a more detailed message, which is that string you just created. The final parameter is the style, which you set to `UIAlertControllerStyle.alert` because you want an alert, not an action sheet. Next, you create a `UIAlertAction` for the alert's cancel button and add it to the controller.

```
let cancelAction = UIAlertAction(title: "Phew!",
                        style: .cancel, handler: nil)
controller2.addAction(cancelAction)
```

Finally, you make the alert appear by presenting the alert view controller.

```
self.present(controller2, animated: true, completion: nil)
```

You can see the alert that's created by this code in Figure 4-4. You'll notice that your code does not attempt to get and configure the alert controller's popover presentation controller. That's because alerts appear in a small, rounded view in the center of the screen on both iPhone and iPad, so there is no popover presentation controller to configure.

Save `ViewController.swift` and then build, run, and try out the completed application.

Summary

In this lengthy chapter, I hope I didn't hit you with too much new stuff, but I went through the use of a good number of controls and showed many different implementation details. You got more practice with outlets and actions, saw how to use the hierarchical nature of views to your advantage, and got some more practice adding Auto Layout constraints. You learned about control states and stretchable images. You also learned how to use both action sheets and alerts.

There's a lot going on in your Control Fun application. Feel free to go back and try things out. Change values, experiment by adding and modifying code, and see what different settings in Interface Builder do. There's no way I could take you through every permutation of every control available in iOS, but the application you just put together is a good starting point and covers a lot of the basics.

In the next chapter, you're going to look at what happens when the user rotates an iOS device from portrait to landscape orientation or vice versa. You're probably well aware that many apps change their displays based on the way the user is holding the device, and I'm going to show you how to do that in your own applications.

CHAPTER 5

Working with Device Rotations

The iPhone and iPad exude amazing engineering in form, fit, and function. Apple engineers found all kinds of ways to squeeze maximum functionality into a very small and elegant package. One example of this exists in the ability of these devices to be used in either portrait (tall and skinny) or landscape (short and wide) mode and how that orientation can be changed at runtime simply by rotating the device. You see an example of this *autorotation* behavior in the iOS Safari browser, as shown in Figure 5-1. In this chapter, I'll cover rotation in detail, starting with an overview of the ins and outs of autorotation and then moving on to different ways of implementing that functionality in your apps.

Figure 5-1. *Like many iOS applications, Mobile Safari changes its display based on how it is held, making the most of the available screen space*

© Molly K. Maskrey 2017
M. K. Maskrey, *Beginning iPhone Development with Swift 4*, https://doi.org/10.1007/978-1-4842-3072-5_5

Prior to iOS 8, if you wanted to design an application that would run on both iPhones and iPads, you created one storyboard with a layout for the iPhone and another one with your iPad layout. In iOS 8, that all changed when Apple added APIs to UIKit and tools in Xcode, making it possible to build an application that runs on (or, using its terminology, adapts to) any device with a single storyboard. You still must design carefully for the different form factor of each type of device, but now you do it all in one place. Even better, using the Preview feature that was introduced in Chapter 3, you see immediately how your application would look on any device without even having to start up the simulator. You'll take a look at how to build adaptive application layouts in the second part of this chapter.

Understanding the Mechanics of Rotation

The ability to run in both portrait and landscape orientations might not work for every application. Several of Apple's iPhone applications, such as the Weather app, may support only a single orientation. However, iPad applications function differently, with Apple recommending that most apps, with the exception of immersive apps like games, should support every orientation, and most of Apple's own iPad apps work fine in both orientations. Many of them use the orientations to show different views of your data. For example, the Mail and Notes apps use landscape orientation to display a list of items (folders, messages, or notes) on the left and the selected item on the right. In portrait orientation, however, these apps let you focus on the details of just the selected item.

For iPhone apps, the base rule is that if autorotation enhances the user experience, you should add it to your application. For iPad apps, the rule is you should add autorotation unless you have a compelling reason not to. Fortunately, Apple did a great job of hiding the complexities of handling orientation changes in iOS and in UIKit, so implementing this behavior in your own iOS applications becomes quite easy.

The view controller authorizes the image to rotate. If the user rotates the device, the active view controller gets asked if it's okay to change to the new orientation (which you'll do in this chapter). If the view controller responds in the affirmative, the application's window and views rotate, and the window and view resize to fit the new orientation.

On the iPhone and iPod touch, a view that starts in portrait mode exists taller than it is wide—you can see the actual available space for any given device by referring to the Software Size column of Table 1-1 in Chapter 1. Note, however, that the vertical screen real estate available for your app decreases by 20 points vertically if your app is showing the status bar, which is the 20-point strip at the top of the screen (see Figure 5-1) that shows information such as signal strength, time, and battery charge.

When the device rotates to landscape mode, the vertical and horizontal dimensions switch around, so, for example, an application running on an iPhone 6/6s would see a screen that's 375 points wide and 667 points high in portrait but that's 667 points wide and 375 points high in landscape. Again, though, on iPads the vertical space actually available to your app gets reduced by 20 points if you're showing the status bar, which most apps do. On iPhones, as of iOS 8, the status bar hides when in landscape orientation.

Understanding Points, Pixels, and the Retina Display

You might be wondering why I'm talking about "points" instead of pixels. Earlier versions of this book did, in fact, refer to screen sizes in pixels rather than points. The reason for this change is Apple's introduction of the Retina display, which is Apple's marketing term for the high-resolution screen on all versions of the iPhone starting with iPhone 4 and later-generation iPod touches, as well as newer variants of the iPad. As you can see by looking back at Table 1-1 again, it doubles the hardware screen resolution for most models and almost triples it for the iPhone 6s/7 Plus.

Fortunately, you don't need to do a thing in most situations to account for this. When you work with on-screen elements, you specify dimensions and distances in *points*, not in pixels. For older iPhones and the iPad, iPad 2, and iPad Mini 1, points and pixels are equivalent—one point is one pixel. On more recent-model Apple devices, however, a point equates to a 4-pixel square (2 pixels wide × 2 pixels high), and the iPhone 5s screen (for example) still appears to be 320 points wide, even though it's actually 640 pixels across. On iPhone 6s/7 Plus, the scaling factor is 3, so each point maps to a 9-pixel square. Think of it as a "virtual resolution," with iOS automatically mapping points to the physical pixels of your screen.

In typical applications, most of the work of actually moving the pixels around the screen is managed by iOS. Your app's main function in all this is making sure everything fits nicely and looks proper in the resized window.

Handling Rotation

To handle device rotation, you need to specify the correct *constraints* for all the objects making up your interface. Constraints tell iOS how the controls should behave when their enclosing view is resized. How does that relate to device rotation? When the device rotates, the dimensions of the screen are (more or less) interchanged—so the area in which your views are laid out changes size.

The simplest way of using constraints is to configure them in Interface Builder (IB). Interface Builder lets you define constraints that describe how your GUI components will be repositioned and resized as their parent view changes or as other views move around. You did a little bit of this in Chapter 4, and you will delve further into the subject of constraints in this chapter. You can think of constraints as equations that make statements about view geometry and the iOS view system itself as a "solver" that will rearrange things as necessary to make those statements true. You can also add constraints in code, but I'm not going to cover that in this book.

Constraints were added to iOS 6 but have been present on the Mac for a bit longer than that. On both iOS and macOS, constraints can be used in place of the old "springs and struts" system that was found in earlier releases. Constraints can do everything the old technology could do, and more.

Creating Your Orientations Project

You'll create a simple app to see how to pick the orientations that you want your app to work with. Start a new Single View App project in Xcode, and call it **Orientations**. Choose Universal from the Devices pop-up, and save it along with your other projects.

Before you lay out your GUI in the storyboard, you need to tell iOS that your view supports interface rotation. There are actually two ways of doing this. You can create an app-wide setting that will be the default for all view controllers, and you can further tweak things for each individual view controller. You'll do both of these things, starting with the app-wide setting.

Understanding Supported Orientations at the App Level

First, you need to specify which orientations your application supports. When your new Xcode project window appeared, it should have opened to your project settings. If not, click the top line in the Project Navigator (the one named after your project) and then make sure you're on the General tab. Among the options available in the summary, you should see a section called Deployment Info, and within that, a section called Device Orientation (see Figure 5-2) with a list of check boxes.

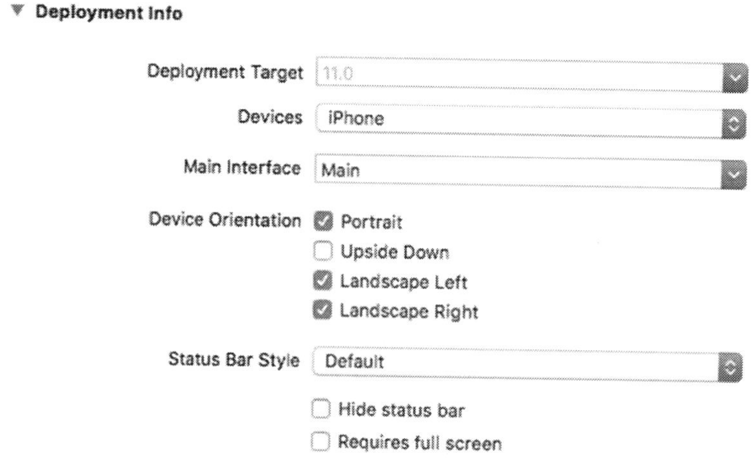

▼ **Deployment Info**

Deployment Target 11.0

Devices iPhone

Main Interface Main

Device Orientation ☑ Portrait
              ☐ Upside Down
              ☑ Landscape Left
              ☑ Landscape Right

Status Bar Style Default
              ☐ Hide status bar
              ☐ Requires full screen

Figure 5-2. *The General tab for your project shows, among other things, the supported device orientations*

This is how you identify which orientations your app supports. It doesn't necessarily mean that every view will use all of the selected orientations, but if you are going to support an orientation in any of the views, that orientation must be selected here. Notice that the Upside Down orientation is off by default. That's because Apple does not encourage the user to hold the phone upside down because if the phone rings while it is in that orientation, the user would have to twist it through a full half-turn to answer it.

Open the Devices drop-down that's just above the check boxes (see Figure 5-3) and you'll see that you can actually configure separate sets of allowed orientations for the iPhone and the iPad. If you choose iPad, you'll see that all four check boxes are selected because the iPad is meant to be used in any orientation.

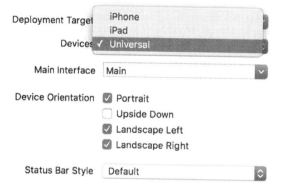

▼ **Deployment Info**

Deployment Target
           iPhone
           iPad
Devices ✓ Universal

Main Interface Main

Device Orientation ☑ Portrait
              ☐ Upside Down
              ☑ Landscape Left
              ☑ Landscape Right

Status Bar Style Default

Figure 5-3. *You can configure different orientations for the iPhone and iPad*

▪ **Note** The four check boxes shown in Figures 5-2 and 5-3 are actually just a shortcut to adding and deleting entries in your application's `Info.plist` file. If you single-click `Info.plist` in the Project Navigator, you should see two entries called "Supported interface orientations" and "Supported interface orientations (iPad)," with subentries for the orientations that are currently selected. Selecting and deselecting those check boxes in the project summary simply adds and removes items from these arrays. Using the check boxes is easier and less prone to error, so using the check boxes is definitely recommended. However, you should know what they do.

Again, you'll work with an iPhone 6s as your device. Now, select Main.storyboard. Find a label in the Object Library and drag it into your view, dropping it so that it's horizontally centered and somewhere near the top, as shown in Figure 5-4. Select the label's text and change it to **This way up**. Changing the text may shift the label's position, so drag it to make it horizontally centered again.

Figure 5-4. *Setting your Portrait orientation label*

You need to add Auto Layout constraints to pin the label in place before running the application, so Control-drag from the label upward until the background of the containing view turns blue and then release the mouse. Hold down the Shift key and select Vertical Spacing to Top Layout Guide and Center Horizontally in Container in the pop-up and then press Return. Now, press ⌘R to build and run this simple app on the iPhone simulator. When it comes up in the simulator, try rotating the device a few times by pressing ⌘-Left Arrow or ⌘-Right Arrow. You'll see that the entire view (including the label you added) rotates to every orientation except upside down, just as you configured it to do. Run it on the iPad simulator to confirm that it rotates to all four possible orientations.

You've identified the orientations your app will support, but that's not all you need to do. You can also specify a set of accepted orientations for each view controller, giving you more fine-grained control over which orientations will work in different parts of your apps.

Understanding Per-Controller Rotation Support

Let's configure your view controller to allow a different, smaller set of accepted orientations. The global configuration for the app specifies a sort of absolute upper limit for allowed orientations. If the global configuration doesn't include upside-down orientation, for example, there's no way that any individual view controller can force the system to rotate the display to upside down. All you can do in the view controller is place further limits on what is acceptable.

In the Project Navigator, single-click ViewController.swift. Here you'll implement a method defined in the UIViewController superclass that lets you specify which subset of the global set of orientations you'll accept *for this view controller*:

```
override func supportedInterfaceOrientations() -> UIInterfaceOrientationMask {
    return UIInterfaceOrientationMask(rawValue:
        (UIInterfaceOrientationMask.portrait.rawValue
            | UIInterfaceOrientationMask.landscapeLeft.rawValue))
}
```

This method lets you return a UIInterfaceOrientationMask that specifies the acceptable orientations. Calling this method is iOS's way of asking a view controller if it's allowed to rotate to a specific orientation. In this case, we're returning a value that indicates that we'll accept two orientations: the default portrait orientation and the orientation you get when you turn your phone 90° clockwise so that the phone's left edge is at the top. You use the Boolean OR operator (the vertical bar symbol) to combine the raw values of these two orientation masks and use the result to create a new UIInterfaceOrientationMask that represents the combined value.

UIKit defines the following orientation masks, which you can combine in any way you like using the OR operator (shown in the preceding example):

- UIInterfaceOrientationMask.portrait.rawValue

- UIInterfaceOrientationMask.landscapeLeft.rawValue

- UIInterfaceOrientationMask.landscapeRight.rawValue

- UIInterfaceOrientationMask.portraitUpsideDown.rawValue

In addition, there are some predefined combinations of these for common use cases. These are functionally equivalent to ORing them together on your own but can save you some typing and make your code more readable.

- UIInterfaceOrientationMask.landscape.rawValue

- UIInterfaceOrientationMask.all.rawValue

- UIInterfaceOrientationMask.allButUpsideDown.rawValue

When the iOS device changes to a new orientation, the supportedInterfaceOrientations() method is called on the active view controller. Depending on whether the returned value includes the new orientation, the application determines whether it should rotate the view. Because every view controller subclass can implement this differently, it is possible for one application to support rotation with some of its views but not with others, or for one view controller to support certain orientations under certain conditions. Run the example application again and verify that you can now rotate the simulator only to the two orientations that are returned by the supportedInterfaceOrientations() method. The .rawValue at the end of each orientation returns the integer value for the orientation to be used in comparison.

▓ **Note**   You can actually rotate the device, but the view itself does not rotate, so the label is back to the top except for the two selected orientations.

CODE COMPLETION IN ACTION

Have you noticed that the defined system constants on the iPhone are always designed so that values that work together start with the same letters? One reason why `UIInterfaceOrientationMask.portrait`, `UIInterfaceOrientationMask.portraitUpsideDown`, `UIInterfaceOrientationMask.landscapeLeft`, and `UIInterfaceOrientationMask.landscapeRight` all begin with `UIInterfaceOrientationMask` is to let you take advantage of Xcode's *code completion* feature.

You've probably noticed that as you type Xcode frequently tries to complete the word you are typing. That's code completion in action.

Developers cannot possibly remember all the various defined constants in the system, but you can remember the common beginning for the groups you use frequently. When you need to specify an orientation, simply type **UIInterfaceOrientationMask** (or even **UIInterf**). You'll see a list of all matches pop up. (In Xcode's preferences, you can configure the list to pop up only when you press the Esc key). You can use the arrow keys to navigate the list that appears and make a selection by pressing the Tab or Return key. This is much faster than needing to look up the values in the documentation or header files.

Feel free to play around with this method by returning different orientation mask combinations. You can force the system to constrict your view's display to whichever orientations make sense for your app, but don't forget the global configuration I talked about earlier. Remember that if you haven't enabled upside down there (for example), none of your views will ever appear upside down, no matter what their view controller's `supportedInterfaceOrientations()` method declares.

▓ **Note**   iOS actually supports two different types of orientations. The one I'm discussing here is the *interface orientation*. There's also a separate but related concept of *device orientation*, which specifies how the device is currently being held. Interface orientation is which way the views on the screen are rotated. If you turn a standard iPhone upside down, the device orientation will be upside down, but the interface orientation will almost always be one of the other three since iPhone apps don't support portrait upside down by default.

Creating Your Layout Project

In Xcode, make another new project based on the Single View App template and name it **Layout**. Select `Main.storyboard` to edit the storyboard in Interface Builder. A great thing about constraints is that they accomplish quite a lot using very little code. To see how this works, drag four labels from the library to your view and place them as shown in Figure 5-5. Use the dashed blue guidelines to help you line up each one near its respective corner. In this example, you're going to use instances of the `UILabel` class to see how to use constraints to build your GUI layout, but the same rules apply to many GUI objects.

Figure 5-5. *Adding four labels to your storyboard*

Double-click each label and assign a title to each one so that you can tell them apart later. I've used UL for the upper-left label, UR for the upper-right label, LL for the lower-left label, and LR for the lower-right label. After setting the text for each label, drag all of them into position so that they are lined up evenly with respect to the container view's corners.

Let's see what happens now, given that you haven't yet set any Auto Layout constraints. Build and run the app on the iPad Air simulator. Once the simulator starts up, you'll find that you can only see the labels on the left—the other two are off-screen to the right. Furthermore, the label at the bottom left is not where it should be—right in the bottom-left corner of the screen. Select Hardware ➤ Rotate Left, which will simulate turning the iPad to landscape mode. You'll find that you can now see the top-left and top-right labels, as shown in Figure 5-6.

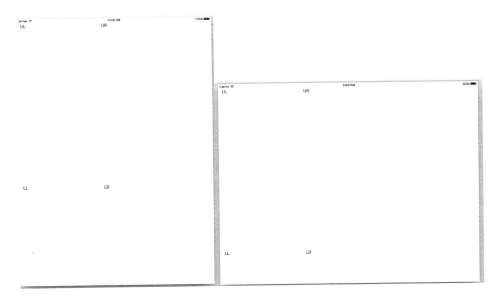

Figure 5-6. *Changing orientation without adding any constraints*

As you can see, things aren't looking so good. The top-left label is in the right spot after rotating, but all of the others are in the wrong places, and some of them aren't visible at all! What's happened is that every object has maintained its distance relative to the upper-left corner of the view in the storyboard. What you really want is to have each label sticking tightly to its nearest corner after rotating. The labels on the right should shift horizontally to match the view's new width, and the labels on the bottom should move vertically to match the new height. Fortunately, you can easily set up constraints in Interface Builder to make these changes happen for you.

As you've seen in earlier chapters, Interface Builder is smart enough to examine this set of objects and create a set of default constraints that will do exactly what you want. It uses some rules of thumb to figure out that if you have objects near edges, you probably want to keep them there. To make it apply these rules, first select all four labels. You can do this by clicking one label and then holding down the Shift key while clicking each of the other three. With all of them selected, choose Editor ➤ Resolve Auto Layout Issues ➤ Add Missing Constraints from the menu (you'll find there are two menu items with this name—in this case, because you have selected all of the labels, you can use either of them). Next, just press the Run button to launch the app in the simulator and then verify that it works.

▦ **Note**   Another way to easily select all the labels is to Shift-click the label names in the Document Outline, as shown in Figure 5-7.

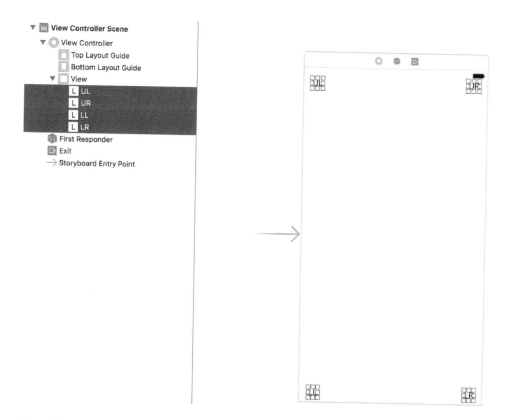

Figure 5-7. *Using the Document Outline view (to the left of the storyboard canvas) can sometimes make it easier to select and work with multiple UI objects*

Knowing that this works is one thing, but to use constraints like this most effectively, it's pretty important to understand how it works, too. So, let's dig into this a bit. Back in Xcode, click the upper-left label to select it. You'll notice that you can see some solid blue lines attached to the label. These blue lines are different from the dashed blue guidelines that you see when dragging objects around the screen, as shown in Figure 5-8.

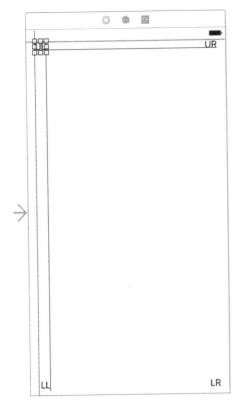

Figure 5-8. *The solid blue lines show constraints that are configured for the chosen object*

Each of those solid blue lines represents a constraint. If you now press ⌥⌘5 to open the Size Inspector, you'll see that it contains a list of constraints. Figure 5-9 shows the constraints that Xcode applied to the UL label in my storyboard, but the constraints that Xcode creates depends on exactly where you placed the labels, so you may see something different.

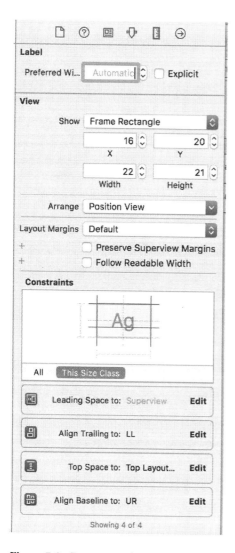

Figure 5-9. *Four constraints generated by Xcode to pin a label in its parent view*

In this case, two of the constraints deal with this label's position relative to its superview, which is the container view: it specifies the *leading space,* which generally means the space to the right, and the *top space,* which means the space above the label. These constraints cause the label to maintain the same distance to the top and right edges of its superview when the superview's size changes, as it does when the device is rotated. The other two constraints keep this label lined up with two of the other labels. Examine each of the other labels to see what constraints they have and make sure that you understand how those constraints work to keep the four labels in the corners of their superview.

You should know that in languages where text is written and read from right to left, leading space is on the right, so adding a trailing constraint will cause a GUI to be laid out in the opposite direction if the user has picked a language such as Arabic for their device. This is, in fact, what the user would expect. It's automatic, so you don't need to do anything special to make it happen.

Overriding Default Constraints

Grab another label from the library and drag it to the layout area. This time, instead of moving toward a corner, drag it toward the left edge of your view, lining up the label's left edge with the left edges of the other labels on the left side and centering it vertically in the view. Dashed lines will appear to help you out. Figure 5-10 shows you what this looks like.

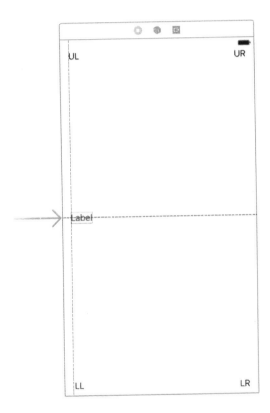

Figure 5-10. *Placing the Left label*

Let's add a new constraint to force this label to stay vertically centered. Select the label, click the Align icon below the storyboard, select Vertically in Container in the pop-up that appears, and then click Add 1 Constraint. Now make sure that the Size Inspector is on display (by pressing ⌥⌘5 if necessary). You'll see that this label now has a constraint aligning its center Y value to that of its superview. The label also needs a horizontal constraint. You can add this by making sure the label is selected and then choosing Editor ➤ Resolve Auto Layout Issues ➤ Add Missing Constraints from the All Views section of the menu. Press ⌘R to run the app again. Do some rotating and you'll see that all the labels now move perfectly into their expected places for the various device types.

Now, let's complete your ring of labels by dragging out a new one to the right side of the view, lining up its right edge with the other labels on the right, and aligning it vertically with the Left label. Change this label's title to Right and then drag it a bit to make sure that the right edge is vertically aligned with the right edges of the other two labels, using the dashed blue line as your guide. You want to use the automatic constraints that Xcode can provide you with, so select Editor ➤ Resolve Auto Layout Issues ➤ Add Missing Constraints to generate them.

Build and run again. Do some rotating again. You'll see that all the labels stay on the screen and are correctly positioned relative to each other (see Figure 5-11). If you rotate back, they should return to their original positions. This technique works great for many applications you're likely to encounter.

Figure 5-11. *The labels in their new positions after rotating*

Using Full-Width Labels

You're going to create some constraints that make sure that your labels stay the same width as each other, with tight spacing to keep them stretched across the top of the view even when the device rotates. Figure 5-12 should give you an idea of what you're trying to do.

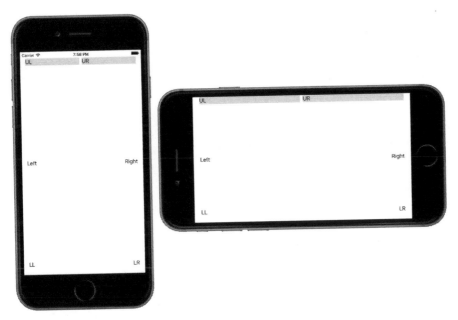

Figure 5-12. *The top labels, spread across the entire width of the display, in both portrait and landscape orientations*

You need to be able to visually verify that you have the result you want—namely, each label is precisely centered within its half of the screen. To make it easier to see whether you have it right, let's temporarily set a background color for the labels. In the storyboard, select both the UL and UR labels, open the Attributes Inspector, and scroll down to the View section. Use the Background control to select a nice, bright color. You'll see that the (currently very small) frame of each label fills with the color you chose.

Drag the resizing control of the UL label from its right edge, pulling it almost to the horizontal midpoint of the view. You don't have to be exact here, for reasons that will become clear soon. After doing this, resize the UR label by dragging its left-edge resizing control to the left until you see the dashed blue guideline appear (if you don't see the guide disappear, just drag it reasonably close), which tells you that it's the recommended width from the label to its left. Now you'll add a constraint to make these labels retain their relative positions. Control-drag from the UL label until the mouse is over the UR label and then release the mouse. In the pop-up, select Horizontal Spacing and press Return. That constraint tells the layout system to hold these labels beside one another with the same horizontal space they have right now. Build and run to see what happens. You should see something like Figure 5-13; the longer label may appear on the left or right depending upon your configuration.

Figure 5-13. *The labels are stretched across the display but not evenly*

That's heading in the right direction but not yet what I had in mind. So, what's missing? You've defined constraints that control each label's position relative to its superview and the allowed distance between the two labels, but you haven't said anything about the sizes of the labels. This leaves the layout system free to size them in whatever way it wants (which, as you've just seen, can be quite wrong). To remedy this, you need to add one more constraint.

Make sure the UL label is selected and then hold down the Shift key (⇧) and click the UR label. With both labels selected, you can make a constraint that affects both of them. Click the Pin icon below the storyboard and select the Equal Widths check box in the pop-up that appears (which you saw in Chapter 3); then click Add 1 Constraint. You'll now see a new constraint appear, as shown in Figure 5-14. You may notice two orange lines have appeared below the labels; this means that the current positions and sizes of the labels in the storyboard do not match what you will see at runtime. To fix this, select the View icon in the Document Outline and then select Editor ➤ Resolve Auto Layout Issues ➤ Update Frames in Xcode's menu. The constraints should change to blue, and the labels will resize themselves so that their widths are equal.

Figure 5-14. *The top labels are now made equal in width by a constraint*

If you run again at this point, you should see the labels spread across the entire screen, in both portrait and landscape orientations (see Figure 5-12).

In this project, all of your labels are visible and are correctly laid out in multiple orientations; however, there is a lot of unused space on the screen. Perhaps it would be better if you also set up the other two rows of labels to fill the width of the view or allowed the height of your labels to change so that there will be less empty space on the interface? Feel free to experiment with the constraints of these six labels and perhaps even add some others. Apart from what I've covered so far, you'll find more actions that create constraints in the pop-ups that appear when you click the Pin and Align icons below the storyboard. And if you end up making a constraint that doesn't do what you want, you can delete it by selecting it and pressing the Delete key, or you can try configuring it in the Attributes Inspector. Play around until you feel comfortable with the basics of how constraints work. You'll use constraints constantly throughout the book, but if you want the full details, just search for *Auto Layout* in the Xcode documentation window.

Creating Adaptive Layouts

The layout for the simple example that you just created works well in portrait and landscape orientations. It also works on both iPhone and iPad, despite their differing screen dimensions. As I already noted, handling device rotation and creating a user interface that works on devices with different screen sizes are really the same problem—after all, from the point of view of your application, when the device rotates, the screen effectively changes size. In the simplest cases, you handle them both at the same time by assigning Auto Layout constraints to make sure that all of your views are positioned and sized where you want them to be. However, that's not always possible. Some layouts work well when the device is in portrait mode but not so well when it's rotated to landscape; similarly, some designs suit the iPhone but not the iPad. When this happens, you really have no choice but to create separate designs for each case. Prior to iOS 8, this meant either implementing your whole layout in code, having multiple storyboards, or doing a combination of the two. Fortunately, Apple has made it possible to design *adaptive* applications that work in both orientations and on different devices while still using only a single storyboard. Let's take a look at how this works.

Creating the Restructure Application

To get started, you'll design a user interface that works well for an iPhone in portrait mode but not so well when the phone is rotated or when the application runs on an iPad. Then you'll see how to use Interface Builder to adapt the design so that it works well everywhere.

Start by making a new Single View app like you've done before, naming this one **Restructure**. You're going to construct a GUI that consists of one large content area and a small set of buttons that perform various (fictional) actions. You'll place the buttons at the bottom of the screen and let the content area take up the rest of the space, as shown in Figure 5-15.

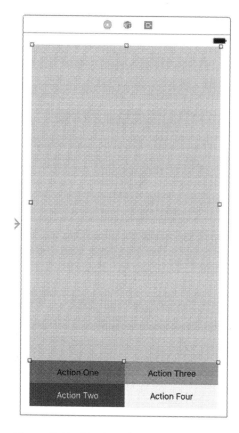

Figure 5-15. *The initial GUI of the Restructure app, in portrait orientation on the iPhone*

■ **Note**   You may have noticed that some of the various illustrations of Apple devices I use in this book have different configurations. While some, such as Figure 5-15, have an appearance closer to a "real" device, others such as Figure 5-11, appear more basic. The differences should not be a concern as you're likely to come across any of them in technical documentation, including that from Apple.

Select Main.storyboard to start editing the GUI. Since you don't really have an interesting content view you want to display, you'll just use a large colored rectangle. Drag a single UIView from the Object Library into your container view. While it's still selected, resize it so that it fills the top part of the available space, leaving a small margin above it and on both sides, as shown in Figure 5-15. Next, switch to the Attributes Inspector and use the Background pop-up to pick some other background color. You can choose anything you like, as long as it's not white, so that the view stands out from the background. In the storyboard in the example source code archive, this view is green, so from now on I'll call it the green view.

Drag a button from the Object Library and place it in the lower left of the empty space below the green view. Double-click to select the text in its label, and change it to **Action One**. Now Option-drag three copies of this button and place them in two columns, like those in Figure 5-15. You don't have to line them up perfectly because you're going to use constraints to finalize their positions, but you should try to place the two button groups approximately equal distances from their respective sides of the containing view. Change their titles to **Action Two**, **Action Three**, and **Action Four**. Also, let's add a different background color to each button so they're easy to see; I've used red, blue, orange, and yellow in order, but you can choose any colors you prefer. If you use a dark background color like blue, you want to make the text lighter as well. Finally, drag the lower edge of the green view downward until it just touches the top row of buttons. Use the blue guidelines to line everything up, as shown in Figure 5-15.

Now let's set up the Auto Layout constraints. Start by selecting the green view. You're going to start by pinning this to the top and to the left and right sides of the main view. That's still not enough to fully constrain it because its height isn't specified yet; you're going to fix that by anchoring it to the top of the buttons, once you've fixed the buttons themselves. Click the Pin button at the bottom right of the storyboard editor. At the top of the pop-up, you'll see the now familiar group of four input fields surrounding a small square. Leave the Constrain to Margins check box selected. Click the red dashed lines above, to the left, and to the right of the small square to attach the view to the top, left, and right sides of its superview (see Figure 5-16). Click Add 3 Constraints.

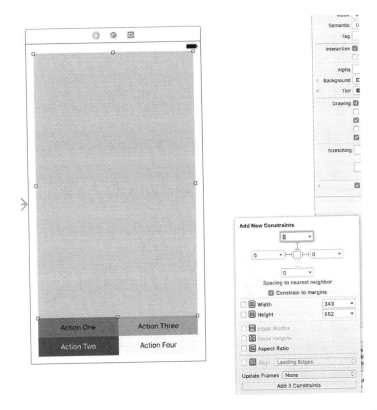

Figure 5-16. Adding constraints to fix the green view to the top, left, and right sides

For now, you'll set a constant height for your buttons, starting with Action One, as shown in Figure 5-17. I've used the value of 43 points simply because that's where it was when I created the button. Anything around this number should be okay for what you're trying to do in this example, which is deal with different devices and orientations. Then repeat the operation for each of the other three buttons.

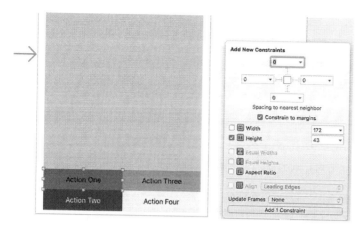

Figure 5-17. *Setting a height value for one of your buttons*

If you performed the operations correctly so far, you should be able to see the results of all the constraints in the Document Outline, as shown in Figure 5-18, where you see each of your four button heights, as well as the three sides for the green view.

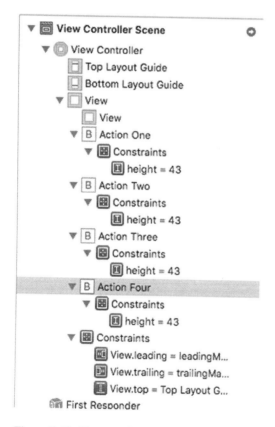

Figure 5-18. *You can always see the progress of setting your constraints in the Document Outline*

Next pin the bottom-left (Action Two) and bottom-right (Action Four) buttons to the lower corners by Control-dragging from each button to the lower left and lower right, respectively. For Action Two, Shift-select the two options, as shown in Figure 5-19.

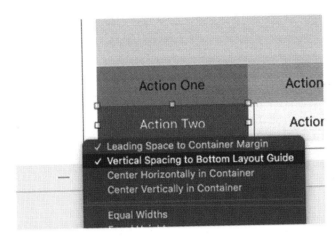

Figure 5-19. *Control-drag down and to the left to pin the Action Two button to the lower left of the container view*

Perform the similar operation, Control-dragging out to the right and down to set the leading and vertical spacing for the Action Four button, as shown in Figure 5-20.

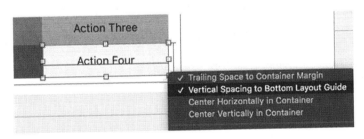

Figure 5-20. *Control-drag down and to the right to pin the Action Four button to the lower right of the container view*

Next, Shift-select all four buttons, click the Pin icon, and set all the widths to be equal (see Figure 5-21). Note that you haven't set a width yet, so they could vary from small to extremely wide; but in a moment, you'll take care of that through additional constraints.

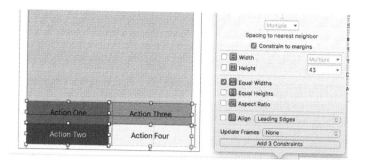

Figure 5-21. *Set all the buttons to be equal widths, although you haven't yet set any value for width in your storyboard*

For the top row of buttons, Action One and Action Three, Control-drag to the left and right, respectively, to set Leading Space to Container Margin and Trailing Space to Container Margin (see Figure 5-22). This ties the left edge of Action One and the right edge of Action Three to the edge of the view, setting one of your width anchor points.

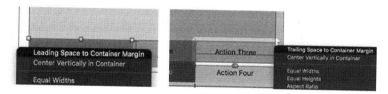

Figure 5-22. *Setting the left edge of Action One and the right edge of Action Three to the edges of the containing view*

These final two constraints will be all you need to make sure that the buttons are half the width of the green view and match each other. Control-drag from Action One to Action Three and set the horizontal spacing. Do the same thing between Action Two and Action Four, as shown in Figure 5-23. What you've done is to set the edge anchor to a fixed location, which is the left and right edges of the container in Figure 5-22. And, as you saw in Figure 5-21, you set the buttons to be equal width. By setting the horizontal spacing so that the buttons on the same row are up against each other, they work out to meet in the center of the view. And since the green view is also pinned to the left and right edges, the buttons meet in the middle of the green view.

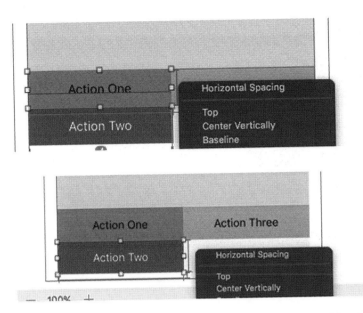

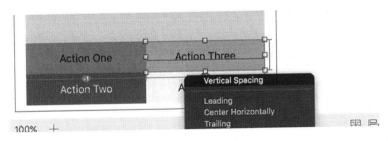

Figure 5-23. *Attach each row of buttons together at the center of the view; this, by default, sets the width of each button to be half the width of the view*

Just a couple more things and you'll be ready to test your app in the various devices. Control-drag from Action Three to Action Four to set the vertical spacing, like you just did with the horizontal spacing of rows, as shown in Figure 5-24. Do the same between Action One and Action Two.

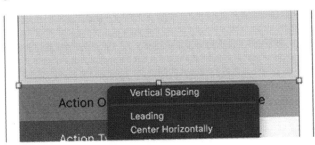

Figure 5-24. *Set the vertical spacing between buttons in the same column like you did with the button rows*

Finally, Control-drag between the green view and the Action One button to set the spacing so that the green view and the top row of buttons are adjacent, as shown in Figure 5-25.

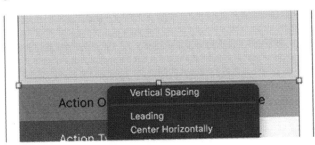

Figure 5-25. *Setting the spacing between your green view and the top row of buttons*

Now you should be able to select any full-screen iPhone or iPad in either portrait or landscape orientation and the buttons should maintain their position, as shown in Figure 5-26.

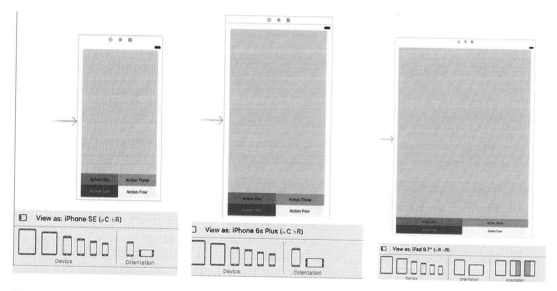

Figure 5-26. *Selecting different devices in portrait orientation; the layouts should maintain their positioning*

One other thing to note when looking at the Issue Navigator in Xcode is that there aren't any issues. By systematically setting just the constraints you needed, you were able to create a layout with minimal effort. However, don't expect it to be this easy all the time.

One last thing to do: let's build and run your project in the simulator before moving forward just to make sure it works as you expect. Figure 5-27 shows the two iPhone 6s orientations, while Figure 5-28 shows the two orientations for a full-screen iPad Air.

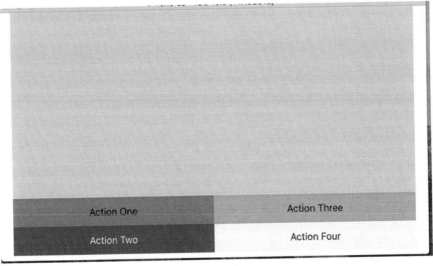

Figure 5-27. *Your two orientations for an iPhone 6s*

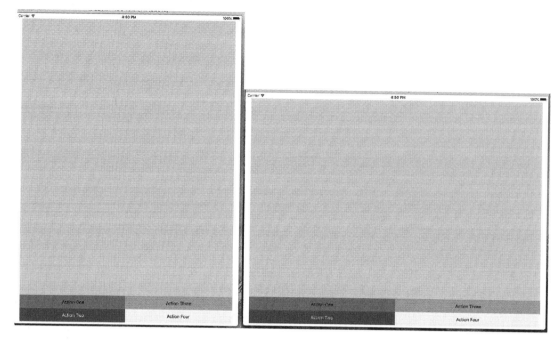

Figure 5-28. *Your two orientations for an iPad Air*

While these look like you would expect them to, they're not what you're after. For an iPhone in landscape, still a wC hC configuration, you want a single column of buttons pressed up against the right side. For an iPad, in any orientation, wR hR, you want a single row of buttons against the bottom of the view.

▨ **Note**   The notation *w- h-* refers to the width and height of the configuration being considered. To simplify things, in Auto Layout this will be either C for compact or R for regular so that you have these options: wC hC, wC hR, wR hC, and wR hR. By looking in the Device Configuration Bar, you can see how these apply to actual Apple devices.

Setting the iPhone Landscape (wC hC) Configuration

You'll get to setting up your wC hC landscape configuration quickly, but first save your work and then close the Xcode project. You can just click the red ball at the upper left of the Xcode window to close this project. You don't have to exit Xcode completely.

Go to Finder on your Mac to locate the Restructure folder and create a compressed version, as shown in Figure 5-29. This creates your "master" copy of the project that you can come back to at any time if, during the following changes, things get out of whack.

Figure 5-29. *Create a master copy of your project as it exists now*

Because you may want to do this again through the course of your following work, rename the `.zip` file to **RestructureBaseline**, as shown in Figure 5-30, so you know that this is the original project you made that works with all devices and orientations in the same manner.

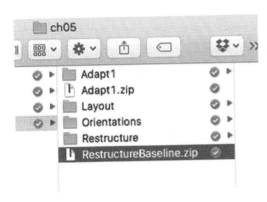

Figure 5-30. *Saving your baseline project under a unique name*

First, let's create your iPhone landscape orientation. Select the iPhone 6s and the landscape orientation. To the right of the Device Configuration Bar, click Vary for Traits and note that the bar turns blue, as shown in Figure 5-31. In the pop-up select both height and width. You should see, again in Figure 5-31, that now only iPhone devices are shown and only in landscape orientation. In this variation of traits, you'll develop your UI just for this configuration.

Figure 5-31. *The starting point for creating the UI for your iPhone landscape configuration*

Next, and yes this will seem scary, click all five UI elements (your green view and the four buttons) and press Delete. Don't worry too much because you saved the project and created a compressed baseline version that you can always get back to later. If you didn't, it might be a good idea to do that now. When completed, your canvas will look, as you'd expect, like Figure 5-32. But, if you look at the Document Outline, you'll still see the elements and even the constraints. That's because they exist for the baseline configuration and you're creating a new configuration or a new trait collection for just your wC hC landscape.

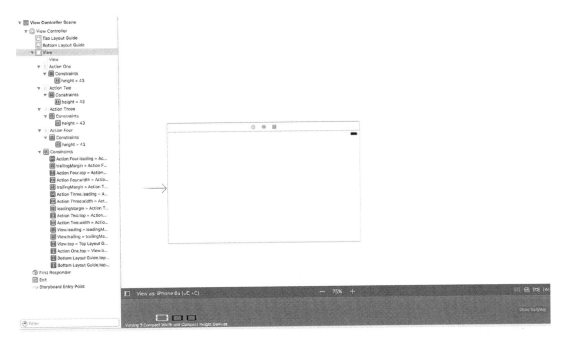

Figure 5-32. Starting over for just your iPhone landscape configuration. Note that you still have all the UI elements and constraints showing in your Document Outline but for your baseline configuration.

As you did for your baseline, drag out a `UIView` and four buttons, setting them up with colors and titles as you did earlier. Place them in the approximate positions shown in Figure 5-33, but don't set any constraints just yet.

Figure 5-33. Drag new UI elements onto the storyboard and position them approximately as shown

In this section, let's make your measurements a little more accurate. Select the green view. Using the Size Inspector, set the dimensions to 500 × 340 points, as shown in Figure 5-34. The width (500pts) is arbitrary; the height is 340, which when divided by 4 comes out to 85, which is what you will set as the height of the buttons. Note that this is not necessarily a constraint but, rather, the appearance on the storyboard. In fact, you don't want any fixed size for the green view since it will vary depending on whether you go up in size to a Plus or down to an SE.

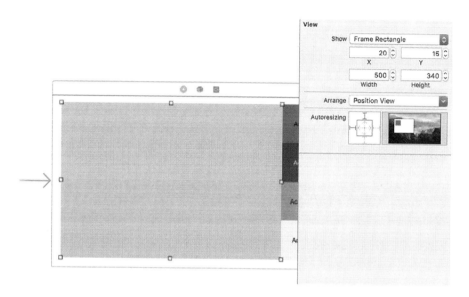

Figure 5-34. Set the dimensions of the green view

Select the green view and pin the top, left, and right sides to the edge, as shown in Figure 5-35.

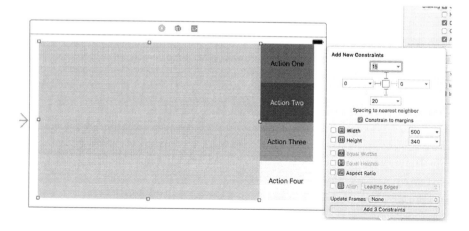

Figure 5-35. Pin the green view to the top, left, and right for the landscape orientation

Next, you're going to fix the width of the Action One button, but you're going to do it a little differently than previously. Inside the Action One button, Control-drag from one point to another both the starting and ending points within the red boundary and release. You're presented with a similar popover (see Figure 5-36), on which you select Width. The width of the Action One button should now be 120 points, as shown in Figure 5-37.

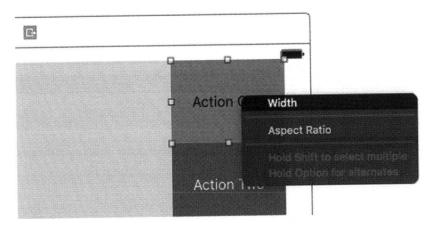

Figure 5-36. *Set the width of the Action One button*

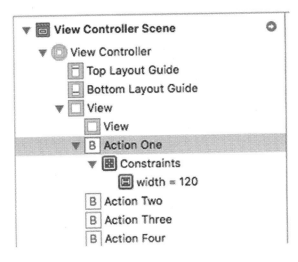

Figure 5-37. *Verify that the Action One button is set to 120 points*

You want all four buttons to be the same width and the same height—the width being 120 points but the height being adjust dynamically based on the available vertical area of the iPhone when in landscape orientation. As before, you'll handle the equal height by setting the spacing between the buttons in the column. For now, Shift-click all four buttons to select them all, click the Pin icon, and set the Equal Widths and Equal Heights constraints, as shown in Figure 5-38.

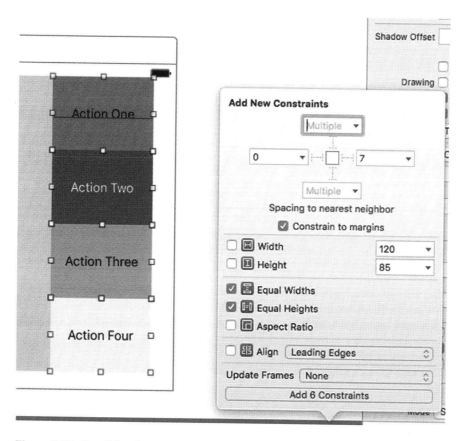

Figure 5-38. *Set all four buttons to equal width and height*

■ **Note**   You may have noticed that although you have four buttons with two constraints each, the actual number of constraints you add is 6. This is because you're actually setting the equal quality of three buttons to the fourth button.

Pin the Action One button to the top and right of its containing view (see Figure 5-39) and the Action Four button to the right and bottom (see Figure 5-40).

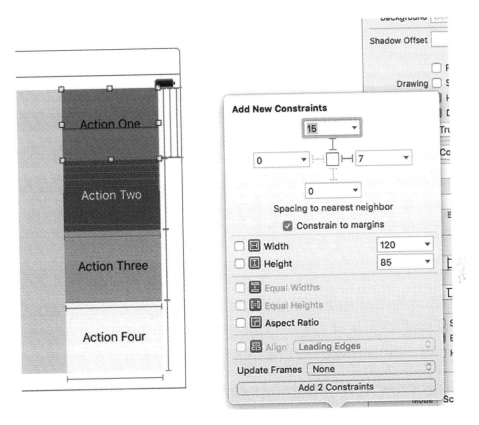

Figure 5-39. *Pinning the Action One button to the top and right*

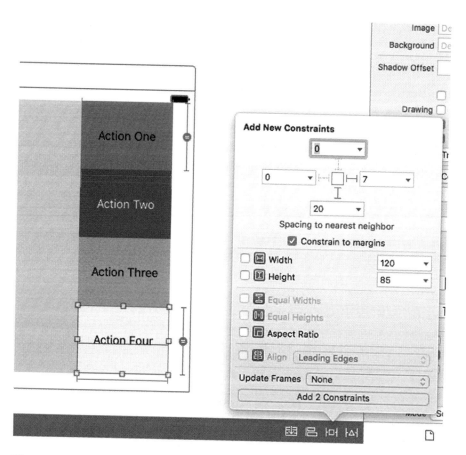

Figure 5-40. *Pinning the Action Four button to the bottom and right*

For the Action Two button, Control-drag to the right and choose Trailing Space to Container Margin to pin it to the right side of the container, as shown in Figure 5-41. Repeat this operation with the Action Three button.

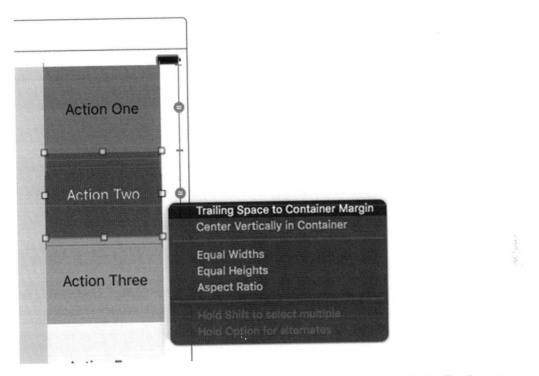

Figure 5-41. *Pin the middle buttons to the right side using Control-drag and set the Trailing Space to Container Margin pop-up, as shown here for Action Two. Do the same operation for the Action Three button.*

Between the Action One and Action Two buttons, Control-drag to set the vertical spacing, as shown in Figure 5-42. Repeat for the spacing between Action Two and Action Three, as well as Action Three and Action Four.

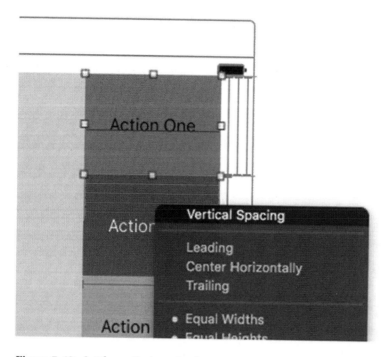

Figure 5-42. *Set the vertical spacing between each of the pairs of buttons in the column. This forces the height of each button to be one-fourth the height of the container.*

Finally, set the horizontal spacing between the green view and the Action One button (you could use any of the four buttons), as shown in Figure 5-43.

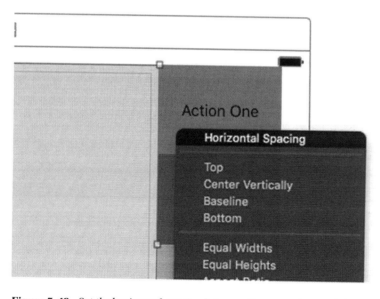

Figure 5-43. *Set the horizontal spacing between the green view and the row of buttons*

Click the Done Varying button in the Device Configuration Bar to finish adding, placing, and setting constraints for this iPhone landscape configuration, as shown in Figure 5-44.

Figure 5-44. *Finish by clicking the Done Varying button in the Device Configuration Bar*

The buttons should now be properly placed for any of the three iPhone wC hC configurations, as shown in Figure 5-45. Note that if you were to select a 6/6s Plus, because that is a wR hC device, you would see the earlier baseline layout.

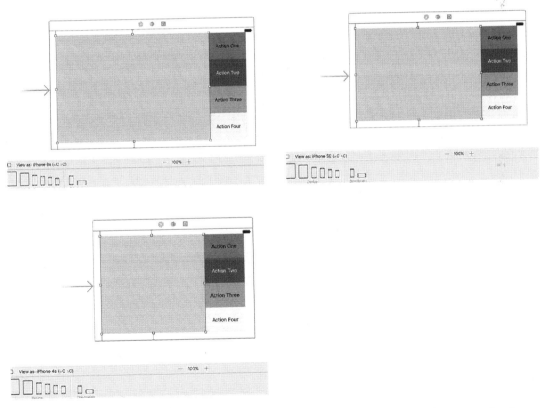

Figure 5-45. *Changing the device type in the Device Configuration Bar shows that you have correctly set up your constraints for the landscape orientation of wC hC iPhone devices*

167

Running the apps in the simulator should yield the results shown in Figure 5-46. Although you could have made the alignment a little tighter to the edges, which would be appropriate for a production app, in this example you wanted to stress the manipulations of UI elements for the various device and orientation configurations. As you become more and more familiar with Auto Layout, you'll naturally get much better with your designs.

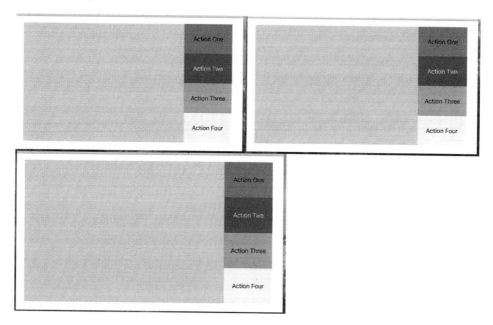

Figure 5-46. *If you've done everything correctly, you should see the proper layout for any iPhone (except 6s/7 Plus) landscape configurations*

The last thing you want to do before moving on to iPad is to save this project version by compressing it for later and assigning a recognizable name. As shown in Figure 5-47, I used the name `Restructure_wChC.zip` for your file, which represents the compact width and height. Feel free to use any naming convention you like, as long as you're able to keep track of the various iterations.

Figure 5-47. *Save this version of the project in case you need to get back to this baseline*

Setting the iPad (iPhone Plus Landscape) (wR hR) Configurations

In the previous two sections, I walked you through each step along the way to creating your layouts for the baseline and iPhone landscape configurations. You need to be able to quickly use Auto Layout when designing your UI, so if you need any review, I suggest running through the preceding sections another couple of times, trying it without looking at the text or figures.

For this configuration, to save space, I've shown the key steps in Table 5-1 along with pointing to the reference figures in case you might need a little help with understanding what the step is about. You'll work this way from now on, at least most of the time unless I need to address something new.

Follow the steps in Table 5-1 to set up the configuration for the iPad in all orientations and the iPhone 6/6s Plus in landscape orientation.

Table 5-1. *Setting Up All Orientations on an iPad and the Landscape Orientation on iPhone 6/6s Plus*

Step	Action	Figure
1	Click Vary For Traits and introduce variations based on width.	5-48
2	Delete the five UI elements in the storyboard. Then add back five new elements from the Object Library as you did in the previous section.	5-49
3	Select the green view you just added and, in the Size Inspector, set the width to 728 and the height to 926. These are not constraints; they'll just help you with visually laying out the elements on the storyboard. (Note: These values work for the iPhone 6s. If using a different device size, you will need to vary your height and width accordingly.)	5-50
4	Select the Action Four button and set its width to 182 using the Size Inspector; again, this is for the iPhone 6s device. This is only for visual placement and not a constraint.	5-51
5	Making sure you still have a blue Device Configuration Bar indicating that you're still in the Vary for Traits mode, align the UI elements as shown: the green view along the top and a single row of buttons along the bottom.	5-52
6	Similar to what you did before, pin the green view to the top, left, and right sides of the containing view.	5-53
7	Pin the Action One button to the lower-left corner of the containing view.	5-54
8	Pin the Action Four button to the lower-right corner of the containing view.	5-55
9	Pin the Action Two button to the bottom edge of the containing view.	5-56
10	Pin the Action Three button to the bottom edge of the containing view.	5-57
11	Add a constraint to set the height of the Action One button to a fixed value. I used 63 points because it fit the layout on my storyboard. There is no "right" answer; adjust it to your needs for your layout.	5-58
12	Shift-select all four action buttons along the bottom row and set them to equal height and width.	5-59
13	Click-drag from the green view to the Action One button and set the vertical spacing. This forces the green view to sit against the row of buttons.	5-60
14	Click-drag from Action One to Action Two setting the horizontal spacing. Repeat for Action Two to Action Three as well as Action Three to Action Four. This causes the buttons to sit next to each other on the sides and to be one-quarter the width of the enclosing container.	5-61
15	Click the Done Varying button to end the modifications for this set of traits.	5-62

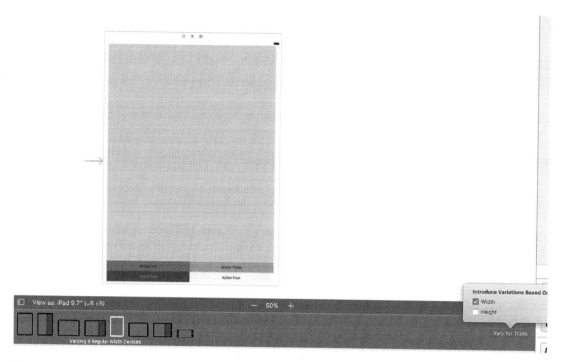

Figure 5-48. *Select an iPad, click Vary For Traits, and choose Width*

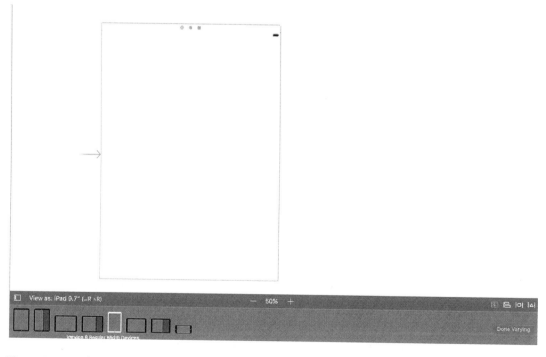

Figure 5-49. *Delete the five UI elements*

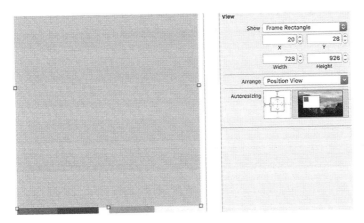

Figure 5-50. *Add in the five new UI elements from the UI Object Library and set the width and height of the green view using the Size Inspector. This does not set constraints, only the visual aspects so you can adjust your storyboard.*

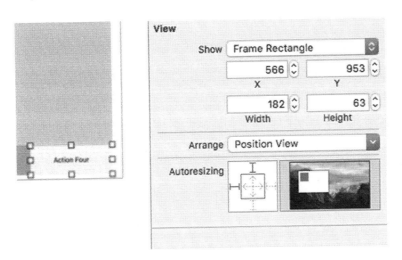

Figure 5-51. *Similarly, set the width and height of the Action Four button so you have a visual reference with which to work and manipulate your storyboard*

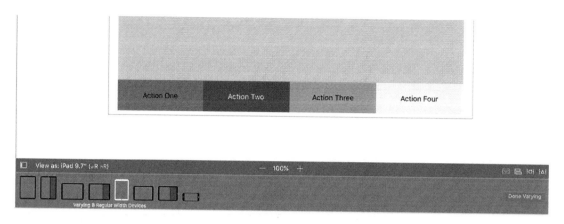

Figure 5-52. *Align everything up as shown, making sure your Device Configuration Bar is still blue indicating you're working with a particular set of traits*

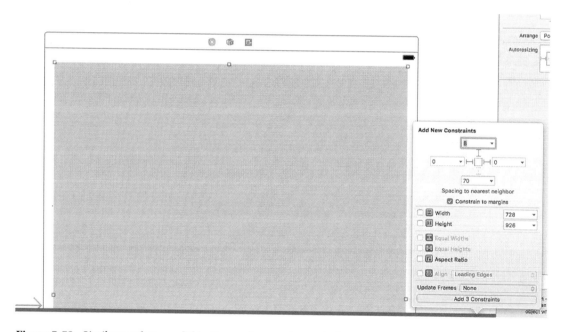

Figure 5-53. *Similar to what you did in the previous sections, pin the green view to the top, left, and right sides of the containing view*

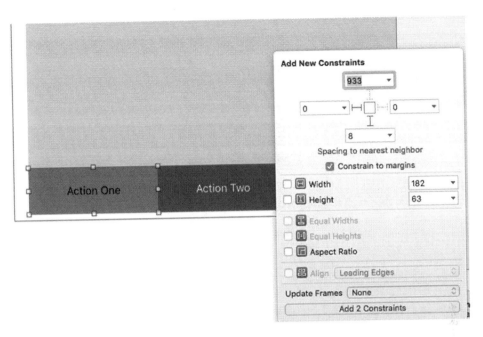

Figure 5-54. *Pin the Action One button to the lower-left corner of the containing view*

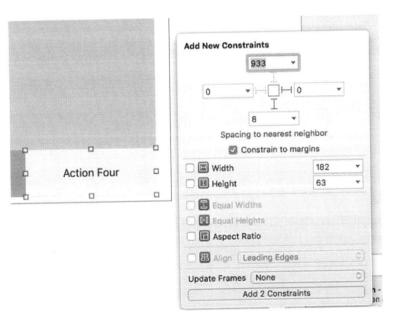

Figure 5-55. *Pin the Action Four button to the lower-right corner of the containing view*

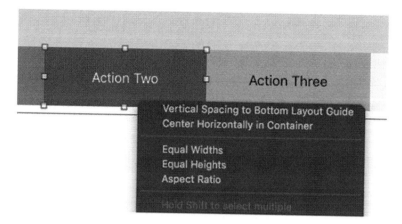

Figure 5-56. *Pin the Action Two button to the bottom edge of the containing view*

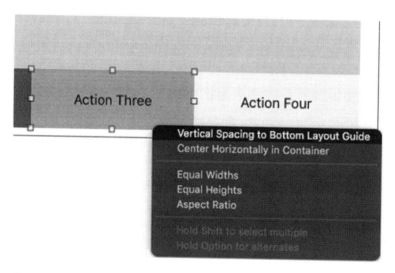

Figure 5-57. *Pin the Action Three button to the bottom edge of the containing view*

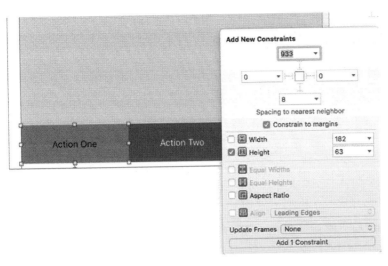

Figure 5-58. *Add a constraint to set the height of the Action One button to a fixed value. I used 63 points because it fit the layout on my storyboard.*

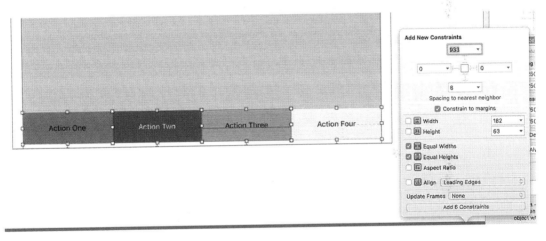

Figure 5-59. *Shift-select all four action buttons along the bottom row and set them to equal height and width*

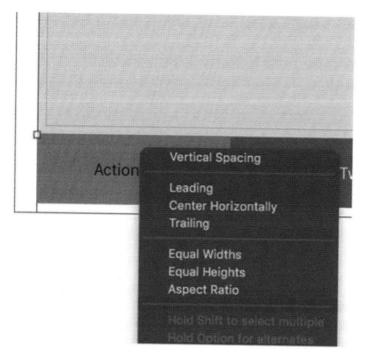

Figure 5-60. *Click-drag from the green view to the Action One button and set the vertical spacing. This forces the green view to sit against the row of buttons.*

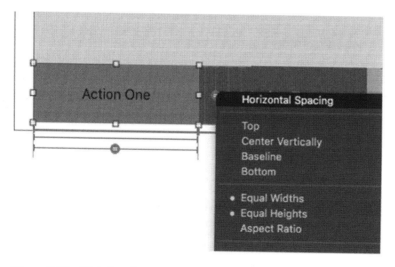

Figure 5-61. *Click-drag from Action One to Action Two, setting the horizontal spacing. Repeat for Action Two to Action Three as well as for Action Three to Action Four.*

Figure 5-62. *Click the Done Varying button to end the modifications for this set of traits*

I hope you were able to follow this abbreviated form of using Auto Layout. If you found any issues, the best thing is to go back, delete your project, and start at the last baseline project. Until you work with Auto Layout for a dozen or so times, you'll most likely make several mistakes and get frustrated. You're not alone. When I'm away from Xcode and especially Auto Layout for a few weeks, I'm often walking away only to restart and re-layout things until I get it the way I need or want it to be.

Assuming you made it to this point successfully, click a few different iPad and orientation configurations to verify that things appear as you expect them, as shown in Figure 5-63.

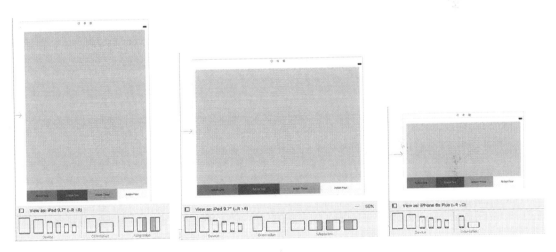

Figure 5-63. *Check to make sure your orientations appear correctly in the storyboard canvas*

Finally, run the simulator for various devices making sure things appear as they should. Figure 5-64 shows what things should look like for an iPad Air in portrait and landscape orientations.

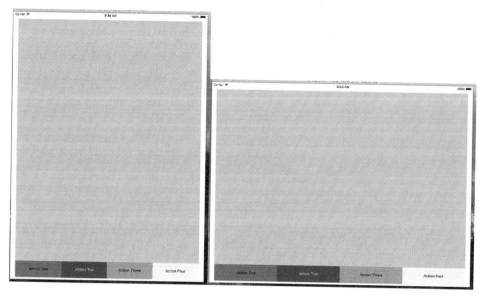

Figure 5-64. *Verify things work as expected by running the simulator using various device types and checking orientations*

Summary

In this chapter, I covered the basics of handling device rotations including getting heavily involved with using the new Xcode 8 Auto Layout and traits editor with the Device Configuration Bar. I started by talking the basics of rotations and what happens when you change orientation on an Apple device. The first project, Orientations, showed the basics of working with simple device rotations and maintaining positioning of labels. In the second project, Layout, you refined your knowledge of label positioning by putting labels into all four corners, as well as the left and right edges, to handle rotations.

Finally, in the Restructure project, you got very deep into understanding the use of Auto Layout for creating device and orientation-specific layout configurations. As you will be using Auto Layout for the rest of this book, as well as your career, make sure that you're comfortable with its use before proceeding. While it can be very daunting at first, through practice, like with anything else, it will become second nature—until Apple changes things next year.

■ ■ ■

CHAPTER 6

Creating a Multiview Application

Up until this point, you've written applications using a single view controller. While single view apps can often do what you need them to, the real power of the iOS platform emerges when you switch out views based on user input. Multiview applications come in several different flavors, but the underlying mechanism functions the same, regardless of how the app appears on the screen. In this chapter, you'll focus on the structure of multiview applications and the basics of swapping content views by building your own multiview app from scratch. By writing your own custom controller class that switches between two different content views, you'll establish a strong foundation for taking advantage of the various multiview controllers provided by Apple.

First, let's look at some examples of your new area of exploration...multiviews.

Looking at Common Types of Multiview Apps

Strictly speaking, you have worked with multiple views in your previous applications, since buttons, labels, and other controls are all subclasses of UIView and they can all go into the view hierarchy. But when Apple uses the term *view* in documentation, it refers to a UIView or one of its subclasses having a corresponding view controller. These types of views are also sometimes referred to as *content views* because they are the primary container for the content of your application.

A utility app provides the simplest example of how a multiview application appears. It focuses primarily on a single view but offers a second view typically used to configure the application or to provide more detail than the primary view. The Stocks application that ships with the iPhone shows a good example of this (see Figure 6-1). By clicking button in the lower-right corner, the view transitions to a new view that lets you set the list of stocks tracked by the application.

© Molly K. Maskrey 2017
M. K. Maskrey, *Beginning iPhone Development with Swift 4*, https://doi.org/10.1007/978-1-4842-3072-5_6

Figure 6-1. *The Stocks application that ships with the iPhone provides two views: one to display the data and another to configure the stock list*

Several tab bar applications ship with the iPhone, including the Phone application (see Figure 6-2) and the Clock application. A tab bar application displays a row of buttons, called the *tab bar*, at the bottom of the screen. Tapping one of the buttons causes a new view controller to become active and a new view to be shown. In the Phone application, for example, tapping Contacts shows a different view than the one shown when you tap Keypad.

Figure 6-2. *The Phone application provides an example of a multiview application using a tab bar*

Another common type of multiview app uses a navigation-based mechanism featuring a navigation controller that uses a bar to control a hierarchical series of views, as shown in the Settings app (see Figure 6-3). In Settings, you first see a series of rows, with each row corresponding to a cluster of settings or a specific app. Touching one of those rows takes you to a new view where you might customize one particular set of settings. Some views present a list that allows you to dive even deeper. The navigation controller keeps track of how deep you go and gives you a control to let you make your way back to the previous view.

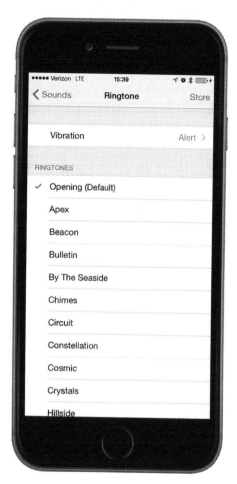

Figure 6-3. *The iPhone Settings application provides a great example of a multiview application using a navigation bar*

For example, selecting the Sounds preference takes you to a view with a list of sound-related options. The top of that view displays a navigation bar with a left arrow labeled Settings that takes you back to the previous view if you tap it. Within the sound options you'll see a row labeled Ringtone. Tap Ringtone. You're taken to a new view featuring a list of ringtones and a navigation bar that takes you back to the main Sounds preference view, as shown in Figure 6-4. A navigation-based application provides a useful mechanism when you want to present a hierarchy of views.

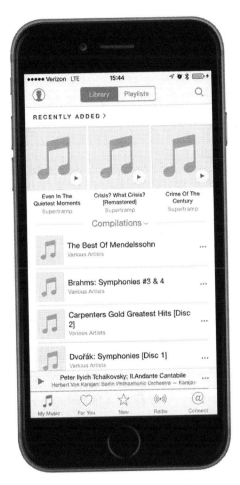

Figure 6-4. *The Music application uses both a navigation bar and a tab bar*

On the iPad, you implement most navigation-based applications, such as Mail, using a split view, where the navigation elements appear on the left side of the screen, and the item you select to view or edit appears on the right. I'll talk about split views in Chapter 11.

Because views are themselves hierarchical in nature, you might combine different mechanisms for swapping views within a single application. For example, the iPhone's Music application uses a tab bar to switch between different methods of organizing your music. It also uses a navigation controller and its associated navigation bar to allow you to browse your music based on that selection. In Figure 6-4, the tab bar is at the bottom of the screen, and the navigation bar is at the top of the screen.

Some applications use a toolbar, which is often confused with a tab bar. A tab bar selects one and only one choice from among two or more options. A toolbar holds buttons and certain other controls, but those items are not mutually exclusive. A perfect example of a toolbar is at the bottom of the main Safari view, as shown in Figure 6-5. If you compare the toolbar at the bottom of the Safari view with the tab bar at the bottom of the Phone or Music application, you'll find the two pretty easy to tell apart. The tab bar has multiple segments, exactly one of which (the selected one) is highlighted with a tint color; but on a toolbar, normally every enabled button is highlighted.

Figure 6-5. *Mobile Safari features a toolbar at the bottom, acting like a free-form bar that allows you to include a variety of controls*

Each of these multiview application types uses a specific controller class from the UIKit. Tab bar interfaces are implemented using the UITabBarController class, and navigation interfaces are implemented using UINavigationController. I'll describe their use in detail in the next few chapters.

Looking at the Architecture of a Multiview Application

The application you're going to build in this chapter, called View Switcher, exhibits a fairly simple appearance; however, in terms of the code, this is the most complex application you've yet tackled. View Switcher consists of three different controllers, a storyboard, and an application delegate.

When first launched, View Switcher appears with a toolbar at the bottom containing a single button, as shown in Figure 6-6. The rest of the view displays a blue background and a button to be pressed.

Figure 6-6. *When you first launch the View Switcher application, you'll see a blue view with a button and a toolbar with its own button*

Pressing the Switch Views button causes the background to turn yellow and the button's title to change, as shown in Figure 6-7.

Figure 6-7. *Pressing the Switch Views button causes the blue view to flip, revealing the yellow view*

If either the Press Me or Press Me, Too button activates, an alert appears indicating which view's button was pressed, as shown in Figure 6-8.

Figure 6-8. *Pressing the Press Me or Press Me, Too button displays the alert*

Although you could achieve this same functionality writing a single-view application, I took this more complex approach to demonstrate the actual mechanics of a multiview application. Three view controllers interact in this simple application: one that controls the blue view, one that controls the yellow view, and a third special controller that swaps the other two in and out when the Switch Views button is pressed.

Before you start building your application, let's discuss how iOS multiview applications get put together. Most multiview applications use the same basic pattern.

Understanding the Root Controller

The storyboard acts as the key player here since it contains all the views and view controllers for your application. You'll create a storyboard with an instance of a controller class that is responsible for managing which other view currently appears to the user. This controller is called the *root controller* (as in "the root of the tree") because it is the first controller the user sees and the controller that is loaded when the application loads. This root controller often acts as an instance of UINavigationController or UITabBarController, although it can also be a custom subclass of UIViewController.

In a multiview application, the root controller takes two or more other views and presents them to the user as appropriate, based on the user's input. A tab bar controller, for example, swaps in different views and view controllers based on which tab bar item was last tapped. A navigation controller does the same thing when the user drills down and backs up through hierarchical data.

■ **Note**   The root controller provides the primary view controller for the application and, as such, specifies whether it is OK to automatically rotate to a new orientation. However, the root controller may pass responsibility for tasks like that to the currently active controller.

In multiview applications, the content view takes up most of the screen and each content view has its own view controller containing outlets and actions. In a tab bar application, for example, taps on the tab bar will go to the tab bar controller, but taps anywhere else on the screen get processed by the controller corresponding to the content view currently displayed.

Content View Anatomy

In a multiview application, each view controller (Swift code) manages a content view, and these content views are where the bulk of your application's user interface resides. Taken together, each of these pairings is called a *scene* within a storyboard. Each scene consists of a view controller and a content view, which may be an instance of UIView or one of its subclasses. Although you can create your interface in code rather than using Interface Builder, the power, flexibility, and stability of the tools preclude ever needing to do that.

In this project, you'll create a new controller class for each content view. Your root controller manages a content view consisting of a toolbar that occupies the bottom of the screen. The root controller then loads a blue view controller, placing the blue content view as a subview to the root controller view. When you press the root controller's Switch Views button (the button is in the toolbar), the root controller swaps out the blue view controller and swaps in a yellow view controller, instantiating that controller if it needs to do so. Let's build the project and see this all become much clearer.

Creating the View Switcher Application

To start your project, in Xcode select File ➤ New ➤ Project or press Shift-⌘N. When the template selection sheet opens, select Single View App and then click Next. On the next page of the assistant, enter **View Switcher** as the product name, set Language to Swift and the Devices pop-up button to Universal. When everything is set up correctly, click Next to continue. On the next screen, navigate to wherever you're saving your projects on disk and click the Create button to create a new project directory.

Renaming the View Controller

As you've already seen, the Single View App template supplies an application delegate, a view controller, and a storyboard. The view controller class is called `ViewController`. In this application, you are going to be dealing with three view controllers, but most of the logic will be in the main view controller. Its task will be to switch the display so that the view from one of the other view controllers is showing at all times. To make the role of the main view controller clear, you probably want to give it a better name, such as `SwitchingViewController`. There are several places in the project where the view controller's class name is referenced. To change its name, you would need to update all of those places. Xcode has a nifty feature called *refactoring* that would do that for you, but, at the time of writing, refactoring is not supported for Swift projects in the Xcode beta I'm using. Instead, you're going to delete the controller that the template created for you and add a new one.

Start by selecting `ViewController.swift` in the Project Navigator. Right-click it and select Delete in the pop-up (see Figure 6-9). When prompted, choose to move the source file to the Trash.

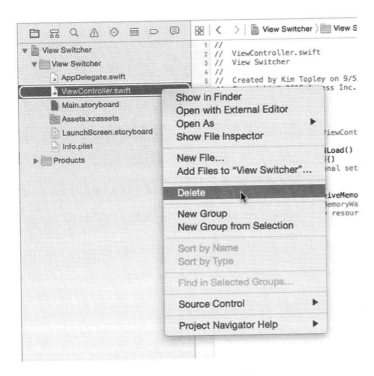

Figure 6-9. *Deleting the template view controller*

Now right-click the View Switcher group and select New File. In the template chooser, select Cocoa Touch Class from the iOS Source section. Name the class `SwitchingViewController` and make it a subclass of `ViewController`. Make sure that "Also create XIB file" is not select since you are going to add this controller to the storyboard a little later and that Language is set to Swift, as shown in Figure 6-10, and then press Next followed by Create.

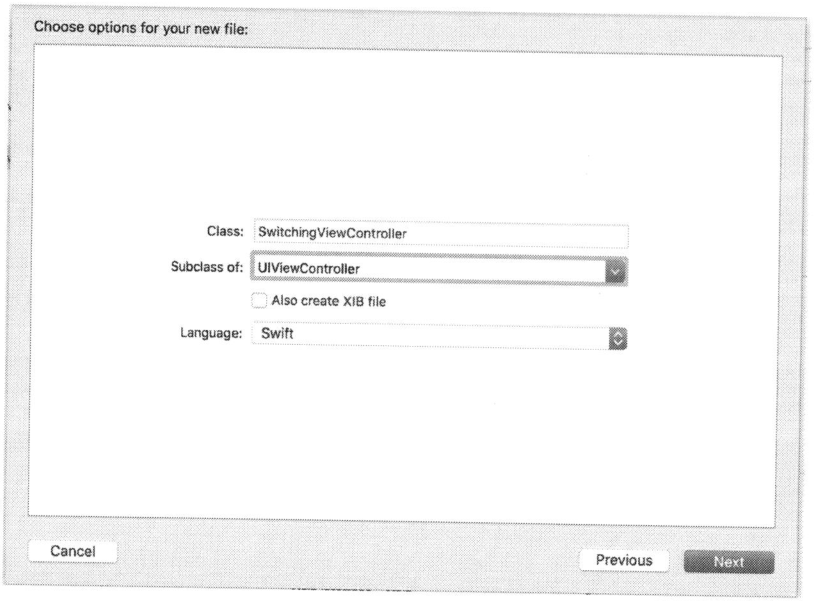

Choose options for your new file:

Class: SwitchingViewController
Subclass of: UIViewController
             ☐ Also create XIB file
Language: Swift

Cancel   Previous   Next

Figure 6-10. *Creating the SwitchingViewController class*

Now that you have your new view controller, you need to add it to the storyboard. Select `Main.storyboard` in the Document Outline to open the storyboard for editing. You'll see that the template created a view controller for you—you just need to link it to your `SwitchingViewController` class. Select the view controller in the Document Outline and open the Identity Inspector. In the Custom Class section, change the class from `UIViewController` to `SwitchingViewController`, as shown in Figure 6-11.

Figure 6-11. *Changing the view controller class in the storyboard*

Now if you check the Document Outline, you should see that the view controller's name has changed to Switching View Controller, as shown in Figure 6-12.

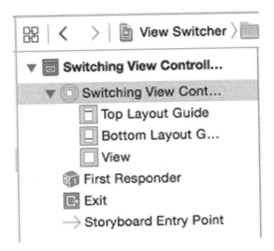

Figure 6-12. *The new view controller in the Document Outline*

Adding the Content View Controllers

You'll need two additional view controllers to display the content views. In the Project Navigator, right-click the View Switcher group and select New File. In the template dialog, choose Cocoa Touch Class from the iOS Source section and click Next. Name the new class `BlueViewController`, make it a subclass of `UIViewController`, and make sure that the "Also create XIB file" check box is not select. Click Next and then Create to save the files for the new view controller. Repeat this process to create the second content view controller, giving it the name `YellowViewController`. To keep things organized, you may want to move the files under the View Switcher folder in the Project Navigator, as shown in Figure 6-13.

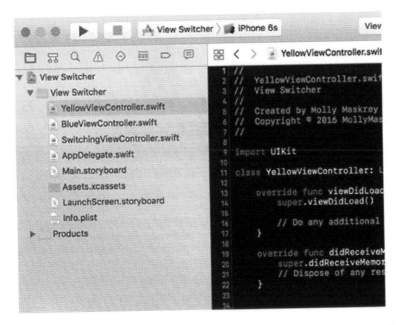

Figure 6-13. *You may want to move the new Swift files under the View Switcher folder in the Xcode Project Navigator*

Modifying SwitchingViewController.swift

The SwitchingViewController class will need an action method that will toggle between the blue and yellow views. You won't create any outlets, but you will need two properties—one for each of the view controllers that you'll be swapping in and out. These don't need to be outlets because you're going to create the view controllers in code rather than in the storyboard. Add the following property declarations to SwitchingViewController.swift:

```
private var blueViewController: BlueViewController!
private var yellowViewController: YellowViewController!
```

Add the following method at the bottom of the class:

```
@IBAction func switchViews(sender: UIBarButtonItem) {
}
```

Previously, you added action methods by Control-dragging from a view to the view controller's source code, but here you'll see that you can work the other way around just as well, since IB can see what outlets and actions are already defined in your source code. Now that you've declared the action you need, you can set up the minimal user interface for this controller in your storyboard.

Building a View with a Toolbar

You now need to set up the view for SwitchingViewController. As a reminder, this view controller will be your root view controller—the controller that is in play when your application is launched. SwitchingViewController's content view will consist of a toolbar that occupies the bottom of the screen and the view from either the yellow or blue view controller. Its job is to switch between the blue view and the yellow view, so it will need a way for the user to change the views. For that, you're going to use a toolbar with a button. Let's build the toolbar now.

In the Project Navigator, select Main.storyboard. In the IB editor view, you'll see your switching view controller. As you can see in Figure 6-14, it's currently empty and quite dull. This is where you'll start building your GUI.

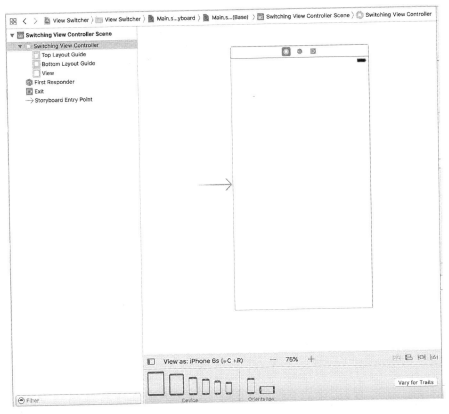

Figure 6-14. *Your empty root view controller (Switching View Controller) storyboard*

Grab a toolbar from the library, drag it onto your view, and place it at the bottom so that it looks like Figure 6-15.

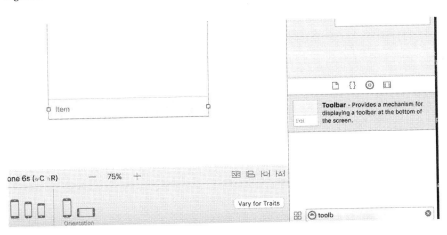

Figure 6-15. *Add a toolbar to the bottom of your root view controller*

You want to keep this toolbar stretched across the bottom of the content view no matter what size the view has. To do that, you need to add three layout constraints—one that pins the toolbar to the bottom of the view and another two that pin it to the view's left and right sides. To do this, select the toolbar in the Document Outline, click the Pin button on the toolbar beneath the storyboard, and change the values in the pop-up, as shown in Figure 6-16.

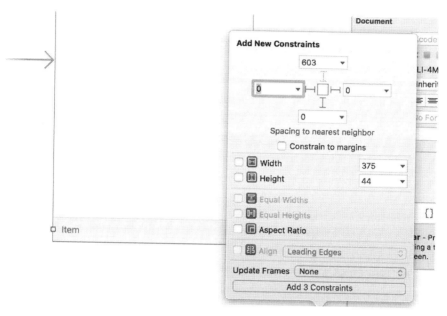

Figure 6-16. *Constrain the toolbar to the bottom, left, and right of its containing view*

Deselect the "Constrain to margins" check box because you want to position the toolbar relative to the edges of the content view, not the blue guidelines that appear near its edges. Next, set the distances to the nearest left, right, and bottom neighbors to zero (if you have correctly positioned the toolbar, they should already be zero). In this case, the nearest neighbor of the toolbar is the content view. You can see this by clicking the small arrow in one of the distance boxes. It opens a pop-up that shows the nearest neighbor and any other neighbors relative to which you could place the toolbar; in this case, there are no neighbors. To indicate that these distance constraints should be active, click the three dashed red lines that link the distance boxes to the small square in the center so that they become solid lines. Finally, change Update Frames to Items of New Constraints (so that the toolbar's representation in the storyboard moves to its new constrained location) and click Add 3 Constraints.

Now, to make sure you're on the right track, click the Run button to make this app launch in the iOS simulator. You should see a plain white app start up, with a pale gray toolbar at the bottom containing a lone button. If not, go back and retrace your steps to see what you missed. Rotate the simulator. Verify that the toolbar stays fixed at the bottom of the view and stretched right across the screen. If this doesn't happen, you need to fix the constraints that you just applied to the toolbar.

Linking the Toolbar Button to the View Controller

You can see that the toolbar has a single button, and you'll use that button to switch between the different content views. Double-click the button in the storyboard, as shown in Figure 6-17, and change its title to **Switch Views**. Press the Return key to commit your change. Now you can link the toolbar button to your action method in `SwitchingViewController`. Before doing that, though, you should be aware that toolbar buttons aren't like other iOS controls. They support only a single target action, and they trigger that action only at one well-defined moment—the equivalent of a Touch Up Inside event on other iOS controls.

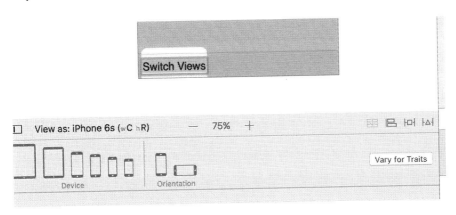

Figure 6-17. *Change the title of the button in the toolbar to Switch Views*

Selecting a toolbar button in Interface Builder can be tricky. The easiest way to do it is to expand the Switching View Controller icon in the Document Outline until you can see the button, which is now labeled Switch Views, and then click it. Once you have the Switch Views button selected, Control-drag from it over to the yellow Switching View Controller icon at the top of the scene, as shown in Figure 6-18. Release the mouse and select the `switchViewsWithSender:` action from the pop-up. If the `switchViewsWithSender:` action doesn't appear and instead you see an outlet called `delegate`, you've most likely Control-dragged from the toolbar rather than the button. To fix it, just make sure you have the button rather than the toolbar selected and then redo your Control-drag.

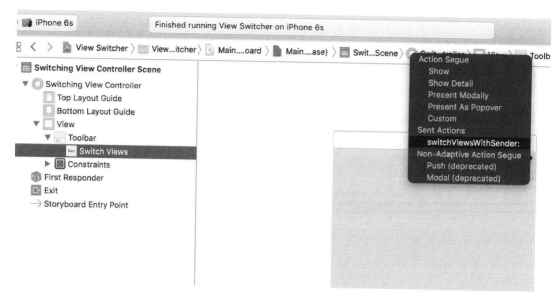

Figure 6-18. *Linking the toolbar button to the switchViewsWithSender: method in the view controller class*

■ **Note** You may have noticed that when you entered the function manually earlier you called it switchViews, but because this is an action, you get the sender parameter added for you whether or not you actually decide to use the parameter.

I have one more thing to point out in this scene, which is SwitchingViewController's view outlet. This outlet is already connected to the view in the scene. The view outlet is inherited from the parent class, UIViewController, and gives the controller access to the view it controls. When you created the project, Xcode created both the controller and its view and hooked them up for you. That's all you need to do here, so save your work. Next, let's get started writing your implementation code in SwitchingViewController.swift.

Writing the Root View Controller Implementation

In the Project Navigator, select SwitchingViewController.swift and modify the viewDidLoad() method to set some things up by adding the lines shown in Listing 6-1.

Listing 6-1. The Code for the viewDidLoad Method of Your Root View Controller

```
override func viewDidLoad() {
    super.viewDidLoad()

    // Do any additional setup after loading the view.
    blueViewController =
        storyboard?.instantiateViewController(withIdentifier: "Blue")
        as! BlueViewController
    blueViewController.view.frame = view.frame
    switchViewController(from: nil, to: blueViewController)  // helper method
}
```

■ **Note**   When you enter the code into the Swift file, as shown in Listing 6-1, you'll get an error on the line containing the call to `switchViewController`. This is because you have not written that helper method yet, which you'll do shortly.

Your implementation of `viewDidLoad()` overrides a `UIViewController` method that is called when the storyboard is loaded. How can you tell? Hold down the `⌥` key (the Option key) and single-click the method named `viewDidLoad()`. A documentation pop-up window will appear, as shown in Figure 6-19. Alternatively, you can select View ➤ Utilities ➤ Show Quick Help Inspector to view similar information in the Quick Help panel. `viewDidLoad()` is defined in your superclass, `UIViewController`, and is intended to be overridden by classes that need to be notified when the view has finished loading.

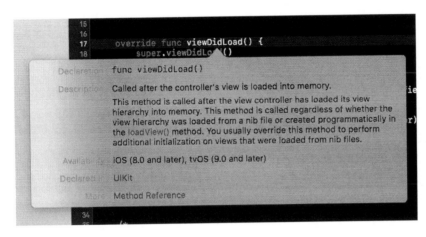

Figure 6-19. *This documentation window appears when you Option-click the viewDidLoad method name*

This version of `viewDidLoad()` creates an instance of `BlueViewController`. You use the `instantiateViewController(withIdentifier:)` method to load the `BlueViewController` instance from the same storyboard that contains your root view controller. To access a particular view controller from a storyboard, you use a string as an identifier—in this case `"Blue"` —which you'll set up when you configure your storyboard a little more. Once the `BlueViewController` is created, you assign this new instance to your `blueViewController` property.

```
blueViewController =
    storyboard?.instantiateViewController(withIdentifier: "Blue")
    as! BlueViewController
```

Next, you set the frame of the blue view controller's view to be the same as that of the switch view controller's content view and switch to the blue view controller so that its view appears on the screen.

```
blueViewController.view.frame = view.frame
switchViewController(from: nil, to: blueViewController)
```

Since you need to perform a view controller switch in several places, the code to do this is in the helper method `switchViewController(from:, to:)` that you'll write shortly.

Now, why didn't you load the yellow view controller here also? You're going to need to load it at some point, so why not do it now? Good question. The answer is that the user may never tap the Switch Views button. The user might just use the view that's visible when the application launches and then quit. In that case, why use resources to load the yellow view and its controller? Instead, you'll load the yellow view the first time you actually need it. This is called *lazy loading*, which is a standard way of keeping memory overhead down. The actual loading of the yellow view happens in the switchViews() method. Fill in the stub of this method that you created earlier by adding the code shown in Listing 6-2.

Listing 6-2. Your switchViews Implementation

```
@IBAction func switchViews(sender: UIBarButtonItem) {
    // Create the new view controller, if required
    if yellowViewController?.view.superview == nil {
        if yellowViewController == nil {
            yellowViewController =
                storyboard?.instantiateViewController(withIdentifier: "Yellow")
                as! YellowViewController
        }
    } else if blueViewController?.view.superview == nil {
        if blueViewController == nil {
            blueViewController =
                storyboard?.instantiateViewController(withIdentifier: "Blue")
                as! BlueViewController
        }
    }

    // Switch view controllers
    if blueViewController != nil
        && blueViewController!.view.superview != nil {
        yellowViewController.view.frame = view.frame
        switchViewController(from: blueViewController,
                                to: yellowViewController)
    } else {
        blueViewController.view.frame = view.frame
        switchViewController(from: yellowViewController,
                                to: blueViewController)
    }
}
```

switchViews() first checks which view is being swapped in by seeing whether the superview of yellowViewController's view is nil. This will be true if one of two things are true.

- If yellowViewController exists, but its view is not being shown to the user, that view will not have a superview because it's not presently in the view hierarchy, and the expression will evaluate to true.

- If yellowViewController doesn't exist because it hasn't been created yet or was flushed from memory, it will also return true.

You then check to see whether yellowViewController exists.

```
if yellowViewController?.view.superview == nil {
```

If the result is nil, that means there is no instance of yellowViewController, so you need to create one. This could happen because it's the first time the button has been pressed or because the system ran low on memory and it was flushed. In this case, you need to create an instance of YellowViewController as you did for BlueViewController in the viewDidLoad method.

```
if yellowViewController == nil {
    yellowViewController =
        storyboard?.instantiateViewController(withIdentifier: "Yellow")
        as! YellowViewController
}
```

If you're switching in the blue controller, you need to perform the same check to see whether it still exists (since it could have been flushed from memory) and create it if it does not. This is just the same code again, referencing the blue controller instead:

```
} else if blueViewController?.view.superview == nil {
    if blueViewController == nil {
        blueViewController =
            storyboard?.instantiateViewController(withIdentifier: "Blue")
            as! BlueViewController
    }
}
```

At this point, you know that you have a view controller instance because either you already had one or you just created it. You then set the view controller's frame to match that of the switch view controller's content view and then you use your switchViewController(from:, to:) method to actually perform the switch, as shown in Listing 6-3.

Listing 6-3. Switching View Controllers Depending On Which One You're Currently Presenting

```
// Switch view controllers
if blueViewController != nil
    && blueViewController!.view.superview != nil {
    yellowViewController.view.frame = view.frame
    switchViewController(from: blueViewController,
                         to: yellowViewController)
} else {
    blueViewController.view.frame = view.frame
    switchViewController(from: yellowViewController,
                         to: blueViewController)
}
}
```

The first branch of the if statement is taken if you are switching from the blue view controller to the yellow and vice versa for the else branch.

In addition to not using resources for the yellow view and controller if the Switch Views button is never tapped, lazy loading gives you the ability to release whichever view is not being shown to free up its memory. iOS will call the UIViewController method didReceiveMemoryWarning(), which is inherited by every view controller, when memory drops below a system-determined level.

Since you know that either view will be reloaded the next time it is shown to the user, you can safely release either controller, provided it is not currently on display. You can do this by adding a few lines to the existing didReceiveMemoryWarning() method, as shown in Listing 6-4.

Listing 6-4. Safely Releasing Unneeded Controllers During Low Memory Conditions

```
override func didReceiveMemoryWarning() {
    super.didReceiveMemoryWarning()
    // Dispose of any resources that can be recreated.

    if blueViewController != nil
        && blueViewController!.view.superview == nil {
        blueViewController = nil
    }
    if yellowViewController != nil
        && yellowViewController!.view.superview == nil {
        yellowViewController = nil
    }
}
```

This newly added code checks to see which view is currently shown to the user and then releases the controller for the other view by assigning nil to its property. This will cause the controller, along with the view it controls, to be deallocated, freeing up its memory.

■ **Tip**   Lazy loading is a key component of resource management on iOS, which you should implement anywhere you can. In a complex, multiview application, being responsible and flushing unused objects from memory can be the difference between an application that works well and one that crashes periodically because it runs out of memory.

The final piece of the puzzle is the switchViewController(from:, to:) method, which is responsible for the view controller switch. Switching view controllers is a two-step process. First, you need to remove the view for the controller that's currently displayed; then, you need to add the view for the new view controller. But that's not quite all—you need to take care of some housekeeping as well. Add the implementation of this method, as shown in Listing 6-5.

Listing 6-5. The switchViewController Helper Method

```
private func switchViewController(from fromVC:UIViewController?,
                                  to toVC:UIViewController?) {
    if fromVC != nil {
        fromVC!.willMove(toParentViewController: nil)
        fromVC!.view.removeFromSuperview()
        fromVC!.removeFromParentViewController()
    }

    if toVC != nil {
        self.addChildViewController(toVC!)
        self.view.insertSubview(toVC!.view, at: 0)
        toVC!.didMove(toParentViewController: self)
    }
}
```

The first block of code removes the outgoing view controller, but let's look at the second block first, where you add the incoming view controller. Here's the first line of code in that block:

```
self.addChildViewController(toVC!)
```

This code makes the incoming view controller a child of the switching view controller. View controllers like SwitchingViewController that manage other view controllers are referred to as *container view controllers*. The standard classes UITabBarController and UINavigationController are both container view controllers, and they have code that does something similar to what the switchViewController(from:, to:) method is doing. Making the new view controller a child of SwitchingViewController ensures that certain events that are delivered to the root view controller are correctly passed to the child controller when required—for example, making sure that rotation is handled properly.

Next, the child view controller's view is added to that of SwitchingViewController.

```
self.view.insertSubview(toVC!.view, atIndex: 0)
```

Note that the view is inserted in the subview's list of SwitchingViewController at index zero, which tells iOS to put this view *behind* everything else. Sending the view to the back ensures that the toolbar you created in Interface Builder a moment ago will always be visible on the screen since you're inserting the content views behind it.

Finally, you notify the incoming view controller that it has been added as the child of another controller.

```
toVC!.didMoveToParentViewController(self)
```

This is necessary in case the child view controller overrides this method to take some action when it becomes the child of another controller.

Now that you've seen how a view controller is added, the code that removes a view controller from its parent is much easier to understand—all you do is reverse each of the steps that you performed when adding it.

```
if fromVC != nil {
    fromVC!.willMoveToParentViewController(nil)
    fromVC!.view.removeFromSuperview()
    fromVC!.removeFromParentViewController()
}
```

Implementing the Content Views

At this point, the code is complete, but you can't run the application yet because you don't have the blue and yellow content controllers in the storyboard. These two controllers are extremely simple. They each have one action method that is triggered by a button, and neither one needs any outlets. The two views are also nearly identical. In fact, they are so similar that they could have been represented by the same class. You chose to make them two separate classes because that's how most multiview applications are constructed.

The two action methods you're going to implement do nothing more than show an alert (as you did in Chapter 4's project), so go ahead and add method in Listing 6-6 to BlueViewController.swift.

Listing 6-6. Pressing the Button on Your Blue Controller Presents an Alert

```
@IBAction func blueButtonPressed(sender: UIButton) {
    let alert = UIAlertController(title: "Blue View Button Pressed",
                          message: "You pressed the button on the blue view",
                          preferredStyle: .alert)
```

```
        let action = UIAlertAction(title: "Yes, I did", style: .default,
                                  handler: nil)
        alert.addAction(action)
        present(alert, animated: true, completion: nil)
}
```

Save the file. Next, switch to `YellowViewController.swift` and add the very similar method shown in Listing 6-7 to that file; save it as well.

Listing 6-7. Pressing the Button on Your Yellow Controller Also Presents an Alert

```
@IBAction func yellowButtonPressed(sender: UIButton) {
    let alert = UIAlertController(title: "Yellow View Button Pressed",
                                 message: "You pressed the button on the yellow view",
                                 preferredStyle: .alert)
    let action = UIAlertAction(title: "Yes, I did", style: .default,
                               handler: nil)
    alert.addAction(action)
    present(alert, animated: true, completion: nil)
}
```

Next, select `Main.storyboard` to open it in Interface Builder so that you can make a few changes. First, you need to add a new scene for `BlueViewController`. Up until now, each storyboard you've dealt with contained just a single controller-view pairing, but the storyboard has more tricks up its sleeve, and holding multiple scenes is one of them. From the Object Library, drag out another view controller and drop it in the editing area next to the existing one. Now your storyboard has two scenes, each of which can be loaded dynamically and independently while your application is running. In the row of icons at the top of the new scene, single-click the yellow View Controller icon and press ⌥⌘3 to bring up the Identity Inspector. In the Custom Class section, the Class menu defaults to `UIViewController`; change it to `BlueViewController`, as shown in Figure 6-20.

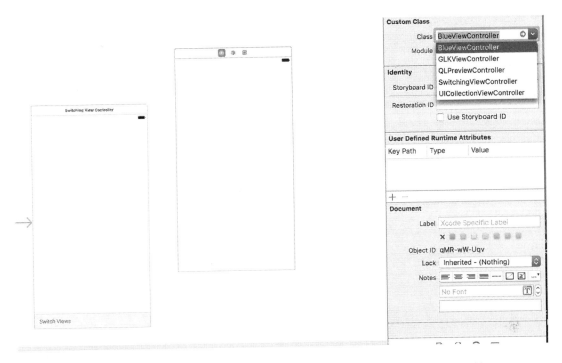

Figure 6-20. *Add your new view controller and associate it with the BlueViewController class file*

You also need to create an identifier for this new view controller so that your code can find it inside the storyboard. Just below the Custom Class section in the Identity Inspector, you'll see a Storyboard ID field. Click there and type **Blue** to match what you used in your code, as shown in Figure 6-21.

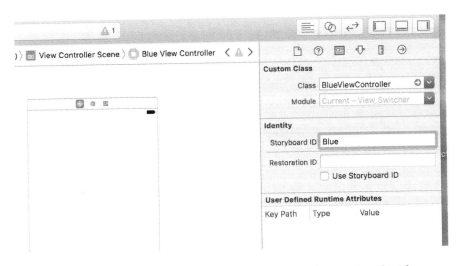

Figure 6-21. *Set the Storyboard ID of your Blue View Controller storyboard to Blue*

So, now you have two scenes. I showed you earlier how to configure your app to load this storyboard at launch time, but I didn't mention anything about scenes there. How will the app know which of these two views to show? The answer lies in the big arrow pointing at the first scene, as shown in Figure 6-22. That arrow points out the storyboard's default scene, which is what the app shows when it starts up. If you want to choose a different default scene, all you have to do is drag the arrow to point at the scene you want.

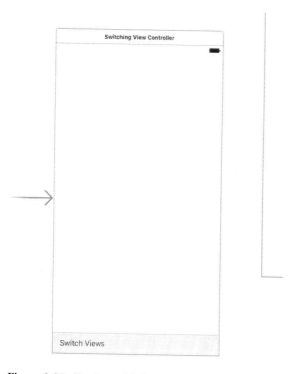

Figure 6-22. *You just added a second scene to your storyboard. The big arrow points at the default scene.*

Single-click the big square view in the new scene you just added and then press ⌥⌘4 to bring up the Attributes Inspector. In the inspector's View section, click the color picker that's labeled Background, and use the pop-up color picker to change the background color of this view to a nice shade of blue. Once you are happy with your blue, close the color picker.

Drag a button from the library to the view, using the guidelines to center it in the view, both vertically and horizontally. You want to make sure that the button stays centered no matter what, so make two constraints to that effect. With the button selected, click the Align icon below the storyboard. In the pop-up, select Horizontally in Container and Vertically in Container, change Update Frames to Items of New Constraints, and then click Add 2 Constraints (see Figure 6-23). It may help to change the background back to white for the alignment and then back to blue once you're finished. Also, because of the blue background, you might want to change the button text to white to be more visible.

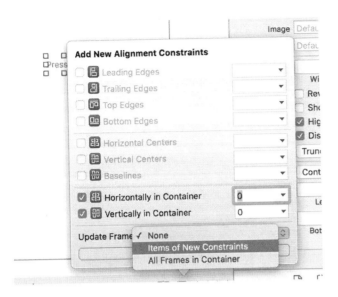

Figure 6-23. Aligning the button to the center of the view

Double-click the button and change its title to **Press Me**. Next, with the button still selected, switch to the Connections Inspector (by pressing ⌥⌘6), drag from the Touch Up Inside event to the yellow View Controller icon at the top of the scene, and connect to the blueButtonPressedWithSender: action method.

Now it's time to do pretty much the same set of things for YellowViewController. Grab yet another view controller from the Object Library and drag it into the editor area. Don't worry if things are getting crowded; you can stack those scenes on top of each other if necessary. Click the View Controller icon for the new scene in the Document Outline and use the Identity Inspector to change its class to YellowViewController and its storyboard ID to Yellow.

Next, select the YellowViewController's view and switch to the Attributes Inspector. There, click the Background color picker, select a yellow, and then close the picker.

Next, drag out a button from the library and use the guidelines to center it in the view. Use the Align icon pop-up to create constraints aligning its horizontal and vertical center, just like for the last button. Now change its title to **Press Me, Too**. With the button still selected, use the Connections Inspector to drag from the Touch Up Inside event to the View Controller icon, and connect to the yellowButtonPressedWithSender action method.

When you're finished, save the storyboard and hit the Run button in Xcode to start the app presenting a full screen of blue. When you tap the Switch Views button, it will change to show the yellow view that you built. Tap it again, and it goes back to the blue view. If you tap the button centered on the blue or yellow view, you'll get an alert view with a message indicating which button was pressed. This alert shows that the correct controller class is being called for the view that is being shown.

The transition between the two views is kind of abrupt, so you're going to animate the transition to give the user a better visual feedback of the change.

Animating the Transition

UIView has several class methods you can call to indicate that the transition between views should be animated, to indicate the type of transition that should be used, and to specify how long the transition should take.

Go back to SwitchingViewController.swift and enhance your switchViews() method by changing it, as shown in Listing 6-8.

Listing 6-8. Your Modified switchViews Method with Animation Added

```swift
@IBAction func switchViews(sender: UIBarButtonItem) {
    // Create the new view controller, if required
    if yellowViewController?.view.superview == nil {
        if yellowViewController == nil {
            yellowViewController =
                storyboard?.instantiateViewController(withIdentifier: "Yellow")
                    as! YellowViewController
        }
    } else if blueViewController?.view.superview == nil {
        if blueViewController == nil {
            blueViewController =
                storyboard?.instantiateViewController(withIdentifier: "Blue")
                    as! BlueViewController
        }
    }

    UIView.beginAnimations("View Flip", context: nil)
    UIView.setAnimationDuration(0.4)
    UIView.setAnimationCurve(.easeInOut)
    // Switch view controllers
    if blueViewController != nil
        && blueViewController!.view.superview != nil {
        UIView.setAnimationTransition(.flipFromRight,
                                    for: view, cache: true)
        yellowViewController.view.frame = view.frame
        switchViewController(from: blueViewController,
                            to: yellowViewController)
    } else {
        UIView.setAnimationTransition(.flipFromLeft,
                                    for: view, cache: true)
        blueViewController.view.frame = view.frame
        switchViewController(from: yellowViewController,
                            to: blueViewController)
    }
    UIView.commitAnimations()
}
```

Build and run this version. When you tap the Switch Views button, instead of the new view just snapping into place, the old view will flip over to reveal the new view.

To tell iOS that you want a change animated, you need to declare an *animation block* and specify how long the animation should take. Animation blocks are declared by using the UIView class method presentViewController(_:animated:completion:), like so:

```swift
UIView.beginAnimations("View Flip", context: nil)
UIView.setAnimationDuration(0.4)
```

presentViewController(_:animated:completion:) takes two parameters. The first is an animation block title. This title comes into play only if you take more direct advantage of Core Animation, the framework behind this animation. For these purposes, you could have used nil. The second parameter is a pointer that allows you to specify an object (or any other C data type) whose address you would like associated with this animation block. It is possible to add some code of your own that will be run during the transition, but you're not doing that here, so you set this parameter to nil. You also set the duration of the animation, which tells UIView how long (in seconds) the animation should last.

After that, you set the *animation curve*, which determines the timing of the animation. The default, which is a linear curve, causes the animation to happen at a constant speed. The option you set here, UIViewAnimationCurve.EaseInOut, specifies that the animation should start slow but speed up in the middle and then slow down again at the end. This gives the animation a more natural, less mechanical appearance.

```
UIView.setAnimationCurve(.easeInOut)
```

Next, you need to specify the transition to use. At the time of this writing, five iOS view transitions are available.

- UIViewAnimationTransition.flipFromLeft

- UIViewAnimationTransition.flipFromRight

- UIViewAnimationTransition.curlUp

- UIViewAnimationTransition.curlDown

- UIViewAnimationTransition.none

You will choose to use two different effects, depending on which view was being swapped in. Using a left flip for one transition and a right flip for the other makes the view seem to flip back and forth. The value UIViewAnimationTransition.none causes an abrupt transition from one view controller to another. Of course, if you wanted that effect, you wouldn't bother creating an animation block at all.

The cache option speeds up drawing by taking a snapshot of the view when the animation begins, and uses that image rather than redrawing the view at each step of the animation. You should always cache the animation unless the appearance of the view needs to change during the animation.

```
UIView.setAnimationTransition(.flipFromRight,
                      forView: view, cache: true)
```

When you're finished specifying the changes to be animated, you call commitAnimations() on UIView. Everything between the start of the animation block and the call to commitAnimations() animates together.

Thanks to Cocoa Touch's use of Core Animation under the hood, you're able to do fairly sophisticated animation with only a handful of code.

Summary

You should now have a very good grasp of how multiview applications are put together, now that you've built one from scratch. Although Xcode contains project templates for the most common types of multiview applications, you need to understand the overall structure of these types of applications so you can build them yourself from the ground up. The standard container controllers (UITabBarController, UINavigationController, and UIPageViewController) are incredible time-savers that you should use when you can, but at times, they simply won't meet your needs.

In the next few chapters, you're going to continue building multiview applications to reinforce the concepts from this chapter and to give you a feel for how more complex applications are put together.

CHAPTER 7

Using Tab Bars and Pickers

In the previous chapter, you built your first multiview application. In this chapter, you'll build another one—this time, creating a full tab bar application with five different tabs and five different content views. Building this application reinforces a lot of what I covered in Chapter 6. You'll use those five content views to demonstrate a type of iOS control not yet covered, a picker view, or just a picker. You may not be familiar with the name, but you've almost certainly used a picker if you've owned an iPhone or iPod touch for more than ten minutes. Pickers contain controls with dials that spin. You use them to input dates in the Calendar application or to set a timer in the Clock application, as shown in Figure 7-1. It is not quite as common on an iPad, since the larger display lets you present other ways of choosing among multiple items, but even there, it's used by the Calendar application.

© Molly K. Maskrey 2017
M. K. Maskrey, *Beginning iPhone Development with Swift 4*, https://doi.org/10.1007/978-1-4842-3072-5_7

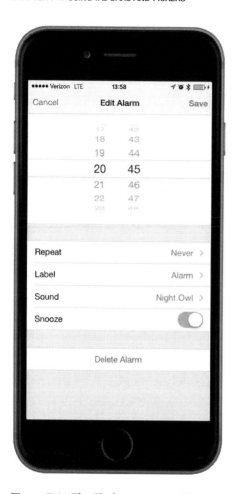

Figure 7-1. *The Clock app uses a picker to set the time the alarm should go off*

Pickers provide a bit more complexity than the iOS controls you've seen so far; as such, they deserve a little more attention. Pickers can be configured to display one dial or many. By default, pickers display lists of text, but they can also be made to display images.

The Pickers Application

This chapter's application, Pickers, features a tab bar, and when you build Pickers, you'll change the default tab bar so that it has five tabs, add an icon to each of the tab bar items, and then create a series of content views and connect each view to a tab. The application's content views feature five different pickers:

- *Date picker*: The first content view you'll build uses a date picker, the easiest type of picker to implement (see Figure 7-2). The view also has a button that, when tapped, displays an alert showing the date that was picked.

Figure 7-2. *The first tab displays a date picker*

- *Single-component picker*: The second tab features a picker with a single list of values, as shown in Figure 7-3, and provides a little more work to implement than the date picker. You'll learn how to specify the values to be displayed in the picker by using a delegate and a data source.

Figure 7-3. *A picker displaying a single list of values*

- *Multicomponent picker*: In the third tab, you'll create a picker with two separate wheels. The technical term is *picker component*. Here, you create a picker with two components. You'll see how to use the data source and delegate by providing two independent lists of data to the picker (see Figure 7-4), each changeable without impacting the other one.

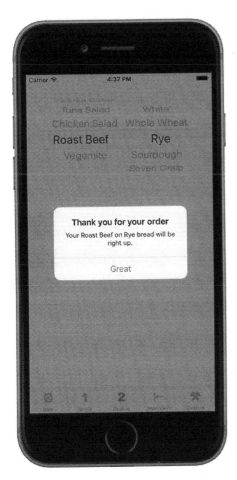

Figure 7-4. *A two-component picker, showing an alert that reflects your selection*

- *Picker with dependent components*: In the fourth content view, you'll build another picker with two components. But this time, the values displayed in the component on the right change based on the value selected in the component on the left. In this example, you're going to display a list of states in the left component and a list of that state's ZIP codes in the right component, as shown in Figure 7-5.

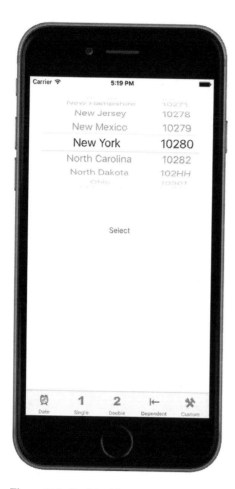

Figure 7-5. *In this picker, one component depends on the other. As you select a state in the left component, the right component changes to a list of ZIP codes in that state.*

- *Custom picker with images*: In the fifth content view, I'll demonstrate how to add image data to a picker, and you're going to do it by writing a little game that uses a picker with five components. Apple's documentation describes the picker's appearance as looking a bit like a slot machine. So, you'll be creating a slot machine, as shown in Figure 7-6. For this picker, the user won't be able to manually change the values of the components but will be able to select the Spin button to make the five wheels rotate to a new, randomly selected value. If three copies of the same image appear in a row, the user wins.

Figure 7-6. *Your fifth component picker uses the picker like a slot machine*

Delegates and Data Sources

Before you start building the application, let's look at what makes pickers more complex than the other controls you've used so far. With the exception of the date picker, you can't use a picker by just grabbing one in the Object Library, dropping it on your content view, and configuring it. You also need to provide each picker with both a delegate and a data source.

You've already used application delegates, and the basic idea works the same for pickers. The control itself defers several jobs to its delegate, the most important of these being the determination of what to actually draw for each of the rows in each of its components. The picker asks the delegate for either a string or a view that will be drawn at a given spot on a given component. The picker gets its data from the delegate.

In addition to the delegate, pickers must have a data source. The data source tells the picker how many components it will be working with and how many rows make up each component. The data source works like the delegate in that its methods are called at certain, prespecified times. Without a data source and a delegate, pickers cannot do their job; in fact, they won't even be drawn.

It's common for the data source and the delegate to be the same object and exist in the same actual Swift file, typically the view controller for the picker's enclosing view. You will use that approach in this application: the view controllers for each of your application's content panes will be the data source and the delegate for their picker.

░ **Note**   The question often arises as to whether the picker data source is part of the model, view, or controller portion of the application. A data source sounds like it must be part of the model, but it's actually part of the controller. The data source isn't usually an object designed to hold data. In simple applications, the data source might hold data, but its true job is to retrieve data from the model and pass it along to the picker.

Creating the Pickers Application

Although Xcode provides a template for tab bar applications, you're going to build yours from scratch. It's not much extra work, and it will be good practice.

Create a new project, select the Single View App template again, and choose Next to go to the next screen. In the Product Name field, type **Pickers**. Make sure the Use Core Data check box is deselected, and set Language to Swift and the Devices pop-up to Universal. Then choose Next again. Xcode will let you select the folder where you want to save your project.

I'm going to walk you through the process of building the whole application, but at any step of the way, if you feel like challenging yourself by moving ahead, by all means do so. If you get stumped, you can always come back.

Creating the View Controllers

In the previous chapter, you created a root view controller (*root controller* for short) to manage the process of swapping your application's other views. You'll be doing that again this time, but you won't need to create your own root view controller class. Apple provides a good class for managing tab bar views, so you're just going to use an instance of UITabBarController as your root controller. First, you need to create five new classes in Xcode: the five view controllers that the root controller will swap in and out. Expand the Pickers folder in the Project Navigator. There, you'll see the source code files that Xcode created to start off the project. Single-click the Pickers folder, and press ⌘N.

Select iOS and then select Source in the left pane of the new file assistant. Then, select the Cocoa Touch Class icon and click Next to continue. The next screen lets you give your new class a name. Enter **DatePickerViewController** in the Class field. Ensure the Subclass of field contains UIViewController. Make sure that the "Also create XIB file" check box is deselected, set Language to Swift, and then click Next.

You'll be shown a folder selection window, which lets you choose where the class should be saved. Choose the Pickers directory, which already contains the AppDelegate class and a few other files. Make sure also that the Group pop-up has the Pickers folder selected and that the target check box for Pickers is selected. After you click the Create button, the file DatePickerViewcontroller.swift will appear in the Pickers folder.

Repeat those steps four more times, using the names SingleComponentPickerViewController, DoubleComponentPickerViewController, DependentComponentPickerViewController, and CustomPickerViewController. At the end of all this, the Pickers folder should contain all the view controller class files, as shown in Figure 7-7.

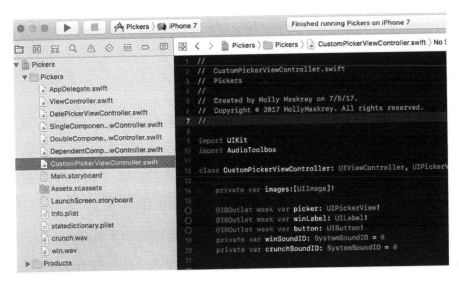

Figure 7-7. *The Project Navigator should contain all these files after creating the five view controller classes*

Creating the Tab Bar Controller

Now, let's create your tab bar controller. The project template already contains a view controller called ViewController, which is a subclass of UIViewController. To convert it to a tab bar controller, all you need to do is change its base class. Open ViewController.swift and make the following change shown in bold:

class ViewController: UITabBarController {

Next, to set up the tab bar controller in the storyboard, open Main.storyboard. The template added an initial view controller, which you're going to replace, so select it in the Document Outline or the Editor Area, and delete it by pressing the Delete key. In the Object Library, locate a tab bar controller and drag it to the editing area (see Figure 7-8).

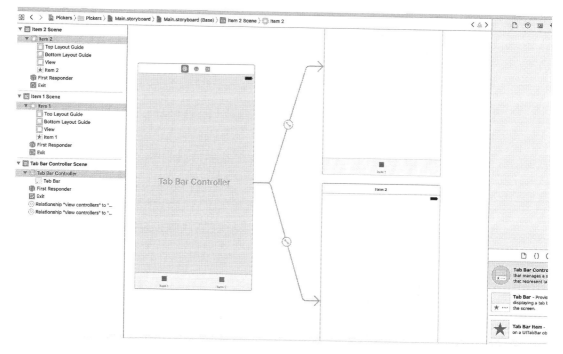

Figure 7-8. *Dragging a tab bar controller from the library onto the canvas*

While you're dragging, you'll see that, unlike the other controllers I've been asking you to drag out from the Object Library, this one actually pulls out three complete view controller pairs at once, all of which are connected to each other with curved lines. This is actually more than just a tab bar controller; it's also two child controllers, already connected and ready to use.

Once you drop the tab bar controller onto the editing area, three new scenes are added to the storyboard. If you expand the document view on the left, you will see a nice overview of all the scenes contained in the storyboard (see Figure 7-8). You'll also see the curvy lines still in place connecting the tab bar controller with each of its children. Those lines will always adjust themselves to stay connected if you move the scenes around, which you are always free to do. The on-screen position of each scene within a storyboard has no impact on your app's appearance when it runs.

This tab bar controller will be your root controller. As a reminder, the root controller controls the very first view that the user will see when your program runs, and it is responsible for switching the other views in and out. Since you'll connect each of your views to one of the tabs in the tab bar, the tab bar controller makes a logical choice as a root controller. You need to tell iOS that the tab bar controller is the one that it should load from `Main.storyboard` when the application starts. To do this, select the Tab Bar Controller icon in the Document Outline and open the Attributes Inspector; then in the View Controller section, select the Is Initial View Controller check box. With the view controller still selected, switch to the Identity Inspector and change the class to `ViewController`.

Tab bars can use icons to represent each of the tabs, so you should also add the icons you're going to use before editing the storyboard. You can find some suitable icons in the `ImageSets` folder of the source code archive for this book. Each subfolder of `ImageSets` contains three images (one for devices with a standard display, two for Retina devices). In the Xcode Project Navigator, select `Assets.xcassets` and drag each subfolder from the `ImageSets` folder and drop it into the left column of the editing area, underneath AppIcon, to copy them all into the project (see Figure 7-9).

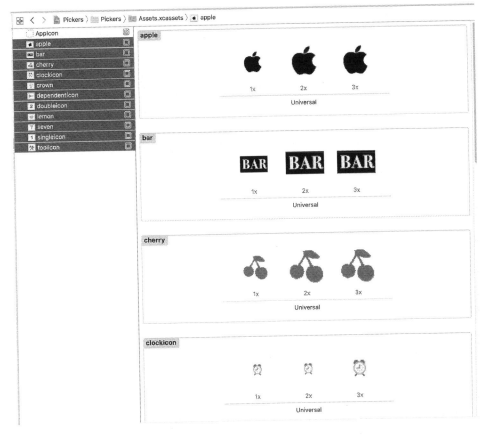

Figure 7-9. *Drag the images below AppIcon within Assets.xcassets in Xcode*

If you want to make your own icons instead, there are some guidelines for how they should be created. The icons you use should be 24 × 24 pixels and saved in PNG format. The icon file should have a transparent background. Don't worry about trying to color the icons so that they match the appearance of the tab bar. Just as it does with the application icon, iOS will take your image and make it look just right.

> **■ Tip** An image size of 24 × 24 pixels is actually for standard displays; for Retina displays on iPhone 4 and later and for the new iPads, you need a double-sized image, or it will appear pixelated. For the iPhone 7/6s Plus, you need to provide an image that's three times the size of the original. This is easy: for any image `foo.png`, you should also provide an image named `foo@2x.png` that is doubled in size and another called `foo@3x.png` that is three times the size. Calling `UIImage(named:"foo")` will return the normal-sized image or the double-sized image automatically to best suit the device on which your app is currently executing.

Back in the storyboard, you can see that each of the child view controllers shows a name like "Item 1" at the top and has a single bar item at the bottom of its view, with a label matching what is present in the tab bar. You might as well set these two up so that they have the right names from the start, so select the Item 1 view controller and then click the tab bar item labeled Item 1 in the Document Outline. Open the Attributes

Inspector and you'll see a text field for setting the title of the bar item, which currently contains the text *Item 1*. Replace the text with **Date** and press the Enter key. This immediately changes the text of the bar item at the bottom of this view controller, as well as the corresponding tab bar item in the tab bar controller. While you're still in the inspector, click the Image pop-up and select "clockicon" to set the icon, too. Now repeat the same steps for the second child view controller, but name this one **Single** and use the "singleicon" image for its bar item.

Your next step is to complete your tab bar controller so it reflects the five tabs shown in Figure 7-2. Each of those five tabs will contain one of your pickers. The way you're going to do this is by simply adding three more view controllers to the storyboard (in addition to the two that were added along with the tab bar controller) and then connecting each of them so that the tab bar controller can activate them. Get started by dragging out a normal view controller from the Object Library and dropping on the storyboard. Next, Control-drag from the tab bar controller to your new view controller, release the mouse button, and select view controllers from the Relationship Segue section of the small pop-up window that appears. This tells the tab bar controller that it has a new child to maintain, so the tab bar immediately acquires a new item. Your new view controller gets a bar item in the bottom of its view and in the Document Outline, just like the others already had. Now do the same steps outlined previously to name this latest view controller's bar item **Double** with "doubleicon" as its image.

Drag out two more view controllers and connect each of them to the tab bar controller, as described previously. One at a time, select each of their bar items, naming one of them **Dependent** with "dependenticon" as its image and naming the other **Custom** with "toolicon" as its image. When finished, you should have one view controller with your tab bar at the bottom and five connected view controllers, as shown in Figure 7-10.

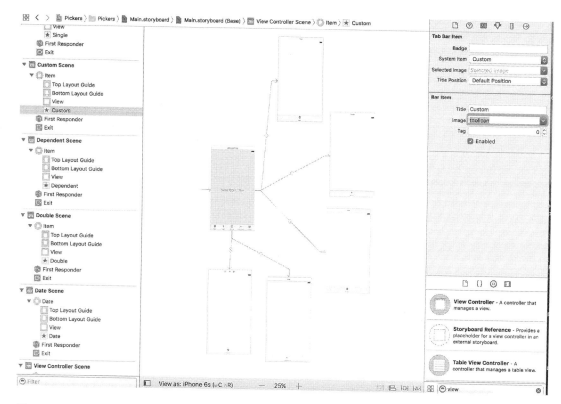

Figure 7-10. *Adding your five view controllers that you'll access using the tab bar from your root view controller*

Now that all your view controllers are in place, it's time to set up each of them with the correct controller class from the set you created earlier. This will let you implement different functionality for each controller. In the Document Outline, select the Date view controller and bring up the Identity Inspector. In the Custom Class section of the inspector, change the class to `DatePickerViewController`, and press Return or Tab to finish (see Figure 7-11).

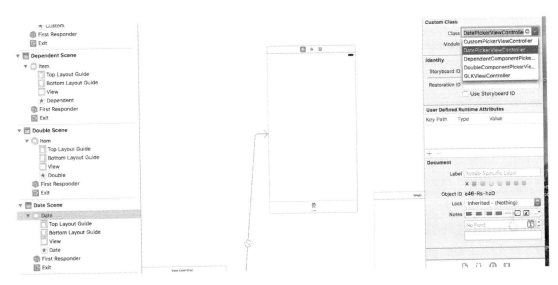

Figure 7-11. *Connecting your Date view to its view controller*

Repeat this same process for the other four view controllers, in the order in which they appear at the bottom of the tab bar controller. You can select each view controller in turn by clicking it in the storyboard, making sure to click in the bar at the top of the controller that contains the controller's name. In the Identity Inspector for each, use the class names `SingleComponentPickerViewController`, `DoubleComponentPickerViewController`, `DependentComponentPickerViewController`, and `CustomPickerViewController`, respectively. Before moving on to the next bit of GUI editing, save your storyboard file.

Initial Simulator Test

At this point, the tab bar and the content views should all be hooked up and working. Compile and run, and your application should launch with a tab bar that functions, as shown in Figure 7-12. Click each of the tabs in turn. Each tab should be selectable.

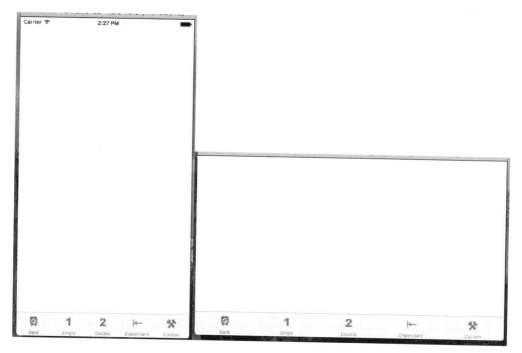

Figure 7-12. *The application with five empty but selectable tabs*

There's nothing in the content views now, so the changes won't be very dramatic. In fact, you won't see any difference at all, except for the highlighting tab bar items. But if everything went correctly, the basic framework for your multiview application is now set up and working. You can start designing the individual content views.

■ **Tip**   If your simulator crashes when you click one of the tabs, most likely you've either missed a step or made a typo. Go back and make sure the connections are right and the class names are all set correctly.

If you want to make doubly sure everything is working, you can add a different label or some other object to each of the content views and then relaunch the application. In that case, you should see the content of the different views change as you select different tabs.

Implementing the Date Picker

To implement the date picker, you'll need a single outlet and a single action. The outlet will be used to grab the value from the date picker. The action will be triggered by a button and will put up an alert to show the date value pulled from the picker. You'll add both of these from inside Interface Builder while editing the Main.storyboard file, so select it in the Project Navigator if it's not already front and center.

The first thing you need to do is find a date picker in the Object Library and drag it to the date scene in the editing area. Click the Date icon in the Document Outline to bring the correct view controller to the front and then drag the date picker from the Object Library and place it at the top of the view, right up against the top of the display. It's okay if it overlaps the status bar because this control has so much built-in vertical padding at the top that no one will notice.

Now you need to apply Auto Layout constraints so that the date picker is correctly sized and placed when the application runs on any kind of device. You want the picker to be horizontally centered and anchored to the top of the view. You also want it to be sized based on its content, so you need three constraints. With the date picker selected, first select Editor ➤ Size to Fit Content from the Xcode menu bar. If this option is not enabled, move the picker slightly and try again. Next, click the Align button below the storyboard, select the Horizontally in Container box, and then click Add 1 Constraint. Click the Pin button (which is next to the Align button). Using the four distance boxes at the top of the pop-up, set the distance between the picker and the top of edge of the view above it to zero by entering **0** in the top box, and below it so that it becomes a solid line. At the bottom of the pop-up, set Update Frames to Items of New Constraints and then click Add 1 Constraint. The date picker will resize and move to its correct position, as shown in Figure 7-13.

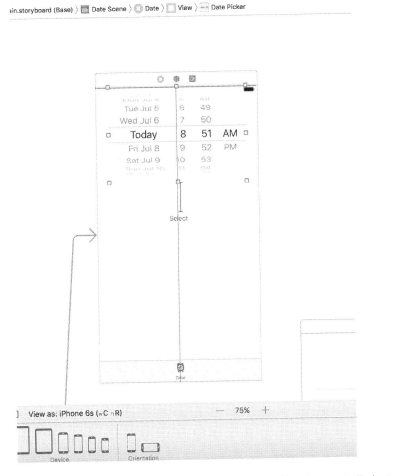

Figure 7-13. *The date picker is positioned at the top of its view controller's view*

Single-click the date picker, if it's not already selected, and go to the Attributes Inspector. As you can see in Figure 7-14, a number of attributes can be configured for a date picker. You're going to leave most of the values at their defaults (but feel free to play with the options when you're finished, to see what they do). The one thing you will do is limit the range of the picker to reasonable dates. Look for the Constraints heading and select the Minimum Date check box. Leave the value at the default of 1/1/1970. Also select the Maximum Date box and set that value to 12/31/2200.

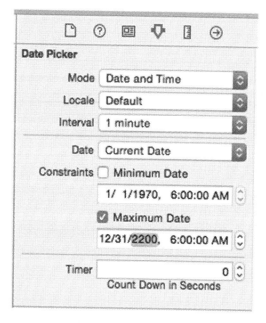

Figure 7-14. *The Attributes Inspector for a date picker. Set the maximum date, but leave the rest of the settings at their default values.*

Now let's connect this picker to its controller. Press ⌥⌘Enter to open the Assistant Editor and make sure the jump bar at the top of the Assistant Editor is set to Automatic. That should make DatePickerViewController.swift show up there. Next, Control-drag from the picker to the blank line between the class declaration and the viewDidLoad() method, releasing the mouse button when the Insert Outlet, Action, or Outlet Collection tooltip appears. In the pop-up window that appears after you let go, make sure Connection is set to Outlet, enter **datePicker** as the name, and then press Enter to create the outlet and connect it to the picker.

Next, grab a button from the library and place it a small distance below the date picker. Double-click the button and give it a title of **Select**. You want this button to be horizontally centered and to stay a fixed distance below the date picker. With the button selected, click the Align button at the bottom of the storyboard, select the Horizontally in Container box, and then click Add 1 Constraint. To fix the distance between them, Control-drag from the button to the date picker and release the mouse. In the pop-up that appears, select Vertical Spacing. Finally, click the Resolve Auto Layout Issues button at the bottom of the storyboard and then click Update Frames in the top section of the pop-up (if this item is not enabled, it means that the button is already in its correct location). The button should move to its correct location, and there should no longer be any Auto Layout warnings.

Make sure that DatePickerViewController.swift is still visible in the Assistant Editor; if it's not, use the Manual selection in the jump bar to locate and open it. Now Control-drag from the button to the line above the closing brace at the end of the class in the Assistant Editor, until you see the Insert Outlet,

Action, or Outlet Collection tooltip appear. Change the Connection type to Action, name the new action **onButtonPressed**, and press Enter to connect it. Doing so creates an empty method called onButtonPressed (), which you should complete with the code in Listing 7-1.

Listing 7-1. Your Select Button Action Code

```
@IBAction func onButtonPressed(_ sender: UIButton) {
    let date = datePicker.date
    let message = "The date and time you selected is \(date)"
    let alert = UIAlertController(
        title: "Date and Time Selected",
        message: message,
        preferredStyle: .alert)
    let action = UIAlertAction(
        title: "That's so true!",
        style: .default,
        handler: nil)
    alert.addAction(action)
    present(alert, animated: true, completion: nil)

}
```

In viewDidLoad(), you create a new NSDate object. An NSDate object created this way will hold the current date and time. You then set datePicker to that date, which ensures that every time this view is loaded from the storyboard, the picker will reset to the current date and time; see Listing 7-2.

Listing 7-2. Setting Your Date in the viewDidLoad() Method

```
override func viewDidLoad() {
    super.viewDidLoad()

    // Do any additional setup after loading the view.
    let date = NSDate()
    datePicker.setDate(date as Date, animated: false)
}
```

And that is all there is. Go ahead and build and run to make sure your date picker checks out. If everything went okay, your application should look like Figure 7-2 when it executes. If you choose the Select button, an alert will pop up, telling you the date and time currently selected in the date picker.

▓ **Note** The date picker does not allow you to specify seconds or a time zone. The alert displays the time with seconds and in Greenwich mean time (GMT). You could have added some code to simplify the string displayed in the alert, but isn't this chapter long enough already? If you're interested in customizing the formatting of the date, take a look at the NSDateFormatter class.

Implementing the Single-Component Picker

Your next picker lets the user select from a list of values. In this example, you'll use an array to hold the values you want to display in the picker. Pickers don't hold any data themselves. Instead, they call methods on their data source and delegate to get the data they need to display. The picker doesn't really care where the underlying data lives. It asks for the data when it needs it, and the data source and delegate (which are often, in practice, the same object) work together to supply that data. As a result, the data could be coming from a static list, as you'll do in this section, or it could be loaded from a file or a URL, or even made up or calculated on the fly.

For the picker class to ask its controller for data, you must ensure that the controller implements the right methods. One part of doing that is declaring in the controller's class definition that it will implement a couple of protocols. In the Project Navigator, single-click `SingleComponentPickerViewController.swift`. This controller class will act as both the data source and the delegate for its picker, so you need to make sure it conforms to the protocols for those two roles. Add the following code:

```
class SingleComponentPickerViewController: UIViewController,
        UIPickerViewDelegate, UIPickerViewDataSource {
```

When you do this, you'll see an error appear in the editor. That's because you haven't yet implemented the required protocol methods. You'll do that soon, so just ignore the error for now.

Building the View

Select `Main.storyboard` again since it's time to edit the content view for the second tab in your tab bar. In the Document Outline, click the Single icon to bring the view controller into the foreground in the Editor Area. Next, bring over a picker view from the library (see Figure 7-15) and add it to your view, placing it snugly into the top of the view, as you did with the date picker view.

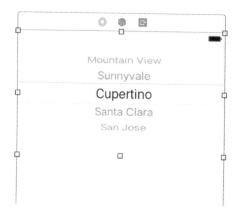

Figure 7-15. *Adding a picker view from the library to your second view*

Now you need to apply Auto Layout constraints so that the picker is correctly sized and placed when the application runs on any kind of device. You want the picker to be horizontally centered and anchored to the top of the view. You also want it to be sized based on its content, so you need three constraints. With the picker selected, first select Editor ➤ Size to Fit Content from the Xcode menu bar. If this option is not enabled, move the picker slightly and try again. Next, click the Align button below the storyboard, select the

Horizontally in Container box, and then click Add 1 Constraint. Click the Pin button (which is next to the Align button). Using the four distance boxes at the top of the pop-up, set the distance between the picker and the top of edge of the view above it to zero by entering **0** in the top box, and then click the dashed red line below it so that it becomes a solid line. At the bottom of the pop-up, set Update Frames to Items of New Constraints and then click Add 1 Constraint. The picker will resize and move to its correct position, as shown in Figure 7-16.

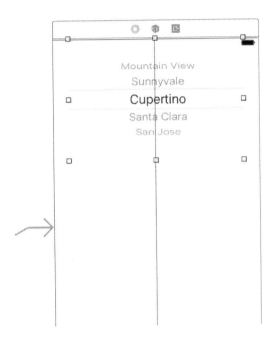

Figure 7-16. *The picker, positioned at the top of its view controller's view*

Now let's connect this picker to its controller. The procedure here is just like for the previous picker view: open the Assistant Editor, set the jump bar to show the `SingleComponentPickerViewController.swift` file, Control-drag from the picker to the top of the `SingleComponentPickerViewController` class, and create an outlet named `singlePicker`.

Next, with the picker selected, press ⌥⌘6 to bring up the Connections Inspector. If you look at the connections available for the picker view, you'll see that the first two items are `dataSource` and `delegate`. If you don't see those outlets, make sure you have the picker selected, rather than the `UIView`. Drag from the circle next to `dataSource` to the View Controller icon at the top of the scene in the storyboard or in the Document Outline (see Figure 7-17) and then drag from the circle next to `delegate` to the View Controller icon. Now this picker knows that the instance of the `SingleComponentPickerViewController` class in the storyboard is its data source and delegate, and the picker will ask it to supply the data to be displayed. In other words, when the picker needs information about the data it is going to display, it asks the `SingleComponentPickerViewController` instance that controls this view for that information.

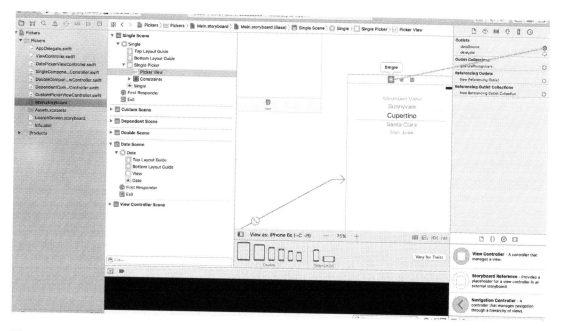

Figure 7-17. *Connecting the dataSource to the view controller*

Drag a button to the view and place it just below the picker. Double-click the button and name it **Select**. Press Return to commit the change. In the Connections Inspector, drag from the circle next to Touch Up Inside to code in the Assistant Editor, releasing it just above the closing bracket at the end of the class definition to make a new action method. Name this action **onButtonPressed** and you'll see that Xcode fills in an empty method. You've just seen another way to add an action method to a view controller and link it to its source view. You want this button to be horizontally centered and to stay a fixed distance below the date picker. With the button selected, click the Align button at the bottom of the storyboard, select the Horizontally in Container box, and then click Add 1 Constraint (see Figure 7-18).

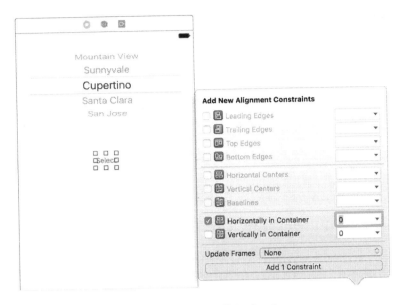

Figure 7-18. Center the button horizontally in the view

To fix the distance between them, Control-drag from the button to the picker and then release the mouse. In the pop-up that appears, select Vertical Spacing (see Figure 7-19). Finally, if you have any layout issues as shown by the Issue Inspector, click the Resolve Auto Layout Issues button at the bottom of the storyboard and then click Update Frames in the top section of the pop-up (if this item is not enabled, it means that the button is already in its correct location). The button should move to its correct location, and there should no longer be any Auto Layout warnings.

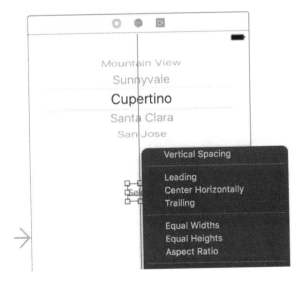

Figure 7-19. Set a consistent vertical spacing from the button to the picker

Implementing the Data Source and Delegate

To make your controller work properly as the picker's data source and delegate, you'll start with some code you should feel comfortable with and then add a few methods that you've never seen before.

Single-click `SingleComponentPickerViewController.swift` in the Project Navigator and add the following property at the top of the class definition. This gives you an array with the names of several well-known movie characters.

```
@IBOutlet weak var singlePicker: UIPickerView!
private let characterNames = [
        "Luke", "Leia", "Han", "Chewbacca", "Artoo",
        "Threepio", "Lando"]
```

Then change the `onButtonPressed()` method to what's shown in Listing 7-3.

Listing 7-3. The onButtonPressed Method for Your Single Picker View

```swift
@IBAction func onButtonPressed(_ sender: UIButton) {
    let row = singlePicker.selectedRow(inComponent: 0)
    let selected = characterNames[row]
    let title = "You selected \(selected)!"

    let alert = UIAlertController(
        title: title,
        message: "Thank you for choosing",
        preferredStyle: .alert)
    let action = UIAlertAction(
        title: "You're welcome",
        style: .default,
        handler: nil)
    alert.addAction(action)
    present(alert, animated: true, completion: nil)
}
```

As you saw earlier, a date picker contains the data you need to get to, but here, your regular picker hands off that job to the delegate and data source. The `onButtonPressed()` method needs to ask the picker which row is selected and then grabs the corresponding data from your `pickerData` array. Here is how you ask it for the selected row:

```
let row = singlePicker.selectedRow(inComponent: 0)
```

Notice that you needed to specify which component you want to know about. You have only one component (i.e., one spinning wheel) in this picker, so you simply pass in **0**, which is the index of the first (and only) component.

In the class declaration, you created an array of character names so that you have data to feed the picker. Usually, your data will come from other sources, like a property list or a web service query. By embedding an array of items in your code the way you've done here, you are making it much harder on yourself if you need to update this list or if you want to have your application translated into other languages. But this approach is the quickest and easiest way to get data into an array for demonstration purposes. Even though you won't usually create your arrays like this, you will almost always configure some form of access to your application's model objects here in the `viewDidLoad()` method so that you're not constantly going to disk or to the network every time the picker asks you for data.

■ **Tip** If you're not supposed to create arrays from lists of objects in your code, as you just did, how should you do it? Embed the lists in property list files and add those files to your project. Property list files can be changed without recompiling your source code, which means there is little risk of introducing new bugs when you do so.

Finally, insert the code shown in Listing 7-4 at the bottom of the file.

Listing 7-4. Picker Data Source and Delegate Methods

```
// MARK:-
// MARK: Picker Data Source Methods

func numberOfComponents(in pickerView: UIPickerView) -> Int {
    return 1
}
func pickerView(_ pickerView: UIPickerView,
                numberOfRowsInComponent component: Int) -> Int {
    return characterNames.count
}

// MARK: Picker Delegate Methods
func pickerView(_ pickerView: UIPickerView, titleForRow row: Int, forComponent component:
Int) -> String? {
    return characterNames[row]
}
```

These three methods are required to implement the picker. The first two methods are from the `UIPickerViewDataSource` protocol, and they are both required for all pickers (except date pickers). Here's the first one:

```
func numberOfComponents(in pickerView: UIPickerView) -> Int {
    return 1
}
```

Pickers can have more than one spinning wheel, or component, and this is how the picker asks how many components it should display. You want to display only one list this time, so you return a value of 1. Notice that a `UIPickerView` is passed in as a parameter. This parameter points to the picker view that is asking you the question, which makes it possible to have multiple pickers being controlled by the same data source. In this case, you know that you have only one picker, so you can safely ignore this argument because you already know which picker is calling you.

The second data source method is used by the picker to ask how many rows of data there are for a given component.

```
func pickerView(_ pickerView: UIPickerView,
                numberOfRowsInComponent component: Int) -> Int {
    return characterNames.count
}
```

Once again, you are told which picker view is asking and which component that picker is asking about. Since you know that you have only one picker and one component, you don't bother with either of the arguments and simply return the count of objects from your sole data array.

// MARK:

Did you notice the following lines of code from `SingleComponentPickerViewController.swift`?

```
// MARK:-
// MARK: Picker Data Source Methods
```

Any line of code that begins with `//` is a comment. Comments that start with `//` `MARK:` are treated specially by Xcode—they tell it to put an entry in the pop-up menu of methods and properties at the top of the editor pane. The first one (with the dash) puts a break in the menu. The second creates a text entry containing whatever the rest of the line holds, which you can use as a sort of descriptive header for groups of methods in your source code.

Some of your classes, especially some of your controller classes, are likely to get rather long, and the methods and functions pop-up menu makes navigating around your code much easier. Putting in `//` `MARK:` comments and logically organizing your code will make that pop-up more efficient to use.

After the two data source methods, you implement one delegate method. Unlike the data source methods, all of the delegate methods are optional. The term *optional* is a bit deceiving because you do need to implement at least one delegate method. You will usually implement the method that you are implementing here. However, if you want to display something other than text in the picker, you must implement a different method instead, as you'll see when you get to the custom picker later in this chapter.

```swift
func pickerView(_ pickerView: UIPickerView, titleForRow row: Int, forComponent component:
Int) -> String? {
    return characterNames[row]
}
```

In this method, the picker asks you to provide the data for a specific row in a specific component. You are provided with a pointer to the picker that is asking, along with the component and row that it is asking about. Since your view has one picker with one component, you simply ignore everything except the `row` argument and use that to return the appropriate item from your data array.

Build and run the application. When the simulator comes up, switch to the second tab—the one labeled Single—and check out your new custom picker, which should look like Figure 7-3.

In the next section you'll implement a picker with two components. If you feel up to a challenge, this next content view is actually a good one for you to attempt on your own. You've already seen all the methods you'll need for this picker, so go ahead if you'd like to give it a try. You might want to start with a good look at Figure 7-4, just to refresh your memory. When you're finished, read on, and you'll see how I tackled this problem.

Implementing a Multicomponent Picker

The next tab will have a picker with two components, or wheels, each independent of the other. The left wheel will have a list of sandwich fillings, and the right wheel will have a selection of bread types. You'll write the same data source and delegate methods that you did for the single-component picker. You'll just need to write a little additional code in some of those methods to make sure you're returning the correct value and row count for each component. Start by single-clicking DoubleComponentPickerViewController.swift and adding the following code:

```
class DoubleComponentPickerViewController: UIViewController,
            UIPickerViewDelegate, UIPickerViewDataSource {
```

Here, you simply conform your controller class to both the delegate and data source. Save this and click Main.storyboard to work on the GUI.

Building the View

Select Double Scene in the Document Outline and click the Double icon to bring its view controller to the front in the Editor Area. Now add a picker view and a button to the view, change the button label to **Select**, and then make the necessary connections. I'm not going to walk you through it this time, but you can refer to the previous section if you need a step-by-step guide, since the two view controllers are identical in terms of connections in the storyboard. Here's a summary of what you need to do:

1. Create an outlet called doublePicker in the class extension of the DoubleComponentPickerViewController class to connect the view controller to the picker.

2. Connect the dataSource and delegate connections on the picker view to the view controller (use the Connections Inspector).

3. Connect the Touch Up Inside event of the button to a new action method called onButtonPressed on the view controller (use the Connections Inspector).

4. Add Auto Layout constraints to the picker and the button to pin them in place.

Make sure that you save your storyboard before you dive back into the code. You may want to bookmark this page because you may be referring to it in a bit.

Implementing the Controller

Select DoubleComponentPickerViewController.swift and add the code in Listing 7-5 at the top of the class definition, below your picker outlet.

Listing 7-5. Parameters Needed for Your Two-Component Picker

```
@IBOutlet weak var doublePicker: UIPickerView!
private let fillingComponent = 0
private let breadComponent = 1
private let fillingTypes = [
    "Ham", "Turkey", "Peanut Butter", "Tuna Salad",
    "Chicken Salad", "Roast Beef", "Vegemite"]
private let breadTypes = [
    "White", "Whole Wheat", "Rye", "Sourdough",
    "Seven Grain"]
```

As you can see, you start by defining two constants that will represent the indices of the two components, which is just to make your code easier to read. Picker components are referred to by number, with the leftmost component being assigned zero and increasing by one with each move to the right. Next, you declare two arrays that hold the data for your two picker components.

Now implement the onButtonPressed() method, as shown in Listing 7-6.

Listing 7-6. What to Do When the Select Button Is Pressed

```
@IBAction func onButtonPressed(_ sender: UIButton) {
    let fillingRow =
        doublePicker.selectedRow(inComponent: fillingComponent)
    let breadRow =
        doublePicker.selectedRow(inComponent: breadComponent)

    let filling = fillingTypes[fillingRow]
    let bread = breadTypes[breadRow]
    let message = "Your \(filling) on \(bread) bread will be right up."

    let alert = UIAlertController(
        title: "Thank you for your order",
        message: message,
        preferredStyle: .alert)
    let action = UIAlertAction(
        title: "Great",
        style: .default,
        handler: nil)
    alert.addAction(action)
    present(alert, animated: true, completion: nil)
}
```

Also, add the data source and delegate methods at the bottom of the class, as shown in Listing 7-7.

Listing 7-7. The dataSource and delegate Methods

```
// MARK:-
// MARK: Picker Data Source Methods
func numberOfComponents(in pickerView: UIPickerView) -> Int {
    return 2
}

func pickerView(_ pickerView: UIPickerView, numberOfRowsInComponent component: Int) -> Int {
    if component == breadComponent {
        return breadTypes.count
    } else {
        return fillingTypes.count
    }
}

// MARK:-
// MARK: Picker Delegate Methods
```

```
func pickerView(_ pickerView: UIPickerView, titleForRow row: Int, forComponent component:
Int) -> String? {
    if component == breadComponent {
        return breadTypes[row]
    } else {
        return fillingTypes[row]
    }
}
```

The onButtonPressed() method is a bit more involved this time, but there's very little there that's new to you. You just need to specify which component you are talking about when you request the selected row using those constants you defined earlier—breadComponent and fillingComponent.

```
let fillingRow =doublePicker.selectedRow(inComponent: fillingComponent)
let breadRow = doublePicker.selectedRow(inComponent: breadComponent)
```

You can see here that using the two constants instead of 0 and 1 makes your code considerably more readable. From this point on, the onButtonPressed() method is fundamentally the same as the last one you wrote.

When you get down to the data source methods, that's where things start to change a bit. In the first method, you specify that your picker should have two components rather than just one.

```
func numberOfComponents(in pickerView: UIPickerView) -> Int {
    return 2
}
```

This time, when you are asked for the number of rows, you need to check which component the picker is asking about and return the correct row count for the corresponding array.

```
func pickerView(_ pickerView: UIPickerView, numberOfRowsInComponent component: Int) -> Int {
    if component == breadComponent {
        return breadTypes.count
    } else {
        return fillingTypes.count
    }
}
```

Next, in your delegate method, you do the same thing. You check the component and use the correct array for the requested component to fetch and return the correct value.

```
func pickerView(_ pickerView: UIPickerView, titleForRow row: Int, forComponent component:
Int) -> String? {
    if component == breadComponent {
        return breadTypes[row]
    } else {
        return fillingTypes[row]
    }
}
```

That wasn't so hard, was it? Compile and run your application, and make sure the Double content pane looks like Figure 7-4.

Notice that the wheels are completely independent of each other. Turning one has no effect on the other. That's appropriate in this case, but there will be times when one component is dependent on another. A good example of this is in the date picker. When you change the month, the dial that shows the number of days in the month may need to change because not all months have the same number of days. Implementing this isn't really hard once you know how, but it's not the easiest thing to figure out on your own, so let's do that next.

Implementing Dependent Components

As you're picking up momentum, I'm not going to hold your hand quite as much when it comes to material I've already covered. Instead, I'll focus on addressing new features. Your new picker will display a list of U.S. states in the left component and a list of corresponding ZIP codes in the right component.

You'll need a separate list of ZIP code values for each item in the left component. You'll declare two arrays, one for each component, as you did last time. You'll also need a *dictionary*. In the dictionary, you're going to store an *array* for each state (see Figure 7-20). Later, you'll implement a delegate method that will notify you when the picker's selection changes. If the value in the left picker wheel changes, you will grab the correct array out of the dictionary and assign it to the array being used for the right-side picker wheel. Don't worry if you didn't catch all that; I'll talk about it more as you get into the code.

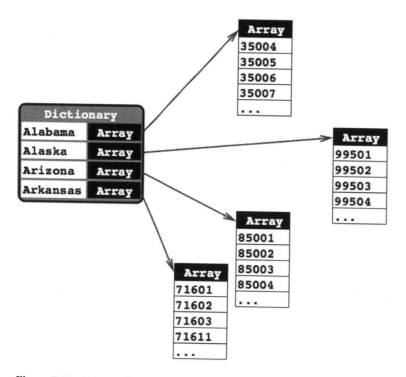

Figure 7-20. *Your application's data. For each state, there will be one entry in a dictionary with the name of the state as the key. Stored under that key will be an Array<String> instance containing all the ZIP codes from that state.*

Add the following code to your `DependentComponentPickerViewController.swift` file:

```
class DependentComponentPickerViewController: UIViewController,
UIPickerViewDelegate, UIPickerViewDataSource {
private let stateComponent = 0
private let zipComponent = 1
private var stateZips:[String : [String]]!
private var states:[String]!
private var zips:[String]!
```

Now it's time to build the content view. That process is identical to the previous two component views you built. If you get lost, flip back to the "Building the View" section for the single-component picker and follow those step-by-step instructions. Here's a hint: start by opening `Main.storyboard`, find the view controller for the `DependentComponentPickerViewController` class, and then repeat the same basic steps you've done for all the other content views in this chapter. You should end up with an outlet property called `dependentPicker` connected to a picker, an empty `onButtonPressed:` method connected to a button, and both the `delegate` and `dataSource` properties of the picker connected to the view controller. Don't forget to add the Auto Layout constraints to both views! When you're finished, save the storyboard.

Now you'll implement this controller class. This implementation may seem a little complicated at first. To make one component dependent on the other, you need to add a whole new level of complexity to your controller class. Although the picker displays only two lists at a time, your controller class must know about and manage 51 lists. The technique you're going to use here actually simplifies that process. The data source methods look almost identical to the one you implemented for the `DoublePickerViewController`. All of the additional complexity is handled elsewhere, between `viewDidLoad` and a new delegate method called `picke rView(_:didSelectRow:inComponent:)`.

Before you write the code, you need some data to display. Up until now, you've created arrays in code by specifying a list of strings. Because you don't want to type in several thousand values, you're going to load the data from a property list. Both `NSArray` and `NSDictionary` objects can be created from property lists.

The data that you need is included in a property list called `statedictionary.plist` in the project archive, under the `Picker Data` folder. Drag that file into the `Pickers` folder in your Xcode project. If you single-click the `.plist` file in the Project Navigator, you can see and even edit the data that it contains (see Figure 7-21).

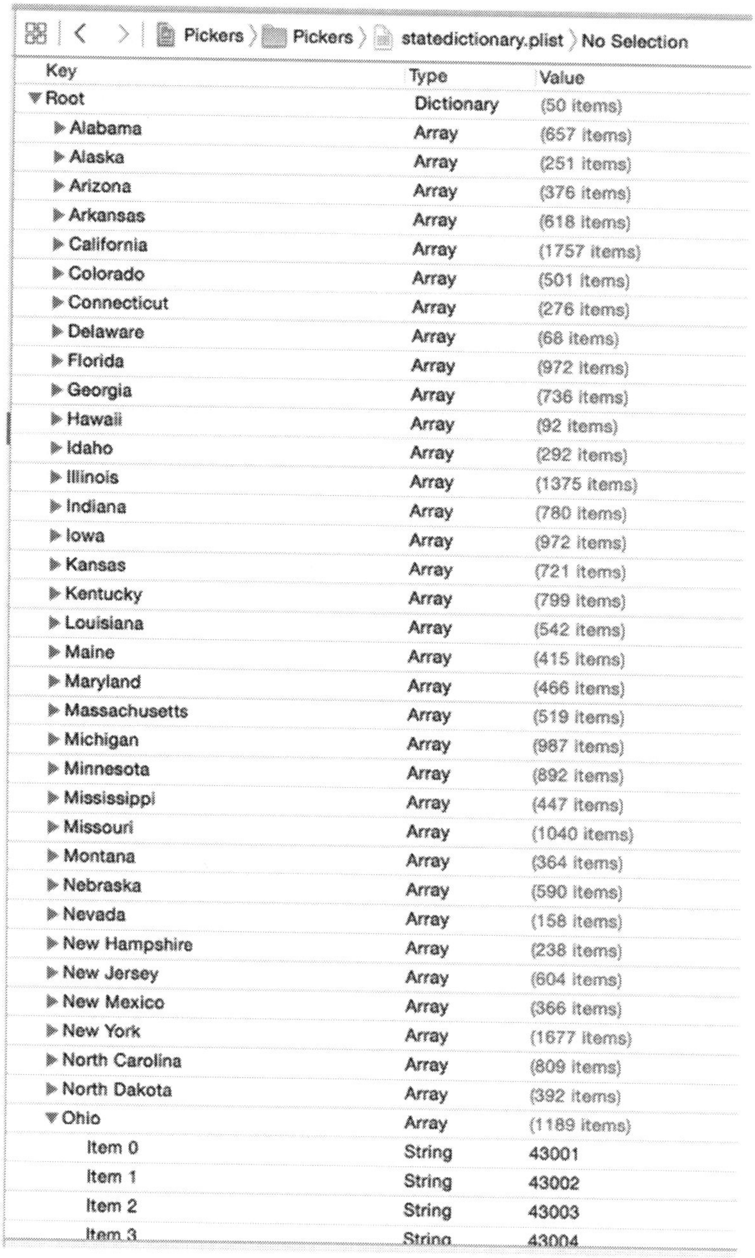

Key	Type	Value
▼ Root	Dictionary	(50 items)
▶ Alabama	Array	(657 items)
▶ Alaska	Array	(251 items)
▶ Arizona	Array	(376 items)
▶ Arkansas	Array	(618 items)
▶ California	Array	(1757 items)
▶ Colorado	Array	(501 items)
▶ Connecticut	Array	(276 items)
▶ Delaware	Array	(68 items)
▶ Florida	Array	(972 items)
▶ Georgia	Array	(736 items)
▶ Hawaii	Array	(92 items)
▶ Idaho	Array	(292 items)
▶ Illinois	Array	(1375 items)
▶ Indiana	Array	(780 items)
▶ Iowa	Array	(972 items)
▶ Kansas	Array	(721 items)
▶ Kentucky	Array	(799 items)
▶ Louisiana	Array	(542 items)
▶ Maine	Array	(415 items)
▶ Maryland	Array	(466 items)
▶ Massachusetts	Array	(519 items)
▶ Michigan	Array	(987 items)
▶ Minnesota	Array	(892 items)
▶ Mississippi	Array	(447 items)
▶ Missouri	Array	(1040 items)
▶ Montana	Array	(364 items)
▶ Nebraska	Array	(590 items)
▶ Nevada	Array	(158 items)
▶ New Hampshire	Array	(238 items)
▶ New Jersey	Array	(604 items)
▶ New Mexico	Array	(366 items)
▶ New York	Array	(1677 items)
▶ North Carolina	Array	(809 items)
▶ North Dakota	Array	(392 items)
▼ Ohio	Array	(1189 items)
Item 0	String	43001
Item 1	String	43002
Item 2	String	43003
Item 3	String	43004

Figure 7-21. *The statedictionary.plist file, showing your list of states. Within Ohio, you can see the start of a list of ZIP codes.*

In DependentComponentPickerViewController.swift, I'm going to first show you some whole methods to implement, and then I'll break it down into more digestible chunks. Start with the implementation of onButtonPressed(),as shown in Listing 7-8.

Listing 7-8. The onButtonPressed Method for Your ZIP Code View

```
@IBAction func onButtonPressed(_ sender: UIButton) {
    let stateRow =
        dependentPicker.selectedRow(inComponent: stateComponent)
    let zipRow =
        dependentPicker.selectedRow(inComponent: zipComponent)

    let state = states[stateRow]
    let zip = zips[zipRow]

    let title = "You selected zip code \(zip)"
    let message = "\(zip) is in \(state)"

    let alert = UIAlertController(
        title: title,
        message: message,
        preferredStyle: .alert)
    let action = UIAlertAction(
        title: "OK",
        style: .default,
        handler: nil)
    alert.addAction(action)
    present(alert, animated: true, completion: nil)
}
```

Next, add the code in Listing 7-9 to the existing viewDidLoad() method.

Listing 7-9. Add to the viewDidLoad() Method

```
override func viewDidLoad() {
    super.viewDidLoad()

    // Do any additional setup after loading the view.
    let bundle = Bundle.main
    let plistURL = bundle.urlForResource("statedictionary",
                    withExtension: "plist")
    stateZips = NSDictionary.init(contentsOf: (plistURL)!) as! [String : [String]]
    let allStates = stateZips.keys
    states = allStates.sorted()
    let selectedState = states[0]
    zips = stateZips[selectedState]
}
```

Finally, add the data source and delegate methods at the bottom of the file, as shown in Listing 7-10.

Listing 7-10. Your dataSource and delegate Methods for Displaying State ZIP Codes

```
// MARK:-
// MARK: Picker Data Source Methods
func numberOfComponents(in pickerView: UIPickerView) -> Int {
    return 2
}
```

```swift
func pickerView(_ pickerView: UIPickerView, numberOfRowsInComponent component: Int) -> Int {
    if component == stateComponent {
        return states.count
    } else {
        return zips.count
    }
}
// MARK:-
// MARK: Picker Delegate Methods
func pickerView(_ pickerView: UIPickerView, titleForRow row: Int, forComponent component:
Int) -> String? {
    if component == stateComponent {
        return states[row]
    } else {
        return zips[row]
    }
}

func pickerView(_ pickerView: UIPickerView, didSelectRow row: Int, inComponent component: Int) {
    if component == stateComponent {
        let selectedState = states[row]
        zips = stateZips[selectedState]
        dependentPicker.reloadComponent(zipComponent)
        dependentPicker.selectRow(0, inComponent: zipComponent,
                                  animated: true)
    }
}
```

There's no need to talk about the onButtonPressed() method since it's fundamentally the same as the previous one. I should talk about the viewDidLoad() method, though. There's some stuff going on there that you need to understand, so pull up a chair and let's chat. The first thing you do in this new viewDidLoad() method is grab a reference to your application's main bundle.

```swift
let bundle = Bundle.main
```

A *bundle* is just a special type of folder, the contents of which follow a specific structure. Applications and frameworks are both bundles, and this call returns a bundle object that represents your application.

■ **Note** In the latest revision of Xcode and the iOS libraries, Apple provided a more user-friendly way of referring to elements such as NSBundle from Swift. Instead of something like let bundle = NSBundle. mainBundle(), you use the much easier and more readable preceding versions.

One of the primary uses of a bundle (NSBundle) is to get to resources that you added to your project. Those files will be copied into your application's bundle when you build your application. If you want to get to those resources in your code, you usually need to use a bundle. You use the main bundle to retrieve the URL of the resource in which you're interested.

```swift
let plistURL = bundle.urlForResource("statedictionary",
                                     withExtension: "plist")
```

This will return a URL containing the location of the `statedictionary.plist` file. You can then use that URL to load your dictionary. Once you do that, the entire contents of that property list will be loaded into the newly created `Dictionary` object; that is, it is assigned to `stateZips`.

```
stateZips = NSDictionary.init(contentsOf: (plistURL)!) as! [String : [String]]
```

The Swift `Dictionary` type has no convenient way to load data from an external source, but the Foundation class `NSDictionary` does. This code takes advantage of that by loading the content of the `statedictionary.plist` file into an `NSDictionary`, which you then cast to the Swift type `[String : [String]]` (that is, a dictionary in which each key is a string representing a state and the corresponding value is an array containing the ZIP codes for that state, as strings). This reflects the structure shown in Figure 7-18.

To populate the array for the left component of the picker, which will display the states, you get the list of all keys from your dictionary and assign those to the `states` array. Before you assign it, though, you sort it alphabetically.

```
let allStates = stateZips.keys
states = allStates.sorted()
```

Unless you specifically set the selection to another value, pickers start with the first row (row 0) selected. To get the `zips` array that corresponds to the first row in the `states` array, you grab the object from the `states` array that's at index 0. That will return the name of the state that will be selected at launch time. You then use that state name to grab the array of ZIP codes for that state, which you assign to the `zips` array that will be used to feed data to the right-side component.

```
let selectedState = states[0]
zips = stateZips[selectedState]
```

The two data source methods are practically identical to the previous version. You return the number of rows in the appropriate array. The same is true for the first delegate method you implemented. The second delegate method is the new one, which is where the magic happens.

```
func pickerView(_ pickerView: UIPickerView, didSelectRow row: Int, inComponent component:
Int) {
    if component == stateComponent {
        let selectedState = states[row]
        zips = stateZips[selectedState]
        dependentPicker.reloadComponent(zipComponent)
        dependentPicker.selectRow(0, inComponent: zipComponent,
                                  animated: true)
    }
}
```

In this method, which is called any time the picker's selection changes, you look at the component and see whether the left component is the one that changed, which would mean that the user selected a new state. If it is, you grab the array that corresponds to the new selection and assign it to the `zips` array. Next, you set the right-side component back to the first row and tell it to reload itself. By swapping the `zips` array whenever the state changes, the rest of the code remains pretty much the same as it was in the `DoublePicker` example.

You're not quite finished yet. Build and run the application and then check out the Dependent tab, as shown in Figure 7-22. The two components are equal in size. Even though the ZIP code will never be more than five characters long, it has been given equal billing with the state. Since state names like Mississippi and Massachusetts won't fit in half of the picker on most iPhone screens, this seems less than ideal.

Figure 7-22. *Do you really want the two components to be of equal size? Notice the clipping of a long state name*

Fortunately, there's another delegate method you can implement to indicate how wide each component should be. Add the method in Listing 7-11 to the delegate section of DependentComponentPickerViewController. swift. You can see the difference in Figure 7-23.

Listing 7-11. Setting the Width of Your Picker's Components

```swift
func pickerView(_ pickerView: UIPickerView, widthForComponent component: Int) -> CGFloat {
    let pickerWidth = pickerView.bounds.size.width
    if component == zipComponent {
        return pickerWidth/3
    } else {
        return 2 * pickerWidth/3
    }
}
```

Figure 7-23. *With the adjustment in width of your picker components, your UI has become more visually useful*

In this method, you return a number that represents how many pixels wide each component should be, and the picker will do its best to accommodate this. I've chosen to give the state component two-thirds of the available width and the rest goes to the ZIP component. Feel free to experiment with other values to see how the distribution of space between the components changes as you modify them. Save, build, and run; the picker on the Dependent tab will look more like the one shown in Figure 7-5.

By this point, you should be fairly comfortable with both pickers and tab bar applications. You have one more thing to do with pickers.

Creating a Simple Game with a Custom Picker

Next up, you're going to create a simulated slot machine. Take a look back at Figure 7-6 before proceeding so you know what you're building.

Preparing the View Controller

Begin by adding the following code to `CustomPickerViewController.swift`:

```
class CustomPickerViewController: UIViewController,
    UIPickerViewDelegate, UIPickerViewDataSource {
private var images:[UIImage]!
```

At this point, all you've added to the class is a property for an array that will hold the images to use for the symbols on the spinners of the slot machine. The rest will come a little later.

Building the View

Even though the picker in Figure 7-6 looks quite a bit fancier than the other ones you've built, there's actually very little difference in the way you'll design your storyboard. All the extra work is done in the delegate methods of your controller.

Make sure that you've saved your new source code and then select `Main.storyboard` in the Project Navigator and use the Document Outline to select the Custom icon in the Custom Scene to edit the GUI. Add a picker view, a label below that, and a button below that. Name the button **Spin**.

With the label selected, bring up the Attributes Inspector. Set the alignment to centered. Then click Text Color and set the color to something bright. Next, let's make the text a little bigger. Look for the Font setting in the inspector, and click the icon inside it (it looks like the letter *T* inside a little box) to pop up the font selector. This control lets you switch from the device's standard system font to another if you like, or you can simply change the size. For now, just change the size to 48 and delete the word *Label* since you don't want any text displayed until the first time the user wins. With the label selected, click Editor ➤ Size to Fit Content to make sure the label is always large enough to display its content.

Now add Auto Layout constraints to center the picker, label, and button horizontally and to fix the vertical gaps between them, between the label and the picker, and between the picker and the top of the view. You'll probably find it easiest to drag from the label in the Document Outline when adding its Auto Layout constraints because the label on the storyboard is empty and difficult to find.

After that, make all the connections to outlets and actions. Create a new outlet called `picker` to connect the view controller to the picker view and another called `winLabel` to connect the view controller to the label. Again, you'll find it easiest to use the label in the Document Outline than the one on the storyboard. Next, connect the button's Touch Up Inside event to a new action method called `spin()`. After that, just make sure to connect the delegate and data source for the picker.

There's one additional thing you need to do. Select the picker and bring up the Attributes Inspector. You need to deselect the User Interaction Enabled within the View settings check box so that the user can't manually change the dial and cheat. Once you've done all that, save the changes you've made to the storyboard.

FONTS SUPPORTED BY IOS DEVICES

Be careful when using the fonts palette in Interface Builder for designing iOS interfaces. The Attribute Inspector's font selector will let you assign from a wide range of fonts, but not all iOS devices have the same set of fonts available. At the time of writing, for instance, there are several fonts that are available on the iPad but not on the iPhone or iPod touch. You should limit your font selections to one of the font families found on the iOS device you are targeting. This post on Jeff LaMarche's excellent iOS blog shows you how to grab this list programmatically: `http://iphonedevelopment.blogspot.com/2010/08/fonts-and-font-families.html`.

In a nutshell, create a view-based application and add this code to the method `application(_: didFinishLaunchingWithOptions:)` in the application delegate:

```
for family in UIFont.familyNames() as [String] {
    println(family)
    for font in UIFont.fontNamesForFamilyName(family) {
        println("\t\(font)")
    }
}
```

Run the project in the appropriate simulator or device, and the available font families and fonts will be displayed in the project's console log.

Implementing the Controller

There is a bunch of new stuff to cover in the implementation of this controller. Select `CustomPickerViewController.swift` and get started by filling in the contents of the `spin()` method, as shown in Listing 7-12.

Listing 7-12. The spin() Method

```
@IBAction func spin(_ sender: UIButton) {
    var win = false
    var numInRow = -1
    var lastVal = -1

    for i in 0..<5 {
        let newValue = Int(arc4random_uniform(UInt32(images.count)))
        if newValue == lastVal {
// numInRow++     *** NOTE THAT increment/decrement operators are deprecated in Swift 3
            numInRow += 1
        } else {
            numInRow = 1
        }
        lastVal = newValue

        picker.selectRow(newValue, inComponent: i, animated: true)
        picker.reloadComponent(i)
```

```
        if numInRow >= 3 {
            win = true
        }
    }
    winLabel.text = win ? "WINNER!" : " "   // Note the space between the quotes
}
```

■ **Note**   The common use of unary increment (foo++) and decrement (foo--) was deprecated in Swift 3 to the use of += and -=, respectively.

Change the viewDidLoad() method to what's shown in Listing 7-13.

Listing 7-13. The Modifications to viewDidLoad() to Set Up the Images and Label

```
override func viewDidLoad() {
    super.viewDidLoad()

    // Do any additional setup after loading the view.
    images = [
        UIImage(named: "seven")!,
        UIImage(named: "bar")!,
        UIImage(named: "crown")!,
        UIImage(named: "cherry")!,
        UIImage(named: "lemon")!,
        UIImage(named: "apple")!
    ]
    winLabel.text = " " // Note the space between the quotes
    arc4random_stir()
}
```

Finally, add the dataSource and delegate code to the end of the class declaration, before the closing brace, as shown in Listing 7-14.

Listing 7-14. Your dataSource and delegate Methods

```
// MARK:-
// MARK: Picker Data Source Methods
func numberOfComponents(in pickerView: UIPickerView) -> Int {
    return 5
}
func pickerView(_ pickerView: UIPickerView, numberOfRowsInComponent component: Int) -> Int {
    return images.count
}
// MARK:-
// MARK: Picker Delegate Methods
func pickerView(_ pickerView: UIPickerView, viewForRow row: Int, forComponent component:
Int, reusing view: UIView?) -> UIView {
    let image = images[row]
    let imageView = UIImageView(image: image)
    return imageView
}
```

```
func pickerView(_ pickerView: UIPickerView, rowHeightForComponent component: Int) -> CGFloat
{
    return 64
}
```

The spin() Method

The spin() method executes when the user taps the Spin button. In it, you first declare a few variables that will help you keep track of whether the user has won. You'll use win to keep track of whether you've found three in a row by setting it to true if you have. You'll use numInRow to keep track of how many of the same value you have in a row so far. You will keep track of the previous component's value in lastVal so that you have a way to compare the current value to the previous value. You initialize lastVal to -1 because you know that value won't match any of the real values.

```
var win = false
var numInRow = -1
var lastVal = -1
```

Next, you loop through all five components and set each one to a new, randomly generated row selection. You get the count from the images array to do that, which is a shortcut you can use because you know that all five columns use the same number of images.

```
for i in 0..<5 {
    let newValue = Int(arc4random_uniform(UInt32(images.count)))
```

You compare the new value to the previous value and increment numInRow if it matches. If the value didn't match, you reset numInRow to 1. You then assign the new value to lastVal, so you'll have it to compare the next time through the loop.

```
if newValue == lastVal {
    numInRow += 1
} else {
    numInRow = 1
}
lastVal = newValue
```

After that, you set the corresponding component to the new value, telling it to animate the change; you tell the picker to reload that component.

```
picker.selectRow(newValue, inComponent: i, animated: true)
picker.reloadComponent(i)
```

The last thing you do each time through the loop is check whether you have three in a row and then set win to true if you do.

```
if numInRow >= 3 {
    win = true
}
```

Once you're finished with the loop, you set the label to say whether the spin was a win.

```
winLabel.text = win ? "WINNER!" : " "
                    // Note the space between the quotes
```

The viewDidLoad() Method

The first thing was to load six different images, which you added to Images.xcassets back at the beginning of the chapter. You did this using the imageNamed() convenience method of the UIImage class.

```
images = [
    UIImage(named: "seven")!,
    UIImage(named: "bar")!,
    UIImage(named: "crown")!,
    UIImage(named: "cherry")!,
    UIImage(named: "lemon")!,
    UIImage(named: "apple")!
]
```

The next thing you did in this method was to make sure the label contains exactly one space. You want the label to be empty, but if you really make it empty, it collapses to zero height. By including a space, you make sure the label is shown at its correct height.

```
winLabel.text = " " // Note the space between the quotes
```

Finally, you called the arc4random_stir() function to seed the random number generator so that you don't get the same sequence of random numbers every time you run the application.

So, what do you do with those six images? If you scroll down through the code you just typed, you'll see that two data source methods look pretty much the same as before; however, if you look further into the delegate methods, you'll see that you're using completely different delegate code to provide data to the picker. The one that you've used up to now returned a string, but this one returns a UIView.

Using this method instead, you can supply the picker with anything that can be drawn into a UIView. Of course, there are limitations on what will work here and look good at the same time, given the small size of the picker. But this method gives you a lot more freedom in what you display, although it is a bit more work.

```
func pickerView(_ pickerView: UIPickerView, viewForRow row: Int, forComponent component:
Int, reusing view: UIView?) -> UIView {
    let image = images[row]
    let imageView = UIImageView(image: image)
    return imageView
}
```

This method returns one UIImageView object initialized with one of the images for the symbols. To do that, you first get the image for the symbol for the row. Next, create and return an image view with that symbol. For views more complex than a single image, it can be beneficial to create all needed views first (e.g., in viewDidLoad()) and then return these precreated views to the picker view when requested. But for your simple case, creating the needed views dynamically works fine.

You got through all of it in one piece, and now you get to take it for a test. So, build and run the application and see how it works (see Figure 7-24).

Figure 7-24. *It's not the prettiest slot machine app, but it gives you an idea of the versatility of working with pickers*

Additional Details for Your Game

Your game works okay, especially when you think about how little effort it took to build it. Now let's improve it with a couple more tweaks. There are two things about this game right now that I should address.

- It's so quiet. Real slot machines aren't quiet, so yours shouldn't be either.

- It tells the user that they've won before the dials have finished spinning, which is a minor thing, but it does tend to eliminate the anticipation. To see this in action, run your application again. It is subtle, but the label really does appear before the wheels finish spinning.

The Picker Sounds folder in the project archive that accompanies the book contains two sound files: crunch.wav and win.wav. Drag both of these files to your project's Pickers folder. These are the sounds you'll play when the users tap the Spin button and when they win, respectively.

To work with sounds, you'll need access to the iOS Audio Toolbox classes. Insert the following AudioToolbox line at a position after the existing import line at the top of CustomPickerViewController.swift:

```
import UIKit
import AudioToolbox
```

Next, you need to add an outlet that will point to the button. While the wheels are spinning, you're going to hide the button. You don't want users tapping the button again until the current spin is all done. Add the following bold line of code to CustomPickerViewController.swift:

```
class CustomPickerViewController: UIViewController,
        UIPickerViewDelegate, UIPickerViewDataSource {
    private var images:[UIImage]!
    @IBOutlet weak var picker: UIPickerView!
    @IBOutlet weak var winLabel: UILabel!
    @IBOutlet weak var button: UIButton!
```

After you type that and save the file, click Main.storyboard to edit the GUI. Open the Assistant Editor and make sure it shows the CustomPickerViewController.swift file. Click and drag from the little ball to the left of the outlet you just added to the button on the storyboard, as shown in Figure 7-25.

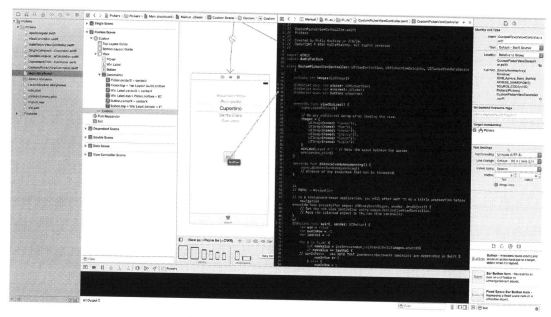

Figure 7-25. *Connecting the button outlet to the button on the storyboard canvas*

Now, you need to do a few things in the implementation of your controller class. First, you need some instance variables to hold references to the loaded sounds. Open `CustomPickerViewController.swift` again and add the following new properties (shown in bold):

```
class CustomPickerViewController: UIViewController,
        UIPickerViewDelegate, UIPickerViewDataSource {
    private var images:[UIImage]!
    @IBOutlet weak var picker: UIPickerView!
    @IBOutlet weak var winLabel: UILabel!
    @IBOutlet weak var button: UIButton!
    private var winSoundID: SystemSoundID = 0
    private var crunchSoundID: SystemSoundID = 0
```

You also need a couple of methods added to your controller class. Add the two methods in Listing 7-15 to the `CustomPickerViewController.swift` file.

Listing 7-15. Hiding the Spin Button and Playing Sounds in Your Slot Machine Game

```
func showButton() {
    button.isHidden = false
}

func playWinSound() {
    if winSoundID == 0 {
        let soundURL = Bundle.main.urlForResource(
            "win", withExtension: "wav")! as CFURL
        AudioServicesCreateSystemSoundID(soundURL, &winSoundID)
    }
    AudioServicesPlaySystemSound(winSoundID)
    winLabel.text = "WINNER!"
    DispatchQueue.main.after(when: .now() + 1.5) {
        self.showButton()
    }
}
```

You use the first method to show the button. As noted previously, you'll need to hide the button when the user taps it because if the wheels are already spinning, there's no point in letting them spin again until they've stopped.

The second method will be called when the user wins. First, you check whether you have already loaded the winning sound. The `winSoundID` and `crunchSoundID` properties are initialized as zero, and valid identifiers for loaded sounds are not zero, so you can check whether a sound is loaded yet by comparing its identifier to zero. To load a sound, you first ask the main bundle for the path to the sound, in this case `win.wav`, just as you did when you loaded the property list for the Dependent picker view. Once you have the path to that resource, the next three lines of code load the sound file in and play it. Next, you set the label to **WINNER!** and call the `showButton()` method; however, you call the `showButton()` method in a special way using a function called `DispatchQueue(when: )`. This is a handy function that lets you run code sometime in the future—in this case, one-and-a-half seconds in the future, which will give the dials time to spin to their final locations before telling the user the result.

▓ **Note** You may have noticed something a bit odd about the way you called the `AudioServicesCreateSystemSoundID()` function. That function takes a URL as its first parameter, but it doesn't want an instance of `NSURL`. Instead, it wants a `CFURL` (previously `CFURLRef`), which is a pointer to a structure that belongs to the C-language Core Foundation framework. `NSURL` is part of the Foundation framework, which is written in Objective-C. Fortunately, many of the C components in Core Foundation are "bridged" to their Objective-C counterparts in the Foundation framework so that a `CFURL` is functionally equivalent to an `NSURL` pointer. That means certain kinds of objects created in Swift or Objective-C can be used with C APIs simply by casting them to the corresponding C type using the `as` keyword.

You also need to make some changes to the `spin()` method. You will write code to play a sound and to call the `playWinSound` method if the player wins. Make the changes to the `spin()` method shown in Listing 7-16.

Listing 7-16. Your Updated spin() Method to Add Sounds

```swift
@IBAction func spin(sender: AnyObject) {
    var win = false
    var numInRow = -1
    var lastVal = -1

    for i in 0..<5 {
        let newValue = Int(arc4random_uniform(UInt32(images.count)))
        if newValue == lastVal {
            numInRow += 1
        } else {
            numInRow = 1
        }
        lastVal = newValue

        picker.selectRow(newValue, inComponent: i, animated: true)
        picker.reloadComponent(i)
        if numInRow >= 3 {
            win = true
        }
    }

    if crunchSoundID == 0 {
        let soundURL = Bundle.main.urlForResource(
            "crunch", withExtension: "wav")! as CFURL
        AudioServicesCreateSystemSoundID(soundURL, &crunchSoundID)
    }
    AudioServicesPlaySystemSound(crunchSoundID)

    if win {
        DispatchQueue.main.after(when: .now() + 0.5) {
            self.playWinSound()
        }
```

```
    } else {
        DispatchQueue.main.after(when: .now() + 0.5) {
            self.showButton()
        }
    }
    button.isHidden = true
    winLabel.text = " " // Note the space between the quotes
}
```

First, you load the crunch sound if needed, just as you did with the win sound before. Now play the crunch sound to let the player know the wheels have been spun. Next, instead of setting the label to **WINNER!** as soon as you know the user has won, you do something tricky. You call one of the two methods you just created, but you do it after a delay using `DispatchQueue.main.after(when: )`. If the user won, you call your playWinSound() method half a second into the future, which will give time for the dials to spin into place; otherwise, you just wait a half-second and reenable the Spin button. While waiting for the result, you hide the button and clear the label's text.

Now you're done, so build and run the app and then click the final tab to see and hear this slot machine in action. Tapping the Spin button should play a little cranking sound, and a win should produce a winning sound.

Summary

By now, you should be comfortable with tab bar applications and pickers. In this chapter, you built a full-fledged tab bar application containing five different content views from scratch. You practiced using pickers in a number of different configurations and creating pickers with multiple components. You even know how to make the values in one component dependent on the value selected in another component. You also saw how to make the picker display images rather than just text.

Along the way, you talked about picker delegates and data sources and saw how to load images, play sounds, and create dictionaries from property lists. It was a long chapter, so congratulations on making it through. In the next chapter, you'll start working with one of the most common elements for iPhone devices: table views.

CHAPTER 8

■ ■ ■

Introducing Table Views

Over the course of the next few chapters, you'll build some hierarchical navigation-based applications similar to the Mail application that ships on iOS devices. Applications of this type, usually called *master-detail applications*, allow the user to drill down into nested lists of data and edit that data. But before you can build these types of applications, you'll need to master the concept of table views.

Table views provide iOS devices with the most common mechanism used to display lists of data to the user. They are highly configurable objects able to look practically any way you want them to. Mail uses table views to show lists of accounts, folders, and messages; however, table views are not limited to just the display of textual data. The Settings, Music, and Clock apps also use table views, even though those applications exhibit very different appearances, as shown in Figure 8-1.

Figure 8-1. *Though they all look different, the Settings, Music, and Clock applications use table views to display their data*

© Molly K. Maskrey 2017
M. K. Maskrey, *Beginning iPhone Development with Swift 4*, https://doi.org/10.1007/978-1-4842-3072-5_8

Understanding Table View Basics

Tables display lists of data, with each item in a table's list known as a *row*. iOS allows tables to have an unlimited number of rows, constrained only by the amount of available memory, but they can be only one column wide.

Using Table Views and Table View Cells

A table view object displays a table's data and functions as instances of the class UITableView; each visible row in a table is implemented by an instance of the class UITableViewCell, as shown in Figure 8-2.

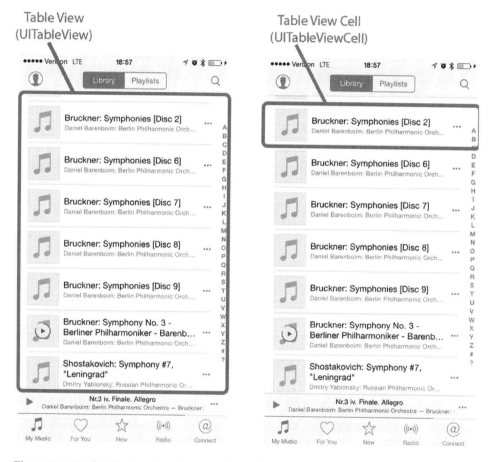

Figure 8-2. *Each table view is an instance of UITableView, and each visible row is an instance of UITableViewCell*

Though not responsible for storing all of your table's data, a table view contains only enough data to draw the rows currently visible. Somewhat like pickers, table views get their configuration data from an object that conforms to the UITableViewDelegate protocol, and they get their row data from an object that conforms to the UITableViewDataSource protocol. You'll see how all this works when developing the sample programs later in the chapter.

As mentioned, all tables contain just a single column. The Clock application, shown on the right side of Figure 8-1, gives the appearance of having two columns, but in reality, that's not the case—each row in the table is represented by a single `UITableViewCell`. By default, a `UITableViewCell` object can be configured with an image, some text, and an optional accessory icon, which is a small icon on the right side, which I'll cover in detail in Chapter 9.

You increase the amount of data in a cell by adding subviews to `UITableViewCell`, which you can do by using one of two basic techniques: adding subviews programmatically when creating the cell or loading them from a storyboard or nib file. You lay out the table view cell however appropriate including any subviews needed. This makes the single-column limitation far less limiting than it sounds at first. You'll explore how to use both of these techniques in this chapter.

Understanding Grouped and Plain Tables

Table views come in two basic styles.

- *Grouped*: A grouped table view contains one or more sections of rows. Within each section, all rows rest tightly together in a compact grouping; but between sections, clear visible gaps exist, as shown in the leftmost picture in Figure 8-3. Note that a grouped table can consist of a single group.

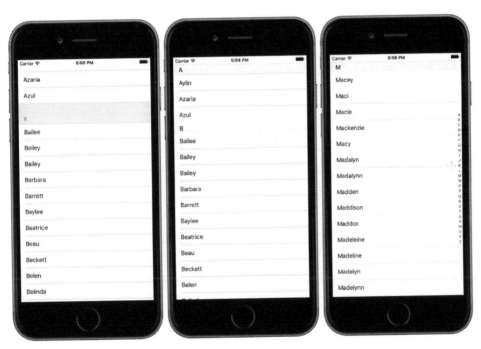

Figure 8-3. One table view displayed as a grouped table (left); a plain table without an index (middle); and a plain table with an index, which is also called an indexed table (right)

- *Plain*: A plain table view (see Figure 8-3, middle), which is the default style, contains sections that are slightly closer together, and each section's header is optionally styled in a custom manner. When an index is used, this style is referred to as *indexed* (see Figure 8-3, right).

If your data source provides the necessary information, the table view allows the user to navigate your list by an index that is displayed along the right side.

iOS breaks up your table into divisions called *sections*. In a grouped table, each section presents itself visually as a group. In an indexed table, Apple refers to each indexed grouping of data as a *section*. For example, in the indexed table shown in Figure 8-3, all the names beginning with *A* would be one section, those beginning with *B* would be another, and so on.

■ **Caution**   Even though it is technically possible to create a grouped table with an index, you should not do so. The *iOS Human Interface Guidelines* specifically state that grouped tables should not provide indexes.

Implementing a Simple Table

Let's look at the simplest possible example of a table view to get a feel for how it works. In this first example, you'll only display a list of text values.

Create a new project in Xcode. For this chapter, you're going back to the Single View App template, so select that one. Call your project **Simple Table**, set Swift as the Language, set the Devices field to Universal, and make sure that Use Core Data is deselected.

Designing the View

In the Project Navigator, expand the top-level Simple Table project and the Simple Table folder. This is such a simple application that you're not going to need any outlets or actions. Go ahead and select Main. storyboard to edit the storyboard. If the View window isn't visible in the layout area, single-click its icon in the Document Outline to open it. Next, look in the Object Library for a table view (see Figure 8-4) and drag that to the View window.

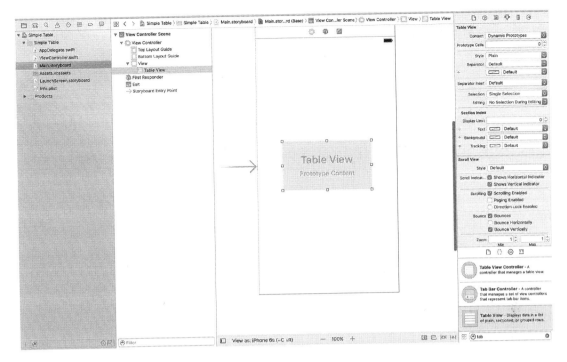

Figure 8-4. *Dragging a table view from the library onto your main view*

Drop the table view onto the view controller and line it up to be more or less centered in its parent view. Now let's add Auto Layout constraints to make sure that the table view is positioned and sized correctly no matter what size the screen is. Select the table in the Document Outline and then click the Pin icon at the bottom right of the storyboard editor (see Figure 8-5).

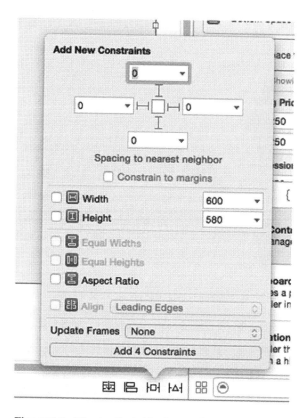

Figure 8-5. *Pinning the table view so that it fits the screen*

At the top of the pop-up, clear the "Constrain to margins" check box, click all four dashed lines, and set the distances in the four input fields to zero. This will have the effect of pinning all four edges of the table view to those of its parent view. To apply the constraints, change Update Frames to Items of New Constraints, and click the Add 4 Constraints button. The table should resize to fill the whole view.

Select the table view again in the Document Inspector and press ⌥⌘6 to bring up the Connections Inspector. You'll notice that the first two available connections for the table view are the same as the first two for the picker views that you used in the previous chapter: dataSource and delegate. Drag from the circle next to each of those connections to the View Controller icon in the Document Outline or above the view controller in the storyboard editor. This makes your controller class both the data source and the delegate for this table, as shown in Figure 8-6.

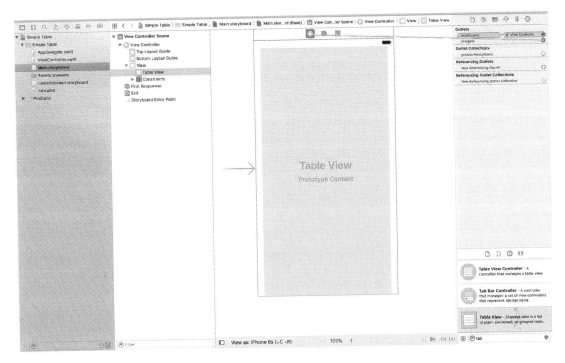

Figure 8-6. *Connecting your table view's dataSource and delegate outlets*

Next, you'll start writing the Swift code for your table view.

Implementing the Controller

If you've gone through the previous chapters, a lot of this will sound familiar and maybe a bit boring. However, because some readers skip ahead, I'm going to try to maintain a consistent approach at least for these early, more basic chapters. Single-click `ViewController.swift` and add the code in Listing 8-1 to the class declaration.

Listing 8-1. Add to the Top of the Class Declaration to Create Your Element Array

```
class ViewController: UIViewController,
            UITableViewDataSource, UITableViewDelegate {
    private let dwarves = [
            "Sleepy", "Sneezy", "Bashful", "Happy",
            "Doc", "Grumpy", "Dopey",
            "Thorin", "Dorin", "Nori", "Ori",
            "Balin", "Dwalin", "Fili", "Kili",
            "Oin", "Gloin", "Bifur", "Bofur",
            "Bombur"
    ]
    let simpleTableIdentifier = "SimpleTableIdentifier"
```

In Listing 8-1 you're conforming your class to the two protocols that are needed for it to act as the data source and delegate for the table view, declaring an array that holds the data that will be displayed in the table and an identifier that you'll use shortly. In a real application, the data would come from another source, such as a text file, a property list, or a web service.

Next, add the code in Listing 8-2 before the closing brace at the end of the file.

Listing 8-2. Your Table View's dataSource Methods

```
// MARK:-
// MARK: Table View Data Source Methods

func tableView(_ tableView: UITableView, numberOfRowsInSection section: Int) -> Int {
    return dwarves.count
}

func tableView(_ tableView: UITableView, cellForRowAt indexPath: IndexPath) ->
UITableViewCell {
    var cell = tableView.dequeueReusableCell(withIdentifier: simpleTableIdentifier)
    if (cell == nil) {
        cell = UITableViewCell(
            style: UITableViewCellStyle.default,
            reuseIdentifier: simpleTableIdentifier)
    }

    cell?.textLabel?.text = dwarves[indexPath.row]
    return cell!
}
```

These methods are part of the UITableViewDataSource protocol. The first one, tableView(_ tableView: UITableView, numberOfRowsInSection section: Int) -> Int, is used by the table to ask how many rows are in a particular section. As you might expect, the default number of sections is one, and this method will be called to get the number of rows in the one section that makes up the list. You just return the number of items in your array.

The next method probably requires a little explanation, so let's look at it more closely.

```
func tableView(_ tableView: UITableView,
               cellForRowAt indexPath: IndexPath) -> UITableViewCell {
```

This method is called by the table view when it needs to draw one of its rows. Notice that the second argument to this method is an NSIndexPath instance. NSIndexPath is a structure that table views use to wrap the section and row indexes into a single object. To get the row index or the section index out of an NSIndexPath, you just access its row property or its section property, both of which return an integer value.

The first parameter, tableView, is a reference to the table that's being constructed. This allows you to create classes that act as a data source for multiple tables.

A table view displays only a few rows at a time, but the table itself can conceivably hold considerably more. Remember that each row in the table is represented by an instance of UITableViewCell, a subclass of UIView, which means each row can contain subviews. With a large table, this could represent a huge amount of overhead if the table were to try to keep one table view cell instance for every row in the table, regardless of whether that row was currently being displayed. Fortunately, tables don't work that way.

Instead, as table view cells scroll off the screen, they are placed into a queue of cells available to be reused. If the system runs low on memory, the table view will get rid of the cells in the queue. But as long as the system has some memory available for those cells, it will hold on to them in case you want to use them again.

Every time a table view cell rolls off the screen, there's a pretty good chance that another one just rolled onto the screen on the other side. If that new row can just reuse one of the cells that has already rolled off the screen, the system can avoid the overhead associated with constantly creating and releasing those views. To take advantage of this mechanism, you'll ask the table view to give you a previously used cell of the specified type using the identifier you declared earlier. In effect, you're asking for a reusable cell of type simpleTableIdentifier.

```
var cell = tableView.dequeueReusableCell(withIdentifier: simpleTableIdentifier)
```

In this example, the table uses only a single type of cell, but in a more complex table, you might need to format different types of cells according to their content or position, in which case you would use a separate table cell identifier for each distinct cell type.

Now, it's completely possible that the table view won't have any spare cells (e.g., when it's being initially populated), so you check the cell variable after the call to see whether it's nil. If it is, you manually create a new table view cell using the same identifier string. At some point, you'll inevitably reuse one of the cells you create here, so you need to make sure that you create it using simpleTableIdentifier.

```
if (cell == nil) {
    cell = UITableViewCell(
        style: UITableViewCellStyle.default,
        reuseIdentifier: simpleTableIdentifier)
}
```

Curious about UITableViewCellStyle.default? You'll get to it when you look at the table view cell styles shortly.

You now have a table view cell that you can return for the table view to use. So, all you need to do is place whatever information you want displayed in this cell. Displaying text in a row of a table is a very common task, so the table view cell provides a UILabel property called textLabel that you can set to display strings. That just requires getting the correct string from your dwarves array and using it to set the cell's textLabel.

To get the correct value, however, you need to know which row the table view is asking for. You get that information from the indexPath's row property. You use the row number of the table to get the corresponding string from the array, assign it to the cell's textLabel.text property, and then return the cell.

```
cell?.textLabel?.text = dwarves[indexPath.row]
return cell!
```

Compile and run your application, and you should see the array values displayed in a table view, as shown on the left of Figure 8-7.

Figure 8-7. *The Simple Table application showing your dwarves array*

You may be wondering why you need all the ? operators in this line of code:

```
cell?.textLabel?.text = dwarves[indexPath.row]
```

Each use of the ? operator is an example of Swift's *optional chaining*, which allows you to write compact code even if you have to invoke the methods or access the properties of an object reference that could be nil. The first ? operator is required because, as far as the compiler is concerned, cell could be nil. The reason for that is you obtained it by calling the dequeueReusableCellWithIdentifier() method, which returns a value of type UITableViewCell?. Of course, the compiler doesn't take into account the fact that you explicitly check for a nil return value and create a new UITableViewCell object if you find one, thus ensuring that cell will, in fact, never be nil when you reach this line of code. If you look at the documentation for the UITableViewCell class, you'll see that its textLabel property is of type UILabel?, so it could also be nil. Again, that won't actually be the case because you are using a default UITableViewCell instance, which always includes a label. Naturally, the compiler doesn't know that, so you use a ? operator when dereferencing it. This is something you'll see throughout your Swift experiences.

Adding an Image

It would be nice if you could add an image to each row. You might think that you would need to create a subclass of `UITableViewCell` or add subviews to do that. Actually, if you can live with the image being on the left side of each row, you're already set. The default table view cell can handle that situation just fine. Let's see how it works.

Drag the files `star.png` and `star2.png` from the `Star Image` folder in the example source code archive to your project's `Assets.xcassets`, as shown in Figure 8-8.

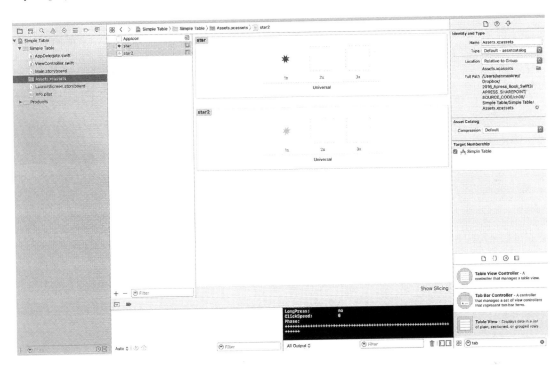

Figure 8-8. *Adding your images to the Assets.xcassests folder*

You're going to arrange for these icons to appear on every row of the table view. All you need to do is create a `UIImage` for each of them and assign it to the `UITableViewCell` when the table view asks its data source for the cell for each row. To do this, in the file `ViewController.swift`, modify the `tableView(_:cellF orRowAtIndexPath:)` method, as shown in Listing 8-3.

Listing 8-3. *Your Modifications to Add the Image to Each Cell*

```
func tableView(_ tableView: UITableView, cellForRowAt indexPath: IndexPath) ->
UITableViewCell {
    var cell = tableView.dequeueReusableCell(withIdentifier: simpleTableIdentifier)
    if (cell == nil) {
        cell = UITableViewCell(
            style: UITableViewCellStyle.default,
            reuseIdentifier: simpleTableIdentifier)
    }
```

```
let image = UIImage(named: "star")
cell?.imageView?.image = image
let highlightedImage = UIImage(named: "star2")
cell?.imageView?.highlightedImage = highlightedImage

cell?.textLabel?.text = dwarves[indexPath.row]
return cell!
}
```

That's it. Each cell has an imageView property of type UIImage, which in turn has properties called image and highlightedImage. The image given by the image property appears to the left of the cell's text and is replaced by the highlightedImage, if one is provided, when the cell is selected. You just set the cell's imageView.image and imageView.highlightedImage properties to whatever images you want to display.

If you compile and run your application now, you should get a list with a bunch of nice little blue star icons to the left of each row, as shown in Figure 8-9. If you select any row, you'll see that its icon switches from blue to green, which is the color of the image in the star2.png file. Of course, you could have included a different image for each row in the table, or, with very little effort, you could have used different icons for the different categories of dwarves.

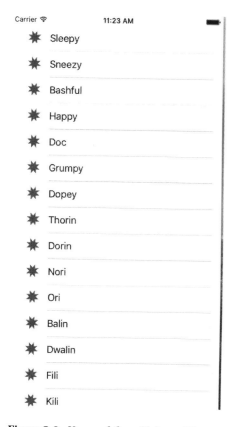

Figure 8-9. *You used the cell's imageView property to add an image to each of the table view's cells*

> ▓ **Note**   UIImage uses a caching mechanism based on the file name, so it won't load a new image property each time UIImage(named:) is called. Instead, it will use the already cached version.

Using Table View Cell Styles

The work you've done with the table view so far has used the default cell style shown in Figure 8-9, represented by the constant UITableViewCellStyle.default. But the UITableViewCell class includes several other predefined cell styles that let you easily add a bit more variety to your table views. These cell styles all use three different cell elements.

- *Image*: If an image is part of the specified style, the image is displayed to the left of the cell's text.

- *Text label*: This is the cell's primary text. In the case of the UITableViewCellStyle. Default style that you have been using so far, the text label is the only text shown in the cell.

- *Detail text label*: This is the cell's secondary text, usually used as an explanatory note or label.

To see what these new style additions look like, add the following code to tableView(_:cellForRow AtIndexPath:) in ViewController.swift:

```
if indexPath.row < 7 {
    cell?.detailTextLabel?.text = "Mr Disney"
} else {
    cell?.detailTextLabel?.text = "Mr Tolkien"
}
```

Place it just before the cell?.textLabel?.text = dwarves[indexPath.row] line in the method.

All you've done here is set the cell's detail text. You use the string "Mr. Disney" for the first seven rows and the string "Mr. Tolkien" for the rest. When you run this code, each cell will look just as it did before (see Figure 8-10). That's because you are using the style UITableViewCellStyle.default, which does not use the detail text.

Figure 8-10. *The default cell style shows the image and text label in a straight line*

Now change UITableViewCellStyle.default to UITableViewCellStyle.subtitle like this:

```
if (cell == nil) {
    cell = UITableViewCell(
        style: UITableViewCellStyle.subtitle,
        reuseIdentifier: simpleTableIdentifier)
}
```

Run the app again. With the subtitle style, both text elements are shown, one below the other, as shown in Figure 8-11.

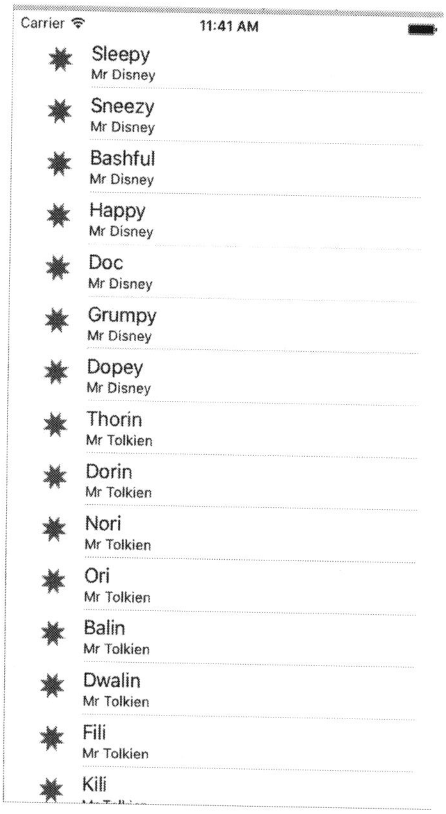

Figure 8-11. *The subtitle style shows the detail text in smaller letters below the text label*

Next, change `UITableViewCellStyle.subtitle` to `UITableViewCellStyle.value1` and then build and run again. This style places the text label and detail text label on the same line but on opposite sides of the cell, as shown in Figure 8-12.

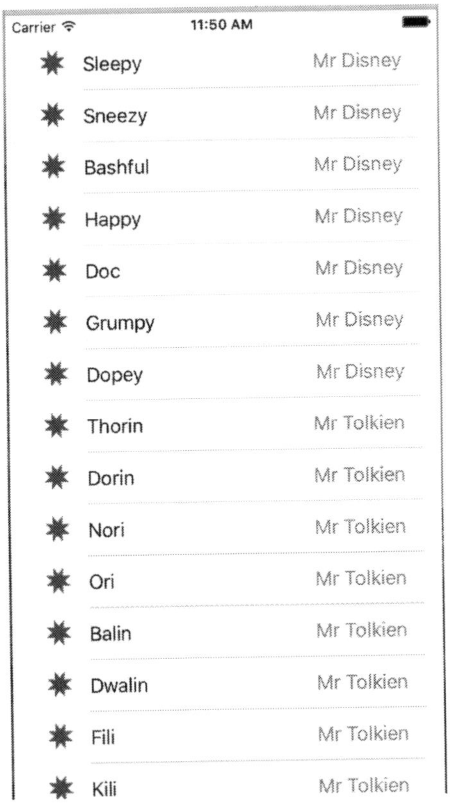

Figure 8-12. *The style value1 places the text label on the left side in black letters and the detail text right-justified on the right side*

Finally, change `UITableViewCellStyle.value1` to `UITableViewCellStyle.value2`. This format is often used to display information along with a descriptive label. It doesn't show the cell's icon but places the detail text label to the left of the text label, as shown in Figure 8-13. In this layout, the detail text label acts as a label describing the type of data held in the text label.

Figure 8-13. *The style value 2 does not display the image and places the detail text label in blue letters to the left of the text label*

Now that you've seen the cell styles that are available, go ahead and change back to the UITableViewCellStyle.default style before continuing. Later in this chapter, you'll see how to create custom table view cells. But before you do that, make sure you consider the available cell styles to see whether one of them will suit your needs.

You may have noticed that you made your controller both the data source and the delegate for this table view; but up until now, you haven't actually implemented any of the methods from the UITableViewDelegate protocol. Unlike picker views, simpler table views don't require the use of a delegate to do their thing. The data source provides all the data needed to draw the table. The purpose of the delegate is to configure the appearance of the table view and to handle certain user interactions. Let's take a look at a few of the configuration options now. I'll discuss a few more in the next chapter.

Setting the Indent Level

The delegate can be used to specify that some rows should be indented. In the file ViewController.swift, add the following method to your code:

```
// MARK:-
// MARK: Table View delegate Methods
func tableView(_ tableView: UITableView, indentationLevelForRowAt indexPath: IndexPath) ->
Int {
    return indexPath.row % 4
}
```

This method sets the *indent level* for each row based on its row number, so row 0 will have an indent level of 0, row 1 will have an indent level of 1, and so on. Because of the % operator, row 4 will revert to an indent level of 0 and the cycle begins again. An indent level is simply an integer that tells the table view to move that row a little to the right. The higher the number, the further to the right the row will be indented. You might use this technique, for example, to indicate that one row is subordinate to another row, as Mail does when representing subfolders.

When you run the application again, you'll see that the rows indent in blocks of four, as shown in Figure 8-14.

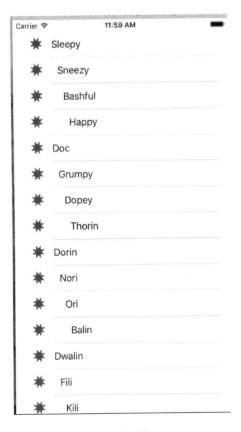

Figure 8-14. *Indented table rows*

Handling Row Selection

The table's delegate has two methods that allow you to handle row selection. One method is called before the row is selected, which can be used to prevent the row from being selected or even to change which row gets selected. Let's implement that method and specify that the first row is not selectable. Add the following method to the end of ViewController.swift:

```swift
func tableView(_ tableView: UITableView, willSelectRowAt indexPath: IndexPath) ->
IndexPath? {
    return indexPath.row == 0 ? nil : indexPath
}
```

This method is passed an indexPath that represents the item that's about to be selected. The code looks at which row is about to be selected. If it's the first row, which is always index zero, then it returns nil to indicate that no row should actually be selected. Otherwise, it returns the unmodified indexPath, which is how you indicate that it's okay for the selection to proceed.

Before you compile and run, let's also implement the delegate method that is called after a row has been selected, which is typically where you'll actually handle the selection. In the next chapter, you'll use this method to handle drill-downs in a master-detail application, but in this chapter, you'll just put up an alert to show that the row was selected. Add the method in Listing 8-4 at the end of ViewController.swift.

Listing 8-4. Pop Up an Alert When the User Taps a Row

```swift
func tableView(_ tableView: UITableView, didSelectRowAt indexPath: IndexPath) {
    let rowValue = dwarves[indexPath.row]
    let message = "You selected \(rowValue)"

    let controller = UIAlertController(title: "Row Selected",
                                       message: message, preferredStyle: .alert)
    let action = UIAlertAction(title: "Yes I Did",
                               style: .default, handler: nil)
    controller.addAction(action)
    present(controller, animated: true, completion: nil)
}
```

Once you've added this method, compile and run the app and then take it for a spin. For example, see whether you can select the first row (you shouldn't be able to) and then select one of the other rows. The selected row should be highlighted. Also, your alert should pop up, telling you which row you selected, while the selected row fades in the background, as shown in Figure 8-15.

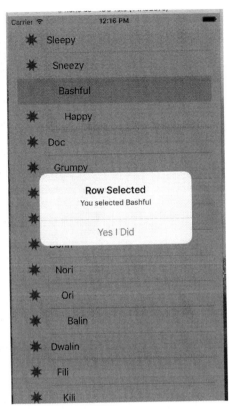

Figure 8-15. *In this example, the first row is not selectable, and an alert is displayed when any other row is selected*

Note that you can also modify the index path before you pass it back, which would cause a different row and/or section to be selected. You won't do that very often, as you should have a very good reason for changing the user's selection. In the vast majority of cases where you use the `tableView(_:willSelectRowAtIndexPath:)` method, you will either return `indexPath` unmodified to allow the selection or return `nil` to disallow it. If you really want to change the selected row and/or section, use the `NSIndexPath(forRow:, inSection:)` initializer to create a new `NSIndexPath` object and return it. For example, the code in Listing 8-5 would ensure that if you tried to select an even-numbered row, you would actually select the row that follows it.

Listing 8-5. Returning the Following Row

```
func tableView(tableView: UITableView,
            willSelectRowAtIndexPath indexPath: NSIndexPath)
    -> NSIndexPath? {
        if indexPath.row == 0 {
            return nil
        } else if (indexPath.row % 2 == 0){
            return NSIndexPath(row: indexPath.row + 1,
                            section: indexPath.section)
        } else {
            return indexPath
        }
}
```

Changing the Font Size and Row Height

Let's say you want to change the size of the font being used in the table view. In most situations, you shouldn't override the default font; it's what users expect to see. But sometimes there are valid reasons to change the font. Change the code for your tableView(_:cellForRowAtIndexPath:) method.

```
func tableView(_ tableView: UITableView, cellForRowAt indexPath: IndexPath) ->
UITableViewCell {
    var cell = tableView.dequeueReusableCell(withIdentifier: simpleTableIdentifier)
    if (cell == nil) {
        cell = UITableViewCell(
            style: UITableViewCellStyle.default,
            reuseIdentifier: simpleTableIdentifier)
    }

    let image = UIImage(named: "star")
    cell?.imageView?.image = image
    let highlightedImage = UIImage(named: "star2")
    cell?.imageView?.highlightedImage = highlightedImage

    if indexPath.row < 7 {
        cell?.detailTextLabel?.text = "Mr Disney"
    } else {
        cell?.detailTextLabel?.text = "Mr Tolkien"
    }

    cell?.textLabel?.text = dwarves[indexPath.row]
    cell?.textLabel?.font = UIFont.boldSystemFont(ofSize: 50) // <- add this line
    return cell!
}
```

When you run the application now, the values in your list are drawn in a really large font size, but they don't exactly fit in the row, as shown in Figure 8-16.

Figure 8-16. *Changing the font used to draw table view cells*

There are a couple of ways to fix this. First, you can tell the table that all of its rows should have a given, fixed height. To do that, you set its `rowHeight` property, like this:

```
tableView.rowHeight = 70
```

If you need different rows to have different heights, you can implement the `UITableViewDelegate`'s `tableView(_:heightForRowAtIndexPath:)` method. Go ahead and add this method to your controller class:

```
func tableView(_ tableView: UITableView, heightForRowAt indexPath: IndexPath) -> CGFloat{
    return indexPath.row == 0 ? 120 : 70
}
```

You've just told the table view to set the row height for all rows to 70 points, except for the first row, which will be a little larger. Compile and run, and your table's rows should be a better fit for their content now, as shown in Figure 8-17.

Figure 8-17. *Changing the row size using the delegate. Notice that the first row is much taller than the rest*

There are more tasks that the delegate handles, but most of the remaining ones come into play when you start working with hierarchical data, which you'll do in the next chapter. To learn more, use the documentation browser to explore the UITableViewDelegate protocol and see what other methods are available.

Customizing Table View Cells

You can do a lot with table views right out of the box; but often, you will want to format the data for each row in ways that simply aren't supported by UITableViewCell directly. In those cases, there are three basic approaches: one that involves adding subviews to UITableViewCell programmatically when creating the cell, a second that involves loading a cell from a nib file, and a third that is similar but loads the cell from a storyboard. You'll take a look at the first two techniques in this chapter, and you'll see an example that creates a cell from a storyboard in Chapter 9.

Adding Subviews to the Table View Cell

To show how to use custom cells, you're going to create a new application with another table view. In each row, you'll display two lines of information along with two labels, as shown in Figure 8-18. Your application displays the name and color of a series of potentially familiar computer models. You'll show both of those pieces of information in the same row by adding subviews to its table view cell.

Figure 8-18. *Adding subviews to the table view cell can give you multiline rows*

Implementing a Custom Table Views Application

Create a new Xcode project using the Single View App template. Name the project **Table Cells** and use the same settings as your last project. Click Main.storyboard to edit the GUI in Interface Builder.

Add a table view to the main view and use the Connections Inspector to set its data source to the view controller, as you did for the Simple Table application. Then, use the Pin button at the bottom of the window to create constraints between the table view's edges and those of its parent view and the status bar. You can actually use the same settings as in Figure 8-5, since the values that you specify in the input boxes at the top of the pop-up are, by default, the distances between the table view and its nearest neighbor in all four directions. Finally, save the storyboard.

Creating a UITableViewCell Subclass

Until this point, the standard table view cells you've been using have taken care of all the details of cell layout for you. Your controller code has been kept clear of the messy details about where to place labels and images; you just pass off the display values to the cell. This keeps presentation logic out of the controller, and that's a really good design to stick to. For this project, you're going to make a new cell UITableViewCell subclass of your own that takes care of the details of the new layout, which will keep your controller as simple as possible.

Adding New Cells

Select the Table Cells folder in the Project Navigator, and press ⌘N to create a new file. In the assistant that pops up, select Cocoa Touch Class from the iOS Source section and click Next. On the following screen, enter **NameAndColorCell** as the name of the new class, select UITableViewCell in the "Subclass of" pop-up list, leave "Also create XIB file" deselected, click Next again, and on the next screen click Create.

Now select NameAndColorCell.swift in the Project Navigator and add the following code:

```
class NameAndColorCell: UITableViewCell {
    var name: String = ""
    var color: String = ""
    var nameLabel: UILabel!
    var colorLabel: UILabel!
```

Here, you've added two properties (name and color) to your cell's interface that your controller will use to pass values to each cell. You also added a couple of properties that you'll use to access some of the subviews you'll be adding to your cell. Your cell will contain four subviews, two of which are labels that have fixed content and another two for which the content will be changed for every row.

Those are all the properties you need to add, so let's move on to the code. You're going to override the table view cell's init(style:reuseIdentifier:) initializer to add some code to create the views that you'll need to display, as shown in Listing 8-6.

Listing 8-6. Your Table View Cell's init() Method

```
override init(style: UITableViewCellStyle, reuseIdentifier: String?) {
    super.init(style: style, reuseIdentifier: reuseIdentifier)

    let nameLabelRect = CGRect(x: 0, y: 5, width: 70, height: 15)
    let nameMarker = UILabel(frame: nameLabelRect)
    nameMarker.textAlignment = NSTextAlignment.right
    nameMarker.text = "Name:"
    nameMarker.font = UIFont.boldSystemFont(ofSize: 12)
    contentView.addSubview(nameMarker)

    let colorLabelRect = CGRect(x: 0, y: 26, width: 70, height: 15)
    let colorMarker = UILabel(frame: colorLabelRect)
    colorMarker.textAlignment = NSTextAlignment.right
```

```
        colorMarker.text = "Color:"
        colorMarker.font = UIFont.boldSystemFont(ofSize: 12)
        contentView.addSubview(colorMarker)

        let nameValueRect = CGRect(x: 80, y: 5, width: 200, height: 15)
        nameLabel = UILabel(frame: nameValueRect)
        contentView.addSubview(nameLabel)

        let colorValueRect = CGRect(x: 80, y: 25, width: 200, height: 15)
        colorLabel = UILabel(frame: colorValueRect)
        contentView.addSubview(colorLabel)
}
```

That should be pretty straightforward. You create four UILabels and add them to the table view cell. The table view cell already has a UIView subview called contentView, which it uses to group all of its subviews. As a result, you don't add the labels as subviews directly to the table view cell but rather to its contentView.

Two of these labels contain static text. The label nameMarker contains the text *Name:*, and the label colorMarker contains the text *Color:*. Those are just labels that you won't change. Both of these labels have right-aligned text using NSTextAlignment.right.

You'll use the other two labels to display your row-specific data. Remember that you need some way of retrieving these fields later, so you keep references to both of them in the properties that you declared earlier.

Since you've overridden a designated initializer of the table view cell class, Swift requires you to also provide an implementation of the init(coder:) initializer. This initializer will never be called in your example application, so just add these three lines of code:

```
required init?(coder aDecoder: NSCoder) {
    fatalError("init(coder:) has not been implemented")
}
```

In Chapter 13, I'll discuss this initializer and why it's sometimes needed.

Now let's put the finishing touches on the NameAndColorCell class by adding some setter logic to the name and color properties. Change the declarations of these properties as follows:

```
var name: String = "" {
    didSet {
        if (name != oldValue) {
            nameLabel.text = name
        }
    }
}
var color: String = "" {
        didSet {
            if (color != oldValue) {
                colorLabel.text = color
            }
        }
    }
```

All you're doing here is adding code to ensure that when the name or color property's value is changed, the text property of the corresponding label in the same custom table view cell is set to the same value.

Implementing the Controller's Code

Now, let's set up the simple controller to display values in your nice new cells. Start off by selecting ViewController.swift and add the code in Listing 8-7.

Listing 8-7. Displaying Values in Your Custom Cell

```
class ViewController: UIViewController, UITableViewDataSource {

    let cellTableIdentifier = "CellTableIdentifier"
    @IBOutlet var tableView:UITableView!
    let computers = [
        ["Name" : "MacBook Air", "Color" : "Silver"],
        ["Name" : "MacBook Pro", "Color" : "Silver"],
        ["Name" : "iMac", "Color" : "Silver"],
        ["Name" : "Mac Mini", "Color" : "Silver"],
        ["Name" : "Mac Pro", "Color" : "Black"]
    ]

    override func viewDidLoad() {
        super.viewDidLoad()
        // Do any additional setup after loading the view, typically from a nib.
        tableView.register(NameAndColorCell.self,
                            forCellReuseIdentifier: cellTableIdentifier)
    }
```

You conformed the view controller to the UITableViewDataSource protocol and added a cell identifier name and an array of dictionaries. Each dictionary contains the name and color information for one row in the table. The name for that row is held in the dictionary under the key Name, and the color is held under the key Color. You also added an outlet for the table view, so you need to connect it in the storyboard. Select the Main.storyboard file. In the Document Outline, Control-drag from the View Controller icon to the Table View icon. Release the mouse and select tableView in the pop-up to link the table view to the outlet.

Now add the code in Listing 8-8 to the end of the ViewController.swift file.

Listing 8-8. Your Table View's Data Source Methods

```
// MARK: -
// MARK: Table View Data Source Methods

func tableView(_ tableView: UITableView, numberOfRowsInSection section: Int) -> Int {
    return computers.count
}

func tableView(_ tableView: UITableView, cellForRowAt indexPath: IndexPath) -> UITableViewCell {
    let cell = tableView.dequeueReusableCell(
        withIdentifier: cellTableIdentifier, for: indexPath)
        as! NameAndColorCell

    let rowData = computers[indexPath.row]
    cell.name = rowData["Name"]!
    cell.color = rowData["Color"]!

    return cell
}
```

You have already seen these methods in your previous example—they belong to the UITableViewDataSource protocol. Let's focus on tableView(_ tableView: UITableView, cellForRowAt indexPath: IndexPath) since that's where you're really getting into some new stuff. Here you're using an interesting feature: a table view can use a sort of registry to create a new cell when needed. That means that as long as you've registered all the reuse identifiers that you're going to use for a table view, you can always get access to an available cell. In your previous example, the dequeue method you implemented also used the registry, but it returned nil if the identifier that you give it isn't registered. The nil return value is used as a signal that you need to create and populate a new UITableViewCell object. The following method that you're using never returns nil:

```
dequeueReusableCell(
            withIdentifier: cellTableIdentifier, for: indexPath)
```

So, how does it get a table cell object? It uses the identifier that you pass to it as the key to its registry. You added an entry to the registry that's mapped to your table cell identifier in the viewDidLoad method.

```
tableView.register(NameAndColorCell.self,
                    forCellReuseIdentifier: cellTableIdentifier)
```

What happens if you pass an identifier that's not registered? In that case, the dequeueReusableCell method crashes. Crashing sounds bad, but in this case, it would be the result of a bug that you would discover right away during development. Therefore, you don't need to include code that checks for a nil return value since that will never happen.

Once you have your new cell, you use the indexPath argument that was passed in to determine which row the table is requesting a cell for and then use that row value to grab the correct dictionary for the requested row. Remember that the dictionary has two key/value pairs: one with name and another with color.

```
let rowData = computers[indexPath.row]
```

Now, all that's left to do is populate the cell with data from the chosen row, using the properties you defined in your subclass.

```
cell.name = rowData["Name"]!
cell.color = rowData["Color"]!
```

As you saw earlier, setting these properties causes the value to be copied to the name and color labels in the table view cell.

Build and run your application. You should see a table of rows, each with two lines of data, as shown in Figure 8-19.

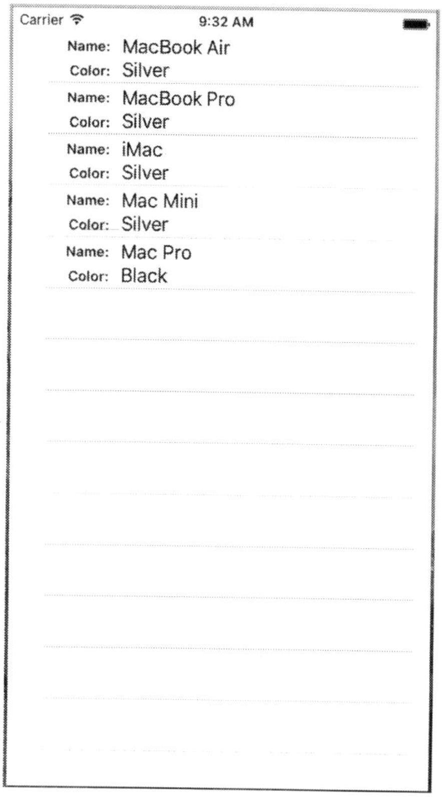

Figure 8-19. *The table view of custom cells created in code*

Being able to add views to a table view cell provides a lot more flexibility than using the standard table view cell alone, but it can get a little tedious creating, positioning, and adding all the subviews programmatically. Gosh, it sure would be nice if you could design the table view cell graphically by using Xcode's GUI editing tools. Well, you're in luck. As mentioned earlier, you can use Interface Builder to design your table view cells and then simply load the views from a storyboard or a XIB file when you create a new cell.

Loading a UITableViewCell from a XIB File

You're going to re-create that same two-line interface you just built in code using the visual layout capabilities that Xcode provides in Interface Builder. To do this, you'll create a new XIB file that will contain the table view cell and lay out its views using Interface Builder. Then, when you need a table view cell to represent a row, instead of creating a standard table view cell, you'll just load the XIB file and use the properties you already defined in your cell class to set the name and color. In addition to using Interface Builder's visual layout, you'll also simplify your code in a few other places. Before proceeding, you might want to make a copy of the Table Cells project in which you can make the changes that follow. As you did previously, exit Xcode and just compress the project file, giving it a suitable name for reference. I called mine Table Cells Orig.zip as a reference to it being the original Table Cells project (see Figure 8-20).

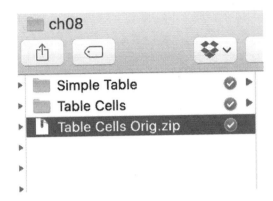

Figure 8-20. *You can compress a project folder to create a version baseline in case you decide to go back to it later*

First, you'll make a few changes to the NameAndColorCell class, in NameAndColorCell.swift. The first step is to mark up the nameLabel and colorLabel properties as outlets so you can use them in Interface Builder.

```
@IBOutlet var nameLabel: UILabel!
@IBOutlet var colorLabel: UILabel!
```

Now, remember that setup you did in init(style: UITableViewCellStyle, reuseIdentifier: String?), where you created your labels? All that can go. In fact, you should just delete the entire method since all that setup will now be done in Interface Builder. And since you are no longer overriding any of the base class initializers, you can delete the init(coder:) method too.

After all that, you're left with a cell class that's even smaller and cleaner than before. Its only real function now is to shuffle data to the labels. Now you need to re-create the cell and its labels in Interface Builder.

Designing the Table View Cell in Interface Builder

Right-click the Table Cells folder in Xcode and select New File from the contextual menu. In the left pane of the new file assistant, click User Interface (making sure to pick it in the iOS section, rather than the watchOS, tvOS, or macOS section). From the upper pane, select User Interface and Empty and then click Next (see Figure 8-21). On the following screen, use the file name NameAndColorCell.xib. Make sure that the main project directory is selected in the file browser and that the Table Cells group is selected in the Group pop-up. Click Create to create a new XIB file.

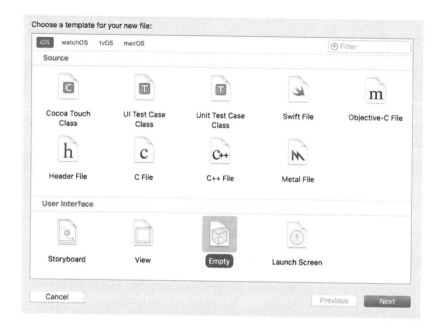

Figure 8-21. *Create an empty UI file that will become your custom cell XIB*

Next, select NameAndColorCell.xib in the Project Navigator to open the file for editing. Until now, you've been doing all of your GUI editing inside of storyboards, but now you're using a nib file instead. Most things are similar and will look very familiar to you, but there are a few differences. One of the main differences is that, while a storyboard file is centered around scenes that pair up a view controller and a view, inside a nib file there's no such forced pairing. In fact, a nib file often doesn't contain a real controller object at all, just a proxy that is called File's Owner. If you open the Document Outline, you'll see it there, right above First Responder.

Look in the library for a table view cell and drag one to the GUI layout area, as shown in Figure 8-22.

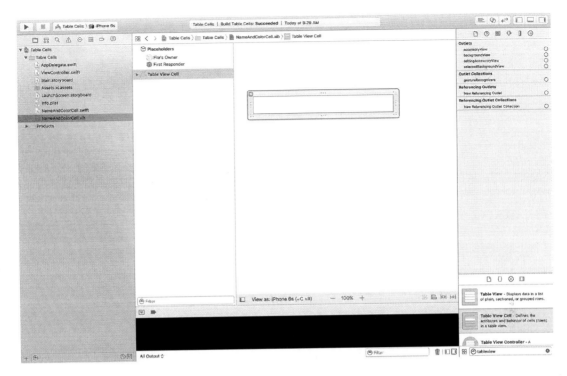

Figure 8-22. *Drag a table view cell from the library onto the canvas*

Next, press ⌥⌘4 to go to the Attributes Inspector (see Figure 8-23). One of the first fields you'll see there is Identifier. That's the reuse identifier you've been using in your code. If this does not ring a bell, scan back through the chapter and look for `CellTableIdentifier`. Set the Identifier value to CellTableIdentifier.

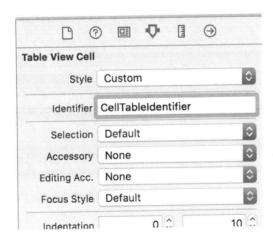

Figure 8-23. *The Attributes Inspector for your table view cell*

The idea here is that when you retrieve a cell for reuse, perhaps because of scrolling a new cell into view, you want to make sure you get the correct cell type. When this particular cell is instantiated from the XIB file, its reuse identifier instance variable will be prepopulated with the name you entered in the Identifier field of the Attributes Inspector—CellTableIdentifier, in this case.

Imagine a scenario where you created a table with a header and then a series of "middle" cells. If you scroll a middle cell into view, it's important that you retrieve a middle cell to reuse and not a header cell. The Identifier field lets you tag the cells appropriately.

The next step is to edit your table cell's content view. First, select the table cell in the editing area and drag down its lower edge to make the cell a little taller. Keep dragging until the height is 65. Go to the library, drag out four labels, and place them in the content view, using Figure 8-24 as a guide. The labels will be too close to the top and bottom for those guidelines to be of much help, but the left guideline and the alignment guidelines should serve their purpose. Note that you can drag out one label and then Option-drag to create copies, if that approach makes things easier for you.

Figure 8-24. *The table view cell's content view, with four labels dragged in*

Next, double-click the upper-left label and change its title to **Name:** and then change the lower-left label to **Color:**.

Now, select both the Name and Color labels and press the small T button in the Attribute Inspector's Font field. This will open a small panel containing a Font pop-up button. Click that and choose Headline as the typeface. If needed, select the two unchanged label fields on the right and drag them a little more to the right to give the design a bit of breathing room; then resize the other two labels so that you can see the text you just set. Next, resize the two right-side labels so that they stretch all the way to the right guideline. Figure 8-25 should give you a sense of your final cell content view.

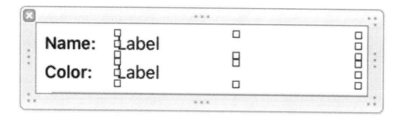

Figure 8-25. *The table view cell's content view with the left label names changed and set to Headline style, which is bold, and with the right labels slightly moved and resized*

As always when you create a new layout, you need to add Auto Layout constraints. The general idea is to pin the left-side labels to the left side of the cell and the right-side labels to its right. You'll also make sure that the vertical separation between the labels and the top and bottom of the cell and between the labels is preserved. You'll link each left-side label to the one on its right. Here are the steps:

1. Click the Name label, hold down Shift, and then click the Color label. Click the Pin icon below the nib editor, select the Equal Widths check box, and click Add 1 Constraint. You'll see some Auto Layout warnings appear when you do this—don't worry about them because you'll fix them as you add more constraints.

2. With the two labels still selected, open the Size Inspector and find the Content Hugging Priority section. If you don't see it, try deselecting and reselecting both labels. The values in these fields determine how resistant the labels are to expanding into extra space. You don't want these labels to expand at all horizontally, so change the value in the Horizontal field from 251 to 500. Any value greater than 251 will do—you just need it to be greater than the Content Hugging Priority value of the two labels on the right so that any extra horizontal space is allocated to them.

3. Control-drag from the Color label up to the Name label, select Vertical Spacing from the pop-up, and press Return.

4. Control-drag diagonally up and left from the Name label toward the top-left corner of the cell until the cell's background turns completely blue. In the pop-up, hold down Shift, select Leading Space to Container Margin and Top Space to Container Margin, and then press Return.

5. Control-drag diagonally down and left from the Color label toward the bottom-left corner of the cell until its background is blue. In the pop-up, hold down Shift, select Leading Space to Container Margin and Bottom Space to Container Margin, and then press Return.

6. Control-drag from the Name label to the label to its right. In the pop-up, hold down Shift, select Horizontal Spacing and Baseline, and then press Return. Control-drag from the top label on the right toward the right edge of the cell until the cell's background turns blue. In the pop-up, select Trailing Space to Container Margin.

7. Similarly, Control-drag from the Color label to the label to its right. In the pop-up, hold down Shift, select Horizontal Spacing and Baseline, and then press Return. Control-drag from the bottom label on the right toward the right edge of the cell until the cell's background turns blue. In the pop-up, select Trailing Space to Container Margin and press Return.

8. Finally, select the Content View icon in the Document Outline and then choose Editor ➤ Resolve Auto Layout Issues ➤ Update Frames from the menu, if it's enabled. The four labels should move to their final locations, as shown in Figure 8-26. If you see something different, delete all the constraints in the Document Outline and try again.

Figure 8-26. *Final label positioning within your custom cell*

Now, you need to let Interface Builder know that this table view cell isn't just a normal cell but an instance of your special subclass. Otherwise, you wouldn't be able to connect your outlets to the relevant labels. Select the table view cell by clicking CellTableIdentifier in the Document Outline, bring up the Identity Inspector by pressing ⌥⌘3, and choose NameAndColorCell from the Class control (see Figure 8-27).

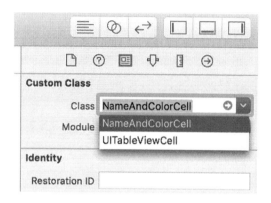

Figure 8-27. *Setting to your custom class*

Next, switch to the Connections Inspector (⌥⌘6), where you'll see the colorLabel and nameLabel outlets (see Figure 8-28).

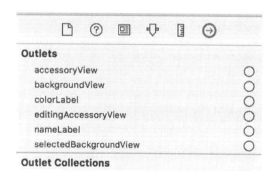

Figure 8-28. *The colorLabel and nameLabel outlets*

Drag from the nameLabel outlet to the top label on the right in the table cell and from the colorLabel outlet to the bottom label on the right, as shown in Figure 8-29.

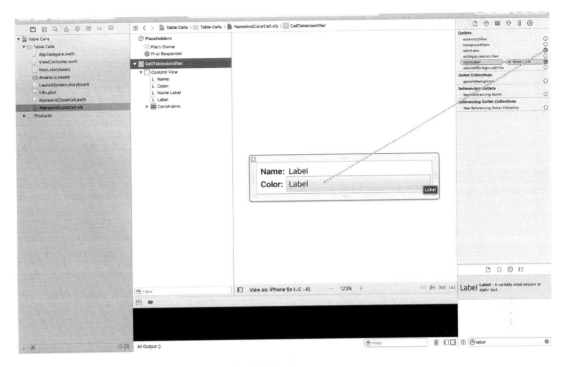

Figure 8-29. *Connecting your name and color label outlets*

Using the New Table View Cell

To use the cell you designed, you just need to make a few pretty simple changes to the `viewDidLoad()` method in `ViewController.swift`, as shown in Listing 8-9.

Listing 8-9. Modifying viewDidLoad() to Use Your New Cell

```
override func viewDidLoad() {
    super.viewDidLoad()
    // Do any additional setup after loading the view, typically from a nib.
    tableView.register(NameAndColorCell.self,
                        forCellReuseIdentifier: cellTableIdentifier)
let xib = UINib(nibName: "NameAndColorCell", bundle: nil)
    tableView.register(xib,
                        forCellReuseIdentifier: cellTableIdentifier)
    tableView.rowHeight = 65
}
```

Just as it can associate a class with a reuse identifier (as you saw in the previous example), a table view can keep track of which nib files are meant to be associated with particular reuse identifiers. This allows you to register cells for each row type you have using classes or nib files once, and `dequeueReusableCell` `(_:forIndexPath:)` will always provide a cell ready for use.

That's it. Build and run. Now your two-line table cells are based on your Interface Builder design skills, as shown in Figure 8-30.

Figure 8-30. *The results of using your custom cell*

Using Grouped and Indexed Sections

The next project will explore another fundamental aspect of tables. You're still going to use a single table view—no hierarchies yet—but you'll divide data into sections. Create a new Xcode project using the Single View App template again, this time calling it **Sections**. As usual, set Language to Swift and Devices to Universal.

Building the View

Open the Sections folder and click Main.storyboard to edit the file. Drop a table view onto the View window, as you did before, and add the same Auto Layout constraints that you used in the Table Cell example. Press ⌥⌘6 and connect the dataSource connection to the View Controller icon.

Next, make sure the table view is selected and press ⌥⌘4 to bring up the Attributes Inspector. Change the table view's style from Plain to Grouped, as shown in Figure 8-31. Save the storyboard.

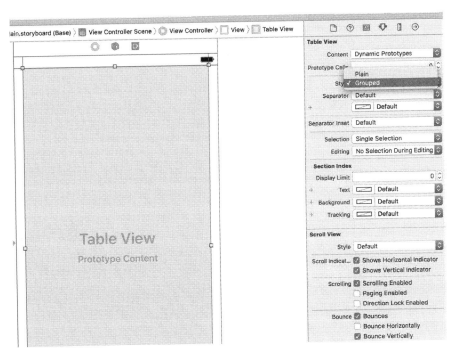

Figure 8-31. *The Attributes Inspector for the table view, showing the Style pop-up with Grouped selected*

Importing the Data

This project needs a fair amount of data. To save you a few hours of typing, I've provided another property list for your tabling pleasure. Grab the file named `sortednames.plist` from the `Sections Data` subfolder in this book's example source code archive and drag it into your project's Sections folder in Xcode.

Once `sortednames.plist` is added to your project, single-click it just to get a sense of what it looks like, as shown in Figure 8-32. It's a property list that contains a dictionary, with one entry for each letter of the alphabet. Underneath each letter is a list of names that start with that letter.

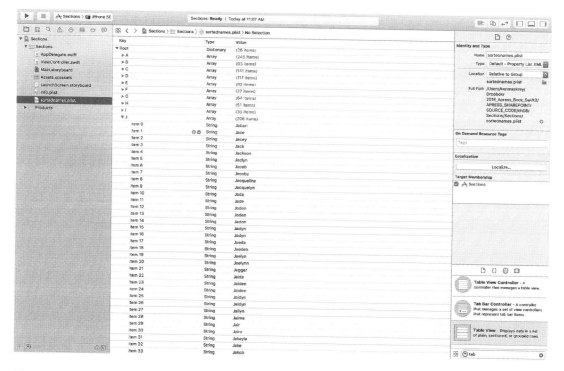

Figure 8-32. *The sortednames.plist property list file. The letter J is open to give you a sense of one of the dictionaries*

You'll use the data from this property list to feed the table view, creating a section for each letter.

Implementing the Controller

Single-click the ViewController.swift file. Make the class conform to the UITableViewDataSource protocol, add a table cell identifier name, and create a couple of properties by adding the following code in bold:

```
class ViewController: UIViewController, UITableViewDataSource {
    let sectionsTableIdentifier = "SectionsTableIndentifier"
    var names: [String: [String]]!
    var keys: [String]!
```

Select the Main.storyboard file again and then bring up the Assistant Editor. If it's not shown, use the jump bar to select the ViewController.swift file. Control-drag from the table view to the Assistant Editor to create an outlet for the table just below the definition of the keys property.

```
@IBOutlet weak var tableView: UITableView!
```

Now modify the viewDidLoad() method, as shown in Listing 8-10.

Listing 8-10. Your New viewDidLoad Method

```swift
override func viewDidLoad() {
    super.viewDidLoad()
    // Do any additional setup after loading the view, typically from a nib.
    tableView.register(UITableViewCell.self,
                            forCellReuseIdentifier: sectionsTableIdentifier)

    let path = Bundle.main.path(forResource:
        "sortednames", ofType: "plist")
    let namesDict = NSDictionary(contentsOfFile: path!)
    names = namesDict as! [String: [String]]
    keys = (namesDict!.allKeys as! [String]).sorted()
}
```

Most of this isn't too different from what you've seen before. Earlier, you added property declarations for both a dictionary and an array. The dictionary will hold all of your data, while the array will hold the sections sorted in alphabetical order. In the viewDidLoad() method, you first registered the default table view cell class that should be displayed for each row, using your declared identifier. After that, you created an NSDictionary instance from the property list you added to your project and assigned it to the names property, casting it to the appropriate Swift dictionary type as you did so. Next, you grabbed all the keys from the dictionary and sorted them to give you an ordered array with all the key values in the dictionary in alphabetical order. Remember that your data uses the letters of the alphabet as its keys, so this array will have 26 letters sorted from *A* to *Z*. You'll use the array to help you keep track of the sections.

Next, add the code in Listing 8-11 to the end of the ViewController.swift file.

Listing 8-11. Your Table View's Data Source Methods

```swift
// MARK: Table View Data Source Methods
func numberOfSections(in tableView: UITableView) -> Int {
    return keys.count
}

func tableView(_ tableView: UITableView, numberOfRowsInSection section: Int) -> Int {
    let key = keys[section]
    let nameSection = names[key]!
    return nameSection.count
}

func tableView(_ tableView: UITableView, titleForHeaderInSection section: Int) -> String? {
    return keys[section]
}

func tableView(_ tableView: UITableView, cellForRowAt indexPath: IndexPath) ->
UITableViewCell {
    let cell = tableView.dequeueReusableCell(withIdentifier: sectionsTableIdentifier,
        for: indexPath)
        as UITableViewCell
    let key = keys[indexPath.section]
    let nameSection = names[key]!
    cell.textLabel?.text = nameSection[indexPath.row]

    return cell
}
```

These are all table data source methods. The first one you added to your class specifies the number of sections. You didn't implement this method in the earlier examples because you were happy with the default setting of 1. This time, you're telling the table view that you have one section for each key in your dictionary.

```
func numberOfSectionsInTableView(tableView: UITableView) -> Int {
    return keys.count
}
```

The next method calculates the number of rows in a specific section. In the previous example, you had only one section, so you just returned the number of rows in your array. This time, you need to break it down by section. You can do this by retrieving the array that corresponds to the section in question and returning the count from that array.

```
func tableView(_ tableView: UITableView, numberOfRowsInSection section: Int) -> Int {
    let key = keys[section]
    let nameSection = names[key]!
    return nameSection.count
}
```

The method `tableView(_:titleForHeaderInSection:)` allows you to specify an optional header value for each section. You simply return the letter for this group, which is the group's key.

```
func tableView(_ tableView: UITableView, titleForHeaderInSection section: Int) -> String? {
    return keys[section]
}
```

In your `tableView(_:cellForRowAtIndexPath:)` method, you need to extract both the section key and the names array using the section and row properties from the index path and then use those to determine which value to use. The section number will tell you which array to pull out of the names dictionary, and then you can use the row to figure out which value from that array to use. Everything else in that method is basically the same as the version in the Table Cells application you built earlier in the chapter.

Build and run the project remembering that you changed the table's Style to Grouped, so you ended up with a grouped table with 26 sections, which should look like Figure 8-33.

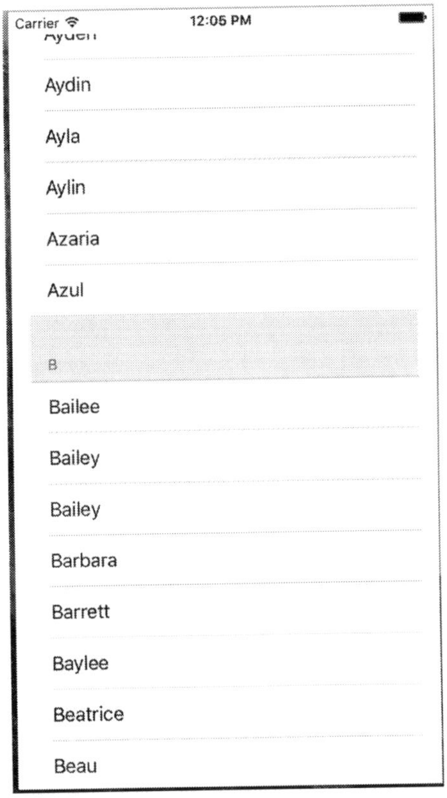

Figure 8-33. *A grouped table with multiple sections*

As a contrast, let's change your table view back to the plain style and see what a plain table view with multiple sections looks like. Select Main.storyboard to edit the file in Interface Builder again. Select the table view and use the Attributes Inspector to switch the view to Plain. Save the project and then build and run it—same data but a different look, as shown in Figure 8-34.

Figure 8-34. *A plain table with sections*

Adding an Index

One problem with your current table is the sheer number of rows. There are 2,000 names in this list. Your finger will get awfully tired looking for Zachariah or Zayne, not to mention Zoie.

One solution to this problem is to add an index down the right side of the table view. Now that you've set your table view style back to Plain, that's relatively easy to do, as shown in Figure 8-35. Add the following method to the bottom of `ViewController.swift` and then build and run the app:

```swift
func sectionIndexTitles(for tableView: UITableView) -> [String]? {
    return keys
}
```

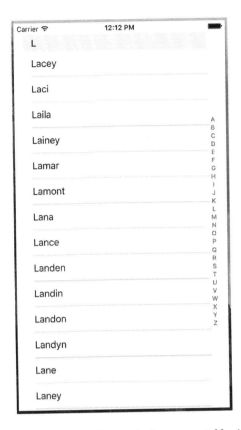

Figure 8-35. *Adding an index to your table view*

Adding a Search Bar

The index is helpful, but even so, you still have a whole lot of names here. If you want to see whether the name Arabella is in the list, for example, you'll need to scroll for a while even after using the index. It would be nice if you could let the user pare down the list by specifying a search term, making it more user-friendly. Well, it's a bit of extra work, but it's not that much. You're going to implement a standard iOS search bar using a search controller, like the one shown on the left in Figure 8-36.

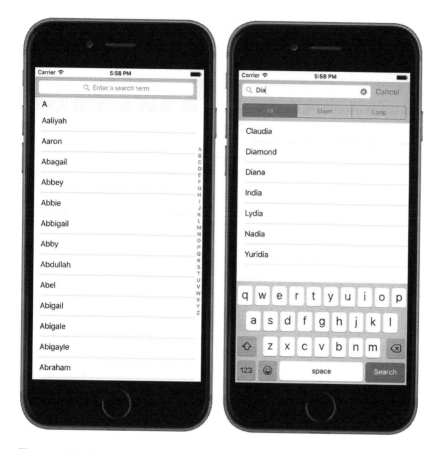

Figure 8-36. *The application with a search bar added to the table*

As the user types into the search bar, the list of names reduces to only those that contain the entered text as a substring. As a bonus, the search bar also allows you to define scope buttons that you can use to qualify the search in some way. You'll add three scope buttons to your search bar—the Short button will limit the search to names that are less than six characters long, the Long button will consider only those names that have at least six characters, and the All button will include all names in the search. The scope buttons appear only when the user is typing into the search bar; you can see them in action on the right of Figure 8-36.

Adding search functionality is quite easy. You need only three things.

- Some data to be searched. In your case, that's the list of names.

- A view controller to display the search results. This view controller temporarily replaces the one that's providing the data. It can choose to display the results in any way, but usually the source data is presented in a table and the results view controller will use another table that looks very similar to it, thus creating the impression that the search is simply filtering the original table. As you'll see, though, that's not actually what's happening.

- A UISearchController that provides the search bar and manages the display of the search results in the results view controller.

Let's start by creating the skeleton of the results view controller. You are going to display your search results in a table, so your results view controller needs to contain a table. You could drag a view controller onto the storyboard and add a table view to it as you have done in the earlier examples in the chapter, but let's do something different this time. You're going to use a `UITableViewController`, which is a view controller with an embedded `UITableView` that is preconfigured as both the data source and the delegate for its table view. In the Project Navigator, right-click the Sections group and select New File from the pop-up menu. In the file template chooser, select Cocoa Touch Class from the iOS Source group and click Next. Name your new class `SearchResultsController` and make it a subclass of `UITableViewController`. Click Next, choose the location for the new file, and let Xcode create it.

Select `SearchResultsController.swift` in the Project Navigator and make the following change to it:

```
class SearchResultsController: UITableViewController,
            UISearchResultsUpdating {
```

You're going to implement the search logic in this view controller, so you conformed it to the `UISearchResultsUpdating` protocol, which allows you to assign it as a delegate of the `UISearchController` class. As you'll see later, the single method defined by this protocol is called to update the search results as the user types into the search bar.

Since it's going to implement the search operation for you, `SearchResultsController` needs access to the list of names that the main view controller is displaying, so you'll need to give it properties that you can use to pass to it the names dictionary and the list of keys that you're using for display in the main view controller. Let's add these properties to `SearchResultsController.swift` now. You've probably noticed that this file already contains some incomplete code that provides a partial implementation of the `UITableViewDataSource` protocol and some commented-out code blocks for other methods that `UITableViewController` subclasses frequently need to implement. You're not going to use these in this example, so delete all of the commented-out code and the two `UITableViewDataSource` methods and then add the following code at the top of the file:

```
class SearchResultsController: UITableViewController, UISearchResultsUpdating  {
    let sectionsTableIdentifier = "SectionsTableIdentifier"
    var names:[String: [String]] = [String: [String]]()
    var keys: [String] = []
    var filteredNames: [String] = []
```

You added the `sectionsTableIdentifier` variable to hold the identifier for the table cells in this view controller. You're using the same identifier as you did in the main view controller, although you could have used any name at all. You also added the two properties that will hold the names dictionary and the list of keys that you'll use when searching and another that will keep a reference to an array that will hold the search results.

Next, add a line of code to the `viewDidLoad()` method to register your table cell identifier with the results controller's embedded table view.

```
override func viewDidLoad() {
    super.viewDidLoad()
    tableView.register(UITableViewCell.self,
                    forCellReuseIdentifier: sectionsTableIdentifier)
}
```

That's all you need to do in the results view controller for now, so let's switch back to your main view controller for a while and add the search bar to it. Select ViewController.swift in the Project Navigator and add a property to hold a reference to the UISearchController instance that will do most of the hard work for you in this example at the top of the file.

```swift
class ViewController: UIViewController, UITableViewDataSource  {
    let sectionsTableIdentifier = "SectionsTableIndentifier"
    var names: [String: [String]]!
    var keys: [String]!
    @IBOutlet weak var tableView: UITableView!
    var searchController: UISearchController!   // ← add this line
```

Next, modify the viewDidLoad() method to add the search controller, as shown in Listing 8-12.

Listing 8-12. Adding the Search Controller to Your Main viewDidLoad method in ViewController.swift

```swift
override func viewDidLoad() {
    super.viewDidLoad()
    // Do any additional setup after loading the view, typically from a nib.
    tableView.register(UITableViewCell.self,
                            forCellReuseIdentifier: sectionsTableIdentifier)

    let path = Bundle.main.pathForResource(
        "sortednames", ofType: "plist")
    let namesDict = NSDictionary(contentsOfFile: path!)
    names = namesDict as! [String: [String]]
    keys = (namesDict!.allKeys as! [String]).sorted()

    let resultsController = SearchResultsController()
    resultsController.names = names
    resultsController.keys = keys
    searchController =
        UISearchController(searchResultsController: resultsController)

    let searchBar = searchController.searchBar
    searchBar.scopeButtonTitles = ["All", "Short", "Long"]
    searchBar.placeholder = "Enter a search term"
    searchBar.sizeToFit()
    tableView.tableHeaderView = searchBar
    searchController.searchResultsUpdater = resultsController
}
```

You start by creating the results controller and set its names and keys properties. Then, you create the UISearchController, passing it a reference to your results controller—UISearchController presents this view controller when it has search results to display:

```swift
let resultsController = SearchResultsController()
resultsController.names = names
resultsController.keys = keys
searchController =
  UISearchController(searchResultsController: resultsController)
```

The next three lines of code get and configure the `UISearchBar`, which is created by the `UISearchController` and which you can get from its `searchBar` property.

```
let searchBar = searchController.searchBar
searchBar.scopeButtonTitles = ["All", "Short", "Long"]
searchBar.placeholder = "Enter a search term"
```

The search bar's `scopeButtonTitles` property contains the names to be assigned to its scope buttons. By default, there are no scope buttons, but here you install the names of the three buttons discussed earlier in this section. You also set some placeholder text to let the user know what the search bar is for. You can see the placeholder text on the left in Figure 8-36.

So far, you have created the `UISearchController` but you haven't connected it to your user interface. To do that, you get the search bar and install it as the header view of the table in your main view controller.

```
searchBar.sizeToFit()
tableView.tableHeaderView = searchBar
```

The table's header view is managed automatically by the table view. It always appears before the first row of the first table section. Notice that you use the `sizeToFit()` method to give the search bar the size that's appropriate for its content. You do this so that it is given the correct height—the width that's set by this method is not important because the table view will make sure that it stretches the whole width of the table and will resize it automatically if the table changes size (typically because the device has been rotated).

The final change to `viewDidLoad` assigns a value to the `UISearchController`'s `searchResultsUpdater` property, which is of type `UISearchResultsUpdating`.

```
searchController.searchResultsUpdater = resultsController
```

Each time the user types something into the search bar, `UISearchController` uses the object stored in its `searchResultsUpdater` property to update the search results. As mentioned, you are going to handle the search in the `SearchResultsController` class, which is why you needed to make it conform to the `UISearchResultsUpdating` protocol.

That's all you need to do to in your main view controller to add the search bar and have the search results displayed. Next, you need to return to `SearchResultsController.swift`, where you have two tasks to complete—add the code that implements the search and the `UITableDataSource` methods for the embedded table view.

Let's start with the code for the search. As the user types into the search bar, the `UISearchController` calls the `updateSearchResultsForSearchController()` method of its search results updater, which is your `SearchResultsController`. In this method, you need to get the search text from the search bar and use it to construct a filtered list of names in the `filteredNames` array. You'll also use the scope buttons to limit the names that you include in the search. Add the following constant definitions at the top of `SearchResultsController.swift`:

```
class SearchResultsController: UITableViewController, UISearchResultsUpdating {
    private static let longNameSize = 6
    private static let shortNamesButtonIndex = 1
    private static let longNamesButtonIndex = 2
```

Now add code in Listing 8-13 to the end of the file.

Listing 8-13. Your Search Results Code

```
// MARK: UISearchResultsUpdating Conformance
func updateSearchResults(for searchController: UISearchController) {
        if let searchString = searchController.searchBar.text {
            let buttonIndex = searchController.searchBar.selectedScopeButtonIndex
            filteredNames.removeAll(keepingCapacity: true)

            if !searchString.isEmpty {
                let filter: (String) -> Bool = { name in
                    // Filter out long or short names depending on which
                    // scope button is selected.
                    let nameLength = name.characters.count
                    if (buttonIndex == SearchResultsController.shortNamesButtonIndex
                        && nameLength >= SearchResultsController.longNameSize)
                        || (buttonIndex == SearchResultsController.longNamesButtonIndex
                            && nameLength < SearchResultsController.longNameSize) {
                        return false
                    }

                    let range = name.range(of: searchString, options: NSString.
                    CompareOptions.caseInsensitive, range: nil, locale: nil)
                    //              let range = name.rangeOfString(searchString,
                    //                                        options: NSString.
                                                              CompareOptions.
                                                              CaseInsensitiveSearch)
                    return range != nil
                }

                for key in keys {
                    let namesForKey = names[key]!
                    let matches = namesForKey.filter(filter)
                    filteredNames += matches
                }
            }
        }
        tableView.reloadData()
}
```

Let's walk through this code to see what it's doing. First, you get the search string from the search bar and the index of the scope button that's selected, and then you clear the list of filtered names. You search only if the text control returns a string; theoretically, it is possible for the text to be nil, so you bracket the rest of the code in an if let construction.

```
if let searchString = searchController.searchBar.text {
    let buttonIndex = searchController.searchBar.selectedScopeButtonIndex
    filteredNames.removeAll(keepingCapacity: true)
```

Next, you check that the search string is not empty—you do not display any matching results for an empty search string.

```
if !searchString.isEmpty {
```

Now you define a closure for matching names against the search string. The closure will be called for each name in the names directory and will be given a name (as a string) and return true if the value matches and false if there's no match. You first check that the length of the name is consistent with the selected scope button and return false if it isn't.

```
let filter: (String) -> Bool = { name in
    // Filter out long or short names depending on which
    // scope button is selected.
    let nameLength = name.characters.count
    if (buttonIndex == SearchResultsController.shortNamesButtonIndex
        && nameLength >= SearchResultsController.longNameSize)
        || (buttonIndex == SearchResultsController.longNamesButtonIndex
            && nameLength < SearchResultsController.longNameSize) {
        return false
    }
```

If the name passes this test, you look for the search string as a substring of the name. If you find it, then you have a match.

```
let range = name.range(of: searchString, options:
NSString.CompareOptions.caseInsensitive,
        range: nil, locale: nil)
        return range != nil
}
```

That's all the code that you need in the closure to handle the name search. Next, you iterate over all the keys in the names dictionary, each of which corresponds to an array of names (key A maps to the names that start with the letter A, and so on). For each key, you get its array of names and filter it using your closure. This gets you a (possibly empty) filtered array of the names that match, which you add to the filteredNames array.

```
for key in keys {
    let namesForKey = names[key]!
    let matches = namesForKey.filter(filter)
    filteredNames += matches
}
```

In this code, namesForKey is of type [String] and contains the names that correspond to whichever key value you are processing. You use the filter() method of Array to apply your closure to each of the elements in namesToKey. The result is another array containing only the elements that match the filter—that is, only the names should match the search text and the selected scope button, which you then add to filteredNames.

Once all the name arrays have been processed, you have the complete set of matching names in the filteredNames array. Now all you need to do is arrange for them to be displayed in the table in your SearchResultsController. You start by telling the table that it needs to redisplay its content.

```
    }
    tableView.reloadData()
}
```

You need the table view to display one name from the filteredNames array in each row. To do that, you implement the methods of the UITableViewDataSource protocol in your SearchResultsController class. Recall that SearchResultsController is a subclass of UITableViewController, so it automatically acts as its table's data source. Add the code in Listing 8-14 to SearchResultsController.swift, above the updateSearchResults method.

Listing 8-14. Your Table View Data Source Methods

```swift
// MARK: Table View Data Source Methods
override func tableView(_ tableView: UITableView, numberOfRowsInSection section: Int) -> Int {
    return filteredNames.count
}

override func tableView(_ tableView: UITableView, cellForRowAt indexPath: IndexPath) ->
UITableViewCell {
    let cell = tableView.dequeueReusableCell(withIdentifier: sectionsTableIdentifier)
    cell!.textLabel?.text = filteredNames[indexPath.row]
    return cell!
}
```

You can now run the app and try filtering the list of names, as shown in Figure 8-37.

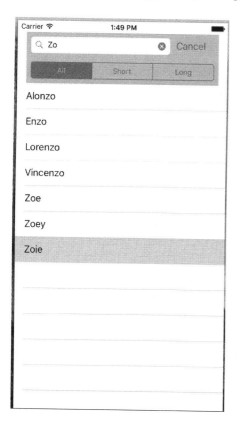

Figure 8-37. *The application with a search bar added to the table*

Using View Debugging

The UISearchController class does a good job of switching between the two tables in your last example—so good that you might find it hard to believe that there is a switch going on at all. Apart from the fact that you've seen all the code, there are also a couple of visual clues—the search table is a plain table, so you don't see the names grouped like they are in the main table. It also has no section index. If you want even more proof, you can get it by using a neat feature of Xcode called View Debugging, which lets you take snapshots of the view hierarchy of a running application and examine them in the Xcode editor area. This feature works on both the simulator and real devices. You'll probably find it invaluable at some point or another when you're trying to find out why one of your views appears to be missing or is not where you expect it to be.

Let's start by looking at what View Debugging makes of your application when it's showing the full name list. Run the application again and in the Xcode menu bar, select Debug ➤ View Debugging ➤ Capture View Hierarchy. Xcode grabs the view hierarchy from the simulator or device and displays it, as shown in Figure 8-38.

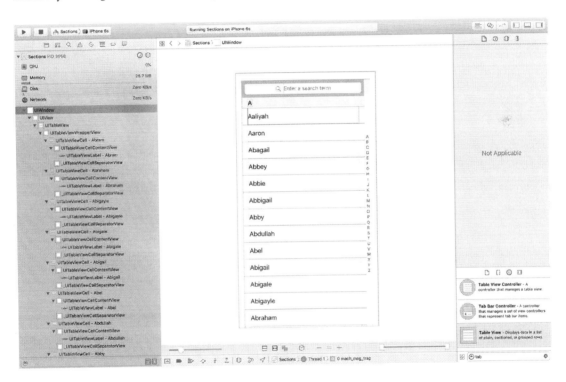

Figure 8-38. *The view hierarchy of the Sections application*

That probably doesn't look very useful—you can't really see anything more than you could in the simulator. To reveal the view hierarchy, you need to rotate the image of the application so that you can look at it "from the side." To do so, click the mouse in the editor area, somewhere just to the left of the captured image, and drag it to the right. As you do so, the layering of views in the application will reveal itself. If you rotate through about 45 degrees, you'll see something like Figure 8-39.

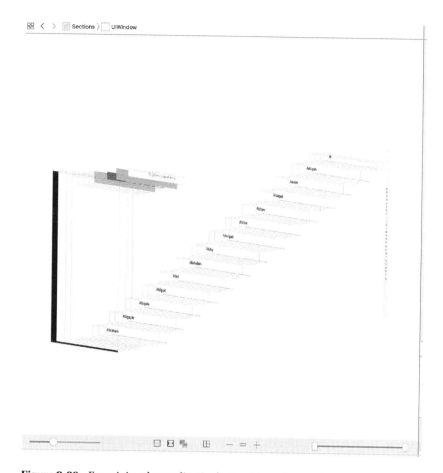

Figure 8-39. Examining the application's view hierarchy

If you click the various views in the stack, you'll see that the jump bar at the top changes to show you the class name of the view that you've clicked and those of all of its ancestor views. Click each of the views from the back to the front to get familiar with how the table is constructed. You should be able to find the view controller's main view, the table view itself, some table view cells, the search bar, the search bar index, and various other views that are part of the table's implementation.

Now let's see what the view hierarchy looks like while you are searching. Xcode pauses your application to let you examine the view snapshot, so first resume execution by clicking Debug ➤ Continue. Now start typing into the application's search bar and capture the view hierarchy again using Debug ➤ View Debugging ➤ Capture View Hierarchy. When the view hierarchy appears, rotate it a little and you'll see something like what's shown in Figure 8-40.

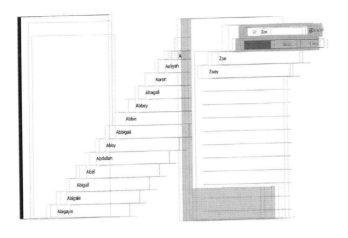

Figure 8-40. Your view hierarchy when searching for Zoe

Now it's pretty clear that there are indeed two tables in use. You can see the original table near the bottom of the view stack, and above (i.e., to the right of) it, you can see the table view that belongs to the search results view controller. Just behind that, there's a translucent gray view that covers the original table—that's the view that dims the original table when you first start typing in the search bar.

Experiment a little with the buttons at the bottom of the editor area—you can use them to turn on and off the display of Auto Layout constraints, reset the view to the top-down view shown earlier, and zoom in and zoom out. You can also use the slider on the left to change the spacing between views, and you can use the one on the right to remove layers at the top or bottom of the hierarchy so that you can see what's behind them. View Debugging is a powerful tool.

Summary

This was a pretty hefty chapter, and you've learned a great deal. You should have a solid understanding of the way that flat tables work. You should know how to customize tables and table view cells, as well as how to configure table views. You also saw how to implement a search bar, which is a vital tool in any iOS application that presents large volumes of data. Finally, you met View Debugging, an extremely useful feature of Xcode. Make sure you understand everything you did in this chapter because you're going to build on it.

You're going to continue working with table views in the next chapter. For example, you'll learn how to use them to present hierarchical data. And you'll see how to create content views that allow the user to edit data selected in a table view, as well as how to present checklists in tables, embed controls in table rows, and delete rows.

■ ■ ■

CHAPTER 9

Adding Navigation Controllers to Table Views

In the previous chapter, you worked through the basics of using table views. In this chapter, you'll go further by adding *navigation controllers*.

Table views and navigation controllers work together, but strictly speaking, a navigation controller doesn't need a table view to function. As a practical matter, however, when using a navigation controller, you normally include at least one or more tables because the strength of the navigation controller lies in the ease with which it handles complex hierarchical data. On the iPhone's small screen, hierarchical data is best presented using a succession of table views.

In this chapter, you'll build an application step by step, just as you did with the Pickers application in Chapter 7. When you have the basic navigation controller and the root view controller working, you'll start adding more controllers and layers to the hierarchy. Each view controller you create reinforces some aspect of table use or configuration.

- How to drill down from table views into child table views

- How to drill down from table views into content views, where detailed data can be viewed and even edited

- How to use multiple sections within a table view

- How to use edit mode to allow rows to be deleted from a table view

- How to use edit mode to let the user reorder rows within a table view

Understanding Navigation Controller Basics

The main tool you'll use to build hierarchical applications, the UINavigationController, functions similarly to the UITabBarController in that it manages, and swaps in and out, multiple content views. The main difference between the two is that the child view controllers of a UINavigationController are organized in a stack, which makes it well suited to working with hierarchies.

If you're a software developer and understand stacks, you may want to skip over the next section or just scan it. But if you're new to stacks, continue reading. Fortunately, stacks are a pretty easy concept to grasp.

© Molly K. Maskrey 2017
M. K. Maskrey, *Beginning iPhone Development with Swift 4*, https://doi.org/10.1007/978-1-4842-3072-5_9

Using Stacks

The stack, a commonly used data structure, functions using the principle of "last in, first out." A common Pez dispenser (see Figure 9-1) provides a great example of a stack. Ever try to load one? According to the little instruction sheet that comes with each and every Pez dispenser, there are a few easy steps. First, unwrap the pack of Pez candy. Second, open the dispenser by tipping its head straight back. Third, grab the stack of candy, holding it firmly between your pointer finger and thumb, and insert the column into the open dispenser.

Figure 9-1. *A Pez dispenser represents a simple implementation of a stack*

Remember that I said a stack was last in, first out? That also means first in, last out. The first piece of candy you push into the dispenser will be the last piece that pops out. The last piece of candy you push in becomes the first piece you pop out. A computer stack follows the same rules:

- When you add an object to a stack, it's called a *push*. You push an object onto the stack.

- The first object you push onto the stack is called the *base* of the stack.

- The object you most recently pushed onto the stack is called the top of the stack (at least until it is replaced by the next object you push onto the stack).

- When you remove an object from the stack, it's called a *pop*. When you pop an object off the stack, it's always the last one you pushed onto the stack. Conversely, the first object you push onto the stack will always be the last one you pop off the stack.

Using a Stack of Controllers

Navigation controllers maintain a stack of view controllers, and when you design your controller, you must specify the very first view the user sees. As discussed previously, you call that view's controller the *root view controller*, or just *root controller*, which becomes the base of the navigation controller's stack. As the user selects a new view to display, another controller gets pushed onto the stack, and its view appears. You refer to these new view controllers as *subcontrollers*. In this chapter's application, Fonts, you'll include a navigation controller and several subcontrollers.

In Figure 9-2, notice the title centered in the navigation bar and the back button on the left side of the navigation bar. The title of the navigation bar gets populated with the title property of the top view controller in the navigation controller's stack, and the title of the back button displays the name of the previous view controller. The back button acts similarly to a web browser's back button. When the user taps that button, the current view controller gets popped off the stack, and the previous view becomes the current view.

Back Button  Title

Figure 9-2. *The Settings application uses a navigation controller. The back button at the upper left pops the current view controller off the stack, returning you to the previous level of the hierarchy. The title of the current content view controller is also displayed*

This design pattern allows you to build complex hierarchical applications iteratively so you don't need to know the entire structure to get everything up and running. Each controller only needs to know about its child controllers, so it can push the appropriate new controller object onto the stack when the user makes a selection. You can build up a large application from many small pieces this way, which you'll be doing in this chapter.

The navigation controller provides the core to many iPhone apps; however, when it comes to iPad apps, the navigation controller plays a more marginal role. The Mail app depicts a typical example featuring a hierarchical navigation controller to let users navigate among all their mail servers, folders, and messages. In the iPad version of Mail, the navigation controller never fills the screen but appears either as a sidebar or as a temporary view covering part of the main view. You'll work with that in Chapter 11.

Fonts: Creating a Simple Font Browser

The application you're about to build shows how to do most of the common tasks associated with displaying a hierarchy of data. When the application launches, you're presented with a list of all the font families that are included with iOS, as shown in Figure 9-3. A font family groups closely related fonts, or fonts that are stylistic variations of one another, such as Helvetica, Helvetica-Bold, Helvetic-Oblique, and other variations all included in the Helvetica font family.

Figure 9-3. *In this project, the root view controller displays accessory icons on the right side of each row in the view. This particular type of accessory icon is called a disclosure indicator, letting you know that touching that row drills down to another view of some kind.*

Selecting any row in this top-level view will push a new view controller onto the navigation controller's stack. The small images on the far right of each row are called *accessory icons*. This particular accessory icon (the gray arrow) displays a disclosure indicator letting the user know that touching that row drills down to another view.

Seeing the Subcontrollers of the Fonts App

Before you actually start working on this chapter's project, let's examine each of the subcontrollers that you'll be using.

Seeing the Font List Controller

Touching any row of the table shown in Figure 9-3 will bring up the child view shown in Figure 9-4.

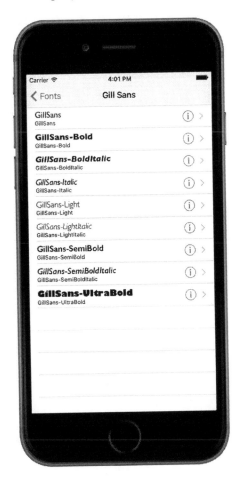

Figure 9-4. *The first of the Fonts application's subcontrollers implements a table in which each row contains a detail disclosure button*

The accessory icon to the right of each row in Figure 9-4, called a *detail disclosure*, functions differently than the arrow you saw previously. Unlike the *disclosure indicator*, the detail disclosure button provides not just an icon but acts as a control that the user can tap independently. This means that you can have two different options available for a given row: one action triggered when the user selects the row and another that is triggered when the user taps the icon. Tapping the small info button within this accessory should allow the user to view, and perhaps edit, more detailed information about the current row. Meanwhile, the presence of the right-pointing arrow should indicate to the user that there is some deeper navigation to be found by tapping elsewhere in the row.

Seeing the Font Sizes View Controller

Touching any row of the table shown in Figure 9-4 brings up the child view shown in Figure 9-5.

Figure 9-5. *Located one layer deeper than the font list view controller, the font sizes view controller shows multiple sizes of the chosen font, one per row*

Using Disclosure Indicators and Detail Disclosure

Here are some guidelines for when to use each of these buttons:

- To offer a single choice for a row tap, don't use an accessory icon if a row tap will only lead to a more detailed view of that row.

- Mark the row with a disclosure indicator (right-pointing arrow) if a row tap leads to a new view listing more items (not a detail view).

- To offer two choices for a row, mark the row with either a detail disclosure indicator or a detail button. This allows the user to tap the row for a new view or the disclosure button for more details.

Seeing the Font Info View Controller

Your final application subcontroller—the only one not a table view—appears (see Figure 9-6) when you tap on the info icon for any row in the font list view controller shown in Figure 9-2.

Figure 9-6. *The final view controller in the Fonts application allows you to view the chosen font at any size you want*

This view lets the user drag a slider to adjust the size of the displayed font. It also includes a switch that allows the user to specify whether this font should be listed among the user's favorites. If any fonts are set as favorites, they appear within a separate group in the root view controller.

Seeing the Fonts Application's Skeleton

Xcode offers a perfectly good template for creating navigation-based applications, and you will likely use it much of the time when you need to create hierarchical applications. However, you're not going to use that template today. Instead, you'll construct your navigation-based application from the ground up so you get a feel for how everything fits together. I'll also walk you through it one piece at a time, so it should be easy to keep up.

In Xcode create a new project. Select Single View App from the iOS template list and then click Next to continue. Set **Fonts** as the product name, set Swift as the Language, and select Universal for Devices. Make sure that Use Core Data is not selected, click Next, and choose the location to save your project.

Setting Up the Navigation Controller

You'll now create the basic navigation structure for your application. At the core of this will be a UINavigationController, managing the stack of view controllers that a user can navigate between, and a UITableViewController, displaying the top-level list of rows you're going to show. As it turns out, Interface Builder makes this easy to create.

Select Main.storyboard. The template has created a basic view controller for you, but you need to use a UINavigationController instead, so select the view controller in either the Editor Area or the Document Outline and delete it to leave the storyboard empty. Now use the Object Library to search for UINavigationController and drag an instance into the editing area. You'll see that you actually get two scenes instead of one, similar to what you saw when creating a tab view controller in Chapter 7. On the left is the UINavigationController itself. Select this controller, open the Attributes Inspector, and check Is Initial View Controller in the View Controller section to make this the controller that appears when the application is launched.

The UINavigationController has a connection wired to the second scene, which contains a UITableViewController. You'll see that the table has the title Root View Controller. Click the Root View Controller icon in the Document Outline (the one below the Table View icon, not the one above it), open the Attributes Inspector, and then set the title to **Fonts**. If you don't see the title change in the storyboard, you chose the wrong Root View Controller icon.

By setting it up this way, you get the view created by the navigation controller, a composite view that contains a combination of two things: the navigation bar at the top of the screen (which usually contains some sort of title and often a back button of some kind on the left) and the content of whatever the navigation controller's current view controller wants to display. In this case, the lower part of the display will be filled with the table view that was created alongside the navigation controller.

You'll see more about how to control what the navigation controller shows in the navigation bar as you go forward. You'll also gain an understanding of how the navigation controller shifts focus from one subordinate view controller to another. For now, I've laid enough groundwork so that you can start defining what your custom view controllers are going to do.

At this point, the application skeleton is essentially complete. You'll see a warning about setting a reuse identifier for a prototype table cell, but you can ignore that for now. Save all your files and then build and run the app. If all is well, the application should launch, and a Fonts navigation bar should appear. You haven't given the table view any information about what to show yet, so no rows will display at this point, as shown in Figure 9-7.

Figure 9-7. *Your application skeleton without any data*

Keeping Track of Favorite Fonts

At several points in this application, you're going to let the user maintain a list of favorite fonts by letting them add chosen fonts, view a whole list of already-chosen favorites, and remove fonts from the list. To manage this list in a consistent way, you're going to make a new class that will hang onto an array of favorites and store them in the user's preference for this application. You'll learn a lot more about user preferences in Chapter 12, but here I'll just touch on some basics.

Start by creating a new class. Select the Fonts folder in the Project Navigator and press ⌘N to bring up the new file assistant. Select Swift File from the iOS Source section and then click Next. On the following screen, name the new file FavoritesList.swift and click Create. Select the new file in the Project Navigator and make the additions shown in Listing 9-1.

Listing 9-1. Your FavoritesList Class File

```
import Foundation
import UIKit

class FavoritesList {
    static let sharedFavoritesList = FavoritesList()
    private(set) var favorites:[String]
```

```
init() {
    let defaults = UserDefaults.standard
    let storedFavorites = defaults.object(forKey: "favorites") as? [String]
    favorites = storedFavorites != nil ? storedFavorites! : []
}

func addFavorite(fontName: String) {
    if !favorites.contains(fontName) {
        favorites.append(fontName)
        saveFavorites()
    }
}

func removeFavorite(fontName: String) {
    if let index = favorites.index(of: fontName) {
        favorites.remove(at: index)
        saveFavorites()
    }
}

private func saveFavorites() {
    let defaults = UserDefaults.standard
    defaults.set(favorites, forKey: "favorites")
    defaults.synchronize()
}
}
```

In Listing 9-1, you declared the API for your new class. For starters, you declared a class property called sharedFavoritesList that returns an instance of this class. No matter how many times this method is called, the same instance will always be returned. The idea is that FavoritesList should work as a singleton. Instead of using multiple instances, you'll just use one instance throughout the application.

Next, you declared a property to hold the names of your favorite fonts. Pay close attention to the definition of this array:

```
private(set) var favorites:[String]
```

The private(set) qualifier means that the array can be read by code outside the class, but only code in the class implementation can modify it. That's exactly what you want because you need users of your class to be able to read the favorites list.

```
let favorites = FavoritesList.sharedFavoritesList.favorites   // Read-access is OK
```

But you don't want either of these to be allowed:

```
FavoritesList.sharedFavoritesList.favorites = []     // Not allowed
FavoritesList.sharedFavoritesList.favorites.append("Comic Sans MS")     // Not allowed
```

The class initializer is responsible for setting the initial content of the favorites array.

```
init() {
    let defaults = UserDefaults.standard
    let storedFavorites = defaults.object(forKey: "favorites") as? [String]
    favorites = storedFavorites != nil ? storedFavorites! : []
}
```

As you'll see shortly, any time you add something to or remove something from this array, you save its contents to the application's user defaults (which is discussed in detail in Chapter 12) so that the content of the list is preserved over application restarts. In the initializer, you check whether you have a stored favorites list, and if so, you use it to initialize the favorites property. If not, you simply make it empty.

The remaining three methods deal with adding to and removing from the favorites array. The implementations should be self-explanatory. Note that the first two methods both call saveFavorites(), which saves the updated value to the user defaults under the same key (favorites) as the initializer uses to read it. You'll learn more about how this works in Chapter 12; but for now, it's enough to know that the UserDefaults (NSUserDefaults) object that you use here acts like a sort of persistent dictionary, and anything that you put in there will be available the next time you ask for it, even if the application has been stopped and restarted.

■ **Note** Previously, in Xcode 8, Apple made many of the former NS- objects more user-friendly for use in Swift; for example, NSUserDefaults is now UserDefaults.

Creating the Root View Controller

Let's get started developing your first view controller. In the previous chapter, you used simple arrays of strings to populate your table rows. You're going to do something similar here, but this time you'll use the UIFont class to get a list of font families and then use the names of those font families to populate each row. You'll also use the fonts themselves to display the font names so that each row will contain a small preview of what the font family contains.

It's time to create the first controller class for this application. The template created a view controller for you, but its name—ViewController—isn't very useful because there are going to be several view controllers in this application. So, first select ViewController.swift in the Project Navigator and click Delete to delete it and move it to the trash. Next, select the Fonts folder in the Project Navigator and press ⌘N to bring up the new file assistant. Select Cocoa Touch Class from the iOS Source section and then click Next. On the following screen, name the new class RootViewController and enter **UITableViewController** for "Subclass of." Click Next and then click Create to create the new class. In the Project Navigator, select RootViewController.swift and add the bold lines in the snippet that follows to add a few properties:

```
class RootViewController: UITableViewController {
    private var familyNames: [String]!
    private var cellPointSize: CGFloat!
    private var favoritesList: FavoritesList!
    private static let familyCell = "FamilyName"
    private static let favoritesCell = "Favorites"
```

You'll assign values to the first three of those properties from the onset and then use them at various times while this class is in use. The `familyNames` array will contain a list of all the font families you're going to display, the `cellPointSize` property will contain the font size that you want to use in all of your table view cells, and `favoritesList` will contain a pointer to the `FavoritesList` singleton. The last two are constants that represent the cell identifiers that you will use for the table view cells in this controller.

Set up all of this class's properties by adding the bold code shown here to the `viewDidLoad()` method, as shown in Listing 9-2.

Listing 9-2. The viewDidLoad() Method for the RootViewController.swift File

```
override func viewDidLoad() {
    super.viewDidLoad()

    familyNames = (UIFont.familyNames() as [String]).sorted()
    let preferredTableViewFont =
        UIFont.preferredFont(forTextStyle: UIFontTextStyleHeadline)
    cellPointSize = preferredTableViewFont.pointSize
    favoritesList = FavoritesList.sharedFavoritesList
    tableView.estimatedRowHeight = cellPointSize
}
```

In Listing 9-2, you populated `familyNames` by asking the `UIFont` class for all known family names and then sorting the resulting array. You then used `UIFont` once again to ask for the preferred font for use in a headline. You did this using a piece of functionality added in iOS 7, which uses a font size setting that can be configured by the user in the Settings app. This dynamic font sizing lets the user set an overall font scaling for systemwide use. Here, you used that font's `pointSize` property to establish a baseline font size that you'll use elsewhere in this view controller. Finally, you grabbed the singleton favorites list object, and you set the `estimatedRowHeight` property of the table view to indicate roughly how tall your table's rows will be. As it turns out, the table will calculate the correct size for each cell based on the cell's content, provided that you set this property, leave the table view's `rowHeight` property set to its default value of `UITableViewAutomaticDimension`, and use default table view cells (or use Auto Layout to construct custom table view cells).

Before you go on, let's delete the `didReceiveMemoryWarning()` method, as well as all of the table view delegate or data source methods that the template gave you—you're not going to use any of them in this class.

The idea behind this view controller is to show two sections. The first section is a list of all available font families, each of which leads to a list of all the fonts in the family. The second section is for favorites and contains just a single entry that will lead the user to a list of their favorite fonts. However, if the user has no favorites (for example, when the app is launched for the first time), you'd rather not show that second section at all since it would just lead the user to an empty list. So, you'll have to do a few things throughout the rest of this class to compensate for this eventuality. The first of these is to implement this method, which is called just before the root view controller's view appears on the screen:

```
override func viewWillAppear(_ animated: Bool) {
    super.viewWillAppear(animated)
    tableView.reloadData()
}
```

The reason for this is that there may be times when the set of things you're going to display might change from one viewing to the next. For example, the user may start with no favorites but then drill down, view a font, set it as a favorite, and then come back out to the root view. At that time, you need to reload the table view so that the second section will appear.

Next, you're going to implement a sort of utility method for use within this class. At a couple of points, while configuring the table view via its data source methods, you'll need to be able to figure out which font you want to display in a cell. You put that functionality into a method of its own, as shown in Listing 9-3.

Listing 9-3. Figuring Out Which Font You Want to Display

```
func fontForDisplay(atIndexPath indexPath: NSIndexPath) -> UIFont? {
    if indexPath.section == 0 {
        let familyName = familyNames[indexPath.row]
        let fontName = UIFont.fontNames(forFamilyName: familyName).first
        return fontName != nil ?
            UIFont(name: fontName!, size: cellPointSize) : nil
    } else {
        return nil
    }
}
```

This method uses the UIFont class to find all the font names for the given family name and then grab the first font name within that family. You don't necessarily know that the first named font in a family is the best one to represent the whole family, but it's as good a guess as any. If the family has no font names, you return nil.

Now, let's move on to the primary code in this view controller: the table view data source methods. First up, let's look at the number of sections:

```
override func numberOfSections(in tableView: UITableView) -> Int {
    return favoritesList.favorites.isEmpty ? 1 : 2
}
```

You use the favorites list to determine whether you want to show the second section. Next, you tackle the number of rows in each section.

```
override func tableView(_ tableView: UITableView, numberOfRowsInSection section: Int) -> Int {
    // Return the number of rows in the section.
    return section == 0 ? familyNames.count : 1
}
```

That one is also pretty simple. You just use the section number to determine whether the section is showing all family names or a single cell linking to the list of favorites. Now let's define one other method, an optional method in the UITableViewDataSource protocol that lets you specify the title for each of your sections.

```
override func tableView(_ tableView: UITableView, titleForHeaderInSection section: Int) ->
String? {
    return section == 0 ? "All Font Families" : "My Favorite Fonts"
}
```

This is another straightforward method. It uses the section number to determine which header title to use. The final core method that every table view data source must implement is the one for configuring each cell, and yours looks like Listing 9-4.

Listing 9-4. Your cellForRow (atIndexPath:) Function

```
override func tableView(_ tableView: UITableView, cellForRowAt indexPath: IndexPath) ->
UITableViewCell {
    if indexPath.section == 0 {
        // The font names list
        let cell = tableView.dequeueReusableCell(withIdentifier: RootViewController.
        familyCell, for: indexPath)
        cell.textLabel?.font = fontForDisplay(atIndexPath: indexPath)
        cell.textLabel?.text = familyNames[indexPath.row]
        cell.detailTextLabel?.text = familyNames[indexPath.row]
        return cell
    } else {
        // The favorites list
        return tableView.dequeueReusableCell(withIdentifier: RootViewController.
        favoritesCell, for: indexPath)
    }
}
```

When you created this class, you defined two different cell identifiers that you use to load two different cell prototypes from the storyboard (much like you loaded a table cell from a nib file in Chapter 8). You haven't configured those cell prototypes yet, but you will soon. Next, you use the section number to determine which of those cells you want to show for the current indexPath. If the cell is meant to contain a font family name, then you put the family name into both its textLabel and its detailTextLabel. You also use a font from the family (the one you get from the fontForDisplay(atIndexPath:) method that you added earlier) within the text label so that you'll see the font family name shown in the font itself, as well as a smaller version in the standard system font.

Doing the Initial Storyboard Setup

Now that you have a view controller that you think should show something, let's configure the storyboard to make things happen. Select Main.storyboard in the Project Navigator. You'll see the navigation controller and the table view controller that you added earlier. The first thing you need to configure is the table view controller. By default, the controller's class is set to UITableViewController. You need to change that to your root view controller class. In the Fonts Scene in the Document Outline, select the yellow Fonts icon, and then use the Identity Inspector to change the view controller's Class to RootViewController.

The other configuration you'll need to do right now is to set up a pair of prototype cells to match the cell identifiers you used in your code. From the start, the table view has a single prototype cell. Select it and press ⌘D to duplicate it, and you'll see that you now have two cells. Select the first one and then use the Attributes Inspector to set its Style to Subtitle, its Identifier to FamilyName, and its Accessory to Disclosure Indicator. Next, select the second prototype cell and then set its Style to Basic, its Identifier to Favorites, and its Accessory to Disclosure Indicator. Also, double-click the title shown in the cell itself and change the text from Title to **Favorites**.

■ **Tip**   The prototype cells that you are using in this example both have standard table view cell styles. If you set Style to Custom, you can design the layout of the cell right in the cell prototype, just like you did when you created a cell in a nib file in Chapter 8.

Now build and run this app, and you should see a nice list of fonts. Scroll around a bit and you'll see that not all of the fonts produce text of the same height, as shown in Figure 9-8. All of the cells are tall enough to contain their content. If you've forgotten why this works, refer to the discussion of the code you added to the viewDidLoad() method earlier in this section.

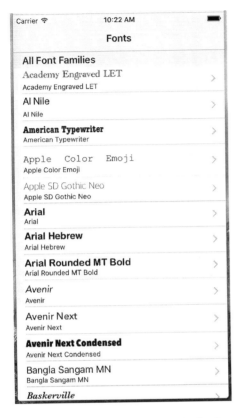

Figure 9-8. *The root view controller displays the installed font families*

First Subcontroller: Creating the Font List View

Your app currently just shows a list of font families, and nothing more. You want to add the ability for a user to touch a font family and see all the fonts it contains, so let's make a new view controller that can manage a list of fonts. Create a new Cocoa Touch class called FontListViewController as a subclass of UITableViewController. In the Project Navigator, select FontListViewController.swift and add the following properties:

```
class FontListViewController: UITableViewController {
    var fontNames: [String] = []
    var showsFavorites:Bool = false
    private var cellPointSize: CGFloat!
    private static let cellIdentifier = "FontName"
```

The fontNames property is what you'll use to tell this view controller what to display. You also created a showsFavorites property that you'll use to let this view controller know if it's showing the list of favorites instead of just a list of fonts in a family since this will be useful later. You'll use the cellPointSize property to hold the preferred display size for displaying each font, once again using UIFont to find the preferred size. Finally, cellIdentifier is the identifier used for the table view cells in this controller.

To initialize the cellPointSize property and set the table view's estimated row height, add the code in Listing 9-5 to the viewDidLoad() method.

Listing 9-5. Your viewDidLoad Method for the FontListViewController.swift File

```
override func viewDidLoad() {
    super.viewDidLoad()

    let preferredTableViewFont =
        UIFont.preferredFont(forTextStyle: UIFontTextStyleHeadline)
    cellPointSize = preferredTableViewFont.pointSize
    tableView.estimatedRowHeight = cellPointSize
}
```

The next thing you want to do is create a little utility method for choosing the font to be shown in each row, similar to what you have in RootViewController. Here it's a bit different, though. Instead of holding onto a list of font families in this view controller, you're holding onto a list of font names in the fontNames property. You'll use the UIFont class to get each named font, like this:

```
func fontForDisplay(atIndexPath indexPath: NSIndexPath) -> UIFont {
    let fontName = fontNames[indexPath.row]
    return UIFont(name: fontName, size: cellPointSize)!
}
```

Now it's time for a small addition in the form of a viewWillAppear() implementation. In RootViewController, you implemented this method in case the list of favorites might change, requiring a refresh. The same applies here. This view controller might be showing the list of favorites, and the user might switch to another view controller, change a favorite (you'll get there later), and then come back here. You need to reload the table view then, and this method takes care of that, as shown in Listing 9-6.

Listing 9-6. Refreshing the View in Case Something Changes

```
override func viewWillAppear(_ animated: Bool) {
    super.viewWillAppear(animated)
    if showsFavorites {
        fontNames = FavoritesList.sharedFavoritesList.favorites
        tableView.reloadData()
    }
}
```

The basic idea is that this view controller, in normal operation, is passed a list of font names before it displays and that the list stays the same the whole time this view controller is around. In one particular case (which you'll see later), this view controller needs to reload its font list.

Moving on, you can delete the numberOfSectionsInTableView() method entirely. You'll have only one section here, and just skipping that method is the equivalent of implementing it and returning 1. Next, you implement the two other main data source methods, as shown in Listing 9-7.

Listing 9-7. Your dataSource Methods

```
override func tableView(_ tableView: UITableView, numberOfRowsInSection section: Int) -> Int {
    // Return the number of rows in the section.
    return fontNames.count
}

override func tableView(_ tableView: UITableView, cellForRowAt indexPath: IndexPath) ->
UITableViewCell {

    let cell = tableView.dequeueReusableCell(
        withIdentifier: FontListViewController.cellIdentifier,
        for: indexPath)

    cell.textLabel?.font = fontForDisplay(atIndexPath: indexPath)
    cell.textLabel?.text = fontNames[indexPath.row]
    cell.detailTextLabel?.text = fontNames[indexPath.row]

    return cell
}
```

Neither of these methods really needs any explanation because they are similar to what you used in RootViewController, but they're even simpler.

You'll add some more to this class later, but first let's see it in action. To make this happen, you'll need to configure the storyboard some more and then make some modifications to RootViewController. Switch to Main.storyboard to get started.

Creating the Font List Storyboard

The storyboard currently contains a table view controller that displays the list of font families, embedded inside a navigation controller. You need to add one new layer of depth to incorporate the view controller that will display the fonts for a given family. Find a table view controller in the Object Library and drag one into the editing area, to the right of the existing table view controller. Select the new table view controller and use the Identity Inspector to set its class to FontListViewController. Select the prototype cell in the table view and open the Attributes Inspector to make some adjustments. Change its Style to Subtitle, its Identifier to FontName, and its Accessory to Detail Disclosure. Using the detail disclosure accessory will let rows of this type respond to two kinds of taps so that users can trigger two different actions, depending on whether they tap the accessory or any other part of the row.

One way to make a user action in one view controller cause the instantiation and display of another view controller is to create a seque connecting the two of them. This is probably an unfamiliar word for many people, so let's get this out of the way: *segue* essentially means "transition." It is sometimes used by writers and filmmakers to describe making a smooth movement from one paragraph or scene to the next. Apple could have been a little straightforward and just called it a transition; but since that word appears elsewhere in the UIKit APIs, maybe Apple decided to use a distinct term to avoid confusion. I should also mention here that the word *segue* is pronounced exactly the same as the name of the Segway personal transportation product (and now you know why the Segway is called what it is).

Often, segues are created entirely within Interface Builder. The idea is that an action in one scene can trigger a segue to load and display another scene. If you're using a navigation controller, the segue can push the next controller onto the navigation stack automatically. You'll be using this functionality in your app, starting right now.

For the cells in the root view controller to make the font list view controller appear, you need to create a couple of segues connecting the two scenes. This is done simply by Control-dragging from the first of the two prototype cells in the Fonts scene to the new scene; you'll see the entire scene highlight when you drag over it, indicating it's ready to connect, as shown in Figure 9-9.

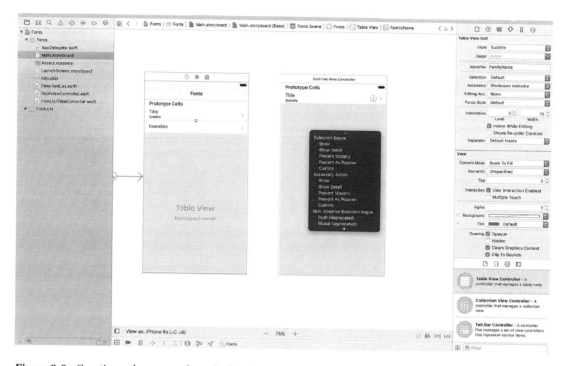

Figure 9-9. *Creating a show segue from the font list controller to the font names controller*

Release the mouse button and select Show from the Selection Segue section of the pop-up menu that appears. Now do the same for the other prototype cell. Creating these segues means that as soon as the user taps any of these cells, the view controller at the other end of the connection will be allocated and made ready.

Making the Root View Controller Prepare for Segues

Save your changes and switch back to RootViewController.swift. Note that I'm not talking about your latest class, FontListViewController, but instead its "parent" controller. This is the place where you'll need to respond to the user's touches in the root table view by preparing the new FontListViewController (specified by one of the segues you just created) for display and by passing it the values it needs to display.

The actual preparation of the new view controller is done using the prepareForSegue(_:sender:) method. Add an implementation of this method, as shown in Listing 9-8.

Listing 9-8. Preparing the New View Controller for Display

```
// MARK: - Navigation

override func prepare(for segue: UIStoryboardSegue, sender: AnyObject?) {
    // Get the new view controller using [segue destinationViewController].
    // Pass the selected object to the new view controller.
    let indexPath = tableView.indexPath(for: sender as! UITableViewCell)!
    let listVC = segue.destinationViewController as! FontListViewController

    if indexPath.section == 0 {
        // Font names list
        let familyName = familyNames[indexPath.row]
        listVC.fontNames = (UIFont.fontNames(forFamilyName: familyName) as [String]).sorted()
        listVC.navigationItem.title = familyName
        listVC.showsFavorites = false
    } else {
        // Favorites list
        listVC.fontNames = favoritesList.favorites
        listVC.navigationItem.title = "Favorites"
        listVC.showsFavorites = true
    }
}
```

This method uses the sender (the UITableViewCell that was tapped) to determine which row was tapped and asks the segue for its destinationViewController, which is the FontListViewController instance that is about to be displayed. You then pass some values along to the new view controller, depending on whether the user tapped a font family (section 0) or the favorites cell (section 1). As well as setting the custom properties for the target view controller, you also access the controller's navigationItem property to set its title. The navigationItem property is an instance of UINavigationItem, which is a UIKit class that contains information about what should be displayed in the navigation bar for any given view controller.

Now run the app. You'll see that touching the name of any font family shows you a list of all the individual fonts it contains (see Figure 9-10). Furthermore, you can tap the Fonts label in the header of the fonts list navigation controller to go back to its parent controller to select another font.

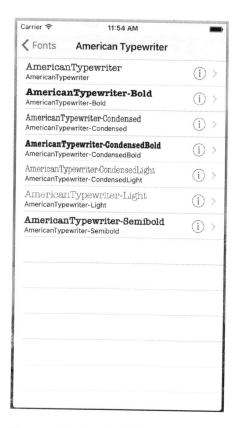

Figure 9-10. *Showing the individual fonts contained in a font family*

Creating the Font Sizes View Controller

What you'll notice, however, is that the app currently doesn't let you go any further. Figures 9-4 and 9-5 show additional screens that let you view a chosen font in various ways; you're not there yet. But soon, you will be! Let's create the view shown in Figure 9-4, which shows multiple font sizes at once. Using the same steps as you used to create FontListViewController, add a new view controller that subclasses UITableViewController and name it FontSizesViewController. The only parameter this class will need from its parent controller is a font. You'll also need a couple of private properties.

For starters, switch to FontSizesViewController.swift and go ahead and delete the didReceiveMemoryWarning and numberOfSectionsInTableView: methods, along with all of the commented-out methods at the bottom. Again, you're not going to need any of those. Now add the following properties at the top of the class definition:

```
import UIKit

class FontSizesViewController: UITableViewController {
    var font: UIFont!
    private static let pointSizes: [CGFloat] = [
        9, 10, 11, 12, 13, 14, 18, 24, 36, 48, 64, 72, 96, 144
    ]
    private static let cellIdentifier = "FontNameAndSize"
```

The font property will be set by FontListViewController before it pushes this view controller onto the navigation controller's stack. The pointSizes property is an array of point sizes in which the font will be displayed. You also need the following utility method, which gets a version of a font with a given size, based on a table row index:

```
func fontForDisplay(atIndexPath indexPath: NSIndexPath) -> UIFont {
    let pointSize = FontSizesViewController.pointSizes[indexPath.row]
    return font.withSize(pointSize)
}
```

You also need to set the table view's estimatedRowHeight property so that the table will automatically calculate the correct row heights for each row based on what it contains. To do that, add the following line to the viewDidLoad() method:

tableView.estimatedRowHeight = FontSizesViewController.pointSizes[0]

It doesn't actually matter what value you assign to this property, so let's arbitrarily choose to use the smallest font point size that the table will need to display.

For this view controller, you're going to skip the method that lets you specify the number of sections to display since you're going to just use the default number (1). However, you must implement the methods for specifying the number of rows and the content of each cell. Listing 9-9 shows these two methods.

Listing 9-9. The dataSource Methods for the FontSizeViewController Table View

```
// MARK: - Table view data source

override func tableView(_ tableView: UITableView, numberOfRowsInSection section: Int) -> Int {
    return FontSizesViewController.pointSizes.count
}

override func tableView(_ tableView: UITableView, cellForRowAt indexPath: IndexPath) ->
UITableViewCell {
    let cell = tableView.dequeueReusableCell(
        withIdentifier: FontSizesViewController.cellIdentifier,
        for: indexPath)

    cell.textLabel?.font = fontForDisplay(atIndexPath: indexPath)
    cell.textLabel?.text = font.fontName
    cell.detailTextLabel?.text =
        "\(FontSizesViewController.pointSizes[indexPath.row]) point"

    return cell
}
```

There's really nothing in any of these methods you haven't seen before, so let's move on to setting up the storyboard for your user interface.

Creating the Font Sizes View Controller Storyboard

Go back to Main.storyboard and drag another table view controller into the editing area. Use the Identity Inspector to set its class to FontSizesViewController. You'll need to make a segue connection from its parent, the FontListViewController. So, find that controller and Control-drag from its prototype cell to the newest view controller and then select Show from the Selection Segue section of the pop-up menu that appears. Next, select the prototype cell in the new scene you just added and then use the Attributes Inspector to set its Style to Subtitle and its Identifier to FontNameAndSize.

Implementing the Font Sizes View Controller Prepare for Segue

Now, just like the last time you extended your storyboard's navigation hierarchy, you need to jump up to the parent controller so that it can configure its child. That means you need to go to FontListViewController. swift and implement the prepareForSegue(_:sender:) method, as shown in Listing 9-10.

Listing 9-10. The FontListViewsController's preparedForSeque Method

```
// MARK: - Navigation

override func prepare(for segue: UIStoryboardSegue, sender: AnyObject?) {
    // Get the new view controller using [segue destinationViewController].
    // Pass the selected object to the new view controller.
    let tableViewCell = sender as! UITableViewCell
    let indexPath = tableView.indexPath(for: tableViewCell)!
    let font = fontForDisplay(atIndexPath: indexPath)

    let sizesVC = segue.destinationViewController as! FontSizesViewController
    sizesVC.title = font.fontName
    sizesVC.font = font
}
```

That probably all looks pretty familiar by now, so I won't dwell on it further.

Run the app, select a font family, and select a font (by tapping a row anywhere except the accessory on the right); you'll now see the multisize listing shown in Figure 9-11.

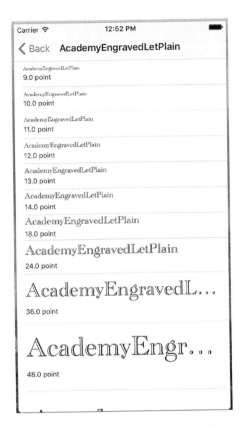

Figure 9-11. *Your multisize table view list*

Creating the Font Info View Controller

The final view controller you're going to create is the one shown in Figure 9-5. This one isn't based on a table view. Instead, it features a large text label, a slider for setting text size, and a switch for toggling whether the font that it uses should be included in the list of favorites. Create a new Cocoa Touch class in your project using UIViewController as the superclass and then name it FontInfoViewController. Like most of the other controllers in this app, this one needs to have a couple of parameters passed in by its parent controller. Enable this by defining these properties and four outlets that you'll use when you construct the user interface in FontInfoViewController.swift:

```
class FontInfoViewController: UIViewController {
    var font: UIFont!
    var favorite: Bool = false
    @IBOutlet weak var fontSampleLabel: UILabel!
    @IBOutlet weak var fontSizeSlider: UISlider!
    @IBOutlet weak var fontSizeLabel: UILabel!
    @IBOutlet weak var favoriteSwitch: UISwitch!
```

Next, implement viewDidLoad() and a pair of action methods that will be triggered by the slider and switch, respectively, as shown in Listing 9-11.

Listing 9-11. Your viewDidLoad(), slider, and switch Methods

```
override func viewDidLoad() {
    super.viewDidLoad()

    // Do any additional setup after loading the view.
    fontSampleLabel.font = font
    fontSampleLabel.text =
        "AaBbCcDdEeFfGgHhIiJjKkLlMmNnOoPpQqRrSsTtUuVv"
        + "WwXxYyZz 0123456789"
    fontSizeSlider.value = Float(font.pointSize)
    fontSizeLabel.text = "\(Int(font.pointSize))"
    favoriteSwitch.isOn = favorite
}
@IBAction func slideFontSize(slider: UISlider) {
    let newSize = roundf(slider.value)
    fontSampleLabel.font = font.withSize(CGFloat(newSize))
    fontSizeLabel.text = "\(Int(newSize))"
}

    @IBAction func toggleFavorite(sender: UISwitch) {
        let favoritesList = FavoritesList.sharedFavoritesList
        if sender.isOn {
            favoritesList.addFavorite(fontName: font.fontName)
        } else {
            favoritesList.removeFavorite(fontName: font.fontName)
        }
    }
}
```

These methods are all pretty straightforward. The viewDidLoad() method sets up the display based on the chosen font; slideFontSize() changes the size of the font in the fontSampleLabel label based on the value of the slider; and toggleFavorite() either adds the current font to the favorites list or removes it from the favorites list, depending on the value of the switch.

Creating the Font Info View Controller Storyboard

Now head back over to Main.storyboard to build the GUI for this app's final view controller. Use the Object Library to find a plain view controller. Drag it into the editing area and use the Identity Inspector to set its class to FontInfoViewController. Next, use the Object Library to find some more objects and drag them into your new scene. You need three labels, a switch, and a slider. Lay them out roughly as shown in Figure 9-12. Don't worry about adding Auto Layout constraints yet—you'll do that later.

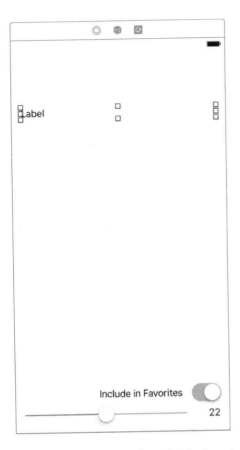

Figure 9-12. *Label, switch, and slider layout*

Notice that I left some space above the upper label since you're going to end up having a navigation bar up there. Also, you want the upper label to be able to display long pieces of text across multiple lines, but by default the label is set to show only one line. To change that, select the label, open the Attributes Inspector, and set the number in the Lines field to 0.

Figure 9-12 also shows changed text in the lower two labels. Go ahead and make the same changes yourself. What you can't see here is that the Attributes Inspector was used to right-align the text in both of them. You should do the same since they will both have layout constraints that essentially tie them to their right edges. Also, select the slider at the bottom and then use the Attributes Inspector to set its Minimum to 1 and its Maximum to 200.

Now it's time to wire up all the connections for this GUI. Start by selecting the view controller and opening the Connections Inspector. When you have so many connections to make, the overview shown by that inspector is pretty nice. Make connections for each of the outlets by dragging from the small circles next to favoriteSwitch, fontSampleLabel, fontSizeLabel, and fontSizeSlider to the appropriate objects in the scene. In case it's not obvious, fontSampleLabel should be connected to the label at the top, fontSizeLabel to the label at the bottom right, and the favoriteSwitch and fontSizeSlider outlets to the only places they can go. To connect the actions to the controls, you can continue to use the Connections Inspector. In the Received Actions section of the Connections Inspector for the view controller, drag from the little circle next to slideFontSize: over to the slider, release the mouse button, and select Value Changed from the context menu that appears. Next, drag from the little circle next to toggleFavorite: over to the switch and again select Value Changed. The connections should look as shown in Figure 9-13.

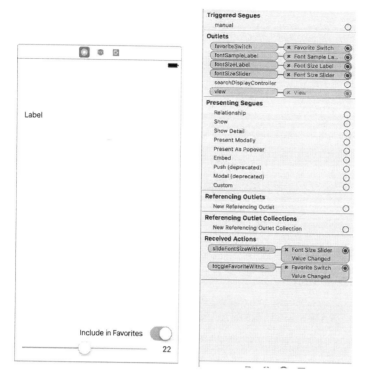

Figure 9-13. *The completed connections for your Font Info View Controller storyboard*

One more thing you need to do here is create a segue so that this view can be shown. Remember that this view is going to be displayed whenever a user taps the detail accessory (the little blue "i" in a circle) when the font list view controller is displayed. So, find that controller, Control-drag from its prototype cell to the new font info view controller you've been working on, and select Show from the Accessory Action section of the context menu that appears. Note that I just said Accessory Action, not Selection Segue (see Figure 9-14). The accessory action is the segue that is triggered when the user taps the detail accessory, whereas the selection segue is the segue that is triggered by a tap anywhere else in the row. You already set this cell's selection segue to open a FontSizesViewController.

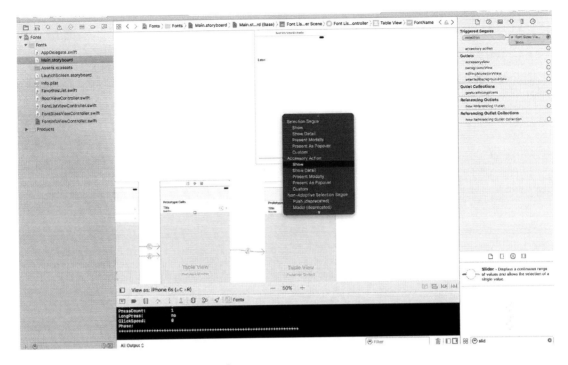

Figure 9-14. *Setting the accessory action show segue*

Now you have two different segues that can be triggered by touches in different parts of a row. Since these will present different view controllers, with different properties, you need to have a way to differentiate them. Fortunately, the `UIStoryboardSegue` class, which represents a segue, has a way to accomplish this: you can use an identifier, just as you do with table view cells.

All you have to do is select a segue in the editing area and use the Attributes Inspector to set its identifier. You may need to shift your scenes around a bit so that you can see both of the segues that are snaking their way out of the right side of the font list view controller. Select the one that's pointing at the font sizes view controller and set its Identifier to ShowFontSizes. Next, select the one that's pointing at the Font Info View Controller and set its Identifier to ShowFontInfo, as shown in Figure 9-15.

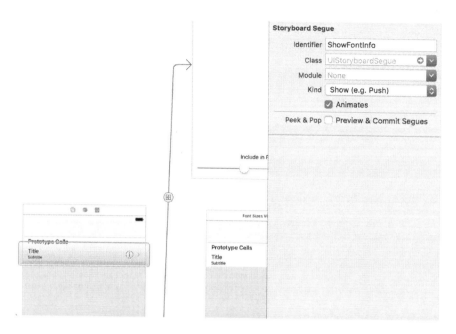

Figure 9-15. *Identifying the segues*

Setting Up Constraints

Setting up that segue lets Interface Builder know that your new scene will be used within the context of the navigation controller like everything else, so it automatically receives a blank navigation bar at the top. Now that the real confines of your view are in place, it's a good time to set up the constraints. This is a fairly complex view with several subviews, especially near the bottom, so you can't quite rely on the system's automatic constraints to do the right thing for you. You'll use the Pin button at the bottom of the editing area and the pop-up window it triggers to build most of the constraints you'll need.

Start with the uppermost label. If you placed it too close to the top, first drag it down until it's a comfortable distance below the navigation bar. Click Pin, and then, in the pop-up window, select the little red bars above, to the left, and to the right of the little square—but not the one below it. Now click the Add 3 Constraints button at the bottom.

Next, select the slider at the bottom and click the Pin button. This time, select the red bars below, to the left, and to the right of the little square—but not the one above it. Again, click Add 3 Constraints to put them in place.

For each of the two remaining labels and for the switch, follow this procedure: select the object, click Pin, select the red bars below and to the right of the little square, turn on the check boxes for Width and Height, and, finally, click Add 4 Constraints. Setting those constraints for all three of those objects will bind them to the lower-right corner.

There's just one more constraint to make. You want the top label to grow to contain its text but to never grow so large that it overlaps the views at the bottom. You can accomplish this with a single constraint. Control-drag from the upper label to the "Include in favorites" label, release the mouse button, and select Vertical Spacing from the context menu that appears. Next, click the new constraint to select it (it's a blue vertical bar connecting the two labels) and open the Attributes Inspector, where you'll see some configurable attributes for the constraint. Change the Relation pop-up to Greater Than or Equal and then set the Constant value to 10. That ensures that the expanding upper label won't push past the other views at the bottom.

Adapting the Font List View Controller for Multiple Segues

Now head back over to good old FontListViewController.swift. Since this class will now be able to trigger segues to two different child view controllers, you need to adapt the prepareForSegue(_:sender:) method, as shown in Listing 9-12.

Listing 9-12. Handling Multiple Segues

```
// MARK: - Navigation

override func prepare(for segue: UIStoryboardSegue, sender: AnyObject?) {
    // Get the new view controller using [segue destinationViewController].
    // Pass the selected object to the new view controller.
    let tableViewCell = sender as! UITableViewCell
    let indexPath = tableView.indexPath(for: tableViewCell)!
    let font = fontForDisplay(atIndexPath: indexPath)

    if segue.identifier == "ShowFontSizes" {
        let sizesVC = segue.destinationViewController as! FontSizesViewController
        sizesVC.title = font.fontName
        sizesVC.font = font
    } else {
        let infoVC = segue.destinationViewController as! FontInfoViewController
        infoVC.title = font.fontName
        infoVC.font = font
        infoVC.favorite =
            FavoritesList.sharedFavoritesList.favorites.contains(font.fontName)
    }
}
```

Build and run the app to see how things worked out. Select a font family that contains many fonts (for example, Gill Sans) and then tap the middle of the row for any font. You'll be taken to the same list you saw earlier, which shows the font in multiple sizes. Press the navigation button at the upper left (it's labeled Gill Sans) to go back and then tap another row; however, this time tap on the right side where the detail accessory is shown. This should bring up the final view controller, which shows a sample of the font with a slider at the bottom that lets you pick whatever size you want.

Also, you can now use the "Include in favorites" switch to mark this font as a favorite. Do that and then hit the navigation button at the top-left corner a couple of times to get back to the root controller view.

Creating My Favorite Fonts

Scroll down to the bottom of the root view controller and you'll see something new: the My Favorite Fonts section is now there. Selecting it shows you a list of all the favorite fonts that have been selected so far, as shown in Figure 9-16.

Figure 9-16. *The list of favorite fonts selected so far*

Adding Features

Now the basic functionality of your app is complete. But before you can really call it a day, there are a couple more features you should implement. If you've been using iOS for a while, you're probably aware that you can often delete a row from a table view by swiping from right to left. For example, in Mail you can use this technique to delete a message in a list of messages. Performing this gesture brings up a small GUI, right inside the table view row. This GUI asks you to confirm the deletion, and then the row disappears and the remaining rows slide up to fill the gap. That whole interaction—including handling the swipe, showing the confirmation GUI, and animating any affected rows—is taken care of by the table view itself. All you need to do is implement two methods in your controller to make it happen.

Also, the table view provides easy-to-use functionality that lets the user reorder rows within a table view by dragging them up and down. As with swipe-to-delete, the table view takes care of the entire user interaction for you. All you have to do is one line of setup (to create a button that activates the reordering GUI) and then implement a single method that is called when the user has finished dragging.

Implementing Swipe-to-Delete

In this app, the FontListViewController class is a typical example of where this feature should be used. Whenever the app is showing the list of favorites, you should let the user delete a favorite with a swipe, saving them the step of tapping the detail accessory and then turning off the switch.

Select `FontListViewController.swift` in Xcode to get started. Start by adding an implementation of the `tableView(_:canEditRowAt: indexPath:)` method.

```
override func tableView(_ tableView: UITableView, canEditRowAt indexPath: IndexPath) -> Bool {
    return showsFavorites
}
```

That method will return `true` if it's showing the list of favorites, and `false` otherwise. This means that the editing functionality that lets you delete rows is enabled only while displaying favorites. If you were to try to run the app and delete rows with just this change, you wouldn't see any difference. The table view won't bother to deal with the swipe gesture because it sees that you haven't implemented the other method that is required to complete a deletion. So, let's put that in place, too. Add an implementation for the `tableView(_: commitEditingStyle:forRowAtIndexPath:)` method, as shown in Listing 9-13.

Listing 9-13. Allowing the Deletion of Rows from Your Favorites List

```
override func tableView(_ tableView: UITableView, commit editingStyle:
UITableViewCellEditingStyle, forRowAt indexPath: IndexPath) {
if !showsFavorites {
    return
}

if editingStyle == UITableViewCellEditingStyle.delete {
    // Delete the row from the data source
    let favorite = fontNames[indexPath.row]
    FavoritesList.sharedFavoritesList.removeFavorite(fontName: favorite)
    fontNames = FavoritesList.sharedFavoritesList.favorites

    tableView.deleteRows(at: [indexPath],
                         with: UITableViewRowAnimation.fade)
}

}
```

This method is called when an editing action in the table is being completed. It's pretty straightforward, but there are some subtle things going on. The first thing you do is check to make sure you're showing the favorites list, and if not, you just bail. Normally, this should never happen since you specified with the previous method that only the favorites list should be editable. Nevertheless, you're doing a bit of defensive programming here. After that, you check the editing style to make sure that the particular edit operation you're going to conclude really was a deletion. It's possible to do insertion edits in a table view but not without additional setup that you're not doing here, so you don't need to worry about that case. Next, you determine which font should be deleted, remove it from your `FavoritesList` singleton, and update your local copy of the favorites list.

Finally, you tell the table view to delete the row and make it disappear with a visual fade animation. It's important to understand what happens when you tell the table view to delete a row. Intuitively, you might think that calling that method would delete some data, but that's not what happens. In fact, you've already deleted the data! This final method call is really your way of telling the table view, "Hey, I've made a change, and I want you to animate away this row. Ask me if you need anything more." When that happens, the table view will start animating any rows that are below the deleted row by moving them up, which means that it's possible that one or more rows that were previously off-screen will now come on-screen, at which time it will indeed ask the controller for cell data via the usual methods. For that reason, it's important that your implementation of the `tableView(_:commitEditingStyle:forRowAtIndexPath:)` method makes necessary changes to the data model (in this case, the `FavoritesList` singleton) *before* telling the table view to delete a row.

Build and run the app again, make sure you have some favorite fonts set up, and then go into the Favorites list and delete a row by swiping from right to left. The row slides partly off-screen, and a Delete button appears on the right (see Figure 9-17). Tap the Delete button so that the row disappears.

Figure 9-17. *A favorite font row with the Delete button showing*

Implementing Drag-to-Reorder

The final feature you're going to add to the font list will let users rearrange their favorites just by dragging them up and down. To accomplish this, you're going to add one method to the `FavoritesList` class, which will let you reorder its items however you want. Open `FavoritesList.swift` and add the following method:

```
func moveItem(fromIndex from: Int, toIndex to: Int) {
    let item = favorites[from]
    favorites.remove(at: from)
    favorites.insert(item, at: to)
    saveFavorites()
}
```

This new method provides the underpinnings for what you're going to do. Now select
`FontListViewController.swift` and add the following lines at the end of the `viewDidLoad` method:

```
if showsFavorites {
    navigationItem.rightBarButtonItem = editButtonItem()
}
```

I've mentioned the navigation item. It's an object that holds the information about what should appear
in the navigation bar for a view controller. It has a property called `rightBarButtonItem` that can hold an
instance of `UIBarButtonItem`, a special sort of button meant only for navigation bars and toolbars. Here,
you're pointing that at `editButtonItem`, a property of `UIViewController` that gives you a special button item
that's preconfigured to activate the table view's editing/reordering GUI.

With that in place, try running the app again and go into the Favorites list. You'll see that there's now
an Edit button in the upper-right corner. Pressing that button toggles the table view's editing GUI, which
right now means that each row acquires a delete button on the left, while its content slides a bit to the right
to make room (see Figure 9-18). This enables yet another way that users can delete rows, using the same
methods you already implemented.

Figure 9-18. *You're added the Edit feature in your favorites table*

But your main interest here is in adding reordering functionality. For that, all you need to do is add the following method in `FontListViewController.swift`:

```
override func tableView(_ tableView: UITableView, moveRowAt sourceIndexPath: IndexPath, to
destinationIndexPath: IndexPath) {
    FavoritesList.sharedFavoritesList.moveItem(fromIndex: sourceIndexPath.row,
                                    toIndex: destinationIndexPath.row)
    fontNames = FavoritesList.sharedFavoritesList.favorites:
}
```

This method is called as soon as the user finishes dragging a row. The arguments tell you which row was moved and where it ended up. All you do here is tell the `FavoritesList` singleton to do the same reordering of its content and then refresh your list of font names, just as you did after deleting an item. To see this in action, run the app, go into the Favorites list, and tap the Edit button. You'll see that the edit mode now includes little "dragger" icons on the right side of each row, which you can use to rearrange items.

Summary

Although you worked a lot with table views in this chapter, your focus was really on the use of navigation controllers and how you drill down into hierarchical content in a limited-width space as you might have on most iPhone devices, especially in portrait orientation.

You created a font list view application that showed you not only how to drill down into more detailed views but how to handle multiple segues from a single table view cell as you did with looking at either font sizes or font information.

Finally, you looked at tweaking your table views a bit to include the capabilities of deleting and moving rows within the view.

CHAPTER 10

Collection Views

For years, iOS developers used the `UITableView` component to create a huge variety of interfaces. With its ability to let you define multiple cell types, create them on the fly as needed, and handily scroll them vertically, `UITableView` became a key component of thousands of apps. While Apple has increased the capability of table views with every major new iOS release, it's still not the ultimate solution for all large sets of data. If you want to present data in multiple columns, for example, you need to combine all the columns for each row of data into a single cell. There's also no way to make a `UITableView` scroll its content horizontally. In general, much of the power of `UITableView` came with a particular trade-off: developers have no control of the overall layout of a table view. You define the look of each individual cell, but the cells are just going to be stacked on top of each other in one big scrolling list.

In iOS 6, Apple introduced a new class called `UICollectionView` addressing these shortcomings. Similar to a table view, `UICollectionView` allows you to display a bunch of "cells" of data and handles functionality such as queuing up unused cells to use later. But unlike a table view, `UICollectionView` doesn't lay these cells out in a vertical stack for you. In fact, `UICollectionView` doesn't lay them out at all. Instead, `UICollectionView` uses a helper class to do layout.

Creating the DialogViewer Project

Let's start by talking about `UICollectionView`. To show some of its capabilities, you're going to use it to lay out some paragraphs of text. Each word will be placed in a cell of its own, and all the cells for each paragraph will be clustered together in a section. Each section will also have its own header. This may not seem too exciting, considering that UIKit already contains other perfectly good ways of laying out text. However, this process will be instructive anyway, since you'll get a feel for just how flexible this thing is. You certainly wouldn't get very far doing something like Figure 10-1 with a table view.

© Molly K. Maskrey 2017
M. K. Maskrey, *Beginning iPhone Development with Swift 4*, https://doi.org/10.1007/978-1-4842-3072-5_10

343

Figure 10-1. Each word is a separate cell, with the exception of the headers, which are, well, headers. All of this is laid out using a single UICollectionView and no explicit geometry calculations of your own.

To make this work, you'll define a couple of custom cell classes, you'll use `UICollectionViewFlowLayout` (the one and only layout helper class included in UIKit at this time), and, as usual, you'll use your view controller class to make it all come together.

Use Xcode to create a new application with the Single View App template, as you've done many times by now. Name your project **DialogViewer** and use the standard settings you've used throughout the book (set Language to Swift and choose Universal for Devices). Open `ViewController.swift` and change its superclass to `UICollectionView`.

class ViewController: UICollectionViewController {

Open `Main.storyboard`. You need to set up the view controller to match what you just specified in `ViewController.swift`. Select the one and only view controller in the Document Outline and delete it, leaving an empty storyboard. Now use the Object Library to locate a collection view controller and drag it into the editing area. If you examine the Document Outline, you'll see that the collection view controller comes with a nested collection view. Its relation to the collection view is very much like the relationship between `UITableViewController` and its nested `UITableView`. Select the icon for the collection view controller and use the Identity Inspector to change its class to ViewController, which you just made into a subclass of UICollectionViewController. In the Attributes Inspector, ensure that the Is Initial View Controller check box is selected. Next, select the collection view in the Document Outline and use the Attributes Inspector to change its background color to white. Finally, you'll see that the collection view has a child called Collection View Cell. This is a prototype cell that you can use to design the layout for your actual cells in Interface Builder, just like you have been doing with table view cells. You're not going to do that in this chapter, so select that cell and delete it.

Defining Custom Cells

Now let's define some cell classes. As you saw in Figure 10-1, you're displaying two basic kinds of cells: a "normal" one containing a word and another that is used as a sort of header. Any cell you're going to create for use in a UICollectionView needs to be a subclass of the system-supplied UICollectionViewCell class, which provides basic functionality similar to UITableViewCell. This functionality includes a backgroundView, a contentView, and so on. Because your two types of cell will have some shared functionality, you'll actually make one a subclass of the other and use the subclass to override some of the functionality of the base class.

Start by creating a new Cocoa Touch class in Xcode. Name the new class ContentCell and make it a subclass of UICollectionViewCell. Select the new class's source file and add declarations for three properties and a stub for a class method, as shown in Listing 10-1.

Listing 10-1. Your ContentCell Class Definition

```
class ContentCell: UICollectionViewCell {
    var label: UILabel!
    var text: String!
    var maxWidth: CGFloat!

    class func sizeForContentString(s: String,
                forMaxWidth maxWidth: CGFloat) -> CGSize {
        return CGSize.zero
    }
}
```

The label property will point at a UILabel. You'll use the text property to tell the cell what to display and the maxWidth property to control the cell's maximum width. You'll use the sizeForContentString(_: forMaxWidth:) method—which you'll implement shortly—to ask how big the cell needs to be to display a given string. This will come in handy when creating and configuring instances of your cell classes.

Now add overrides of the UIView init(frame:) and init(coder:) methods, as shown in Listing 10-2.

Listing 10-2. Init Override Routines for Your Cell ContentCell Class

```
override init(frame: CGRect) {
    super.init(frame: frame)
    label = UILabel(frame: self.contentView.bounds)
    label.isOpaque = false
    label.backgroundColor =
        UIColor(red: 0.8, green: 0.9, blue: 1.0, alpha: 1.0)
    label.textColor = UIColor.black()
    label.textAlignment = .center
    label.font = self.dynamicType.defaultFont()
    contentView.addSubview(label)
}
```

```
required init?(coder aDecoder: NSCoder) {
    super.init(coder: aDecoder)
}
```

The code in Listing 10-2 is pretty simple. It creates a label, sets its display properties, and adds the label to the cell's contentView. The only mysterious thing here is that it uses the defaultFont() method to get a font, which is used to set the label's font. The idea is that this class should define which font will be used for displaying content, while also allowing any subclasses to declare their own display font by overriding the defaultFont() method. We haven't created the defaultFont() method yet, so let's do so.

```
class func defaultFont() -> UIFont {
    return UIFont.preferredFontForTextStyle(UIFontTextStyleBody)
}
```

It's pretty straightforward. It uses the preferredFontForTextStyle() method of the UIFont class to get the user's preferred font for body text. The user can use the Settings app to change the size of this font. By using this method instead of hard-coding a font size, you make your apps a bit more user-friendly. Notice how this method is called:

```
label.font = self.dynamicType.defaultFont()
```

The defaultFont() method is a type method of the ContentCell class. To call it, you would normally use the name of the class, like this:

```
ContentCell.defaultFont()
```

In this case, that won't work—if this call is made from a subclass of ContentCell (such as the HeaderCell class that you will create shortly), you want to actually call the subclass' override of defaultFont(). To do that, you need a reference to the subclass's type object. That's what the expression self.dynamicType gives you. If this expression is executed from an instance of the ContentCell class, it resolves to the type object of ContentCell, and you'll call the defaultFont() method of that class; but in the HeaderCell subclass, it resolves to the type object for HeaderCell, and you'll call HeaderCell's defaultFont() method instead, which is exactly what you want. To finish off this class, let's implement the method that you added a stub for earlier, the one that computes an appropriate size for the cell, as shown in Listing 10-3.

Listing 10-3. Compute an Approximate Cell Size

```
class func sizeForContentString(s: String,
                                forMaxWidth maxWidth: CGFloat) -> CGSize {
    let maxSize = CGSize(width: maxWidth, height: 1000.0)
    let opts = NSStringDrawingOptions.usesLineFragmentOrigin

    let style = NSMutableParagraphStyle()
    style.lineBreakMode = NSLineBreakMode.byCharWrapping
    let attributes = [ NSFontAttributeName: defaultFont(),
                       NSParagraphStyleAttributeName: style]

    let string = s as NSString
    let rect = string.boundingRect(with: maxSize, options: opts,
                                   attributes: attributes, context: nil)

    return rect.size
}
```

The method in Listing 10-3 does a lot of things, so it's worth walking through it. First, you declare a maximum size so that no word will be allowed to be wider than the value of the maxWidth argument, which will be set from the width of the UICollectionView. You also create a paragraph style that allows for character wrapping, so in case your string is too big to fit in your given maximum width, it will wrap around to a subsequent line. You also create an attributes dictionary that contains the default font you defined for this class and the paragraph style you just created. Finally, you use some NSString functionality provided in UIKit that lets you calculate sizes for a string. We pass in an absolute maximum size and the other options and attributes that you set up, and you get back a size.

All that's left for this class is some special handling of the text property. Instead of letting this use an implicit instance variable as you normally do, you're going to define methods that get and set the value based on the UILabel you created earlier, basically using the UILabel as storage for the displayed value. By doing so, you can also use the setter to recalculate the cell's geometry when the text changes. Replace the definition of the text property in ContentCell.swift with the code in Listing 10-4.

Listing 10-4. The Text Property Definition in the ContentCell.swift File

```swift
var label: UILabel!
var text: String! {
    get {
        return label.text
    }
    set(newText) {
        label.text = newText
        var newLabelFrame = label.frame
        var newContentFrame = contentView.frame
        let textSize = type(of: self).sizeForContentString(s: newText,
                                                    forMaxWidth: maxWidth)

        newLabelFrame.size = textSize
        newContentFrame.size = textSize
        label.frame = newLabelFrame
        contentView.frame = newContentFrame
    }
}
```

The getter is nothing special, but the setter is doing some extra work. Basically, it's modifying the frame for both the label and the content view, based on the size needed for displaying the current string.

That's all you need for your base cell class. Now let's make a cell class to use for a header. Use Xcode to make another new Cocoa Touch class, naming this one HeaderCell and making it a subclass of ContentCell. Let's open HeaderCell.swift and make some changes. All you're going to do in this class is override some methods from the ContentCell class to change the cell's appearance, making it look different from the normal content cell, as shown in Listing 10-5.

Listing 10-5. The HeaderCell Class

```swift
class HeaderCell: ContentCell {

    override init(frame: CGRect) {
        super.init(frame: frame)
        label.backgroundColor = UIColor(red: 0.9, green: 0.9,
                                            blue: 0.8, alpha: 1.0)
        label.textColor = UIColor.black()
    }
```

```
    required init?(coder aDecoder: NSCoder) {
        super.init(coder: aDecoder)
    }

    override class func defaultFont() -> UIFont {
        return UIFont.preferredFont(forTextStyle: UIFontTextStyleHeadline)
    }

}
```

That's all you should have to do to give the header cell a distinct look, with its own colors and font.

Configuring the View Controller

Select `ViewController.swift` and start by declaring an array to contain the content you want to display, as shown in Listing 10-6.

Listing 10-6. Your Content to Be Displayed— Place This in the ViewController.swift File

```
private var sections = [
    ["header": "First Witch",
     "content" : "Hey, when will the three of us meet up later?"],
    ["header" : "Second Witch",
     "content" : "When everything's straightened out."],
    ["header" : "Third Witch",
     "content" : "That'll be just before sunset."],
    ["header" : "First Witch",
     "content" : "Where?"],
    ["header" : "Second Witch",
     "content" : "The dirt patch."],
    ["header" : "Third Witch",
     "content" : "I guess we'll see Mac there."]
]
```

The `sections` array contains a list of dictionaries, each of which has two keys: `header` and `content`. You'll use the values associated with those keys to define your display content.

Much like `UITableView`, `UICollectionView` lets you register the class of a reusable cell based on an identifier. Doing this lets you call a dequeuing method later, when you're going to provide a cell. If no cell is available, the collection view will create one for you—just like `UITableView`. Add this line to the end of the `viewDidLoad()` method to make this happen:

```
self.collectionView?.register(ContentCell.self, forCellWithReuseIdentifier: "CONTENT")
```

Since this application has no navigation bar, the content of the main view will be visible beneath the status bar. To prevent that, add the following lines to the end of `viewDidLoad()`:

```
var contentInset = collectionView!.contentInset
contentInset.top = 20
collectionView!.contentInset = contentInset
```

That's enough configuration in `viewDidLoad()` for now. Before you get to the code that populates the collection view, you need to write one little helper method. All of your content is contained in lengthy strings, but you're going to need to deal with them one word at a time to be able to put each word into a cell. So, let's create an internal method of your own to split those strings apart. This method takes a section number, pulls the relevant content string from your section data, and splits it into words.

```swift
func wordsInSection(section: Int) -> [String] {
    let content = sections[section]["content"]
    let spaces = NSCharacterSet.whitespacesAndNewlines
    let words = content?.components(separatedBy: spaces)
    return words!
}
```

Providing Content Cells

Now it's time to create the group of methods that will actually populate the collection view. These next three methods are all defined by the `UICollectionViewDataSource` protocol, which is adopted by the `UICollectionViewController` class. The `UICollectionViewController` assigns itself as the data source of its nested `UICollectionView`, so these methods will be called automatically by the `UICollectionView` when it needs to know about its content.

First, you need a method to let the collection view know how many sections to display:

```swift
override func numberOfSections(in collectionView: UICollectionView) -> Int {
    return sections.count
}
```

Next, you have a method to tell the collection how many items each section should contain. This uses the `wordsInSection()` method you defined earlier.

```swift
override func collectionView(_ collectionView: UICollectionView, numberOfItemsInSection
section: Int) -> Int {
    let words = wordsInSection(section: section)
    return words.count
}
```

Listing 10-7 shows the method that actually returns a single cell, configured to contain a single word. This method also uses your `wordsInSection()` method. As you can see, it uses a dequeuing method on `UICollectionView`, similar to the one in `UITableView`. Since you've registered a cell class for the identifier you're using here, you know that the dequeuing method always returns an instance.

Listing 10-7. Setting Up the Collection View Cell

```swift
override func collectionView(_ collectionView: UICollectionView, cellForItemAt indexPath:
IndexPath) -> UICollectionViewCell {
    let words = wordsInSection(section: indexPath.section)

    let cell = collectionView.dequeueReusableCell(
        withReuseIdentifier: "CONTENT", for: indexPath) as! ContentCell
    cell.maxWidth = collectionView.bounds.size.width
    cell.text = words[indexPath.row]
    return cell
}
```

Judging by the way that UITableView works, you might think that at this point you'd have something that works, in at least a minimal way. Build and run the app. You'll see that you're not really at a useful point yet, as shown in Figure 10-2.

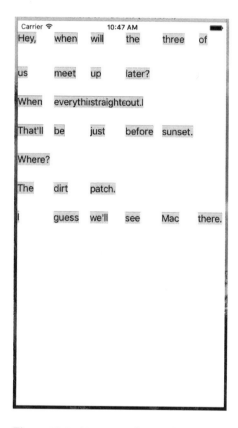

Figure 10-2. *Not quite what you're looking for…yet*

You can see some of the words, but there's no "low" going on here. Each cell is the same size, and everything is all jammed together. The reason for this is that you have some collection view delegate responsibilities you have to take care of to make things work.

Creating the Layout Flow

Until now, you've been dealing with the UICollectionView, but this class has a sidekick that takes care of the actual layout. UICollectionViewFlowLayout, which is the default layout helper for UICollectionView, includes delegate methods of its own that it will use to try to pull out more information from you. You're going to implement one of these right now. The layout object calls this method for each cell to find out how large it should be. Here you're once again using your wordsInSection() method to get access to the word in question and then using a method you defined in the ContentCell class to see how large it needs to be.

When the UICollectionViewController is initialized, it makes itself the delegate of its UICollectionView. The collection view's UICollectionViewFlowLayout will treat the view controller as its own delegate if it declares that it conforms to the UICollectionViewDelegateFlowLayout protocol. The first thing you need to do is change the declaration of your view controller in ViewController.swift so that it declares conformance to that protocol.

```
class ViewController: UICollectionViewController,
          UICollectionViewDelegateFlowLayout {
```

All of the methods of the UICollectionViewDelegateFlowLayout protocol are optional, and you need to implement only one of them. Add the method in Listing 10-8 to ViewController.swift.

Listing 10-8. Resizing the Cells Using the UICollectionViewDelegateFlowLayout Protocol

```
func collectionView(collectionView: UICollectionView,
          layout collectionViewLayout: UICollectionViewLayout,
          sizeForItemAtIndexPath indexPath: NSIndexPath) -> CGSize {
    let words = wordsInSection(indexPath.section)
    let size = ContentCell.sizeForContentString(words[indexPath.row],
                    forMaxWidth: collectionView.bounds.size.width)
    return size
}
```

Now build and run the app again. You'll see that you've taken a step forward, as shown in Figure 10-3.

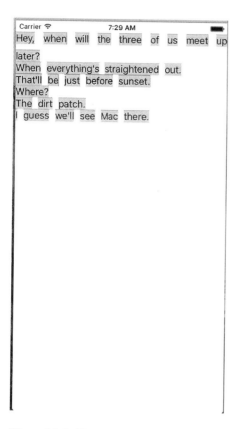

Figure 10-3. Your paragraph flow begins taking shape

You can see that the cells are now flowing and wrapping around so that the text is readable and that the beginning of each section drops down a bit. But each section is jammed really tightly against the ones before and after it. They're also pressing all the way out to the sides, which doesn't look too nice. Let's fix that by adding a bit more configuration. Add these lines to the end of the viewDidLoad() method:

```
let layout = collectionView!.collectionViewLayout
let flow = layout as! UICollectionViewFlowLayout
flow.sectionInset = UIEdgeInsetsMake(10, 20, 30, 20)
```

Here you're grabbing the layout object from your collection view. You assign this first to a temporary variable, which will be inferred to be of type UICollectionViewLayout. You do this primarily to highlight a point: UICollectionView knows only about this generic layout class, but it's really using an instance of UICollectionFlowLayout, which is a subclass of UICollectionViewLayout. Knowing the true type of the layout object, you can use a typecast to assign it to another variable of the correct type, enabling you to access properties that only that subclass has. In this case, you use the sectionInset property to tell the UICollectionViewLayout to leave some empty space around each item in the collection view. In this case, that means there will now be a little space around every word, as you'll see if you run the example again (see Figure 10-4).

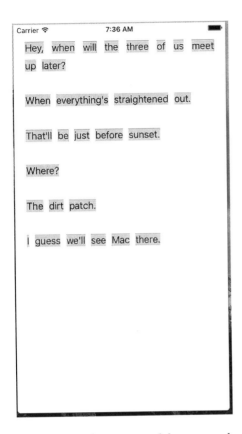

Figure 10-4. Things are much less cramped

Implementing the Header Views

The only thing missing now is the display of your header objects, so it's time to fix that. You will recall that UITableView has a system of header and footer views, and it asks for those specifically for each section. UICollectionView has made this concept a bit more generic, allowing for more flexibility in the layout. The way this works is that, along with the system of accessing normal cells from the delegate, there is a parallel system for accessing additional views that can be used as headers, footers, or anything else. Add this bit of code to the end of viewDidLoad() to let the collection view know about your header cell class:

```
self.collectionView?.register(HeaderCell.self,
                forSupplementaryViewOfKind: UICollectionElementKindSectionHeader,
                withReuseIdentifier: "HEADER")
```

As you can see, in this case not only are you specifying a cell class and an identifier, but you're also specifying a "kind." The idea is that different layouts may define different kinds of supplementary views and may ask the delegate to supply views for them. UICollectionFlowLayout is going to ask for one section header for each section in the collection view, which you'll supply, as shown in Listing 10-9.

Listing 10-9. Getting Your Header Cell View

```
override func collectionView(_ collectionView: UICollectionView,
viewForSupplementaryElementOfKind kind: String, at indexPath: IndexPath) ->
UICollectionReusableView {
    if (kind == UICollectionElementKindSectionHeader) {
        let cell =
            collectionView.dequeueReusableSupplementaryView(
                ofKind: kind, withReuseIdentifier: "HEADER",
                for: indexPath) as! HeaderCell
        cell.maxWidth = collectionView.bounds.size.width
        cell.text = sections[indexPath.section]["header"]
        return cell
    }
    abort()
}
```

Note the abort() call at the end of this method. This function causes the application to terminate immediately. It's not the sort of thing you should use frequently in production code. Here, you only expect to be called to create header cells, and there is nothing you can do if you are asked to create a different kind of cell—you can't even return nil because the method's return type does not permit it. If you are called to create a different kind of header, it's a programming error on your part or a bug in UIKit.

Build and run. You'll see...wait! Where are those headers? As it turns out, UICollectionFlowLayout won't give the headers any space in the layout unless you tell it exactly how large they should be. So, go back to viewDidLoad() and add the following line at the end:

flow.headerReferenceSize = CGSize(width: 100, height: 25)

Build and run once more. You'll see the headers in place, as Figure 10-1 showed earlier and Figure 10-5 shows again.

Figure 10-5. *The completed DialogViewer app*

Summary

In this chapter, I've really just touched on `UICollectionView` and what can be accomplished with the default `UICollectionFlowLayout` class. You can get even fancier with it by defining your own layout classes, but that is a topic for another book.

Stack views are something else you should look into when considering applications using collection views. They may offer an alternative approach that could save you time. As this book is tending to get larger and larger with the new Swift, Xcode, and iOS features, I'm leaving stack views as an exercise for you.

CHAPTER 11

Split Views and Popovers for iPad Apps

Chapter 9 dealt with app navigation based on selections in table views, where each selection causes the top-level view, which filled the entire screen, to slide left and bring in the next view in the hierarchy. Many iPhone and iPod touch apps work this way such as Mail, which lets you drill down through mail accounts and folders until you make your way to the message. Although this approach works on the iPad, it leads to a user interaction problem.

On a screen the size of the iPhone or iPod touch, having a screen-sized view slide away to reveal another screen-sized view works well. But with an iPad, that same interaction can seem less smooth, perhaps a little exaggerated, and even a little overwhelming. Consuming such a large display with a single table view wastes space. As a result, you'll see that the built-in iPad apps don't behave this way. Instead, any drill-down navigation functionality, like that used in Mail, becomes relegated to a narrow column whose contents slide left or right as the user drills down into or backs out of the hierarchy. With the iPad in landscape mode, the navigation column stays at a fixed position on the left, with the content of the selected item displayed on the right in what's known as a **split view** (see Figure 11-1), and applications built this way are called **master-detail** applications.

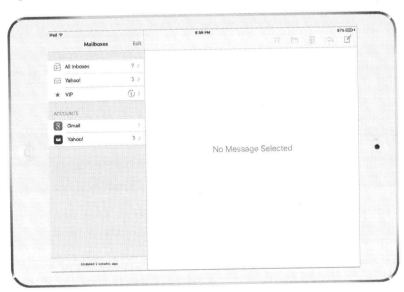

Figure 11-1. *This iPad, in landscape mode, shows a split view with the navigation column on the left. Tap an item in the navigation column, and that item's content displays in the area on the right.*

© Molly K. Maskrey 2017
M. K. Maskrey, *Beginning iPhone Development with Swift 4*, https://doi.org/10.1007/978-1-4842-3072-5_11

Split view provides a perfect visual for developing master-detail applications like Mail. Prior to iOS 8, the split view class, UISplitViewController, was available only on the iPad, meaning that if you wanted to build a universal master-detail application, you had to do it one way on the iPad and another way on the iPhone. Now, with UISplitViewController available everywhere, you no longer need to write special code to handle the iPhone.

When used on the iPad, the left side of the split view provides a width of 320 points by default. The split view itself, with navigation and content side by side, typically appears only in landscape mode. If you turn the device to portrait orientation, the split view still functions, but it's no longer visible in the same way. The navigation view loses its permanent location. It can be activated only by swiping in from the left side of the view or by pressing a toolbar button, causing it to slide in from the left in a view that floats in front of everything else on the screen, as shown in Figure 11-2.

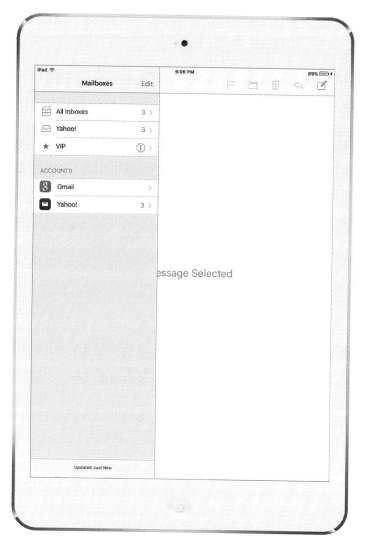

Figure 11-2. *Split view on an iPad in portrait mode appears differently from landscape mode, in that the information from the left side of the split view in landscape mode appears only when the user swipes in from the left or taps a toolbar button*

Some applications don't strictly follow this rule such as the iPad Settings app, which uses a split view visible all the time. The left side neither disappears nor covers the content view on the right. But for this chapter's project, you'll stick to the standard usage pattern.

You'll create a master-detail application using a split view controller, and then you'll test the application on the iPad simulator. But when it's finished, you'll see that the same code also works on the iPhone, although it doesn't quite look the same. You'll learn how to customize the split view's appearance and behavior and create and display a popover that's like the one that you saw in Chapter 4 when I discussed alert views and action sheets. Unlike the popover in Figure 4-29, which wrapped an action sheet, this one will contain content that is specific to the example application—specifically, a list of presidents, as shown in Figure 11-3.

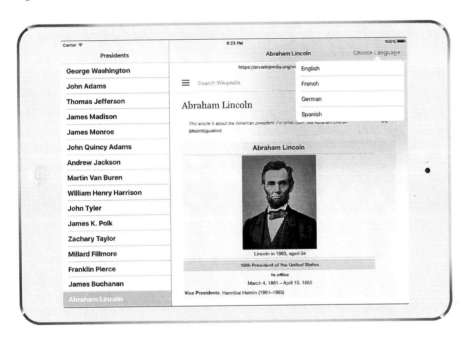

Figure 11-3. *A popover visually appears to sprout from the button that triggered it*

Building Master-Detail Applications with UISplitViewController

You're going to start off with an easy task: taking advantage of one of Xcode's predefined templates to create a split view project. You'll build an app that lists all the U.S. presidents and shows the Wikipedia entry for whichever one you select.

Open Xcode and select File ➤ New ➤ Project. From the iOS Application section, select Master-Detail Application and click Next. On the next screen, name the new project **Presidents**, set Language to Swift, and set Devices to Universal. Make sure that all of the check boxes are deselected. Click Next, choose the location for your project, and then click Create. Xcode will do its usual thing, creating a handful of classes and a storyboard file for you, and then showing the project. If it's not already open, expand the Presidents folder and take a look at what it contains.

From the start, the project contains an app delegate (as usual), a class called `MasterViewController`, and a class called `DetailViewController`. Those two view controllers represent, respectively, the views that will appear on the left and right sides of the split view in landscape orientation. `MasterViewController` defines the top level of a navigation structure, and `DetailViewController` defines what's displayed in the larger area when a navigation element is selected. When the app launches, both of these are contained inside a split view, which, as you may recall, does a bit of shape-shifting as the device is rotated.

To see what this particular application template gives you in terms of functionality, build the app and run it in the iPad simulator. If the application launches into portrait mode, you'll see just the detail view controller, as shown on the left in Figure 11-4. Tap the Master button on the toolbar or swipe from the left edge of the view to the right to slide in the master view controller over the top of the detail view, as shown on the right in Figure 11-4.

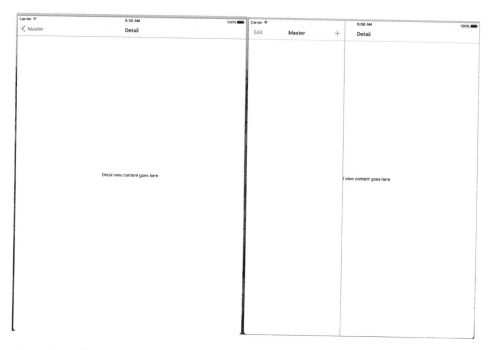

Figure 11-4. *The default master-detail application in portrait mode. The layout on the right is similar to Figure 11-2.*

Rotate the simulator left or right, into landscape orientation. In this mode, the split view works by showing the navigation view on the left and the detail view on the right, as shown in Figure 11-5.

Figure 11-5. *The default master-detail application in landscape mode. Note the similar layouts shown in this figure and Figure 11-1*

Understanding How the Storyboard Defines the Structure

From the onset, you have a pretty complex set of view controllers in play.

- A split view controller that contains all the elements

- A navigation controller to handle what's happening on the left side of the split

- A master view controller (displaying a master list of items) inside the navigation controller

- A detail view controller on the right

- Another navigation controller as a container for the detail view controller on the right

In the default master-detail application template that you used, these view controllers are set up and interconnected in the main storyboard file, rather than in code. Apart from doing GUI layout, Interface Builder functions as a way of letting you connect different components without writing a bunch of code establishing relationships. Let's look at the project's storyboard to see how things are set up.

Select Main.storyboard to open it in Interface Builder. This storyboard really has a lot of stuff going on. You'll definitely want to open the Document Outline for the best results, as shown in Figure 11-6. Zooming out can also help you see the big picture.

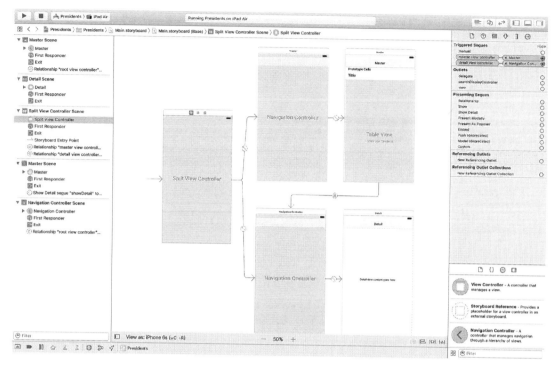

Figure 11-6. *Main.storyboard open in Interface Builder. This complex object hierarchy can be best viewed using the Document Outline on the left.*

To get a better sense of how these controllers relate to one another, open the Connections Inspector, and then spend some time clicking each of the view controllers in turn. Here's a quick summary of what you'll find:

- The `UISplitViewController` has relationship segues called *master view controller* and *detail view controller* to two `UINavigationControllers`. These are used to tell the `UISplitViewController` what it should use for the narrow strip it displays on the left (the master view controller) and for the larger display area (the detail view controller).

- The `UINavigationController` linked via the master view controller segue has a root view controller relationship to its own root view controller, which is the `MasterViewController` class generated by the template. The master view controller is a subclass of `UITableViewController`, which you should be familiar with from Chapter 9.

- Similarly, the other `UINavigationController` has a root view controller relationship to the detail view controller, which is the template's `DetailVIewController` class. The detail view controller generated by the template is a plain `UIViewController` subclass, but you are at liberty to use any view controller that meets your application's requirements.

- There is a storyboard segue from the cells in the master view controller to the detail view controller, of type showDetail. This segue causes the item in the clicked cell to be shown in the detail view. You'll learn more about this later when you take a more detailed look at the master view controller.

At this point, the content of Main.storyboard provides a definition of how the app's various controllers are interconnected. As in most cases where you're using storyboards, this eliminates a lot of code, which is usually a good thing.

Understanding How Code Defines the Functionality

One of the main reasons for keeping the view controller interconnections in a storyboard is that they don't clutter up your source code with configuration information that doesn't need to be there. What's left is just the code that defines the actual functionality. Let's look at what you have as a starting point. Xcode defined several classes for you when the project was created. You're going to peek into each of them before you start making any changes.

Creating the App Delegate

First up is AppDelegate.swift, the application delegate. Its source file starts something like Listing 11-1.

Listing 11-1. AppDelegate.swift

```
import UIKit


@UIApplicationMain
class AppDelegate: UIResponder, UIApplicationDelegate, UISplitViewControllerDelegate {

    var window: UIWindow?

    func application(_ application: UIApplication, didFinishLaunchingWithOptions
    launchOptions: [NSObject: AnyObject]?) -> Bool {
        // Override point for customization after application launch.
        let splitViewController = self.window!.rootViewController as! UISplitViewController
        let navigationController = splitViewController.viewControllers[splitViewController.
        viewControllers.count-1] as! UINavigationController
        navigationController.topViewController!.navigationItem.leftBarButtonItem =
        splitViewController.displayModeButtonItem()
        splitViewController.delegate = self
        return true
    }
```

Let's look at the last part of this code first:

```
splitViewController.delegate = self;
```

This line sets the UISplitViewController's delegate property, pointing it at the application delegate itself. But why make this connection here in code, instead of having it hooked up directly in the storyboard? After all, just a few paragraphs ago, you were told that elimination of boring code—"connect this thing to that thing"—is one of the main benefits of both XIBs and storyboards. And you've hooked up delegates in Interface Builder plenty of times, so why can't you do that here?

To understand why using a storyboard to make the connections can't really work here, you need to consider how a storyboard differs from a XIB file. A XIB file is really a frozen object graph. When you load a XIB into a running application, the objects it contains all "thaw out" and spring into existence, including all the interconnections specified in the file. The system creates a fresh instance of every single object in the file, one after another, and connects all the outlets and connections between objects. A storyboard, however, is something more than that. You could say that each scene in a storyboard corresponds roughly to a XIB file. When you add in the metadata describing how the scenes are connected via segues, you end up with a storyboard. However, unlike a single XIB, a complex storyboard is not normally loaded all at once. Instead, any activity that causes a new scene to be activated will end up loading that particular scene's frozen object graph from the storyboard. This means that the objects you see when looking at a storyboard won't necessarily all exist at the same time.

Since Interface Builder has no way of knowing which scenes will coexist, it actually forbids you from making any outlet or target/action connections from an object in one scene to an object in another scene. In fact, segues are the only connection that it allows you to make from one scene to another.

You can try this for yourself. First, select the split view controller in the storyboard (you'll find it within the dock in the split view controller scene). Now bring up the Connections Inspector and try to drag a connection from the delegate outlet to another view controller or object. You can drag all over the layout view and the list view, and you won't find any spot that highlights (which would indicate it was ready to accept a drag). The only way to make this connection is in code. All in all, this extra bit of code is a small price to pay, considering how much other code is eliminated by your use of storyboards.

Now let's rewind and look at what happens at the start of the `application(_:didFinishLaunchingWith Options:)` method:

```
let splitViewController = self.window!.rootViewController as! UISplitViewController
```

This grabs the window's `rootViewController`, which is the one indicated in the storyboard by the free-floating arrow. If you look back at Figure 11-6, you'll see that the arrow points at your `UISplitViewController` instance. This code comes next:

```
let navigationController = splitViewController.viewControllers[splitViewController.viewControllers.count-1] as! UINavigationController
```

On this line, you dig into the `UISplitViewController`'s `viewControllers` array. When the split view is loaded from the storyboard, this array has references to the navigation controllers, wrapping the master and detail view controllers. You grab the last item in this array, which points to the `UINavigationController` for your detail view. Finally, you see this:

```
navigationController.topViewController!.navigationItem.leftBarButtonItem =
    splitViewController.displayModeButtonItem()
```

This assigns the `displayModeButtonItem` of the split view controller to the navigation bar of the detail view controller. The `displayModeButtonItem` is a bar button item that is created and managed by the split view itself. This code is actually adding the Master button that you can see on the navigation bar on the left in Figure 11-4. On the iPad, the split view shows this button when the device is in portrait mode and the master view controller is not visible. When the device rotates to landscape orientation or the user presses the button to make the master view controller visible, the button is hidden.

Creating the Master View Controller

Now, let's take a look at `MasterViewController`, which controls the setup of the table view containing the app's navigation. Listing 11-2 shows the code from the top of the file `MasterViewController.swift`.

Listing 11-2. MasterViewController.swift

```swift
import UIKit

class MasterViewController: UITableViewController {

    var detailViewController: DetailViewController? = nil
    var objects = [AnyObject]()

    override func viewDidLoad() {
        super.viewDidLoad()
        // Do any additional setup after loading the view, typically from a nib.
        self.navigationItem.leftBarButtonItem = self.editButtonItem()

        let addButton =
UIBarButtonItem(barButtonSystemItem: .add, target: self, action:
#selector(insertNewObject(_:)))
        self.navigationItem.rightBarButtonItem = addButton
        if let split = self.splitViewController {
            let controllers = split.viewControllers
            self.detailViewController = (controllers[controllers.count-1] as!
            UINavigationController).topViewController as? DetailViewController
        }
    }
}
```

The main point of interest here is the viewDidLoad() method. In previous chapters, when you implemented a table view controller that responded to a user row selection, you typically created a new view controller and pushed it onto the navigation controller's stack. In this app, however, the view controller you want to show is already in place, and it will be reused each time the user makes a selection on the left. It's the instance of DetailViewController contained in the storyboard file. Here, you're grabbing that DetailViewController instance and saving it in a property, anticipating that you'll want to use it later, although this property is not used in the rest of the template code.

The viewDidLoad() method also adds a button to the toolbar. This is the + button that you can see on the right of master view controller's navigation bar in Figure 11-4 and Figure 11-5. The template application uses this button to create and add a new entry to the master view controller's table view. Since you don't need this button in your Presidents application, you'll be removing this code shortly.

There are several more methods included in the template for this class, but don't worry about those right now. You're going to delete some of those and rewrite the others, but only after taking a look at the detail view controller.

Creating the Detail View Controller

The final class created for you by Xcode is DetailViewController, which takes care of the actual display of the item the user chooses from the table in the master view controller. Listing 11-3 shows what you'll find in DetailViewController.swift.

Listing 11-3. DetailViewController.swift

```swift
import UIKit

class DetailViewController: UIViewController {

    @IBOutlet weak var detailDescriptionLabel: UILabel!

    func configureView() {
        // Update the user interface for the detail item.
        if let detail = self.detailItem {
            if let label = self.detailDescriptionLabel {
                label.text = detail.description
            }
        }
    }

    override func viewDidLoad() {
        super.viewDidLoad()
        // Do any additional setup after loading the view, typically from a nib.
        self.configureView()
    }

    override func didReceiveMemoryWarning() {
        super.didReceiveMemoryWarning()
        // Dispose of any resources that can be recreated.
    }

    var detailItem: NSDate? {
        didSet {
            // Update the view.
            self.configureView()
        }
    }
}
```

The detailDescriptionLabel property is an outlet that connects to a label in the storyboard. In the template application, the label simply displays a description of the object in the detailItem property. The detailItem property itself is where the view controller stores its reference to the object that the user selected in the master view controller. Its property observer (the code in the didSet block), which is called after its value has been changed, calls configureView(), another method that's generated for you. All it does is call the description method of the detail object and then uses the result to set the text property of the label in the storyboard.

```swift
func configureView() {
    // Update the user interface for the detail item.
    if let detail = self.detailItem {
        if let label = self.detailDescriptionLabel {
            label.text = detail.description
        }
    }
}
```

The `description` method is implemented by every subclass of `NSObject`. If your class doesn't override it, it returns a default value that's probably not very useful. However, in the template code, the detail objects are all instances of the `NSDate` class, and `NSDate`'s implementation of the `description` method returns the date and time, formatted in a generic way.

Understanding How the Master-Detail Template Application Works

Now you've seen all of the pieces of the template application, but you're probably still not very clear on how it works, so let's run it and take a look at what it actually does. Run the application on an iPad simulator and rotate the device to landscape mode so that the master view controller appears. You can see that the label in the detail view controller currently has the default text that's assigned to it in the storyboard. What you're going to see in this section is how the act of selecting an item in the master view controller causes that text to change. There currently aren't any items in the master view controller. To fix that, press the + button at the top right of its navigation bar a few times. Every time you do that, a new item is added to the controller's table view, as shown in Figure 11-7.

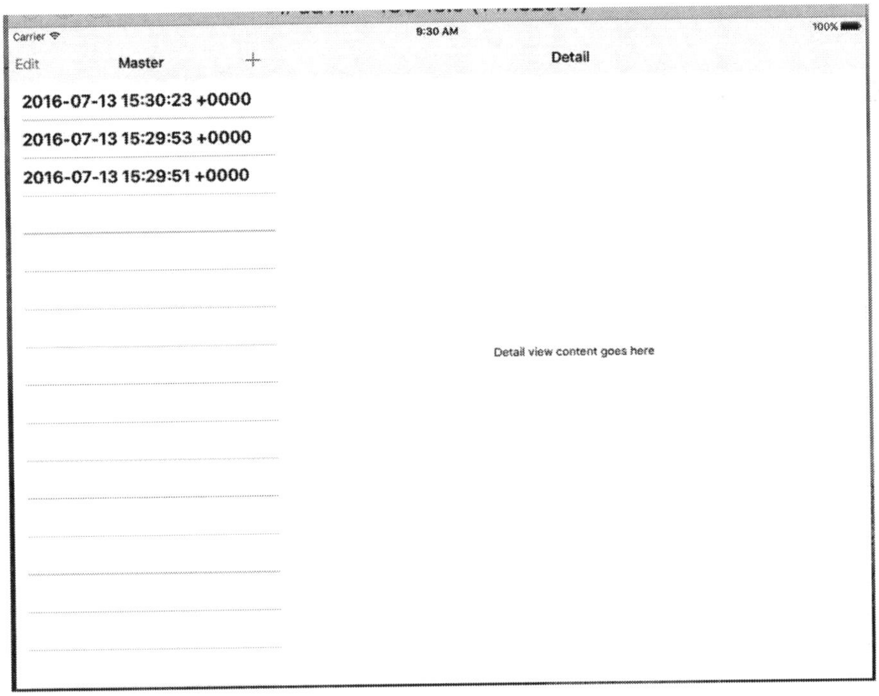

Figure 11-7. *The template application with an item selected in the master view controller and displayed in the detail view controller*

All of the items in the master view controller table are dates. Select one of them, and the label in the detail view updates to show the same date. You've already seen the code that does this—it's the `configureView` method in `DetailViewController.swift`, which is called when a new value is stored in the detail view controller's `detailItem` property. What is it that causes a new value of the `detailItem` property to be set? Take a look back at the storyboard in Figure 11-6. There's a segue that links the prototype table cell in the master view controller's table cell to the detail view controller. If you click this segue and open the Attributes Inspector, you'll see that this is a Show Detail segue with the identifier `showDetail`, as shown in Figure 11-8.

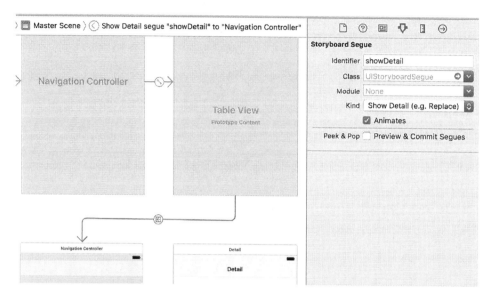

Figure 11-8. The Show Detail segue linking the master and detail view controllers

As you saw in Chapter 9, a segue that's linked to a table view cell is triggered when that cell is selected, so when you select a row in the master view controller's table view, iOS performs the Show Detail segue, with the navigation controller wrapping the detail view controller as the segue destination. This causes two things to happen.

- A new instance of the detail view controller is created, and its view is added to the view hierarchy.

- The prepareForSegue(_:sender:) method in the master view controller is called.

The first step takes care of making sure the detail view controller is visible. In the second step, your master view controller needs to display the object selected in the master view controller in some way. Here's how the template code in MasterViewController.swift handles this, as shown in Listing 11-4.

Listing 11-4. The MasterViewcontroller.swift File's prepare(forSegue:)

```
// MARK: - Segues

override func prepare(for segue: UIStoryboardSegue, sender: AnyObject?) {
    if segue.identifier == "showDetail" {
        if let indexPath = self.tableView.indexPathForSelectedRow {
            let object = objects[indexPath.row] as! NSDate
            let controller = (segue.destinationViewController as! UINavigationController).
            topViewController as! DetailViewController
            controller.detailItem = object
            controller.navigationItem.leftBarButtonItem = self.splitViewController?.
            displayModeButtonItem()
            controller.navigationItem.leftItemsSupplementBackButton = true
        }
    }
}
```

First, the segue identifier is checked to make sure that it's the one that is expected and that the NSDate object from the selected object in the view controller's table is obtained. Next, the master view controller finds the DetailViewController instance from the topViewController property of the destination view controller in the segue that caused this method to be called. Now that you have both the selected object and the detail view controller, all you have to do is set the detail view controller's detailItem property to cause the detail view to be updated. The final two lines of the prepare(forSegue:) method add the display mode button to the detail view controller's navigation bar. When the device is in landscape mode, this doesn't do anything because the display mode button isn't visible, but if you rotate to portrait orientation, you'll see that the button (it's the Master button) appears.

So, now you know how the selected item in the master view controller gets displayed in the detail view controller. Although it doesn't look like much is going on here, in fact there is a great deal happening under the hood to make this work correctly on both the iPad and the iPhone, in portrait and landscape orientations. The beauty of the split view controller is that it takes care of all the details and leaves you free to worry about how to implement your custom master and detail view controllers.

That concludes the overview of what the Xcode Master-Detail Application template provides. It might be a lot to understand at first, but, ideally, presenting it one piece at a time has helped you understand how all the pieces fit together.

Adding the President Data

Now that you've seen the basic layout of your project, it's time to fill in the blanks and turn the template app into something all your own. Start by looking in the book's source code archive, where the folder Presidents Data contains a file called PresidentList.plist. Drag that file into your project's Presidents folder in Xcode to add it to the project, making sure that the check box telling Xcode to copy the file itself is selected. This file contains information about all the U.S. presidents so far, consisting of just the name and the Wikipedia entry URL for each of them.

Now, let's look at the master view controller and see how you need to modify it to handle the presidential data properly. It's going to be a simple matter of loading the list of presidents, presenting them in the table view, and passing a URL to the detail view for display. In MasterViewController.swift, start off by adding the bold line shown here at the top of the class and removing the crossed-out line:

```
class MasterViewController: UITableViewController {
    var detailViewController: DetailViewController? = nil
    var objects = [AnyObject]()
    var presidents: [[String: String]]!
```

Now look at the viewDidLoad() method, where the changes are a little more involved (but still not too bad). You're going to add a few lines to load the list of presidents and then remove a few other lines that set up edit and insertion buttons in the toolbar, as shown in Listing 11-5.

Listing 11-5. The MasterViewController.swift viewDidLoad Method

```
override func viewDidLoad() {
    super.viewDidLoad()
    // Do any additional setup after loading the view, typically from a nib.
    let path = Bundle.main.path(forResource: "PresidentList", ofType: "plist")
    let presidentInfo = NSDictionary(contentsOfFile: path)!
    presidents = presidentInfo["presidents"]! as! [[String: String]]
```

```
    if let split = self.splitViewController {
        let controllers = split.viewControllers
        self.detailViewController = (
controllers[controllers.count-1] as! UINavigationController).topViewController as?
DetailViewController
    }
}
```

This code may be a little confusing at first.

```
let path = Bundle.main.path(forResource:"PresidentList", ofType: "plist")!
let presidentInfo = NSDictionary(contentsOfFile: path)!
presidents = presidentInfo["presidents"]! as! [[String: String]]
```

The Bundle.main pathForResource(_:ofType:) method gets the path to the PresidentList.plist file, the content of which is then loaded into an NSDictionary. This dictionary has one entry, with the key presidents. The value of that entry is an array, which has one NSDictionary for each president; that dictionary contains key-value pairs, where both the key and the value are strings. You cast the array to the correct Swift type, [[String: String]], and assign it to the presidents variable.

This template-generated class also includes a method called insertNewObject() for adding items to the objects array. You don't even have that array anymore, so delete the entire method.

Also, you have a couple of data source methods that deal with letting users edit rows in the table view. You're not going to allow any editing of rows in this app, so let's just remove the canEditRowAt and commit editingStyle: methods.

Now it's time to get to the main table view data source methods, adapting them for your purposes. Let's start by editing the method that tells the table view how many rows to display.

```
override func tableView(_ tableView: UITableView, numberOfRowsInSection section: Int) -> Int {
        return presidents.count
    }
```

After that, edit the tableView(_:cellForRowAtIndexPath:) method to make each cell display a president's name.

```
override func tableView(_ tableView: UITableView, cellForRowAt indexPath: IndexPath) ->
UITableViewCell {
    let cell = tableView.dequeueReusableCell(withIdentifier: "Cell", for: indexPath)

    let president = presidents[indexPath.row]
    cell.textLabel!.text = president["name"]
    return cell
}
```

Finally, edit the prepareForSegue(_:sender:) method to pass the data for the selected president (which, as described earlier, is a dictionary of type [String: String]) to the detail view controller, as in Listing 11-6.

Listing 11-6. The prepare (forSegue:) Method

```
// MARK: - Segues

override func prepare(for segue: UIStoryboardSegue, sender: AnyObject?) {
    if segue.identifier == "showDetail" {
        if let indexPath = self.tableView.indexPathForSelectedRow {
            let object = presidents[indexPath.row]
            let controller = (segue.destinationViewController
                as! UINavigationController).topViewController as! DetailViewController
            controller.detailItem = object
            controller.navigationItem.leftBarButtonItem =
                self.splitViewController?.displayModeButtonItem()
            controller.navigationItem.leftItemsSupplementBackButton = true
        }
    }
}
```

■ **Note** If your template for the `DetailViewController.swift` file's `detailItem` method had the value `NSDate` or similar, you should change it to `AnyObject?` to remove potential errors.

That's all you need to do in the master view controller.

Next, select `Main.storyboard`, click the Master icon in the master scheme in the Document Outline to select the master view controller (it's the one on the right of the top row of the storyboard), double-click its title bar, replace Master with **Presidents**, and save the storyboard.

At this point, you can build and run the app. Switch to landscape mode to bring up the master view controller, showing a list of presidents, as in Figure 11-9. Tap a president's name to display a not-very-useful string in the detail view.

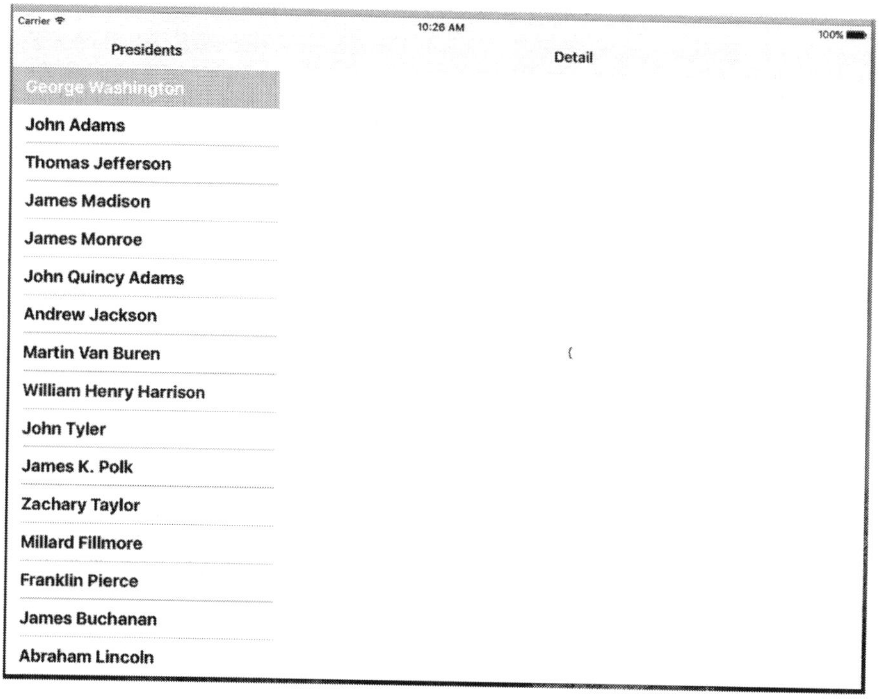

Figure 11-9. Your first run of the app, showing a list of presidents in the master view controller, but nothing in the detail view

Let's finish this example by making the detail view do something a little more useful with the data that it's given. Add the following line shown in bold to `DetailViewContoller.swift` to create an outlet for a web view to display the Wikipedia page for the selected president:

```
class DetailViewController: UIViewController {
    @IBOutlet weak var detailDescriptionLabel: UILabel!
    @IBOutlet weak var webView: UIWebView!
```

Next, scroll down to the `configureView()` method and replace it with the code in Listing 11-7.

Listing 11-7. The configureView Method

```
func configureView() {
    // Update the user interface for the detail item.
    if let detail = self.detailItem {
if let label = self.detailDescriptionLabel {
            let dict = detail as! [String: String]
            let urlString = dict["url"]!
            label.text = urlString

            let url = NSURL(string: urlString)!
            let request = URLRequest(url: url as URL)
            webView.loadRequest(request)
```

372

```
            let name = dict["name"]!
            title = name
        }
    }
}
```

The detailItem that was set by the master view controller is a dictionary containing two key-value pairs: one with a key name that stores the president's name and another with a key url that gives the URL of the president's Wikipedia page. You use the URL to set the text of the detail description label and to construct an URLRequest that the UIWebView will use to load the page. You use the name to set the detail view controller's title. When a view controller is a container in a UINavigationController, the value in its title property is displayed in the navigation controller's navigation bar. That's all you need to get your web view to load the requested page.

The final changes you need to make are in Main.storyboard. Open it for editing and find the detail view at the lower right. Let's first take care of the label in the GUI (the text of which reads "Detail view content goes here"). Start by selecting the label. You might find it easiest to select the label in the Document Outline, in the section labeled Detail Scene. Once the label is selected, drag it to the top of the window. The label should run from the left-to-right blue guideline and fit snugly under the navigation bar (resize it to make sure that is the case). This label is being repurposed to show the current URL. But when the application launches, before the user has chosen a president, you want this field to give the user a hint about what to do.

Double-click the label and change its text to **Select a President**. You should also use the Size Inspector to make sure that the label's position is constrained to both the left and right sides of its superview, as well as the top edge, as shown in Figure 11-10. If you need to adjust these constraints, use the methods described earlier to set them up. You can probably get almost exactly what you want by selecting the label and then choosing Editor ➤ Resolve Auto Layout Issues ➤ Reset to Suggested Constraints from the menu.

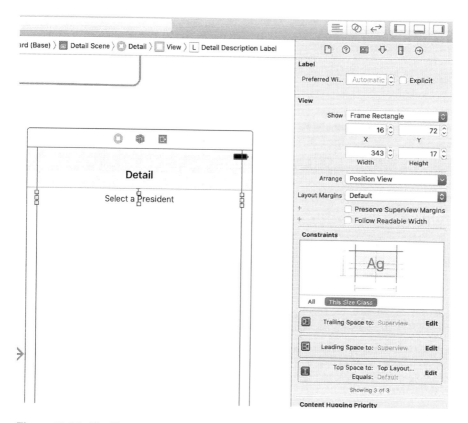

Figure 11-10. *The Size Inspector, showing the constraints settings for the "Select a President" label*

Next, find a UIWebView in the Object Library and drag it into the space below the label you just moved. After dropping the web view there, use the resize handles to make it fill the rest of the view below the label. Make it go from the left edge to the right edge and from the blue guideline just below the bottom of the label all the way to the very bottom of the window. Now use the Size Inspector to constrain the web view to the left, bottom, and right edges of the superview, as well as to the label for the top edge. Once again, you can probably get exactly what you need by selecting Editor ➤ Resolve Auto Layout Issues ➤ Reset to Suggested Constraints from the menu.

Now select the master view controller in the Document Outline and open the Attributes Inspector. In the View Controller section, change the title from Master to **Presidents**. This changes the title of the navigation button at the top of the detail view controller to something more useful.

You have one last step to complete. To hook up the outlet for the web view that you created, Control-drag from the Detail icon (the one immediately below the Detail Scene icon in the Document Outline) to your new web view (same section, just below the label in the Document Outline, or in the storyboard) and connect the webView outlet. Save your changes.

Now you can build and run the app. It will let you see the Wikipedia entries for each of the presidents, as shown in Figure 11-11. Rotate the display between the two orientations. You'll see how the split view controller takes care of everything for you, with a little help from the detail view controller.

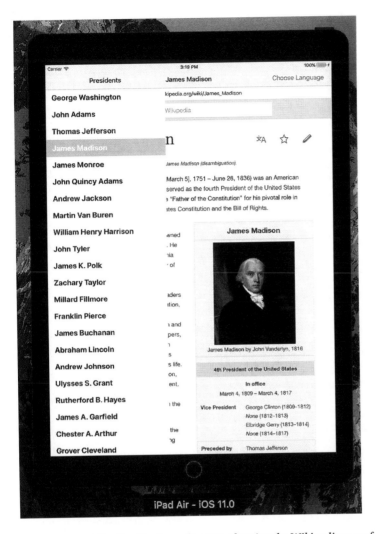

Figure 11-11. *The Presidents application, showing the Wikipedia page for James Madison*

Creating Your Own Popover

In Chapter 4, you saw that you can display an action sheet in what looks like a cartoon speech bubble (see Figure 4-29). That speech bubble is the visual representation of a *popover controller*, or *popover* for short. The popover that you get with an action sheet is created for you when the action sheet is presented by a UIPopoverPresentationController. It turns out that you can use the same controller to create popovers of your own.

To see how this works, you're going to add a popover that will be activated by a permanent toolbar item (unlike the one in the UISplitView, which is meant to come and go). This popover will display a table view containing a list of languages. If the user picks a language from the list, the web view will load whatever Wikipedia entry that was already showing, in the new language. This is simple enough to do since switching from one language to another in Wikipedia is just a matter of changing a small piece of the URL that contains an embedded country code. Figure 11-3 shows what you are aiming for.

▪ **Note**   In this example, you're using a `UIPopoverPresentationController` to display a table view controller, but don't let that mislead you—it can be used to handle the display of any view controller content you like. I'm sticking with table views for this example because it's a common use case, it's easy to show in a relatively small amount of code, and it's something with which you should already be quite familiar.

Start by right-clicking the `Presidents` folder in Xcode and selecting New File from the pop-up menu. When the assistant appears, select Cocoa Touch Class from the iOS Source section and then click Next. On the next screen, name the new class `LanguageListController` and select `UITableViewController` from the "Subclass of" field. Click Next, double-check the location where you're saving the file, and click Create.

The `LanguageListController` will be a pretty standard table view controller class. It will display a list of items and let the detail view controller know when a choice is made by using a pointer back to the detail view controller. Edit `LanguageListController.swift`, adding the three lines shown after the class name:

```
class LanguageListController: UITableViewController {
    weak var detailViewController: DetailViewController? = nil
    private let languageNames: [String] = ["English", "French", "German", "Spanish"]
    private let languageCodes: [String] = ["en", "fr", "de", "es"]
```

These additions define a pointer back to the detail view controller (which you'll set from code in the detail view controller itself when you're about to display the language list), as well as a pair of arrays containing the values that will be displayed (English, French, etc.) and the underlying values that will be used to build an URL from the chosen language (`en`, `fr`, and so on).

If you copied and pasted this code from the book's source archive (or e-book) into your own project or typed it yourself a little sloppily, you may not have noticed an important difference in how the `detailViewController` property was declared earlier. Unlike most properties that reference an object pointer, you declared this one using `weak` instead of `strong`. This is something you must do to avoid a *retain cycle*.

What's a retain cycle? It's a situation where a set of two or more objects have references to each other, in a circular fashion. Each object is keeping the memory of the other object from being freed. Most potential retain cycles can be avoided by carefully considering the creation of your objects, often by trying to figure out which object "owns" which. In this sense, an instance of `DetailViewController` owns an instance of `LanguageListController` because it's the `DetailViewController` that actually creates the `LanguageListController` to get a piece of work done. Whenever you have a pair of objects that need to refer to one another, you'll usually want the owner object to retain the other object, while the other object should specifically not retain its owner. Since you're using the ARC feature that Apple introduced way back in Xcode 4.2, the compiler does most of the work for you. Instead of paying attention to the details about releasing and retaining objects, all you need to do is declare a property that refers to an object that you do not own with the `weak` keyword instead of `strong`. ARC does the rest.

Next, scroll down a bit to the `viewDidLoad()` method and add this setup code:

```
override func viewDidLoad() {
    super.viewDidLoad()

    clearsSelectionOnViewWillAppear = false
    preferredContentSize = CGSize(width: 320, height: (languageCodes.count * 44))
    tableView.register(UITableViewCell.self, forCellReuseIdentifier: "Cell")
}
```

Here, you define the size that the view controller's view will use if shown in a popover (which, as you know, it will be). Without defining the size, you would end up with a popover stretching vertically to fill nearly the whole screen, even if it can be displayed in full with a much smaller view. And finally, you register a default table view cell class to use, as explained in Chapter 8.

Further down, you have a few methods generated by Xcode's template that don't contain particularly useful code—just a warning and some placeholder text. Let's replace those with something real.

```
override func numberOfSections(in tableView: UITableView) -> Int {
    return 1
}
override func tableView(_ tableView: UITableView, numberOfRowsInSection section: Int) -> Int {
    return languageCodes.count
}
```

Now implement the `tableView(_:cellForRow atIndexPath:)` method to get a cell object and put a language name into a cell, as shown in Listing 11-8.

Listing 11-8. Getting Your Cell for the Table View

```
override func tableView(_ tableView: UITableView, cellForRowAt indexPath: IndexPath) ->
UITableViewCell {
    let cell = tableView.dequeueReusableCell(withIdentifier: "Cell", for: indexPath)
    // Configure the cell...
    cell.textLabel!.text = languageNames[indexPath.row]

    return cell
}
```

Next, implement `tableView(_:didSelectRowAtIndexPath:)` so that you can respond to a user's touch by passing the language selection back to the detail view controller and dismissing the presented LanguageListController by calling its `dismissViewControllerAnimated(_:completion:)` method.

```
override func tableView(_ tableView: UITableView, didSelectRowAt indexPath: IndexPath) {
    detailViewController?.languageString = languageCodes[indexPath.row]
    dismiss(animated: true, completion: nil)
}
```

■ **Note** DetailViewController doesn't actually have a languageString property yet, so you will see a compiler error. You'll take care of that in just a bit.

Now it's time to make the changes required for `DetailViewController` to display the popover, as well as to generate the correct URL whenever the user either changes the display language or picks a different president. Start by adding the following three lines of code in `DetailViewController.swift` after the UIWebView declaration:

```
private var languageListController: LanguageListController?
private var languageButton: UIBarButtonItem?
var languageString = ""
```

You added some properties to keep track of the GUI components required for the popover and the user's selected language. All that you need to do now is fix `DetailViewController.swift` so that it can handle the language popover and the URL construction.

Start by adding a function that takes as arguments a URL pointing to a Wikipedia page and a two-letter language code and then returns a URL that combines the two. You'll use this at appropriate spots in your controller code later, as shown in Listing 11-9.

Listing 11-9. Function to Get Your Language-Specific URL

```
private func modifyUrlForLanguage(url: String, language lang: String?) -> String {
    var newUrl = url

    // We're relying on a particular Wikipedia URL format here. This
    // is a bit fragile!
    if let langStr = lang {
        // URL is like https://en.wikipedia...
        let range = NSMakeRange(8, 2)
        if !langStr.isEmpty && (url as NSString).substring(with: range) != langStr {
            newUrl = (url as NSString).replacingCharacters(in: range,
                                                           with: langStr)
        }
    }


    return newUrl
}
```

Your next move is to update the `configureView()` method. This method will use the function you just defined to combine the URL that's passed in with the chosen `languageString` to generate the correct URL, as shown in Listing 11-10.

Listing 11-10. Update configureView Method for the Language-Specific URL

```
func configureView() {
    // Update the user interface for the detail item.
    if let detail = self.detailItem {
        if let label = self.detailDescriptionLabel {
            let dict = detail as! [String: String]
            // let urlString = dict["url"]!
            let urlString = modifyUrlForLanguage(url: dict["url"]!, language:
            languageString)
            label.text = urlString

            let url = URL(string: urlString)!
            let request = URLRequest(url: url )
            webView.loadRequest(request)
            let name = dict["name"]!
            title = name
        }
    }
}
```

Now let's update the viewDidLoad() method. Here, you're going to create a UIBarButtonItem and put it into the UINavigationItem at the top of the screen. The button will call the controller's showLanguagePopover() method, which you'll implement shortly, when it is clicked, as shown in Listing 11-11.

Listing 11-11. The Modified viewDidLoad Method

```
override func viewDidLoad() {
    super.viewDidLoad()
    // Do any additional setup after loading the view, typically from a nib.
    self.configureView()
    languageButton = UIBarButtonItem(title: "Choose Language", style: .plain,
                                        target: self, action:
            #selector(DetailViewController.showLanguagePopover))
    navigationItem.rightBarButtonItem = languageButton
}
```

Next, you implement a property observer for the languageString property, which is called when the value of the property is changed. The property observer calls configureView() so that the URL is regenerated to include the selected language and the new page loaded.

```
var languageString = "" {
    didSet {
        if languageString != oldValue {
            configureView()
        }
    }
}
```

Now, let's implement the method that's called when the user taps the Choose Language button. Simply put, you display the LanguageListController, creating it the first time you do so. Then, you get its popover presentation controller and set the properties that control where the popover will appear. Place this method after the viewDidLoad() method, as shown in Listing 11-12.

Listing 11-12. The showLanguagePopover Method

```
@objc func showLanguagePopover() {
    if languageListController == nil {
        // Lazy creation when used for the first time
        languageListController = LanguageListController()
        languageListController!.detailViewController = self
        languageListController!.modalPresentationStyle = .popover
    }
    present(languageListController!, animated: true, completion: nil)
    if let ppc = languageListController?.popoverPresentationController {
        ppc.barButtonItem = languageButton
    }
}
```

In the first part of this method, you check whether you have already created the LanguageListController. If you haven't, you create an instance and then set its detailViewController property to point to itself. You also set its modalPresentationStyle property to .popover. This property determines how the controller is displayed when it is modally presented. There are several possible values, which you can read about on the documentation page for the UIViewController class. Not surprisingly, the value .popover is the one you need to use if you want the controller to be presented in a popover.

Next, you use the `presentViewController(_:animated:completion:)` method to make the `LanguageListController` visible, just as you did when displaying an alert in Chapter 4. Calling this method does not make the controller visible immediately—UIKit does that when it's finished processing the button click event—but it does create the `UIPopoverPresentationController` that will manage the controller's popover. Before the popover appears, you need to tell the UIKit framework where it should appear. In Chapter 4, you used this technique to place a popover near a specific view by setting its `UIPopoverPresentationController`'s `sourceRect` and `sourceView` properties. In this example, you want the popover to appear near the language button, and you can do that by assigning a reference to that button to the controller's `barButtonItem` property.

Now run the example on the iPad simulator and press the Choose Language button. You'll find that the language list controller is displayed in a popover, as shown in Figure 11-12. You should be able to use the language pop-up to select any of the four available languages and watch the web view update to show the version of the president's page for that language.

Figure 11-12. *Choosing to load a page in a different language*

Switching from one language to another should always leave the chosen president intact. Likewise, switching from one president to another should leave the language intact—but actually, it doesn't. Try this: choose a president, change the language to (say) Spanish, and then choose another president. Unfortunately, the language is no longer Spanish.

Why did this happen? The Show Detail segue creates a new instance of the detail view controller every time it's called. That means that the language setting, which is stored as a property of the detail view controller, is going to be lost each time a new president is selected. To fix it, you need to add a few lines of code in the master view controller. Open `MasterViewController.swift` and make the changes in Listing 11-13 to the `prepareForSegue` method.

Listing 11-13. Updated prepareForSegue Method

```
override func prepare(for segue: UIStoryboardSegue, sender: AnyObject?) {
    if segue.identifier == "showDetail" {
        if let indexPath = self.tableView.indexPathForSelectedRow {
            let object = presidents[indexPath.row]
            let controller = (segue.destinationViewController as!
                UINavigationController).topViewController as! DetailViewController
            if let oldController = detailViewController {
                controller.languageString = oldController.languageString
            }
            controller.detailItem = object
            controller.navigationItem.leftBarButtonItem =
                self.splitViewController?.displayModeButtonItem()
            controller.navigationItem.leftItemsSupplementBackButton = true
            detailViewController = controller
        }
    }
}
```

Summary

In this chapter, you learned about the split view controller and its role in the creation of master-detail applications. You also saw that a complex application with several interconnected view controllers can be configured entirely within Interface Builder. Although split views are now available on all devices, they are probably still most useful in the larger screen space of the iPhone 7/6s Plus and the iPad.

CHAPTER 12

■ ■ ■

App Customization with Settings and Defaults

Typically, all but the simplest apps you're likely to use include a preferences window where the user sets application-specific options. On macOS, you'll usually find a Preferences menu item in the application's menu. Selecting it brings up a window where the user enters and changes various options. The iPhone and iPad include a dedicated application called Settings that you've likely used before. In this chapter, I'll show you how to add settings for your iOS application to the Settings app and how to access those settings from within your application.

Exploring the Settings Bundle

The Settings application lets the user enter and change preferences for any application that includes a settings bundle. The settings bundle contains a group of files built in to an application that tells the Settings application which preferences the application want to collect from the user, as shown in Figure 12-1. The Settings application acts as a common user interface for the iOS User Defaults mechanism. User Defaults stores and retrieves preferences for the application.

© Molly K. Maskrey 2017
M. K. Maskrey, *Beginning iPhone Development with Swift 4*, https://doi.org/10.1007/978-1-4842-3072-5_12

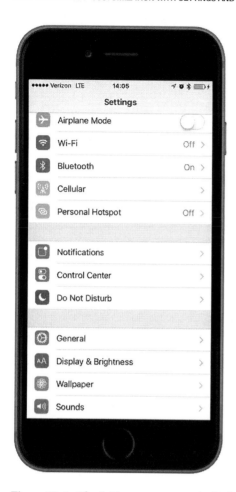

Figure 12-1. *The Settings app on a typical iPhone display*

In an iOS application, the NSUserDefaults class provides the User Defaults service. If you've programmed in Cocoa on macOS, you're probably already familiar with NSUserDefaults because it's the same class used to store and read preferences on macOS. Your applications use NSUserDefaults to read and store preference data using pairs of keys and values, just as you would access keyed data from a dictionary. The difference is that NSUserDefaults data persists to the file system rather than stored in an object instance in memory. In this chapter, you'll create an application, add and configure a settings bundle, and then access and edit those preferences from the Settings application and from within your own application.

Because the Settings app provides a standard interface, you don't need to design your own UI for your app's preferences. You create a property list describing your application's available settings, and the Settings app creates the interface for you. Immersive applications, such as games, generally should provide their own preferences view so that the user doesn't need to quit to make a change. Even utility and productivity applications might, at times, have preferences that a user should be able to change without leaving the application. I'll also show you to how to collect preferences from the user directly in your application and store those in iOS's User Defaults.

iOS allows the user to switch from one application to the Settings app, change a preference, and then switch back to your still-running application. You'll see how to do this at the end of the chapter.

Creating the Bridge Control Application

In this chapter, you're going to build a simple application that keeps track of some aspects of managing the bridge of a simulated starship. First, you'll create a settings bundle so that when the user launches the Settings application, there will be an entry for your app, Bridge Control, as shown in Figure 12-2.

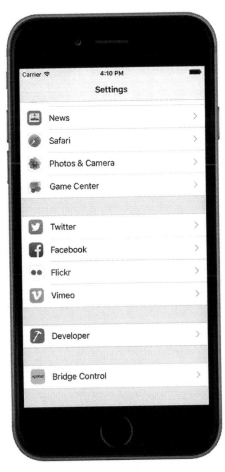

Figure 12-2. *The Settings application shows an entry for your Bridge Control application in the simulator*

If the user selects your application from the display in Figure 12-2, Settings drills down into a view showing the preferences relevant to your application. The Settings application uses text fields, secure text fields, switches, and sliders to update values, as shown in Figure 12-3.

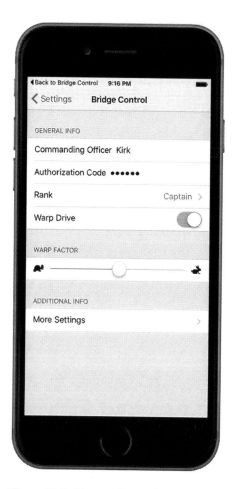

Figure 12-3. *Your application's primary settings view*

Notice that two items in the view contain disclosure indicators. The first one, Rank, takes the user to another table view that displays the options available for that item. From that table view, the user selects a single value, as shown in Figure 12-4.

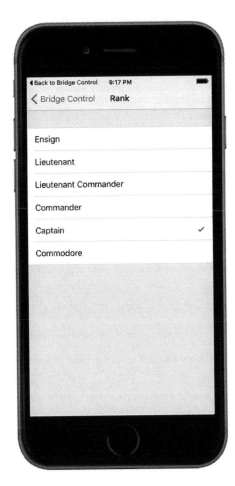

Figure 12-4. *Selecting a single preference item from a list*

The More Settings disclosure indicator allows the user to drill down to another set of preferences, as shown in Figure 12-5. This child view can have the same kinds of controls as the main settings view or even its own child views. The Settings application uses a navigation controller, which it needs because it supports the construction of hierarchical preference views.

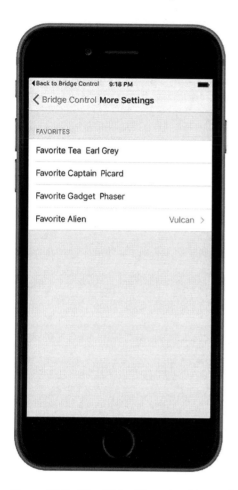

Figure 12-5. *The child settings view for your Bridge Control application*

When users launch Bridge Control, it presents a list of the preferences gathered in the Settings application, as shown in Figure 12-6.

Figure 12-6. *The app's main view presents the list of preferences to the user*

To show how to update preferences from within your application, Bridge Control provides a second view where the user can change additional preferences directly in the application, as shown in Figure 12-7.

Figure 12-7. *Bridge Control allows setting some preferences from within the app itself*

Creating the Bridge Control Project

In Xcode, open a new project, and when the assistant comes up, select Application from under the iOS heading in the left pane, click the Tabbed Application icon, and then click Next. On the next screen, name your project **Bridge Control**. Set Devices to Universal and then click the Next button. Finally, choose a location for your project and click Create.

The Bridge Control application is based on the UITabBarController class that you used in Chapter 7. The template creates two tabs, which is all you'll need. Each tab requires an icon. You'll find these in the 12 - Images folder in the example source code archive. In Xcode, select Assets.xcassets, and then delete the first and second images that were added by the Xcode template. Now add the replacement images by dragging the singleicon.imageset and doubleicon.imageset folders from Images into the editing area.

Next, you'll assign the icons to their tab bar items. Select `Main.storyboard`. You'll see the tab bar controller and the two child controllers for its tabs: one labeled First View and the other Second View. Select the first child controller and then click its tab bar item, which currently shows a square and the title First. In the Bar Item section of the Attributes Inspector, change Title to **Main** and Image to singleicon, as shown in Figure 12-8. Now select the tab bar item for the second child controller and change the title from Second to **Settings** and the image from second to doubleicon. That's enough work on the application itself for now—before doing anything more, let's create its settings bundle.

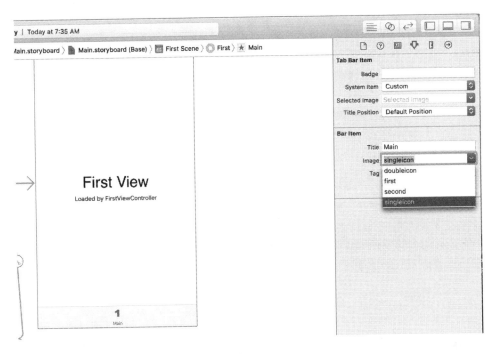

Figure 12-8. *Setting the icon for the first tab bar item*

Working with the Settings Bundle

The Settings application uses the contents of each application's settings bundle to construct a settings view for that application. If an application has no settings bundle, then the Settings app doesn't show anything for it. Each settings bundle must contain a property list called `Root.plist` that defines the root-level preferences view. This property list must follow a very precise format, which I'll talk about when you set up the property list for your app's settings bundle.

When the Settings application starts up, it checks each application for a settings bundle and adds a settings group for each application that includes a settings bundle. If you want your preferences to include any subviews, you need to add property lists to the bundle and add an entry to `Root.plist` for each child view. You'll see exactly how to do that in this chapter.

Adding a Settings Bundle to Your Project

In the Project Navigator, click the Bridge Control folder and then select File ➤ New ➤ File or press ⌘N. In the left pane, select Resource under the iOS heading and then select the Settings Bundle icon (see Figure 12-9). Click the Next button, leave the default name of Settings.bundle, and click Create.

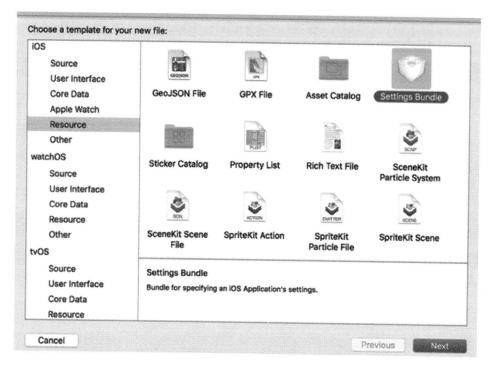

Figure 12-9. *Adding a settings bundle to your project*

You should now see a new item in the project window called Settings.bundle. Expand the Settings. bundle item. You should see two subitems: a folder named en.lproj, containing a file named Root.strings, and another named Root.plist. I'll discuss en.lproj later when I talk about localizing an application into other languages. Here, you'll concentrate on Root.plist.

Select Root.plist and take a look at the editor pane. You're looking at the Xcode property list editor, as shown in Figure 12-10.

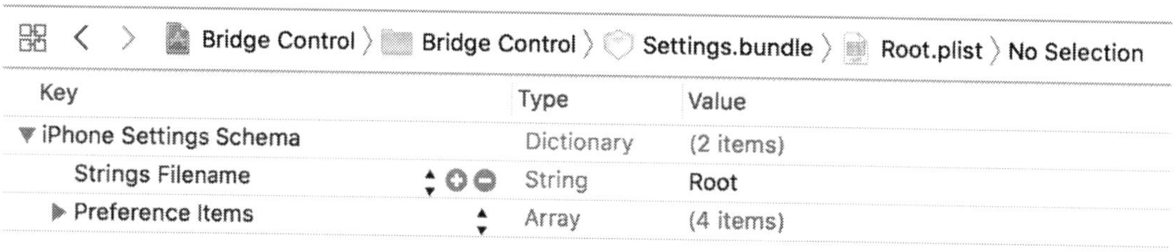

Key		Type	Value
▼ iPhone Settings Schema		Dictionary	(2 items)
Strings Filename	⬍ ⊕ ⊖	String	Root
▶ Preference Items	⬍	Array	(4 items)

Figure 12-10. *Root.plist in the property list editor pane. If your editing pane looks slightly different, don't panic. Simply Control-click in the editing pane and select Show Raw Keys/Values from the contextual menu that appears.*

Notice the organization of the items in the property list. Property lists are essentially dictionaries, storing item types and values and using a key to retrieve them, just as a Dictionary does. Several different types of nodes can be put into a property list. The Boolean, Data, Date, Number, and String node types are meant to hold individual pieces of data, but you also have a couple of ways to deal with whole collections of nodes, as well. In addition to Dictionary node types, which allow you to store other dictionaries, there are Array nodes, which store an ordered list of other nodes similar to an array. The Dictionary and Array types are the only property list node types that can contain other nodes.

■ **Note**   Although you can use most kinds of objects as keys in a Dictionary node type, keys in property list dictionary nodes must be strings. However, you are free to use any node type for the values.

When creating a settings property list, you need to follow a very specific format. Fortunately, Root. plist, the property list that came with the settings bundle you just added to your project, follows this format exactly. Let's take a look.

In the Root.plist editor pane, names of keys can be displayed either in their true, "raw" form or in a slightly more human-readable form. I'm a big fan of seeing things as they truly are whenever possible, so right-click anywhere in the editor and make sure that the Show Raw Keys/Values option in the contextual menu is selected, as shown in Figure 12-11. The rest of the discussion here uses the real names for all the keys I'm going to talk about, so this step is important.

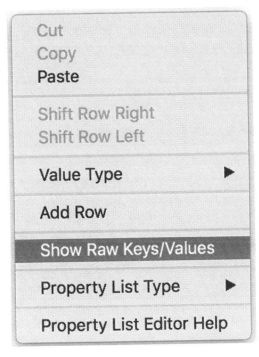

Figure 12-11. *Right-click or Control-click anywhere in the property list editing pane and make sure the Show Raw Keys/Values item is selected. This will ensure that real names are used in the property list editor, which makes your editing experience more precise.*

▓ **Caution**   Leaving the property list, either by editing a different file or by quitting Xcode, may reset the Show Raw Keys/Values item to be deselected. If your text suddenly looks a little different, take another look at that menu item and make sure it is selected.

One of the items in the dictionary is StringsTable. A strings table is used in translating your application into another language. You won't be using it in this chapter, but feel free to leave it in your project since it won't do any harm. In addition to StringsTable, the property list contains a node named PreferenceSpecifiers, which is an array. This array node is designed to hold a set of dictionary nodes, where each node represents either a single preference item that the user can modify or a single child view that the user can drill down into.

Click the disclosure triangle to the left of PreferenceSpecifiers to expand that node. You'll notice that Xcode's template kindly gave you four child nodes, as shown in Figure 12-12. Those nodes don't reflect the preferences that you need in this example, so delete Item 1, Item 2, and Item 3 (select each one and press the Delete key, one after another), leaving just Item 0 in place.

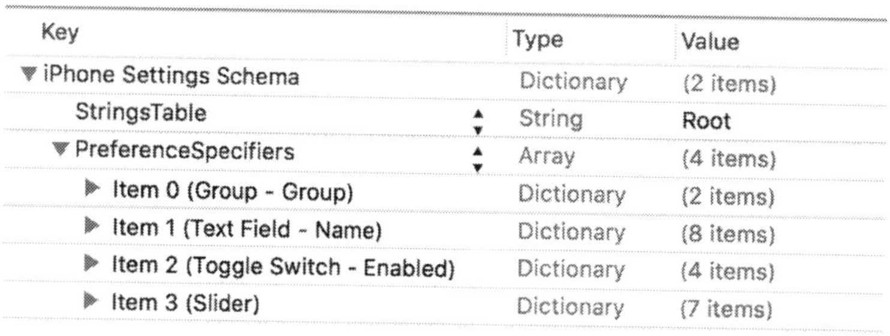

Key	Type	Value
▼ iPhone Settings Schema	Dictionary	(2 items)
StringsTable	String	**Root**
▼ PreferenceSpecifiers	Array	(4 items)
▶ Item 0 (Group - Group)	Dictionary	(2 items)
▶ Item 1 (Text Field - Name)	Dictionary	(8 items)
▶ Item 2 (Toggle Switch - Enabled)	Dictionary	(4 items)
▶ Item 3 (Slider)	Dictionary	(7 items)

Figure 12-12. Root.plist in the editor pane, this time with PreferenceSpecifiers expanded

▓ **Note**   To select an item in the property list, it is best to click one side or the other of the Key column to avoid bringing up the Key column's drop-down menu.

Single-click Item 0, but don't expand it. The Xcode property list editor lets you add rows simply by pressing the Return key. The current selection state—including which row is selected and whether it's expanded—determines where the new row will be inserted. When an unexpanded array or dictionary is selected, pressing Return adds a sibling node after the selected row. In other words, it will add another node at the same level as the current selection. If you were to press Return (but don't do that now), you would get a new row called Item 1 immediately after Item 0. Figure 12-13 shows an example of hitting Return to create a new row. Notice the drop-down menu that allows you to specify the kind of preference specifier this item represents—more on this in a bit.

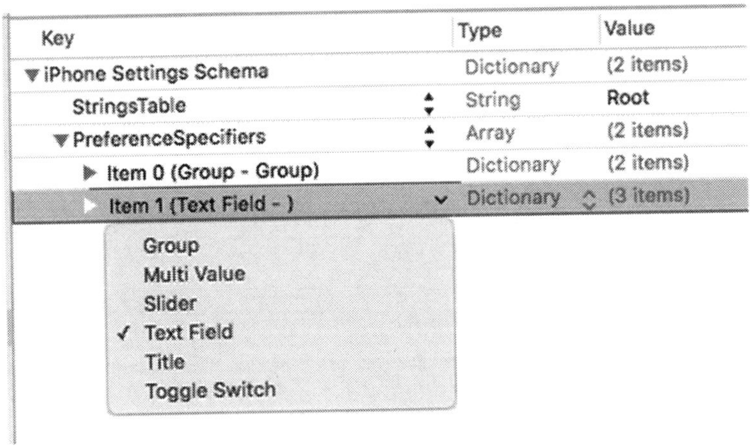

Key	Type	Value
▼ iPhone Settings Schema	Dictionary	(2 items)
StringsTable	String	Root
▼ PreferenceSpecifiers	Array	(2 items)
▶ Item 0 (Group - Group)	Dictionary	(2 items)
▶ Item 1 (Text Field -)	Dictionary	(3 items)

> Group
> Multi Value
> Slider
> ✓ Text Field
> Title
> Toggle Switch

Figure 12-13. *You selected Item 0 and hit Return to create a new sibling row. Note the drop-down menu that appears, allowing you to specify the kind of preference specifier this item represents.*

Now expand Item 0 and see what it contains, as shown in Figure 12-14. The editor is now ready to add child nodes to the selected item. If you were to press Return at this point (again, don't actually press it now), you would get a new first child row inside Item 0.

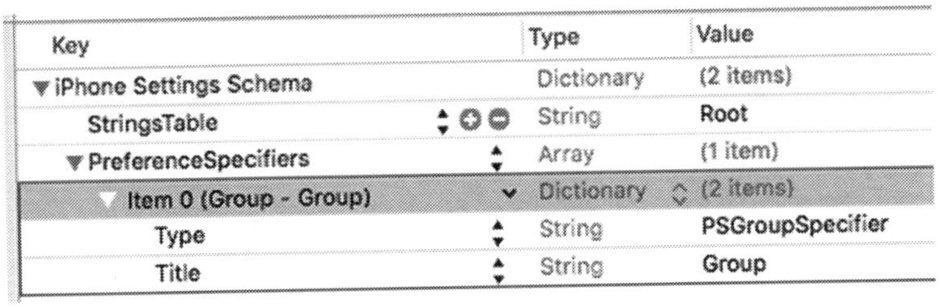

Key	Type	Value
▼ iPhone Settings Schema	Dictionary	(2 items)
StringsTable	String	Root
▼ PreferenceSpecifiers	Array	(1 item)
▼ Item 0 (Group - Group)	Dictionary	(2 items)
Type	String	PSGroupSpecifier
Title	String	Group

Figure 12-14. *When you expand Item 0, you'll find a row with a key of Type and a second row with a key of Title. This represents a group with a title of Group.*

One of the items inside Item 0 has a key of Type. Every property list node in the PreferenceSpecifiers array must have an entry with this key. The Type key tells the Settings application what type of data is associated with this item. In Item 0, the Type item has a value of PSGroupSpecifier. This indicates that the item represents the start of a new group. Each item that follows will be part of this group—until the next item with a Type of PSGroupSpecifier. If you look back at Figure 12-3, you'll see that the Settings application presents the application settings in a grouped table. Item 0 in the PreferenceSpecifiers array in a settings bundle property list should always be a PSGroupSpecifier so that the settings start in a new group. This is important because you need at least one group in every Settings table.

The only other entry in Item 0 has a key of Title, and this is used to set an optional header just above the group that is being started. Now take a closer look at the Item 0 row itself, and you'll see that it's actually shown as Item 0 (Group – Group). The values in parentheses represent the value of the Type item (the first Group) and the Title item (the second Group). This is a nice shortcut that Xcode gives you so that you can visually scan the contents of a settings bundle.

As shown in Figure 12-3, you called your first group General Info. Double-click the value next to Title, and change it from Group to General Info (see Figure 12-15). When you enter the new title, you may notice a slight change to Item 0. It's now shown as Item 0 (Group – General Info) to reflect the new title. In the Settings application, the title is shown in uppercase, so the user will actually see GENERAL INFO instead. You can see this in Figure 12-3.

Key		Type	Value
▼ iPhone Settings Schema		Dictionary	(2 items)
StringsTable	↕	String	Root
▼ PreferenceSpecifiers	↕	Array	(1 item)
▼ Item 0 (Group - General Info)		Dictionary	(2 items)
Type	↕	String	PSGroupSpecifier
Title	↕⊕⊖	String	◇ General Info

Figure 12-15. *You changed the title of the Item 0 group from Group to General Info*

Adding a Text Field Setting

You now need to add a second item in this array, which will represent the first actual preference field. You're going to start with a simple text field. If you were to single-click the PreferenceSpecifiers row in the editor pane (don't do this, just keep reading) and press Return to add a child, the new row would be inserted at the beginning of the list, which is not what you want. You want to add a row at the end of the array.

To add the row, click the disclosure triangle to the left of Item 0 to close it and then select Item 0 and press Return. This gives you a new sibling row after the current row, as shown in Figure 12-16. As usual, when the item is added, a drop-down menu appears, showing the default value of Text Field.

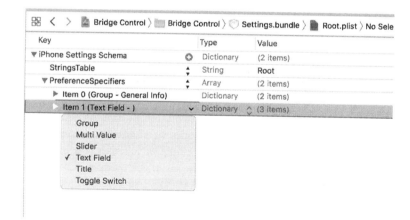

Figure 12-16. *Adding a new sibling row to Item 0*

Click somewhere outside the drop-down menu to make it go away and then click the disclosure triangle next to Item 1 to expand it. You'll see that it contains a Type row set to PSTextFieldSpecifier. This is the Type value used to tell the Settings application that you want the user to edit this setting in a text field. It also contains two empty rows for Title and Key, as shown in Figure 12-17.

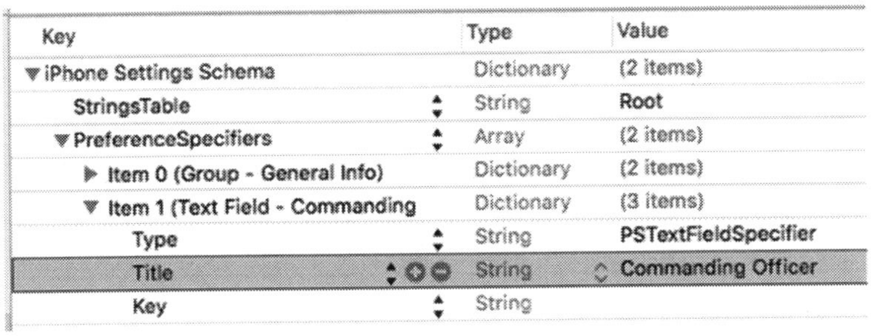

Key	Type	Value
▼ iPhone Settings Schema	Dictionary	(2 items)
StringsTable	String	Root
▼ PreferenceSpecifiers	Array	(2 items)
▶ Item 0 (Group - General Info)	Dictionary	(2 items)
▼ Item 1 (Text Field - Commanding	Dictionary	(3 items)
Type	String	PSTextFieldSpecifier
Title	String	Commanding Officer
Key	String	

Figure 12-17. *The text field item, expanded to show the type, title, and key*

Select the Title row and then double-click in the whitespace of the Value column. Type in **Commanding Officer** to set the Title value. This is the text that will appear in the Settings app.

Now do the same for the Key row (no, that's not a misprint; you're really looking at a key called **Key**). In the value field, type **officer** (note the lowercase first letter), which is the key to use when it stores the value entered in this text field.

Recall what I said about NSUserDefaults? It lets you store values using a key, similar to a Dictionary. Well, the Settings application does the same thing for each of the preferences it saves on your behalf. If you give it a key value of foo, then later in your application, you can request the value for foo, and it will give you the value the user entered for that preference. You will use key value officer later to retrieve this setting from the user defaults in your application.

■ **Note**   Title has a value of Commanding Officer, and Key has a value of officer. This uppercase/ lowercase difference will happen frequently, and here you're even compounding the difference by using two words for the displayed title and a single word for the key. The Title value is what appears on the screen, so using the capital *C* and *O* and putting a space between the words all makes sense. The Key value is a text string you'll use to retrieve preferences from the user defaults, so all lowercase makes sense there. Could you use all lowercase for Title? Of course. And you could use all capitals for Key. As long as you capitalize it the same way when you save and when you retrieve, it doesn't matter which convention you use for your preference keys.

Now select the last of the three Item 1 rows (the one with a key of Key) and press Return to add another entry to the Item 1 dictionary, giving this one a key of AutocapitalizationType. Note that, as soon as you start typing **AutocapitalizationType**, Xcode presents you with a list of matching choices, so you can simply pick one from the list instead of typing the whole name. After you've entered AutocapitalizationType, press the Tab key or click the small up/down arrow icon on the right of the Value column to open a list where you can select from the available options. Choose Words. This specifies that the text field should automatically capitalize each word that the user types in this field.

Create one last new row and give it a key of AutocorrectionType and a value of No. This will tell the Settings application not to autocorrect values entered into this text field. In any situation where you do want the text field to use autocorrection, you would set the value in this row to Yes. Again, Xcode presents you with a list of matching choices as you begin entering **AutocorrectionType**. It shows you a list of valid options in a pop-up.

When you're finished, your property list should look like the one shown in Figure 12-18.

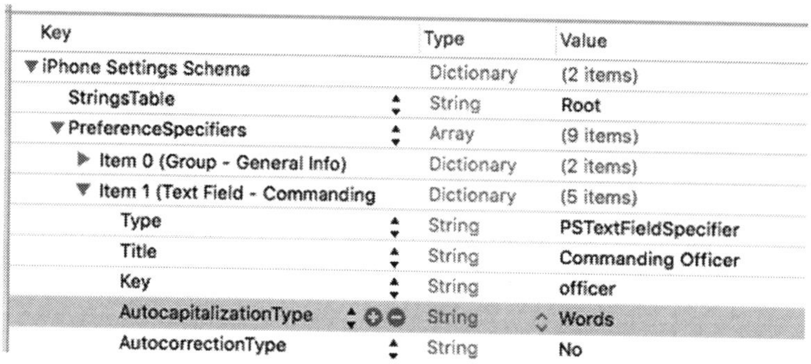

Key		Type	Value
▼ iPhone Settings Schema		Dictionary	(2 items)
StringsTable	⬍	String	Root
▼ PreferenceSpecifiers	⬍	Array	(9 items)
▶ Item 0 (Group - General Info)		Dictionary	(2 items)
▼ Item 1 (Text Field - Commanding		Dictionary	(5 items)
Type	⬍	String	PSTextFieldSpecifier
Title	⬍	String	Commanding Officer
Key	⬍	String	officer
AutocapitalizationType	⬍ ⊕ ⊖	String	⬍ Words
AutocorrectionType	⬍	String	No

Figure 12-18. *The finished text field specified in Root.plist*

That's it. Build and run the application by selecting Product ➤ Run. You haven't built any sort of GUI for the app yet, so you'll just see the first tab of the tab bar controller. Press the Home button (or press ⌥⌘H on the simulator) and then tap the icon for the Settings application. Scroll down and you will find an entry for your application, which uses the icon added earlier (see Figure 12-2). Click the Bridge Control row. You will be presented with a simple settings view with a single text field, as shown in Figure 12-19.

Figure 12-19. *Your root view in the Settings application after adding a group and a text field*

You're not finished yet, but you should now have a sense of how easy it is to add preferences to your application. Let's add the rest of the fields for your root settings view. The first one you'll add is a secure text field for the user's authorization code.

Adding a Secure Text Field Setting

Go back to Xcode and click Root.plist to return to your setting specifiers (don't forget to turn on Show Raw Keys/Values, assuming Xcode's editing area has reset this). Collapse Item 0 and Item 1 and then select Item 1. Press ⌘C to copy it to the clipboard and then press ⌘V to paste it back. This will create a new Item 2 that is identical to Item 1. Expand the new item and change the Title value to Authorization Code and the Key value to authorizationCode. Remember that the Title value is what's shown in an on-screen label, and the Key value is what's used for saving the value.

Next, add one more child to the new item. Remember that the order of items does not matter, so feel free to place it directly below the Key item you just edited. To do this, select the Key/authorizationCode row and then hit Return.

Give the new item a Key value of IsSecure (note the leading uppercase *I*) and press Tab. You'll see that Xcode automatically changes the Type to Boolean. Now change its Value from NO to YES, which tells the Settings application that this field needs to hide the user's input like a password field, rather than behaving like an ordinary text field. Finally, change AutocapitalizationType to None. Figure 12-20 shows the finished Item 2.

Key	Type	Value
器 〈 〉 📄 Bridge Control 〉 Bridge Control 〉 Settings.bundle 〉 Root.plist 〉 No Selection		
▼ iPhone Settings Schema	Dictionary	(2 items)
StringsTable	String	Root
▼ PreferenceSpecifiers	Array	(3 items)
▶ Item 0 (Group - General Info)	Dictionary	(2 items)
▶ Item 1 (Text Field - Commanding	Dictionary	(5 items)
▼ Item 2 (Text Field - Authorization	Dictionary	(6 items)
Type	String	PSTextFieldSpecifier
Title	String	Authorization Code
Key	String	authorizationCode
IsSecure	Boolean	YES
AutocapitalizationType	String	None
AutocorrectionType	String	No

Figure 12-20. *Your finished Item 2, a text field designed to accept an authorizationCode*

Adding a Multivalue Field

The next item you're going to add is a **multivalue field**. This type of field will automatically generate a row with a disclosure indicator. Clicking it will let users drill down to another table, where they can select one of several rows. Collapse Item 2, select the row, and then press Return to add Item 3. Use the pop-up attached to the Key field to select Multi Value and then expand Item 3 by clicking the disclosure triangle.

The expanded Item 3 already contains a few rows. One of them, the Type row, is set to PSMultiValueSpecifier. Look for the Title row and set its value to Rank. Then find the Key row and give it a value of rank. The next part is a little tricky, so let's talk about it before you do it.

You're going to add two more children to Item 3, but they will be Array type nodes, not String type nodes, as follows:

- One array, called **Titles**, will hold a list of the values from which the user can select.

- The other array, called **Values**, will hold a corresponding list of the values that are stored in the user defaults.

So, if the user selects the first item in the list, which corresponds to the first item in the Titles array, the Settings application will actually store the first value from the Values array. This pairing of Titles and Values lets you present user-friendly text to the user but actually stores something else, like a number, date, or different string. Both of these arrays are required. If you want them to be the same, you can create one array, copy it, paste it back in, and then change the key so that you have two arrays with the same content but stored under different keys. You'll actually do just that.

Select Item 3 (leave it open) and press Return to add a new child. You'll see that, once again, Xcode is aware of the type of file you're editing and even seems to anticipate what you want to do: the new child row already has Key set to Titles and is configured to be an Array, which is just what you wanted! Press Return to stop editing the Key field and then expand the Titles row and hit Return to add a child node. Repeat this five more times so you have a total of six child nodes. All six nodes should be the String type and should be given the following values: Ensign, Lieutenant, Lieutenant Commander, Commander, Captain, and Commodore.

Once you've created all six nodes and entered their values, collapse Titles and select it. Next, press ⌘C to copy it and press ⌘V to paste it back. This will create a new item with a key of Titles - 2. Double-click the key Titles - 2 and change it to Values.

You're almost finished with your multivalue field. There's just one more required value in the dictionary, which is the default value. Multivalue fields must have one—and only one—row selected. So, you need to specify the default value to be used if none has yet been selected; it needs to correspond to one of the items in the Values array (not the Titles array, if they are different). Xcode already added a DefaultValue row when you created this item, so all you need to do now is give it a value of Ensign. Go ahead and do that now. Figure 12-21 shows the finalized version of Item 3.

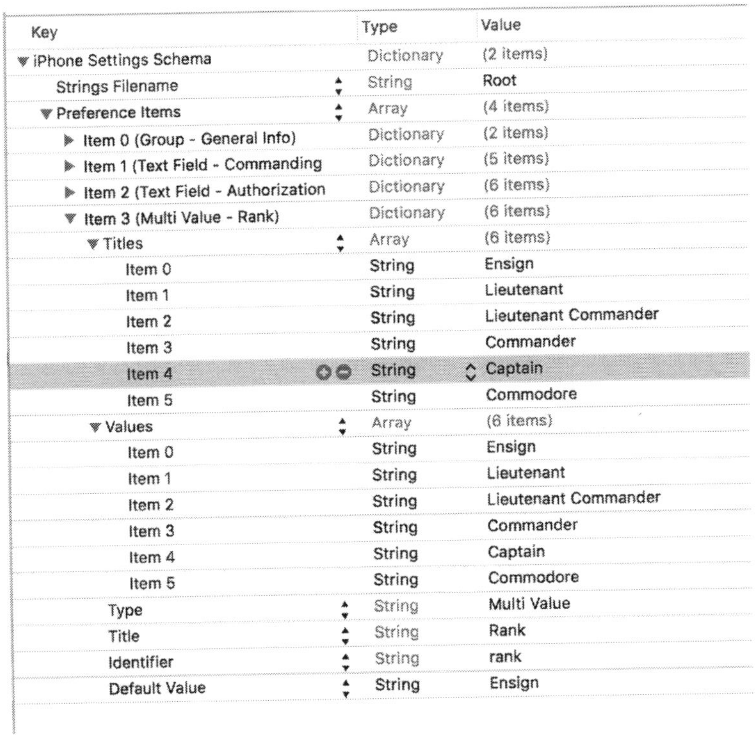

Key	Type	Value
▼ iPhone Settings Schema	Dictionary	(2 items)
Strings Filename	String	Root
▼ Preference Items	Array	(4 items)
▶ Item 0 (Group - General Info)	Dictionary	(2 items)
▶ Item 1 (Text Field - Commanding	Dictionary	(5 items)
▶ Item 2 (Text Field - Authorization	Dictionary	(6 items)
▼ Item 3 (Multi Value - Rank)	Dictionary	(6 items)
▼ Titles	Array	(6 items)
Item 0	String	Ensign
Item 1	String	Lieutenant
Item 2	String	Lieutenant Commander
Item 3	String	Commander
Item 4	String	Captain
Item 5	String	Commodore
▼ Values	Array	(6 items)
Item 0	String	Ensign
Item 1	String	Lieutenant
Item 2	String	Lieutenant Commander
Item 3	String	Commander
Item 4	String	Captain
Item 5	String	Commodore
Type	String	Multi Value
Title	String	Rank
Identifier	String	rank
Default Value	String	Ensign

Figure 12-21. *Your finished Item 3, a multivalue field designed to let the user select from one of six possible values*

Let's check your work. Save the property list and build and run the application again. When your application starts, press the Home button and launch the Settings application. When you select Bridge Control, you should see three fields on your root-level view, as shown in Figure 12-22. Go ahead and play with it a bit and then let's move on.

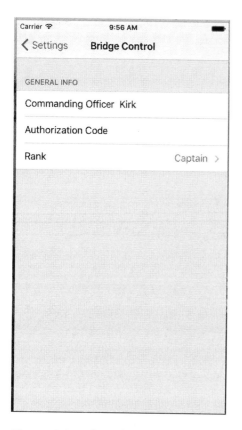

Figure 12-22. Three of your fields have been implemented.

Adding a Toggle Switch Setting

The next item you need to get from the user is a Boolean value that indicates whether your warp engines should be turned on. To capture a Boolean value in your preferences, you are going to tell the Settings application to use a UISwitch by adding another item to your PreferenceSpecifiers array with a type of PSToggleSwitchSpecifier.

Collapse Item 3 if it's currently expanded and then single-click it to select it. Press Return to create Item 4. Use the drop-down menu to select Toggle Switch and then click the disclosure triangle to expand Item 4. You'll see there's already a child row with a Key of Type and a Value of PSToggleSwitchSpecifier. Give the empty Title row a value of Warp Drive and set the value of the Key row to warp.

You have one more required item in this dictionary, which is the default value. Just as with the Multi Value setup, here Xcode has already created a DefaultValue row for you. Let's turn on your warp engines by default by giving the DefaultValue row a value of YES. Figure 12-23 shows your completed Item 4.

Key	Type	Value
▼ iPhone Settings Schema	Dictionary	(2 items)
Strings Filename	String	Root
▼ Preference Items	Array	(5 items)
▶ Item 0 (Group - General Info)	Dictionary	(2 items)
▶ Item 1 (Text Field - Commanding	Dictionary	(5 items)
▶ Item 2 (Text Field - Authorization	Dictionary	(6 items)
▶ Item 3 (Multi Value - Rank)	Dictionary	(6 items)
▼ Item 4 (Toggle Switch - Warp	Dictionary	(4 items)
Type	String	Toggle Switch
Title	String	Warp Drive
Identifier	String	warp
Default Value	Boolean	YES

Figure 12-23. *Your finished Item 4, a toggle switch to turn the warp engines on and off*

Adding the Slider Setting

The next item you need to implement is a slider. In the Settings application, a slider can have a small image at each end, but it can't have a label. Let's put the slider in its own group with a header so that the user will know what the slider does. Start by collapsing Item 4. Now single-click Item 4 and press Return to create a new row. Use the pop-up to turn the new item into a Group and then click the item's disclosure triangle to expand it. You'll see that Type is already set to `PSGroupSpecifier`. This will tell the Settings application to start a new group at this location. Double-click the value in the row labeled Title and change the value to Warp Factor.

Collapse Item 5 and select it and then press Return to add a new sibling row. Use the pop-up to change the new item into a Slider, which indicates to the Settings application that it should use a `UISlider` to get this information from the user. Expand Item 6 and set the value of the Key row to warpFactor so that the Settings application knows which key to use when storing this value.

You're going to allow the user to enter a value from 1 to 10. You'll set the default to warp 5. Sliders need to have a minimum value, a maximum value, and a starting (or default) value; and all of these need to be stored as numbers, not strings, in your property list. Fortunately, Xcode has already created rows for all these values. Give the DefaultValue row a value of 5, the MinimumValue row a value of 1, and the MaximumValue row a value of 10.

If you want to test the slider, go ahead. You're going to do just a bit more customization. As noted, you can place an image at each end of the slider. Let's provide little icons to indicate that moving the slider to the left slows you down and moving it to the right speeds you up.

Adding Icons to the Settings Bundle

In the Images folder in the project archive that accompanies this book, you'll find two icons called rabbit. png and turtle.png. You need to add both of these to your settings bundle. Because these images need to be used by the Settings application, you can't just put them in your Bridge Control folder; you need to put them in the settings bundle so the Settings application can access them. To do that, you'll need to open the settings bundle in the Finder. Control-click the Settings.bundle icon in the Project Navigator, and when the contextual menu appears, select Show in Finder (see Figure 12-24) to show the bundle in the Finder.

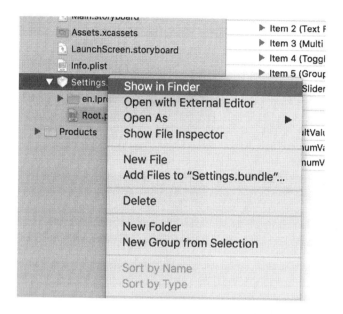

Figure 12-24. *The Settings.bundle contextual menu*

Remember that bundles look like files in the Finder, but they are really folders. When the Finder window opens to show the Settings.bundle file, Control-click the file and select Show Package Contents from the contextual menu that appears. This will open the settings bundle in a new Finder window. You should see the same two items that you see in Settings.bundle in Xcode. Copy the two icon files, rabbit.png and turtle.png, from the Images folder into the Settings.bundle package contents in the Finder window, next to en.proj and Root.plist. You can leave this window open in the Finder, as you'll need to copy another file here soon. Now you'll return to Xcode and tell the slider to use these two images.

Back in Xcode, return to Root.plist and add two more child rows under Item 6. Give one a key of MinimumValueImage and a value of turtle. Give the other a key of MaximumValueImage and a value of rabbit. Figure 12-25 shows your finished Item 6.

Key		Type	Value
▼ iPhone Settings Schema		Dictionary	(2 items)
StringsTable	⬍	String	Root
▼ PreferenceSpecifiers	⬍	Array	(7 items)
▶ Item 0 (Group - General Info)		Dictionary	(2 items)
▶ Item 1 (Text Field - Commanding		Dictionary	(5 items)
▶ Item 2 (Text Field - Authorization		Dictionary	(6 items)
▶ Item 3 (Multi Value - Rank)		Dictionary	(6 items)
▶ Item 4 (Toggle Switch - Warp		Dictionary	(4 items)
▶ Item 5 (Group - Warp Factor)		Dictionary	(2 items)
▼ Item 6 (Slider)		Dictionary	(7 items)
Type	⬍	String	PSSliderSpecifier
Key	⬍	String	warpFactor
DefaultValue	⬍	Number	5
MinimumValue	⬍	Number	1
MaximumValue	⬍	Number	10
MinimumValueImage	⬍	String	turtle
MaximumValueImage	⬍	String	rabbit

Figure 12-25. *Your finished Item 6: a slider with turtle and rabbit icons to represent slow and fast*

Save your property list and then build and run the app to make sure everything functions as expected. You should be able to navigate to the Settings application and find the slider waiting for you, with the sleepy turtle and the happy rabbit at their respective ends, as shown in Figure 12-26.

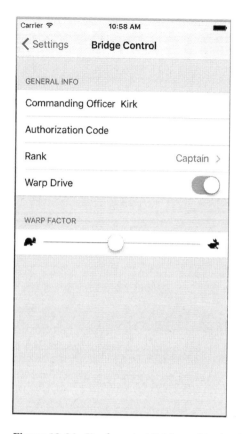

Figure 12-26. *You have text fields, multivalue fields, a toggle switch, and a slider*

Adding a Child Settings View

You're going to add another preference specifier to tell the Settings application that you want it to display a child settings view. This specifier will present a row with a disclosure indicator that, when tapped, will take the user down to a whole new view full of preferences.

Since you don't want this new preference to be grouped with the slider, first you'll copy the group specifier in Item 0 and paste it at the end of the PreferenceSpecifiers array to create a new group for your child settings view. In Root.plist, collapse all open items; then single-click Item 0 to select it and press ⌘C to copy it to the clipboard. Next, select Item 6 and then press ⌘V to paste in a new Item 7. Expand Item 7 and double-click the Value column next to the key Title, changing it from General Info to Additional Info.

Now collapse Item 7 again. Select it and press Return to add Item 8, which will be your actual child view. Expand it by clicking the disclosure triangle. Find the Type row, give it a value of PSChildPaneSpecifier, and then set the value of the Title row to More Settings. You need to add one final row to Item 8, which will tell the Settings application which property list to load for the More Settings view. Add another child row and give it a key of File (you can do this by changing the key of the last row in the group from Key to File) and a value of More (see Figure 12-27). The file extension .plist is assumed and must not be included (if it is, the Settings application won't find the .plist file).

Key	Type	Value
▼ iPhone Settings Schema	Dictionary	(2 items)
StringsTable	String	Root
▼ PreferenceSpecifiers	Array	(9 items)
▶ Item 0 (Group - General Info)	Dictionary	(2 items)
▶ Item 1 (Text Field - Commanding	Dictionary	(5 items)
▶ Item 2 (Text Field - Authorization	Dictionary	(6 items)
▶ Item 3 (Multi Value - Rank)	Dictionary	(6 items)
▶ Item 4 (Toggle Switch - Warp	Dictionary	(4 items)
▶ Item 5 (Group - Warp Factor)	Dictionary	(2 items)
▶ Item 6 (Slider)	Dictionary	(7 items)
▶ Item 7 (Group - Additional Info)	Dictionary	(2 items)
▼ Item 8 (Child Pane - More	Dictionary	(4 items)
Type	String	PSChildPaneSpecifier
Title	String	More Settings
Key	String	
File	String	More

Figure 12-27. *Your finished Items 7 and 8, setting up the new Additional Info settings group and providing the child pane link to the file, More.plist*

You are adding a child view to your main preference view. You've configured the settings bundle to indicate that the settings in that child view are specified in the More.plist file so you need to add a file called More.plist into the settings bundle. You can't add new files to the bundle in Xcode, and the Property List Editor's Save dialog will not let you save into a bundle, so you need to create a new property list, save it somewhere else, and then drag it into the Settings.bundle window using the Finder. When you create your own child settings views, the easiest approach is to make a copy of Root.plist, give it a new name, and then delete all of the existing preference specifiers except the first one and add whatever preference specifiers you need for that new file. To save yourself the trouble of doing all this, you can grab the More.plist file in the Images folder in the project archive that accompanies this book and then drag it into that Settings.bundle window you left open earlier, alongside Root.plist.

You're now finished with your settings bundle. Feel free to build, run, and test the Settings application. You should be able to reach the child view and set values for all the other fields. Go ahead and play with it, and make changes to the property list if you want.

▓ **Tip** I've covered almost every configuration option available (at least at the time of this writing). You can find the full documentation of the settings property list format in the document called *Settings Application Schema Reference* in the iOS Dev Center. You can get that document, along with a ton of other useful reference documents, from this page: http://developer.apple.com/library/ios/navigation/.

Before continuing, select the Assets.xcassets item in Xcode's Project Navigator and then copy the rabbit.png and turtle.png icons from the Images folder in the project archive into the left side of the editor area. This will add these icons to the project as new images resources, ready for use. You'll be using them in your application to show the value of the current settings.

You might have noticed that the two icons you just added are exactly the same ones you added to your settings bundle earlier. You might be wondering why you've added them to your Xcode project twice. Remember that iOS applications can't read files out of other applications' sandboxes. The settings bundle doesn't become part of your application's sandbox—it becomes part of the Settings application's sandbox. Since you also want to use those icons in your application, you need to add them separately to Assets. xcassets so they are copied into your application's sandbox too.

Reading Settings in Your Application

You've now solved half of your problem. The user can use the Setting app to declare their preferences, but how do you get to them from within your application? As it turns out, that's the easy part. Before you write the code to retrieve your settings, open the Settings application, locate your application's settings, and set a value for every setting so that the application has something to display in the user interface that you're about to create.

Retrieving User Settings

You'll use a class called UserDefaults (NSUserDefaults) to access the user's settings. UserDefaults is implemented as a singleton, which means there is only one instance of UserDefaults that holds the settings for your application. To get access to that one instance, you call the class method standard, like so:

```
let defaults = UserDefaults.standard
```

Once you have a pointer to the standard user defaults, you use it much like a Dictionary. To get a value from it, you can call object(forKey:), which will return an object, a String, or a Foundation object such as a date (NSDate) or NSNumber. If you want to retrieve the value as a scalar—like an int, float, or Boolean—you can use another method, such as int(forKey:), float(forKey:), or bool(forKey:).

While you were creating the property list for this application, you were actually creating an array of PreferenceSpecifiers inside a .plist file. Within the Settings application, some of those specifiers were used to create groups, while others were used to create interface objects for user interaction. Those are the specifiers you are really interested in because they hold the keys for the real settings data. Every specifier that was tied to a user setting has a Key named Key. Take a minute to go back and check. For example, the Key for your slider has a value of warpFactor and the Key for your Authorization Code field is authorizationCode. You'll use those keys to retrieve the user settings.

Instead of using strings for each key directly in your methods, you'll define some constants for those values. That way, you can use these constants in your code instead of inline strings, where you would run the risk of mistyping something. You'll set these up in a separate Swift file since you're going to use some of them in more than one class later. So, in Xcode, press ⌘N and, from the iOS section of the file creation window, choose Source and then Swift File. Click Next, call the file Constants.swift, and click Create. Open the newly created file and add code in Listing 12-1.

Listing 12-1. Your Constants

```
let officerKey = "officer"
let authorizationCodeKey = "authorizationCode"
let rankKey = "rank"
let warpDriveKey = "warp"
let warpFactorKey = "warpFactor"
let favoriteTeaKey = "favoriteTea"
let favoriteCaptainKey = "favoriteCaptain"
let favoriteGadgetKey = "favoriteGadget"
let favoriteAlienKey = "favoriteAlien"
```

These constants are the keys that you used in your .plist file for the different preference fields. Now that you have a place to display the settings, let's quickly set up your main view with a bunch of labels. Before going over to Interface Builder, let's create outlets for all the labels you'll need. Single-click FirstViewController.swift, and make the changes in Listing 12-2.

Listing 12-2. Adding Outlets to the FirstViewController.swift File

```
class FirstViewController: UIViewController {
    @IBOutlet var officerLabel:UILabel!
    @IBOutlet var authorizationCodeLabel:UILabel!
    @IBOutlet var rankLabel:UILabel!
    @IBOutlet var warpDriveLabel:UILabel!
    @IBOutlet var warpFactorLabel:UILabel!
    @IBOutlet var favoriteTeaLabel:UILabel!
    @IBOutlet var favoriteCaptainLabel:UILabel!
    @IBOutlet var favoriteGadgetLabel:UILabel!
    @IBOutlet var favoriteAlienLabel:UILabel!
```

There's nothing new here—we declared nine properties, all of them labels with the @IBOutlet keyword to make them connectable in Interface Builder. Save your changes. Now that you have your outlets declared, let's head over to the storyboard file to create the user interface.

Creating the Main View

Select Main.storyboard to edit it in Interface Builder. When it comes up, you'll see the tab bar view controller on the left and the view controllers for the two tabs on the right, one above the other. The upper one is for the first tab, corresponding to the FirstViewController class, and the lower one is for the second tab, which will be implemented in the SecondViewController class.

You're going to start by adding a bunch of labels to the view of FirstViewController so it looks like the one shown in Figure 12-28. You'll need a grand total of 18 labels. Half of them, on the left side of the screen, will be right-aligned and bold; the other half, on the right side of the screen, will be used to display the actual values retrieved from the user defaults and will have outlets pointing to them. All of the changes that you make here will be to the view controller for the first tab, which is the upper one on the right of the storyboard.

Figure 12-28. *The view controller for the first tab in Interface Builder, showing the 18 labels you added*

Start by expanding the node for Main Scene in the Document Outline and then expand the View item. You'll find two child views already in place—delete them both. Now drag a label from the Object Library and drop it near the top left of the view in the storyboard. Drag it all the way to the left of the window (or at least to the left blue guideline) and then widen it by dragging its right edge toward the center of the view, like the Officer label in Figure 12-28. In the Attributes Inspector, make the text right aligned and change the font to System Bold 17. Now Option-drag the label downward to create eight more copies, lining them up neatly to form the left column. Change the label texts so that they match the ones in Figure 12-28.

Building the right column is slightly easier. Drag another label onto the view and place it to the right of the Officer label, leaving a small gap between them. In the Attributes Inspector, set the font to System 17. Option-drag this label downward to create eight more copies, each of them lined up with the corresponding label in the left column.

Now you need to set the Auto Layout constraints. Let's start by linking the top two labels together. Control-drag from the Officer label to the label to its right. Release the mouse and hold down the Shift key. In the pop-up menu, select Horizontal Spacing and Baseline and then click outside the pop-up. Do the same for the other eight rows to link each pair of labels together.

Next, you'll fix the positions of the labels in the left column relative to the left and top of the view. In the Document Outline, Control-drag from the Officer label to its parent view. Release the mouse, hold down the Shift key, select Leading Space to Container Margin and Vertical Spacing to Top Layout Guide, and then press Return to apply the constraints. Do the same with the other eight labels in the left column.

410

Finally, you need to fix the widths of the labels in the left column. Select the Officer label and click the Pin button below the storyboard editor. In the pop-up, select the Width check box followed by Add 1 Constraint. Repeat this process for all of the labels in the left column.

All of the labels should now be properly constrained, so select the view controller Main in the Document Outline and then click Editor ➤ Resolve Auto Layout Issues ➤ Update Frames in the Xcode menu. (If this option is not enabled, all of the labels are already in their correct positions in the storyboard.) If all is well, the labels will move to their final positions.

The next thing you need to do is link the labels in the right column to their outlets. Open `FirstView Controller.swift` in the Assistant Editor and Control-drag from the top label in the right column to the `officerLabel` outlet to connect them. Control-drag from the second label in the right column to `authorizationLabel` and repeat this process until all nine labels in the right column are connected to their outlets. Save the `Main.storyboard` file.

Updating the First View Controller

In Xcode, select `FirstViewController.swift` and add the code in Listing 12-3 at the bottom of the class.

Listing 12-3. Displaying Data in Your Label Fields

```swift
func refreshFields() {
    let defaults = UserDefaults.standard
    officerLabel.text = defaults.string(forKey: officerKey)
    authorizationCodeLabel.text = defaults.string(forKey: authorizationCodeKey)
    rankLabel.text = defaults.string(forKey: rankKey)
    warpDriveLabel.text = defaults.bool(forKey: warpDriveKey)
        ? "Engaged" : "Disabled"
    warpFactorLabel.text = defaults.object(forKey: warpFactorKey)?.stringValue
    favoriteTeaLabel.text = defaults.string(forKey: favoriteTeaKey)
    favoriteCaptainLabel.text = defaults.string(forKey: favoriteCaptainKey)
    favoriteGadgetLabel.text = defaults.string(forKey: favoriteGadgetKey)
    favoriteAlienLabel.text = defaults.string(forKey: favoriteAlienKey)
}

override func viewWillAppear(_ animated: Bool) {
    super.viewWillAppear(animated)
    refreshFields()
}
```

There's not really much here that should throw you. The `refreshFields()` method does two things. First, it grabs the standard user defaults. Second, it sets the text properties of all the labels to the appropriate object from the user defaults using the same key values that you put in your `.plist` file. Notice that for `warpFactorLabel`, you're calling `string` on the object returned. Most of your other preferences are strings, which come back from the user defaults as `String` objects. The preference stored by the slider, however, comes back as an `NSNumber`, but you need a string for display purposes, so you call `string` on it to get a string representation of the value it holds.

After that, you overrode your superclass's `viewWillAppear()` method, and there you called your `refreshFields()` method. This causes the displayed values to be updated whenever the view appears—which includes when the application starts and when the user switches from the second tab to the first tab.

Now run the application. You should see the user interface that you built for the first tab, with most of the fields filled with the values that you entered into the Settings application earlier. However, some of the fields will be empty. Don't worry, this is not a bug. It is correct behavior, believe it or not. You'll see why, and how to fix it, in the upcoming "Registering Default Values" section.

Changing Defaults from Your Application

Now that you have the main view up and running, let's build the second tab. As you can see in Figure 12-29, the second tab features your warp drive switch, as well as the warp factor slider. You'll use the same controls that the Settings application uses for these two items: a switch and a slider. In addition to declaring your outlets, you'll also declare a method called refreshFields(), just as you did in FirstViewController, and two action methods that will be triggered by the user touching the controls.

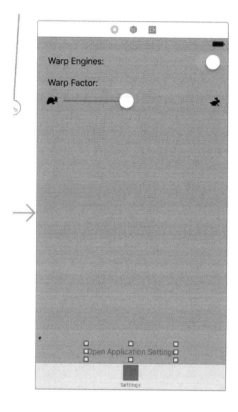

Figure 12-29. *Designing the second view controller in Interface Builder*

Select SecondViewController.swift and make the following changes:

```
class SecondViewController: UIViewController {
    @IBOutlet var engineSwitch:UISwitch!
    @IBOutlet var warpFactorSlider:UISlider!
```

Now, save your changes and select Main.storyboard to edit the GUI in Interface Builder, this time focusing on Settings Scene in the Document Outline. Hold down the Option key and click the disclosure triangle to expand Settings Scene and everything below it. Locate the View node and delete both of its child nodes. Next, select the View node and then bring up the Attributes Inspector. Change the background color by using the Background pop-up to select Light Gray Color.

Next, drag two labels from the library and place them on the view in the storyboard. Make sure you drag them onto the Settings Scene controller, which is the one at the bottom right of the storyboard. Double-click one of them and change it to read **Warp Engines:**. Double-click the other and call it **Warp Factor:**. Place both labels against the left guideline, one above the other. You can use Figure 12-29 as a placement guide.

Next, drag over a switch from the library and place it against the right side of the view, across from the Warp Engines label. Control-drag from the View Controller icon (it's the yellow one) at the top of the settings scene to the new switch and connect it to the engineSwitch outlet. Next, open SecondViewController in the Assistant Editor and Control-drag from the switch to a point just above the closing brace at the bottom of the file. Release the mouse and create an action called onEngineSwitchTapped, leaving all the other selections in the pop-up at their default values.

Drag over a slider from the library and place it below the Warp Factor label. Resize the slider so that it stretches from the blue guideline on the left margin to the one on the right. Now Control-drag from the View Controller icon at the top of the settings scene to the slider and then connect it to the warpFactorSlider outlet. Next, Control-drag from the slider to the end of the SecondViewController class and create an action called onWarpSliderDragged, leaving all the other selections in the pop-up at their default values.

Single-click the slider, if it's not still selected, and then bring up the Attributes Inspector. Set Minimum to 1.00, Maximum to 10.00, and Current to 5.00. Next, select **turtle** for Min Image and **rabbit** for Max Image. If those don't show up in the pop-up buttons, make sure you dragged the images into the Assets.xcassets assets catalog.

To complete the user interface, drag a button from the Object Library, drop it at the bottom of the view, and change its name to **Open Settings Application**. Control-drag from the button to just below the onWarpSliderDragged method in SecondViewController and create an action called onSettingsButtonTapped. You'll use this button at the end of the chapter.

It's time to add the Auto Layout constraints. Start by selecting Main.storyboard. In the Document Outline, Control-drag from the Warp Engines label to its parent view and release the mouse. Hold down the Shift key, select Leading Space to Container Margin and Vertical Spacing to Top Layout Guide, and then press the Return key to apply the constraints. Repeat this for the Warp Factor label.

Next, Control-drag from the switch to Main View and release the mouse. Hold down the Shift key, select Trailing Space to Container Margin and Vertical Spacing to Top Layout Guide, and then press Return. Control-drag from the slider to Main View and release the mouse. Hold down the Shift key and this time select Leading Space to Container Margin, Trailing Space to Container Margin, and Vertical Spacing to Top Layout Guide; then press Return.

Finally, you need to fix the position of the button at the bottom of the view. Control-drag from the button to Main View, release the mouse, select Vertical Spacing to Bottom Layout Guide and Center Horizontally in Container while holding down the Shift key, and then press Return. That completes the Auto Layout constraints, so go ahead and select the view controller Main in the Document Outline, and then click Editor ➤ Resolve Auto Layout Issues ➤ Update Frames in the Xcode menu. Make sure that everything is where it should be in the view.

Now, let's finish the settings view controller. Select SecondViewController.swift and add the code in Listing 12-4 at the bottom of the class.

Listing 12-4. Your refreshFields and viewWillAppear Methods for the SecondViewController

```
override func viewWillAppear(_ animated: Bool) {
    super.viewWillAppear(animated)
    refreshFields()
}

func refreshFields() {
    let defaults = UserDefaults.standard
    engineSwitch.isOn = defaults.bool(forKey: warpDriveKey)
    warpFactorSlider.value = defaults.float(forKey: warpFactorKey)
}
```

Next, add the following code in the onEngineSwitchTapped() and onWarpSliderDragged() methods:

```
@IBAction func onEngineSwitchTapped(_ sender: AnyObject) {
    let defaults = UserDefaults.standard
    defaults.set(engineSwitch.isOn, forKey: warpDriveKey)
}
@IBAction func onWarpSliderDragged(_ sender: AnyObject) {
    let defaults = UserDefaults.standard
    defaults.set(warpFactorSlider.value, forKey: warpFactorKey)
}
```

When the view controller's view appears (e.g., when the tab is selected), you call your refreshFields() method. This method's three lines of code get a reference to the standard user defaults and then use the outlets for the switch and slider to make them display the values stored in the user defaults. You also implemented the onEngineSwitchTapped() and onWarpSliderDragged() action methods so that you could stuff the values from your controls back into the user defaults when the user changes them.

Now you should be able to run the app, switch to the second tab, edit the values presented there, and see them reflected in the first tab when you switch back.

Registering Default Values

You've created a settings bundle, including some default settings for a few values, to give the Settings app access to your app's preferences. You've also set up your own app to access the same information, with a GUI to let the user see and edit it. However, one piece is missing: your app is completely unaware of the default values that you specified in the settings bundle. You can see this for yourself by deleting the Bridge Control app from the iOS simulator or the device you're running on (thereby deleting the preferences stored for the app) and then running it from Xcode again. At the start of a fresh launch, the app will show you blank values for most of the settings. Even the default values for the warp drive settings, which you defined in the settings bundle, are nowhere to be seen. If you then switch over to the Settings app, you'll see the default values; however, unless you actually change the values there, you'll never see them back in the Bridge Control app.

The reason your default settings disappeared is that your app knows nothing about the settings bundle it contains. So, when it tries to read the value from UserDefaults for warpFactor and finds nothing saved under that key, it has nothing to show you. Fortunately, UserDefaults includes a method called register() that lets you specify the default values that you should find if you try to look up a key/value that hasn't been set. To make this work throughout the app, it's best if this is called early during app startup. Select AppDelegate.swift and modify the application(_:didFinishLaunchingWithOptions:) method.

```
func application(application: UIApplication,
            didFinishLaunchingWithOptions launchOptions: [NSObject: AnyObject]?) -> Bool {
    // Override point for customization after application launch.

    let defaults = [warpDriveKey: true, warpFactorKey: 5, favoriteAlienKey: "Vulcan"]
    UserDefaults.standard.register(defaults)
    return true
}
```

The first thing you do here is create a dictionary that contains three key/value pairs, one for each of the keys available in Settings that requires a default value. You're using the same key names you defined earlier to reduce the risk of mistyping a key name. You pass the entire dictionary to the standard NSUserDefaults instance's registerDefaults() method. From that point on, NSUserDefaults will give you the values you specify here, as long as you haven't set different values either in your app or in the Settings app.

This class is complete. Delete the Bridge Control application and run it again. It will look something like Figure 12-6, except yours will be showing whatever values you entered in your Settings application, of course.

▓ **Note** To remove an app, click an app icon from the main device screen and hold until the icons start wiggling. Then, release the mouse and click the X on the app that you want to delete.

Keeping It Real

Now you should be able to run your app, view the settings, and then press the Home button and open the Settings app to tweak some values. Hit the Home button again to launch your app again from the home screen. You may be in for a surprise. When you go back to your app, you won't see the settings change. They'll remain as they are, showing the old values.

In iOS, hitting the Home button while an app is running doesn't actually quit the app. Instead, the operating system suspends the app in the background, leaving it ready to be quickly fired up again. This is great for switching back and forth between applications since the amount of time it takes to reawaken a suspended app is much shorter than what it takes to launch it from scratch. However, in this case, you need to do a little more work, so that when your app wakes up, it effectively gets a slap in the face, reloads the user preferences, and redisplays the values they contain.

I'll give you a sneak peek at the basics of how to make your app notice that it has been brought back to life. To do this, you're going to sign up each of your controller classes to receive a notification that is sent by the application when it wakes up from its state of suspended execution.

A *notification* is a lightweight mechanism that objects can use to communicate with each other. Any object can define one or more notifications that it will publish to the application's *notification center*, which is a singleton object that exists only to pass these notifications between objects. Notifications are usually indications that some event occurred, and objects that publish notifications include a list of notifications in their documentation. The UIApplication class publishes a number of notifications (you can find them in the Xcode documentation viewer, toward the bottom of the UIApplication page). The purpose of most notifications is usually pretty obvious from their names, but the documentation contains further information if you're unclear about a given notification's purpose.

Your application needs to refresh its display when the application is about to come to the foreground, so you are interested in the notification called UIApplicationWillEnterForeground. You'll modify the viewWillAppear() method of your view controllers to subscribe to that notification and tell the notification center to call another method when that notification happens. Add the following code to both FirstViewController.swift and SecondViewController.swift:

```
@objc func applicationWillEnterForeground(notification:NSNotification) {
    let defaults = UserDefaults.standard
    defaults.synchronize()
    refreshFields()
}
```

The method itself is quite simple. First, it gets a reference to the standard user defaults object and calls its synchronize() method, which forces the User Defaults system to save any unsaved changes and also reload any unmodified preferences from storage. In effect, you're forcing it to reread the stored preferences so that you can pick up the changes that were made in the Settings app. Next, the applicationWillEnterForeground() method calls the refreshFields() method, which each class uses to update its display.

Now you need to make each of your controllers subscribe to the notification. Add the following two lines of code to the viewWillAppear: method in both FirstViewController.swift and SecondViewController.swift:

```
let app = UIApplication.shared()
NotificationCenter.default.addObserver(self, selector: #selector(self.applicationWillEnterFore
ground(notification:)), name: Notification.Name.UIApplicationWillEnterForeground, object: app)
```

You start by getting a reference to your application instance and then use that to subscribe to the applicationWillEnterForeground notification, using the default NotificationCenter instance and a method called addObserver(_:selector:name:object:). You then pass the following to this method:

- For the observer, you pass self, which means that your controller class (each of them individually, since this code is going into both of them) is the object that needs to be notified.

- For selector, you pass a selector to the applicationWillEnterForeground() method you just wrote, telling the notification center to call that method when the notification is posted.

- The third parameter, applicationWillEnterForeground, is the name of the notification that you're interested in receiving.

- The final parameter, app, is the object from which you're interested in getting the notification. You use a reference to your own application for this. If you passed nil for the final parameter instead, you would get notified any time any application posted the UIApplicationWillEnterForeground.

That takes care of updating the display, but you also need to consider what happens to the values that are put into the user defaults when the user manipulates the controls in your app. You need to make sure that they are saved to storage before control passes to another app. The easiest way to do that is to call synchronize as soon as the settings are changed by adding one line to the first two of your action methods in SecondViewController.swift.

```
@IBAction func onEngineSwitchTapped(_ sender: AnyObject) {
    let defaults = UserDefaults.standard
    defaults.set(engineSwitch.isOn, forKey: warpDriveKey)
    defaults.synchronize()
}
@IBAction func onWarpSliderDragged(_ sender: AnyObject) {
    let defaults = UserDefaults.standard
    defaults.set(warpFactorSlider.value, forKey: warpFactorKey)
    defaults.synchronize()
}
```

▓ **Note**   Calling the synchronize() method is a potentially expensive operation because the entire contents of the user defaults in memory must be compared with what's in storage. When you're dealing with a whole lot of user defaults at once and want to make sure everything is in sync, it's best to try to minimize calls to synchronize() so that this whole comparison isn't performed over and over again. However, calling it once in response to each user action, as you're doing here, won't cause any noticeable performance problems.

There's one more thing to take care of to make this work as cleanly as possible. You already know that you must clean up your memory by setting properties to `nil` when they're no longer in use, as well as performing other cleanup tasks. The notification system is another place where you need to clean up after yourself by telling the default `NotificationCenter` that you don't want to listen to any more notifications. In this case, where you've registered each view controller to observe this notification in its `viewWillAppear()` method, you should unregister in the matching `viewDidDisappear()` method. So, in both `FirstViewController.swift` and `SecondViewController.swift`, add the following method:

```swift
override func viewDidDisappear(_ animated: Bool) {
    super.viewDidDisappear(animated)
    NotificationCenter.default.removeObserver(self)
}
```

Note that it's possible to unregister for specific notifications using the `removeObserver(_:name:object:)` method by passing in the same values that were used to register your observer in the first place. In any case, the preceding line is a handy way to make sure that the notification center forgets about your observer completely, no matter how many notifications it was registered for.

With that in place, it's time to build and run the app and see what happens when you switch between your app and the Settings app. Changes you make in the Settings app should now be immediately reflected in your app when you switch back to it.

Switching to the Settings Application

To switch from the Bridge Control application to its settings, you need to go to the home screen, launch the Settings application, find the Bridge Control entry, and select it. That's a lot of steps. It's so tiresome that many applications have opted to include their own settings screen rather than make the user go through all of that. Wouldn't it be much nicer if you could just take the user directly to screen for your settings in the Settings application? Well, it turns out that you can do just that. Remember the Open Settings Application button you added to `SecondViewController` in Figure 12-30? You wired it up to the `onSettingsButtonTapped()` method in the view controller, but you didn't put any code in that method. Let's fix that now. Add the following code shown to the `onSettingsButtonTapped()` method:

```swift
@IBAction func onSettingsButtonTapped(_ sender: AnyObject) {
    let application = UIApplication.shared()
    let url = URL(string: UIApplicationOpenSettingsURLString)! as URL
    if application.canOpenURL(url) {
        application.open(url, options:["":""] , completionHandler: nil)
    }
}
```

This code uses a system-defined URL stored in the external constant `UIApplicationOpenSettings URLString` (the value is actually `app-settings:`) to launch the Settings application right from your view controller. Run the application, switch to the second tab, and click the Open Settings Application button—you'll be taken directly to your settings screen, the one shown in Figure 12-3. That's a great improvement. Even better, as of iOS 9, at the top of the Settings screen, you'll see a small button that lets you return directly to your application (see Figure 12-30). Now you can easily navigate back and forth between the Bridge Control and Settings applications, changing values and seeing the effect on your application's user interface.

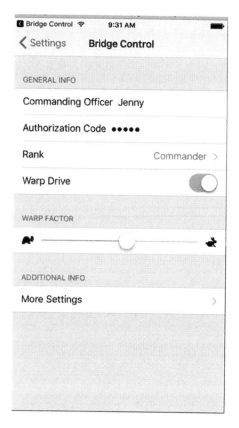

Figure 12-30. *When the Settings application is opened from Bridge Control, there's a button in the status bar that lets you go right back to your application*

Summary

At this point, you should have a solid grasp on both the Settings application and the User Defaults mechanism. You know how to add a settings bundle to your application and how to build a hierarchy of views for your application's preferences. You also learned how to read and write preferences using UserDefaults, as well as how to let the user change preferences from within your application. You even got a chance to use a new project template in Xcode. There really shouldn't be much in the way of application preferences that you are not equipped to handle now.

■ ■ ■

CHAPTER 13

Persistence: Saving Data Between App Launches

So far, you've focused on the controller and view aspects of the MVC paradigm. Although several of your applications read data from their own application bundle, only the Bridge Control example in Chapter 12 places any data in persistent storage. When any of your other apps launched, they appeared with exactly the same data they had when first launched. That approach worked up to this point, but in the real world, your apps need to persist data. When users make changes, they want to see those changes when they launch the program again.

A number of different mechanisms exist for persisting data on an iOS device. If you've programmed in Cocoa for macOS, you've likely used some or all of these techniques. In this chapter, you'll look at four mechanisms for persisting data to the iOS file system.

- Property lists

- Object archives (or archiving)

- SQLite3 (iOS's embedded relational database)

- Core Data (Apple's provided persistence tool)

■ **Note**   Property lists, object archives, SQLite3, and Core Data are not the only ways you can persist data on iOS; they are just the most common and easiest. You always have the option of using traditional C I/O calls like `fopen()` to read and write data. You can also use Cocoa's low-level file-management tools. In almost every case, doing so will result in a lot more coding effort and is rarely necessary, but those tools are there if you want them.

Your Application's Sandbox

All four of this chapter's data-persistence mechanisms share an important common element: your application's Documents folder. Every application gets its own Documents folder, and applications are allowed to read and write from their own Documents directory.

First, let's look at how applications are organized in iOS by examining the folder layout used by the iPhone simulator. To see this, you'll need to look inside the Library directory contained in your home directory. On OS X 10.6 and earlier, this was no problem; however, starting with OS X 10.7, Apple decided to make the Library folder hidden by default, so there's a small extra hoop to jump through. Open a Finder window and navigate to your home directory. If you can see your Library folder, that's great. If not, hold down the Option key (⌥) and select Go ➤ Library. The Library option is hidden unless you hold down the Option key.

Within the Library folder, drill down into Developer/CoreSimulator/Devices/. Within that directory, you'll see one subdirectory for each simulator in your current Xcode installation. The subdirectory names are globally unique identifiers (GUIDs) that are generated automatically by Xcode, so it's impossible to know just by looking at them which directory corresponds to which simulator. To find out, look for a file called device.plist in any of the simulator directories and open it. You'll find a key that maps to the simulated device's name. Figure 13-1 shows the device.plist file for the iPad Pro simulator.

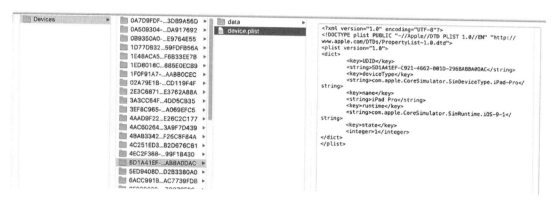

Figure 13-1. *Using the device.plist file to map a directory to a simulator*

Choose a device and drill down into its data directory until you reach the subdirectory data/ Containers/Data/Application. Here again you'll see subdirectories with names that are GUIDs. In this case, each one of them represents either a preinstalled application or an application that you have run on that simulator. Select one of the directories and open it. You'll see something like Figure 13-2.

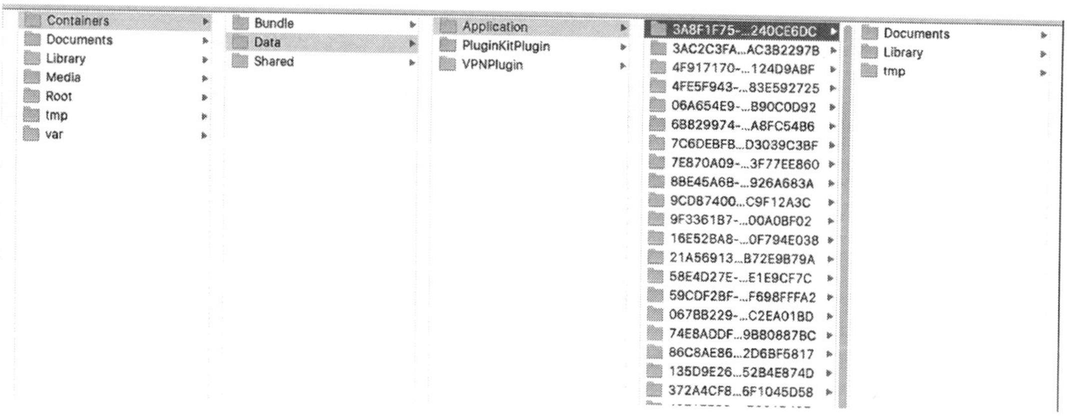

Figure 13-2. *The sandbox for an application on the simulator*

■ **Note** It may take a little searching when starting from the Devices in Figure 13-1 to find a Containers subdirectory. If you don't see it at first, keep going down the list of device GUIDs, and you should eventually find your way to the Containers subdirectory.

Although the previous listing represents the simulator, the file structure functions similarly to what's on an actual device. To see the sandbox for an application on a device, plug it onto your Mac and open the Xcode Devices window (Window ➤ Devices). You should see your device in the window sidebar. Select it and then choose an application from the Installed Apps table. Near the bottom of the window on the right side, you'll see a section called Installed Apps (you may have to click a down arrow near the bottom of the window to see this section) that contains a table with a row for each of the apps you have installed from Xcode. Below the table, there's an icon that looks like a gear. Click it and select Show Container from the pop-up to see the contents of the sandbox for whichever application you select in the table (see Figure 13-3). You can also download everything in the sandbox to your Mac. Figure 13-4 shows the application sandbox for an application called townslot2 from my book *App Development Recipes for iOS and watchOS* (Apress, 2016).

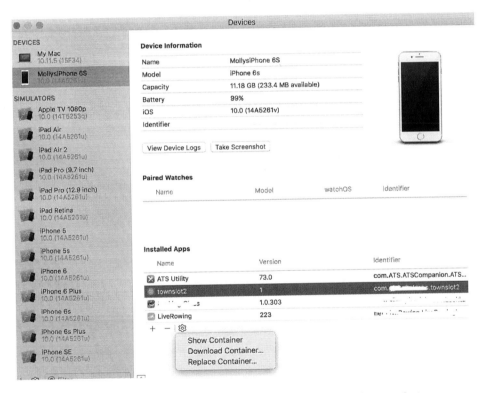

Figure 13-3. *Configuration and contents of an actual device showing the townslot2 app*

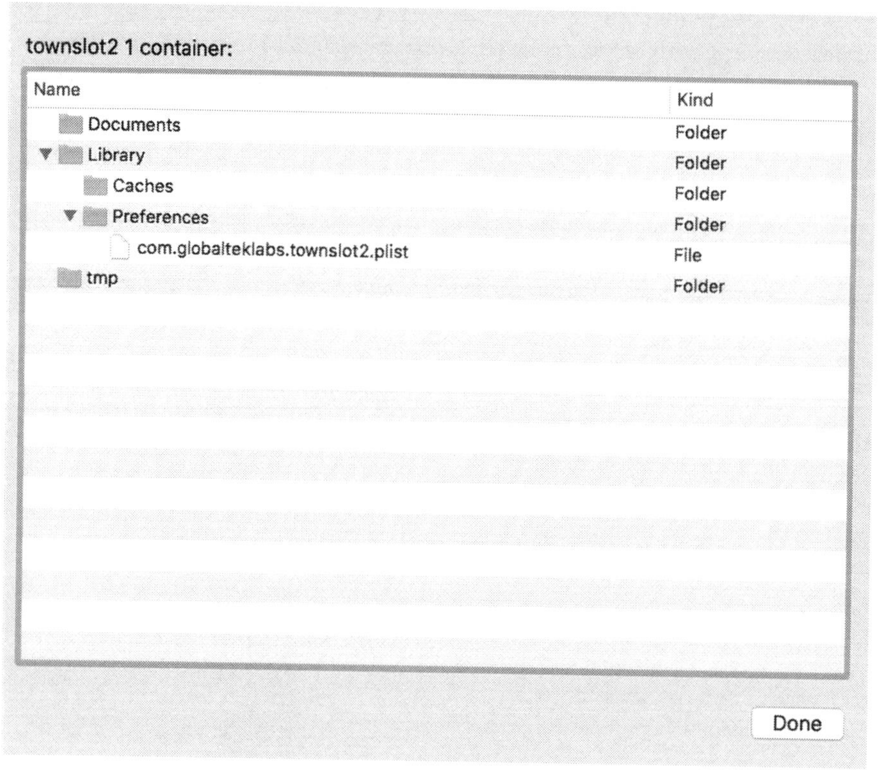

Figure 13-4. *The sandbox for the townslot2 application on an iPhone 6s*

Every application sandbox contains these three directories.

- Documents: Your application stores data in the Documents directory. If you enable iTunes file sharing for your application, the user can see the contents of this directory (and any subdirectories that your application creates) in iTunes and may upload files to it.

■ **Tip** To enable file sharing for your application, open its Info.plist file and add the key "Application supports iTunes file sharing" with the value YES.

- Library: This provides another place that your application stores data. Use it for files that you do not want to share with the user. You can create your own subdirectories if required. As you can see in Figure 13-4, the system creates subdirectories called Cache and Preferences; Preferences contains the .plist file storing the application's preferences and sets using the UserDefaults class, which I discussed in Chapter 12.

- tmp: The tmp directory offers a place where your application can store temporary files. Files written into tmp will not be backed up by iTunes when your iOS device syncs; but to avoid filling up the file system, your application does need to take responsibility for deleting the files in tmp once they are no longer needed.

Getting the Documents and Library Directories

Although your application exists in a folder with a seemingly random name, it's quite easy to retrieve the full path to the Documents directory so that you can read and write your files using the method urls(for:in:) of the FileManager class locates the various directories for you. FileManager is a Foundation class, so it is shared with Cocoa for OS X. Many of its available options are designed for macOS and some of the return values on iOS that aren't very useful because your application doesn't have rights to access the directory due to iOS's sandboxing mechanism. Listing 13-1 shows an example code snippet in Swift 4 to access the iOS Documents directory.

Listing 13-1. Code to Get an NSURL that Points to the Documents Directory

```
let urls = FileManager.default.urls(for:
    .documentDirectory, ins: .userDomainMask)
if let documentUrl = urls.first {
    print(documentUrl)
```

The first argument to the urlsForDirectory(_:in:) method specifies which directory you are looking for. The searchPathDirectory enumeration defines the possible values; here, you use the value SearchPathDirectory.documentDirectory (shortened to .documentDirectory) indicating that you are looking for the Documents directory. The second argument gives the domain or domains (called the *domainMask* in the Apple documentation) to be used for the search. The possible domains are all values of the SearchPathDomainMask enumeration, and here you specify .userDomainMask. On iOS, this domain maps to the running application's sandbox. The urls(for: in:) method returns an array containing one or more URLs that map to the requested directory in the specified domain. On iOS, there is always only one Documents directory for each application, so you can safely assume that exactly one NSURL object will be returned, but just be on the safe side, you use an if let construction to safely access the first element of the NSURL array, just in case it happens to be empty. On a real iOS device, the URL for the Documents directory would be something like file:///var/mobile/Containers/Data/Application/69BFDDB0-E4A8-4359-8382-F6DDDF031481/Documents/.

You can create a URL for a file in the Documents directory by appending another component onto the end of the URL you just retrieved. You'll use an NSURL method called appendingPathComponent(), which was designed for just that purpose.

```
let fileUrl = try documentUrl.appendingPathComponent("theFile.txt")
```

▓ **Note**   Error handling in Swift 4 operates similar to other languages that use the try, catch, and throw keywords.

After this call, fileUrl should contain the full URL (see Listing 13-2) for a file called theFile.txt in your application's Documents directory, and you can use this URL to create, read, and write from that file. It's important to note that the file doesn't need to exist for you to be able to get an NSURL object for it.

Listing 13-2. You can use the same method with first argument .libraryDirectory to locate the app's library directory

```
let urls = FileManager.default.urls(for:
    .libraryDirectory, in: .userDomainMask)
if let libraryUrl = urls.first {
    print(libraryUrl)
}
```

This code would return a URL like this:

```
file:///var/mobile/Containers/Data/Application/69BFDDB0-E4A8-4359-8382-F6DDDF031481/Library/.
```

It's possible to specify more than one search domain. When you do so, FileManager looks for the directory in all of the domains and may return more than one NSURL. For reasons already explained, this is not really very useful on iOS, but for the sake of completeness, consider the example in Listing 13-3.

Listing 13-3. Getting Multiple URLs

```
let urls = FileManager.default.urls(for:
    .libraryDirectory,in: [.userDomainMask, .systemDomainMask])
print(urls)
```

Here, you ask FileManager to look for the Library directory in both the user and system domains, and the result is that you get back an array containing two NSURLs:

- `file:///var/mobile/Containers/Data/Application/69BFDDB0-E4A8-4359-8382-F6DDDF031481/Library/`

- `file:///System/Library/`

The second URL refers to the system's Library directory, which, of course, you can't access. When more than one URL is returned, the order in which they appear in the returned array is undefined.

Notice how you wrote the value of the inDomains argument in Listing 13-3.

```
[.userDomainMask, .systemDomainMask]
```

This might look like an initializer for an array, but it's actually creating a set—the syntax for initializing an array and a set in Swift are the same.

Getting the tmp Directory

Getting a reference to your application's temporary directory is even easier than getting a reference to the Documents directory. The Foundation function called NSTemporaryDirectory() returns a string containing the full path to your application's temporary directory. To create an NSURL for a file that will be stored in the temporary directory, first find the temporary directory.

```
let tempDirPath = NSTemporaryDirectory()
```

Next, convert the path to a URL and create a path to a file in the temporary directory by appending a path component to it as you did before, as shown in Listing 13-4.

Listing 13-4. Appending a Path Component to a URL

```
let tempDirUrl = NSURL(fileURLWithPath: tempDirPath)
let tempFileUrl = tempDirUrl.appendingPathComponent("tempFile.txt")
```

The resulting URL will be something like this:

```
file:///private/var/mobile/Containers/Data/Application/29233884-23EB-4267-8CC9-86DCD507D84C/
tmp/tempFile.txt
```

File-Saving Strategies

All the persistence approaches you're going to look at in this chapter use the iOS file system. In the case of SQLite3, you'll create a single SQLite3 database file and let SQLite3 worry about storing and retrieving your data. In its simplest form, Core Data takes care of all the file system management for you. With the other two persistence mechanisms—property lists and archiving—you need to put some thought into whether you are going to store your data in a single file or in multiple files.

Single-File Persistence

Using a single file for data storage provides the easiest approach and, with many applications, a perfectly acceptable one. You start by creating a root object, usually an `Array` or `Dictionary` (your root object can also be based on a custom class when using archiving). Next, you populate your root object with all the program data that needs to be persisted. Whenever you need to save, your code rewrites the entire contents of that root object to a single file. When your application launches, it reads the entire contents of that file into memory. When it quits, it writes out the entire contents. This is the approach you'll use.

The downside of using a single file is that you need to load all of your application's data into memory and that you must write all of it to the file system for even the smallest changes. But if your application isn't likely to manage more than a few megabytes of data, this approach works fine, and its simplicity certainly makes things easier.

Multiple-File Persistence

Using multiple files for persistence provides another approach. For example, an e-mail application might store each e-mail message in its own file.

There are obvious advantages to this method. It allows the application to load only data that the user has requested (another form of lazy loading); and when the user makes a change, only the files that changed need to be saved. This method also gives you the opportunity to free up memory when you receive a low-memory notification. Any memory that is being used to store data that the user is not currently viewing can be flushed and then simply reloaded from the file system the next time it's needed. The downside of multiple-file persistence is that it adds a fair amount of complexity to your application. For now, you'll work with single-file persistence.

Next, you'll get into the specifics of each of your persistence methods: property lists, object archives, SQLite3, and Core Data. You'll explore each of these in turn and build an application that uses each mechanism to save some data to the device's file system. You'll start with property lists.

Using Property Lists

Several of your sample applications have used property lists, most recently when you created a property list to specify your application settings and preferences in Chapter 12. Property lists provide convenience in that they can be edited manually using Xcode or the Property List Editor application. Also, both `Dictionary` and `Array` instances can be written to and created from property lists, as long as they contain only specific serializable objects.

Property List Serialization

A *serialized object* is one that has been converted into a stream of bytes so that it can be stored in a file or transferred over a network. Although any object can be made serializable, only certain objects can be placed into a collection class, such as an NSDictionary or NSArray, and then stored to a property list using the collection class's writeToURL(_:atomically:) or writeToFile(_:atomically:) methods. The following classes can be serialized this way:

- Array or NSArray
- NSMutableArray
- Dictionary or NSDictionary
- NSMutableDictionary
- NSData
- NSMutableData
- String or NSString
- NSMutableString
- NSNumber
- Date or NSDate

If you can build your data model from just these objects, you can use property lists to save and load your data.

▓ **Note**   The writeToURL(_:atomically:) and writeToFile(_:atomically:) methods do the same thing, but the first requires you to give the file location as an NSURL, the second as a String. Previously, file locations were always given as string paths, but more recently Apple started preferring to use NSURLs instead, so the examples in this book do the same, except where there is only an API that requires a path. You can easily get the path for a file-based NSURL from its path property, as you'll see in the first example in this chapter.

If you're going to use property lists for persisting application data, use either an Array or a Dictionary to hold the data that needs to be persisted. Assuming that all the objects that you put into the Array or Dictionary are serializable objects from the preceding list, you can write out a property list by calling the write(to url: URL, atomically: Bool) -> Bool method on the dictionary or array instance, as shown in Listing 13-5.

Listing 13-5. Writing to a Property List

```
let array: NSArray = [1,2,3]
let tempDirPath = NSTemporaryDirectory()
let tempDirUrl = NSURL(fileURLWithPath: tempDirPath)
let tempFileUrl = tempDirUrl.appendingPathComponent("tempFile.txt")
array.write(to: tempFileUrl!, atomically:true)
```

▨ **Note** The `atomically` parameter causes the method to first write the data to an auxiliary file, not to the specified location, and after successfully being written to that file, it gets a copy to the location specified by the first parameter. This provides a safer way to write a file because if the application crashes during the save, the existing file (if there was one) will not be corrupted. It adds a bit of overhead, but in most situations, it's worth the cost.

One problem with the property list approach is that custom objects cannot be serialized into property lists. You also can't use other classes from Cocoa Touch, which means that classes like NSURL, UIImage, and UIColor cannot be used directly.

Apart from the serialization issue, keeping all your model data in the form of property lists means you can't easily create derived or calculated properties (such as a property that is the sum of two other properties), and some of your code that really should be contained in model classes must be moved to your controller classes. Again, these restrictions work for simple data models and apps. But most of the time your app will be much easier to maintain by creating dedicated model classes.

Simple property lists still provide usefulness in complex applications as they are a great way to include static data in your application. For example, when your application includes a picker, often the best way to include the list of items for it is to create a .plist file, placing that file into your project's Resources folder and causing it to be compiled into your application.

You'll now build a simple application that uses property lists to store its data.

Creating the First Version of a Persistence Application

You're going to build a program that lets you enter data into four text fields, saves those fields to a .plist file when the application quits, and then reloads the data back from that .plist file the next time the application launches (see Figure 13-5).

Figure 13-5. *Your Persistence application*

■ **Note** In this chapter's applications, you won't be taking the time to set up all the user interface niceties that you have added in previous examples. Tapping the Return key, for example, will neither dismiss the keyboard nor take you to the next field. If you want to add such polish to the application, doing so would be good practice, so I encourage you to do that on your own.

In Xcode, create a new project using the Single View App template and name it **Persistence**. Before you build the view with the four text fields, let's create the single outlet you need. In the Project Navigator, single-click the ViewController.swift file and add the following outlet:

```
class ViewController: UIViewController {
    @IBOutlet var lineFields:[UITextField]!
```

Designing the Persistence Application View

Now select `Main.storyboard` to edit the GUI. Once Xcode switches over to Interface Builder mode, you'll see the view controller scene in the editing pane. Drag a text field from the library and place it against the top and right blue guidelines. Bring up the Attributes Inspector. Make sure the Clear When Editing Begins box is deselected.

Now drag a label to the window and place it to the left of the text field using the left blue guideline; then use the horizontal blue guideline to line up the label's vertical center with that of the text field. Double-click the label and change it to say **Line 1:**. Finally, resize the text field using the left resize handle to bring it close to the label. Use Figure 13-6 as a guide. Next, select the label and text field, hold down the Option key, and drag down to make a copy below the first set. Use the blue guidelines to guide your placement. Now select both labels and both text fields, hold down the Option key, and drag down again. You should now have four labels next to four text fields. Double-click each of the remaining labels and change their names to Line 2:, Line 3:, and Line 4:. Again, compare your results with Figure 13-6.

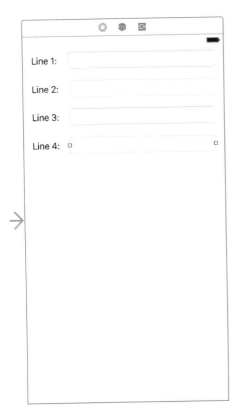

Figure 13-6. *Designing the Persistence application's view*

Once you have all four text fields and labels placed, Control-drag from the View Controller icon in the Document Outline to each of the four text fields. Connect them all to the lineFields outlet collection, making sure to connect them in order from top to bottom. Save the changes you made to Main.storyboard.

Now let's add the Auto Layout constraints to make sure that the design works the same way on all devices. Starting by Control-dragging from the Line 1 label to the text field to its right and then release the mouse. Hold down the Shift key and select Horizontal Spacing and Baseline and then click the Return key. Do the same for the other three labels and text fields.

Next, you'll fix the positions of the text fields. In the Document Outline, Control-drag from the top text field to its parent View icon, release the mouse, hold down the Shift key, and select Trailing Space to Container Margin and Vertical Spacing to Top Layout Guide. Do the same for the other three text fields.

We need to fix the widths of the labels so that they don't resize if the user types more text than will fit in any of the text fields. Select the top label and click the Pin button below the storyboard editor. In the pop-up, select the Width check box and click Add 1 Constraint. Do the same for all of the labels.

Finally, back in the Document Outline, Control-drag from the Line 1 label to the View icon, release the mouse, and select Leading Space to Container Margin. Do the same for all of the labels and that's it—all the required Auto Layout constraints have been set. Select the view controller icon in the Document Outline followed by Editor ➤ Resolve Auto Layout Issues ➤ Update Frames in the menu to remove the warnings in the Xcode Activity View. Now build and run the application and compare the result with Figure 13-6.

Editing the Persistence Classes

In the Project Navigator, select ViewController.swift and add the code in Listing 13-6.

Listing 13-6. Getting the URL for Your data.plist File

```
func dataFileURL() -> NSURL {
    let urls = FileManager.default.urls(for:
        .documentDirectory, in: .userDomainMask)
    var url:NSURL?
    url = URL(fileURLWithPath: "")        // create a blank path
    do {
        try url = urls.first!.appendingPathComponent("data.plist")
    } catch  {
        print("Error is \(error)")
    }
    return url!
}
```

The dataFileURL() method returns the URL of the data file that you'll be creating in this example by finding the Documents directory and appending the file name to it. This method will be called from any code that needs to load or save data. You are playing it a little loose here with the URL. Note that you've encapsulated the appendingPathComponent method within a Swift do-catch block. You have to do this because the append method throws an error that needs to be caught. But since you know that your app bundle must have a document directory and you're creating the data.plist file yourself, you're not going to see this error as long as you write the code correctly. Normally, you want to handle things a little more securely so your customers don't see crashes, but for the sake of brevity you're not going to deal with that here since it's not the subject of your discussion.

■ **Note**   In Swift you use a `do-catch` block (which can be found in the Xcode code snippet library) to try a method call that throws an exception (an error) and then "catch" that exception and handle it in some way that prevents the app from crashing.

Find the `viewDidLoad()` method and add the following code to it, as well as a new method for receiving notifications named `applicationWillResignActive()` just below it, as shown in Listing 13-7.

Listing 13-7. The viewDidLoad Method in the ViewController.swift File and the applicationWillResignActive Method

```swift
override func viewDidLoad() {
    super.viewDidLoad()
    // Do any additional setup after loading the view, typically from a nib.
    let fileURL = self.dataFileURL()
    if (FileManager.default.fileExists(atPath: fileURL.path!)) {
        if let array = NSArray(contentsOf: fileURL as URL) as? [String] {
            for i in 0..<array.count {
                lineFields[i].text = array[i]
            }
        }
    }

let app = UIApplication.shared()
    NotificationCenter.default.addObserver(self, selector: #selector(self.applicationWill
ResignActive(notification:)), name: Notification.Name.UIApplicationWillResignActive,
object: app)
}

@objc func applicationWillResignActive(notification:NSNotification) {
    let fileURL = self.dataFileURL()
    let array = (self.lineFields as NSArray).value(forKey: "text") as! NSArray
    array.write(to: fileURL as URL, atomically: true)
}
```

In the `viewDidLoad()` method, you do a few more things. First, you use the `fileExists(atPath:)` method of the `FileManager` class to check whether your data file already exists, which would be the case if you have already run the application at least once. This method requires the file's path name, which you get from the path property of its URL (unfortunately, there isn't a variant of this method that accepts a URL argument). If there isn't one, you don't want to bother trying to load it. If the file does exist, you instantiate an array with the contents of that file and then copy the objects from that array to your four text fields. Because arrays are ordered lists, you copy them in the same order as you saved them.

To read the file, you use an `Array` initializer that creates an NSArray object from the contents of a file at a given URL. The `Array` initializer expects the file content to be in property list format, which is fine because that's the form in which it is saved, in the code you'll write shortly.

The application needs to save its data before it is terminated or sent to the background, so you are interested in the notification called `applicationWillResignActive`. This notification is posted whenever an app is no longer the one with which the user is interacting. This happens when the user taps the Home button, as well as when the application is pushed to the background by some other event, such as an incoming phone call. You can find out that this has happened by registering for a notification from iOS's notification center. The notification center delivers a notification by calling a method that you register with it, passing an argument of type Notification that includes the details of the event that's being notified. To register for this notification, you get a reference to your application instance and use that to subscribe to UIApplicationWillResignActive, using the default NotificationCenter instance and a method called addObserver(_:selector:name:object:). You pass self as the first parameter, specifying that your ViewController instance is the observer that should be notified. For the second parameter, you pass a selector to the applicationWillResignActive() method, telling the notification center to call that method when the notification is posted. The third parameter, UIApplicationWillResignActive, is the name of the notification that you're interested in receiving. This is a string constant defined by the UIApplication class.

Finally, you add the implementation of the applicationWillResignActive() method, which the notification center will call:

```
@objc func applicationWillResignActive(notification:NSNotification) {
    let fileURL = self.dataFileURL()
    let array = (self.lineFields as NSArray).value(forKey: "text") as! NSArray
    array.write(to: fileURL as URL, atomically: true)
}
```

This method is pretty short but really does a lot with just a few method calls. You construct an array of strings by calling the text method on each of the text fields in your lineFields array. To accomplish this, you use a clever shortcut: instead of explicitly iterating through your array of text fields, asking each for its text value and adding that value to a new array, you cast the Swift lineFields array (of UITextFields) to an NSArray and call value(forKey:) on it, passing "text" as a parameter. The NSArray implementation of valueForKey() does the iteration for you, asks each UITextField instance it contains for its text value, and returns a new NSArray containing all the values. After that, you write the contents of that array out to your .plist file in property list format using the write(_ to:atomically:) method. That's all there is to saving your data using property lists.

Let's summarize how this works. When your main view is finished loading, you look for a .plist file. If it exists, you copy data from it into your text fields. Next, you register to be notified when the application becomes inactive (either by quitting or by being pushed to the background). When that happens, you gather the values from your four text fields, place them in a mutable array, and write that mutable array to a property list.

Build and run the application. It should build and then launch in the simulator. Once it comes up, you should be able to type into any of the four text fields. When you've typed something in them, press Command-Shift-H to return to the home screen. It's very important that you do this. If you just exit the simulator, that's the equivalent of forcibly quitting your application. In that case, the view controller will never receive the notification that the application is going inactive, and your data will not be saved. After returning to the home screen, you may then quit the simulator or stop the app from Xcode and run it again. Your text will be restored and will appear in the text fields the next time the app starts.

■ **Note**   It's important to understand that returning to the home screen doesn't typically quit the app—at least not at first. The app is put into a background state, ready to be instantly reactivated in case the user switches back to it.

Property list serialization is pretty cool and easy to use. However, it's a little limiting since only a small selection of objects can be stored in property lists. Let's look at a somewhat more robust approach.

Archiving Model Objects

In the Cocoa world, the term **archiving** refers to another form of serialization, but it's a more generic type that any object can implement. Any model object specifically written to hold data should support archiving. The technique of archiving model objects lets you easily write complex objects to a file and then read them back in. As long as every property you implement in your class is either a scalar (e.g., Int or Float) or an instance of a class that conforms to the NSCoding protocol, you can archive your objects completely. Since most Foundation and Cocoa Touch classes capable of storing data do conform to NSCoding (though there are a few noteworthy exceptions, such as UIImage), archiving is relatively easy to implement for most classes.

Although not strictly required to make archiving work, another protocol should be implemented along with NSCoding: the NSCopying protocol, which allows your object to be copied. Being able to copy an object gives you a lot more flexibility when using data model objects.

Conforming to NSCoding

The NSCoding protocol declares two methods, which are both required. One encodes your object into an archive; the other one creates a new object by decoding an archive. Both methods are passed an instance of NSCoder, which you work with in very much the same way as NSUserDefaults, introduced in the previous chapter. You can encode and decode both objects and native data types like Int and Float values using *key-value coding*.

To support archiving in an object, you need to make it a subclass of NSObject (or any other class that is derived from NSObject), and you need to encode each of your instance variables into encoder using the appropriate encoding method. Let's see how this works. Suppose you create a simple container class, like this:

```
class MyObject : NSObject, NSCoding, NSCopying {
    var number = 0;
    var string = ""
    var child: MyObject?

    override init() {
    }
}
```

This class contains an integer property, a string property, and a reference to another instance of the same class. It is derived from NSObject and conforms to the NSCoding and NSCopying protocols. The NSCoding protocol method to encode an object of type MyObject might look like this:

```
func encode(with aCoder: NSCoder) {
    aCoder.encode(string, forKey: "stringKey")
    aCoder.encode(32, forKey: "intKey")
    if let myChild = child {
        aCoder.encode(myChild, forKey: "childKey")
    }
}
```

If MyObject were a subclass of a class that also conforms to NSCoding, you would need to make sure that also you called encodeWithCoder() on its superclass to ensure that the superclass encodes its data. In that case, this method would look like this instead:

```
func encode(with aCoder: NSCoder) {
    super.encode(with aCoder: NSCoder)
    aCoder.encode(string, forKey: "stringKey")
    aCoder.encode(32, forKey: "intKey")
    if let myChild = child {
        aCoder.encode(myChild, forKey: "childKey")
    }
}
```

The NSCoding protocol also requires you to implement an initializer that initializes an object from an NSCoder, allowing you to restore an object that was previously archived. Implementing this method is similar to implementing encodeWithCoder(). If your object has no base class or you are subclassing some other class that doesn't conform to NSCoding, your initializer would look something like the following:

```
required init?(coder aDecoder: NSCoder) {
        string = aDecoder.decodeObject(forKey: "stringKey") as! String
        number = aDecoder.decodeInteger(forKey: "intKey")
        child = aDecoder.decodeObject(forKey: "childKey") as? MyObject
}
```

The initializer sets the properties of the object being initialized by decoding values from the passed-in instance of NSCoder. Since you are allowing the child property of the original object to be nil, you need to use conditional casting when assigning to the decoded object's child property because the archived object may not have a stored child object.

When implementing NSCoding for a class with a superclass that also conforms to NSCoding, you need to add an extra line to allow the superclass to initialize its own state.

```
required init?(coder aDecoder: NSCoder) {
    string = aDecoder.decodeObject(forKey: "stringKey") as! String
    number = aDecoder.decodeInteger(forKey: "intKey")
    child = aDecoder.decodeObject(forKey: "childKey") as? MyObject
    super.init(code: aDecoder)
}
```

That's basically it. As long as you implement these two methods to encode and decode all your object's properties, your object is archivable and can be written to and read from archives.

Implementing NSCopying

As mentioned earlier, conforming to NSCopying is a good idea for any data model objects. NSCopying has one method, called copyWithZone(), which allows objects to be copied. Implementing NSCopying is similar to implementing init(coder:). You just need to create a new instance of the same class and then set all of that new instance's properties to the same values as this object's properties. Even though you implement the copy(with zone:) method, the application code actually calls a method called copy(), which forwards the operation to copy(with zone:).

```
let anObject = MyObject()
let objectCopy = anObject.copy() as! MyObject
```

Here's what the copy(withZone:) method for the MyObject class would look like:

```
func copy(with zone: NSZone? = nil) -> AnyObject {
    let copy = MyObject()
    copy.number = number
    copy.string = string
    copy.child = child?.copy() as? MyObject
    return copy
}
```

Notice that with this implementation, if there is a property that references a child object (such as the child property in this example), the new object will have a copy of that child, not the original one. If the child object is of a type that is immutable or if you only need to provide a shallow copy of the object, then you would simply assign the original child object reference to the new object.

▒ **Note**   Don't worry too much about the NSZone parameter. This pointer is to a struct that is used by the system to manage memory. Only in rare circumstances did developers ever need to worry about zones or create their own, and nowadays, it's almost unheard of to have multiple zones. Calling copy on an object is the same as calling copy(with zone:) using the default zone, which is always what you want. In fact, on the modern iOS, zones are completely ignored. The fact that NSCopying uses zones at all is a historical oddity for the sake of backward compatibility.

Archiving and Unarchiving Data Objects

Creating an archive from an object (or objects) that conforms to NSCoding is relatively easy. First, you create an instance of the Foundation class NSMutableData to hold the encoded data, and then you create an NSKeyedArchiver instance to archive objects into that NSMutableData instance.

```
let data = NSMutableData()
let archiver = NSKeyedArchiver(forWritingWith: data)
```

After creating both of those, you then use key-value coding to archive any objects you want to include in the archive, like this:

```
archiver.encode(anObject, forKey: "keyValueString")
```

Once you've encoded all the objects you want to include, you just tell the archiver you're finished, and then you write the NSMutableData instance to the file system.

```
archiver.finishEncoding()
let success = data.write(to: archiveUrl as URL, atomically: true)
```

If you're feeling a little overwhelmed by archiving, don't worry. It's actually fairly straightforward. You're going to retrofit your Persistence application to use archiving, so you'll get to see it in action. Once you've done it a few times, archiving will become second nature, as all you're really doing is storing and retrieving your object's properties using key-value coding.

The Archiving Application

Let's redo the Persistence application so that it uses archiving instead of property lists. You're going to be making some fairly significant changes to the Persistence source code, so you should make a copy of your entire project folder before continuing. I've compressed it before making any changes—using the property list technique—to `PersistencePL.zip`.

Implementing the FourLines Class

Once you're ready to proceed and have a copy of your Persistence project open in Xcode, press ⌘N or select File ➤ New ➤ File. When the new file assistant comes up, from the iOS section, select Swift File and click Next. On the next screen, name the file `FourLines.swift`, choose the Persistence folder to save it, and then click Create. This class is going to be your data model. It will hold the data that you're currently storing in a dictionary in the property list application.

Single-click `FourLines.swift` and add the code in Listing 13-8.

Listing 13-8. Your FourLines Class

```
class FourLines : NSObject, NSCoding, NSCopying {
    private static let linesKey = "linesKey"
    var lines:[String]?

    override init() {
    }
    required init?(coder aDecoder: NSCoder) {
        lines = aDecoder.decodeObject(forKey: FourLines.linesKey) as? [String]
    }
    func encode(with aCoder: NSCoder) {
        if let saveLines = lines {
            aCoder.encode(saveLines, forKey: FourLines.linesKey)
        }
    }
    func copy(with zone: NSZone? = nil) -> AnyObject {
        let copy = FourLines()
        if let linesToCopy = lines {
            var newLines = Array<String>()
            for line in linesToCopy {
                newLines.append(line)
            }
            copy.lines = newLines
        }
        return copy
    }
}
```

We just implemented all the methods necessary to conform to the NSCoding and NSCopying protocols. You encoded the lines property in encode(with aCoder:) and decoded it using the same key value in init(with aCoder:). In copy(with zone:), you created a new FourLines object and copied the string array to it, carefully making a deep copy so that changes to the original will not affect the new object. See? It's not hard at all; just make sure you did not forget to change anything if you did a lot of copying and pasting.

Implementing the ViewController Class

Now that you have an archivable data object, let's use it to persist your application data. Select ViewController.swift and make the changes in Listing 13-9.

Listing 13-9. Your Save and Retrieve Code for Archiving Object in ViewController.swift

```
override func viewDidLoad() {
    super.viewDidLoad()
    // Do any additional setup after loading the view, typically from a nib.
    let fileURL = self.dataFileURL()
    if (FileManager.default.fileExists(atPath: fileURL.path!)) {
        if let array = NSArray(contentsOf: fileURL as URL) as? [String] {
            for i in 0..<array.count {
                lineFields[i].text = array[i]
            }
        }
        let data = NSMutableData(contentsOf: fileURL as URL)
        let unarchiver = NSKeyedUnarchiver(forReadingWith: data as! Data)
        let fourLines = unarchiver.decodeObject(forKey: ViewController.rootKey)
                        as! FourLines
        unarchiver.finishDecoding()
        if let newLines = fourLines.lines {
            for i in 0..<newLines.count {
                lineFields[i].text = newLines[i]
            }
        }
    }
    let app = UIApplication.shared()
    NotificationCenter.default.addObserver(self, selector: #selector(self.applicationWill
    ResignActive(notification:)), name: Notification.Name.UIApplicationWillResignActive,
    object: app)
}

@objc func applicationWillResignActive(notification:NSNotification) {
    let fileURL = self.dataFileURL()
    let fourLines = FourLines()
    let array = (self.lineFields as NSArray).value(forKey: "text")
        as! [String]
    fourLines.lines = array
```

```
    let data = NSMutableData()
    let archiver = NSKeyedArchiver(forWritingWith: data)
    archiver.encode(fourLines, forKey: ViewController.rootKey)
    archiver.finishEncoding()
    data.write(to: fileURL as URL, atomically: true)
}

func dataFileURL() -> NSURL {
    let urls = FileManager.default.urls(for:
        .documentDirectory, in: .userDomainMask)
    var url:NSURL?
    url = URL(fileURLWithPath: "")        // create a blank path
    do {
        try url = urls.first!.appendingPathComponent("data.archive")
    } catch {
        print("Error is \(error)")
    }
    return url!
}
```

Save your changes and then build and run this version of the app. Not very much has changed really. You started off by specifying a new file name in the dataFileURL() method so that your program doesn't try to load the old property list as an archive. You also defined a new constant that will be the key value you use to encode and decode your object. Next, you redefined the loading and saving by using FourLines to hold the data and using its NSCoding methods to do the actual loading and saving. The GUI is identical to the previous version.

This new version takes several more lines of code to implement than property list serialization, so you might be wondering if there really is an advantage to using archiving over just serializing property lists. For this application, the answer is simple: no, there really isn't any advantage. But imagine you had an array of archivable objects, such as the FourLines class that you just built. You could archive the entire array by archiving the array instance itself. Collection classes like Array, when archived, archive all of the objects they contain. As long as every object you put into an array or dictionary conforms to NSCoding, you can archive the array or dictionary and restore it so that all the objects that were in it when you archived it will be in the restored array or dictionary. The same is not true of property link persistence, which works only for a small set of Foundation object types—you cannot use it to persist custom classes without writing additional code to convert instances of those classes to and from a Dictionary, with one key for each object property.

In other words, the NSCoding approach scales beautifully (in terms of code size, at least). No matter how many objects you add, the work to write those objects to disk (assuming you're using single-file persistence) is exactly the same. With property lists, the amount of work increases with every object you add.

Using iOS's Embedded SQLite3

The third persistence option I'm going to discuss is using iOS's embedded SQL database, called SQLite3. SQLite3 is very efficient at storing and retrieving large amounts of data. It's also capable of doing complex aggregations on your data, with much faster results than you would get doing the same thing using objects. Consider a couple scenarios. What if you need to calculate the sum of a particular field across all the objects in your application? Or, what if you need the sum from just the objects that meet certain criteria? SQLite3 allows you to get this information without loading every object into memory. Getting aggregations from SQLite3 is several orders of magnitude faster than loading all the objects into memory and summing their values. Being a full-fledged embedded database, SQLite3 contains tools to make it even faster by, for example, creating table indexes that can speed up your queries.

SQLite3 uses the Structured Query Language (SQL), the standard language used to interact with relational databases. Whole books have been written on the syntax of SQL (hundreds of them, in fact), as well as on SQLite itself. So if you don't already know SQL and you want to use SQLite3 in your application, you have a little work ahead of you. I'll show you how to set up and interact with the SQLite database from your iOS applications. I'll also show you some of the basics of the syntax in this chapter. But to really make the most of SQLite3, you'll need to do some additional research and exploration. A couple of good starting points are "An Introduction to the SQLite3 C/C++ Interface" (`www.sqlite.org/cintro.html`) and "SQL As Understood by SQLite" (`www.sqlite.org/lang.html`).

Relational databases (including SQLite3) and object-oriented programming languages use fundamentally different approaches to storing and organizing data. The approaches are different enough that numerous techniques and many libraries and tools for converting between the two have been developed. These different techniques are collectively called **object-relational mapping** (ORM). There are currently several ORM tools available for Cocoa Touch. In fact, you'll look at one ORM solution provided by Apple, called Core Data, later in the chapter.

But before you do that, you're going to focus on the SQLite3 basics, including setting it up, creating a table to hold your data, and using the database in an application. Obviously, in the real world, an application as simple as the one you're working on wouldn't warrant the investment in SQLite3. But this application's simplicity is exactly what makes it a good learning example.

Creating or Opening the Database

Before you can use SQLite3, you must open the database. The function that's used to do that, `sqlite3_open()`, will open an existing database; or, if none exists at the specified location, the function will create a new one. Here's what the code to open a database might look like:

```
var database:OpaquePointer? = nil
let result = sqlite3_open("/path/to/database/file", &database)
```

If `result` is equal to the constant `SQLITE_OK`, then the database was successfully opened. Notice the type of the database variable. In the SQLite3 API, this variable is a C language structure of type `sqlite3`. When this C API is imported into Swift, this variable is mapped to `UnsafeMutablePointer<COpaquePointer>`, which is how Swift expresses the C pointer type `void *`. This means you have to treat it as an opaque pointer. That's OK because you won't need to access the internals of this structure from your Swift code—you just need to pass the pointer to other SQLite3 functions, like `sqlite3_close()`.

```
sqlite3_close(database)
```

Databases store all their data in tables. You can create a new table by crafting an SQL `CREATE` statement and passing it in to an open database using the function `sqlite3_exec`, like so:

```
let createSQL = "CREATE TABLE IF NOT EXISTS PEOPLE" +
                "(ID INTEGER PRIMARY KEY AUTOINCREMENT, FIELD_DATA TEXT)"
var errMsg:UnsafeMutablePointer<Int8> = nil
result = sqlite3_exec(database, createSQL, nil, nil, &errMsg)
```

The function `sqlite3_exec` is used to run any command against SQLite3 that doesn't return data, including updates, inserts, and deletes. Retrieving data from the database is a little more involved. You first need to prepare the statement by feeding it your SQL `SELECT` command.

```
let createSQL = "SELECT ID, FIELD_DATA FROM FIELDS ORDER BY ROW"
var statement: OpaquePointer? = nil
result = sqlite3_prepare_v2(database, createSQL, -1, &statement, nil)
```

If result equals SQLITE_OK, your statement was successfully prepared, and you can start stepping through the result set. This code shows another instance where you have to treat a SQLite3 structure as an opaque pointer—in the SQLite3 API, the statement variable would be of type sqlite3_stmt.

Here is an example of stepping through a result set and retrieving an Int and a String from the database:

```
while sqlite3_step(statement) == SQLITE_ROW {
    let row = Int(sqlite3_column_int(statement, 0))
    let rowData = sqlite3_column_text(statement, 1)
    let fieldValue = String(cString:rowData!)
    lineFields[row].text = fieldValue!
}
sqlite3_finalize(statement)
```

Using Bind Variables

Although it's possible to construct SQL strings to insert values, it is common practice to use something called *bind variables* for this purpose. Handling strings correctly—making sure they don't have invalid characters and that quotes are inserted properly—can be quite a chore. With bind variables, those issues are taken care of for you.

To insert a value using a bind variable, you create your SQL statement as normal but put a question mark (?) into the SQL string. Each question mark represents one variable that must be bound before the statement can be executed. Next, you prepare the SQL statement, bind a value to each of the variables, and execute the command.

Here's an example that prepares a SQL statement with two bind variables, binds an Int to the first variable and a string to the second variable, and then executes and finalizes the statement:

```
var statement:OpaquePointer? = nil
let sql = "INSERT INTO FOO VALUES (?, ?);"
if sqlite3_prepare_v2(database, sql, -1, &statement, nil)
        == SQLITE_OK {
    sqlite3_bind_int(statement, 1, 235)
    sqlite3_bind_text(statement, 2, "Bar", -1, nil)
}
if sqlite3_step(statement) != SQLITE_DONE {
    print("This should be real error checking!")
}
sqlite3_finalize(statement);
```

There are multiple bind statements available, depending on the data type that you want to use. Most bind functions take only three parameters:

- The first parameter to any bind function, regardless of the data type, is a pointer to the sqlite3_stmt used previously in the sqlite3_prepare_v2() call.

- The second parameter is the index of the variable to which you're binding. This is a one-indexed value, meaning that the first question mark in the SQL statement has index 1, and each one after it is one higher than the one to its left.

- The third parameter is always the value that should be substituted for the question mark.

A few bind functions, such as those for binding text and binary data, have two additional parameters.

- The first additional parameter is the length of the data being passed in the third parameter. In the case of C strings, you can pass -1 instead of the string's length, and the function will use the entire string. In all other cases, you need to tell it the length of the data being passed in.

- The final parameter is an optional function callback in case you need to do any memory cleanup after the statement is executed. Typically, such a function would be used to free memory allocated using malloc().

The syntax that follows the bind statements may seem a little odd since you're doing an insert. When using bind variables, the same syntax is used for both queries and updates. If the SQL string had a SQL query, rather than an update, you would need to call sqlite3_step() multiple times until it returned SQLITE_DONE. Since this is an update, you call it only once.

Creating the SQLite3 Application

In Xcode, create a new project using the Single View App template and name it **SQLite Persistence**. This project will start off identical to the previous project, so begin by opening the ViewController.swift file and add an outlet:

```
class ViewController: UIViewController {
    @IBOutlet var lineFields:[UITextField]!
```

Next, select Main.storyboard. Design the view and connect the outlet collection by following the instructions in the "Designing the Persistence Application View" section earlier in this chapter. Once your design is complete, save the storyboard file.

You've covered the basics, so let's see how this would work in practice. You're going to modify your Persistence application again, this time storing its data using SQLite3. You'll use a single table and store the field values in four different rows of that table. You'll also give each row a row number that corresponds to its field. For example, the value from the first line will get stored in the table with a row number of 0, the next line will be row number 1, and so on. Let's get started.

Linking to the SQLite3 Library

SQLite 3 is accessed through a procedural API that provides interfaces to a number of C function calls. To use this API, you'll need to link your application to a dynamic library called libsqlite3.dylib. Select the SQLite Persistence item at the very top of the Project Navigator list (leftmost pane) and then select SQLite Persistence from the TARGETS section in the main area (see Figure 13-7, middle pane). (Be careful that you have selected SQLite Persistence from the TARGETS section, not from the PROJECT section.)

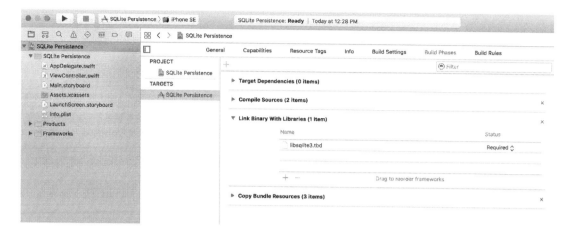

Figure 13-7. *Selecting the SQLite Persistence project in the Project Navigator; selecting the SQLite Persistence target; and finally, selecting the Build Phases tab*

With the SQLite Persistence target selected, click the Build Phases tab in the rightmost pane. You'll see a list of items, initially all collapsed, which represent the various steps Xcode goes through to build the application. Expand the item labeled Link Binary With Libraries. This section contains the libraries and frameworks that Xcode links with your application. By default, it's empty because the compiler automatically links with any iOS frameworks that your application uses, but the compiler doesn't know anything about the SQLite3 library, so you need to add it here.

Click the + button at the bottom of the linked frameworks list, and you'll be presented with a sheet that lists all available frameworks and libraries. Find `libsqlite3.tbd` in the list (or use the handy search field) and click the Add button. Note that there may be several other entries in that directory that start with libsqlite3. Be sure you select `libsqlite3.tbd`. It is an alias that always points to the latest version of the SQLite3 library.

Modifying the Persistence View Controller

Next, you need to import the header files for SQLite3 into the view controller so that the compiler can see the function and other definitions that make up the API. There is no way to directly import the header file into Swift code because the SQLite3 library is not packaged as a framework. The easiest way to deal with this is to add a **bridging header** to the project. Once you have a bridging header, you can add other header files to it, and those header files will be read by the Swift compiler. There are a couple of ways to add a bridging file. You'll use the simpler of the two, which is to temporarily add an Objective-C class to the project. Let's do that now.

Press ⌘N or select File ➤ New ➤ File. In the iOS Source section of the dialog, choose Cocoa Touch Class and click Next. Name the class `Temporary`, make it a subclass of `NSObject`, change the language to Objective-C, and click Next. In the next screen, click the Create button. When you do this, Xcode will pop up a window asking whether you want to create a bridging header. Click Create Bridging Header. Now, in the Project Navigator, you'll see the files for the new class (`Temporary.m` and `Temporary.h`) and the bridging header, which is called `SQLite Persistence-Bridging-Header.h`. Delete the `Temporary.m` and `Temporary.h` files—you don't need them anymore. Select the bridging header to open it in the editor and then add the following line to it:

```
#import <sqlite3.h>
```

Now that the compiler can see the SQLite3 library and header files, you can write some more code. Select ViewController.swift and make the changes shown in Listing 13-10.

Listing 13-10. Using SQLite3 to Save and Retrieve Your Information

```swift
override func viewDidLoad() {
    super.viewDidLoad()
    // Do any additional setup after loading the view, typically from a nib.
    var database:OpaquePointer? = nil
    var result = sqlite3_open(dataFilePath(), &database)
    if result != SQLITE_OK {
        sqlite3_close(database)
        print("Failed to open database")
        return
    }
    let createSQL = "CREATE TABLE IF NOT EXISTS FIELDS " +
                        "(ROW INTEGER PRIMARY KEY, FIELD_DATA TEXT);"
    var errMsg:UnsafeMutablePointer<Int8>? = nil
    result = sqlite3_exec(database, createSQL, nil, nil, &errMsg)
    if (result != SQLITE_OK) {
        sqlite3_close(database)
        print("Failed to create table")
        return
    }

    let query = "SELECT ROW, FIELD_DATA FROM FIELDS ORDER BY ROW"
    var statement:OpaquePointer? = nil
    if sqlite3_prepare_v2(database, query, -1, &statement, nil) == SQLITE_OK {
        while sqlite3_step(statement) == SQLITE_ROW {
            let row = Int(sqlite3_column_int(statement, 0))
            let rowData = sqlite3_column_text(statement, 1)
            let rowData = sqlite3_column_text(statement, 1)
            let fieldValue = String(cString:rowData!)
            lineFields[row].text = fieldValue
        }
        sqlite3_finalize(statement)
    }
    sqlite3_close(database)

    let app = UIApplication.shared()
    NotificationCenter.default.addObserver(self, selector: #selector(self.applicationWill
    ResignActive(notification:)), name: Notification.Name.UIApplicationWillResignActive,
    object: app)
}

func dataFilePath() -> String {
    let urls = FileManager.default.urls(for:
        .documentDirectory, in: .userDomainMask)
    var url:String?
    url = ""        // create a blank path
```

```
        do {
            try url = urls.first?.appendingPathComponent("data.plist").path!
        } catch {
            print("Error is \(error)")
        }
        return url!
    }


    func applicationWillResignActive(notification:NSNotification) {
        var database:OpaquePointer? = nil
        let result = sqlite3_open(dataFilePath(), &database)
        if result != SQLITE_OK {
            sqlite3_close(database)
            print("Failed to open database")
            return
        }
        for i in 0..<lineFields.count {
            let field = lineFields[i]
            let update = "INSERT OR REPLACE INTO FIELDS (ROW, FIELD_DATA) " +
            "VALUES (?, ?);"
            var statement:OpaquePointer? = nil
            if sqlite3_prepare_v2(database, update, -1, &statement, nil) == SQLITE_OK {
                let text = field.text
                sqlite3_bind_int(statement, 1, Int32(i))
                sqlite3_bind_text(statement, 2, text!, -1, nil)
            }
            if sqlite3_step(statement) != SQLITE_DONE {
                print("Error updating table")
                sqlite3_close(database)
                return
            }
            sqlite3_finalize(statement)
        }
        sqlite3_close(database)
    }
```

The first piece of new code is in the viewDidLoad() method. You begin by getting the path to the database file using the dataFilePath() method that you added. This is just like the dataFileURL() method that you added to your earlier examples, except that it returns the file's path, not its URL. That's because the SQLite3 APIs that work with files require paths, not URLs. Next, you use the path to open the database, creating it if it does not exist. If you hit a problem with opening the database, you close it, print an error message, and return.

```
var database:OpaquePointer? = nil
var result = sqlite3_open(dataFilePath(), &database)
if result != SQLITE_OK {
    sqlite3_close(database)
    print("Failed to open database")
    return
}
```

Next, you need to make sure that you have a table to hold your data. You use an SQL CREATE TABLE statement to do that. By specifying IF NOT EXISTS, you prevent the database from overwriting existing data—if there is already a table with the same name, this command quietly completes without doing anything. That means it's safe to use it every time your application launches without explicitly checking to see if a table exists.

```
let createSQL = "CREATE TABLE IF NOT EXISTS FIELDS " +
                      "(ROW INTEGER PRIMARY KEY, FIELD_DATA TEXT);"
var errMsg:UnsafeMutablePointer<Int8>? = nil
result = sqlite3_exec(database, createSQL, nil, nil, &errMsg)
if (result != SQLITE_OK) {
    sqlite3_close(database)
    print("Failed to create table")
    return
}
```

Each row in the database table contains an integer and a string. The integer is the number of the row in the GUI from which the data was obtained (starting from zero), and the string is the content of the text field on that row. Finally, you need to load your data. You do this using a SQL SELECT statement. In this simple example, you create a SQL SELECT statement that requests all the rows from the database and then you ask SQLite3 to prepare your SELECT. You also tell SQLite3 to order the rows by the row number so that you always get them back in the same order. Absent this, SQLite3 will return the rows in the order in which they are stored internally.

```
let query = "SELECT ROW, FIELD_DATA FROM FIELDS ORDER BY ROW"
var statement:OpaquePointer? = nil
if sqlite3_prepare_v2(database, query, -1, &statement, nil) == SQLITE_OK {
```

Next, you use the sqlite3_step() function to execute the SELECT statement and step through each of the returned rows.

```
while sqlite3_step(statement) == SQLITE_ROW {
```

Now you grab the row number, store it in an int, and then grab the field data as a C string, which you then convert to a Swift String, as described earlier in the chapter.

```
let row = Int(sqlite3_column_int(statement, 0))
let rowData = sqlite3_column_text(statement, 1)
let fieldValue = String(cString:rowData!)
```

Next, you set the appropriate field with the value retrieved from the database.

```
lineFields[row].text = fieldValue
```

Finally, you close the database connection, and you're finished.

```
    }
    sqlite3_finalize(statement)
}
sqlite3_close(database)
```

Note that you close the database connection as soon as you're finished creating the table and loading any data it contains, rather than keeping it open the entire time the application is running. It's the simplest way of managing the connection; and in this little app, you can just open the connection those few times you need it. In a more database-intensive app, you might want to keep the connection open all the time.

The other changes you made are in the applicationWillResignActive() method, where you need to save your application data.

The applicationWillResignActive() method starts by once again opening the database. To save the data, you loop through all four fields and issue a separate command to update each row of the database.

```
for i in 0..<lineFields.count  {
    let field = lineFields[i]
```

You craft an INSERT OR REPLACE SQL statement with two bind variables. The first represents the row that's being stored; the second is for the actual string value to be stored. By using INSERT OR REPLACE instead of the more standard INSERT, you don't need to worry about whether a row already exists.

```
let update = "INSERT OR REPLACE INTO FIELDS (ROW, FIELD_DATA) " +
             "VALUES (?, ?);"
```

Next, you declare a pointer to a statement, prepare your statement with the bind variables, and bind values to both of the bind variables.

```
var statement:OpaquePointer? = nil
if sqlite3_prepare_v2(database, update, -1, &statement, nil) == SQLITE_OK {
    let text = field.text
    sqlite3_bind_int(statement, 1, Int32(i))
    sqlite3_bind_text(statement, 2, text!, -1, nil)
}
```

Now you call sqlite3_step to execute the update, check to make sure it worked, and finalize the statement, ending the loop.

```
if sqlite3_step(statement) != SQLITE_DONE {
    print("Error updating table")
    sqlite3_close(database)
    return
}
sqlite3_finalize(statement)
```

Notice that you simply print an error message here if anything goes wrong. In a real application, if an error condition is one that a user might reasonably experience, you should use some other form of error reporting, such as popping up an alert box.

```
sqlite3_close(database)
```

▪ **Note**   There is one condition that could cause an error to occur in the preceding SQLite code that is not a programmer error. If the device's storage is completely full—to the extent that SQLite can't save its changes to the database—then an error will occur here, as well. However, this condition is fairly rare and will probably result in deeper problems for the user, outside the scope of your app's data. Your app probably wouldn't even launch successfully if the system were in that state. So, you're going to just sidestep the issue entirely.

Build and run the app. Enter some data and then press the iPhone simulator's Home button. Quit the simulator (to force the app to actually quit) and then relaunch the SQLite Persistence application. That data should be right where you left it. As far as the user is concerned, there's absolutely no difference between the various versions of this application; however, each version uses a different persistence mechanism.

Using Core Data

The final technique demonstrated in this chapter shows how to implement persistence using Apple's Core Data framework. Core Data is a robust, full-featured persistence tool. Here, I will show you how to use Core Data to re-create the same persistence you've seen in your Persistence application so far.

■ **Note**   For more comprehensive coverage of Core Data, check out *Pro iOS Persistence: Using Core Data* by Michael Privet and Robert Warner (Apress, 2014).

In Xcode, create a new project. Select the Single View App template from the iOS section and click Next. Name the product **Core Data Persistence**, make sure that Swift is selected as the language, choose Universal in the Devices control, but don't click the Next button just yet. If you look just below the Devices control, you'll see a Use Core Data check box. There's a certain amount of complexity involved in adding Core Data to an existing project, so Apple has kindly provided an application project template to do much of the work for you. Deselect the Use Core Data check box (see Figure 13-8) and then click the Next button. When prompted, choose a directory to store your project and then click Create.

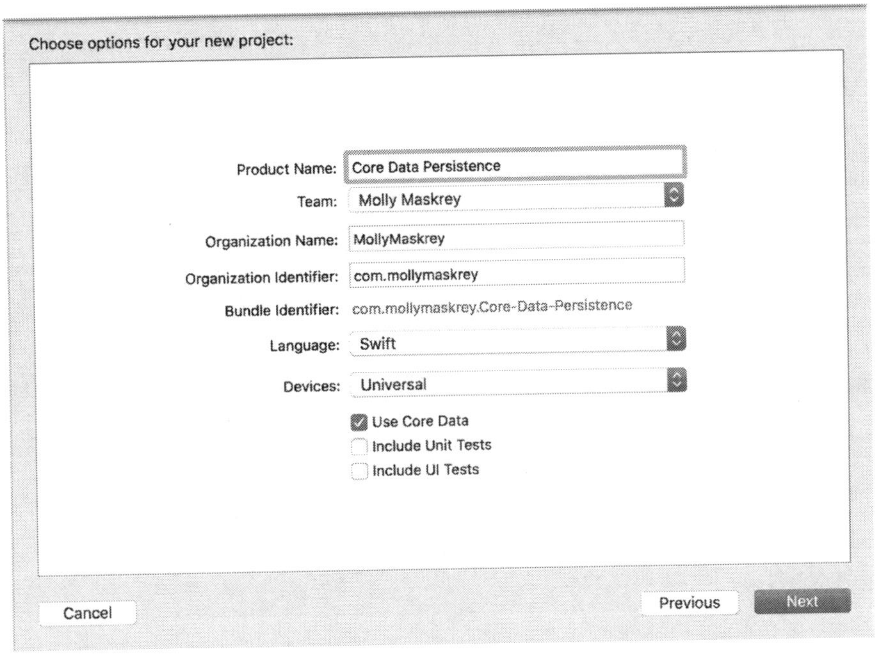

Choose options for your new project:

Product Name:	Core Data Persistence
Team:	Molly Maskrey
Organization Name:	MollyMaskrey
Organization Identifier:	com.mollymaskrey
Bundle Identifier:	com.mollymaskrey.Core-Data-Persistence
Language:	Swift
Devices:	Universal

☑ Use Core Data
☐ Include Unit Tests
☐ Include UI Tests

Cancel   Previous   Next

Figure 13-8. Select Single View App and the option to use Core Data for persistence

Before you move on to your code, let's take a look at the project window, which contains some new items. Expand the `Core Data Persistence` folder if it's closed (see Figure 13-9).

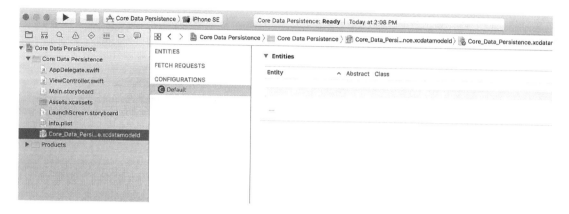

Figure 13-9. *Your project template with the files needed for Core Data. The Core Data model is selected, and the data model editor is shown in the editing pane.*

Entities and Managed Objects

Most of what you see in the Project Navigator should be familiar: the application delegate, the view controller, two storyboards, and the assets catalog. In addition, you'll find a file called `Core_Data_Persistence.xcdatamodeld`, which contains your data model. Within Xcode, Core Data lets you design your data models visually, without writing code, and stores that data model in the `.xcdatamodeld` file.

Single-click the `.xcdatamodeld` file now, and you will be presented with the **data model editor** (see the right side of Figure 13-9). The data model editor gives you two distinct views into your data model, depending on the setting of the Editor Style control in the lower-right corner of the project window. In Table mode, the mode shown in Figure 13-9, the elements that make up your data model will be shown in a series of editable tables. In Graph mode, you'll see a graphical depiction of the same elements. At the moment, both views reflect the same empty data model.

Before Core Data, the traditional way to create data models was to create subclasses of `NSObject` and conform them to `NSCoding` and `NSCopying` so that they could be archived, as you did earlier in this chapter. Core Data uses a fundamentally different approach. Instead of classes, you begin by creating *entities* here in the data model editor and then, in your code, you create *managed objects* from those entities.

■ **Note**   The terms *entity* and *managed object* can be a little confusing since both refer to data model objects. Entity refers to the description of an object. Managed object refers to actual concrete instances of that entity created at runtime. So, in the data model editor, you create entities; but in your code, you create and retrieve managed objects. The distinction between entities and managed objects is similar to the distinction between a class and instances of that class.

An entity is made up of properties. There are three types of properties:

- *Attributes*: An attribute serves the same function in a Core Data entity as a property does in a Swift class. They both hold the data.

- *Relationships*: As the name implies, a relationship defines the relationship between entities. For example, to create a Person entity, you might start by defining a few attributes such as hairColor, eyeColor, height, and weight. You might also define address attributes, such as state and zipCode, or you might embed them in a separate HomeAddress entity. Using the latter approach, you would then create a relationship between a Person and a HomeAddress. Relationships can be *to-one* and *to-many*. The relationship from Person to HomeAddress is probably to-one since most people have only a single home address. The relationship from HomeAddress to Person might be to-many since there may be more than one Person living at that HomeAddress.

- *Fetched properties*: A fetched property is an alternative to a relationship. Fetched properties allow you to create a query that is evaluated at fetch time to see which objects belong to the relationship. To extend the earlier example, a Person object could have a fetched property called Neighbors that finds all HomeAddress objects in the data store that have the same ZIP code as the Person's own HomeAddress. Because of the nature of how fetched properties are constructed and used, they are always one-way relationships. Fetched properties are also the only kind of relationship that lets you traverse multiple data stores.

Typically, attributes, relationships, and fetched properties are defined using Xcode's data model editor. In your Core Data Persistence application, you'll build a simple entity so you can get a sense of how this all works together.

Key-Value Coding

In your code, instead of using accessors and mutators, you will use key-value coding to set properties or retrieve their existing values. Key-value coding may sound intimidating, but you've already used it quite a bit in this book. Every time you used Dictionary, for example, you were using a form of key-value coding because every object in a dictionary is stored under a unique key value. The key-value coding used by Core Data is a bit more complex than that used by Dictionary, but the basic concept is the same. When working with a managed object, the key you will use to set or retrieve a property's value is the name of the attribute you want to set. So, here's how to retrieve the value stored in the attribute called name from a managed object:

```
let name = myManagedObject.valueForKey("name")
```

Similarly, to set a new value for a managed object's property, do this:

```
myManagedObject.setValue("Gregor Overlander", forKey:"name")
```

Putting It All in Context

So, where do these managed objects live? They live in something called a *persistent store*, also referred to as a *backing store*. Persistent stores can take several different forms. By default, a Core Data application implements a backing store as a SQLite database stored in the application's Documents directory. Even though your data is stored via SQLite, classes in the Core Data framework do all the work associated with loading and saving your data. If you use Core Data, you don't need to write any SQL statements like the ones you saw in the SQLite Persistence application. You just work with objects, and Core Data figures out what it needs to do behind the scenes.

SQLite isn't the only option Core Data has for storage. Backing stores can also be implemented as binary flat files or even stored in an XML format. Another option is to create an in-memory store, which you might use if you're writing a caching mechanism; however, it doesn't save data beyond the end of the current session. In almost all situations, you should just leave it as the default and use SQLite as your persistent store.

Although most applications will have only one persistent store, it is possible to have multiple persistent stores within the same application. If you're curious about how the backing store is created and configured, take a look at the file AppDelegate.swift in your Xcode project. The Xcode project template you chose provided you with all the code needed to set up a single persistent store for your application.

Other than creating it, you generally won't work with your persistent store directly. Rather, you will use something called a *managed object context*, often referred to as just a *context*. The context manages access to the persistent store and maintains information about which properties have changed since the last time an object was saved. The context also registers all changes with the *undo manager*, which means that you always have the ability to undo a single change or roll back all the way to the last time data was saved.

■ **Note**   You can have multiple contexts pointing to the same persistent store, though most iOS applications will use only one.

Many Core Data method calls require an NSManagedObjectContext as a parameter or must be executed against a context. With the exception of more complicated, multithreaded iOS applications, you can just use the managedObjectContext property provided by your application delegate, which is a default context that is created for you automatically, also courtesy of the Xcode project template.

You may notice that in addition to a managed object context and a persistent store coordinator, the provided application delegate contains an instance of NSManagedObjectModel. This class is responsible for loading and representing, at runtime, the data model you will create using the data model editor in Xcode. You generally won't need to interact directly with this class. It's used behind the scenes by the other Core Data classes so they can identify which entities and properties you've defined in your data model. As long as you create your data model using the provided file, there's no need to worry about this class at all.

Creating New Managed Objects

Creating a new instance of a managed object is pretty easy, though not quite as straightforward as creating a normal object instance. Instead, you use the insertNewObject(forEntityName: into:) factory method in a class called NSEntityDescription. NSEntityDescription's job is to keep track of all the entities defined in the app's data model and to let you create instances of those entities. This method creates and returns an instance representing a single entity in memory. It returns either an instance of NSManagedObject that is set up with the correct properties for that particular entity or, if you've configured your entity to be implemented with a specific subclass of NSManagedObject, an instance of that class. Remember that entities are like classes. An entity is a description of an object and defines which properties a particular entity has.

To create a new object, do this:

```
let thing = NSEntityDescription.insertNewObject (forEntityName: "Thing",
                          into:managedObjectContext)
```

The method is called insertNewObject(forEntityName: into:) because, in addition to creating the object, it inserts the newly created object into the context and then returns that object. After this call, the object exists in the context but is not yet part of the persistent store. The object will be added to the persistent store the next time the managed object context's save() method is called.

Retrieving Managed Objects

To retrieve managed objects from the persistent store, you'll use a *fetch request*, which is Core Data's way of handling a predefined query. For example, you might say, "Give me every Person whose eyeColor is blue." To create a fetch request, you provide it with an NSEntityDescription that specifies the entity of the object or objects you want to retrieve. Here is an example that creates a fetch request:

```
let context = appDelegate.managedObjectContext
let request: NSFetchRequest<NSFetchRequestResult> = NSFetchRequest(entityName:"Thing")
```

You *execute* the fetch request using an instance method on NSManagedObjectContext.

```
do {
    let objects = try context.fetch(request)
    // No error - use "objects"
} catch {
    // Error - the "error" variable contains an NSError object
  print(error)
}
```

fetch() will load the specified objects from the persistent store and return them in an optional array. If an error is encountered, fetch() throws an NSError object that describes the specific problem. You need to either catch this error and handle it if at all possible or let it propagate to the caller of the function that contains this code. Here, you just write the error to the console. If you are not familiar with Swift's error handling mechanisms, refer to the section "Error Handling" in the appendix. If no error occurs, you will get a valid array, though it may not have any objects in it since it is possible that none meets the specified criteria. From this point on, any changes you make to the managed objects returned in that array will be tracked by the managed object context you executed the request against and saved when you send that context a save: message.

The Core Data Application

Before getting into the code, you'll create your data model.

Designing the Data Model

Select Core_Data_Persistence.xcdatamodel to open Xcode's data model editor. The data model editing pane shows all the entities, fetch requests, and configurations that are contained within your data model.

■ **Note**   The Core Data concept of *configurations* lets you define one or more named subsets of the entities contained in your data model, which can be useful in certain situations. For example, if you want to create a suite of apps that shares the same data model but some apps shouldn't have access to everything (perhaps there's one app for normal users and another for administrators), this approach lets you do that. You can also use multiple configurations within a single app as it switches between different modes of operation. In this book, you're not going to deal with configurations at all, but since the list of configurations (including the single default configuration that contains everything in your model) is right there, staring you in the face beneath the entities and fetch requests, I thought it was worth a mention here.

As shown in Figure 13-9, those lists are empty now because you haven't created anything yet. Remedy that by clicking the plus icon labeled Add Entity in the lower-left corner of the editor pane. This will create a new entity with the name Entity, as shown in Figure 13-10.

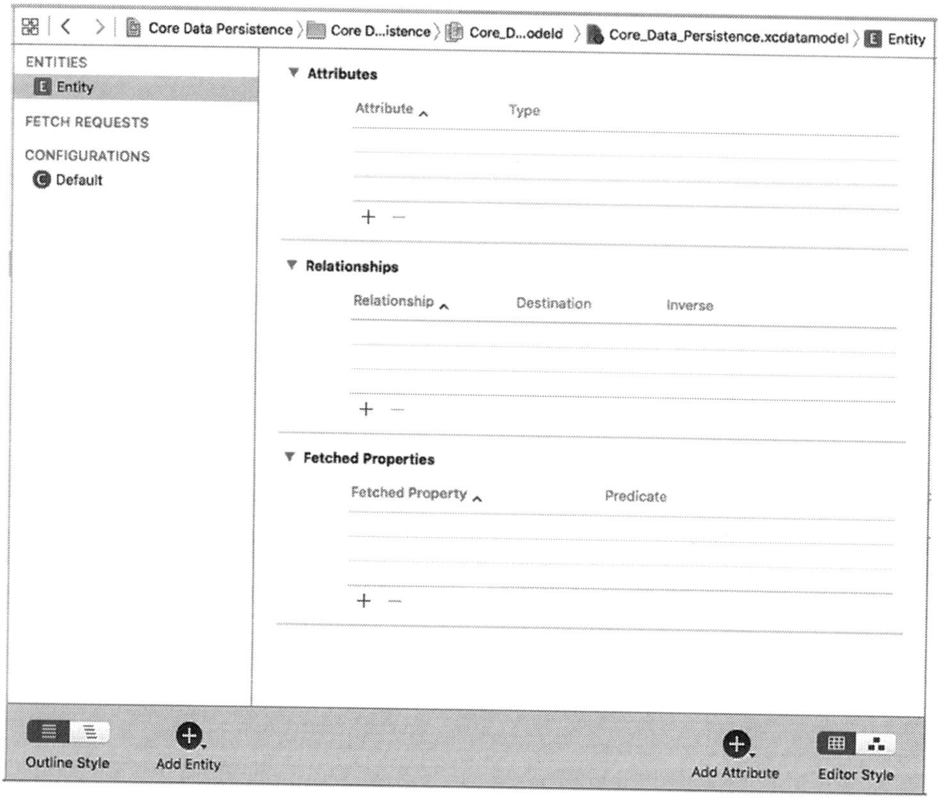

Figure 13-10. *The data model editor, showing your newly added entity*

As you build your data model, you'll probably find yourself switching between Table view and Graph view using the Editor Style control at the bottom right of the editing area. Switch to Graph view now. Graph view presents a little box representing your entity, which itself contains sections for showing the entity's attributes and relationships, also currently empty (see Figure 13-11). Graph view is really useful if your model contains multiple entities because it shows a graphic representation of all the relationships between your entities.

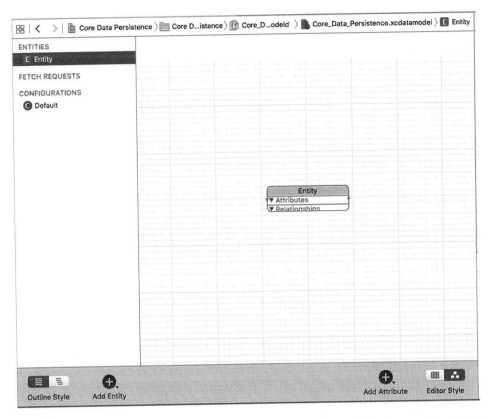

Figure 13-11. *Using the control in the lower-right corner, you switched the data model editor into Graph mode. Note that Graph mode shows the same entities as Table mode, just in a graphic form. This is useful if you have multiple entities with relationships between them.*

▓ **Note** If you prefer working graphically, you can actually build your entire model in Graph view. You're going to stick with Table view in this chapter because it's easier to explain. When you're creating your own data models, feel free to work in Graph view if that approach suits you better.

Whether you're using Table view or Graph view for designing your data model, you'll almost always want to bring up the Core Data data model inspector. This inspector lets you view and edit relevant details for whatever item is selected in the data model editor—whether it's an entity, attribute, relationship, or anything else. You can browse an existing model without the data model inspector; but to really work on a model, you'll invariably need to use this inspector, much as you frequently use the Attributes Inspector when editing nib files.

Press ⌥⌘3 to open the data model inspector. At the moment, the inspector shows information about the entity you just added. The single entity in your model contains the data from one line on the GUI, so you'll call it Line. Change the Name field from Entity to **Line**, as shown in Figure 13-12.

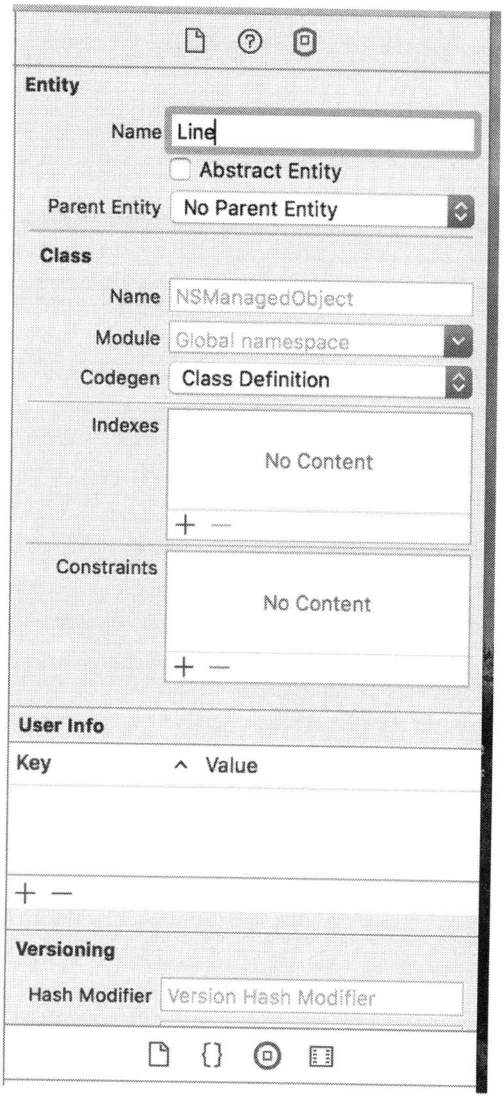

Figure 13-12. *Using the data model inspector to change your entity's name to Line*

If you're currently in Graph view, use the Editor Style control to switch back to Table view. Table view shows more details for each piece of the entity you're working on, so it's usually more useful than Graph view when creating a new entity. In Table view, most of the data model editor is taken up by the table showing the entity's attributes, relationships, and fetched properties. This is where you'll set up your entity.

Notice that at the lower right of the editing area, next to the Editor Style control, there's an icon containing a plus sign, labeled Add Attribute. If you select your entity and then hold down the mouse button over this control, a pop-up menu will appear, allowing you to add an attribute, relationship, or fetched property to your entity (see Figure 13-13). Alternatively, if you just want to add an attribute, you can simply click the plus icon.

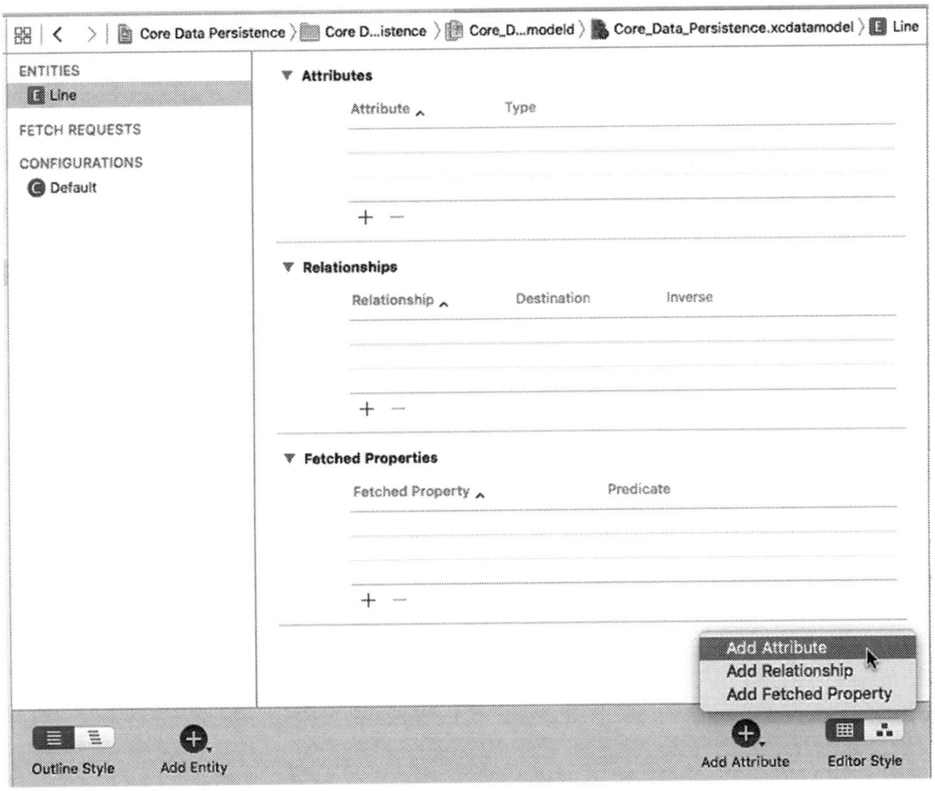

Figure 13-13. *With an entity selected, press and hold the right plus-sign icon to add an attribute, relationship, or fetched property to your entity*

Go ahead and use this technique to add an attribute to your Line entity. A new attribute, creatively named `attribute`, is added to the Attributes section of the table and selected. In the table, you'll see that not only is the row selected but the attribute's name is selected. This means that immediately after clicking the plus sign, you can start typing the name of the new attribute without further clicking. Change the new attribute's name from attribute to lineNumber, and click the pop-up next to the name to change its Type from Undefined to Integer 16. Doing so turns this attribute into one that will hold an integer value. You will be using this attribute to identify which of the managed object's four fields holds data. Since you have only four options, you selected the smallest integer type available.

Now direct your attention to the data model inspector, which is in the pane to the right of the editor area. Here, additional details can be configured. The inspector should be showing properties for the attribute you just added. If it's still showing details of the Line entity, click the attribute row in the editor to select it, and the inspector should switch its focus to the attribute. The check box below the Name field on the right, Optional, is selected by default. Click it to deselect it. You don't want this attribute to be optional—a line that doesn't correspond to a label on your interface is useless.

Selecting the Transient check box creates a transient attribute. This attribute is used to specify a value that is held by managed objects while the app is running but is never saved to the data store. You do want the line number saved to the data store, so leave the Transient check box deselected. Selecting the Indexed check box will cause an index in the underlying SQL database to be created on the column that holds this attribute's data. Leave the Indexed check box deselected. The amount of data is small, and you won't provide the user with a search capability; therefore, there's no need for an index.

Beneath that are more settings that allow you to do some simple data validation by specifying minimum and maximum values for the integer, a default value, and more. You won't be using any of these settings in this example.

Now make sure the Line entity is selected and click the Add Attribute control to add a second attribute. Change the name of your new attribute to `lineText` and change its Type to String. This attribute will hold the actual data from the text field. Leave the Optional check box selected for this one; it is altogether possible that the user won't enter a value for a given field.

▓ **Note**   When you change Type to String, you'll notice that the inspector shows a slightly different set of options for setting a default value or limiting the length of the string. Although you won't be using any of those options for this application, it's nice to know they're there.

Your data model is complete. That's all there is to it. Core Data lets you point and click your way to an application data model. Let's finish building the application so you can see how to use your data model from your code.

Modifying the AppDelegate.swift File

Locate the following line in the `AppDelegate.swift` file:

```
// MARK: - Core Data stack
```

Below this line you should see two sections of code. The first creates an `NSPersistentContainer`, a new feature that essentially provides a wrapper around a lot of the Core Data structure. You won't be using that in this example, so delete that section of code.

▓ **Note**   The new container feature is a good thing that will eventually make life easier as you develop Core Data applications, however, at the time of writing, I found it to not be consistently stable and as such will follow the methods of creating your project as was done in the previous version of this book. The approach you'll be using works just fine.

Also delete the template `saveContext` method and replace it with that shown in Listing 13-11. This is where all your "stuff" gets saved. You'll call it from your view controller when you are ready to resign active status of your app.

Listing 13-11.   Your saveContext Method in the AppDelegate.swift File

```
func saveContext () {
    if managedObjectContext.hasChanges {
        do {
            try managedObjectContext.save()
        } catch {
            // Replace this implementation with code to handle the error appropriately.
            // abort() causes the application to generate a crash log and terminate. You
                should not use this function in a shipping application, although it may be
                useful during development.
```

```
            let nserror = error as NSError
            NSLog("Unresolved error \(nserror), \(nserror.userInfo)")
            abort()
        }
    }
}
```

Next, add the following methods in Listing 13-12 to the AppDelegate.swift file after the following line:

```
// MARK: - Core Data stack
```

Listing 13-12. Your Core Data Stack

```
// MARK: - Core Data stack

lazy var applicationDocumentsDirectory: URL = {
    // The directory the application uses to store the Core Data store file. This code uses
        a directory in the application's documents Application Support directory.
    let urls = FileManager.default.urls(for: .documentDirectory, in: .userDomainMask)
    return urls[urls.count-1]
}()

lazy var managedObjectModel: NSManagedObjectModel = {
    // The managed object model for the application. This property is not optional. It is a
        fatal error for the application not to be able to find and load its model.
    let modelURL = Bundle.main.url(forResource: "Core_Data_Persistence", withExtension:
    "momd")!
    return NSManagedObjectModel(contentsOf: modelURL)!
}()

lazy var persistentStoreCoordinator: NSPersistentStoreCoordinator = {
    // The persistent store coordinator for the application. This implementation creates and
    returns a coordinator, having added the store for the application to it. This property
    is optional since there are legitimate error conditions that could cause the creation of
    the store to fail.
    // Create the coordinator and store
    let coordinator = NSPersistentStoreCoordinator(managedObjectModel: self.
    managedObjectModel)
    let url = try! self.applicationDocumentsDirectory.appendingPathComponent("SingleViewCor
    eData.sqlite")
    var failureReason = "There was an error creating or loading the application's saved data."
    do {
        try coordinator.addPersistentStore(ofType: NSSQLiteStoreType, configurationName:
        nil, at: url, options: nil)
    } catch {
        // Report any error we got.
        var dict = [String: AnyObject]()
        dict[NSLocalizedDescriptionKey] = "Failed to initialize the application's saved data"
        dict[NSLocalizedFailureReasonErrorKey] = failureReason
        dict[NSUnderlyingErrorKey] = error as NSError
        let wrappedError = NSError(domain: "YOUR_ERROR_DOMAIN", code: 9999, userInfo: dict)
        // Replace this with code to handle the error appropriately.
```

457

```
        // abort() causes the application to generate a crash log and terminate. You should
            not use this function in a shipping application, although it may be useful during
            development.
        NSLog("Unresolved error \(wrappedError), \(wrappedError.userInfo)")
        abort()
    }

    return coordinator
}()

lazy var managedObjectContext: NSManagedObjectContext = {
    // Returns the managed object context for the application (which is already bound to the
        persistent store coordinator for the application.) This property is optional since
        there are legitimate error conditions that could cause the creation of the context to
        fail.
    let coordinator = self.persistentStoreCoordinator
    var managedObjectContext = NSManagedObjectContext(concurrencyType:
    .mainQueueConcurrencyType)
    managedObjectContext.persistentStoreCoordinator = coordinator
    return managedObjectContext
}()
```

The following line defines the path to the Core Data store file:

```
lazy var applicationDocumentsDirectory: URL = {
```

This variable represents your managed object model:

```
lazy var managedObjectModel: NSManagedObjectModel = {
    // The managed object model for the application.
    // This property is not optional. It is a fatal error for
    //the application not to be able to find and load its model.
    let modelURL = Bundle.main.url(forResource: "Core_Data_Persistence", withExtension:
    "momd")!
    return NSManagedObjectModel(contentsOf: modelURL)!
}()
```

Similarly, the following section of code provides the reference to your persistent store coordinator:

```
lazy var persistentStoreCoordinator: NSPersistentStoreCoordinator = {
    // The persistent store coordinator for the application. This implementation creates
        and returns a coordinator, having added the store for the application to it. This
        property is optional since there are legitimate error conditions that could cause the
        creation of the store to fail.
    // Create the coordinator and store
    let coordinator = NSPersistentStoreCoordinator(managedObjectModel: self.
    managedObjectModel)
    let url = try! self.applicationDocumentsDirectory.appendingPathComponent("SingleViewCor
    eData.sqlite")
    var failureReason = "There was an error creating or loading the application's saved data."
```

```
    do {
        try coordinator.addPersistentStore(ofType: NSSQLiteStoreType, configurationName:
        nil, at: url, options: nil)
    } catch {
        // Report any error we got.
        var dict = [String: AnyObject]()
        dict[NSLocalizedDescriptionKey] = "Failed to initialize the application's saved
        data"
        dict[NSLocalizedFailureReasonErrorKey] = failureReason
        dict[NSUnderlyingErrorKey] = error as NSError
        let wrappedError = NSError(domain: "YOUR_ERROR_DOMAIN", code: 9999, userInfo: dict)
        // Replace this with code to handle the error appropriately.
        // abort() causes the application to generate a crash log and terminate. You should
            not use this function in a shipping application, although it may be useful during
            development.
        NSLog("Unresolved error \(wrappedError), \(wrappedError.userInfo)")
        abort()
    }

    return coordinator
}()
```

Finally, the last remaining piece is your managed object context shown here:

```
lazy var managedObjectContext: NSManagedObjectContext = {
    // Returns the managed object context for the application (which is already bound to the
        persistent store coordinator for the application.) This property is optional since
        there are legitimate error conditions that could cause the creation of the context
        to fail.
    let coordinator = self.persistentStoreCoordinator
    var managedObjectContext = NSManagedObjectContext(concurrencyType: .mainQueue
    ConcurrencyType)
    managedObjectContext.persistentStoreCoordinator = coordinator
    return managedObjectContext
}()
```

That's really all you need for your application delegate. You create the various bits and pieces needed so the rest of your app can have access to the Core Data capabilities.

Creating the Persistence View

Select ViewController.swift and make the following change shown in bold:

```
class ViewController: UIViewController {
    @IBOutlet var lineFields:[UITextField]!
```

Save this file. Next, select Main.storyboard to edit the GUI in Interface Builder. Design the view and connect the outlet collection by following the instructions in the "Designing the Persistence Application View" section earlier in this chapter. You might also find it useful to refer to Figure 13-6. Once your design is complete, save the storyboard file.

Now go back to ViewController.swift and make the changes in Listing 13-13.

Listing 13-13. Modifying Your ViewController.swift File to Use Core Data

```
import UIKit
import CoreData

class ViewController: UIViewController {
    private static let lineEntityName = "Line"
    private static let lineNumberKey = "lineNumber"
    private static let lineTextKey = "lineText"
    @IBOutlet var lineFields:[UITextField]!

    override func viewDidLoad() {
        super.viewDidLoad()
        // Do any additional setup after loading the view, typically from a nib.

        let appDelegate =
                    UIApplication.shared().delegate as! AppDelegate
        let context = appDelegate.managedObjectContext
        let request: NSFetchRequest<NSFetchRequestResult> = NSFetchRequest(entityName:
        ViewController.lineEntityName)

        do {
            let objects = try context.fetch(request)
            for object in objects {
                let lineNum: Int = object.value(forKey: ViewController.lineNumberKey)! as! Int
                let lineText = object.value(forKey: ViewController.lineTextKey) as? String
                ?? ""
                let textField = lineFields[lineNum]
                textField.text = lineText
            }

            let app = UIApplication.shared()
            NotificationCenter.default.addObserver(self,
                        selector: #selector(UIApplicationDelegate.
                        applicationWillResignActive(_:)),
                        name: NSNotification.Name.UIApplicationWillResignActive,
                        object: app)
        } catch {
            // Error thrown from executeFetchRequest()
            print("There was an error in executeFetchRequest(): \(error)")
        }
    }

    func applicationWillResignActive(_ notification:Notification) {
        let appDelegate =
            UIApplication.shared().delegate as! AppDelegate
        let context = appDelegate.managedObjectContext
        for i in 0 ..< lineFields.count {
            let textField = lineFields[i]

            let request: NSFetchRequest<NSFetchRequestResult> = NSFetchRequest(entityName:
            ViewController.lineEntityName)
```

```
            let pred = Predicate(format: "%K = %d", ViewController.lineNumberKey, i)
            request.predicate = pred

            do {
                let objects = try context.fetch(request)
                var theLine:NSManagedObject! = objects.first as? NSManagedObject
                if theLine == nil {
                    // No existing data for this row - insert a new managed object for it
                    theLine =
                        NSEntityDescription.insertNewObject(
                                forEntityName: ViewController.lineEntityName,
                                into: context)
                                as NSManagedObject
                }

                theLine.setValue(i, forKey: ViewController.lineNumberKey)
                theLine.setValue(textField.text, forKey: ViewController.lineTextKey)
            } catch {
                print("There was an error in executeFetchRequest(): \(error)")
            }
        }
        appDelegate.saveContext()
    }
}
```

So that you can use Core Data, you imported the Core Data framework. Next, you modified the viewDidLoad() method, which needs to check whether there is any existing data in the persistent store. If there is, it should load the data and populate the text fields with it. The first thing you do in that method is get a reference to your application delegate, which you then use to get the managed object context (of type NSManagedObjectContext) that was created for you.

```
let appDelegate =
            UIApplication.shared().delegate as! AppDelegate
let context = appDelegate.managedObjectContext
```

The next order of business is to create a fetch request and pass it the entity name so it knows which type of objects to retrieve.

```
let request: NSFetchRequest<NSFetchRequestResult> =
NSFetchRequest(entityName: ViewController.lineEntityName)
```

Since you want to retrieve all Line objects in the persistent store, you do not create a predicate. By executing a request without a predicate, you're telling the context to give you every Line object in the store. Having created the fetch request, you use the fetch() method of the managed object context to execute it. Since fetch() can throw an error, you place the call and the code that uses its results in a do-catch block so that you can log the error, if there is one.

```
do {
    let objects = try context.fetch(request)
```

Next, you loop through the array of retrieved managed objects, pull the lineNum and lineText values from each managed object, and use that information to update one of the text fields on your user interface.

```
for object in objects {
    let lineNum: Int = object.value(forKey: ViewController.lineNumberKey)! as! Int
    let lineText = object.value(forKey: ViewController.lineTextKey) as? String ?? ""
    let textField = lineFields[lineNum]
    textField.text = lineText
}
```

Of course, the first time you execute this code, you won't have saved anything in the data store, so the objects list will be empty.

Next, just as with all the other applications in this chapter, you register to be notified when the application is about to move out of the active state (either by being shuffled to the background or by exiting completely), so you can save any changes the user has made to the data.

```
let app = UIApplication.shared()
NotificationCenter.default.addObserver(self,
        selector: #selector(UIApplicationDelegate.applicationWillResignActive(_:)),
        name: NSNotification.Name.UIApplicationWillResignActive,
        object: app)
```

Finally, the catch clause prints any error that is thrown from the fetch() method.

```
} catch {
    // Error thrown from executeFetchRequest()
    print("There was an error in executeFetchRequest(): \(error)")
}
```

Now let's look at applicationWillResignActive(). You start out the same way as the previous method: by getting a reference to the application delegate and using that to get a pointer to your application's default managed object context.

```
let appDelegate =
    UIApplication.shared().delegate as! AppDelegate
let context = appDelegate.managedObjectContext
```

After that, you go into a loop that executes once for each text field and then get a reference to the correct field.

```
for i in 0 ..< lineFields.count {
    let textField = lineFields[i]
```

Next, you create your fetch request for your Line entry. You need to find out whether there's already a managed object in the persistent store that corresponds to this field, so you create a predicate that identifies the correct object for the field by using the index of the text field as the record key.

```
let request: NSFetchRequest<NSFetchRequestResult> =
let pred = Predicate(format: "%K = %d", ViewController.lineNumberKey, i)
request.predicate = pred
```

Now you execute the fetch request against the context. As before, you wrap this code in a do-catch block so that you can report any error that is reported by Core Data.

```
do {
    let objects = try context.fetch(request)
```

After that, you declare a variable called theLine of type NSManagedObject that will reference the managed object for this row's data. You may not have previously stored any data for this row, so at this point, you don't know whether you're going to get a managed object for it from the persistent store. For that reason, theLine needs to be declared as optional. But for convenience, you'll make it force unwrapped since you're going to use the insertNewObject (forEntityName: inManagedObjectContext:) method to create a new managed object for this row in the persistent store if you didn't get one. You'll use that managed object to initialize theLine in that case.

```
var theLine:NSManagedObject! = objects.first as? NSManagedObject
if theLine == nil {
    // No existing data for this row – insert a new managed object for it
    theLine =
        NSEntityDescription.insertNewObject(
                forEntityName: ViewController.lineEntityName,
                into: context)
            as NSManagedObject
```

Next, you use key-value coding to set the line number and text for this managed object. You log any error that was caught in the catch clause.

```
theLine.setValue(i, forKey: ViewController.lineNumberKey)
theLine.setValue(textField.text, forKey: ViewController.lineTextKey)
```

Finally, once you're finished looping, you tell the context to save its changes.

```
appDelegate.saveContext()
```

That's it. Build and run the app to make sure it works. The Core Data version of your application should behave the same as the previous versions.

Summary

You should now have a solid handle on four different ways of preserving your application data between sessions—five ways if you include the user defaults that you learned how to use in the previous chapter. You built an application that persisted data using property lists and modified the application to save its data using object archives. You then made a change and used the iOS's built-in SQLite3 mechanism to save the application data. Finally, you rebuilt the same application using Core Data. These mechanisms are the basic building blocks for saving and loading data in almost all iOS applications.

CHAPTER 14

Graphics and Drawing

You've constructed all your application UIs so far using views and controls that are part of the UIKit framework. You can do a lot with UIKit, and a great many applications are constructed using only its predefined objects. Some visual elements (see Figure 14-1), however, can't be fully realized without going beyond what the UIKit stock components offer.

Figure 14-1. *Graphics-intense apps can require more drawing control than UIKit offers*

For example, sometimes an application needs to be able to do custom drawing. iOS includes the Core Graphics framework, allowing you to perform a wide array of drawing tasks. In this chapter, you'll explore a small part of this powerful graphics environment. I'll also show how to build sample applications demonstrating key features of Core Graphics and explain the main concepts.

© Molly K. Maskrey 2017
M. K. Maskrey, *Beginning iPhone Development with Swift 4*, https://doi.org/10.1007/978-1-4842-3072-5_14

Quartz 2D

Core Graphics includes a main set of APIs called Quartz 2D, which is a collection of functions, data types, and objects designed to let you draw directly into a view or an image in memory. Quartz 2D provides the view or image that is being drawn into as a virtual canvas. It follows what's called a *painter's model*, which means that the drawing commands are applied in much the same way that paint is applied to a canvas.

If a painter paints an entire canvas red and then paints the bottom half of the canvas blue, the canvas will be half red and half either blue, if the blue paint is opaque, or purple if the blue paint is semitransparent. Quartz 2D's virtual canvas works the same way. If you paint the whole view red and then paint the bottom half of the view blue, you'll have a view that's half red and half either blue or purple, depending on whether the second drawing action was fully opaque or partially transparent. Each drawing action gets applied to the canvas on top of any previous drawing actions.

Quartz 2D provides a variety of line, shape, and image drawing functions. Though easy to use, Quartz 2D is limited to two-dimensional drawing. You'll start with the basics of how Quartz 2D works and then build a simple drawing application using it.

The Quartz 2D Approach to Drawing

When using Quartz 2D (Quartz for short), you'll usually add the Swift graphics code to the view doing the drawing. For example, you might create a subclass of UIView and add Quartz function calls to that class's **draw(_ rect:)** method. The **draw(_ rect:)** method is part of the UIView class definition and is called every time a view needs to redraw itself. If you insert your Quartz code in **draw(_ rect:)**, that code will be called, and then the view redraws itself.

Quartz 2D's Graphics Contexts

In Quartz, as in the rest of Core Graphics, drawing happens in a *graphics context*, usually referred to simply as a *context*. Every view includes an associated context. You retrieve the current context, use that context to make various Quartz drawing calls, and let the context handle rendering the drawing onto the view. You can think of this context as a sort of canvas. The system provides you with a default context where the contents will appear on the screen. However, it's also possible to create a context of your own for doing drawing that you don't want to appear immediately but that you want to save for later or use for something else. You'll focus on using the default context, which you get from within **draw(_ rect:)** by writing let context = UIGraphicsGetCurrentContext().

The graphics context is of type CGContext. This is the Swift mapping for the C-language pointer type CGContextRef, the native Core Graphics representation of a context. The actual inferred type of the context variable in the preceding code is CGContext!. It's optional because C-language calls can theoretically return NULL (although UIGraphicsGetCurrentContext() doesn't, provided you only use it where there is guaranteed to be a current context), and it's unwrapped so that you don't have to unwrap every reference to the context.

■ **Note**   Core Graphics is a C-language API. All the functions with names starting with CG that you see in this chapter are C functions, not Swift functions.

Once you have a graphics context, you can draw into it by passing the context to a variety of Core Graphics drawing functions. For example, the sequence in Listing 14-1 creates a path describing a simple line and then draws that path.

Listing 14-1. Drawing into a Graphics Context

```
context?.setLineWidth(4.0)
context?.setStrokeColor(UIColor.red.cgColor)
context?.move (to: CGPoint(x: 10.0, y: 10.0))
context?.addLine (to: CGPoint(x: 20.0, y: 20.0))
context?.strokePath()
```

The first call specifies that any subsequent drawing commands that create the current path should be performed with a brush that is 4 points wide. Think of this as selecting the size of the brush you're about to paint with. Until you call this function again with a different number, all lines will have a width of 4 points when drawn in this context. You then specify that the stroke color should be red. In Core Graphics, two colors are associated with drawing actions.

- The *stroke color* is used in drawing lines and for the outline of shapes.

- The *fill color* is used to fill in shapes.

A context has a sort of invisible pen associated with it that does the line drawing. As drawing commands are executed, the movements of this pen form a path. When you call .moveTo(x: , y:), you lift the virtual pen and move to the location you specify, without actually drawing anything. Whatever operation comes next, it will do its work relative to the point to which you last moved the pen. In the earlier example, for instance, you first moved the pen to (10, 10). The next function call added a line from the current pen location (10, 10) to the specified location (20, 20), which became the new pen location.

When you draw in Core Graphics, you're not drawing anything you can actually see—at least not immediately. You're creating a path, which can be a shape, a line, or some other object; however, it contains no color or other features to make it visible. It's like writing in invisible ink. Until you do something to make it visible, your path can't be seen. So, the next step is to call the .strokePath() function, which tells Quartz to draw the path you've constructed. This function will use the line width and the stroke color you set earlier to actually color (or "paint") the path and make it visible.

The Coordinate System

In Listing 14-1, you passed a pair of floating-point numbers as parameters to context!.moveTo(x:, y:) and context!.addLineTo(x:, y:). These numbers represent positions in the Core Graphics coordinate system. Locations in this coordinate system are denoted by their x and y coordinates, which you usually represent as (x, y). The upper-left corner of the context is (0, 0). As you move down, the y increases. As you move to the right, the x increases. What this code did was draw a diagonal line from (10, 10) to (20, 20), which would look like the one shown in Figure 14-2.

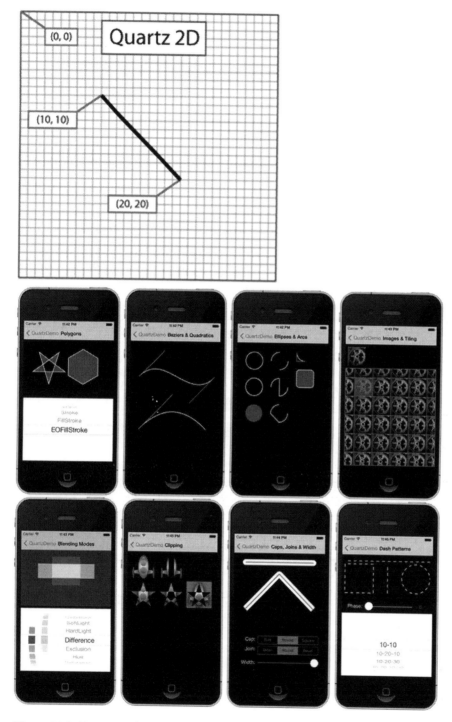

Figure 14-2. *Drawing a line using Quartz 2D's coordinate system*

The Quartz coordinate system can be a little confusing on iOS because its vertical component is flipped from what many graphics libraries use and from the traditional Cartesian coordinate system. In other systems such as OpenGL or the macOS version of Quartz, (0, 0) is in the lower-left corner; and as the y coordinate increases, you move toward the top of the context or view, as shown in Figure 14-3.

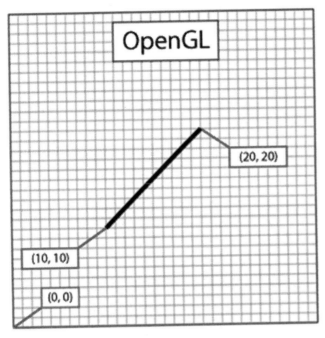

Figure 14-3. *In many graphics libraries, including OpenGL, drawing from (10, 10) to (20, 20) would produce a line that looks like this instead of the line in Figure 14-2*

To specify a point in the coordinate system, some Quartz functions require two floating-point numbers as parameters. Other Quartz functions ask for the point to be embedded in a CGPoint, which is a struct that holds two floating-point values: x and y. To describe the size of a view or other object, Quartz uses CGSize, which is a struct that also holds two floating-point values: width and height. Quartz also declares a data type called CGRect, which is used to define a rectangle in the coordinate system. A CGRect contains two elements: a CGPoint called origin, with x and y values that identify the top left of the rectangle; and a CGSize called size, which identifies the width and height of the rectangle, as shown in Listing 14-2.

Listing 14-2. Creating a Rectangle

```
var startingPoint = CGPoint(x: 1.0, y: 1.0)
var sizeOfrect = CGSize(width: 10.0, height: 10.0)
var rectangle = CGRect(origin: startingPoint, size: sizeOfrect)
```

Specifying Colors

An important part of drawing is color, so understanding the way colors work on iOS is critical. UIKit provides a class that represents a color: UIColor. You can't use a UIColor object directly in Core Graphic calls. However, UIColor is just a wrapper around a Core Graphics structure called cgColor (which is what the Core Graphic functions require). You can retrieve a cgColor reference from a UIColor instance by using its cgColor property, as I showed earlier, context!.setStrokeColor(UIColor.red.cgColor).

You got a reference to a predefined UIColor instance using a type method called red and then retrieved its cgColor property and passed that into the function. If you look at the documentation for the UIColor class, you'll see that there are several convenience methods like redColor() that you can use to get UIColor objects for some commonly used colors.

A Bit of Color Theory for Your iOS Device's Display

In modern computer graphics, any color displayed on the screen has its data stored in some way based on something called a color model. A *color model* (sometimes called a *color space*) is simply a way of representing real-world color as digital values that a computer can use. One common way to represent colors is to use four components: red, green, blue, and alpha. In Quartz, each of these values is represented as CGFloat. These values should always contain a value between 0.0 and 1.0.

■ **Caution**   On 32-bit systems, CGFloat is a 32-bit floating-point number and therefore maps directly to the Swift Float type. However, on 64-bit systems, it is a 64-bit value, corresponding to the Swift Double type. Be careful when manipulating CGFloat values in Swift code.

The red, green, and blue components are fairly easy to understand, as they represent the *additive primary colors*, or the *RGB color model*, as shown in Figure 14-4. If you add together the light of these three colors in equal proportions, the result appears to the eye as either white or a shade of gray, depending on the intensity of the light mixed. Combining the three additive primaries in different proportions gives you a range of different colors, referred to as a *gamut*.

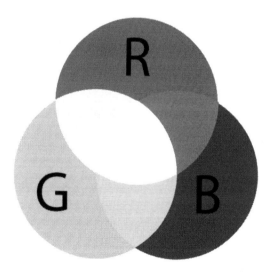

Figure 14-4. *A simple representation of the additive primary colors that make up the RGB color model*

You've probably learned that the primary colors are red, yellow, and blue, which are known as the *historical subtractive primaries*, or the *RYB color model*, and have little application in modern color theory and are almost never used in computer graphics. The color gamut of the RYB color model is much more limited than the RGB color model, and it also doesn't lend itself easily to mathematical definition. For these purposes, the primary colors are red, green, and blue, not red, yellow, and blue.

In addition to red, green, and blue, Quartz uses another color component, called *alpha*, which represents how transparent a color is. When drawing one color on top of another color, alpha is used to determine the final color that is drawn. With an alpha of 1.0, the drawn color is 100 percent opaque and obscures any colors beneath it. With any value less than 1.0, the colors below will show through and mix with the color above. If the alpha is 0.0, then this color will be completely invisible, and whatever is behind it will show through completely. When an alpha component is used, the color model is sometimes referred to as the *RGBA color model*, although technically speaking, the alpha isn't really part of the color; it just defines how the color will interact with other colors when it is drawn.

Other Color Models

Although the RGB model is the most commonly used in computer graphics, it is not the only color model. Several others are in use, including the following:

- Hue, saturation, value (HSV)

- Hue, saturation, lightness (HSL)

- Cyan, magenta, yellow, black (CMYK), which is used in four-color offset printing

- Grayscale

There are also different versions of some of these models, including several variants of the RGB color space. Fortunately, for most operations, you don't need to worry about the color model that is being used. You can just call `cgColor` on your `UIColor` objects, and in most cases, Core Graphics will handle any necessary conversions.

Drawing Images in Context

Quartz allows you to draw images directly into a context. This is another example of a UIKit class (`UIImage`) that you can use as an alternative to working with a Core Graphics data structure (`cgImage`). The `UIImage` class contains methods to draw its image into the current context. You'll need to identify where the image should appear in the context using either of the following techniques:

- By specifying a `CGPoint` to identify the image's upper-left corner

- By specifying a `CGRect` to frame the image, resized to fit the frame if necessary

You can draw a `UIImage` into the current context as shown in Listing 14-3.

Listing 14-3. Draw a UIImage into the Current Context

```
var image:UIImage  = UIImage() // assuming this exists and points at a UIImage instance
let drawPoint = CGPoint(x: 100.0, y: 100.0)
image.draw(at: drawPoint)
```

Drawing Shapes: Polygons, Lines, and Curves

Quartz provides a number of functions to make it easier to create complex shapes. To draw a rectangle or a polygon, you don't need to calculate angles, draw lines, or do any math at all. You can just call a Quartz function to do the work for you. For example, to draw an ellipse, you define the rectangle into which the ellipse needs to fit and let Core Graphics do the work, as shown in Listing 14-4.

Listing 14-4. Drawing a Rectangle in the Current Context

```
let startingPoint = CGPoint(x: 1.0, y: 1.0)
let sizeOfrect = CGSize(width: 10.0, height: 10.0)
let theRect = CGRect(origin: startingPoint, size:sizeOfrect)
context!.addEllipse(inRect: theRect)
context!.addRect(theRect)
```

You use similar methods for rectangles. Quartz also provides methods that let you create more complex shapes, such as arcs and Bezier paths.

■ **Note**   You won't be working with complex shapes in this chapter's examples. To learn more about arcs and Bezier paths in Quartz, check out the *Quartz 2D Programming Guide* in the iOS Dev Center at http://developer.apple.com/documentation/GraphicsImaging/Conceptual/drawingwithquartz2d/ or in Xcode's online documentation.

Quartz 2D Tool Sampler: Patterns, Gradients, and Dash Patterns

Quartz offers quite an impressive array of tools. For example, Quartz supports filling polygons not only with solid colors but also with gradients. In addition to drawing solid lines, it can also use an assortment of dash patterns. Take a look at the screenshots in Figure 14-5, which are from Apple's QuartzDemo sample code, to see a sampling of what Quartz can do for you.

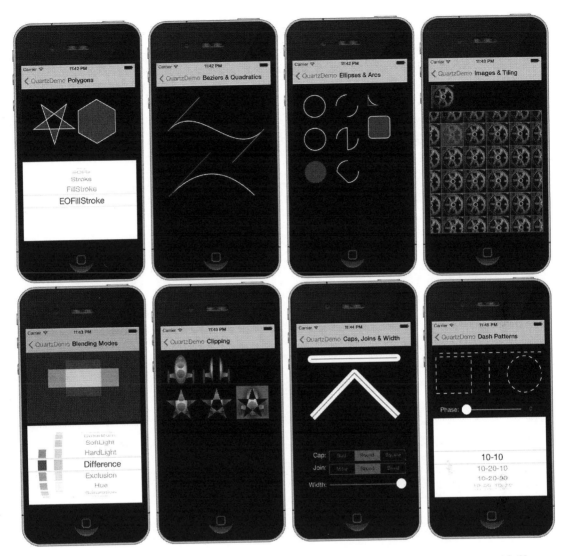

Figure 14-5. *Some examples of what Quartz 2D can do from the QuartzDemo sample project provided by Apple*

Now that you have a basic understanding of how Quartz works and what it is capable of doing, let's try it.

The QuartzFun Application

For your next application, you'll build a simple drawing program (see Figure 14-6) using Quartz to give you a feel for how the concepts I've been describing fit together.

Figure 14-6. *The QuartzFun application in action*

Creating the QuartzFun Application

In Xcode, create a new project using the Single View App template and call it **QuartzFun**. The template has already provided you with an application delegate and a view controller. You're going to be executing your custom drawing in a custom view, so you need to also create a subclass of UIView where you'll do the drawing by overriding the **draw(_ rect:)** method. With the QuartzFun folder selected (the folder that currently contains the app delegate and view controller files), press ⌘N to bring up the new file assistant and then select Cocoa Touch Class from the iOS Source section. Name the new class **QuartzFunView** and make it a subclass of UIView.

You're going to add a couple of enumerations—one for the types of shapes that can be drawn and another for the available colors. Also, since one of the color selections is Random, you'll also need a method that returns a random color each time it's called. Let's start by creating that method and the two enumerations.

Creating a Random Color

You could define a global function that returns a random color, but it's better to add this function as an extension to the UIColor class. Open the QuartzFunView.swift file and add the following code near the top:

```
// Random color extension of UIColor
extension UIColor {
    class func randomColor() -> UIColor {
        let red = CGFloat(Double(arc4random_uniform(255))/255)
        let green = CGFloat(Double(arc4random_uniform(255))/255)
        let blue = CGFloat(Double(arc4random_uniform(255))/255)
        return UIColor(red: red, green: green, blue: blue, alpha:1.0)
    }
}
```

This code is fairly straightforward. For each color component, you use the arc4random_uniform() function to generate a random floating-point number in the range 0 to 255. Each component of the color needs to be between 0.0 and 1.0, so you simply divide the result by 255. Why 255? Quartz 2D on iOS supports 256 different intensities for each of the color components, so using the number 255 ensures that you have a chance to randomly select any one of them. Finally, you use those three random components to create a new color. You set the alpha value to 1.0 so that all generated colors will be opaque.

Defining Shape and Color Enumerations

The possible shapes and drawing colors are represented by enumerations. Add the following definitions to the QuartzFunView.swift file:

```
enum Shape : Int {
    case line = 0, rect, ellipse, image
}

// The color tab indices
enum DrawingColor : Int {
    case red = 0, blue, yellow, green, random
}
```

Both enumerations are derived from UInt because, as you'll see later, you will need to use the raw enumeration values to map between a shape or a color and the selected segment of a segmented control.

Implementing the QuartzFunView Skeleton

Since you're going to do your drawing in a subclass of UIView, let's set up that class with everything it needs, except for the actual code to do the drawing, which you'll add later. Start out by adding the following six properties to the QuartzFunView class:

```
// Application-settable properties
var shape = Shape.line
var currentColor = UIColor.red
var useRandomColor = false

// Internal properties
private let image = UIImage(named:"iphone")
private var firstTouchLocation = CGPoint.zero
private var lastTouchLocation = CGPoint.zero
```

The shape property keeps track of the shape the user wants to draw, the currentColor property is the user's selected drawing color, and the useRandomColor property will be true if the user chooses to draw with a random color. These properties are all meant to be used outside the class (in fact, they will be used by the view controller).

The next three properties are required only by the class implementation and are therefore marked as private. The first two properties will track the user's finger as it drags across the screen. You'll store the location where the user first touches the screen in firstTouchLocation. You'll store the location of the user's finger while dragging and when the drag ends in lastTouchLocation. Your drawing code will use these two variables to determine where to draw the requested shape. The image property holds the image to be drawn on the screen when the user selects the rightmost toolbar item on the bottom toolbar, as shown in Figure 14-7.

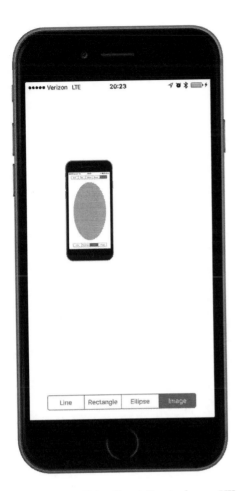

Figure 14-7. *Using QuartzFun to draw a UIImage*

Now on to the implementation itself. Let's first add a few methods to respond to the user's touches. After the property declarations, insert the three methods in Listing 14-5.

Listing 14-5. The Touch Methods for the QuartFunView.swift File

```
override func touchesBegan(_ touches: Set<UITouch>, with event: UIEvent?) {
if let touch = touches.first {
    if useRandomColor {
        currentColor = UIColor.randomColor()
    }
    firstTouchLocation = touch.location(in: self)
    lastTouchLocation = firstTouchLocation
    setNeedsDisplay()
}
}
```

```
    override func touchesMoved(_ touches: Set<UITouch>, with event: UIEvent?) {
    if let touch = touches.first {
        lastTouchLocation = touch.location(in: self)
        setNeedsDisplay()
    }
}

    override func touchesEnded(_ touches: Set<UITouch>, with event: UIEvent?) {
    if let touch = touches.first {
        lastTouchLocation = touch.location(in: self)
        setNeedsDisplay()
    }
}
```

These three methods are inherited from UIView, which in turn inherits them from its parent, UIResponder. They can be overridden to find out where the user is touching the screen. They work as follows:

- touchesBegan(_:withEvent:) is called when the user's finger first touches the screen. In that method, you change the color if the user has selected a random color using the new randomColor method you added to UIColor earlier. After that, you store the current location so that you know where the user first touched the screen, and you indicate that your view needs to be redrawn by calling setNeedsDisplay() on self.

- touchesMoved(_:withEvent:) is continuously called while the user is dragging a finger on the screen. All you do here is store the new location in lastTouchLocation and indicate that the screen needs to be redrawn.

- touchesEnded(_:withEvent:) is called when the user lifts the finger off the screen. Just as in the touchesMoved(_:withEvent:) method, all you do is store the final location in the lastTouchLocation variable and indicate that the view needs to be redrawn.

You'll come back to this class once you have your application skeleton up and running. That **draw(_ rect:)** method, which is currently commented out, is where you will do this application's real work, and you haven't written that yet. Let's finish setting up the application before you add your drawing code.

Creating and Connecting Outlets and Actions

Before you can start drawing, you need to add the segmented controls to your GUI and then hook up the actions and outlets. Single-click Main.storyboard to set these things up. The first order of business is to change the class of the view. In the Document Outline, expand the items for the scene and for the view controller it contains and then single-click the View item. Press ⌥⌘3 to bring up the Identity Inspector and change the class from UIView to QuartzFunView.

Now use the Object Library to find a segmented control and drag it to the top of the view, just below the status bar. Place it somewhere near the center. You don't need to be too accurate with this because you'll shortly add a layout constraint that will center it.

With the segmented control selected, bring up the Attributes Inspector and change the number of segments from 2 to 5. Double-click each segment in turn, changing each label to (from left to right) Red, Blue, Yellow, Green, and Random, in that order. Now let's apply layout constraints. In the Document Outline, Control-drag from the segmented control item to the Quartz Fun View item, release the mouse, hold down the Shift key, select Vertical Spacing to Top Layout Guide and Center Horizontally in Container, and then press Return. In the Document Outline, select the View Controller icon; then back in the storyboard editor, click the Resolve Auto Layout Issues button (the one to the right of the Pin button) and select Update Frames. If this option is not enabled, make sure you have View Controller selected in the Document Outline. The segmented control should now be properly sized and positioned, as shown in Figure 14-8.

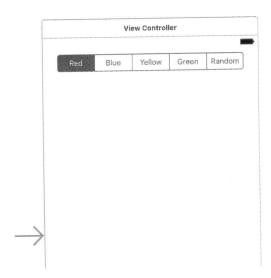

Figure 14-8. *Your correctly labelled and positioned color segment control*

Bring up the assistant editor, if it's not already open, and select ViewController.swift from the jump bar. Now Control-drag from the segmented control in the Document Outline to the ViewController.swift file on the right to the line below the class declaration and release the mouse to create a new outlet. Name the new outlet colorControl, and leave all the other options at their default values. Your class should now look like this:

```
class ViewController: UIViewController {
    @IBOutlet weak var colorControl: UISegmentedControl!
```

Next, let's add an action. Open ViewController.swift in the assistant editor, select Main.storyboard again, and Control-drag from the segmented control over to the bottom of the class definition in the view controller file, directly above the closing brace. In the pop-up, change the connection type to Action and the name to changeColor. The pop-up should default to using the Value Changed event, which is what you want. You should also set the type to UISegmentedControl.

Now let's add a second segmented control. This one will be used to choose the shape to be drawn. Drag a segmented control from the library and drop it near the bottom of the view. Select the segmented control in the Document Outline, bring up the Attributes Inspector, and change the number of segments from 2 to 4. Now double-click each segment and change the titles of the four segments to Line, Rectangle, Ellipse, and Image, in that order. Now you need to add layout constraints to fix the size and position of the control, just like you did with the color selection control. Here's the sequence of steps that you need:

1. In the Document Outline, Control-drag from the new segmented control item to the Quartz Fun View item and release the mouse. Hold down the Shift key and select Vertical Spacing to Bottom Layout Guide and Center Horizontally in Container; then press Return.

2. In the Document Outline, select the View Controller icon; then back in the editor, click the Resolve Auto Layout Issues button and select Update Frames.

Once you've done that, open ViewController.swift in the assistant editor again and then Control-drag from the new segmented control to the bottom of ViewController.swift to create another action. Change the connection type to Action, name the action **changeShape**, change the type to UISegmentedControl, and click Connect. The storyboard should now look like Figure 14-9. Your next task is to implement the action methods.

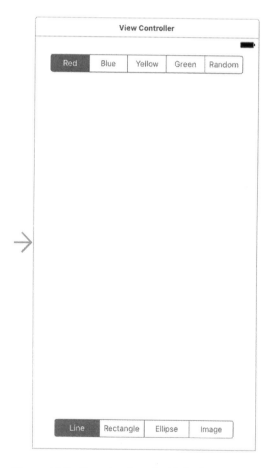

Figure 14-9. *Your storyboard with both segmented controls in place*

Implementing the Action Methods

Save the storyboard and feel free to close the assistant editor. Now select ViewController.swift, look for the stub implementation of changeColor() that Xcode created for you, and add the code in Listing 14-6.

Listing 14-6. The changeColor Method Goes in the ViewController.swift File

```swift
@IBAction func changeColor(_ sender: UISegmentedControl) {
    let drawingColorSelection =
            DrawingColor(rawValue: UInt(sender.selectedSegmentIndex))
    if let drawingColor = drawingColorSelection {
        let funView = view as! QuartzFunView
        switch drawingColor {
        case .red:
            funView.currentColor = UIColor.red
            funView.useRandomColor = false

        case .blue:
            funView.currentColor = UIColor.blue
            funView.useRandomColor = false

        case .yellow:
            funView.currentColor = UIColor.yellow
            funView.useRandomColor = false

        case .green:
            funView.currentColor = UIColor.green
            funView.useRandomColor = false

        case .random:
            funView.useRandomColor = true
        }
    }
}
```

This is pretty straightforward. You simply look at which segment was selected and create a new color based on that selection to serve as your current drawing color. To map from the segmented control's selected index to the enumeration value for the corresponding color, you use the enumeration's constructor that takes a raw value.

```swift
let drawingColorSelection =
        DrawingColor(rawValue: UInt(sender.selectedSegmentIndex))
```

After that, you set the currentColor property so that your class knows which color to use when drawing, unless a random color has been selected. In that case, you set the useRandomColor property to true, and a new color will be chosen each time the user starts a new drawing action (you'll find in this code in the touchesBegan(_:withEvent:) method, which you added a few pages ago). Since all the drawing code will be in the view itself, you don't need to do anything else in this method.

Next, look for the existing implementation of changeShape() and add the following code to it:

```
@IBAction func changeShape(_ sender: UISegmentedControl) {
    let shapeSelection = Shape(rawValue: UInt(sender.selectedSegmentIndex))
    if let shape = shapeSelection {
        let funView = view as! QuartzFunView
        funView.shape = shape
        colorControl.isHidden = shape == Shape.image
    }
}
```

In this method, all you do is set the shape type based on the selected segment of the control. The four elements of the Shape enumeration correspond to the four toolbar segments at the bottom of the application view. You set the shape to be the same as the currently selected segment, and you also hide or show the color selection control based on whether the Image segment was selected.

Make sure that everything is in order by compiling and running your app. You won't be able to draw shapes on the screen yet, but the segmented controls should work; and when you tap the Image segment in the bottom control, the color controls should disappear.

Now that you have everything working, let's do some drawing.

Adding Quartz 2D Drawing Code

You're ready to add the code that does the drawing. You'll draw a line, some shapes, and an image. You're going to work incrementally, adding a small amount of code, and then run the app to see what that code does.

Drawing the Line

Let's do the simplest drawing option first: drawing a single line. Select QuartzFunView.swift and replace the commented-out **draw(_ rect: CGRect)** method with the one shown in Listing 14-7.

Listing 14-7. The draw(rect:) Method

```
override func draw(_ rect: CGRect) {
    let context = UIGraphicsGetCurrentContext()
    context!.setLineWidth(2.0)
    context!.setStrokeColor(currentColor.cgColor)

    switch shape {
    case .line:
        context?.move(to: CGPoint(x: firstTouchLocation.x,
                                  y: firstTouchLocation.y))
        context?.addLine(to: CGPoint(x: lastTouchLocation.x,
                                     y: lastTouchLocation.y))
        context?.strokePath()

    case .rect:
        break

    case .ellipse:
        break
```

```
    case .image:
        break
    }
}
```

You start things off by retrieving a reference to the current context, which will let you draw onto your QuartzFunView.

```
let context = UIGraphicsGetCurrentContext()
```

Next, you set the line width to 2.0, which means that any line that you stroke will be 2 points wide.

```
context!.setLineWidth(2.0)
```

After that, you set the color for stroking lines. Since UIColor has a CGColor property, which is what this function needs, you use that property of your currentColor property to pass the correct color on to this function.

```
context!.setStrokeColor(currentColor.cgColor)
```

You use a switch to jump to the appropriate code for each shape type. As mentioned earlier, you'll start off with the code to handle drawing a line, get that working, and add code for each shape in turn as you make your way through this example.

```
switch shape {
case .line:
```

To draw a line, you tell the graphics context to create a path starting at the first place the user touched. Remember that you stored that value in the touchesBegan(_:withEvent:) method, so it will always reflect the starting point of the most recent touch or drag.

```
context?.move (to: CGPoint(x: firstTouchLocation.x,
                           y: firstTouchLocation.y))
```

Next, you draw a line from that spot to the last spot the user touched. If the user's finger is still in contact with the screen, lastTouchLocation contains the finger's current location. If the user is no longer touching the screen, lastTouchLocation contains the location of the user's finger when it was lifted off the screen:

```
context?.addLine(to: CGPoint(x: lastTouchLocation.x,
                             y: lastTouchLocation.y))
```

This function doesn't actually draw the line—it just adds it to the context's current path. To make the line appear on the screen, you need to stroke the path. This function will stroke the line you just drew, using the color and width you set earlier.

```
context?.strokePath()
```

That's it for now. At this point, you should be able to compile and run the app once more. The Rectangle, Ellipse, and Shape options won't work, but you should be able to draw lines just fine using any of the color choices (see Figure 14-10).

Figure 14-10. *The line-drawing part of your application is now complete. Here, you are drawing using a random color.*

Drawing the Rectangle and Ellipse

Let's write the code to draw the rectangle and the ellipse at the same time since Quartz implements both of these objects in basically the same way. Change the existing **draw(_ rect:)** method as shown in Listing 14-8.

Listing 14-8. Changes to draw(_ rect:) to Handle the Rectangle and Ellipse

```
override func draw(_ rect: CGRect) {
    let context = UIGraphicsGetCurrentContext()
    context?.setLineWidth(2.0)
    context?.setStrokeColor(currentColor.cgColor)
    context?.setFillColor(currentColor.cgColor)
    let currentRect = CGRect(x: firstTouchLocation.x,
                             y: firstTouchLocation.y,
                             width: lastTouchLocation.x - firstTouchLocation.x,
                             height: lastTouchLocation.y - firstTouchLocation.y)
```

```
    switch shape {
    case .line:
        context?.move(to: CGPoint(x: firstTouchLocation.x,
                            y: firstTouchLocation.y))
        context?.addLine(to: CGPoint(x: lastTouchLocation.x,
                            y: lastTouchLocation.y))
        context?.strokePath()

    case .rect:
        context?.addRect(currentRect)
        context?.drawPath(using: .fillStroke)

    case .ellipse:
        context?.addEllipse(inRect: currentRect)
        context?.drawPath(using: .fillStroke)

    case .image:
        break
    }
}
```

Because you want to paint both the outline of the ellipse and the rectangle and to fill their interiors, you add a call to set the fill color using currentColor.

```
context?.setFillColor(currentColor.cgColor)
```

Next, you declare a CGRect variable. You do this here because both the rectangle and ellipse are drawn based on a rectangle. You'll use currentRect to hold the rectangle described by the user's drag. Remember that a CGRect has two members: size and origin. A function called CGRect(x: y: width: height:) lets you create a CGRect by specifying the values needed to make your rectangle. The code to create the rectangle is pretty straightforward. You use the point stored in firstTouchLocation to create the origin. Next, you figure out the size by getting the difference between the two x values and the two y values. Note that, depending on the direction of the drag, one or both size values may end up with negative numbers, but that's okay. A CGRect with a negative size will simply be rendered in the opposite direction of its origin point (to the left for a negative width; upward for a negative height).

```
let currentRect = CGRect(x: firstTouchLocation.x,
        y: firstTouchLocation.y,
        width: lastTouchLocation.x - firstTouchLocation.x,
        height: lastTouchLocation.y - firstTouchLocation.y)
```

Once you have this rectangle defined, drawing either a rectangle or an ellipse is as easy as calling two functions: one to draw the rectangle or ellipse in the CGRect you defined and the other to stroke and fill it:

```
case .rect:
    context?.addRect(currentRect)
    context?.drawPath(using: .fillStroke)

case .ellipse:
    context?.addEllipse(inRect: currentRect)
    context?.drawPath(using: .fillStroke)
```

Build and run your application. Try the Rectangle and Ellipse tools to see how you like them. Don't forget to change colors, including using a random color.

Drawing the Image

For the last trick, let's draw an image. The 16 - Image folder contains three images named iphone.png, iphone@2x.png, and iphone@3x.png that you can add to your project's asset catalog. Select Assets.xcassets in the Project Navigator to open it in the editor; then select all three images in the Finder and drag them onto the editor area to create a new image group called iphone in the asset catalog. Now modify the draw(_ rect:) method as shown in Listing 14-9.

Listing 14-9. Your Modified draw(_ rect:) Method to Handle Images

```swift
override func draw(_ rect: CGRect) {
    let context = UIGraphicsGetCurrentContext()
    context?.setLineWidth(2.0)
    context?.setStrokeColor(currentColor.cgColor)
    context?.setFillColor(currentColor.cgColor)
    let currentRect = CGRect(x: firstTouchLocation.x,
                             y: firstTouchLocation.y,
                             width: lastTouchLocation.x - firstTouchLocation.x,
                             height: lastTouchLocation.y - firstTouchLocation.y)

    switch shape {
    case .line:
        context?.move(to: CGPoint(x: firstTouchLocation.x,
                         y: firstTouchLocation.y))
        context?.addLine(to: CGPoint(x: lastTouchLocation.x,
                         y: lastTouchLocation.y))
        context?.strokePath()

    case .rect:
        context?.addRect(currentRect)
        context?.drawPath(using: .fillStroke)

    case .ellipse:
        context?.addEllipse(inRect: currentRect)
        context?.drawPath(using: .fillStroke)

    case .image:
        let horizontalOffset = image!.size.width / 2
        let verticalOffset = image!.size.height / 2
        let drawPoint =
            CGPoint(x: lastTouchLocation.x - horizontalOffset,
                     y: lastTouchLocation.y - verticalOffset)
        image!.draw(at: drawPoint)
    }
}
```

First, you calculate the center of the image since you want the image drawn centered on the point where the user last touched. Without this adjustment, the image would be drawn with the upper-left corner at the user's finger, also a valid option. Then, you make a new `CGPoint` by subtracting these offsets from the x and y values in `lastTouchLocation`:

```
let horizontalOffset = image!.size.width / 2
let verticalOffset = image!.size.height / 2
let drawPoint =
    CGPoint(x: lastTouchLocation.x - horizontalOffset,
            y: lastTouchLocation.y - verticalOffset)
```

Now you tell the image to draw itself. This line of code does that:

```
image!.draw(at: drawPoint)
```

Build and run the application, select Image from the segmented control, and check that you can place an image on the drawing canvas. For a little extra fun, move your finger around the screen and observe that the image follows it.

Optimizing the QuartzFun Application

Your application does what you want, but you should consider a bit of optimization. In your little application, you won't notice a slowdown; however, in a more complex application that is running on a slower processor, you might see some lag. The problem occurs in `QuartzFunView.swift`, in the methods `touchesMoved(_:withEvent:)` and `touchesEnded(_:withEvent:)`. Both methods include this line of code:

```
setNeedsDisplay()
```

Obviously, this is how you tell your view that something has changed and that it needs to redraw itself. This code works, but it causes the entire view to be erased and redrawn, even if only a tiny bit has changed. You do want to erase the screen when you get ready to drag out a new shape, but you don't want to clear the screen several times a second as you drag out your shape.

Rather than forcing the entire view to be redrawn many times during your drag, you can use the `setNeedsDisplayInRect()` method instead. `setNeedsDisplayInRect()` is a `UIView` method that marks just one rectangular portion of a view's region as needing redisplay. By using this method, you can be more efficient by marking only the part of the view that is affected by the current drawing operation as needing to be redrawn.

You need to redraw not just the rectangle between `firstTouchLocation` and `lastTouchLocation` but any part of the screen encompassed by the current drag. If the user touched the screen and then scribbled all over but you redrew only the section between `firstTouchLocation` and `lastTouchLocation`, then you would leave a lot of stuff drawn on the screen by the previous redraw that you don't want to remain.

The solution is to keep track of the entire area that has been affected by a particular drag in a `CGRect` instance variable. In `touchesBegan(_:withEvent:)`, you would reset that instance variable to just the point where the user touched. Then, in `touchesMoved(_:withEvent:)` and `touchesEnded(_:withEvent:)`, you would use a Core Graphics function to get the union of the current rectangle and the stored rectangle and store the resulting rectangle. You would then use it to specify which part of the view needs to be redrawn. This approach gives you a running total of the area impacted by the current drag.

At the moment, you calculate the current rectangle in the `draw(_ rect: )` method for use in drawing the ellipse and rectangle shapes. You'll move that calculation into a new method so that it can be used in all three places without repeating code. Let's try it.

Add a new property called redrawRect to the QuartzFunView class.

```
// Internal properties
private let image = UIImage(named:"iphone")
private var firstTouchLocation = CGPoint.zero
private var lastTouchLocation = CGPoint.zero
private var redrawRect = CGRect.zero
```

You will use this property to keep track of the area that needs to be redrawn. You also need to move the calculation of the current redraw rectangle to a separate method, which you should add at the end of the QuartzFunView class.

```
func currentRect() -> CGRect {
    return CGRect(x: firstTouchLocation.x,
        y: firstTouchLocation.y,
        width: lastTouchLocation.x - firstTouchLocation.x,
        height: lastTouchLocation.y - firstTouchLocation.y)
}
```

Now, in the draw(_ rect:) method, change all references of currentRect to currentRect() so that the code uses that new method you just created. Next, delete the lines of code where you calculated currentRect, as shown in Listing 14-10.

Listing 14-10. Your Final Modifications to draw(_ rect:)

```
override func draw(_ rect: CGRect) {
    let context = UIGraphicsGetCurrentContext()
    context?.setLineWidth(2.0)
    context?.setStrokeColor(currentColor.cgColor)
    context?.setFillColor(currentColor.cgColor)

    switch shape {
    case .line:
        context?.move(to: CGPoint(x: firstTouchLocation.x,
                                  y: firstTouchLocation.y))
        context?.addLine(to(CGPoint(x: lastTouchLocation.x,
                                    y: lastTouchLocation.y))
        context?.strokePath()

    case .rect:
        context?.addRect(currentRect())
        context?.drawPath(using: .fillStroke)

    case .ellipse:
        context?.addEllipse(inRect: currentRect())
        context?.drawPath(using: .fillStroke)
```

```
case .image:
    let horizontalOffset = image!.size.width / 2
    let verticalOffset = image!.size.height / 2
    let drawPoint =
        CGPoint(x: lastTouchLocation.x - horizontalOffset,
                    y: lastTouchLocation.y - verticalOffset)
    image!.draw(at: drawPoint)
    }
}
```

You also need to make some changes to touchesBegan(_:withEvent:), touchesEnded(_:withEvent:), and touchesMoved(_:withEvent:). You will recalculate the space impacted by the current operation and use that to indicate that only a portion of your view needs to be redrawn. Replace the existing touchesEnded(_:withEvent:) and touchesMoved(_:withEvent:) methods with the new versions shown in Listing 14-11.

Listing 14-11. The Updated Touches Routines

```
override func touchesBegan(_ touches: Set<UITouch>, with event: UIEvent?) {
    if let touch = touches.first {
        if useRandomColor {
            currentColor = UIColor.randomColor()
        }
        firstTouchLocation = touch.location(in: self)
        lastTouchLocation = firstTouchLocation
        redrawRect = CGRect.zero
        setNeedsDisplay()
    }
}

override func touchesMoved(_ touches: Set<UITouch>, with event: UIEvent?) {
    if let touch = touches.first {
        lastTouchLocation = touch.location(in: self)

        if shape == .image {
            let horizontalOffset = image!.size.width / 2
            let verticalOffset = image!.size.height / 2
            redrawRect = redrawRect.union(CGRect(x: lastTouchLocation.x - horizontalOffset,
                    y: lastTouchLocation.y - verticalOffset,
                    width: image!.size.width, height: image!.size.height))
        } else {
            redrawRect = redrawRect.union(currentRect())
        }
        setNeedsDisplay(redrawRect)
    }
}
```

```
override func touchesEnded(_ touches: Set<UITouch>, with event: UIEvent?) {
    if let touch = touches.first {
        lastTouchLocation = touch.location(in: self)

        if shape == .image {
            let horizontalOffset = image!.size.width / 2
            let verticalOffset = image!.size.height / 2
            redrawRect = redrawRect.union(CGRect(x: lastTouchLocation.x - horizontalOffset,
                        y: lastTouchLocation.y - verticalOffset,
                        width: image!.size.width, height: image!.size.height))
        } else {
            redrawRect = redrawRect.union(currentRect())
        }
        setNeedsDisplay(redrawRect)
    }
}
```

Build and run the application again to see the final result. You probably won't see any difference, but with only a few additional lines of code, you reduced the amount of work necessary to redraw your view by getting rid of the need to erase and redraw any portion of the view that hasn't been affected by the current drag. Being kind to your iOS device's precious processor cycles like this can make a big difference in the performance of your applications, especially as they get more complex.

▨ **Note**   If you're interested in a more in-depth exploration of Quartz 2D topics, you might want to take a look at *Beginning iPad Development for iPhone Developers: Mastering the iPad SDK* by Jack Nutting, Dave Wooldridge, and David Mark (Apress, 2010). This book covers a lot of Quartz 2D drawing. All the drawing code and explanations in that book apply to the iPhone as well as the iPad.

Summary

In this chapter, you've really just scratched the surface of the drawing capabilities built into iOS. You should feel pretty comfortable with Quartz 2D now, and with some occasional references to Apple's documentation, you can probably handle most any drawing requirement that comes your way.

APPENDIX A

▪▪▪

An Introduction to Swift

Until recently, writing an iPhone or iPad application meant working with Objective-C. Because of its unusual syntax, Objective-C is one of the most polarizing of programming languages—people tend to love it or hate it. At the World Wide Developer Conference in 2014, Apple changed all that by unveiling an alternative—a new language called Swift. Swift's syntax is designed to be easily recognizable to programmers who are used to some of the more popular object-oriented programming languages like C++ and Java, therefore making it easier for them to start writing applications for iOS (and for Macs since Swift is also fully supported as a development language on macOS). This appendix covers the parts of Swift that you'll need to know in order to understand the example code in this book. I assume that you already have some programming experience and that you know what variables, functions, methods, and classes are. This appendix is neither a reference nor an exhaustive guide to the language—for that, there are numerous other resources, some of which are listed in Chapter 1.

Swift Basics

One of the most useful new features introduced in Xcode 6 alongside Swift is the *playground*. As the name suggests, a playground is a place where you can go to play with code without having to create an environment in which to run it—just open a playground, type in some code, and see the results. Playgrounds are a great place to prototype something new, and they are also an ideal place to start learning a new language, so you're going to use them throughout this appendix.

Let's begin by creating a new playground. Start Xcode and go to File ➤ New ➤ Playground. In the dialog that opens, choose an iOS playground of Blank type (Figure A-1). Then choose a name for your playground (something like SwiftBasics) and make sure that Platform is iOS. Then press Next. Choose the folder in which your playground will be saved and then click Create. Xcode creates the playground and opens it in a new window, as shown in Figure A-2. As you read through the examples in this appendix, feel free to experiment by adding code of your own to the playground or by modifying the examples to see what happens.

© Molly K. Maskrey 2017
M. K. Maskrey, *Beginning iPhone Development with Swift 4*, https://doi.org/10.1007/978-1-4842-3072-5

Figure A-1. *Choose a Blank iOS playground*

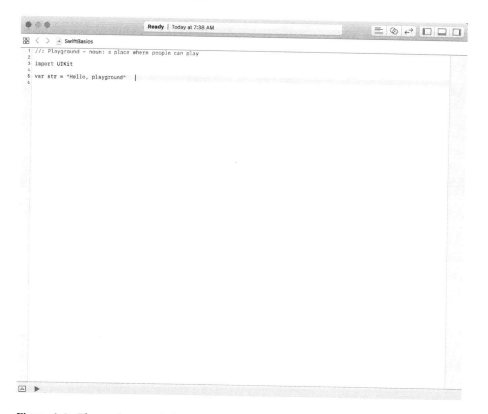

Figure A-2. *The newly created playground*

Playgrounds, Comments, Variables, and Constants

Let's take a moment to look at what you've got in your playground. It's divided into two areas—code is on the left, and results appear on the right. As you type code, the Swift compiler compiles and executes it and shows you the result almost immediately. The code in Figure A-1 declares a new variable called str and initializes it with the string "Hello, playground". You can see this string in the results column on the right. Try changing the value and notice that the result updates to match as soon as you stop typing.

The code on line 1 in Figure A-1 is a comment. Anything following the character sequence // up to the end of the line is ignored by the compiler. Here, the comment occupies the whole line, but that's not the only option. You could add a comment to the end of a line of code too:

```
var str = "Hello, playground"   // my comment for this line
```

To write a comment that's longer than one line, start it with /* and end it with */, like this:

```
/*
This is a comment that occupies
More than one line.
*/
```

There are various different ways to write a multiline comment. Some people like to make it clear that a line is part of a comment by starting each line with a * character.

```
/*
 * This is a comment that occupies
 * More than one line.
 */
```

Other people like to write single-line comments like this:

```
/* This is another way to write a single-line comment. */
```

The import statement on line 3 of Figure A-1 makes Apple's UIKit framework available for use in the playground.

```
import UIKit
```

IOS includes many frameworks, some of which you'll read about in this book. UIKit is the user interface framework, which you'll be using in all of your code examples. Another framework that you'll frequently make use of is Foundation, which contains classes that provide basic functionality like date and time handling, collections, file management, networking, and much more. To get access to this framework, you need to import it, like this:

```
import Foundation
```

However, UIKit automatically imports Foundation, so any playground that imports UIKit gets access to Foundation for free, without having to add an explicit import for it.

Line 5 is the first (and only) line of executable code in this playground.

```
var str = "Hello, playground"
```

The var keyword declares a new variable with a given name. Here, the variable is called str, which is appropriate because it's a string. Swift is very liberal with variable names: you can use almost any character you like in the name, with the exception of the first character, which is somewhat restricted. You can find the precise rules in Apple's documentation at https://developer.apple.com/library/ios/documentation/Swift/Conceptual/Swift_Programming_Language.

Following the declaration of the variable comes an expression that assigns its initial value. You don't have to initialize a variable when you declare it, but you must do so before you use it (i.e., before you execute any code that reads its value). However, if you choose to assign a value, then Swift can infer the variable's type, saving you the trouble of stating it explicitly. In this example, Swift infers that str is a string variable because it was initialized with a string literal. If you choose not to provide an initializer (perhaps because there is no fixed initial value), you must declare the variable's type by appending it to the name and separated from it by a colon, like this:

```
var str2: String          // an uninitialized variable
```

Try changing the code on line 5 of the playground to this:

```
var str: String
str = "Hello, playground"
```

This is completely equivalent to the original code, but now you've had to explicitly state that str is a string variable (String is the Swift type that represents a string). In most cases, it's easier to combine the declaration and initialization and allow the compiler to infer the variable's type.

Here's another example that makes use of Swift's type inference feature:

```
var count = 2
```

Here, the compiler infers that the count variable is an integer. Its actual type is Int (you'll cover the numeric types that Swift provides in the next section). How can you be sure that this is the case? Easy. Let Swift tell you. Type the preceding code into the playground, hover the mouse over count, and hold down the ⌥ (Option) key. The cursor changes to a question mark. Now click the mouse and Swift shows you the type that it's inferred for the variable in a pop-up, as shown in Figure A-3.

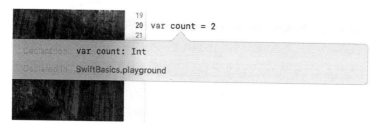

Figure A-3. *Getting the inferred type of a variable*

The fact that you haven't explicitly declared the type of a variable doesn't mean that it doesn't have one or that you can play fast and loose with it. Swift assigns a type when the variable is declared, and then you have to stick with that type. Unlike dynamic languages like JavaScript, you can't change the type of a variable simply by assigning a new value to it. Try doing this:

```
var count = 2
count = "Two"
```

Attempting to assign a string value to an integer variable is an error; you'll see a red marker in the margin on the left of the playground. Click it, and Swift displays a message explaining the problem (see Figure A-4).

Figure A-4. Swift is not a dynamic language. You can't change the type of a variable.

If you've programmed before, you may notice that you aren't bothering to add semicolons at the end of your statements. That's one of the many nice little features of Swift: it's almost never necessary to end a statement with a semicolon. If you're used to writing in C, C++, Objective-C, or Java, that will probably feel a bit strange at first, but after a while, you'll get used to it. Of course, you *can* type the semicolon if you want, but most likely you'll wind up not doing so. The only time you must use a semicolon is if you want to write two statements on the same line. This code is not valid:

```
var count = 2 count = 3
```

Add a semicolon, and the compiler is happy again.

```
var count = 2; count = 3
```

As the preceding line of code shows, you can change the value of a variable. That's why it's called a *variable*, after all. What if you just want to give a name to a fixed value? In other words, you want to create a constant and give it a name. For that, Swift provides the let statement, which is just like var, except that you must provide an initial value.

```
let pi = 3.14159265
```

As with variables, Swift can infer the type of the constant (or you can explicitly state it if you want), but you can't reassign the value of a constant, which is, of course, the point of making it constant.

```
pi = 42        // Error - Cannot assign to value: 'pi' is a 'let' constant
```

Naturally, you can initialize the value of a variable from a constant.

```
let pi = 3.14159265
var value = pi
```

As you've seen, Swift prints the results of executable statements to the right of the corresponding code. You can also create output using the print() function from the Swift standard library. For example, try this:

```
print("Hello, world")
```

The string "Hello, world" followed by a newline character appears in the playground output area, as usual, but you can also make it appear inline with the code. To do that, hover the mouse over the results area, and you'll see a couple of circular controls appear. Click the control on the right, and the result appears right below the `print()` statement, as shown in Figure A-5. Also notice at the bottom is the debug area where the output also appears. You can open or close the debug area using the triangle disclosure button to the left of the bottom of the playground.

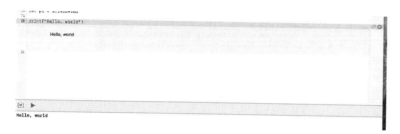

Figure A-5. *Viewing output inline with the code and in the debug area*

If you don't want the newline to be automatically appended to the string, you can get rid of it or replace it with another string by using a slightly different version of `print()` that takes an additional argument. Try this:

```
print("Hello, world", terminator: "")
```

This code replaces the newline with an empty string, and if you check in the results area, you'll see that the newline is no longer there.

■ **Tip**   `print()` is a function from the Swift standard library. You'll find documentation for the library at `https://developer.apple.com/library/ios/documentation/General/Reference/ SwiftStandardLibraryReference`. Another way to see what's in the standard library is to add the line `import Swift` to your playground and then hold down the ⌘ (Cmd) key and click the word *Swift*. The playground switches to a listing of the content of the standard library. There's a lot of information here, and you'll need to know a lot more about Swift to understand all of it, but it's worth looking it over to get a feel for what's available.

Predefined Types, Operators, and Control Statements

Swift comes with a set of basic, predefined types. In later sections, you'll see that you can add to these by defining your own classes, structures, and enumerations. You can even add functionality to an existing type by creating an extension of that type. Swift also has operators and control statements that will no doubt be familiar to you from other languages. Let's start with a quick overview of the basic types.

Numeric Types

Swift has four basic numeric types—`Int`, `Uint`, `Float`, and `Double`—and a collection of more specialized integer types. The full set of integer types, together with their sizes (in bits) and the ranges of values that they can represent, is listed in Table A-1.

Table A-1. *Integer Types*

Type	Size in Bits	Maximum Value	Minimum Value
Int	32 or 64	As Int32 or Int64	As Int32 or Int64
UInt	32 or 64	As UInt32 or UInt64	0
Int64	64	9,223,372,036,854,775,807	−9,223,372,036,854,775,808
UInt64	64	18,446,744,073,709,551,615	0
Int32	32	2,147,483,647	−2,147,483,648
UInt32	32	4,294,967,295	0
Int16	16	32767	−32768
Uint16	16	65535	0
Int8	8	127	−128
UInt8	8	255	0

Int and its derivatives are signed values, whereas the types related to UInt are unsigned. The default type for integer values (i.e., the type that's inferred when you write something like var count = 3) is Int and is the recommended type to use, unless you have a specific reason to use one of the others.

As you can see from the table, the range of values that Int and UInt can represent depends on the platform. On 32-bit systems (e.g., some iPads and all iPhones before the iPhone 4s, and the iPhone 5c), these are both 32-bit values, whereas on 64-bit systems, they are 64 bits wide. If you need a value that's definitely 32-bit or definitely 64-bit, then use Int32 or Int64 instead. The Int8 and UInt8 types can be used to represent bytes.

You can discover the maximum and minimum values for each of these types programmatically by using their max and min properties. For example, try entering these lines into your playground (without the comments, which show the results):

```
print(Int8.max)     //  127
print(Int8.min)     //  -128
print(Int32.max)    //  2,147,483,647
print(Int32.min )   //  -2,147,483,648
print(UInt32.max)   //  4,294,967,295
```

Integer literals can be written in decimal, hexadecimal, binary, or octal number bases. Try out these examples:

```
let decimal = 123       // Value is 123
let octal = 0o77        // Octal 77 = decimal 63
let hex = 0x1234        // Hex 1234 = decimal 4660
let binary = 0b1010     // Binary 1010 = decimal 10
```

The prefix 0o indicates octal, 0x indicates hexadecimal, and 0b indicates binary. For readability, you can also use an underscore character (_) anywhere to separate number groups.

```
let v = -1_234      // Same as -1234
let w = 12_34_56    // Same as 123456
```

Notice that you don't have to stick with the normal rule of grouping by units of three digits.

The Float and Double types are respectively 32-bit and 64-bit floating-point numbers. You assign a value to a floating-point variable by using a floating-point literal. Swift infers a type of Double, unless otherwise specified.

```
let a = 1.23            // This is inferred to be a Double
let b: Float = 1.23     // Forced to be Float
```

You can also use exponential (or scientific) notation, which is convenient for large numbers.

```
let c = 1.23e2          // Evaluated as 123.0
let d = 1.23e-1         // Evaluated as 0.123
let e = 1.23E-1         // Same as 1.23e-1
```

By their nature, floating-point numbers are not completely precise. One reason for this is that fractional values cannot be accurately represented in binary floating-point form. You can see this if you enter the following into the playground (where, as before, the comment shows the result):

```
let f: Float = 0.123456789123        // 0.1234568
let g: Double = 0.123456789123       // 0.123456789123
```

You can see that the Float representation of this value is less accurate than the Double representation. If you make the fractional part longer, you'll exceed the precision of the Double format as well.

```
let g: Double = 0.12345678912345678   // 0.1234567891234568
```

Floating-point numbers also lose precision when their value is large.

```
let f: Float = 123456789123456           // Inaccurate: 1.234568e+14
let g: Double = 123456789123456          // Accurate: 123,456,789,123,456.0
let h: Double = 123456789123456789       // Inaccurate: 1.234567891234568e+17
```

Unlike other languages, Swift does not provide implicit type conversion when you assign a variable (or expression) of one numeric type to a variable of another numeric type. For example, this code does not compile, as shown in Figure A-6:

```
let a = 123
let b = 0.456
let c = a + b
```

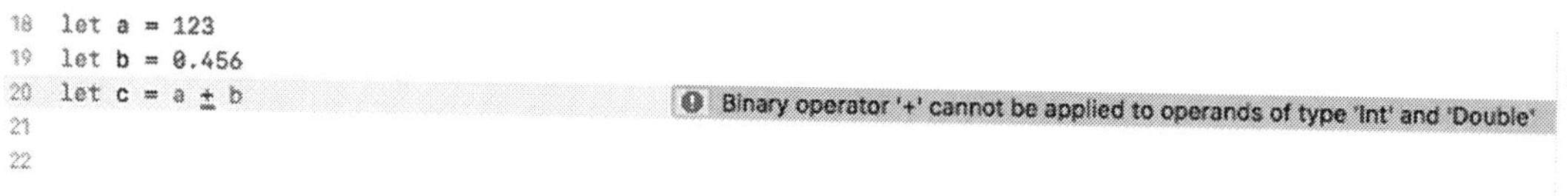

```
18  let a = 123
19  let b = 0.456
20  let c = a + b              ● Binary operator '+' cannot be applied to operands of type 'Int' and 'Double'
21
22
```

Figure A-6. Swift does not allow you to combine variables of different types

Variable a is of type Int, and b is a Double. Swift could convert the Int to a Double and perform the addition, but it does not. You have to perform the conversion yourself.

```
let a = 123
let b = 0.456
let c = Double(a) + b
```

The expression Double(a) invokes an initializer of the Double type with an integer argument. The numeric types all provide initializers that let you perform conversions of this kind.

Another example that arises frequently involves the CGFloat type. CGFloat is a floating-point type defined by the Core Graphics framework. It's used to represent coordinates and sizes, among other things. Depending on whether your application is running on a 32-bit or 64-bit platform, it's equivalent to either Float or Double. To perform operations that involve a mix of CGFloats and other types, you need to explicitly convert one to the other. For example, the following code adds a Double and a CGFloat, producing a CGFloat result by converting the Double to CGFloat:

```
let a: CGFloat = 123
let b: Double = 456
let c = Double(a) + b     // Result is of type Double
```

On 32-bit platforms, CGFloat is less precise than Double, so this operation may lose information, but that's inevitable if you need a value of type CGFloat. If you need a result of type Double, you can convert the CGFloat to Double without losing accuracy.

It's important to note that Swift allows you to mix numeric types when all of the values concerned are literals. Here's an example:

```
1 + 0.5     // Evaluated as 1.5
```

You'll find all of the usual binary arithmetic operators in Swift. You can use them to combine numbers of the same type, and you can apply them to numbers of different types if you explicitly convert one of the operands, as you have just seen. Table A-2 lists the arithmetic operators that are available. Operators are listed in decreasing order of precedence.

Table A-2. *Predefined Binary Arithmetic Operators*

Operator	Meaning
<<	Bitwise left shift
>>	Bitwise right shift
, &	Multiplication
/, &/	Division
%, &%	Remainder
&	Bitwise AND
+, &+	Addition
-, &-	Subtraction
|	Bitwise OR
^	Bitwise XOR

The arithmetic operations +, -, *, /, and % detect overflow. If you want overflow to be ignored, use &+, &-, &*, &/, or &% instead. For example, enter this code into the playground:

```
let a = Int.max
let b = 1
let c = Int.max + b
```

You're adding 1 to the largest representable integer value, which will trigger overflow. In the playground, you'll see an error message for the line containing the assignment to the variable c, but if you execute this same code in an application, it would crash. To allow the operation to proceed ignoring the overflow, use &+ instead.

```
let a = Int.max
let b = 1
let c = a &+ b
```

The << and >> operators perform a left and right shift of the left operand by the amount specified by their right operand. This is equivalent to multiplication and division by a power of two. Here's an example:

```
let a = 4
let b = a << 2    // Result is 16
let c = b >> 1    // Result is 8
```

When the left operand is negative, the sign of the result is preserved.

```
let a = -4
let b = a << 2    // Result is -16
let c = b >> 1    // Result is -8
```

The &, |, and ^ operations perform bitwise AND, OR, and XOR operations on their operands. This is not to be confused with the operators && and ||, which are logical operators that give a Boolean result (see the "Booleans" section later in this appendix). Here are some examples:

```
let a = 7          // Value 0b111
let b = 3          // Value 0b011
let c = a & b      // Result is 0b011 = 3

let a = 7          // Value 0b111
let b = 3          // Value 0b011
let c = a | b      // Result is 0b111 = 7

let a = 7          // Value 0b111
let b = 3          // Value 0b011
let c = a ^ b      // Result is 0b100 = 4
```

There are also compound variants of these operators that perform the operation followed by an assignment, with the target of the assignment acting as the left operand of the operation. Here's an example:

```
var a = 10
a += 20         // Shorthand for a = a + 20, result = 30
```

```
var b = 7
b &= 3          // Shorthand for b = b & 3, result = 3
```

■ **Note**   Starting in Swift 3, the unary operators ++ and -- are no longer available. You'll need to use a format to replace something like a++ with a += 1. This also means you'll need to be aware, when converting code with these unary types, of the order of the operator (i.e., ++a vs. a++ and so on).

The ~ unary operator performs bitwise inversion of the bits of its integer operand.

```
let a = 0b1001
let b = ~a
```

The result of this operation in 32 bits is 0b11111111111111111111111111110110, which is the same as -10.

Strings

A string, represented by the String type, is a sequence of Unicode characters. The fact that Swift uses Unicode in strings makes it possible to build applications that support many different character sets without requiring special code. However, it has some complications, some of which are mentioned here. For a full discussion on the implications of the use of Unicode, refer to *The Swift Programming Language*, which you'll find on Apple's Developer web site at the URL shown earlier, or in iBooks.

A string literal is a sequence of characters enclosed in double quotes, like this example that you've already seen:

```
let str = "Hello, playground"
```

If you need to include a " character in a string, escape it with a \ character, like this:

```
let quoted = "Contains \"quotes\""      // Contains "quotes"
```

To get a \, escape it with another \, like this:

```
let backslash = "\\"       // Result is \
```

Any Unicode character can be embedded in a string by giving its hexadecimal representation (or *code point*), surrounded by \u{}. For example, the @ symbol has code point 0x40, so the following example shows two ways to represent @ in a Swift string:

```
let atSigns = "@\u{40}"      // Result is @@
```

Certain characters have special escape representations. For example, \n and \t represent the new line and tab characters, respectively.

```
let specialChars = "Line1\nLine2\tTabbed"
```

Strings have the useful ability to interpolate expressions enclosed in the escape sequence \(). Here's an example:

```
print("The value of pi is \(Double.pi)")    // Prints "The value of pi is 3.14159265358979\n"
```

This code interpolates the value of the predefined constant `.pi` into the string and then prints the result. The interpolated value can also be an expression, and there can be more than one of them.

```
// This code prints: "Area of a circle of radius 3.0 is 28.2743338823081\n"
let r = 3.0
print("Area of a circle of radius \(r) is \(Double.pi * r * r)")
```

The + operator can be used to concatenate strings. This is the only way to combine strings that you want to split over more than one line of a source code file.

```
let s = "That's one small step for man, " +
        "one giant leap for mankind"
print(s)   // "That's one small step for man, one giant leap for mankind\n"
```

You can compare two strings using the == and != operators (see the "Booleans" section), which effectively perform a character-by-character comparison of their operands. Here's an example:

```
let s1 = "String one"
let s2 = "String two"
let s3 = "String " + "one"
s1 == s2     // false: strings are not the same
s1 != s2     // true: strings are different
s1 == s3     // true: strings contain the same characters.
```

The seemingly simple task of getting the length of a string is complicated by the fact that strings are composed of Unicode characters because not every Unicode character is represented by a single code point. You're going to skip a detailed discussion of this subject here, but there are two things to be aware of. First, if you want to get an accurate count of the number of characters in a string, which works under all circumstances, use the string's characters property and then get its length.

```
s3.characters.count      // 10
```

If you know that the string only contains characters that are represented by a single Unicode code point, you can use get a count of a UTF-16 view of the string instead, which may be faster under some circumstances.

```
s3.utf16.count        // 10
```

The `String` type itself provides quite a few useful string operations, which you'll find documented in the Swift library reference cited earlier in this appendix. You can also make use of the fact that Swift automatically bridges the `String` type to the `NSString` class in the Foundation framework, which means that methods defined by `NSString` can be used as if they were also defined on `String` itself.

The `Character` type can be used to hold a single character from a string. This allows iteration over the individual characters of a string via its `characters` property.

```
let s = "Hello"
for c in s.characters {
    print(c)
}
```

The body of the for loop in this example (the syntax of which is discussed later) is executed once for each character in the string, with the character assigned to the variable c, which is inferred to be of type Character. In the playground, you can't directly see the result of this loop in the results column—only that it was executed five times. Instead, click the leftmost of the two controls that appear when you hover over the result in the results column (the one that looks like an eye) to get a pop-up and then right-click the pop-up and select Value History from the menu that appears to see all of the characters, as shown in Figure A-7.

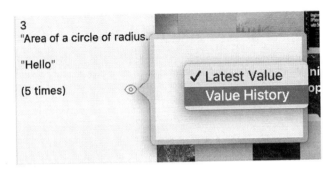

***Figure A-7.** Value History pop-up*

▦ **Tip** If you don't see the results column, hover the mouse over the right edge until you see the column-width drag bar and then use it to widen the width of the results panel.

You can create and initialize a Character in the same way as a String, but you need to explicitly state the type to avoid the inference of String, and the initializer must consist of exactly one character:

```
let c: Character = "s"
```

There's not much you can do with Characters other than compare them with other Characters. You can't append them to each other, and you can't directly add them to Strings. You have to use the append() method of String instead.

```
let c: Character = "s"
var s = "Book"   // "var" because we want to modify it
s += c           // Error - illegal
s.append(c)      // "Books" - Legal
```

Strings in Swift are not immutable, but they are *value objects*, which means that whenever you assign a string to a variable or use one as a function argument or return value, the string is copied. Modifications made to the copy do not affect the original.

```
var s1 = "Book"
var s2 = s1      // s2 is now a copy of s1
s2 += "s"        // Appends to s2; s1 is unchanged
s1               // "Book"
s2               // "Books"
```

■ **Note**   For the sake of efficiency, the actual copy of a string's content does not happen immediately upon assignment. In the preceding example, the strings s1 and s2 share the same copy of their character content after the assignment s1 = s2, until the statement s2 += "s" is executed. At this point, a copy of the shared content is made and installed in s2 before the character "s" is appended to it. All of this happens automatically.

Booleans

Booleans are represented by the Bool type, with possible values of true or false.

```
var b = true              // Inferred type is Bool
var b1: Bool
b1 = false
```

Swift has the usual set of comparison operators (==, !=, >, <, >=, <=) that return a Bool value when applied to numeric values.

```
var a = 100
var b = 200
var c = a

a == c        // true
a == b        // false
a != b        // true
a > b         // false
a < b         // true
a >= c        // true
```

Incidentally, these operators can also be applied to strings.

```
let a = "AB"
let b = "C"
let c = "CA"
let d = "AB"
a == b      // false - strings have different content
a == d      // true - strings have the same content
a != c      // true - strings have different content
a > b       // false: uses sorting order
a < c       // true: both start with C, but string c is longer than a
```

You can negate a Boolean value with the unary ! operator.

```
var a = 100
var b = 200
a == b          // false
!(a == b)       // !false == true
```

Boolean expressions can be combined using the ==, !=, &&, and || operators. The && and || operators are short-circuiting, which means they evaluate their second operand only if the result is not determined by the value of the first operand. Specifically, the second operand of a || operator does not need to be evaluated if the first is true, and the second operand of && is not evaluated if the first is false.

```
var a = 100
var b = 200
var c = 300

a < b && c > b    // true; both expression are evaluated
a < b || c > b    //  true: second expression is not evaluated
a > b && c > b    // false: second expression is not evaluated
```

Enumerations

Enumerations let you give meaningful names to the values of types where that set of values is fixed and known in advance. To define an enumeration, you give it a name and list all of the possible values as cases.

```
enum DaysOfWeek {
    case Sunday, Monday, Tuesday, Wednesday,
        Thursday, Friday, Saturday
}
```

You can also define each case separately.

```
enum DaysOfWeek {
    case Sunday
    case Monday
    case Tuesday
    case Wednesday
    case Thursday
    case Friday
    case Saturday
}
```

To refer to an enumeration value, use the enumeration name and the case name, separated by a period.

```
var day = DaysOfWeek.Sunday     // "day" is inferred to be of type "DaysOfWeek"
```

When the context is clear, you can omit the enumeration name. In the following example, the compiler already knows that the variable day is of type DaysOfWeek, so there is no need to explicitly say so when assigning to it.

```
day = .Friday     // Note that the "." Is required
```

In Swift, you can also give an associated value to an enumeration case. Try this example in your playground.

```
enum Status {
    case OK
    case ERROR(String)
}
```

```
let status = Status.OK
let failed = Status.ERROR("That does not compute")
```

Here, the ERROR case has an associated value—a string that describes the error. You can recover the associated value in a switch statement, as you'll see in upcoming "Control Statements" section.

In some cases, it is useful to map each enumeration case to a value, referred to as a *raw value*. To do this, specify the type of the value along with the enumeration name and then assign individual values to each case as it is defined. Here's a variant of the DaysOfWeek enum that assigns an integer value to each case:

```
enum DaysOfWeek : Int {
    case Sunday = 0
    case Monday
    case Tuesday
    case Wednesday
    case Thursday
    case Friday
    case Saturday
}
```

Raw values can be strings or any of the numeric types. When the raw value type is an integer, you don't need to assign an explicit value to each case; unassigned values are inferred by adding 1 to the previous raw value. In the preceding example, Sunday was assigned the raw value 0, and as a result, Monday is automatically given the raw value 1, Tuesday is assigned the raw value 2, and so on. You can override the automatic assignment of values, as long as each case has a unique value.

```
enum DaysOfWeek : Int {
    case Sunday = 0
    case Monday          // 1
    case Tuesday         // 2
    case Wednesday       // 3
    case Thursday        // 4
    case Friday = 20     // 20
    case Saturday        // 21
}
```

You can get the raw value for a case by accessing its rawValue property.

```
var day = DaysOfWeek.Saturday
let rawValue = day.rawValue            // 21. DaysOfWeek.Saturday.rawValue is also valid
```

Here's another example, using String as the raw value type.

```
enum ResultType : String {
    case SUCCESS = "Success"
    case WARNING = "Warning"
    case ERROR = "Error"
}
let s = ResultType.WARNING.rawValue     // s = "Warning"
```

Given a raw value, you can construct the corresponding case value by passing it to an initializer.

```
let result = ResultType(rawValue: "Error")
```

In this example, the type of the result variable is not ResultType, but ResultType?, an example of an *optional*. Since it's possible to pass an invalid raw value to the initializer, there has to be some way to indicate that there is no valid case with that value. Swift does this by returning the special value nil; but nil cannot be assigned to an ordinary variable, only to an optional. Optional types are indicated by a trailing ?, and you need to be careful when manipulating them. I will discuss optionals in more detail later.

Arrays, Ranges, and Dictionaries

Swift provides three basic collection types (arrays, dictionaries, and sets) and a range syntax that provides a convenient way to represent a (possibly large) range of values. Ranges are particularly useful when accessing arrays.

Arrays and Ranges

Swift supports the creation of an array of values using the syntax [type], where type is the type of the array value. The following code creates and initializes an array of integers and an array of strings:

```
var integers = [1, 2, 3]
var days = ["Sunday", "Monday", "Tuesday", "Wednesday",
            "Thursday", "Friday", "Saturday"]
```

You can, of course, separate the declaration and initialization of an array, as long as it's initialized before it is used. This requires explicit specification of the array type.

```
var integers: [Int]        // [Int] means "ar
ray of Ints"
integers = [1, 2, 3]
```

Use [] to initialize an empty array.

```
var empty: [String] = []
```

To access the elements of an array, use a numeric subscript as an index. The first element of the array has index 0.

```
integers[0]        // 1
integers[2]        // 3
days[3]            // "Wednesday"
```

Use the same syntax to assign a new value to an element of the array.

```
integers[0] = 4            // [4, 2, 3]
days[3] = "WEDNESDAY"      // Replaces "Wednesday" with "WEDNESDAY"
```

To extract or modify part of an array, use the Swift *range syntax*. This can result in a change in the number of elements in the array.

```
var integers = [1, 2, 3]
integers[1..<3]            // Get elements 1 and 2 as an array. Result is [2, 3]
integers[1..<3] = [4]      // Replace elements 1 and 2 with [4]. Result is [1, 4]
```

```
integers = [1, 2, 3]
integers[0...1] = [5, 4]      // Replace elements 0 and 1 with [5, 4]. Result is [5, 4, 3]
```

▓ **Note**   If you view this in the results column, you won't see the correct answer; you'll need to expand the result as I showed earlier or view it in the debug panel at the bottom.

The range syntax a..<b means all the values from a to b, excluding b; so 1..<5 is the same as 1, 2, 3, 4. The syntax a...b (note that there are three consecutive periods) includes b in the range so that 1...5 means 1, 2, 3, 4, 5. The range a..<a is always empty, whereas the range a...a contains exactly one element (a itself). The value of b must be greater than or equal to the value of a, and there is an implicit increment of 1.

To get the number of elements in an array, use its count property.

```
var integers = [1, 2, 3]
integers.count                  // 3
integers[1..<3] = [4]
integers.count                  // 2
```

To add an element to an array, use the append() method or the insert(_:atIndex:) method.

```
var integers = [1, 2, 3]
integers.append(4)                    // Result is [1, 2, 3, 4]
integers.insert(-1, atIndex: 0)    // Result is [-1, 1, 2, 3, 4]
```

You can also use the + operator to concatenate two arrays and the += operator to add one array to another.

```
var integers = [1, 2, 3]
let a = integers + [4, 5]  // a = [1, 2, 3, 4, 5]; integers array unchanged
integers += [4, 5]          // Now integers = [1, 2, 3, 4, 5]
```

Use the remove(), removeSubrange(), and removeAll() methods to remove all or some of the elements of an array.

```
var days = ["Sunday", "Monday", "Tuesday", "Wednesday",
            "Thursday", "Friday", "Saturday"]

days.remove(at: 3)                        // Removes "Wednesday" and returns it to the caller
days.removeSubrange(0..<4)                 // Leaves ["Friday", "Saturday"]
days.removeAll(keepingCapacity: false)     // Leaves an empty array
```

The keepingCapacity argument passed to removeAll() indicates whether the space allocated for the array's elements should be kept (value true) or released (value false).

You can iterate over a whole array or over a part of an array using the for statement, which is discussed in the "Control Statements" section.

If an array is created using a let statement, neither it nor its contents can be modified in any way.

```
let integers = [1, 2, 3]                  // Constant array
integers = [4, 5, 6]                      // Error: cannot replace the array
integers[0] = 2                           // Error: cannot reassign elements
integers.removeAll(keepingCapacity: false)  // Error: cannot modify content
```

Like strings, arrays are value objects, so assigning them or passing them to or from functions creates a copy.

```
var integers = [1, 2, 3]
var integersCopy = integers    // Creates a copy of "integers"
integersCopy[0] = 4            // Does not change "integers"
integers                       // [1, 2, 3]
integersCopy                   // [4, 2, 3]
```

You can use the contains() method to find out whether an array contains a given element.

```
let integers = [1, 2, 3]
integers.contains(2)    // true
integers.contains(4)    // false
```

To get the index of an element in an array, use the index(of:) method.

```
let integers = [1, 2, 3]
integers.index(of: 3)        // Result is 2
```

If the element is not found in the array, the result is nil.

```
let integers = [1, 2, 3]
integers.index(of: 5)        // Result is nil
```

Dictionaries

You can create a *dictionary*, a data structure mapping instances of a key to a corresponding value, using a syntax that is similar to that used for an array. You'll sometimes see dictionaries referred to as *maps*. The following code creates a dictionary in which the keys are strings and the values are integers:

```
var dict = ["Red": 0,
            "Green": 1,
            "Blue": 2]
```

The formal type of this dictionary is [String: Int]. You may also see this referred to as Dictionary<String, Int>, using *generics* syntax, which I'm not going to cover in this appendix. Similarly, you may see an array of type [Int] referred to as Array<Int>.

If you don't use an initializer, you need to explicitly state the type of the dictionary when you declare it.

```
var dict: [String: Int]
dict = ["Red": 0, "Green": 1,  "Blue": 2]
```

To get the value of a dictionary entry given its key, use subscript notation, like this:

```
let value = dict["Red"]  // Result is 0, the value mapped to the key "Red"
```

You can modify a dictionary in much the same way as you modify an array.

```
dict["Yellow"] = 3    // Adds a new value with key Yellow
dict["Red"] = 4       // Updates the value with key Red
```

To remove an element from the dictionary, use the removeValue(forKey:) method; to remove all values, use removeAll().

```
var dict = ["Red": 0, "Green": 1,  "Blue": 2]
dict.removeValue(forKey: "Red")    // Removes value with key "Red"
dict.removeAll()                   // Empties the dictionary
```

Dictionaries created using the let statement cannot be modified.

```
let fixedDict = ["Red": 0,  "Green": 1, "Blue": 2]
fixedDict["Yellow"] = 3               // Illegal
fixedDict["Red"] = 4                  // Illegal
fixedDict = ["Blue", 7]               // Illegal
fixedDict.removeValue(forKey:"Red")   // Illegal
```

You can iterate over the keys of a dictionary using the for statement, as you'll see in the "Control Statements" section. To get the number of key-value pairs in dictionary, use the count property.

```
var dict = ["Red": 0, "Green": 1, "Blue": 2]
dict.count       // 3
```

Like arrays, dictionaries are value types and are copied on assignment or when passed to and from functions. Modifications to the copy do not affect the original.

```
var dict = ["Red": 0, "Green": 1, "Blue": 2]
var dictCopy = dict
dictCopy["Red"] = 4    // Does not affect "dict"
dict                   // "Red":0, "Green": 1, "Blue": 2
dictCopy               // "Red":4, "Green": 1, "Blue": 2
```

Sets

The third and final Swift collection type is Set. A Set is a collection of elements that has no defined ordering and in which each element can appear only once. Adding another instance of an element that is already present does not change the content of the set. In most other respects, a set is much like an array.

The syntax for initializing a set is the same as that used for arrays. To disambiguate, you need to explicitly state that you are creating a Set. Here are two (equivalent) ways to do that:

```
let s1 = Set([1, 2, 3])
let s2: Set<Int> = [1, 2, 3]
```

The contains() method returns a Bool that indicates whether a set contains a given element, and the count property holds the number of elements in the set.

```
s1.contains(1)    // true
s2.contains(4)    // false
s1.count          // 3
```

As you'll see later, you can enumerate the elements of a set using a for loop.
To add an element to or remove an element from a set, use the insert() and remove() methods.

```
var s1 = Set([1, 2, 3])    // [2, 3, 1] (note that order does not matter in a set)
s1.insert(4)               // [2, 3, 1, 4]
s1.remove(1)               // [2, 3, 4]
s1.removeAll()             // [] (empty set)
```

NSArray, NSDictionary, and NSSet

The Foundation framework has Objective-C classes that represent arrays, dictionaries and sets—NSArray, NSDictionary, and NSSet. The relationship between these classes and their Swift counterparts is similar to that between NSString and String. In general, you can treat a Swift array as an NSArray, a Swift dictionary as an NSDictionary, and a Swift set as an NSSet. As an example, suppose you had an NSString like this:

```
let s: NSString  = "Red,Green,Blue"
```

Suppose also that you want to separate this into three separate parts, each containing one color name. NSString has a method called components(separatedBy:) that will do exactly what you want (and so does String, but you have an NSString in this case, not a String). This method takes the separator string as an argument and returns an NSArray containing the individual components.

```
let s: NSString = "Red,Green,Blue"
let components = s.components(separatedBy: ",")// Calls the NSString method
components        // ["Red", "Green", "Blue"]
```

Even though this method returns an NSArray, Swift is clever enough to map it to the corresponding Swift collection—an array of Strings—so the inferred type of components is [String], not [NSString]. You can confirm this by hovering the mouse over the variable name and clicking while holding down the ⌥ (Option) key.

You can directly create NSDictionary, NSSet, and NSArray instances in Swift code. Here's an example:

```
let d = NSDictionary()
```

The inferred type of the variable d is, of course, NSDictionary. You can explicitly cast an NSDictionary (whether you created it or obtained it from a method in the Foundation framework or another framework) to the Swift Dictionary type using the as keyword (which I'll say more about later).

```
let e = d as Dictionary
```

Now if you ⌥-click the name e, you'll see that Swift infers a type of Dictionary<NSObject, AnyObject> for this variable, which is another way of saying its type is [NSObject: AnyObject]. What are these key and value types and where did they come from? An NSDictionary created in the preceding Swift code is type-free: the compiler does not know the types of the keys and values that might be added to it (the same applies to NSSet and NSArray). The compiler has no choice but to infer a couple of general types: NSObject is the base class for all Foundation objects, and AnyObject is a Swift protocol (discussed later) that corresponds to any Swift class type—the type signature [NSObject: AnyObject] says "I have almost no idea what this dictionary contains." When you retrieve elements from an NSDictionary or an NSArray in Swift, you usually have to use the as! operator (more on this later) to cast them explicitly to the correct types or cast the NSDictionary itself to the type that you know it must be. For example, if you know that an NSDictionary instance maps strings to strings, you can do this:

```
let d = NSDictionary()
let e = d as! [String: String]
```

Here, you cast the NSDictionary to [String: String]. This code works even if the dictionary actually contains NSStrings instead of Strings because Swift automatically maps between String and NSString. Beware, though: if the NSDictionary key and value types are not both what you claim they are, your application will crash. You may have noticed that in this example you performed the cast using as! instead of as. I'll explain the difference between these two operators shortly.

There is a safer way to handle all of this that involves optionals, which is the subject of the next section.

Optionals

Let's go back to an example that you used in the previous section on dictionaries.

```
var dict: [String: Int]
dict = ["Red": 0, "Green": 1,  "Blue": 2]
let value = dict["Red"]
```

Although the values in this dictionary are all of type Int, the inferred type for value is not Int, but Int?—an *optional integer*. The ? signals the optional nature of the type. What does *optional* mean and why is it being used here? To answer that, think about what should happen if you access the dictionary with a key for which there is no value.

```
let yellowValue = dict["Yellow"]
```

What value should be assigned to yellowValue? Most languages address this by having a distinguished value that means, by convention, "no value." In Objective-C this value is referred to as nil (which is really just a redefinition of 0); in C and C++ it's NULL (again, a redefinition of 0); and in Java it's null. The problem with this is that it can be dangerous to use a nil (or equivalent) value. In Java, for example, using a null reference causes an exception; in C and C++, the application is likely to crash. What's worse, there's no way to know from its declaration whether a variable might contain a null (or nil or NULL) value. Swift solves this problem in a neat way: it has a nil value, but a variable (or constant) can be set to nil only if it's declared as an optional or its type is inferred to be optional. As a result, you can tell immediately whether a variable or constant could be nil by examining its type: if it's not optional, it can't be nil. Further, Swift requires you to take that into account explicitly whenever you use the value.

Let's look at some examples to make this clearer. Suppose you define a variable called color, like this:

```
var color = "Red"
```

Because of the way it's defined, the inferred type is String, which is not optional. Therefore, it's illegal to attempt to assign nil to this variable.

```
color = nil   // Illegal: color is not an optional type.
```

Because of this, you know for sure that you don't need to worry about color having a nil value, ever. It also means that you can't use this variable to hold a value returned from a dictionary, even if you know that value will not be nil.

```
let dict = [0: "Red", 1: "Green", 2: "Blue"]
color = dict[0]!    // Illegal: value of dict[0] is optional string, color is not optional.
```

To make this assignment legal, you have to change the type of color from `String` to optional `String`.

```
let dict = [0: "Red", 1: "Green", 2: "Blue"]
var color: String?      // "String?" means optional String
color = dict[0]         // Legal
print(color)            // What does this print?
```

How do you make use of the value assigned to the `color` variable? Enter the preceding code into the playground and you'll see that what's printed is not `"Red"` but `Optional("Red")`. The dictionary access doesn't return the actual value; it returns the value "wrapped" as an optional. To get the string value, you need to "unwrap" the optional using the `!` operator, like this:

```
let actualColor = color!    // "color!" means unwrap the optional
```

The inferred type of `actualColor` is `String` and the value that gets assigned to it is Red. It follows from this that whenever you retrieve a value from a dictionary, it's going to be of optional type, and you have to unwrap it to get the value that you want. But remember, I said that `nil` references are dangerous; in Swift that translates as unwrapping optionals can be dangerous. Change your playground code to this:

```
let dict = [0: "Red", 1: "Green", 2: "Blue"]
let color = dict[4]
let actualColor = color!
```

Swift correctly infers that the type of `color` is `String?`, but when you unwrap the result of the dictionary access to assign the value to `actualColor`, you get an error. In the playground, this error is just reported to you; in an application, it would cause a crash. Why did this happen? Well, there is no entry in the dictionary with key 4, so the `color` variable was assigned the value `nil`. If you try to unwrap `nil`, you crash. You're probably thinking that this is no improvement on what happens in other languages, but that's not true. First, the fact that `color` is of optional type tells you that you must expect that it could be `nil`—and the converse (which is equally valuable). Second, Swift gives you a way to handle the case where the optional value is `nil`. In fact, it gives you several ways.

The first thing you can do is check whether you got `nil` from the dictionary access and only unwrap the value if you didn't.

```
if color != nil {
    let actualColor = color!
}
```

This construction is so common that Swift has shorthand for it. Here's the second way to handle optional unwrapping:

```
if let actualColor = color {
    // Executed only if color was not nil
    print(actualColor)
}
```

The code block associated with the `if` statement is executed only if `color` is not `nil`, and the unwrapped value is assigned to the constant `actualColor`. You can even make `actualColor` a variable by changing `let` to `var`.

```swift
if var actualColor = color {
    // Executed only if color was not nil. actualColor can be modified
    print(actualColor)
}
```

In these examples, you defined the new variable actualColor to receive the unwrapped value, which requires you to give it a new name. Sometimes, it can seem artificial to have to use a different name for what is really the same thing and, in fact, it isn't necessary—we can actually give the new variable the same name as the optional variable that's being unwrapped, like this:

```swift
if var color = color {
    // Executed only if the value of the original color variable was not nil
    print(color)    // Refers to the new variable, holding the unwrapped value
}
```

It's important to realize that the new color variable is not related to the existing one and, indeed, it has a different type (String instead of String?). In the body of the if statement, the name color refers to the new, unwrapped variable, not the original one.

```swift
let dict = [0: "Red", 1: "Green", 2: "Blue"]
let color = dict[0]
if var color = color {
    // Executed only if color was not nil
    print(color)                        // "Red"
    color = "Green"                     // Reassigns the local variable
}                                       // New color variable is now out of scope
color                                   // Refers to the original value: "Red"
```

How about if you want to use a default value for a key that's not present in the dictionary? Swift gives you a convenient way to do that too. Here's the third way to handle optional unwrapping:

```swift
let dict = [0: "Red", 1: "Green", 2: "Blue"]
let color = dict[4]
let actualColor = color ?? "Blue"
```

The ?? operator (called the *coalescing operator*) unwraps its left operand, if it's not nil, and returns its value; otherwise, it returns its second operand. In this case, since color is nil, actualColor would be assigned the value Blue. Of course, you can contract the preceding code into two statements to make it slightly easier to read.

```swift
let dict = [0: "Red", 1: "Green", 2: "Blue"]
let actualColor = dict[4] ?? "Blue"
```

Dictionaries are not the only context in which optionals are used. If you look through the Swift API documentation, you'll see plenty of methods that return optional values. It's even possible for a type initializer to return an optional value. You've already seen an example of this; if you try to initialize an instance of an enumeration using an invalid raw value, the result is nil.

```
enum ResultType : String {
    case SUCCESS = "Success"
    case WARNING = "Warning"
    case ERROR = "Error"
}
let result = ResultType(rawValue: "Invalid")
```

The inferred type of result is ResultType?, and in this case, its value would be nil because there is no enumeration case that has the raw value Invalid.

You've learned that you have to be careful when unwrapping optionals, but sometimes that can be both inconvenient and unnecessary. As you'll see as you try the examples in this book, it's common to define a variable in a class that cannot be given a useful value while the class itself is being initialized, but that you know will have a valid value before your code needs to use it. In cases like that, you could define the variable as optional and unwrap it every time you use it. That keeps the compiler happy, but it means you have to keep adding ! operators everywhere or wrap the access in an if let construction, even though you know that the unwrapping will always succeed.

Fortunately, Swift lets you sidestep this. All you have to do is tell Swift that you want it to automatically unwrap the optional whenever you access it. Here's how you would do that in your dictionary example:

```
let dict = [0: "Red", 1: "Green", 2: "Blue"]

var color: String!      // Notice the !
color = dict[0]         // Assigns Optional("Red")
print(color)            // Automatically unwraps the optional
```

The key to this code is that the color variable was declared to be of type String!, not String?. Variables declared this way are called *implicitly unwrapped optionals*. The ! tells Swift that you want it to assume that the variable will always have a non-nil value whenever you use it and to go ahead and unwrap it. That means you can write print(color) instead of print(color!). Although you're not saving much here, if you had to access the result more than once, you would end up typing fewer characters by using this feature.

Beware, however. You've now told Swift that color will never be nil. If it turns out that it is nil when you try to use it, Swift will unwrap it, and your application will crash.

You can use optionals to address another issue that came up while discussing dictionaries: how to handle values obtained from an NSDictionary. Let's set the problem up by creating a Foundation dictionary with some initial values.

```
let d = NSDictionary(objects: ["Red", "Green", "Blue"], forKeys: [0 as NSCopying, 1 as
NSCopying, 2 as NSCopying])
```

This code initializes an NSDictionary with a mapping from Ints to Strings. In reality, of course, you wouldn't create an NSDictionary and cast it like this; you would just create a Swift dictionary. But suppose you got the dictionary from a call to a Foundation method—perhaps it was populated from the content of a file. As long as the dictionary really does map Ints to Strings, this code works fine, and you can access its content in the usual way:

```
let color = d[1]     // Gets an optional, wrapping "Green"
```

Note, however, that Swift doesn't really know the type of the value that it got from the dictionary; it infers AnyObject?, which is an optional wrapping some kind of object. You can do better by explicitly casting the result to the correct type.

```
let color = d[1] as! String
```

But what if you got the type of the dictionary wrong? Maybe what you've actually got is a [Int: Int]. To see what happens, change the types of the keys in the first line from numbers to strings, like this:

```
let d = NSDictionary(objects: [ 0, 1, 2], forKeys: [0 as NSCopying, 1 as NSCopying, 2 as
NSCopying])
let value = d[1] as! String
```

This code crashes when casting the value obtained from the dictionary to String. That's a little drastic. You really want to be able to detect this condition and take some corrective action instead of crashing. You can do that by using the as? operator instead of as. The as? operator returns an optional: if its first operand is not of the type given by its second operand, it returns nil instead of crashing. So now you can do something like this:

```
let d = NSDictionary(objects: [ 0, 1, 2], forKeys: [0 as NSCopying, 1 as NSCopying, 2 as
NSCopying])
if let value = d[1] as? String {  // as? returns nil if d is not of type String?
    print("OK")                    // As expected - use value as normal
} else {
    print("Incorrect types")      // Executed if d is not of type [Int: String]
}
```

There is another way to achieve the same effect. You can use the is keyword to check whether the dictionary is of the expected type before using it.

```
if d is [Int: String] {   // Evaluate to true if d maps Ints to Strings
    print("Is [Int: String]")
} else {
    print("Incorrect types")
}
```

You've probably noticed that you use both the as and as! operators when casting. What's the difference? Roughly speaking, you use as when the cast is guaranteed to work and as! when it's not—the ! expresses the fact that you are forcing the compiler to accept code that it would otherwise report an error for, such as when downcasting. Here's an example of a safe cast, where you can use as:

```
let s = "Fred"
let n = s as NSString
```

The inferred type of s is String and you're trying to cast it to NSString. Swift performs this bridging operation automatically, so you can use as in this case. Similarly, any upcast can be done with the as operator.

```
let label = UILabel()
let view = label as UIView
```

Here, label is of type UILabel, a UIKit class that represents a label, which is a user interface component that displays text. Every UIKit user interface component is a subclass of UIView, so you can freely upcast the label to its base class UIView with the as operator. The converse, however, is not true.

```
let view: UIView = UILabel()
let label = view as! UILabel    // Downcast requires !
```

This time, you created a UILabel, but you assigned it to a variable of type UIView. To cast this variable back to the type UILabel, you need to use the as! operator, because there is no guarantee that a variable of type UIView refers to a UILabel—it could be referencing another type of UIKit component, such as a UIButton. Here's another example that you have already seen:

```
let d = NSDictionary(objects: ["Red", "Green", "Blue"], forKeys: [0 as NSCopying, 1 as
NSCopying, 2 as NSCopying])
let color = d[1] as! String
```

As you saw earlier, when you recover a value from an NSDictionary, its type is inferred to be AnyObject?, which could refer to any Swift object type. To cast the value to String, you need to use the as! operator.

That's enough about optionals for now. I'll have more to say about this topic when I discuss calling methods in the upcoming "Properties" and "Methods" sections.

Control Statements

You've seen Swift's data types and how you can initialize them and perform operations on them. Now let's look at Swift's control statements. Swift supports all of the control statements you find in most other languages and adds some interesting new features to some of them.

The if Statement

Swift's if statement works just like it does in most other languages: you test a Boolean condition and execute some code only if it evaluates to true. You can optionally include an else block that executes if the condition is false. Here's an example:

```
let random = arc4random_uniform(10)
if random < 5 {
    print("Hi")
} else {
    print("Ho")
}
```

The arc4random_uniform() function returns a random integer between 0 (inclusive) and its argument value (exclusive), so in this case any integer from 0 to 9. You test the returned value and print "Hi" if it's less than 5 but print "Ho" if it's not. Notice that Swift does not require you to put the test condition in parentheses, so either of these will work:

```
if random < 5 {  // Parentheses not required
}
if (random < 5) { // But can be used
}
```

By contrast to other languages, the code to be executed *must* be enclosed in braces, even if it's only a single line. That means that this code is not valid in Swift:

```
if random < 5
    print("Hi")        // Invalid: must be in braces
else
    print("Ho")        // Invalid: must be in braces
```

Swift also has the ternary operator ?:, which may be familiar to you and which you probably either love or hate. This operator evaluates the Boolean expression before the ? and executes either the statement between the ? and the : if the result is true or the statement after the : if the result is false. You can use it to write the preceding code like this:

```
let random = arc4random_uniform(10)
random < 5 ? print("Hi") : print("Ho")
```

In this case, you can shorten the code even more by observing that all you're doing is printing one string or the other and write this instead:

```
let random = arc4random_uniform(10)
print(random < 5 ? "Hi" : "Ho")
```

Depending on your point of view, either that's much clearer than the code you started with or it's impossible to read.

You've already seen that there is a special form of the if statement that simplifies the handling of optionals.

```
let dict = [0: "Red", 1: "Green", 2: "Blue"]
let color = dict[0]
if let color = color {
    // Executed only if color was not nil
    print(color)                            // "Red"
}
```

You can actually unwrap more than one optional in a single if let or if var statement.

```
let dict = [0: "Red", 1: "Green", 2: "Blue", 3: "Green", 4: "Yellow"]
let color1 = dict[Int(arc4random_uniform(6))]
let color2 = dict[Int(arc4random_uniform(6))]
if let color1 = color1, color2 = color2 {
    // Executed only if both colors were not nil
    print("color1: \(color1), color2: \(color2)")
}
```

This code generates a pair of random keys in the range 0 through 5 and uses them to get color strings from the dictionary. Since there is no entry with key 5, it's possible that either (or both) of the values that you get are nil. The compound if let statement lets you safely unwrap both values and executes its body only if both were not nil. You can also include a test condition by adding a where clause.

```
let dict = [0: "Red", 1: "Green", 2: "Blue", 3: "Green", 4: "Yellow"]
let color1 = dict[Int(arc4random_uniform(6))]
let color2 = dict[Int(arc4random_uniform(6))]
if let color1 = color1, color2 = color2 where color1 == color2 {
    // Executed only if both colors were the same
    print("color1: \(color1), color2: \(color2)")
}
```

You can even include a test before unwrapping the optionals.

```
let dict = [0: "Red", 1: "Green", 2: "Blue", 3: "Green", 4: "Yellow"]
let color1 = dict[Int(arc4random_uniform(6))]
let color2 = dict[Int(arc4random_uniform(6))]
if dict.count > 3, let color1 = color1, color2 = color2 where color1 == color2 {
    print("color1: \(color1), color2: \(color2)")
}
```

The for Statement

Swift used to contain two variants of the `for` statement. The first, very much like the one that will be familiar to anybody who has worked with a C-based language, has been deprecated in Swift 3 and is no longer valid.

```
for var i = 0; i < 10; i += 1 {
    print(i)
}
```

The current acceptable form allows you to iterate over a sequence of values, such as a range or a collection. This code produces the same result as the `for` loop shown earlier.

```
for i in 0..<10 {
    print(i)
}
```

Notice that you don't need to use `var` to introduce the variable when using this form. You can create and iterate over a more general range by using the `stride()` method. Here's an example that prints the even integers from 10 down to 0, inclusively:

```
for i in stride(from: 10, through: 0, by: -2) {
    print(i)
}
```

Looping over the elements of an array is very simple, and the intent of the code is more obvious than it would be with an indexed loop.

```
let strings = ["A", "B", "C"]
for string in strings {
    print(string)
}
```

The same construction also works for sets, although the iteration order is undefined since sets do not provide any ordering.

```
let strings = Set<String>(["A", "B", "C"])
for string in strings {
    print(string)
}
```

You can iterate over the keys of a dictionary by using its keys property. As with sets, the iteration order is undefined.

```
let d = [ 0: "Red", 1: "Green", 2: "Blue"]
for key in d.keys {
    print("\(key) -> \(d[key])")
}
```

You can do the same thing more directly by iterating the dictionary as a set of key-value pairs.

```
for (key, value) in d {
    print("\(key) -> \(value)")
}
```

Each key-value pair is returned as *tuple* with two elements, where the name key is linked to the first element of the tuple and the name value to the second. Refer to the *Swift Programming Language* book for further discussion of tuples.

The repeat and while Statements

The repeat and while statements are the same as the do and while statements in C, C++, Java, and Objective-C. They both execute a body of code until a condition is met; the difference is that the while statement tests the condition before each pass of the loop, whereas repeat tests it at the end of each pass.

```
var i = 10
while i > 0 {
    print(i)
    i -= 1
}

var j = 10
repeat {
    print(j)
    j -= 1
} while j > 0
```

The switch Statement

The Swift switch statement is very powerful. I don't have space here to talk about all of its features, but you should definitely read about it in more detail in Apple's *Swift Programming Language* book. I'll illustrate just the most important features with a few examples.

You can use the switch statement to select a code path based on one of several possible values of a variable or expression. For example, this code prints something different based on the value of the value variable:

```
let value = 11
switch value {
case 2, 3, 5, 7, 11, 13, 17, 19:
    print("Count is prime and less than 20")
```

```
case 20...30:
    print("Count is between 20 and 30")

default:
    print("Greater than 30")
}
```

There are several points to note about this code. First, a case can have multiple possible values, separated by commas. The case is executed if the switch expression has any of the listed values. Second, the case value can be a range. In fact, the switch statement is capable of some very powerful pattern matching, the details of which are covered in Apple's documentation. Third, control does not pass from one case into another, as it does in most other languages. That means that the preceding example will execute only one case and print only once; it is not necessary to include a break statement between cases in a switch. If you really want to continue execution from one case into the following case, you can do so by adding a fallthrough statement at the end of the first case.

The case list must be exhaustive: if the default case had not been included in the preceding code, the compiler would have flagged an error. Furthermore, every case must have at least one line of executable code. That means that the following code is not legal (and is also misleading):

```
switch (value) {
case 2:
case 3:  // Illegal - previous case is empty.
    print("Value is 2 or 3")
default:
    print("Value is neither 2 nor 3")
}
```

The correct way to write that code is to include both 2 and 3 in the same case.

```
switch (value) {
case 2, 3:   // Correct: catches value 2 and value 3
    print("Value is 2 or 3")
default:
    print("Value is neither 2 nor 3")
}
```

Alternatively, you can use fallthrough.

```
switch (value) {
case 2: fallthrough
case 3:  // Illegal - previous case is empty.
    print("Value is 2 or 3")
default:
    print("Value is neither 2 nor 3")
}
```

The `switch` expression does not have to be numeric. Here's an example that switches based on the value of a string:

```
let s = "Hello"
switch s {
case "Hello":
    print("Hello to you, too")

case "Goodbye":
    print("See you tomorrow")

default:
    print("I don't understand")
}
```

The next example uses the `Status` enumeration that defined earlier and shows how to get access to the associated value of an enumeration case that has one:

```
enum Status {
    case OK
    case ERROR(String)
}
let result = Status.ERROR("Network connection rejected")
switch (result) {
case .OK:
    print("Success!")

case .ERROR(let message):
    print("Ooops: \(message)")
}
```

Since the compiler knows that the type of the `switch` expression is `Status`, there is no need to fully qualify the case values; you can say case `.OK` instead of case `Status.OK`. The compiler also knows that the enumeration has only two possible values, and since both of those values are listed as cases, there is no need to add a default case. Notice the form of the `.ERROR` case; the `.ERROR(let message)` causes the compiler to extract the associated value of the `ERROR` and assign it to a constant called `message`, which is valid only in the scope of the case itself. If the enumeration has more than one associated value, you can get all of the values by including one `let` statement for each, separated by commas.

Functions and Closures

Unlike many other languages, Swift uses a keyword (`func`) to denote a function. To define a function, you need to give its name, its argument list, and its return type. This function calculates and returns the area of a rectangle given the lengths of its sides.

```
func areaOfRectangle(width: Double, height: Double) -> Double {
    return width * height
}
```

The function arguments are enclosed in parentheses, separated by commas, and written in the same way as variable declarations—that is, name followed by type. Unlike variable declarations, though, specifying the type of an argument is not optional. If the function has no arguments, the parentheses must be empty.

```swift
func hello() {
    print("Hello, world")
}
```

If the function returns a value, the type of that value must be given, preceded by the symbol ->. In this case, the arguments are both Doubles, as is the return value. If the function doesn't return anything, you can either omit the return type (as shown in the definition of the preceding hello() function) or write it as -> Void. Here's a function that either does nothing or prints its argument, depending on the value of the debug variable, and returns nothing:

```swift
let debug = true    // Enables debugging
func debugPrint(value: Double) {
    if debug {
        print(value)
    }
}
```

The definition of this function could also be written slightly more verbosely, like this:

```swift
func debugPrint(value: Double) -> Void {  // "-> Void" is optional
```

To invoke a function, refer to it by name and supply the appropriate arguments.

```swift
let area = areaOfRectangle(width: 20, height: 10)
```

Prior to Swift 3, it was acceptable to omit the name of the first argument as follows:

```swift
let area = areaOfRectangle(20, height: 10)    // no longer valid as of Swift 3
```

Another feature of Swift is that function arguments can have two names—an *external* name (the name that's used by the function's caller) and an *internal* name (the name that's used in the body of the function). It's always optional to supply an external name. If you don't supply one, the external name is taken to be the same as the internal one. Here's another way to write the areaOfRectangle() function, this time with both external and internal argument names:

```swift
func areaOfRectangle(width w: Double, height h: Double) -> Double {
    return w * h
}
```

When you specify both an external and an internal argument name, the external name comes first; if you supply only one argument name, then it is the internal argument name, and there is no external name. Notice that the body of the code uses the internal argument names (w and h), not the external names (width and height). So, why would you want to use external argument names? This feature is partly motivated by the naming conventions used for Objective-C methods, which need to be mapped by the compiler so that they can be called from Swift. You'll say more about that when you examine Swift classes later in this appendix. In this example, the only benefit of adding external names is that if they exist, the caller is required to supply them when invoking the function, which makes the code more readable.

```
let area = areaOfRectangle(width: 20, height: 10)    // Now "width" and "height" are
mandatory
```

You can provide a default value for a function argument by including it in the argument list. The following function breaks an input string into components separated by the given delimiter and defaults the delimiter to a space if it's not given:

```
func separateWords(str: String, delimiter: String = " ") -> [String] {
    return str.components(separatedBy: delimiter)
}
```

You can call this function without supplying an explicit delimiter, in which case a single space is used as the delimiter.

```
let result = separateWords(str:"One small step")
print(result)    // [One, small, step]
```

Swift automatically supplies an external name for an argument with a default value, making it the same as the internal name (although you can override this by supplying your own external name). That means the argument name must be used if its value is not defaulted.

```
let result = separateWords(str: "One. Two. Three", delimiter: ". ")  // "delimiter" is
required
print(result)    // [One, Two, Three]
```

If you really don't want to force the user to include the argument name, you can write the external name as _, although this is not recommended because it reduces readability.

```
func separateWords(str: String, _ delimiter: String = " ") -> [String] {
    return str.components(separatedBy: delimiter)
}
let result = separateWords(str: "One. Two. Three",  ". ")  // "delimiter" is required
print(result)     // [One, Two, Three]
```

You can use this to change the areaOfRectangle() function so that neither argument name needs to be supplied.

```
func areaOfRectangle(_ w: Double, _ h: Double) -> Double {
    return w * h
}
let area = areaOfRectangle(20, 10)
```

Notice that it is necessary to precede the first argument with an _ if you want to use an unnamed argument first.

```
func areaOfRectangle(_ w: Double, _ h: Double) -> Double {
    return w * h
}
```

In Swift, functions are types, so you can create a variable of function type, assign a reference to a function to it, and use that variable to call the function. Similarly, you can pass a function as an argument to another function or return a function from a function.

524

To declare a function variable, you specify the function's signature as the type of the variable. The signature consists of the function's argument types in parentheses (unless there is just one argument, when the parentheses can be omitted), followed by ->, followed by the return type. The following code creates a variable that can hold a reference to a function that performs an unspecified operation on a Double and returns another Double:

```
var operation: (Double) -> Double
```

For one function arguments, previous versions of Swift allowed omitting the parentheses, but this is no longer valid.

```
var operation: Double -> Double                    // No Longer valid as of Swift 3
```

You can write functions that operate on a Double and assign any of those functions to the variable. Here's an example:

```
func doubleMe(number: Double) -> Double {
    return 2 * number
}
operation = doubleMe
```

Now you can invoke the function using the function variable, supplying the argument as if you were directly calling the function.

```
operation(2)     // Result is 4
```

You can make the operation variable refer to a different function and perform a different operation using the same call expression.

```
func quadrupleMe(number: Double) -> Double {
    return 4 * number
}
operation = quadrupleMe
operation(2)     // Result is 8
```

The ability to pass functions around in this way is very powerful. There are several Swift methods that accept function arguments. One of them is the sort(by:) method, which sorts an ordered collection based on an ordering provided by a function that's passed as its argument. The ordering function is required to accept two arguments, which are elements of the collection being sorted, and return the Bool value true if the first argument is less than the second and false otherwise. Here's an example of such a function that compares two Ints:

```
func compareInts(_ first: Int, _ second: Int) -> Bool {
    return first < second
}
```

Now you can create an array of Ints and use sort() and the compareInts() function to sort them. To do so, pass the compareInts() function an argument to sort(), like this:

```
var values = [12, 3, 5, -4, 16, 18]
let sortedValues = values.sort(by: compareInts)
sortedValues     // Result: [-4, 3, 5, 12, 16, 18]
```

525

This probably looks ridiculously complex at first, so let's break it down. The comparison function must be enclosed in braces. After that, the first part of the definition is just its argument list and its return type, followed by the keyword in, which separates the arguments and return type from the function body.

```
{(first: Int, second: Int) -> Bool in
```

Next, you have the body of the function, which is the same as the original code from the compareInts() function, followed by the closing brace and the parenthesis that closes the argument list of the sorted() method.

```
    return first < second
})
```

There's a name for this kind of anonymous function that's written in place: it's called a *closure*. Once you're used to how it works, you'll probably find yourself making a lot of use of closures. Other languages also support this capability such as in Python where it would be called a *lambda*.

If a closure is the final argument of a function, Swift lets you clean the syntax up a bit by taking it outside the function's argument list, like this:

```
let sortedValues = values.sorted() {    // The closure is now outside the parentheses
        (first: Int, second: Int) -> Bool in
            return first < second
    }
```

That's still quite a lot of code. Fortunately, you can clean it up a little more. Swift can infer that the closure requires two Int arguments and must return a Bool. It knows this because of the way in which the sort() method is defined in the standard library. Because of this, you can omit the argument types, the parentheses around the argument names, and the return type, leaving you with just this:

```
let sortedValues = values.sorted() {
    first, second in    // Swift infers the argument types and return type!
    return first < second
}
```

That's much better. But you can take it one step further by omitting the argument names too. Swift knows there are two arguments, and if you don't name them, it calls them $0 and $1 (and $2, $3, etc., if there were more). That lets you reduce your closure to just one line of code.

```
let sortedValues = values.sorted() { return $0 < $1 }
```

That's not quite the end. Swift also lets you drop the return keyword. So, finally you get to this:

```
let sortedValues = values.sorted() { $0 < $1 }
```

I think you'll agree, that's a lot more expressive than what you started with. Or at least it is once you're used to reading the somewhat terse syntax. Experiment with this in the playground, try out some variations, and see what works and what doesn't.

If you're wondering why closures are called closures, it's because they "close over" variables that are in their scope when they are created. That means that they can read and even write those variables. It's difficult to appreciate how useful this is without the correct context. You'll see examples in the rest of the book that illustrate the point. For now, let's just demonstrate that you can write a closure that uses a value that's defined outside of that closure. Take a look at the following code:

```
func getInterestCalculator(rate: Double) -> (Double, Int) -> Double {
    let calculator = {
        (amount: Double, years: Int) -> Double in rate * amount * Double(years)
    }
    return calculator
}
```

The function signature tells you that the getInterestCalculator() function requires an argument of type Double and returns a function. The returned function requires two arguments—a Double and an Int— and it returns a Double.

What you're actually doing here is passing an interest rate to the getInterestCalculator() function, and it's going to return to you a function that will calculate simple interest at that given rate.

Inside the getInterestCalculator() function, you create a closure and assign it to the calculator variable.

```
let calculator = {
        (amount: Double, years: Int) -> Double in rate * amount * Double(years)
    }
```

As you can see, the closure function requires the amount as a Double, and the period over which interest will be calculated in years as an Int. The most important point to notice is that the body of the closure uses the rate argument that was passed to the getInterestCalculator() function. Finally, the closure is returned to the caller of getInterestCalculator().

Now let's write some code that calls this function and uses the function that it returns.

```
let calculator = getInterestCalculator(rate: 0.05)
calculator(100.0, 2)    // Result is 10: interest at 5% on $100 over 2 years.
```

The returned function is assigned to the calculator constant, and then it's invoked to compute the interest on $100 over two years, at an interest rate of 5 percent. So, what's so interesting about this? Well, think about what is happening here. The returned closure is referencing the value of the rate argument of the getInterestCalculator() function, but it's doing so after that function has returned. How is that possible? It works because the closure *captures* the function argument by referencing it. When a variable is captured by a closure as the closure is being created, a copy of its value is taken, and that copy is used when the closure is executed. That's how the interest rate value that was passed as an argument to getInterestCalculator() is made available to the closure after the argument itself no longer exists.

Error Handling

If you scan through the Xcode documentation page for the NSString class, you'll come across several methods declarations that include a throws clause, like this one:

```
init(contentsOfFile path: String, encoding enc: UInt) throws
```

Whenever you see a throws clause, it means that the method reports an error that you can choose to ignore or to handle by catching it. You'll first of all see how you might ignore it, and then you'll look at how to catch and handle the error. Let's try to ignore it by just pretending the throws clause is not there.

```
let s = String(contentsOfFile: "XX", encoding: String.Encoding.utf8)
```

If you type that into the playground, you'll see the "Call can throw but is not marked with 'try'" error. To make the compiler accept this call, you have to add a try clause. There are three variants of try, two of which allow you to ignore the error and a third that is used when you intend to catch it. Let's continue to ignore the potential error.

```
let s = try? String(contentsOfFile: "XX", encoding: String.Encoding.utf8)
```

That gets rid of the compilation error. Now the playground executes the statement and shows the result nil. When you use try?, you're converting the return type of the method that you're calling into an optional. Since this method is actually an initializer for the String class (which String actually gets from NSString), the return type is converted to String?, and that is the inferred type of the variable s. In this case, the value is nil because the file XX doesn't actually exist.

You can use a try? clause in an if statement to do something only if the file exists and its content was successfully loaded.

```
if let s = try? String(contentsOfFile: "XX", encoding: String.Encoding.utf8) {
    print("Content loaded")
} else {
    print("Failed to load contents of file")
}
```

If you're sure that the file you are trying to read exists and its content can be read, you can replace try? with try!, like this:

```
let s = try! String(contentsOfFile: "XX", encoding: String.Encoding.utf8)
```

Although this is legal syntax, it's not good practice because your application would crash if anything went wrong—you can see that by trying this statement in the playground.

Catching Errors

You've seen that if you use try? as part of an if let statement, you can find out whether the operation completed correctly, and you can take some different action if it wasn't. The try? statement implicitly tells you that an error occurred by returning a nil value, but there is no way to find out what that error was. To do that, you have to use the try statement and wrap it in a do-catch block, like this:

```
do {
    let s = try String(contentsOfFile: "XX", encoding: String.Encoding.utf8)
    print("Loaded content \(s)")
} catch {
    print(error)
}
```

The statements inside the do block are executed to completion or until one of them throws an error, at which point control transfers to the catch block. The init(contentsOfFile:encoding:) initializer throws a value of type NSError, which is the Foundation framework's generic error type. Inside the catch block, you can get the value of the error from the error variable, as shown in the preceding example.

Throwing an Error

Any function or method can throw an error, provided that it declares that it does so by including a throws clause in its definition. The thrown value can be any type that adopts the ErrorType protocol, as NSError does—in fact, if you check the inferred type of the error variable in the preceding example, you'll find that it is ErrorType. Errors thrown by methods in the Foundation framework (and other Apple frameworks) are of type NSError, but you are free to define custom error types in your own code. It's common to use an enumeration for this purpose because it can conveniently represent one or more error cases and even include additional information about the error.

As an example, let's write a function that calculates the length of the third side of a triangle given the lengths of the other two sides and the angle between them. You're going to insist that the values of the arguments that correspond to the lengths of the sides must both be positive and the angle must be between 0 and π radians. Let's start by writing the function without any error checking.

```
func calcThirdSide(_ side1: Double, side2: Double, angle: Double) -> Double {
    return sqrt(side1 * side1 + side2 * side2 - 2 * side1 * side2 * cos(angle))
}
```

You're using the cosine rule to calculate the length of the third side. To check that the implementation is correct, let's try it out on a right-angled triangle with sides of length 3 and 4.

```
let side3 = calcThirdSide(3, side2: 4, angle: Doule.pi /2)
print(side3)
```

Pythagoras's theorem tells you that the length of the third side in this case should be 5, and that's the result you'll see in the playground if you run this code. Now let's start adding error checking. You have two different types of condition that you need to check—the lengths of the sides and the value of the angle. This is a natural fit for an enumeration, so let's define one.

```
enum TriangleError : Error {
    case SideInvalid(reason: String)
    case AngleInvalid(reason: String)
}
```

Since you're going to throw instances of this enumeration, it is required to conform to Error. You defined cases for each of the types of error that you'll check to provide an error message, so both cases have an associated string value.

Before you can add error checking to your function, you have to tell the compiler that it might throw an error. To do that, you add the throws keyword to the function definition. This keyword must be placed after the function's argument list and before its return type (if it has one).

```
func calcThirdSide(_ side1: Double, side2: Double, angle: Double) throws  -> Double {
    return sqrt(side1 * side1 + side2 * side2 - 2 * side1 * side2 * cos(angle))
}
```

As soon as you add the throws keyword, the compiler starts complaining that the function call is not made in a try statement. Let's fix that by adding some code to catch the error.

```
do {
    let side3 = try calcThirdSide( 3, side2: 4, angle: Doule.pi /2)
    print(side3)
```

```
} catch {
    print(error)
}
```

Now you can start adding error checks to the calcThirdSide(side1:side2:angle:) function. Modify the function definition to the following:

```
func calcThirdSide(_ side1: Double, side2: Double, angle: Double) throws  -> Double {
    if side1 <= 0 {
        throw TriangleError.SideInvalid(reason: "Side 1 must be >= 0, not \(side1)")
    }
    return sqrt(side1 * side1 + side2 * side2 - 2 * side1 * side2 * cos(angle))
}
```

The if statement tests whether the value of the side1 argument is zero or negative and, if so, uses the throw keyword to throw an instance of your TriangleError enumeration with an appropriate message. To test whether this works, change the value of the side1 argument in the test code from 3 to -1.

```
let side3 = try calcThirdSide(-1, side2: 4, angle: Doule.pi /2)
```

You should see the text SideInvalid("Side 1 must be >= 0, not -1.0") in the playground's results area, indicating that the correct error was thrown and caught.

Now let's add the other three error checks to the calcThirdSide(side1:side2:angle:) function.

```
func calcThirdSide(_ side1: Double, side2: Double, angle: Double) throws -> Double {
    if side1 <= 0 {
        throw TriangleError.SideInvalid(reason: "Side 1 must be >= 0, not \(side1)")
    }

    if side2 <= 0 {
        throw TriangleError.SideInvalid(reason: "Side 2 must be >= 0, not \(side2)")
    }

    if angle < 0 {
        throw TriangleError.AngleInvalid(reason: "Angle must be >= 0, not \(angle)")
    }

    if angle >= Doule.pi {
        throw TriangleError.AngleInvalid(reason: "Angle must be <= π, not \(angle)")
    }

    return sqrt(side1 * side1 + side2 * side2 - 2 * side1 * side2 * cos(angle))
}
```

Experiment with the arguments passed to the calcThirdSide(side1:side2:angle:) function to verify that these checks work.

The guard Statement

It's quite common to have argument checking code like this at the start of a function. Swift gives you another way to express these error tests—you can use the guard statement instead of an if statement. Here's how you would rewrite the calcThirdSide(side1:side2:angle:) function to use guard instead of if:

```swift
func calcThirdSide(_ side1: Double, side2: Double, angle: Double) throws  -> Double {
    guard side1 > 0 else {
        throw TriangleError.SideInvalid(reason: "Side 1 must be >= 0, not \(side1)")
    }

    guard side2 > 0 else {
        throw TriangleError.SideInvalid(reason: "Side 2 must be >= 0, not \(side2)")
    }

    guard angle >= 0 else {
        throw TriangleError.AngleInvalid(reason: "Angle must be >= 0, not \(angle)")
    }

    guard angle < Double.pi else {
        throw TriangleError.AngleInvalid(reason: "Angle must be <= &#x00F0;, not \(angle)")
    }

    return sqrt(side1 * side1 + side2 * side2 - 2 * side1 * side2 * cos(angle))
}
```

The body of the guard statement must be preceded by the keyword else and is executed only if the tested condition is not met. You can think of the meaning of guard as "unless this condition is met, execute the statement body." Because of that, the sense of test must be the opposite of what would be tested by an if statement. For example, the condition tested by the first if statement was side1 <=0, whereas the condition for the equivalent guard statement is side1 > 0. This might seem strange at first, but once you get used to it, you'll see that the guard version of the code is clearer because you're stating the conditions that need to be met in order for execution to proceed, not the inverse condition.

The general form of the guard statement is as follows:

```swift
guard expression else {
    // Guard body statements
    // Transfer of control outside the scope containing the guard
}

// Control must not reach here if the guard body was executed
```

The guard body can include as many separate statements as required, provided that one condition is met—at the end of the statement body, control must transfer outside the immediate scope of the guard statement. In the preceding example, the guard statement is in the scope of the calcThirdSide(side1:side2:angle:) function, so control must be transferred out of that function at the end of the guard block. Here, you achieve that by throwing an error, but you could also return from the function. If the guard block is contained in a for statement, the immediate scope is the for statement, and you can use either a continue statement or a break statement to meet the requirements of the guard statement. The same applies to repeat and while statements. If you allow the flow of control to continue from the end of the guard block into the statements that follow it, you will get a compiler error.

More on Error Catching

So far, you've used a single, generic catch block to capture and print any error that's thrown from the calc ThirdSide(side1:side2:angle:) function. More generally, a do-catch statement can have multiple catch blocks, and each catch block can have an expression that is matched against the error that is thrown to select the block that should be executed. If none of the catch block expressions matches the error, then the block without an expression is used; if there is no such block, the error is thrown to the caller of the function or method containing the do-catch statement, and that function or method must declare that this may happen by including a throws clause in its definition. Let's look at some examples.

Change the do-catch block in the playground as follows:

```swift
do {
    let side3 = try calcThirdSide( -1, side2: 4, angle: Doule.pi /2)
    print(side3)
} catch let e as TriangleError {
    print(e)
}
```

Here, you've added an expression to the catch block that causes it to catch only errors that are of type TriangleError. The error itself is assigned to the variable e, which is in scope only in the catch block. Since the calcThirdSide(side1:side2:angle:) function only throws errors of this type, you don't need any further catch blocks. If you wanted to handle specific types of error differently, you simply add more cases. Here's an example:

```swift
do {
    let side3 = try calcThirdSide( -1, side2: 4, angle: Doule.pi /2)
    print(side3)
} catch TriangleError.SideInvalid(let reason) {
    print("Caught invalid side: \(reason)")
} catch {
    print("Caught \(error)")
}
```

The first catch block handles the SideInvalid case and assigns the error message from the enumeration value to the variable reason so that it can be used in the body of the catch block. The second catch block has no expression, so it captures any error that's not handled by earlier blocks. In this case, that corresponds to the AngleInvalid case. When a catchall block like this last one is present, it must be the final catch block, so this is invalid:

```swift
do {
    let side3 = try calcThirdSide(-1, side2: 4, angle: Doule.pi /2)
    print(side3)
} catch {  // Invalid - this must be the last catch block
    print("Caught: \(error)")
} catch TriangleError.SideInvalid(let reason) {
    print("Caught invalid side: \(reason)")
}
```

To handle each case individually, just give each one its own `catch` block.

```
do {
    let side3 = try calcThirdSide(-1, side2: 4, angle: - Doule.pi /2)
    print(side3)
} catch TriangleError.AngleInvalid(let reason) {
    print("Caught invalid angle: \(reason)")
} catch TriangleError.SideInvalid(let reason) {
    print("Caught invalid side: \(reason)")
}
```

Since you have explicitly handled both of the possible errors that the `calcThirdSide(side1:side2:ang le:)` function may throw, there is no need to add a catchall `catch` block.

Classes and Structures

Swift provides two different ways to create custom types—classes and structures. Both may contain properties, initializers, and methods. A *property* is a variable defined within the body of a class or structure, a *method* is a function defined in a class or structure, and an *initializer* is a special type of method that is used to establish the initial state of a class or structure instance while it's being created.

Structures

Here's an example of a structure that represents a circle with a given radius:

```
struct CircleStruct {
    var radius: Double

    func getArea() -> Double {
        return Double.pi * radius * radius
    }

    func getCircumference() -> Double {
        return 2 * Double.pi * radius
    }
}
```

The circle has one property that holds its radius and two methods that return its area and circumference.

Swift automatically creates an initializer for a structure that assigns values to its properties using the initializer's arguments. Here's how you would use that initializer to create an instance of `CircleStruct`:

```
var circleStruct = CircleStruct(radius: 10)
```

The synthesized initializer for a structure has one argument for each property. The argument names are the same as the property names, and they appear in the order that the properties are defined in the structure itself. Notice that the argument names are required when using the initializer because the initializer arguments have both external and internal names.

Once you have created a structure instance, you can directly read and modify the properties using the property name. This code reads the radius of the circle and then doubles it.

```
var circleStruct = CircleStruct(radius: 10)
let r = circleStruct.radius          // Reads the radius property - result = 10
circleStruct.radius = 2 * r          // Doubles the radius.
```

Structures are value objects, so the following code creates a copy of the original CircleStruct object and assigns it to the newCircleStruct variable. Changes made to the radius property using the newCircleStruct variable do not affect the original, and vice versa.

```
var newCircleStruct = circleStruct   // Copies the structure
newCircleStruct.radius = 32           // Affects only the copy
newCircleStruct.radius                // New value: 32
circleStruct.radius                   // Old value: 20
```

If you assign a structure to a constant using a let statement, all of its properties become read-only.

```
let constantCircleStruct = CircleStruct(radius: 5)
constantCircleStruct.radius = 10     // Invalid: constantCircleStruct is constant
```

Swift requires that all properties of a structure (or class) be initialized before the initializer finishes execution. You can choose to set property values in the initializer itself or as part of the property definition. Here's a slightly different implementation of the CircleStruct structure that initializes the radius to a default value of 1 when it's defined:

```
struct CircleStruct {
    var radius: Double = 1

    init() {
    }

    init(radius: Double) {
        self.radius = radius
    }

    func getArea() -> Double {
        return Doule.pi * radius * radius
    }

    func getCircumference() -> Double {
        return 2 * Doule.pi * radius
    }
}
```

Notice that the structure now has two initializers (initializers are always called init): one that takes no arguments and another that takes the radius as its argument. The first initializer lets you create an instance of the structure using the default radius set by the definition of the radius property.

```
let circleStructDefault = CircleStruct()
circleStructDefault.radius      // Result is 1
```

The second initializer assigns its argument to the radius property.

```
init(radius: Double) {
    self.radius = radius
}
```

Before you added the zero-argument initializer, you didn't need to write this one because Swift created it for you; but it does not do that if you add initializers of your own. Notice that the assignment to the property uses the form self.radius. The self variable represents the instance of the structure that's being initialized. In method calls, it represents the instance on which the method was invoked. Usually, you don't need to qualify the property access with self, but in this case you need to do so because the initializer argument has the same name as the property.

As noted, by default, Swift requires you to use the initializer argument name when creating a structure instance (as you'll soon see, the same applies to classes). When you define your own initializer, you can opt out of this by using an underscore (_) as an external argument name, as shown by the following modification to the second CircleStruct initializer:

```
init(_ radius: Double) {
    self.radius = radius
}
```

With this change, you must use the initializer like this:

```
var circleStruct = CircleStruct(10)    // Argument name must be omitted
```

The implementations of the getArea() and getCircumference() methods don't introduce anything new; they just perform a simple calculation using the value of the radius property. Notice that here you don't use self when reading the property value, although you could. This version of the getArea() method is equivalent to the one shown previously:

```
func getArea() -> Double {
    return Doule.pi * self.radius * self.radius   // Explicit use of "self" - not recommended
}
```

You invoke these methods just like any other function, except that an instance of the structure is required.

```
let circleStructDefault = CircleStruct()
circleStructDefault.getArea()           // Returns the area
circleStructDefault.getCircumference()  // Returns the circumference
```

Classes

Creating a class is syntactically similar to creating a structure, but there are a few differences to be aware of. Here's an implementation of a circle as a class:

```
class CircleClass {
    var radius: Double = 1

    init() {
    }
```

```
    init(radius: Double) {
        self.radius = radius
    }

    func getArea() -> Double {
        return M Double.pi * radius * radius
    }

    func getCircumference() -> Double {
        return 2 * Double.pi * radius
    }
}
```

The only syntactic difference between this and the structure version is the keyword class instead of struct, but there are some differences in the way that Swift handles class and structure initializers.

- Swift does not create an initializer that sets the initial values of the properties of a class. Instead, it creates an empty init() initializer.

- As with structures, if you add initializers of your own, you no longer get the free init() initializer.

In the case of CircleClass, the presence of the init(radius: Double) initializer means that Swift would not generate the init() version, so you had to add it yourself.

You can use either initializer to create a CircleClass instance, depending on whether you want to set the radius.

```
var circleClassDefault = CircleClass()      // Sets the default radius
circleClassDefault.radius                   // Result is 1
var circleClass = CircleClass(radius: 10)   // Explicitly set the radius
circleClass.radius                          // Result is 10
```

Classes are not value objects, so assigning a class instance to a variable or passing one to a function does not create a copy, as the following code demonstrates:

```
var newCircleClass = circleClass     // Does not copy
newCircleClass.radius = 32           // Only one copy, so this change is visible...
newCircleClass.radius                // ...through both references. Result is 32
circleClass.radius                   // Result is 32
```

Properties

The radius property of your circle is called a *stored property* because the value is stored with the class or structure. It's also possible to have *computed properties*, which don't have storage of their own. Instead, you calculate the value of the property every time it's read. The area and circumference of a circle could be regarded as properties, so you could reasonably reimplement them as computed properties. Here's how you would do that for CircleClass (the implementation would be the same for CircleStruct):

```
class CircleClass {
    var radius: Double = 1
    var area: Double {
        return Double.pi * radius * radius
    }
```

```
    var circumference: Double {
        return 2 * Double.pi * radius
    }

    init() {
    }

    init(radius: Double) {
        self.radius = radius
    }
}
```

The syntax is very simple: you state the property name and its type (which is mandatory for a computed property), followed by a code block containing the code required to calculate the property value. With area and circumference as properties, you can get their values with slightly fewer keystrokes than when using a method.

```
let circleClass = CircleClass(radius: 10)
circleClass.area
circleClass.circumference
```

You are actually using a shortcut in the implementation of these properties; the full form of the area property, for example, would be as follows:

```
var area: Double {
    get {
        return Double.pi * radius * radius
    }
}
```

The difference is the get keyword and the additional set of braces around the code that calculates the property value. Since area is a read-only property, you haven't implemented a setter, so Swift allows you to omit this extra boilerplate.

It's perfectly possible to regard area as a settable property. If a new area is set, you can calculate and store the corresponding radius—and similarly for circumference. To make a property settable, you need to add a set block and put back the get boilerplate if you omitted it. Here's how you would implement the setters for area and circumference:

```
var area: Double {
    get {
        return Double.pi * radius * radius
    }

    set {
        radius = sqrt(newValue/Doule.pi)
    }
}

var circumference: Double {
    get {
        return 2 * Double.pi * radius
    }
```

```
    set {
        radius = newValue/(2 * DOUBLE.PI)
    }
}
```

In the implementation of the setter, you get the value that's being set from a variable called newValue. If you don't like that name, you can choose one of your own by declaring it after the set keyword.

```
set (value) {
    radius = value/(2 * Double.pi)
}
```

Now that these properties are settable, you can use them to find out the radius for a given circumference or area.

```
circleClass.area = 314
circleClass.radius          // Radius for area 314 is 9.997
circleClass.circumference = 100
circleClass.radius          // Radius for circumference 100 is 15.915
```

Swift supports adding code to observe changes to a stored (but not computed) property. To do so, you add a willSet or didSet block (or both) to the property definition. These blocks are called whenever the property value is being set, even if the new and old values are the same, except when the property is being initialized. The willSet block is called before the new value is assigned to the property, and didSet is called after the assignment. A typical use for a property observer is to ensure that the property can be assigned only valid values. Here's how you would modify the radius property in CircleClass to make sure that only non-negative values can be assigned:

```
class CircleClass {
    var radius: Double = 1 {
        didSet {
            if (radius < 0) {
                radius = oldValue
            }
        }
    }
}
```

When the didSet block is called, the new value has already been stored in the radius property. If it's negative, you set it back to the previous value, which you can get from the oldValue variable. As with property setter blocks, you can change the name of this variable if you want. Setting the property value from within the didSet block does not cause the property observer blocks to be invoked again. With this change, an attempt to set a negative radius is ignored.

```
circleClass.radius = 10     // Valid: radius set to 10
circleClass.radius          // Result: 10.0
circleClass.radius = -1     // Invalid - trapped by didSet block
circleClass.radius          // Result: 10.0
```

Methods

As you have seen, classes and structures can both have methods. Methods behave just like functions, except that they have access to an implicitly defined value called self that refers to the instance of the class or structure on which the method was invoked. Methods defined on a class can change the value of its properties, but by default, structure methods cannot. Let's see how this works adding a new method to CircleClass called adjustRadiusByAmount(_:times:), which adjusts the circle's radius by a given amount a specified number of times. Here's the method definition:

```
func adjustRadiusByAmount(amount: Double, times: Int = 1) {
    radius += amount * Double(times)
}
```

With this definition, you call this method as follows:

```
var circleClass = CircleClass(radius: 10)
circleClass.radius                          // Result: 10
circleClass.adjustRadiusByAmount(5, times: 3)
circleClass.radius                          // Result = 10 + 3 * 5 = 25
circleClass.adjustRadiusByAmount(5)         // "times" is defaulted to 1
circleClass.radius                          // Result = 30
```

Now try to add the same method to the CircleStruct structure.

```
struct CircleStruct {
    var radius: Double = 1

    init() {
    }

    init(radius: Double) {
        self.radius = radius
    }

    func getArea() -> Double {
        return Doule.pi * radius * radius
    }

    func getCircumference() -> Double {
        return 2 * Doule.pi * radius
    }

    func adjustRadiusByAmount(amount: Double, times: Int = 1) {
        radius += amount * Double(times)
    }
}
```

Unfortunately, this does not compile. By default, structure methods cannot mutate the structure's state. This is because you are encouraged to make value objects immutable, if possible. If you really want to add a mutating method like this one, you have to add the mutating keyword to its definition.

```
mutating func adjustRadiusBy(amount: Double, times: Int = 1) {
    radius += amount * Double(times)
}
```

Optional Chaining

How do you call a method or access a property of an optional? You first have to unwrap the optional. You need to be very careful when doing this because, as you already know, unwrapping an optional that is nil causes your application to crash. Suppose you have the following variable and you want to get the radius of whatever circle it's pointing at:

```
var optionalCircle: CircleClass?
```

Since the value of optionalCircle could be nil (and, in this case, it is), you can't just do this:

```
optionalCircle!.radius        // CRASH!
```

Instead, you need to check whether optionalCircle is nil before unwrapping it, like this:

```
if optionalCircle != nil {
    optionalCircle!.radius
}
```

This is safe, but it's really too much code. There's a better way, which is called *optional chaining*. Instead of using ! to unwrap the optional, you use ?. Using optional chaining, you can go back to writing just one line of code.

```
var optionalCircle: CircleClass?
var radius = optionalCircle?.radius
```

When optional chaining is in use, the property access occurs only if optionalCircle is not nil, and since there may be no value to assign to the radius variable, Swift infers its type as Double? instead of Double. It's common to use this technique in conjunction with the if let construction, like this:

```
var optionalCircle: CircleClass?
if let radius = optionalCircle?.radius {
    print("radius = \(radius)")
}
```

The real value of this comes if you have objects embedded in other objects, where the references to the embedded objects are optionals. To follow the chain of objects to the value that you want, you would have had to make a nil check for each reference. With optional chaining, you can let Swift do the hard work for you by using an expression like this:

```
outerObject?.innerObject?.property
```

Optional chaining also works for method calls:

```
var optionalCircle: CircleClass?
optionalCircle?.adjustRadiusByAmount(5, times: 3)
```

The method call happens only if optionalCircle is not nil; if it is nil, the call is skipped.

Subclassing and Inheritance

So you've got a fairly useful class that represents a circle. What if you wanted to add something new to it? For example, let's say you want to add a color property. Well, you would just add the property to the existing class definition and you're done. But what if you don't own the CircleClass class? Maybe it's part of a third-party framework. You can't modify the source code. In many cases like this, you might be able to add an *extension* to the class. Extensions let you add functionality to any class—even classes that you don't own, and sometimes that's the right thing to do. In this case, though, it's not the right thing because you want to add a stored property. Instead, you'll extend the class by creating a *subclass*. Subclasses inherit the properties and methods of the class from which they are derived (their *base class*). If what the subclass provides isn't quite right, you can override its behavior, keeping what you want and changing what you need to (subject, of course, to the base class being properly designed).

In this section, you're going to extend CircleClass and create ColoredCircleClass. ColoredCircleClass will have the same features as CircleClass—it will still have the radius, area, and circumference properties—and it will have a new color property. Before you get started on that, let's add a few more things to CircleClass so that you can see how to override them in a derived class.

Clear everything from your playground and enter the following modified definition of CircleClass:

```swift
class CircleClass {
    var radius: Double = 1 {
        didSet {
            if (radius < 0) {
                radius = oldValue
            }
        }
    }
    var area: Double {
        get {
            return M Doule.pi * radius * radius
        }

        set {
            radius = sqrt(newValue/ Doule.pi)
        }
    }

    var circumference: Double {
        get {
            return 2 * Doule.pi * radius
        }
        set {
            radius = newValue/(2 * Doule.pi)
        }
    }

    var description: String {
        return "Circle of radius \(radius)"
    }

    required init() {
    }
```

```
    init(radius: Double) {
        self.radius = radius
    }

    func adjustRadiusByAmount(amount: Double, times: Int = 1) {
        radius += amount * Double(times)
    }

    func reset() {
        radius = 1;
    }
}
```

First, you added a computed `description` property that just returns a description of the class in string form. It's a computed property because you want the return value to contain the current radius, which can change. In your `ColoredCircleClass`, you'll want to add the circle's color to this description and, as you'll see, you'll do so by overriding the version of the property.

Next, you added the keyword `required` to the initializer with no arguments. It's very useful to have an initializer like this one that sets every property to a default value. The designer of this class thought it was so useful that he wanted to ensure that any subclass that's created from it also provides such an initializer. Adding `required` to the initializer achieves that because the Swift compiler will ensure that subclasses also implement an `init()` initializer; furthermore, it will ensure that it's also marked as required so that subclasses of the subclass have the same obligation. In `ColoredCircleClass`, you'll set a default `color` in your version of this initializer.

Finally, you added a `reset()` method that reverts the radius property to its default value. You'll need to override this in your subclass to also reset the circle's new `color` property.

You know what you have to do. Let's do it. As you read through what follows, add the new code to your playground. As you go along, you will encounter errors and warnings; don't worry about those because you'll fix them as you go along.

First, you need to create your subclass and tell the Swift compiler that its base class is `CircleClass`. Here's how you do that:

```
class ColoredCircleClass : CircleClass {
}
```

This is the normal way to start a class definition, which tells Swift that `ColoredCircleClass` has `CircleClass` as its base class. Any class can have exactly one base class, which must be declared in this way. As you'll see soon, it can also claim conformance to one or more `protocols`, which would also be listed here.

Next, you add the new stored property.

```
class ColoredCircleClass : CircleClass {
    var color: UIColor = UIColor.black
}
```

The type of your property is `UIColor`—a class from the UIKit framework that represents a color. You've initialized the property to a `UIColor` instance that represents black. Next, let's override the `description` property to add your color to the returned string. Here's how you do that:

```
class ColoredCircleClass : CircleClass {
    var color: UIColor = UIColor.black
```

```
    override var description: String {
        return super.description + ", color \(color)"
    }
}
```

The first thing to notice is the `override` keyword, which tells the compiler that you are aware that there is already a definition of a `description` property in the base class and you are intentionally overriding it. In some languages, it's very easy to accidentally create a method or a property of the same name as something in the base class without realizing it. That can lead to bugs that are hard to find.

The new implementation of this property first calls the base class version using the expression `super. description`. The keyword super tells the compiler that you want to reference the description property of your superclass (the one from which you are derived), not your own. Having done that, it then adds a string representation of your color property. The result will be that the description will include both the radius (from the super class) and the color (from this class).

Moving on, you need to add the `required` override of the `init()` initializer. Here it is:

```
required init() {
    super.init()
}
```

Every initializer is required to ensure that all the properties of its own class are initialized and then ensure that its base class does the same. You have only the `color` property, and it is initialized at the point of declaration. So, all you have to do is give the base class an opportunity to initialize its own state, which you do by calling `super.init()`. If you had any other properties that you needed to initialize, the compiler requires you to set them before calling `super.init()`. Also, note the `required` keyword, which is necessary because the base class `init()` is marked as `required`.

■ **Note**   I said earlier that marking the base class `init()` initializer as required makes it mandatory for any subclass to implement the same initializer. Up to this point, your `ColoredCircleClass` did not have an explicit `init()` initializer, yet there was no error. Why? The reason is that since `ColoredCircleClass` has no other initializers, the compiler created the `init()` initializer for you, which satisfies the base class requirement.

Next, you need an initializer that sets nondefault `radius` and `color` values. Add the following code to the class:

```
init(radius: Double, color: UIColor) {
    self.color = color
    super.init(radius: radius)
}
```

You first set the value of your `Color` property from the initializer argument, and then you pass the radius value to the initializer of the base class. That's all you need to do.

The last thing you need to do is override the `reset()` method to reset the color property to black. By now, you should be familiar with what's required.

```
override func reset() {
    super.reset()
    color = UIColor.black
}
```

As before, the override key tells the compiler that you are overriding a method from the base class (by the way, if you mistyped the name and called it, say, resets, the compiler would complain that there is no such method in the base class; that's another benefit you get from the override keyword). The rest of this method follows the pattern you've seen before; do your part of the work—and delegate to the base class to do its part using the super keyword to invoke the base class method. Here, it doesn't matter whether you do your part first or call the base class method first. In other words, this version would also work:

```
override func reset() {
    color = UIColor.black
    super.reset()
}
```

That's it. Let's try the default initializer:

```
var coloredCircle = ColoredCircleClass()
coloredCircle.radius          // Result: 1
coloredCircle.color           // Result: black
coloredCircle.description
        // Result: "Circle of radius 1.0, color UIDeviceWhiteColorSpace 0 1"
```

Now let's try the other initializer:

```
coloredCircle = ColoredCircleClass(radius: 20, color: UIColor.red())
coloredCircle.radius        // Result: 20
coloredCircle.color         // Result: red
coloredCircle.description  // Result: "Circle of radius 20.0, color
UIDeviceRGBColorSpace 1 0 0 1"
```

Subclassing is a very useful technique. Every example that you see in this book will use at least one subclass! It's worth taking the time to review the "Initialization" and "Inheritance" sections in Apple's *Swift Programming Language* book. There are a lot of subtle details that I didn't have time to cover here.

Protocols

A *protocol* is the declaration of a group of methods, initializers, and properties to which a class, structure, or enumeration can conform by providing implementations of them. As you'll see throughout this book, protocols are frequently used to define objects known as *delegates*, which provide hooks that allow you to customize the behavior of framework classes, react to events, and so forth.

Here's the definition of a protocol called Resizable:

```
protocol Resizable {
    var width: Float { get set }
    var height: Float { get set }

    init(width: Float, height: Float)
    func resizeBy( wFactor: Float, hFactor: Float) -> Void
}
```

The Resizable protocol requires any type that claims conformance to it to provide the two properties, one initializer, and one function that it declares. Notice that the protocol itself does not define anything; it simply dictates what a conforming type must do. Here's a class called Rectangle that conforms to the Resizable protocol:

```swift
class Rectangle : Resizable, CustomStringConvertible {
    var width: Float
    var height: Float
    var description: String {
        return "Rectangle, width \(width), height \(height)"
    }

    required init(width: Float, height: Float) {
        self.width = width
        self.height = height
    }

    func resizeBy( wFactor: Float, hFactor: Float) -> Void {
        width *= wFactor
        height *= hFactor
    }
}
```

A type declares that it conforms to a protocol by including the protocol name after the name of its base class, if any, in its declaration. This class conforms to both the `Resizable` protocol and the `CustomStringConvertible` protocol, which is defined in the Swift standard library.

As you can see, the class provides the actual implementation of the features required by the `Resizable` protocol. If a protocol requires the implementation of an initializer, then that initializer must be marked as `required`, as shown here. Instances of types that conform to a protocol can be assigned to variables of the protocol's type, like this:

```swift
let r: Resizable = Rectangle(width: 10, height: 20)
```

Conformance to the `CustomStringConvertible` protocol requires the type to provide a `String` property called `description`, which is used when a human-readable representation of the type is required. In particular, this property is used when an instance of the conforming type is passed as an argument to the `print()` function.

```swift
let rect = Rectangle(width: 10, height: 20)
print(rect)    // Prints "Rectangle, width 10.0, height 20.0"
```

Extensions

Extensions are a powerful feature that Swift shares with Objective-C. An extension allows you to add functionality to any class, structure, or enumeration, including those in the standard Swift library or the system frameworks. The syntax of an extension definition is similar to that of classes and structures. The extension is introduced by the keyword `extension` followed by the name of the extended type and then the extensions themselves. You can add computed (but not stored) properties, methods, initializers, nested types, and protocol conformance to the extended type.

In Chapter 14, you used an extension to add a method to the `UIColor` class (from the UIKit framework) that returns a random color. Here's how the extension is defined:

```swift
extension UIColor {
    class func randomColor() -> UIColor {
        let red = CGFloat(Double((arc4random() % 256))/255)
        let green = CGFloat(Double(arc4random() % 256)/255)
```

545

```
        let blue = CGFloat(Double(arc4random() % 256)/255)
        return UIColor(red: red, green: green, blue: blue, alpha:1.0)
    }
}
```

Here's how it's used:

```
let randomColor = UIColor.randomColor()
```

Summary

Now you've had a tour of the most important features of Swift. What you've seen here is by no means everything there is to know. I've left out quite a lot (and simplified some of the rest), and you should read the official documentation (or one of the books listed in Chapter 1) to expand your knowledge, when you have the time. In the meantime, turn back to Chapter 3 (or where you left off in the main part of this book) and start writing your first iOS application with Swift.

Index

Get the eBook for only $5!

Why limit yourself?

With most of our titles available in both PDF and ePUB format, you can access your content wherever and however you wish—on your PC, phone, tablet, or reader.

Since you've purchased this print book, we are happy to offer you the eBook for just $5.

To learn more, go to http://www.apress.com/companion or contact support@apress.com.

Apress®

85325342R00321

Made in the USA
San Bernardino, CA
18 August 2018